D1526715

GEORGE BURNS AND GRACIE ALLEN

George and Gracie in San Francisco, taking in the view from the Hotel Mark Hopkins, August 1939. (Photo courtesy of the San Francisco Public Library)

GEORGE BURNS AND GRACIE ALLEN

A Bio-Bibliography

Cynthia Clements
and Sandra Weber

Bio-Bibliographies in the Performing Arts, Number 72
James Robert Parish, Series Adviser

GREENWOOD PRESS
Westport, Connecticut • London

Library of Congress Cataloging-in-Publication Data

Clements, Cynthia.
George Burns and Gracie Allen : a bio-bibliography / Cynthia Clements and Sandra Weber.
p. cm.—(Bio-bibliographies in the performing arts, ISSN 0892–5550 ; no. 72)
Filmography: p.
Discography: p.
Includes bibliographical references and index.
ISBN 0–313–26883–5 (alk. paper)
1. Burns, George, 1896– . 2. Allen, Gracie, 1902–1964. 3. Burns, George,—1896– —Bibliography. 4. Allen, Gracie,—1902–1964—Bibliography. 5. Comedians—United States—Biography. 6. Entertainers—United States—Biography. I. Weber, Sandra. II. Title. III. Series.
PN2287.B87C64 1996
792.7′028′092273—dc20
[B] 96–4970

British Library Cataloguing in Publication Data is available.

Library of Congress Catalog Card Number: 96–4970
ISBN: 0–313–26883–5
ISSN: 0892–5550

First published in 1996

Greenwood Press, 88 Post Road West, Westport, CT 06881
An imprint of Greenwood Publishing Group, Inc.

Printed in the United States of America

The paper used in this book complies with the Permanent Paper Standard issued by the National Information Standards Organization (Z39.48–1984).

10 9 8 7 6 5 4 3 2 1

In memory of Dorothy Maye Cofer Clements

and

Dedicated to Ashleigh Cooley

CONTENTS

Photo Essay Follows Page 194.

PREFACE

In the eyes and minds of today's audiences, George Burns was a solo act. But in the hearts of those fortunate enough to remember and in the annals of show business, he will be forever linked with his partner on stage and off, Gracie Allen.

Nathan Birnbaum may not sound like the name of a well-known and much-loved entertainer, but it is. Nathan, who seemed no different from and destined for no more success than any of the thousands of other young boys who grew up in the tenement buildings of New York City's Lower East Side, would one day become one of the most famous men in the world. Three critical factors were to make Nathan "Natty" Birnbaum a success: he learned to smoke a cigar, he changed his name to George Burns, and he met and married Gracie Allen.

Of course, those things took time, and fame did not come quickly or easily. George was over thirty years old before he reached a certain level of success in show business, having been an entertainer nearly his whole life. For him, show business was the only career he sought.

Of all people, Gracie would have been the one not surprised by the accolades George garnered in the years since her death. Knowing how much George loved show business, she wouldn't have broken up the team if she hadn't believed he could make it without her. Incredible as it might have seemed to fans of the Burns and Allen team, George Burns was even more popular in his last two decades than he was at the height of his career as straight man to Gracie Allen and better known than practically anyone else in show business. He was born before most areas of show business that are popular today existed. So was Gracie. In vaudeville, they finally "made it" when they played the Palace in New York City in 1926; and, as radio, records, film and television developed, they were there, carrying their act from one medium to the next until Gracie ended the act in 1958. Few entertainers had the necessary talent and luck to achieve success in every show business medium. But George and Gracie did. And George went on to other venues. His nightclub, college-circuit and convention appearances didn't stop until he was in his late nineties. He made commercials, a music video, an exercise video; he wrote books and won an Oscar, an Emmy and a Grammy. He was even booked into the London Palladium and Caesar's

Palace in Las Vegas on his 100th birthday in 1996, bookings that were sold out. He did more than one-man shows; he *was* a one-man show business phenomenon.

Show business. The allure of those two words is so strong that some people will do anything to be part of it. George Burns spent years trying to get into show business; Gracie Allen spent years trying to get out. Today's presumably sophisticated audiences sometimes seem to prefer confusing the actor with his onscreen alter ego. For our own reasons we want to think that the actor is the character, which is nothing new. The press perpetuated the myth that the "reel" Gracie was the "real" Gracie years ago. One newspaper report, a hard news story about George's troubles with the law over smuggled jewelry and his subsequent fine and suspended prison sentence, described him as "(the) spouse of goofy Gracie Allen." People too often didn't honor her in the way she deserved--as a talented actress playing a part. No wonder Gracie felt that no one wanted to know anything about her as a person, only as a fictitious character.

The fact that Gracie Allen was a private person who revealed little of her true self to reporters and the public helped to perpetuate the "dumb Dora" character image she portrayed in the Burns and Allen comedy act. Although articles were written noting that Gracie Allen in real life was not dumb at all, but in fact was an intelligent woman and a very good actress, this did not dispel her public image. The team had adopted the "dumb Dora" characterization shortly after they first began working in vaudeville in late 1922. They had many predecessors, such as Ryan and Lee (Benny Ryan and Harriet Lee) and Joe and Aleen (Joe Laurie, Jr. and Aleen Bronson), in which the woman played the "not too bright" female role versus her "intelligent" male partner.

Burns and Allen began to make real strides in their climb to show business success in 1929 and in the early 1930s, just as vaudeville was going into its decline. They were signed in 1929 by film studios to work in shorts and, eventually, features, joining other popular comedians in the movies. In 1932 they were able to move into the new broadcasting medium of radio, joining Guy Lombardo's show as comedians and later hosting their own radio shows from 1934 to 1950. Burns and Allen were among the handful of vaudevillians who were able to translate their act into a radio format. Their competitors in radio were also good friends, including husband and wife teams Jack Benny and Mary Livingstone (**The Jack Benny Program** [1932-1955]), Fred Allen and Portland Hoffa (**The Fred Allen Show** [1932-1949]) and Jim and Marion Jordan (**Fibber McGee & Molly** [1935-1956]).

While George Burns's role, both as an actor onstage and the mastermind offstage, was an important part in the success of the Burns and Allen act, it was Gracie's portrayal of the "Gracie Allen" character that really made the shows a success. It was Gracie who brought millions of radio listeners back to the show week after week, year after year. The same was true when Burns and Allen made the bold move in 1950 to television, the first comedy team to do so with success (Lum and Abner tried in 1949 but couldn't get past the pilot stage; Amos 'n' Andy didn't go on the air until June 28, 1951). The medium showcased their talents to the best advantage. Unlike the majority of their feature films, television turned the camera full force on them, and their talents outshone even the brightest spotlight. Audiences loved George's bemused tolerance and Gracie's charming lunacy. While they basically brought their radio show characters to television, their show was also an innovator. They introduced the "fourth wall" technique, whereby George spoke directly to the audience, delivering monologues outside of the plot. Using multi-cameras to film the show, previewing the shows for live audiences and recording their reactions, putting a television set in George's office, which enabled him to watch the other actors on the show, revealing what he saw to the television audience--all are techniques that are taken for granted now, but were certainly pioneering ideas more than forty years ago. Other television comedy team shows would be more successful in the ratings than **The George Burns and Gracie Allen Show** such as **I Love Lucy** with Lucille Ball and Desi Arnaz--but it was Burns and Allen who paved the way. Their television show came to an end not because of poor ratings but due to Gracie's decision to retire in 1958.

In detailing the careers of Burns and Allen, it must be noted that these people were multitalented performers who could sing, dance and act and did so on the stage, in film, in radio and on television. After Gracie's retirement and continuing after her death in 1964, George was able to find success as a single act for the next thirty-one years, ending a year shy of his 100th birthday when ill health forced him to cancel any future performances.

This volume attempts to document the careers of George Burns and Gracie Allen as a male/female comedy team from 1922-1958 and continues with George's stage, television and film work from 1958-1995. The authors have compiled factual information from primary sources whenever available. Unfortunately, Mr. Burns (through his manager and publicist, Irving Fein) politely declined to assist the authors. More successful were the contacts made with actors, writers and producers who worked with Burns and Allen and who were able to contribute some insight into how the team worked and about their true personalities.

The authors wish to thank especially Ned Comstock of the USC Cinema-Television Library and Archives of Performing Arts for his assistance in gaining access to the George Burns and Gracie Allen archives and to the staff of the Film and Television Archives at UCLA for their willingness to allow the viewing of several Burns and Allen films that are not in current release.

Spellings of the words "theater" and "theatre" are used interchangeably.

The book is arranged as follows:

(1) a **chronology** of major events in the life and careers of George Burns and Gracie Allen;

(2) a **biography** section which attempts to clarify and flesh out dates, times and events in their lives;

(3) **vaudeville** appearances from 1922 to the 1930s delineated by date, length of booking, theater name and location;

(4) a **filmography** which lists the films made by Burns and Allen as a team and separately are preceded by the letter "F" and are divided into shorts and features. The film's title, running time, studio, year of release, Motion Picture Association of America ratings, selected production credits, cast, synopsis, reviews and commentary are included;

(5) **radio** series and radio guest appearances from 1929 to the 1960s as a team and separately, beginning with their first radio performance in England and continuing with some of George's radio interviews in the 1960s. Each entry in their series is preceded by the letter "R" and includes the airdate and a synopsis; entries in the guest appearance section may include program title, network, original airdate and synopsis;

(6) **television** series and television guest appearances from 1950 to 1995 as a team and separately are preceded by the letter "T" and contain the original airdate and synopsis as well as syndicated title of the filmed episodes; guest appearances include program title, network, airdate and synopsis;

(7) a **discography** offering a wide spectrum of recordings on album, cassette and compact disc produced of Burns and Allen as a team and separately; entries are preceded by the letter "D" and include compilations and books on tape as well as various packagings of their radio shows and other material;

(8) a **videography** listing videotapes and laserdiscs of Burns and Allen films and television shows and of George's stage shows and other videos that are available through distributors are preceded by the letters "VG";

(9) **awards and honors** presented to Burns and Allen, separately and as a team (including those given to Gracie posthumously), many of their **personal appearances** made as a team and separately and **research centers** where the majority of research materials on George Burns and Gracie Allen is located are included as appendices;

(10) an annotated **bibliography**, which is arranged with lists of individual articles and books written by Gracie Allen and George Burns, followed by articles and books written about them as a team and as individuals. Also included in this section are interviews as well as books that provide the reader with insight into the eras of vaudeville, film, radio, television and comedy during the times in which Burns and Allen performed (in George Burns's case, this encompassed almost the entire twentieth century); all entries are preceded by the letter "B";

(11) an **index**.

Also included are photographs and illustrations of Burns and Allen during their four decades of working as a comedy team.

This book had been completed at the time of George Burns' death on March 9, 1996. The authors have added pertinent material as of April 1996 in an "Addendum" at the end of the various book sections. Any additions or corrections for future editions may be sent to the authors in care of Greenwood Press.

ACKNOWLEDGMENTS

Academy of Television Arts and Sciences and Foundation; BBC Written Archives Centre; the late Ralph Bellamy; William T. Benedict, Theatre Historical Society of America; James M. Blakely, KKHJ Radio; Hendrik (Hank) Booraem, Jr.; Frank Bresee; Herb Browar; Marilyn Brownstein; George F. Butler; Cable News Network; Judy Cantor, **San Francisco Examiner** Library; Sister Rosemarie Carroll and Carmel Tickler, Star of the Sea Elementary School; Stephen A. Carvell, Kraft General Foods; CBS; **Cleveland Plain Dealer**; Lisa Cohen; Ned Comstock, USC Cinema-Television Library and Archives of Performing Arts; Gary W. Coville; Dallas County Community College District Libraries; Dallas Public Library; Paul Dane, Society of Wireless Pioneers, Inc.; Louise Danton, TV Library of the Academy of Television Arts and Sciences; Ronald L. Davis; Fred de Cordova; Mary Diltz, KNX-AM; Sally Dumaux, Frances Howard Goldwyn Library; Ralph Edwards; Family History Library; Film and Television Archive, UCLA; Ellen G. Gartrell, J. Walter Thompson Company Archives of Duke University; Samuel A. Gill and Howard H. Prouty of the Margaret Herrick Library, Special Collections, Academy of Motion Picture Arts and Sciences; John and Larry Gassman, SPERDVAC; Golden Age Radio; Jim Harmon; Richard K. Hayes; Amy Henderson, Smithsonian Institution; Paul and Ruth Henning; Jay Hickerson; Indiana University Library; Institut National de L'Audiovisuel; Marty Jacobs, The Museum of the City of New York; Scott Jones, North American Radio Archives; Kent State Libraries Special Collections; KFI Radio; Walid Khaldi, Southwest Film/Video Archives, SMU; King Features; Tom Kleinschmidt; Kristine Krueger, National Film Information Service of the Academy of Motion Picture Arts and Sciences; Chris Lembesis; London Palladium; Los Gatos Chamber of Commerce and Public Library; Leonard Maltin; Peggy McCay; Ann V. McVee, Tinsletown Titles; Eleanor J. Mish, American Museum of the Moving Image; Charles Michelson; Motion Picture, Broadcasting and Recorded Sound Division, Performing Arts Library, The Library of Congress; Motorola Corporation; Museum of Broadcast Communications; Museum of Television and Radio; NBC; Newark Public Library; Olathe, Kansas, Public Library; **Omaha World-Herald** Library; Oral History Collection, SMU; Palm Springs Historical Society; James Robert Parish; Roger C. Paulson, Archives of the Airwaves; Art Pierce; Playbill Inc.; Popular Culture Library, Bowling Green State University; Tom

Price, Priceless Sound Productions; Joel Rane, American Film Institute; Bob Reed; Richmond Branch, San Francisco Public Library; Barry Rivadue; Mike Rophone, Radio Yesteryear; San Francisco Performing Arts Library and Museum; San Francisco Public Library; Richard Schnyder, Hollywood Center Studios; Margie Schultz; Dean Siegal, Block Drug Company; D. Lynn Siegelman, Sanofi-Winthrop; Al Simon; Anthony Slide; Charles Smith; Southern Methodist University Libraries; Special Collections, UCLA; Robin Steiner, Shea's Buffalo Center for the Performing Arts; Vincent Terrace; Peter Tatchell, **Laugh Magazine**; Lynn Taylor; **The Pat Sajak Show**; **The Tonight Show**; Theatre Arts Library, UCLA; Theatre Collection, Free Library of Philadelphia; Julie Thomas-Lowe, Carnation; Stephen Vallillo; Gene Ward; Pat Willis; Wisconsin Center for Film and Theater Research; Ron Wolf, Pacific Pioneers Broadcasters.

CHRONOLOGY

1895 July 26	Grace Ethel Cecile Rosalie Allen is born in San Francisco, California, to George and Margaret Allen.
1896 January 20	Nathan Birnbaum is born in New York City to Louis and Dorothy Birnbaum.
1898	Grace makes her first appearance on stage at a church social.
1903 or 1904	Louis Birnbaum dies in New York City.
1905	Margaret Allen marries Edward G. Pidgeon.
1906 or 1907	Nathan quits school. He and some friends form the "Pee Wee Quartet."
1907-1910	Nathan wins several dancing contests in the New York City area with different female partners.
1909-1914	During summer vacations Grace's song and dance act is booked into local motion picture houses.
1910	Nathan, who has chosen the name George Burns, works as a dancing instructor and is a partner in "B. B.'s College of Dancing" in Brooklyn, New York.
1910-1919	George works at various jobs and at times gets bookings in vaudeville theaters under numerous names.
1914 June 19	Grace graduates from the Star of the Sea School in San Francisco.
1914-1915	Grace works as a dancing instructor in the Allen sisters' dancing school in San Francisco.

1916 Grace gets a job with Larry Reilly in his Irish vaudeville act. Later, "The Three Allen Sisters" (Grace, Hazel and Bessie) join the tour billed as "Larry Reilly and Company."

1918 Bessie and Hazel leave the act and return to San Francisco.

1919 In New Jersey, Grace quits the Reilly act in a dispute over her billing.

1919-1920 George teams with singer Sid Gary.

1920-1921 Grace is hired by Benny Ryan to replace his ill partner (and wife), Harriet Lee, in their comedy and dance act.

Grace works with various male partners in a comedy skit written by Benny Ryan.

1921-1922 Grace attends secretarial school in New York City, where she rooms with friends Mary Kelly and Rena Arnold.

George teams up with singer Billy Lorraine and, as "The Two Broadway Thieves," they are booked fourteen weeks on the Pantages vaudeville circuit.

1922 Fall Burns and Lorraine play their last appearance as a team at the Jefferson Theater in Union Hill, New Jersey. George is introduced to Grace Allen by Rena Arnold.

Grace decides to quit secretarial school and agrees to work in a comedy act with George Burns.

Billed as George N. Burns and Grace Allen they appear for the first time as a team at the Hill Theater in Newark, New Jersey.

1923 George and Grace's act, "Sixty-Forty," is booked as a vaudeville "disappointment act" in theaters across the country.

1924 May Grace is hospitalized in San Francisco for appendicitis.

1925 George works on a new act, "Lamb Chops," with comedy writer Al Boasberg.

December 25 Grace agrees to marry George.

1926 January 7 George and Grace are married at the City Hall in Cleveland, Ohio, while touring their new act, "Lamb Chops."

	January 18	Appearing in "Lamb Chops," George and Grace break all house records at the Keith Theater in Syracuse, New York.
	February 24	Burns and Allen sign a five-year contract with the Keith-Orpheum circuit.
	August 23	Burns and Allen make their first appearance at the Palace Theater in New York City.
1929	Feb. 25-Oct. 4	Burns and Allen tour the British Isles with their vaudeville act.
	June 10	Burns and Allen appear for the first time on radio as one of the acts of the BBC radio show **Vaudeville**. They are asked to perform for fifteen weeks on the BBC.
	October	Burns and Allen return to New York City and are signed by Warner Bros. to do a motion picture film short. The film is titled **Burns and Allen in Lambchops**; in it they perform part of their vaudeville act of the same name.
	n.d.	Burns and Allen sign with Paramount to do several film shorts. George writes the script for what becomes **Fit To Be Tied**.
1931	January 8	Their Radio-Keith-Orpheum vaudeville contract ends.
	January 9	Burns and Allen are signed to a three-year contract with Paramount-Publix to make four film shorts a year and to appear in vaudeville shows at the Publix theaters.
	August 5	Margaret Allen dies at St. Francis Hospital in San Francisco. George and Gracie are appearing in the city at the time.
	October 3	Burns and Allen appear at the Palace Theater with headliners Eddie Cantor and George Jessel in a nine-week engagement which breaks all records for length of run (ends on January 8, 1932) and box office receipts. Their latest act is called "Dizzy."
	November 15	Gracie Allen appears for the first time on American radio as a guest on Eddie Cantor's **Chase & Sanborn Hour**.
1932	January 28	Burns and Allen are guests on Rudy Vallee's radio show, the **Fleischmann Yeast Hour**.
	February 15	Burns and Allen appear on radio with Guy Lombardo on **The Robert Burns Panatela Program**. They are asked to return the next week and are signed to become regulars on the show. This is the beginning of their eighteen-year series career on American radio.

	Summer	Burns and Allen begin filming **The Big Broadcast**, their first feature film.
1933	January 4	The first radio show that mentions Gracie's "missing brother" is broadcast.
	May 24	The radio show becomes known as **The White Owl Program**.
	October	This is Burns and Allen's last month to work in vaudeville, ending when their contract expires.
1934	September	Burns and Allen adopt a baby girl, Sandra Jean, from The Cradle in Evanston, Illinois.
		The Robert Burns Panatela Program is renamed **The Adventures of Gracie** after Guy Lombardo leaves the show. It will later be called **The Vintage White Owl Program**.
	October 3	Burns and Allen's radio show is broadcast on its first coast-to-coast hookup from New York City.
1935	January	Burns and Allen present their first radio broadcast in front of a studio audience at the Figueroa Playhouse in Los Angeles, California.
	September	Burns and Allen adopt a second child, Ronald Jon, from the same Catholic foundling home from which they had adopted their daughter.
	October 2	George and Gracie's first program for a new sponsor, the Campbell Soup Company,is broadcast.
1936	December	The Burnses move permanently to California and purchase a home in Beverly Hills.
1937	April 12	George and Gracie's first program for General Foods and Grape-Nuts Cereal is broadcast.
1938	September 30	Liggett and Myers Tobacco (Chesterfield Cigarettes) becomes Burns and Allen's new radio sponsor on tonight's show.
	Fall	George and Jack Benny are accused of smuggling jewelry into the United States.
1939	January 31	George pleads guilty to two federal indictments for smuggling. He is fined and given a suspended sentence.
	October 4	Burns and Allen begin their radio association with Hinds Honey and Almond Cream in their first broadcast for Lehn and Fink.
1940	February 7	The first mention of Gracie running for president occurs on their radio show.

		Nebraska for the Surprise Party Convention.
	May 15	**The Burns and Allen Show** is broadcast from the Ak-sar-ben Coliseum in Omaha, Nebraska, during the three-day Surprise Party Convention for presidential candidate Gracie Allen.
	June 29	Gracie donates all proceeds from her book, **How to Become President**, to the American Red Cross.
	July 1	The Hormel Packing Company takes over as their radio show sponsor.
1941	October 7	Burns and Allen begin their series for Swan Soap. The association will last for nearly four years.
1943	March 16	Gracie performs her "One Finger Concerto" at Carnegie Hall, New York City.
1945	September 20	George and Gracie kick off their next radio show, this time for Maxwell House Coffee.
1949	September 21	The last Burns and Allen radio series debuts; its sponsor is the Block Drug Company for Amm-i-dent Toothpaste.
1950	May 17	This is George and Gracie's last regular radio broadcast before moving their show to television.
	October 12	**The George Burns and Gracie Allen Show** makes its television debut.
1954	October 4	The first and only Burns and Allen show produced in color is broadcast.
1955	Fall	**The Burns and Allen** television show begins showing in London, England, over the BBC.
	October 30	George's first book, **I Love Her, That's Why!**, is published.
1958	February 18	Gracie Allen announces her retirement from show business.
	September 15	The last first-run episode of George and Gracie's television show is broadcast.
	September 22	The last Burns and Allen network television show signs off of CBS with a rerun episode.
	October 21	**The George Burns Show** debuts on NBC. It ends on April 14, 1959. Its demise causes George to turn serious attention to his nightclub act.
1964	August 27	Gracie dies of a heart attack at Cedars of Lebanon Hospital in Los Angeles, California.

August 31 Gracie is buried at Forest Lawn Memorial Park in Glendale, California.

September 14 **Wendy and Me**, starring George and Connie Stevens, debuts on ABC. Its last telecast (a rerun) is September 6, 1965.

1966 January 20 George's beloved brother and business associate, Willy, dies.

1974 August 9 George Burns enters Cedars of Lebanon Hospital in Los Angeles for open heart surgery. He is released on September 25.

December George's best friend, comedian Jack Benny, dies the week after Christmas.

1975 George returns to motion pictures in a part orginally set to be played by Jack Benny. His role in **The Sunshine Boys** earns him an Oscar for Best Supporting Actor. His show business career is rejuvenated upon the audience's "rediscovery" of his talent.

1979 September 24 George is involved in an automobile accident.

1981 George donates a piece of property to the Motion Picture and Television Fund that nets the recipient, the Motion Picture and Television Country House and Hospital in Woodland Hills, California, $500,000.

1984 It's reported in November that George has recently signed a multiyear contract with Caesar's Palace for "a series of annual dates in Las Vegas, Lake Tahoe, Nevada and Atlantic City, New Jersey."

1985 September 18 George returns to television as host/narrator for thirteen episodes of **George Burns' Comedy Week**. The series' last broadcast is December 25, 1985.

Fall George donates $1 million to the Motion Picture and Television Country House and Hospital in Woodland Hills, California. He promises future donations, joking he'll need a place to go when he gets old.

1986 Reports indicate that George has signed a five-year contract with Caesar's Palace for a semiannual six-night stand, one show per night.

George contributes $1 million to the Cedars-Sinai Medical Center in Los Angeles, California.

1988		George's second book devoted to his wife is published. This one is called **Gracie: A Love Story**.
1989		George makes another $1 million donation to the Cedars-Sinai Medical Center, Los Angeles, California.
1990		According to published reports, George has signed a five-year contract with Caesar's Palace.
1991	March 19	It's reported that George has signed an exclusive two-year contract with the Riviera Hotel and Casino in Las Vegas. No mention is made of his previously reported five-year contract with Caesar's from 1990.
1992		It's reported that George has re-signed with Caesar's Palace for three years.
1994	July 13	George is admitted to Cedars-Sinai Medical Center in Los Angeles, California, for observation after suffering a fall in his home in Las Vegas, Nevada. He is released on July 22.
	September 12	George undergoes surgery to remove fluid from around his brain.
	September 22	George is released from the hospital to continue the recuperation process at home in Beverly Hills, California.
1995	August	George's manager, Irving Fein, announces that George "has scaled back plans for performances marking his 100th birthday."
	September	George's office announces that he has cancelled future performances.
1996	January 20	George celebrates his 100th birthday at his home. He makes no public appearances due to ill health.
	March 9	George Burns dies at his home in Beverly Hills, California.
	March 12	George is buried at Forest Lawn Memorial Park, Glendale, California in a private service.

BIOGRAPHY

Burns and Allen. George and Gracie. Petite Gracie Allen, queen of the *non sequitur*, and her "straight man" husband and partner, George Burns, became the longest running successful comedy team in entertainment history, winning over fans of vaudeville, radio, film, and television during their thirty-five year career. George and Gracie were a good team, George says, because "I would think of it; Gracie was able to do it." George Burns and Gracie Allen were born and grew up on opposite ends of the country, married in the middle, and proceeded to make the whole world laugh. Grace Ethel Cecile Rosalie Allen (reordered, the first letters of each name spell Grace) was born first, on July 27, 1895 in San Francisco, California. At that time her parents, George and Margaret Allen, were living at 17th and 346 Castro Streets in the city and were already the parents of four children, Bessie (b. 1884), Pearl (b. 1886), George (b. 1888) and Hazel (b. 1889). Gracie's siblings would later become known to Burns and Allen radio and television audiences as their names were often incorporated into the comedy team's routines.

Her father, George Allen, of Scottish descent, was born in San Francisco in 1862 and was a successful song and dance man who performed in vaudeville on the West Coast. His future wife, Margaret (Maggie) Darragh was born in 1867 in California where her parents had settled. Her father Patrick (nicknamed Patle or Patsl) had emigrated from Ireland and her mother Clara had been born in Massachusetts. The Darraghs later moved to San Francisco where Maggie and her brothers and sister were born.

George met his future wife, Margaret Darragh in San Francisco through her brothers, who had hired George Allen to teach them ballroom dancing. They were married in 1883 in that same city. Throughout their marriage, George continued to teach dancing and physical education; and in 1898 he was employed as an instructor with W. C. Bean, "teachers of gymnastics" in San Francisco. But he also worked as an iron molder and was at times unemployed.

The Allen family moved several times after Grace's birth in 1895, to 208 Fifth Street and later to 224 Fifth Street in San Francisco. Grace's widowed maternal grandmother, Clara Darragh, always lived on nearby streets.

Gracie Allen said that she never saw her father on the stage performing his dancing act. But at the age of three he led her onto a stage for the first time at a church benefit where she sang an Irish song. Grace was dressed in a man's full dress suit coat with a top hat and carried a red beard, which she had refused to wear. Her first performance granted her mention in the newspaper as "la petite Grace."

As a child, Grace Allen experienced two serious accidents. When she was a year and a half old, she pulled a boiling pot of water off the stove and the liquid spilled, scalding her right arm and shoulder. She was hospitalized while the doctors attempted to save her arm. They were successful, and the young Grace recovered with some limitation of arm movement. She would wear long sleeved dresses and blouses the remainder of her life to hide the scars.

Not long after recovering from this accident she pulled over a lamp, which caused glass fragments to fall into her eye. Most of the fragments were removed and her eyesight was saved, but her vision was somewhat affected from that point forward, and her eyes became very sensitive to bright light.

The Allens' homelife was not unlike that of other Irish-American families in the late 19th and early 20th centuries in San Francisco, which had a large Irish Catholic population. But it suddenly was upheaved at the early turn of the century when George Allen left his wife and five children. Gracie Allen never related this event to interviewers, but it clearly made an impression on her life, as her father neglected to keep in touch with her. George and Margaret later divorced.

While still a child, Grace, who was much younger than her brother and sisters, went to live with her mother's sister, Clara Burke, in Los Gatos, California, a farming community in Santa Clara County, south of San Francisco. She would live there with her aunt and uncle for some years but would see her mother and sisters as often as was possible.

As a single mother, Margaret Allen had to work to support her children. In 1904 she moved to 311 Shotwell Street, below Market Street. Several blocks away, at 1011 Shotwell, lived a San Francisco police patrol driver, Edward Pidgeon, who Margaret would marry in 1905.

The area below Market Street where Grace and her family lived was destroyed during the 1906 San Francisco earthquake and fire. The family moved either before or after the fire, to 668 Fourth Avenue, near Golden State Park. Thousands of single-family middle-class homes would be built in this area of San Francisco, known as the Richmond District, beginning in 1910.

Grace's stepfather, Edward Pigeon, was a 6'4" policeman of Irish descent and a hero to many San Franciscans. The city newspapers of 1917 had front-page stories about his heroism in saving drowning swimmers and boaters from the waters of San Francisco Bay. He was also recognized several times for saving people from fires and counseling potential suicide victims. On December 6, 1923, at the age of 47, he died suddenly of pleurisy only a week after winning a horse jumping contest. Captain Pigeon's funeral was attended by all of San Francisco's city officials. At the time of his death his step daughter Grace was in New York City working in a vaudeville act with her partner, George "Nat" Burns.

Although George Allen had long been separated from their lives, his daughters had inherited his dancing talents and the Allen sisters continued his occupation of teaching dance. By

1907 Pearl Allen was teaching dancing in the basement of their Fourth Avenue home. All of the sisters would help out in the teaching and running of the dance studio, but it would be Pearl who would continue and keep it opened until 1948.

Bessie was the first Allen sister to work in show business. After teaching dancing in San Francisco (Allen & Hickman, 1133 Mission Street) she was employed on the Sullivan Considine vaudeville circuit as a singer, dancer, and magician's assistant. At the age of six, Grace went to see her oldest sister perform onstage and prior to Bessie's stage entrance boasted that she could give a better performance. Calling her bluff, Bessie pulled her on the stage where Grace began to cry and than ran offstage. But not willing to let her sister get away without proving her point, Bessie pushed her back on the stage and the youngest Allen managed to dance an Irish jig and a sailor's hornpipe, crying all the time. At the conclusion of Grace's performance the audience broke out in applause.

Throughout her youth Grace Allen performed at many local dance recitals, as did her sisters. To publicize the "May Pole Dance" at the Golden Gate Park in 1909, her photograph was reproduced in the **San Francisco Chronicle** along with that of another young dancer. For two years in a row Pearl and Hazel Allen were directors of this event, which featured fifty young dancers who had been training at the Juvenile Gaelic dancing club at the Allens' dance studio. The three eldest Allen sisters were known as the most talented Irish dancers in the San Francisco Bay Area. They also won numerous contests and awards up and down the Pacific Coast.

While her sisters and brother were working, (George Allen, Grace's brother, was never involved in show business), Grace, who was seven years younger than Hazel, her nearest sibling in age, was still in school. After attending the Hawthorne Elementary School in San Francisco, Grace was enrolled in the Star of the Sea Convent School on Ninth Avenue and Geary Street near her home in the Richmond District. In speaking of her youth, Gracie Allen would remark that she was a star stuck child who spent every afternoon after school and weekends going downtown to every theater lobby to look at the pictures of the entertainers. She wasn't interested in school and really wanted to quit and go into show business.

As a teenager, during school vacations, Grace's act was booked by Ella Weston, who worked in one of the local booking houses. She would perform a little song and dance act and also sing in motion picture houses to accompany color slides illustrating what was seen on the screen. Margaret Allen, and sometimes Hazel, accompanied the youngest Allen on these occasions, and encouraged Grace to continue in show business.

When Grace was a little older, she, Pearl and Hazel would join Bessie at various times on vaudeville circuits in a dancing act, billed as "The Allen Sisters." They would perform an "illusion" act in which the four would appear on stage on a platform covered by fog, do a Highland reel, and then disappear in the fog. Grace succeeded in getting the show cancelled at one booking. She kept slipping on the spot where talcum powder from the previous act had been left on the stage. The act got a lot of laughs from the audience when she kept falling down. But during their next performance, and after the floor was cleaned, they didn't receive laughs and the theater manager cancelled their act.

School was not of much interest nor importance to Grace but at her mother's insistence she managed to complete her high school education at the Star of the Sea School. Grace Cecile Allen was a commercial class student and was granted a business diploma on June 19, 1914. She was almost nineteen years old and eager to begin her career in show business.

~~~~~

While Grace Allen was growing up in comfortable surroundings in California, Nathan Birnbaum (i.e., George Burns) found life difficult in the Lower East Side of New York City. Born on January 20, 1896, at 95 Pitt Street, he was the son of Louis (Lippe) Phillip and Dorothy (Bluth) Birnbaum, immigrant Jews who had left their homelands for a better life in America.

Like so many fleeing from poverty and persecution in 19th century Europe, they were only one family from the midst of a large wave of immigrants to America. Louis (b. 1855) was originally from Poland and Dorothy (Dora b. 1857), from Austria. Their arranged marriage took place when they were in their early teens.

In 1886 Louis immigrated to the United States and he found a job working as a coat presser in New York City. Two years later his wife and their two children were able to join him in America. Eventually there would be fourteen children (twelve survived) born to the couple: (Morris b. ?), Annie (b. 1880), Isadore (b. 1881), Esther (b. 1883), Sarah (b. 1885), Sophie (b. 1883), Mamie (b. 1889), Goldie (b. 1894), Nathan (b. 1896), Theresa (b. 1897), Sammy (b. 1899), William (b. 1903). Only William (Willy) would join his brother Nathan in show business when he became Burns and Allen's business manager. His contribution to their success grew as the years passed, and he eventually wore many hats, including a writer and producer of their radio shows as well as writer for their television series. Exactly why and when he adopted George's new last name of "Burns" is a matter of speculation.

Louis Birnbaum, the father, had a difficult time finding work and spent most of his time at the local synagogue where he was a part-time cantor. Like many Jewish immigrants, most of the family worked for the garment industry in New York City.

When Nathan was five years old, the family moved to nearby 259 Rivington Street, into four small rooms on the third floor of a tenement house. The Birnbaums, like most of their neighbors in the East Side area of New York City, had trouble earning enough money to keep their family fed and clothed. All of the children worked at various jobs to bring money into the household. Although Louis Birnbaum was well respected in his community he could never earn enough money working in the garment district nor the synagogue to support his family. The situation worsened for the Birnbaum household when he died suddenly around the turn of the century at the age of forty-seven, leaving his wife with several young children to raise and support. Nathan, only seven years old, was in the room when his father slumped over in his chair and died.

To help support the family, Nathan tried all sorts of jobs, such as selling newspapers on the street, shining shoes and mixing syrup for ice cream sodas.
~~~~~

In the slums of New York City the residents had to struggle to exist, and there was little, if any, money spent on amusements. Organ grinders who would walk the neighborhoods with their playful monkeys provided entertainment for young children like Nathan, who loved to sing and dance and would follow alongside making their own fun.

As the son of a cantor, Nathan had inherited a love of singing. Always thinking of ways to earn money for the family, he organized a group of his friends together and the "Peewee Quartet" was born. The members were Moishe Friedman (Toda), brothers Heshy and Mortzy Weinberger, and Nathan. Lew Farley, the local mailman, who helped the boys by teaching the group to sing harmony. The "Peewee Quartet" began trying to make money by walking into saloons on the Lower East Side and attempted to sing their songs before they were tossed out of the bars. They then tried street corners, backyards, amusement parks and the Staten Island Ferry, where they had a somewhat captive audience. They even won some amateur night prizes with their performances.

After two years the "Peewee Quartet" disbanded, but Nathan had fallen in love with show business and was determined to continue with his singing and dancing. Although George Burns's singing was the brunt of jokes, in fact young Nathan had a fine tenor voice. But as a child he contacted diphtheria, an illness that affects the throat and larynx. Although he recovered from the illness, it left him with a gravelly sounding voice. At some point his speech also began being punctuated by a slight stammer.

On occasion he attended school at P.S. 22 in New York City, but he quit in the fourth grade to help earn more money for his family. He was never a good student, was dyslexic, and showed little interest in school. Like his future wife, all young Nathan could think about was a career in show business.

Concentrating all of his time and energy on earning more money, Nathan worked on getting a booking for amateur night at the local Cannon Street picture house. He began a friendship with Abie Kaplan, whom he had met at the neighborhood's Hamilton Fish Park, where local dancers would meet to practice their dance steps. Nathan learned some additional dances from Abie, which he added to his repertoire and would show off at amateur shows.

It was about this time that Nathan would change his first name to George and his last name to Burns. The story he told about this name change is that "George" was borrowed from his older brother, who, disliking his own name of Isadore, changed it to George. The "Burns" came from the Burns Brothers Coal yard, where George and his friend Al "Burns" would pick up the coal that had fallen from the trucks and fill up their knickers to carry it home. Thus Nathan Birnbaum became George "Nat" Burns, later changing his name legally.

George and his friend worked together at local picture houses like Seiden's Theatre on Columbus Street where they pulled the house curtain up and down for the vaudeville acts. Motion picture production was increasing in the United States and films were becoming popular with public audiences. In the early 1900s picture houses would show a silent film feature on the same bill with live vaudeville acts. Grace Allen was singing at similar theaters in San Francisco during school vacations at this same time.

George's chum decided to leave show business, so George next joined up with an entertainer named Mac Fry. This act didn't last long, and George next became Williams of "Brown and Williams", a singing and dancing act. This partnership lasted long enough for George to earn enough money to buy a gold tooth to replace a missing tooth.

With no additional offers to team up with anyone else, thirteen-year-old George had to leave show business. He found work as a size ticket boy and later as a pattern cutter at various companies in the garment industry in New York City. But George did not have an interest in working at any job not connected with show business. He spent most of his time thinking of how to put a song and dance act together and entertaining audiences. Any time he could work in show business, George considered himself happy and on the road to success, even if it meant working in a song and dance act at the burlesque houses in the Bowery section of New York City. Although it was a rough and dangerous area of the city and he would become acquainted with various criminals, George was more interested in show business and trying out new dance steps and learning new songs than joining a gang and doing favors for gangsters. His mother also kept an eye on him, although she was afraid that he might become a criminal. She had cause to be concerned. Once during his youth George and his friends were used by gangsters to sing as a cover for the real activity when the police raided their illegal gambling houses. Always trying out new acts, George next teamed up with two friends, Hymie Goldberg and Nat Fields. The boys decided to do a singing and dancing act calling themselves "Goldie, Fields and Glide," which led to their entertaining audiences around New York City. The act was short-lived and the boys all went back to their regular jobs--except George--who was unemployed. He would sit in the waiting room of a booking agency and hope to hear news of a possible job.

This went on for a year or so until George was signed for a touring act named "The Fourth of July Kids." It was an imitation act based on the successful Gus Edwards Revues, whose players included future stars like Eddie Cantor and George Jessel. The nine boys and girls in the "Fourth of July Kids" sang, danced and performed in short sketches. George, who had a tendency to stutter on stage in front of an audience, was hired as a singer. According to George, he started using a cigar onstage at the age of fourteen because he needed something to do with his hands to overcome his stage fright. Unfortunately the young troup was left stranded by the manager on their first tour and the group disbanded.

Returning home to New York City, George, now in his mid-teens, was able to get a job as a dancing instructor at Bennie Bernstein's Dancing School at Second Street and Avenue B. George eventually became a partner in the business, which became B.B.'s College of Dancing and moved to Brooklyn. The school was soon closed by the police when they discovered that a robber had ditched his stolen property in the school there.

Even so, George decided to concentrate on his dancing, and started entering various dance hall contests around New York City. These contests were often Friday night exhibition dances. He had various women partners and usually teamed up with one he thought would help him win the contest. With one partner, Nettie Gold, he danced the Peabody, a popular dance of the day, and performed an "eccentric fox trot."

George later teamed up with Hannah Siegal. The two were so successful in winning dancing contests, that George decided they should tour in vaudeville. He named their act "José and Burns" (he had renamed Hannah, Hermosa José) for which they dressed in Spanish costumes. In recounting his early years in vaudeville, George said that the team received a booking for thirty-six weeks, but suddenly Hannah's parents insisted that she couldn't go on the road with him unless they were married. Ever practical, George and Hannah married, played the booking and were divorced and broke up the act upon their return to New York. (In his 1979 interview with Barbara Walters, George revealed that several years earlier he had called Hannah during a visit to New York and that they both got a kick out of her introducing him to her friends as her ex-husband). **SEE T528**.

Although not very successful, George was traveling around the country, playing in vaudeville theaters no matter how small the town. He became a trick roller skater and even filled in for three days working with a seal in the animal act "Flipper and Friend." In order to keep working, he was always changing his name as well as the act--anything to stay in show business.

But work wasn't consistent, and when a vaudeville job ended, George would return home to New York City. For a time he lived with a friend, Mike Marx, in the city. His mother and some of his sisters had moved into an apartment building on Eastern Parkway in Brooklyn.

In 1920, when in his early twenties, George met singer Sid Gary. They formed a vaudeville act which was successful enough to keep them employed and traveling for two years on the West Coast and in Loew's vaudeville circuits. It was when they were touring in Oklahoma City that George received the following comment in a review from the local newspaper, "George Burns has a nice gold tooth."

George and Sid decided to break up their partnership, and George next teamed up with New York singer Billy Lorraine. The two men formed the team of Nat Burns and Billy Lorraine, billing themselves as "The Two Broadway Thieves." They were at least honest. Their twelve-minute act consisted of impersonations of Broadway stars they had never seen on stage. Most of the audiences hadn't seen the stars either, so they didn't know that they weren't seeing an original act. Billy, as the singer, would do Al Jolson, Eddie Cantor and Harry Lauder; and George, as the dancer, would imitate the styles of George White and Eddie Leonard. The act finished with the two of them doing George M. Cohan (**B157: 347**). In 1921 Burns and Lorraine accepted a fourteen-week contract with the Pantages Circuit for $237.50 a week.

After a year, George and Billy decided to end their partnership. For some time, George had been collecting jokes from humor magazines such as **College Humor** and **Whiz Bang**. He was also thinking about forming a talking act with a female partner. George wasn't too worried about changing partners. In vaudeville, teams were always breaking up and it was fairly easy to find someone interested in joining an act.

~~~~~

Burns and Lorraine's last scheduled appearance as a team was in the fall of 1922 in Union Hill, New Jersey. Also on the bill was a comedienne named Rena Arnold, who was the
~~~~~

headliner in the act "Rena Arnold and Company." Between performances, George and Billy mentioned to Rena that they were ending their act and would be looking for other partners. Always joking and looking for laughs, George told Rena a risqué joke which she did not appreciate.

By chance, Rena's unemployed friend and roommate Grace Allen had skipped secretarial school that day to see Rena's act. Grace had been unable to find work in vaudeville for almost a year and was attending secretarial school. She was twenty-six years old, single, and had to think of her future--and it appeared not to be in show business. She had been able to stay in New York only because her family was sending her money. Grace realized that in order to stay in New York she had to get steady employment. Rena knew that her friend disliked the thought of becoming a secretary and wanted to get back into vaudeville. She mentioned to Grace Allen that Burns and Lorraine were splitting up and maybe Grace would want to work with Lorraine, the singer in the act. Although Billy was a stutterer when he spoke, and thus wouldn't be able to work in a talking act, Rena didn't think George "Nat" Burns would be a very good choice as a partner, considering his risqué jokes and manner. Grace went with her friend to watch the vaudeville show and afterwards Rena took her backstage to meet Burns and Lorraine.

In later years when discussing their first meeting, George described the petite 5-foot, 100-pound Grace Allen as "looking stringy and peaked from twelve workless months in New York...acted uppity and tossed her long black curls from her shoulders" when introduced to Burns and Lorraine. **SEE B392.**

Grace's impression of her future partner wasn't all glowing either--"George acted outrageously conceited over a split week engagement in a five-a-day grind house and wore a loud checked suit and used out of date slang." **SEE B392.**

But George was impressed by her, despite her "uppity" manner, and hoped that she would work with him in a new act. Grace had decided that she would rather try to work out an act with George than Billy, and they agreed to give it a try. George later phoned her to set up a time when they could get together and decide on an act. Grace did require one change--that George replace his gold tooth--before she would work with him.

Grace never did return to secretarial school. In fact, the owner of the school was quite perplexed at her abrupt disappearance. Five years later he saw Burns and Allen perform on a New York stage and his concerns were put to rest.

~~~~~

Grace Allen's years after graduation from the Star of the Sea School had been first spent in teaching young children to dance in the Allens' dancing school. As each sister had graduated from high school, she took over the management of their school. Her sisters were ready to turn over the school to Grace when her time came around after graduation. But Grace really wanted to be on the stage and did not look forward to teaching little girls how to dance as a lifetime vocation.

After a year or so of working in the dancing school, Grace was offered a part as one of the colleens in Irishman Larry Reilly's vaudeville act with Florence Printy. Reilly's act was becoming successful in touring the West Coast, performing Irish jigs and dances with some dramatic sketches
~~~~~

from Irish plays. Grace Allen was not a comedienne in the act but a dramatic stage actress.

Florence and another girl who also played in the act eventually quit to get married, and that left two openings for Larry Reilly to fill The act was getting ready to go on tour for several weeks and Grace's sisters and mother weren't too happy about her going around the country in a vaudeville act. So Bessie and Hazel quit their jobs, left Pearl in San Francisco to run the dancing school, and joined Grace in the "Larry Reilly and Company" act on the Keith Circuit. They would be touring in New England, the South and Midwest. Their tour started in Chicago at the Hippodrome where the three Allen sisters received favorable reviews from the local newspaper critics.

The act eventually made its way to the mecca of show business in America--New York City. Grace was elated. She had finally made it to Broadway. Although she was excited about being in show business, her sisters were not. They soon left the act and returned to San Francisco--Bessie to marry Ed Myers, a successful inventor, and Hazel to find secretarial work.

After a year or two touring with Larry Reilly and being billed as the part of the act titled "and Company", Grace was surprised to find that the "and Company" was left off the playbill when they were about to open at the U.S. Theater in Hoboken, New Jersey. She questioned Larry Reilly and said that she was going to quit the act if she did not get billing. When refused, Grace Allen quit on the spot and returned to New York City to contemplate working with someone else.

Many of her friends gave her advice on how to get a new act together. One of these friends was Ben (Benny) Ryan, a successful dancer, song writer and partner with his wife in the vaudeville comedy team of "Ryan and Lee."

Ryan wrote an act for Grace and she teamed up with some male dance partners who didn't seem to work out. One, named Boylan Brazil, constantly sent their trunks and scenery to the wrong town. While playing in Montreal, Canada, he lost the scenery they used in their act as well as Grace's trunk and the key to the trunk. She returned alone to New York City with only the dress she was wearing. She then had to wait two weeks before the officials at Grand Central Station would return her trunk, not sure she was the rightful owner as she had no identification.

The act that Benny Ryan had written had Grace playing the part of a young girl from the country named "Sally Simpkins." In the role she flirted with a city jewelry salesman and played the part of a dumb woman labeled a "dumb Dora." In this type of comedy act, the man would act as a straight man and the woman became the comedienne. The "dumb Dora" act initiated with Ryan and Lee around 1914. This vaudeville act was based on an earlier one from around the turn of the century, when the male-female vaudeville team of

> Wilbur Mack and Nella Walker started a new craze called the 'bench act'... where they would do flirtation stuff, exchange wisecracks and finish up with a neat song and dance...Their act was copied by many and started a trend that led to making 'funny women' without funny clothes. Later, Ryan and Lee,

> Laurie and Bronson brought a new type of mixed act to vaude--a dumb girl type of comedienne and a smart cracking, straight man, depending on cross-fire comedy using a song and dance finish."
> **SEE B295: 228.**

This would be the basis for the comedic style that Burns and Allen would adopt. George Burns took credit for putting together the act for Burns and Allen, but it is interesting to note the personal relationship of Benny Ryan and Grace Allen, who would become engaged sometime before the meeting of George Burns and Grace Allen in late 1922, and the possible influence he may have had on the beginning of the "Burns and Allen" vaudeville act.

Benny Ryan was formerly the dancing partner of George White, (i.e., of "George White's Scandals"). Their teaming had some success in vaudeville in the early 1900s. In 1911, Ryan teamed up with Harriet Lee, a young woman who had been working in musical comedy. They toured the country in vaudeville but it wasn't until 1914 that their comedy skit, called "You've Spoiled It," brought the team success. The act included songs, comedy and dancing and was described as being different from other traditional vaudeville comedy teams. They included some physical comedy in their act, evident by a publicity photo of the time which shows Harriet ready to hit Ryan, who looks like he has already lost the fight, with his hair mussed, his right hand up above his head in surrender, and his hat under Miss Lee's shoe. What made their act different from others was the cross talk between the two, both of whom were acting the part of comedians, and their song and dance finish.

Harriet Lee was an attractive woman who wore fashionable clothes when performing on stage. This was unusual for comediennes of the day, who were mostly loud and dressed outrageously for their performances. Harriet also spoke in a type of baby talk, which a **Variety** reviewer found irritating in a December 8, 1916, review of the "Ryan and Lee" act. But they went on to play in B. F. Keith's famous New York City's Palace Theater that same year to applauding audiences and soon became known as one of the most successful vaudeville comedy teams of the day using the "dumb Dora" characterization.

Ryan and Lee married, but by 1918 their act and marriage seemed to be in trouble as Ryan walked out after a matinee performance at the Colonial Theater in New York City (**New York Star**, September 11. 1918). They would eventually divorce but would reunite for a radio broadcast in 1937. Ryan would also be at his ex-wife's bedside when she died of pneumonia in a New York hospital in 1943. He would continue to work as a song and contract writer for films and a writer of special material for comedians until his death in 1968. Some of the songs he wrote were "The Gang that Sang Heart of My Heart," "Inka Dinka Doo," "M-I-S-S-I-S-S-I-P-P-I," and "When Frances Dances with Me."

Many acts borrowed from Ryan and Lee's characterizations. Seemingly, Burns and Allen were among them or at least shared some of the Ryan and Lee commonalities in their act. The smart dress style of Gracie Allen (on and off stage), her baby-talk voice, George Burns as the straight man, and Gracie Allen as the "dumb Dora" who got all of the laughs are all reminiscent of "Ryan and Lee." In their early days as a team,

"Burns and Allen" would be noted by one reviewer as a comedy team who worked like "Ryan and Lee" (**Variety**, March 3, 1927).

~~~~~

When George "Nat" Burns arrived on time at the thirty-dollar-a-week apartment Grace shared with Rena Arnold and her new friend Mary Kelly in the Hotel Endicott in New York City, Grace Allen was astonished and told her friends that this one must be all right as he was actually there and at the time when he said he would be. She had been disappointed so often with teaming up with bad partners that she wasn't really expecting George to show up and ask her to form an act.

Grace had an act she wanted them to use. It was the "Sally Simpkins" act written for her by Benny Ryan. But it required scenery, which neither she nor George had nor could afford to purchase. Instead they decided on George's idea for an act as it didn't require any stage scenery or props. He had been thinking of doing a comedy act in which he would be the comedian and his female partner would act as a "straight man" and feed him the jokes.

They rehearsed for the next few weeks, sometimes in music publishers' rehearsal halls. George was unsure of Grace as a potential partner. She did not seem to rehearse very well and had a thick Irish brogue, which she had picked up while working in the act with Larry Reilly. In that act she had over emphasized her normal Irish speech by learning stage Irish. George was concerned that the audience wouldn't be able to understand her when she spoke. Also, compared with George's experience in vaudeville, Grace Allen had very little. She had started performing at a young age, but had only really worked full time in vaudeville with her sisters as "The Allen Sisters", a year or so with Larry Reilly in a one-act sketch and a few other acts.

In his autobiography (**B396**) actor/comedian Benny Rubin, who was a good friend of Benny Ryan's, notes that Grace Allen worked with Benny as a dancer during a period of time when Harriet Lee was ill. Other acts in which Grace Allen may have been a participant cannot be documented. Exactly what she did from the time she left San Francisco around 1915 or 1916 to 1922 when she met George Burns in New York City can only be generalized.

But in 1922, George was prepared to take a gamble, and after about three weeks of rehearsing, he and Grace were ready to put the act to a test. They were signed for their first booking as a team. Billed as George N. Burns and Grace Allen in "Sixty-Forty." George felt that it was his act and he should get first billing. The "Sixty-Forty" had no meaning according to George, although he admitted that he was going to get sixty percent of their salary and Grace forty percent because he had written the act and thought he was of more value to the team. This was to change later to a fifty-fifty split, when it was obvious that Grace Allen was the secret of the team's success.

Their first appearances as a team were in Newark (the Hill Theater) and Boonton, New Jersey. During these first apppearances on a stage, the audiences continued to react the same way. They laughed at Grace's high-pitched voice and delivery more than they did at George's jokes. He was dressed the part as a comedian in baggy pants, short coat and a swivel
~~~~~

tie. This was similar to the outfit worn by comedian Joe E. Brown, which George had copied. Grace, as the straight woman in the act, wore a nice dress. She only owned two at the time, one for daily wear and the other for her stage appearances. She had grown up dressing well (her mother made most of her stage and dance costumes when she was a child) and didn't change this aspect of her person just for show business.

After several other performances, it became evident to George that he would have to relinquish his role as the jokester in the act. Grace was getting more laughs with her straight lines than he was in acting as the comedian. George decided to write lines to make Gracie the comedic character. Now "Gracie Allen" became the scatterbrained woman and George the suffering boyfriend in their comedy act. It was their audiences which led to Grace Allen becoming "Gracie Allen." George Burns often remarked that it was the "audience which finds the character for you. Grace had a funny delivery on stage--she was very sharp, quick and cute and they laughed at her straight lines--and they didn't laugh at my jokes." **SEE B497: 137**.

During these years and lasting until the 1930s the team was billed as George N. Burns (or George Nat Burns) and Grace (later Gracie) Allen. In real life his wife always called George "Nat" or "Nattie" as his real name was Nathan. After their marriage, George nicknamed Gracie "Googie."

The new team played in any theater that would give them a job, and stayed mostly on the East Coast. "Burns and Allen" in 1923 were among those "disappointment acts" (also known as a "dissy act), which were called on short notice to fill in when the booked act wasn't able to appear. They would wait in their separate hotel rooms on Monday and Thursday nights for a phone call which would hopefully have a job offer at the other end. Then they would hop on a bus or train to the town or city where they would perform. Automobiles weren't always reliable transportation in the 1920s as evidenced by a stamped notice on a contract Burns and Allen signed in February 25, 1926: "As motoring to your next stand is liable to delay your arrival in time to fulfill your contract, artists will please take the trains." However, they were also advised not to rely on the railroad for "prompt transportation of equipment" and were requested to carry enough with them to open their engagements on the scheduled time. Finding just the right mode of travel in those days could be very confusing.

And travel they did. Although Burns and Allen would find success in vaudeville near its decline, there were still over 4,000 theaters across the country and Canada where some 20,000 vaudeville artists could find work. **SEE B400: 4**.

Small time vaudevillians, like Burns and Allen in 1923, signed weekly contracts, if they were lucky, for three or four shows a day. The big time artists were offered and signed long-term contracts with the larger vaudeville promoters and played on theater circuits. The bigger star you were the fewer shows you played--only two a day--and your salary was higher. Burns and Allen started at five dollars a day and would play for many years averaging $350 a week for the team. They had to pay their agents and all transportation costs, and barely broke even at the end of the month. They lived in separate rooms all around the country when touring, and when returning to New York City, they rented rooms at hotels like the Coolidge or the Princeton. When they received a new booking they started the routine again--traveling to different vaudeville houses, playing the bill and moving on to the next town or city.

It was far from a glamorous life, and only those hopelessly in love with show business could put up with the vagaries of the business and the responsibilities heaped upon their heads. The Fire Prevention Bureau in Chicago required that all scenery be fireproof and declared that "artists will hereafter not be permitted to present their act in Chicago unless they have complied with the law." Those who played the Orpheum circuit were forbidden to perform within fifty miles of any city where an Orpheum theater was located at anytime between the date of their next contract and the date of their last engagement. Showing up late for rehearsals could result in overtime pay for the orchestra being deducted from the artist's pay. Acts had to provide their own photos, billing, and advertising material; if they failed to do so the Photo and Press Bureau would obtain the materials and, again, deduct the cost from their pay. If the venue was changed the manager would pick up the extra transportation charges, but any extra stagehands, electricity, or props were provided at the artist's expense. The artist was strictly an independent contract and not an employee of the booking agency.

Performers could also be obligated to turn down radio concerts or radio broadcasts during the period of their contracts. By this time George, who always said he performed under a variety of names in his early days in vaudeville, had even more reason to be thankful he had teamed up with Gracie. Contracts could include a stipulation that "said act has never...played or advertised under any other name than the name set forth above." Acts were booked nearly a year in advance at times, but it could be one or two months--or a day. And, finally, no matter how many cinders blew in the artist's eyes on those train trips, they had to keep their sheet music tucked safely away, because their contract required them to "furnish clean and complete orchestration of music for two first violins, a second violin, viola, cello, bass, flute, clarinet, cornet, trombone, drums, and piano." One of the few protections the artist received, and it was double-edged, was that "No statement or promise by the manager or its representative or the Artist or his representative concerning the Artist's position on the bill, dressing room, advertising or any other thing...should be binding on the Artist or the Circuit unless endorsed in writing on the face of the contract."

In the 1920s the largest chain of vaudeville theaters in North America was owned by promoters B. F. Keith and his manager (later chief executive), Edward F. Albee. Their three major theater circuit competitors were the Orpheum, Pantages and Loew's. Next in importance were the smaller vaudeville talent promoters like Gus Sun, Fally Markus, and B. S. Moss, whose artists often played only one-a-day (one show per day) bills in small towns. In 1927 the monopoly of the Keith-Albee circuit become even more powerful when they merged with the Orpheum theaters, forming the Keith-Albee-Orpheum circuit. Burns and Allen received their first booking as a team through Fally Markus. They would eventually sign contracts with all of the major promoters, performing at theaters on vaudeville circuits ranging from the East to West coasts.

These larger chains had some theaters that could seat several hundred people. By 1911, there were twenty-six vaudeville theaters in New York City alone, with most seating over 1,000. Keith and Proctor's at 58th Street, could seat 2,000 at a time when ticket prices ranged from 5 cents to $1.50. **SEE B323: 47.**

The standard vaudeville show was structured and consisted of eight acts. The opening number would always be a nonspeaking act, like animals or acrobatics, because the audiences were just coming into the theater and wouldn't be able to hear a talking act. Then two or three acts followed, generally a fast-talking comedy or a dancing act. This wasn't considered a good spot on the bill. Next came the headliner, right before intermission. After the break there would be several acts before the closing number, the worst spot to be on the bill, because the audience was leaving the theater at this time. In the years he played in vaudeville before teaming up with Gracie, George was usually the second act on a bill, and performed only twelve minutes. The better acts did seventeen minutes and were listed on a higher spot on the show. Burns and Allen also played in "one," which was the front of a stage in front of the curtain, nearest the audience.

In 1923 Burns and Allen's first vaudeville act was one in which Gracie would play the role of a "dumb Dora." In the act she wasn't smart and misunderstood almost everything. "Sixty-Forty" started with Gracie coming onto a dark stage with a spotlight following her movements. She was looking for George. He entered from the dark and Gracie started telling him how "low" he was. George remained silent throughout her complaining about him. She finally stopped talking to ask George why he wasn't saying anything. George replied with two words "hello babe." The laughs were based on how he delivered these two words and George worried about it constantly. He worried so much that one afternoon while playing at the Columbia Theater in New York City he was speechless when it came time to say his lines. Gracie just carried on without his saying a word. She was a natural on the stage and seemed to be able to carry the team. George felt that he wasn't very good and this type of performance only emphasized his faults. But Gracie stuck by him and eventually he would improve his delivery and overcome his stage fright and stuttering.

Personally, George and Gracie got along well. In fact, George was in love with her, but he wouldn't tell her this because he was afraid she would quit the act. She was engaged to marry Benny Ryan, who was pressing her to quit and marry him. Mary Kelly noted that

> it was obvious from the very first that he was head over heels in love with Gracie. He waited on her hand and foot. Half the time she didn't know at what theater they were playing. George did everything but carry her there. After he had arranged a booking for them, he would phone Gracie, tell her when to start for the theater, what subway to take, where to get off, where the stage entrance was and the number of her dressing room. Once a week they'd go dancing at a night club. As they grew to know each other better, they would have dinner together every night--but Gracie was very strict about paying her check, unless George had

invited her out. **SEE B267**.

Gracie kept putting the wedding date off with Benny Ryan. With more experience, the team of Burns and Allen improved and they began to play in better vaudeville theaters like the Fifth Avenue in New York City and the Bushwick in Brooklyn. This last theater is where, for the first time, Burns and Allen were booked to play a two-a-day (two shows) theater. They were having some success with the audiences and now thought that they had finally broken through to the big time. There would be no more days of three and four shows a day. The next week they were booked into the Orpheum Theater in Brooklyn and, for the first time, not as a "disappointment act."

But it led to a big disappointment. Ethel Barrymore, the great stage actress, was headlining the bill in the "Twelve Pound Look." Legitimate stage actors often toured in vaudeville--it helped keep them in front of the public eye and they were often paid huge salaries. Burns and Allen were booked next to closing after Miss Barrymore and it proved disastrous. The audiences came to see the stage star and got up to leave after she performed. So, when Burns and Allen came on stage, the audiences were leaving and making so much noise that no one could hear the act. Eventually, George and Gracie didn't even bother to go on the stage--they just sat in their dressing rooms until everyone else had left the theater.

After this experience, they found that they were back on the road as a "disappointment act." The big break that they were looking for had not come with the Orpheum Theater booking.

A revealing look at Gracie's personality was brought out around this time. George had received a phone call that offered them more money than they had ever been offered, $450 a week, to play the Cosmos Theater in Washington, D.C. But when he told Gracie, she said no. He would have to cancel the booking. She later explained that she didn't want to play in that theater because her sister Hazel Boyston's husband was just starting out in the diplomatic service in Washington D. C. and they might be embarrassed by having a sister playing in vaudeville. As throughout the centuries, theatrical players were thought of as lower class citizens. Signs still were posted in some towns saying they would not rent rooms to actors. George was from a poverty background, which was common among vaudevillians. In fact, many were orphans with no history of family and had grown up in slum neighborhoods (**B400: 5**). Fellow vaudevillians were their family and the true vaudevillian's life and personality was unlike that of the average person. George Burns was a true vaudevillian, but Gracie Allen was not. She was a young woman who had grown up loving performing on stage, but it wasn't the major emphasis in her life--it was her job.

In their personal lives, Gracie was still engaged to Benny Ryan, but he was often out on tour which was fine with her partner. When Ryan was out of town, George and Gracie would often double date with her roommate Mary Kelly and Mary's boyfriend, comedian Jack Benny. Jack and George had been friends since their first meeting in 1921 and they would become lifelong best friends. Like Gracie, Mary was an Irish Roman Catholic, and Jack, like George, was Jewish. Mary and Jack came close to marrying but their different faiths, among other personal reasons, eventually led to the end of their relationship.

In 1924 Gracie was ready to marry Benny Ryan and break up the act with George. George was crushed. He was about to lose not only the woman he loved but also a great partner who was leading the couple to success in vaudeville. But his luck held. They were offered a multiweek tour on the Orpheum circuit, which would include the San Francisco Orpheum theater. It had been Gracie's lifelong wish to play that theater in her hometown. But she was confused about marrying Benny Ryan and giving up her career with George. Mary Kelly, who liked George and thought Gracie would be better off with him than Benny, tried to push Gracie into going on the tour with George. She kept suggesting to Gracie that she would get her wish to play the Orpheum in San Francisco and could then return to New York and marry Ryan.

Before any contracts were signed, with Mary Kelly's help, George was able to get the team of Burns and Allen four hundred dollars a week, fifty dollars more than they had been making. Mary was dating the Orpheum booker, Ray Myers (they later married), and was able to get the raise by telling Ray she wouldn't date him again unless he gave Burns and Allen the extra money.

Gracie was now in a spot and felt she couldn't say no to the tour, but she had a hard time convincing Benny Ryan to put off the wedding date for several months. They were supposed to be married the day that she and George were leaving to start the tour. At New York City's Grand Central Station, George and Jack Benny waited for Gracie to show up. She finally did arrive--running--as the train was pulling out from the station. George realized that he was very lucky and that he had to make the most of this tour--not only to save the team of "Burns and Allen," but to convince Gracie to marry him.

The Orpheum circuit began in Vancouver, Canada, and continued down the West Coast to California. Weeks passed and in May, 1924 Burns and Allen were booked into the Oakland Orpheum Theater before going on to San Francisco across the bay. But Gracie became ill and had to be rushed to the hospital. She was diagnosed with appendicitis and had emergency surgery. The Orpheum booking had to be cancelled as well as the next five weeks of dates while Gracie recovered. Luckily, she became ill near her hometown and her family was able to help her. After the hospital stay, she went home to convalesce at her mother's home in San Francisco.

When she fell ill, Gracie knew that George would be hard pressed for money during the time she was recovering as he would not be working, so she arranged to have him stay at her family's home. It allowed George to have Gracie's complete attention. Also, she didn't hear from Benny Ryan because he was still angry with her for walking out on him right before their wedding.

After Gracie's recovery, Burns and Allen continued their Orpheum tour, picking it up in July at the Golden Gate Theatre in San Francisco on their way back East. At first, Gracie left out the dancing segment of their routine due to her recent surgery and the act was criticized by some critics for the omission. The tour ended in New York City around Christmastime.

The new year saw Burns and Allen continue to perform around the East Coast, and in March, 1925 they began a twenty-five week tour on the Loew's circuit. On this tour they were booked in New York, Massachusetts, Rhode Island, Pennsylvania, Alabama, Louisiana, Illinois, Wisconsin, New Jersey, Tennessee, Canada, Georgia, New Jersey and Ohio.

Always thinking of new ways to improve their act, George was working on a new seventeen-minute act he planned to name "Lamb Chops" after a joke in their vaudeville routine written by jewelry salesman Al Boasberg, who was on his way to becoming one of the top vaudeville comedy writers--later moving on to radio. It was quite popular during the late 1920s to do jokes about women's appetites, and "Lamb Chops" was tailor-made for the times. George had worked with Al on the new act. He was excited about the script as well as about being considered a serious suitor in Gracie's eyes. He continued to propose to Gracie about once a week to no avail. But his hopes were dashed when he learned that she still was planning to marry Benny Ryan and break up the act when they returned to New York City at the end of their Loew's contract in November, 1925. In desperation, he gave her an ultimatum the week before Christmas--either marry him or *he* would break up the act.

At a Christmas Eve party with their friends, George was admittedly not in the best of humor, knowing that Gracie had been late to the party because she had been waiting for a call from Benny. When he mocked Gracie's gift card that read, "To Nattie, with all my love," by accusing her of not even knowing what love meant, a tearful Gracie fled the room and George left the party. Before the sun rose on that Christmas morning, Gracie phoned George to say she would marry him. A few hours earlier, when Benny Ryan had phoned her to ask why she hadn't called to wish him Merry Christmas, Gracie had broken off their engagement. After talking it over with Mary Kelly, she realized it was George she loved, not Benny. George had been carrying around a little ring that he was ready to give Gracie anytime she accepted his proposal. The day Gracie said "yes" was the happiest day of George's life. Gracie's decision affected not only their personal lives, it ensured that the professional pairing of "Burns and Allen" would continue. **SEE B22, T528.**

After learning of the couple's decision to marry, George's and Gracie's mothers both approved of the forthcoming marriage. Coming from an Orthodox Jewish background, it would not have been surprising for George's mother to object to his marriage to an Irish Roman Catholic. Even though George was twenty-nine years old and Gracie thirty, they were concerned that their families might not approve of the mixed marriage. But both of their mothers seemed to leave this decision to the couple. In future interviews George often noted that Gracie was a "nice girl" for the three years they traveled together as vaudeville partners before their marriage. "But I don't think either her parents or mine gave us the benefit of the doubt. You know how it is when people of the theater travel together. The outside world always imagines the worst (**B73**)." Gracie would remain a practicing Roman Catholic throughout her life. Years later George remarked that his religion was to "be nice to other people and be ready when they play your music." **SEE B22: 64.**

At this important time in their personal lives, Burns and Allen continued to perfect their new act, "Lamb Chops." George and Gracie were already booked into some small towns in

Ohio for several weeks on the Gus Sun Time and were anxious to get audience's reactions to lines like:

George: "Do you like to love?"
Gracie: "No".
George: "Do you like to kiss?"
Gracie: "No".
George: "What do you like?"
Gracie: "Lamb chops."

On January 7, 1926, near the end of their five-week tour in Ohio, George and Gracie arrived in Cleveland around five o'clock in the morning after sitting up in a "milk run" train all night. After catching a taxi to the Statler Hotel they waited in the hotel lobby for two hours for the next day's rates to go into effect before they could check in. They then rushed off to get married at the Cleveland City Hall. Mary Kelly and George's brother Isadore and his family, who lived in Ohio, arrived at the hotel for a wedding celebration. The Burnses had a three-day honeymoon before continuing their vaudeville tour. Accoring to George, the wedding ring he had bought for Gracie cost twenty dollars (**B22**). She wore it until the day she died.

On January 11th they began a short week at the Colonial Theater in Detroit where the audience kept them on stage for thirty-four minutes. The theater manager sent in a glowing report about the act to B.F. Keith's offices in Syracuse, New York. Burns and Allen were then asked to appear in Syracuse with their *new* act "Lamb Chops." At the same time, a theater in Pittsburg, Pennsylvania, wanted the team to perform their old established act there. George took a chance and accepted the Syracuse offer. Burns and Allen arrived to find their names on the outside marquee of the Keith theater. Ironically, their friends Larry Reilly and Rena Arnold were appearing at the theater the same week in different acts. Burns and Allen presented their new act "Lamb Chops" for one week at the Keith Syracuse and broke all house records.

The week of February 24, 1926, saw them booked into the Jefferson Theater on 44th Street in New York City, which was known for tough audiences who sometimes threw objects at the performers if they didn't like them. But Burns and Allen were a success with their new act, and between the first and second shows they were offered a five-year contract with the Keith-Orpheum Circuit, the longest vaudeville contract ever offered up to that time, for a minimum of forty weeks a year. Their salaries for 1926-1927 would be three hundred seventy-five to four hundred dollars a week, with a guaranteed four of twenty weeks to be played at three hundred fifty dollars. They signed their new contract as "George N. Burns and Grace Allen, individually and as copartners doing business under the firm name and style of Burns and Allen of Hotel Claridge, Broadway and 44th Street, New York." For his wife's birthday in July, George held a large party for Gracie in the ballroom of Castle Edward, at a summer resort overlooking Lake Hopatcong in New Jersey. With friends like Mary Kelly and Jack Benny, George and Gracie had often visited there on weekend outings.

~~~~~

A few months after their marriage, Burns and Allen finally received the booking that every vaudevillian hoped
~~~~~

for--the Palace Theater in New York City at 47th Street and Broadway, the greatest theater in vaudeville, which featured the biggest names in show business. Burns and Allen played there for the first time on August 23, 1926. They were now working alongside the top acts in vaudeville.

Having signed their new contract, the Keith-Orpheum vaudeville circuit had the team booked in dozens of different theaters in 1926. For the next few years Burns and Allen played in B. F. Keith vaudeville theaters across the country. Sometimes they played at one theater for a week and other times they had split weeks, with three or four days at each theater, before moving on to the next city. Burns and Allen received mostly glowing reviews from the local newspapers, such as this one in May 1927 when they were signed with the Keith-Orpheum circuit:

> "The first note of the sort I have ever written to any artist since I have been (a) reviewer of shows...swing around the (Portland, Oregon) Orpheum again sometime and keep me from being bored to death by other team acts."

"Lamb Chops" was a clean act (many vaudeville theaters forbade profanity anyway as well as the use of liquor and drugs and cancelled acts who didn't comply), with funny jokes based on the "suffering" George and the "scatterbrained" Gracie, who always answered everything seriously, adding to the humor. Her delivery of lines and personal appearance made the audiences fall in love with her, which helped to lead to their success as a team. It was Gracie who was noticed, not George. To audiences, George's only purpose in being on stage with Gracie seemed to be to feed her lines, as she was the one who got the laughs. In recounting this period of their work as a comedy team, George always said that it was Gracie who carried the act.

But George was responsible for making the business arrangements and taking care of the behind-the-scenes work for their act, which was an important part of making Burns and Allen successful performers. Burns and Allen had a personal routine when they arrived in a town for a performance. As George was always concerned with their billing, the music being correct, etc., he would send Gracie ahead to the hotel with the luggage, and he would head straight to the theater to check the arrangements with the manager. He protected Gracie from all of these concerns so that she simply went to the theaters and performed. As they became more sucessful, Willy Burns, George's brother who was working in the insurance business, was asked by his older brother to help Burns and Allen on their business decisions.

In October 1928 the Radio Corporation of America (RCA) purchased the Keith-Albee-Orpheum circuit; and, upon the merger, Radio-Keith-Orpheum (RKO) was born with the purpose of introducing motion pictures into vaudeville theaters. Edward F. Albee's name did not survive the corporate intertwining.

In 1929 Burns and Allen received an offer to perform in London's Palladium Theatre. Gracie was excited about what would be their first trip abroad. They played their last RKO date stateside and then sailed from New York City to Southhampton, England, for their first show in London, scheduled for the end of February.

Upon arrival, George discovered that they were allotted only eleven minutes for their act. He tried to get more time for their entire sketch, but was unsuccessful. Nevertheless, this didn't hurt their acceptance by the British audiences as the "American Musical Comedy Couple."

At first, some of their lines from "Lamb Chops" didn't get the laughs they'd had with American audiences. It seemed that the English didn't know what lamp chops were--they called them lamb cutlets. So George changed a few words in their routine to fit the British meanings. They received good reviews, though at times the columnists commented more on the expensive and elegant dresses Gracie wore on stage than on their act.

Burns and Allen performed at several London theaters in addition to the Palladium, including the Alhambra in Leicester Square and the Coliseum in Charing Cross, and also in night clubs and cafés such as Chez Henri and the Trocadero Restaurant. They also performed in other cities in England, Scotland, and Wales.

It was on this first tour in 1929 that Burns and Allen were introduced to radio broadcasting. Commercial radio stations had been increasing in numbers in the United States since 1920. In 1922 the British Broadcasting Company (BBC) had been formed in Great Britain. Seven years later in 1929 variety performers were broadcasting three or four times a week on the BBC.

Burns and Allen were a success the moment they made their first appearances in England. As their comedy had been so well received, they were asked to perform five broadcasts on the BBC radio show **Vaudeville**. On June 10, 1929, at 8:41 P.M., broadcasting from Savoy Hill, London, they were introduced as the "American Musical Comedy Duo." They presented thirteen minutes of "Lamb Chops" and sang the song "I Do," which was part of the routine. **SEE B385**.

They were asked back the next week, and the weeks stretched into months as they continued their broadcasts for the BBC. They would return to the broadcast studio each week to transmit their act across the radio air waves to different regions throughout Great Britain.

George realized that this was a new entertainment medium that they needed to try to break into. Motion pictures and radio were fast replacing vaudeville as the main entertainment media. Burns and Allen had unfortunately found success at the beginning of the end of vaudeville. As early as 1913, a survey taken in Waltham, Massachusetts, illustrated that weekly attendance at silent moving picture shows was almost the same as attendance at vaudeville and burlesque theaters (**B323**: **88**). By the early 1920s the feature film was becoming standard in cities and towns across the nation. In the 1927-1928 season over 1,900 films were released in the United States, almost one-third were comedy shorts (**B289**: **115**). These comedy one-reelers were produced by motion picture companies such as the Educational Film Corporation of America, Warner Bros. and Sennett.

After a successful long-term engagement in Great Britain, (which they would repeat by returning for several summer seasons in the 1930s) George and Gracie came home to New York City in October 1929.

As guests at a party soon after they arrived home, they met theatrical agent Arthur Lyons. He mentioned that an actor was needed to replace an ailing Fred Allen, who was to start filming a motion picture short the next day at the Warner Bros. Vitaphone Studios for short subjects on Long Island. The actor would have to appear the next morning with a nine minute act for which he would be paid $1,700. George immediately said that Burns and Allen would be willing to accept such an offer and Lyons gave them the job.

After Gracie learned of the agreement, she didn't want to go. Her experience was on the stage, not in film. George had to convince her to do it, knowing that it wouldn't work without her performance. Although they were both very apprehensive, they arrived at the studio the next day and had to improvise their performance because the set's hotel room scenery did not fit their act, which was supposed to be taking place on a street corner. This first film short was titled **Burns and Allen in Lamb Chops** (**F1**) and consisted of lines from their vaudeville act. George would ask Gracie a question and she would have a "dumb Dora" answer. Then they would sing and dance in between the dialogue. At the end of this short, George tells Gracie to "get off" and nudges her offstage out of camera range.

Warner Bros. was not impressed by their performance and did not offer them a contract for another motion picture short. But after receiving $1,700 for less than ten minutes work, George wanted to make more film appearances. So he worked on a script, which became **Fit To Be Tied** (**F2**), and tried to sell it to another studio. Paramount Studios bought it and George and Gracie made this film short later that year. In it Gracie sings to George, who wants to ask her for a date, and after the nine-minute film is over, Burns and Allen can't decide how to end the scene. They stop acting and speak to each other as performers, making it evident that they had just given a performance and now were speaking to each other outside of the storyline. George looks at the camera, and tells Gracie to just say "goodbye" to the audience by looking at the camera. This ending would later develop into "Say good night, Gracie," which was Burns and Allen's closing remark for many of their radio and television shows and would become a famous "catch phrase" identified with the team. (Contrary to some reports, however, Gracie does not parrot him; she merely smiles sweetly and says, "good night.")

In 1929, with George and Gracie three years into their Keith-Orpheum (now RKO) vaudeville circuit contract, Paramount-Publix, the leading theater operating company in the world with over twelve hundred theaters, signed Burns and Allen to a three-year contract to make four film shorts a year for the studio. The team would eventually make fourteen film shorts for Paramount at their East Coast Studios in Astoria, Long Island, New York. (Years later those shorts, along with hundreds of others, were sold to UM&M TV Corp. for $3 million.) Theaters were increasingly showing motion pictures on the same stage as vaudeville shows and there was a growing business enterprise in producing film shorts. During these early years in film a theater would present a ten-minute film short followed by a vaudeville show. Actors like Burns and Allen were sometimes performing in vaudeville theaters at the same time that their film shorts were being viewed at a nearby theater. On at least one occasion Burns and Allen were performing in a vaudeville theater at the same time one of their film shorts was being shown across the street at another theater, their names on both marquees.

Although Burns and Allen had become very popular and were finding some success in the film industry as actors, their vaudeville contract at times prevented them from doing other work. One example was when they were offered the parts of Eva Puck and Sammy White in a theatrical production of **Showboat** but could not get out of their vaudeville obiligations to play on the stage.

By 1931 Burns and Allen had played the Palace Theater in New York City several times, appearing with top vaudeville headliners such as Eddie Cantor and George Jessel. One evening that same year George was asked if Gracie would remain another week to act as mistress of ceremonies, the first woman asked to perform in that role. George said no, as it would mean that they would have to change their act. He mentioned turning down the booking to George Jessel, a good friend, who immediately left to phone the Palace booker that Burns and Allen had decided to accept the offer. He returned to tell George that he had accepted on their behalf as the opportunity was too great for the team to reject.

George and Gracie were fearful of changing their act. Vaudevillians performed the same act for years once they had one that was successful. But with Jessel's acceptance for them they had no choice but to agree to change their act. George did a little thinking and went back to Al Boasberg, who had already brought them success in "Lamb Chops." They included more jokes and worked on developing Gracie's stage character. The routine included lines like:

> George: "Gracie, you're dizzy."
> Gracie: "I know I'm dizzy."
> George: "You're the only dizzy girl I know that's glad she's dizzy."
> Gracie: "I'm glad I'm a dizzy girl because boys like dizzy girls and I like boys."
>
> ("Dizzy" routine, January 18, 1933 radio script, Burns and Allen.)

At the end of their performance George would ask the orchestra leader for "music," he and Gracie would dance a little, George would say "stop" and he would tell a joke. This went on for a few lines and ended with the team dancing off the stage. This same waltz-talk routine had flopped with audiences just a few years before, but now it was met with applause. The audiences certainly *should* have been applauding considering how much talent their money was buying. In January 1931 a vaudeville show ticket in San Francisco cost thirty cents (fifteen cents for children) if a patron visited the theater between 11:00 A.M. and 1:00 P.M.

The merits of the Boasberg-Burns and Allen collaboration are apparent in this March 25, 1931, review by **Variety** of the new seventeen-minute routine. The writer first noted the success of the earlier "Lamb Chops" routine by Al Boasberg. Almost deceptively simple at first glance, "Lamb Chops" had been an audience pleaser for several years on both sides of the Atlantic Ocean. The combination of Burns and Allen's "showmanlike" delivery and Boasberg's writing had apparently produced another winner:

> The new offering, presented along similar lines, with Grace Allen the dumb-dora,

is, however, without any props but stronger than the previous act.

That same year, on October 31, 1931, billed as "America's Foremost Conversation Act," Burns and Allen returned to the Palace to join headliners Eddie Cantor and George Jessel in a nine-week engagement that would break all records for its length of run and box office receipts (averaging $35,000 a week). It was the last straight vaudeville show at the Palace Theater and helped mark the end of vaudeville. It was also Burns and Allen's last weeks on their RKO contract, which had apparently been extended by one year at some point during their original five-year agreement. Two weeks after the end of the booking the Palace Theater closed. A **Variety** review commented on Gracie's appearance as well as her acting: "Shy Gracie Allen, with a nice new dress that doesn't fit as expertly as its demure predecessors, remains the most facile and subtle of all vaudeville's dumb ladies." **SEE B338**.

~~~~~

With the closing of the Palace Theater, it was clear that vaudevillians who wanted to continue their livelihood would have to penetrate another area of show business. In addition to moving pictures, radio was leading to vaudeville's demise. The National Broadcasting Company (NBC), part of the Radio Corporation of America (RCA), began broadcasting from the East Coast of the United States on November 15, 1926. A second NBC network began six weeks later. By 1931 more stations were operating across the United States and talent was needed for the shows. The first stars of radio were former vaudevillians. Going to a radio broadcast soon became an event, and some vaudeville theater managers persuaded audiences to purchase a ticket for a stage show by offering them a free ticket for a radio broadcast.

Burns and Allen had tried to enter American radio after their success in broadcasting for the BBC in Great Britain, but they were turned down. Some broadcasters felt that the team had only a seventeen-minute act and would not be able to come up with material for a weekly radio show. Other advertisers felt that Gracie's high-pitched, childlike voice, although unique, would not be tolerated by audiences. Gracie used a stage voice that was about an octave higher than her real voice. In a 1935 study of sex differences in radio voices, results showed that "contralto voices were preferred by audiences...and that most comediennes...have voices that are low pitched and that female voices which gave the impression of culture and refinement were not popular" (**B115**: **137**). Gracie's voice didn't fit either category, yet hers became one of radio's most popular and easily recognizable.

In 1931 Eddie Cantor and Rudy Vallee were two top entertainers who hosted popular radio variety shows featuring various guest performers. After the successful Palace Theater nine-week run, Cantor had asked several of the performers from that Palace bill, including Burns and Allen, to join his stage show in various venues. Burns and Allen were still under contract to RKO but were granted permission to join this show.

It was during this tour that Cantor asked George if Gracie would appear on his **Chase & Sanborn Hour** radio show. George said yes, but only if Cantor would let Gracie use material that George had written. He agreed and on Sunday,
~~~~~

November 15, 1931, at 8:00 P.M. Gracie Allen debuted on American radio. She appeared in a short routine with Cantor, acting the part of a newspaper reporter interviewing him for a story. **SEE R804**.

Gracie's appearance met with favorable response according to the Crossley radio rating polls. After her appearance on his show, Eddie Cantor noted that "George wasn't about to let anyone else use Gracie again" (**B114**). On January 28, 1932, Burns and Allen were booked on Rudy Vallee's show for Standard Brands, the **Fleischmann Yeast Hour**, and polls indicated that they were well received by radio listeners. **SEE R805**.

Only weeks later, on February 15, 1932, Burns and Allen appeared on the top rated radio show, popularly known as **The Guy Lombardo Show**, (but technically **The Robert Burns Panatela Program**, sponsored by Robert Burns Panatela Cigars). **SEE R806**. They were asked back the next week (**R1**) and from that date forward remained a permanent act on the show until Lombardo left and they became its stars. George and Gracie had appeared with Guy Lombardo and His Royal Canadians the previous year while on tour with Paramount-Publix, working seven days a week doing seven shows a day. When the advertising agency representing the General Cigar Company began looking for other entertainers to help sell their cigars on the Lombardo show, Guy recommended his friends, George and Gracie. Guy noted that Burns and Allen had helped make bearable the grueling tour of the previous year. "Unflappable George and down to earth Gracie were not always good for a laugh but were fascinating companions." **SEE B302: 160**.

Prior to the team's appearance, the radio musical show featured Guy Lombardo and His Royal Canadians (they were the number one dance band of the 1920s and 1930s) playing "the sweetest music this side of heaven." (Decades later New Year's Eve revelers still pay homage to Guy Lombardo when "Auld Lang Syne" is played, whether they realize it or not. Although the band didn't introduce the song, it became absolutely identified with it). Referred to as "one of the most listened-to, talked-about and imitated big bands of all time," the Lombardo brothers' band began to develop its distinctive style in their hometown of London, Ontario, Canada, in the early 1920s. **SEE B421**.

When Burns and Allen joined the broadcast, they appeared in two separate one-minute spots, while the band continued playing in the background. The sponsor's advertising agency, J. Walter Thompson, received letters from college students complaining about the interruption of the music. George was afraid that Burns and Allen would be taken off the program. But John U. Reber of the agency told George not to be concerned. He felt that at least someone was listening to the program, even if they were complaining. A few weeks later, the agency received more letters from the students but this time they said that they were getting used to the comedians and now felt that they improved the show. This acceptance from radio listeners allowed Burns and Allen to remain on the show.

Burns and Allen were now beginning their careers in radio comedy, which would last for eighteen years and lead to international recognition. George and Gracie had already spent almost a decade in vaudeville as a team and had been a success, but not to the extent they would become in radio. In this new medium they would eventually be heard by millions of radio listeners each week in comparison to the largest vaudeville theaters, which might have two thousand to three thousand seats and in which they played almost nightly.

As in vaudeville, the success of Burns and Allen was based largely on the love the audiences had for the "Gracie" character. They felt sorry for her, even if she did get into messes of her own making. She made silly remarks, but she would say them so seriously that audiences believed she really thought what she was saying was true. As George Burns often remarked, it was the audience that determined if a performer would became a success.

~~~~~

Radio holds pleasant memories for many people who remember sitting around the set with their families. Maybe this is because it was the premier "medium of imagination" (**B86**) or maybe because it evokes thoughts of simpler times, when "making love" meant talking romantically or kissing or holding hands in a balcony. The ubiquitous commercials were woven into the fabric of the show and the products nearly became another character in the minds of the audience, sometimes too much so as indicated by this letter from a listener who "had always enjoyed George Burns and Gracie Allen" but "was tired of their announcer making continuous references to soap throughout the show" (i.e., Bill Goodwin for Swan Soap; see **The New York Times**, February 25, 1944, sec. 2: 7).

But radio was still a business--a competitive one. Early radio programing was controlled by the sponsors (advertisers) as indicated in this assessment by Hank Booraem, a radio writer, director and producer turned advertising agency executive.

> In the final analysis, the advertiser was IT. What he said went. The networks really had very, very little to say about it. The networks had what they called a Continuity Acceptance Office which approved or disapproved jokes basically on the basis of moral considerations, never as a question of show biz. It wasn't until television was well underway... that the networks got in and really finally got control of their own business. The agencies had the expertise which the clients did not, by the way. They had the experts on staff to produce and to direct the programs. **SEE B86**.

When Burns and Allen signed their radio contract, the J. Walter Thompson Agency assigned one of their writers, Carroll Carroll, to work on the show. Carroll, who had been a successful magazine and stage writer and would become a writer for many major show business entertainers, would remain with the Burnses for many years. He noted in his autobiography that he "spent so much time with Nat, Gracie, and Willy Burns that I was almost a member of the family" (**B117: 14**). He also remarked that he fell in love with Gracie the first time they met, echoing what audiences also felt hearing her on the radio or seeing her on the stage or in films.

With their entry into radio, George Burns knew that he would have to add writers to help write the dialogue for the
~~~~~

shows. In vaudeville they had used only three basic routines. Radio required thirty or sixty minutes of material (including commercials) each week. Writers Harry Conn and John P. Medbury, who had sold jokes to George in vaudeville, were signed to work on the shows along with Carroll Carroll. Later they added Harvey Helm after Harry Conn left to work with Jack Benny. All of these writers wrote for other radio shows and like the other radio stars George Burns would pay the writers a weekly salary for jokes. Willy Burns, George's youngest brother, also did some of the writing.

Burns and Allen would continue to follow the vaudevillian's premise that if a script is good, don't change it. Throughout their careers in interviews, radio, motion pictures and television performances, some of their same routines were used time and time again, for the most part successfully. On those occasions when something went wrong in the broadcast studio or on stage (once Gracie accidentally dropped her radio script on a live broadcast) or they needed to "fill time" for a broadcast, George would just mention an opening line from one of their vaudeville routines like "How's your brother?" and Gracie would talk for as long as necessary, about her imaginary sibling. Other Burns and Allen catch phrases which would become known to audiences were "Oh, there you go again," "I know, and I'm pretty too," "Hello, are you there? Well, we're here," "Georgie Porgie," "I bet you say that to all the girls," "Oh, that's silly," and "Oh, go away." None would ever become as much a part of popular entertainment folklore, however, as did the previously mentioned "Say good night, Gracie."

In radio, as in vaudeville, Gracie had nothing to do with the writing of the shows or any of the business aspects. Throughout their careers George made all of the decisions and she trusted him. She simply looked over the scripts and read her lines on the air. It was George who knew which lines were good for Gracie to say, and he was "almost unique in being able to pick out the good line from the babble of a group of guys (writers) pitching gags." **SEE B117: 15**.

In explaining their work in radio George attributed some of their success to the fact that they "planned all of the radio sketches for an intimate audience...That's why it is difficult for people to imitate us. The material is hard to appropriate." **SEE B436**.

But no matter how good the writing was, it was Gracie Allen's acting ability and performances that sold the shows and brought in the listening and viewing audiences. However, Burns and Allen were still very much a team. The combination of George's ability to help find the words for Gracie to say--and her talent as an actress to sell the act to the public--made them a success. At times, Gracie Allen the actor would refuse to say certain lines--and George would have to change them with his writers. She, too, knew what was good for Gracie Allen the actress and the real Gracie Allen to say. But she never openly criticized nor complained to others about the script changes. She simply would express her concerns privately to her husband, who, consulting with his writers, had the script lines rewritten. George noted that there was only one time when Gracie refused to do an entire script. Of course, it was rewritten. If Gracie refused to do a show, there would be no show.

Taking into account the number of annual appearances they made and shows broadcast, it is surprising that Gracie actually missed very few performances. She suffered from migraine headaches but was able to do a show many times while, in fact, she was ill. But all of this was not realized by the audiences because of her capability as an actress to cover up her true feelings. Gracie Allen's delivery was almost always perfect. In a medium such as live radio and with many actors on one stage during a performance, she rarely made an error

As early as the 1930s, and especially after the adoption of her two children, Gracie Allen often was quoted as saying she could leave show business with no regrets. The fact was that Gracie Allen, even after a lifetime of work on the stage, in films, on radio, and later on television, seemingly did not actually like show business. When she was "onstage" she was a performer. Once the curtain dropped, she was "offstage" and out of show business and never spoke about the theater nor her performances. Those who knew her, including George, labeled Gracie Allen as "the most completely untheatrical woman in existence" (**B228: 91**). It was a quote that would be echoed over and over.

The real Gracie Allen Burns was completely unlike the "Gracie" character she portrayed. She was a quiet, reserved, private individual who usually let her husband speak to the interviewers for both of them. One rare occasions a reporter would get an insight into her style of performing. In one interview, Gracie revealed that "a sense of timing is the greatest essential for a successful comedienne" (**B327**). She continued to explain that timing was a gift and wasn't something that could be taught. To her, knowing how long to wait for an audience to finish laughing before going on to the next line was an art. It is interesting to note that Gracie titled herself as a comedienne in this interview. In many interviews George referred to his wife not as a comedienne, but as an actress who played the part of a funny woman. Their son, Ronnie, echoed the thought when he took his father's place during a 1978 tribute to his mother at the University of California. Guy Lombardo, a close friend of the couple, noted that "George Burns was first and foremost a vaudevillian...but Gracie Allen on the other hand may have been a favorite next door neighbor, sweet, compliant, practical and never onstage when she was off it" (**B302: 160**). In fact, both George and Gracie were well-liked individuals whose personalities never changed, even after they became famous and wealthy show business entertainers.

~~~~~

To announce a time change for the **The Robert Burns Panatela Program** a publicity stunt had been suggested by Robert Taplinger, the head of publicity at CBS Radio. The idea was that Gracie should begin looking for a lost brother. So on the show that inaugurated their time change (January 4, 1933 [**R46**]), Gracie mentioned that her brother was missing and, at the same time of the radio broadcast, newspaper stories were planted across the United States. Suddenly radio listeners began talking about Gracie's lost brother and started to offer suggestions to help find him. CBS widened their publicity by having Gracie walk in on other radio shows during their broadcasts, simply interrupting the actors and beginning to talk about her brother. This was one of the first times that a radio actor burst into other shows when they were on the air.
~~~~~

This stunt even managed to cut short another network's broadcast. Rudy Vallee again booked Burns and Allen on his NBC radio show (**R810**), and the plan was to have Gracie talk about her missing brother. But NBC was not aggreeable to offer a rival network, CBS, free publicity. The script was altered for the show, but Rudy Vallee supposedly accidentally (or perhaps purposely) picked up the wrong script and asked "Hello, Gracie, have you found your missing brother yet?" The show's director frantically signalled to the engineer to "cut," and the program went off the air for half a minute while people rushed around to see if everybody had the original or the altered script (**B322**). This gained their own show even more publicity as headlines mentioned that Gracie Allen had shut down the NBC network. The J. Walter Thompson agency estimated that they received free publicity worth $125,000 when newspaper columns across the country reported the incident.

Gracie's "missing brother" was a major topic of conversation on their own show off and on until mid-May 1933 and heightened Burns and Allen's popularity enormously. "Where's My Brother?" became the title of their stage show revue when they made personal appearances to promote the radio show. George Allen, Gracie's real brother in San Francisco, was located and people began to bother him--making jokes that they had found Gracie's "lost brother." The newspapers printed his photograph around the country. Being a quiet and reserved man, he finally grew tired of all the publicity and constant kidding from his friends and fled from all the attention by taking a vacation from his job at the Standard Oil Company for a month. He also sent his younger sister a telegram asking her did she really have to do this for a living? Seemingly, due to the unhappiness this caused her real brother, Burns and Allen would not use the name of George Allen as a character in their radio and later television routines, although they would continue talk about her "brother" in general terms. In contrast, Burns and Allen incorporated Gracie Allen's sisters' names (Hazel, Bessie and Pearl) constantly as character names in scripts, as well as the names of George's siblings.

The publicity stunt led to something not quite as funny for the Burnses in real life. While appearing in Chicago in October 1933, their last week in vaudeville, newspaper accounts (**San Francisco Chronicle**, October 22, 1933) reported that George had paid money to some Chicago gangsters who threatened to kidnap Gracie and hold her for ransom unless twenty-five hundred dollars was paid up front. This appeared to be a rather common practice in Chicago, and many entertainers paid the money rather than take chances. George reportedly denied that he had paid any money and said that he was just buying benefit tickets for a charity.

During the years when George and Gracie were signed with the General Cigar Company (1932-1934), Guy Lombardo and His Royal Canadians often broadcast from different cities than the Burnses, thus becoming the first radio show in the United States to do remote broadcasts on the same show. Burns and Allen were still traveling around the country appearing at theaters and elsewhere honoring their Paramount-Publix contract. George was already singing "Ain't Misbehavin'" at these appearances, a song that would appear to be his own theme song as much as sixty years later.

Having a cigar company for a sponsor meant more than the fact that George would be well supplied with his trademark prop. The commercials definitely equated smoking with success, a sense of satisfaction and well-being, confidence and belonging. Though obviously tilted toward the young male audience, the commercials also let the female members know this was something they could and would want to buy for their men. Smoking a cigar, after all, made him a more gracious man. (George remained adamant, however, that he only smoked inexpensive cigars, ones that could be purchased for thirty-five cents apiece in the early 1980s).

On May 17, 1933, George and Gracie broadcast their last show for Robert Burns Panatelas (**R65**). The next week (**R66**) they were sponsored by White Owl Cigars, still for the General Cigar Company, in a show called **The White Owl Program**. In June 1934, Guy Lombardo and His Royal Canadians left for a new show. When George and Gracie returned from their summer vacation the show was renamed **The Adventures of Gracie**, although it would also be referred to as **The Vintage White Owl Program**. This new show was based for a time on Gracie's "travels" around the United States and Europe, debuted on September 19, 1934 (**R122**), and lasted until September 25, 1935. On that same date a **Variety** reviewer wrote that the success of Burns and Allen was based on "Gracie Allen's delivery as one of the few dependable elements of this undependable show business." This comment would be essentially repeated throughout Burns and Allen's careers. To be a success on radio was not a given, and many established vaudeville performers failed in their attempts to move their acts to radio. It was George and Gracie's talents that gained them success on radio, aided by the business-minded George, who hired and was willing to pay for the best writers. Theirs was a success that could be measured in more than dollars and cents; it could also be measured in sacks of mail. The 1935 **Blue Book of Radio Entertainers** (**B82**) reported that they once received 360,000 fan letters in four days during the time of the "missing brother"; other reports varied in the amount of letters and the time frame. Regardless of exact numbers, the team had obviously touched a very responsive chord in the American audience, and it was just the beginning. George and Gracie lent themselves quite well to highly publicized stunts of that sort, and the coming years would see three more major ratings coups.

In their first years on radio, George and Gracie's shows consisted not of one major script plot but of quick routines that jumped from topic to topic. Also, they portrayed two single people, who appeared to be friends and sometimes gave the impression that they did date. Burns and Allen would not "wed" on the radio until late 1941, when their show changed and they began to portray a married couple. With their radio program rated as one of the top ten shows and their salaries reportedly now $5,000 a week, George and Gracie moved from a New York City hotel to the twenty-second floor of the Essex House, 160 Central Park South. Because they traveled so much they seemed not to want to put down roots and purchase a home, but instead lived in residential hotels. George was quoted in some interviews that he and Gracie might buy a farm and settle in the country after their show business success ended. Little were they to know how much longer it would continue.

~~~~~
~~~~~

In 1932, Burns and Allen were offered and signed a two-year contract with Paramount Studios to act in feature films. Because they were also honoring their radio contract at the same time, this necessitated that Burns and Allen travel from New York City to the Paramount Studios in Hollywood and do the radio show from California. They would be acting in their film scenes on days they were not broadcasting their radio show.

So, in June 1932, they began filming their first full-length picture, **The Big Broadcast** (**F19**), in Hollywood. This movie featured various radio stars, including Bing Crosby, and allowed the radio listener to see his or her favorite performers. According to newspaper reports at the time, Guy Lombardo and His Royal Canadians were also signed for the film but declined after learning they would be billed under Bing Crosby. Reportedly Guy feared that his reputation would be damaged.

The successful film **The Big Broadcast** (**F19**) was followed by **The Big Broadcast of 1936** (**F27**) and **The Big Broadcast of 1937** (**F28**)--films which also included Burns and Allen in the cast. George and Gracie always had small parts in these films, mostly because George thought that this was better than being headlined. He felt that the audiences might get tired of Burns and Allen if they saw too much of them. So he preferred that the team perform in short sequences in the films. Usually George wrote their lines, often drawing from their vaudeville routines.

Dissatisfied with the script, they did not appear in **The Big Broadcast of 1938**. It is often more interesting to hear of the roles actors turn down than the ones they accept, and George and Gracie were not immune to that that phenomenon. Reportedly, George turned down several film offers which other actors would make famous, including **The Road to Singapore**, which would star Bing Crosby, Bob Hope and Dorothy Lamour and become a highly successful film series. At least one other source, however, states that the picture was intended as a vehicle for George and Fred MacMurray, and that MacMurray backed out (**B417**). Assuming the story is not apocryphal, there is no way to know if the film would have been a hit without Crosby and Hope or whether it really would have been a suitable property for Burns and Allen or Burns and MacMurray.

In June 1934 George and Gracie left on a much publicized trip to Europe, including the Balkans and the Soviet Union. On their return home to New York City onboard the deck of the ship "Rex," a newsreel interview filmed George and Gracie gagging it up with reporters, telling how they loved Italy (**R819**, **VG74**). Gracie hugs and kisses one of the photographers, a takeoff from Burns and Allen's vaudeville act in which she opened the act by kissing a stranger in the wings of a stage.

Gracie and George almost always "performed" for their interviews and often included short routine answers from their vaudeville act. Because of her reserved nature, this was probably the easiest way for Gracie to handle interviewers as she was unwilling to reveal very much of her inner self to others, especially to reporters. She let George do most of the talking to reporters, even when she was present. According to her husband, Gracie's private life with her family was the most important part of her life. For George Burns, replies to an interviewer's questions meant a chance to get a laugh, so his answers were seldom serious. On rare occasions, when George and Gracie replied seriously to questions about their careers, the answers they gave often differed from interview to interview. Whether they did this on purpose or why they did so is not known.

During the filming of one of their first feature films for Paramount, the importance of Grace's feelings about her marriage was revealed when she became very upset at being asked to take off her wedding ring. She always wore a large ring over her wedding ring when performing in vaudeville and in films to give the impression that she and George were single, which they portrayed as part of their act.

While working in Hollywood in 1934, the Burnses lived at the elegant Chateau Elysee on Franklin Street, which was near Hollywood Boulevard and Vine Street. This location was near where they did their radio broadcast from the CBS studios. They later would lease an estate off of Sunset Boulevard.

In September 1934, a month after their return from their overseas vacation, the Burnses announced the adoption of a six-week-old baby girl from The Cradle, a Catholic Foundling home in Evanston, Illinois. They named the baby Sandra Jean (Sandy) and a year later, when they returned to the Cradle legally to finalize the adoption, they adopted a five-week-old premature baby boy, and named him Ronald Jon (Ronnie).

The practice of infant adoption in Hollywood had varying degrees of success, as it does anywhere. George and Gracie's experience appears to have been among the stories with happy endings. After they adopted the children, George and Gracie mentioned them in many of their interviews, and the children appear with their parents in many publicity photographs and on vacations. In fact, when the Burnses were shooting a film on Catalina Island in 1935, they so missed Sandy that they had the nurse fly with the baby from Los Angeles to the island. Sandy Burns became the first baby to fly in an airplane to Catalina Island.

~~~~~

On January 16, 1935, Burns and Allen presented their first broadcast before a studio audience (**R139**). In the early years of radio, live audiences did not attend the broadcasts. Many of the performers, like Gracie, were terrified at the thought of speaking into a microphone. Having a live audience watch their performance at the same time was even more frightening, notwithstanding the fact that they had been performing before live audiences for years in vaudeville and during personal appearances. Apparently it was the addition of a microphone--and its implications--that caused these feelings of terror. Gracie once said, "The onstage Gracie may look poised and steady but the real Gracie is shy, a little self-conscious, and before every performance of my life, panicky" (**B8**). Comedian Ed Wynn was the first radio performer to allow an audience to watch his radio broadcast. He felt he needed the live reaction of an audience. To perform comedy with no reaction is difficult, as in the case of Burns and Allen, who depended on the audiences to aid in the timing of their lines when they were in vaudeville. George found that smoking cigars on stage helped his timing. If the audience was applauding, George puffed on his cigar, waiting for the applause to die down before he continued on to the next line in the script or routine. Burns and Allen also used the word
~~~~~

"yeah" in their dialogues to help keep them on track. Other radio performers eventually agreed with Wynn and many of the radio broadcasts, Burns and Allen's among them, would include studio audiences, with the top shows filling large studios with hundreds of people.

In the 1930s several radio programs began to move their casts and shows from New York City to the West Coast in order to join the firmly transplanted motion picture industry. More important to the radio industry was the development of a circuit by the engineers of the American Telephone and Telegraph (AT&T) company. This circuit made it possible for radio programs to be heard nationwide and for broadcasts to originate from the West Coast by switching a circuit (**B402**: **3**). This made national coast-to-coast programming possible. Up to this time radio broadcasts were broadcast at one hour (Eastern Standard Time) for the East Coast listeners and then the performers returned three hours later to rebroadcast the same program for the West Coast (Pacific Standard Time) listeners. In the early days of radio, in the late 1920s, East Coast programs were heard only as far west as Denver, Colorado.

October 2, 1935 (**R176**) found George and Gracie with a new sponsor, the Campbell Soup Company, in a program titled **Campbell's Tomato Juice Program**. During the time they were with Campbell's they would switch back and forth between extolling the virtues of Campbell's tomato juice and chicken soup. Their last show for this sponsor was broadcast March 24, 1936 (**R253**).

The increase in the market value of the Burns and Allen act is a particularly revealing indicator of the power of the exposure of a weekly radio show. During their last days in vaudeville they commanded the sum of $750 a week for an appearance in Cleveland; less than four years later an appearance at the Cleveland Auto Show (coincidentally, at the same venue) paid them $8,000 for eight days' work (**B321**).

Realizing that their futures were in California and not New York, George and Gracie decided to move permanently to the West Coast in 1936. It was a predictable move. In the late 1930s both NBC and CBS held grand openings for their new West Coast studios in Hollywood, which equaled their studios in New York City. Most of the New York radio stars moved to California in these years.

Gracie had found a home under construction that she liked and that she and George decided to purchase. During Christmas week of 1936 they moved into the only home they were to own--a seventeen-room Gregorian-styled structure at 720 North Maple Drive in Beverly Hills. Due to her migraine headaches, which she continued to suffer from, Gracie had the rooms painted in soft shades of rose and green. Although a native Californian, Gracie actually preferred New York City, while George, a native New Yorker, preferred California. But they both felt that California had a better lifestyle in which to bring up their children in addition to the fact that the entertainment field was now becoming centralized in California.

~~~~~

George and Gracie were now "stars" living in Beverly Hills, home of the wealthiest entertainers in motion pictures and radio. Jack Benny and his wife, Mary (Livingstone) Benny, (born Sadie Marks), who were the Burnses' closest friends,
~~~~~

lived nearby, and, in fact, Jack visited the Burnses almost daily. Their daughter, Joan Benny, was Sandy Burns's best friend and the children spent a lot of time together. Gracie once tossed Mary a birthday party in June 1938 at their home (and George had a script written for it), and the Burnses spent many New Year's Eves with the Bennys. It wasn't until years later that George revealed that Mary Benny envied Gracie her public and private successes and would try to outdo her (**B22**). Whether it involved a house, a fur coat or a fainting spell, Mary wasn't satisfied with merely "keeping up with the Joneses." She had to be "Mrs. Jones." Joan Benny delved into her mother's insecurities in her own book (**B70**), indicating that the resulting lifelong competition wasn't limited to Gracie but involved a number of different people.

George and Gracie's personal lives and performances were featured in radio and motion picture magazines and national newspapers and newsreels. Everywhere they went there seemed to be a photographer. Every social event they attended--private or public--was chronicled. They were among the highest paid radio entertainers of the 1930s and 1940s, and requests for personal appearances ran the gamut from Gracie christening a ship to Hollywood's Santa Claus Lane Parade to the opening of a donut shop. They would never be known as famous motion picture actors (until George revived his film career decades later), but their appearances in feature films were well received by audiences.

To the public, Burns and Allen were best known as major radio stars. The Burns and Allen radio show would change format, sponsors, networks, and supporting casts throughout the eighteen years it was broadcast on radio. But the basics of their "act" of Gracie's illogical logic never changed. Although their ratings experienced the usual peaks and valleys, they continued to have millions of listeners throughout their years in radio. Life was sweet when legendary Abe Lastfogel was your agent. They reportedly earned salaries of $5,000 a week in the 1930s and by 1943 were earning a reported $9,000 a week just for their weekly radio show.

Burns and Allen were also popular in other countries. Always well received in England where they had started their careers in radio, their humor was also enjoyed by the French. In 1936 a French broadcasting company asked Burns and Allen for permission to revise some of their old radio scripts and allow them to be rebroadcast by French actors. George Burns and Gracie Allen agreed, although they did not receive much compensation for this. Even as late as the 1950s some of their early films were just being released to audiences in Africa.

In 1936 there were only four comedy teams broadcasting on the networks' evening programming schedule. The next year saw an increase to six comedy teams (**B484: 316-317**). George remarked that Burns and Allen were always in the top ten radio shows, because there wasn't even a total of ten competitors. But it is a reality that a sponsor would never had allowed their radio show to continue unless there were millions of Burns and Allen listeners who were buying the products the show was advertising. According to the National Association of Broadcasters, total radio revenue for the 1936-1937 period was over $107,000,000. For that same period Burns and Allen's sponsors, the Campbell Soup Company, had the highest client revenue of $1,294,854. (**SEE B484: 281**).

In March 1937, their association with Campbell's coming to a close, General Foods Corporation stepped in to offer George and Gracie a contract for a show for Grape-Nuts Cereal, an association that would last from April of that year until August 1938. **The Grape-Nuts Program** was the first of two Burns and Allen radio shows sponsored by the well-known corporation.

~~~~~

Continuing to honor their Paramount contracts during the 1930s, Burns and Allen, as previously noted, usually performed briefly on the screen with short routines woven into the film script. But one film allowed audiences to see the multiple talents of the team. In 1937 Burns and Allen were loaned out for the RKO film **A Damsel in Distress** (**F30**), with Fred Astaire and Joan Fontaine. This musical comedy was the first Astaire would make without Ginger Rogers after several successful pictures featuring the two as a team.

George and Gracie showed Fred a dance routine with whisk brooms which George had seen in vaudeville, hoping that this would convince Fred that they could dance and appear in the film. George in fact had found the original team member (from "Evans and Evans") who had performed the dance and paid him to teach him and Gracie the routine. She and George practiced the number at home, showed it to Fred, and he agreed that it should be a part of the film. Upon the release of the film, audiences and critics alike acknowledged that they were surprised at George and Gracie's dancing ability. What they did not know nor remember was that both George and Gracie had started their careers as dancers. Even though the film did not do as well financially as had past Astaire films, this was one of the few opportunities that Burns and Allen were given to display their acting and dancing abilities and Gracie's singing talents in a motion picture.

This film also called for some additional lighting effects because Gracie eyes were two different colors--one was brown and the other blue. In film, the camera would be able to distinguish between the two colors, so the lighting technicians on the set had to compensate their lighting on Gracie's eyes so that the eye color would seem to be the same to viewers.

~~~~~

The year 1938 turned out not to be a happy one for the couple, although it started off with the announcement in January that S. S. Van Dine (pseudonym of W. H. Wright), author of the popular Philo Vance detective mysteries, had been assigned to write the script for a new MGM motion picture, **The Gracie Allen Murder Case** (**F33**). The movie would be based on the book by the same title which was published that same year.

A studio executive had come up with the idea of a mystery story combining Philo Vance and Gracie Allen. Burns and Allen met with Wright, who wanted their permission to use their names in a book. George agreed as this would bring Burns and Allen publicity, always an ongoing element in show business.

Although not a top film star, Gracie's talents were such that the industry executives were very much aware that her name would be a box office draw. Parker Brothers even came out with a board game based on the film.

While the character of George Burns does appear in the book, the actor George Burns does not appear in the motion picture. He did join his wife on the set and helped Gracie with her lines and other matters, so that his influence on her performance was still evident to those who saw how they worked together. To most audiences as well as those who worked in show business, it was Gracie Allen who was the one and only star of the team. But those who had the opportunity to see how they worked realized that George was an important part of the team, working behind the scenes with his wife in advising her. One comment at the time was that George Burns was an excellent dialogue writer. George had been writing for the team since their vaudeville days and he worked weekly with his radio writers.

George and Gracie had signed with Chesterfield Cigarettes beginning in the fall 1938 season for **The Chesterfield Program**, leaving General Foods for a time. Although they had a regular radio show and were making films and guest appearances on other shows in their spare time, George and his publicity agency still made sure that Gracie's name stayed constantly in the news. On September 27, 1938, the Manhattan art gallery of Julien Levy, who sponsored the Spanish surrealist artist Salvador Dali, opened an exhibition at his 15 East 57th street gallery with ten surrealistic pastel paintings by Gracie Allen. Twenty-five percent of the proceeds from the show were to be donated to the China Aid Council's medical relief fund. Gracie did not actually paint the art work, which had such titles as "Behind the Before Yet Under the Vase," "About the World as in Tears and Tomorrow is Tuesday," "Man with Mike Fright," "Eyes Adrift as Sardines Wrench at Your Heartstrings," and "Moon over Manicurist." All of the paintings sold and were sent on an exhibition tour across the United States. One of the paintings was stolen from a Los Angeles gallery, but it was returned the next day. The publicity gimmick worked. Gracie and "her" paintings were covered by radio and the print media across the country.

The latter part of 1938 brought Burns and Allen the most unfavorable press they would receive in their lifetimes. There had never been any scandal about Burns and Allen. They were loved by their audiences and were known to have a strong and happy marriage. But their popularity and success, along with that of their best friend, Jack Benny, were jeopardized in the fall of 1938 by newspaper headlines revealing that Jack Benny and George Burns had been accused of smuggling jewelry into the United States for their wives. According to press accounts of the time, the Burnses and Bennys had become friends with a man named Albert Nathaniel Chapereau (alias Shapiro), who portrayed himself around Hollywood as a Nicaraguan diplomat. While dining with the Chapereaus, George expressed his wish to buy a bracelet for Gracie similar to one he had admired being worn by Mrs. Chapereau. On the spot, Chapereau sold George that bracelet, although more pieces would eventually be involved. In the summer of 1938, the Bennys were vacationing in the south of France when Chapereau appeared at their hotel. Mary Benny had purchased some jewelry in Paris, and, as a favor, Chapereau asked Jack Benny if he would allow him to bring the jewelry into the United States in a diplomatic pouch. That way, the Bennys would not have to pay import custom taxes on the purchase. Jack agreed and when Chapeareau appeared in New York, he gave the smuggled jewelry to George Burns for delivery. The customs officials were led on to the case after Chapereau's maid, Rosa Weber, who was reportedly an admirer of Adolf Hitler, heard a conversation in which the Chapereaus denounced the dictator. This angered Weber and she reported Chapereau's jewelry delivery to the New York police officials.

Burns and Allen radio audiences tuned in on December 16, 1938 (**R334**) for the first radio broadcast since the indictments. Audiences attending the show at CBS's enormous Studio A in Hollywood waited to see how George and especially Gracie would perform.

> Gracie Allen walked out from the wings to face them with the same chipper smile and the same laughing eyes as ever. Only the farsighted and the shrewdly observant saw that tonight, additionally the smile held a determined quality and that the wide eyes sparkled with a new, unrecognizable light...She read her lines with the same ineffable timing and finesse that have, through the years, been the wonder of show business. It was a miracle of control considering the condition of her nerves ....The audience stood and yelled their acclaim, applauding until their hands were sore and muscles ached. It was one of the most magnificent performances from the point of delivery and stage presence she had ever given. **SEE B239: 33**.

George's case, at its resolution, involved two bracelets and a ring with a total value of $4,885. To better place the financial implications in perspective, one newspaper reported that George and Gracie were earning $9,875 a week from their radio show and roughly that amount from the films they worked on twelve or so weeks during the year (**New York World Telegram**, February 1, 1939); **The New York Post** estimated their weekly income at that time to be $11,000. George cooperated fully with the legal system, making several flights to New York from California at his own expense. Having been charged with three counts in two indictments, he pleaded guilty on the advice of his lawyer, Carl Newton. Although storms had forced down his plane in Kansas City on his way to New York for sentencing, he did manage to arrive on time for his appearance before Federal Court Judge William Bondy on January 31, 1939.

The professional notoriety he suffered was substantial and was part of the request for leniency by George's attorney, but the judge apparently was largely unmoved as he imposed his sentence. "A great many people with money can take a chance on smuggling and compromising with Washington if they get caught, but the poor man doesn't have a chance. All people, rich and poor, will be treated alike in my court room." To George's visible relief he received suspended concurrent prison sentences of one year and a day on each of the three counts and was fined $8,000 (as opposed to the $12,000 fine asked for by the Assistant United States Attorney). He could have received a maximum sentence of eighteen years in prison and a $45,000 fine and had, in fact, already paid $9,770 in customs penalties. Jack Benny, whose own case involved $2,131 worth of jewelry, felt that he and his friend had been used by Chapereau and was at first determined to plead not guilty at his April 1939 trial. But, he, too, was advised by his attorney to take his punishment and put the ordeal behind him. His guilty plea was accepted, and he, too, was given a suspended sentence and fined. **SEE B22, B70, B137**. However, in February 1945 there was a report that Chapereau was naming the Bennys and the Burnses in a lawsuit because he had acted on their behalf by bringing the jewelry into this country. The defendants' attorneys made plans to move for a dismissal of the suit; the end result is unknown.

For the months of May and June 1939, before the end of the radio season, their radio sponsors asked that the Burns and Allen show broadcast from the CBS studio in New York City to coincide with the World's Fair opening in that city. It also timed with the opening of **The Gracie Allen Murder Case** (**F33**) in April.

On the last show before leaving for New York the strain of all that had come before and the stress of temporarily uprooting the family for a move to New York seemed to express itself in the April 28th (**R353**) broadcast as attested by this May 3, 1939, review appeared in **Variety**:

> ...listened in on a shipshod job...the material was substandard and more surprising was the way they kicked the material around. The show was seemingly unrehearsed. Lapses were particularly notable in the case of Gracie Allen. The comedienne was at a disadvantage for she got tangled up in her lines on numerous occasions and was way off in her timing. Extraordinary for a performer of her experience and standing.

Because of Gracie's perfection in her craft, a poor performance caused astonishment. This could have been an occasion when she was ill, or there hadn't been enough time for rehearsal.

Still popular with the public, on her arrival in New York City, Gracie nearly caused a riot when she stood outside of the CBS studio before their show, selling tickets to passers-by. A few days later on the opening day of the fair, George and Gracie were there with their two children visiting the fairgrounds.

On June 20, 1939, Gracie stepped out of character when she appeared without George on the quiz show **Information Please** (**R850**). Gracie joined the regular panelists and attempted to answer questions sent in by listeners. Gracie surprised audiences and even the panelists with her number of correct answers. It was one of the few times that Gracie would appear as herself on radio and not as the character "Gracie Allen." After her appearance a number of colleges wanted to recommend her for an honarary degree.

~~~~~

Although Burns and Allen's careers survived the negative publicity from George's trial, for whatever reason, at the end of the radio season Burns and Allen were not renewed by their radio sponsor, the Liggett and Myers Tobacco Company. But there were other sponsors who were willing to take a risk and
~~~~~

sign them to a new contract. In late May the press had released the news that Burns and Allen had signed a new contract with Lehn and Fink for Hinds Honey and Almond Cream. The new show would not start until October 1939 and the Burnses would have complete control over the half-hour show. This meant that in addition to receiving $13,500 a program, a thousand dollars more than from their previous sponsor, George and Gracie would be selecting the supporting cast for the shows.

Editorials were written at the time indicating that, while technically George had been guilty of breaking the law, he had openly admitted that he had made a mistake and had pleaded guilty. The average radio listener accepted this and admired George for his honesty. Prior to the filming of **The Gracie Allen Murder Case** (**F33**), George had been released from Paramount. Gracie's contract with the studio ended after the film's release, either because Paramount no longer felt her services were profitable for the company or because Gracie wanted to spend more time with her children at home. Although each would go on to separate film projects, Burns and Allen would never again appear together in a motion picture.

George and Gracie returned to California and vacationed for a time before the new 1939-1940 radio season began. They had a little cabin in the mountains of the High Sierras that was so inaccessible that Gracie remarked that the family got lost the first time they drove looking for the "shack."

~~~~~

October 4, 1939 saw the premiere of the new **Burns and Allen Show, The Hinds Honey and Almond Cream Program** (**R362**). Broadcasting from Hollywood, the new cast members included the character of "Bubbles," a friend of Gracie's. The character was portrayed by George and Gracie's friend, Mary Kelly. Mary had continued to act in vaudeville ("Swift and Kelly") and on the stage but had fallen on hard times, losing her money in the stock market crash of 1929. She had married Ray Myers, the former booker for the Orpheum, but they eventually separated. For many years Mary worked as the telephone operator at the Academy of Vaudeville Artists in New York City. Once a tall, slim, beautiful woman, she now weighed over two hundred pounds. But Gracie never forgot her friend and she continued to correspond with Mary through the years and in fact visited here whenever she was in New York. It was Gracie who had a hand in getting a part for Mary on the Burns and Allen radio show. This led to an upswing in Mary's show business career, as she also appeared on other radio programs, including that of her former boyfriend, Jack Benny. She also had bit parts in a few motion pictures. For a time, Mary even lived with George and Gracie in Beverly Hills. Although she was reported to be in reasonably good health, (despite problems with alcohol), she died in her sleep in her Hollywood apartment on June 7, 1941, at the age of forty-six.

George and Gracie's new show still portrayed the Burnses as unmarried friends, and the plots were similar to those of their previous shows. On February 7, 1940, Burns and Allen began yet another publicity stunt, which was to equal that of Gracie's "lost brother" in the 1930s. On that evening's show Gracie mentioned on the air that she might run for the highest office in the land, president of the United States of America. The J. Walter Thompson Advertising Agency, which represented
~~~~~

Burns and Allen, had decided that Gracie should run for president against the incumbent, Franklin D. Roosevelt, and his challenger, lawyer and political leader Wendell Willkie.

Within the month the campaign had established its own political party, the Surprise Party, a mascot--a kangaroo named Laura--and a slogan, "It's in the Bag." The entire campaign, together with songs, and Laura, became a part of the weekly Burns and Allen radio show during the remainder of the season. Gracie even "wrote" a book (ghostwritten) called **How to Become President**, "Prepared by the Gracie Allen Self-Delusion Institute" (**B7**). Each copy sold for a dollar, and such was Gracie's celebrity that the slim (96 pages) volume, although written in jest, did not escape the reviewer's pen. Recognizing the identity of the true author ("Dean" Charles Palmer) and calling the contents "ectoplasmic," the newspaper critic lamented

> "the book doesn't quite come off...We suggest that when (Gracie) runs again...she be more discriminating in her choice of campaign manager (and literary mentor!)" (**PM**, June 23, 1940).

There was even a campaign song, "Vote for Gracie," written by Charles Henderson, which Gracie sang to announce her candidacy. The song had several choruses, asking voters to vote for her (**Radio Mirror**, July, 1940). Listeners of the Burns and Allen radio show heard it regularly on the program during the campaign.

To aid in the publicity, Gracie would walk in and interrupt other radio broadcasts to mention her campaign, a repeat of the mechanics of 1933s "missing brother" stunt. During one week period she appeared on so many different broadcasts that she went home physically exhausted. Sandy reportedly walked over to her reclining mother, patted her head and said, "Poor Mommy, are you working for all the networks now?" Gracie's schedule was so hectic that present-day historians cannot agree on exactly how many programs she might have appeared.

The nation began to act as if this were not a stunt but a real campaign for the presidency. Gracie received eight hundred signatures in forty minutes on a petition nominating her for president. A fraternity at Harvard University endorsed her. Everyone realized that Gracie was not really serious about the campaign, but it was great fun for everyone concerned--everyone, that is, except Gracie. She was doing a lot of work to publicize her running for election in addition to performing weekly on her radio show. She did as much work as the real presidental canidates.

In March 1940, Gracie was the honored guest at the Women's National Press Club dinner in Washington, D.C. In April she received a number of votes from a few small towns during the Wisconsin primaries. She was very successful in her role of an actual candidate.

Gracie began to get letters from around the country supporting her campaign. It was eventually decided that she should have a convention for her Surprise Party. Several cities wanted to host the convention, but the honor went to Omaha, Nebraska. The convention would coincide with the Golden Spike Days Celebration, which commemorated the opening of the transcontinental railroad in the nineteenth century. The Union Pacific Railroad offered Burns and Allen a campaign train which would leave Los Angeles on its way to Omaha, with "whistle stops" at many cities along the way.

The train started its journey on May 9, 1940. Burns and Allen had an entourage with them that included her sister Hazel, publicity people, writers and actors who would be broadcasting on the radio program from the convention. Gracie was so unsure of herself acting this part as presidential candidate, giving campaign speeches at stops along the way, that at first she needed reassurance from George and Hazel. After all, no actor had ever attempted to carry a mock candidacy to this extreme. She carried most of the weight for the success of the stunt and this affected her physically. George feared that all of the stress might bring cause her to have migraine attacks: besides worrying about his wife's health, he was concerned that the convention would have to be cancelled.

Like an actual candidate traveling around the country on a train and giving speeches from the rear platform at thirty-one stops along the way, Gracie spoke to crowds that sometimes numbered in the thousands. She and the cast were dressed in period costumes that would fit with the Omaha festivities of the Golden Spike Days. The first stop on the tour was Riverside, California, where several hundred people showed up at the station to hear Gracie's opinions on what she would do as president. Upon their train's arrival in Omaha, the celebration began in earnest. It was a four-day festival of parades, awards, appearances, and dances, with the Surprise Party's political convention the climax of the week. Gracie was honored at several events, including being given the Indian name of Chief Wau-La-Shja-wa, "She who says funny things." The Burns and Allen radio broadcast that week played to a live audience of over fifteen thousand people in Omaha in addition to radio listeners around the country.

While seemingly most of the public enjoyed this publicity stunt, there was some criticism that Gracie Allen running for president was a mockery of the nation's highest office. After the Omaha convention, Gracie broadcast a direct and rather serious speech on the stunt, saying that it was not meant to be disrespectful of the presidency.

Nationally elected officials acknowledged Gracie's candidacy. In June 1940, just days after her Omaha convention, she was invited to be a guest at The White House in Washington, D.C. Photographs of the event show Gracie with the First Lady, Eleanor Roosevelt, Mrs. Thomas E. Dewey and Mrs. Ruby Black. But it was time to put an end to something that had, once again, taken on a life of its own. During an American Red Cross broadcast on June 29, 1940 (**R865**), Gracie withdrew from the race and announced that the proceeds from her book **How to Become President** (**B7**) would be donated to the Red Cross. Her words were uncharacteristically "Gracie Allen," but they came straight from the real Gracie Allen's heart. "On every occasion when I faced the microphone before, it has been in the character of a comedienne...I speak to you tonight as an American woman, a woman with children of my own whom I am doing my best to bring up in a world of terrible uncertainty." Although Gracie "lost" the election to Franklin D. Roosevelt, she sent him a congratulatory letter for which she received a personal reply from the newly re-elected president of the United States.

Worldwide the news was quite serious, with Europe already at war and the United States soon to be brought into World War

II. In fact, Hitler's blitzkrieg into Holland and Belgium started the day the Burns and Allen train left Hollywood. There had been some talk about the trip being cancelled due to the war news in Europe. But comedy teams such as Burns and Allen gave the public something to laugh about in times of such duress. They would bring humor and entertainment into people's lives during a period when another world war was looming.

~~~~~

In mid-summer 1940 **The Burns and Allen Show** changed networks and sponsors when the principals signed a contract with NBC and Hormel, makers of Spam, as their new sponsor. This radio contract for **The Hormel Program** would tie with the one with Chesterfield as the shortest Burns and Allen ever signed--nine months. Their audience ratings would begin to slip week after week and Hormel did not renew their show.

George and his staff tried to figure out what they were doing wrong. Burns and Allen had been on radio for eight years doing basically the same act--Gracie getting into trouble and misunderstanding everyone. The conclusion was finally reached that audiences were tired of Burns and Allen acting as an unmarried couple and with the "Gracie" character continuing to flirt with the men on the show. The radio audience knew that the actors Burns and Allen were a married couple with two children, and Gracie's onstage antics seemed unrealistic to listeners.

Hubbell Robinson of Young and Rubicam had already come up with the idea of putting George and Gracie on the air as husband and wife, a departure from the stand-up routines (sans plot lines) they had been doing during their William Morris Agency days. Even when he started working with Burns and Allen in 1932 writer Carroll Carroll could never understand why the team continued to play unmarried characters and George seemingly never offered an explanation. Hendrik (Hank) Booraem, Jr., who now lives in North Carolina and is the guiding hand for the Blue Ridge Radio Players (a group of volunteers who produce thirty-minute radio dramas for broadcast and cassette, targeting the visually handicapped and functionally illiterate), directed the Burns and Allen radio show between April 1942 and the late summer of 1943. He muses about the decision to alter George and Gracie's onscreen relationship in an effort to short up ratings.

> It seems terribly obvious at this point, but in those days it [portraying George and Gracie as husband and wife on the air] was very surprising. The same thing happened with Benny. Benny really did stand-up routines, vaudeville routines, the kind of thing they'd done at The Palace. This is how these fellas had become famous. They had just translated those [stand-up routines] to radio and, frankly, they were getting a little worn out. The idea of doing situation comedy, which was unheard of at that time, at least for comedians of their stature, really changed their whole lives; it made it possible for them to be the household figures that they've become over the decades...the
~~~~~

eons, it seems like (**SEE B86**).

After months of trying to find another sponsor, in October 1941, Lever Brothers, the maker of Swan Soap, offered them a new contract of $7,500 a week for the entire show, which included Burns and Allen and all the other cast members. George agreed, knowing that this was the only offer they had. The major change in the show's format to a domestic situation comedy was now cast in stone. When they began **The Swan Soap Show**, George and Gracie were forty-five and forty-six years old, respectively, although she appeared much younger in age. In fact, Gracie always gave her birthdate incorrectly. George Burns said that he never asked Gracie Allen how old she was, and she never told him.

Rehearsals for the show were held on Sunday mornings, with the final rehearsal set for all day on Tuesdays, the day the show was broadcast. During the program George would go back and forth between the control room (where the engineer, agency executive and producers could be found) and the stage, checking timing and conferring with his brother, Willy, and others. Gracie spent her time repeatedly looking over her lines. The addition of venerable orchestra leader Paul Whiteman to the cast was considered a major boost. **SEE B103**.

That same year MGM signed Gracie for a film, **Mr. and Mrs. North** (**F34**), based on the popular stage play and book of a married couple always getting involved in mysteries. The play later become a long-running radio program as well as a television series (which was less successful, although it starred the very capable and attractive Richard Denning and Pamela Britton). George was not offered a part in this film and Gracie noted that this was the first time he did not help her to prepare for a performance. This was a departure from their years of working together as a team.

When they were working on their first film shorts while still in vaudeville, George had written the scripts out in longhand. But because he could not spell very well, having left school in the fourth grade, Gracie would take the scripts and type them, correcting the spelling. In radio the writers worked independently and three weeks before a broadcast they would get together with George and work out the scripts. George then showed them to Gracie, who would go to rehearsal and then give a perfect performance on the air. There were many comments at the time that the Burns and Allen radio show was one of the easiest shows to work on--due to the professionalism of George and especially Gracie, who never complained nor became angry in front of others. She came to the studio, gave her performance and went home. When they worked in feature films George noted that he would never let Gracie read the movie scripts. George would teach her the lines verbally.

In **Mr. and Mrs. North** (**F34**) Gracie played Pamela North opposite William Post, Jr., in the role of her husband. When George brought Ronnie and Sandy to the studio one day to watch their mother filming, Ronnie remarked, after Gracie had slapped William Post in a scene, "It doesn't seem very lifelike--I've never seen you do that at home."

~~~~~

After December 7, 1941, and the bombing of Pearl Harbor, which caused the entrance of the United States into World War
~~~~~

II, all the radio shows began to mention the war effort on their shows. Gracie and George often ended their radio show during these years with a mention to their radio listeners to "save paper", "save waste fat", "buy war bonds", or "dig a victory garden." Joining other radio performers, Burns and Allen would sometimes broadcast their show from military training centers in California and would perform at many of the war rallies broadcast during the war. The previous year Gracie had "delivered" 5,000 trainees to the United States Navy at San Diego to help with the naval recruiting drive. This show was broadcast around the world to over 170,000 listeners of the Armed Forces Radio. Naval officers noted that it was one of the finest contributions to recruiting ever staged. Burns and Allen had received no pay for their performance, and they paid the cost of taking their supporting cast to the show. The American Women's Voluntary Services even dedicated a "Gracie Allen Canteen" in her honor. At one point Gracie made a speech to Consolidated Aircraft and gave the company a flag courtesy of the Treasury Department.

The war had another far-reaching impact on radio production. Hank Booraem describes the ramifications brought about in the industry.

> It was incredible, the effect the war had on the shows. In the first place, about half the writers got drafted. The Armed Forces Radio Service [formerly known as the Army Radio Service] was formed to provide entertainment to the troops overseas. All these guys that got drafted were immediately grabbed by the AFRS to write comedy shows for the troops overseas. But what really happened was that they were moonlighting on the shows they had just left and sometimes at incredible prices. Some of these guys were getting two or three thousand dollars a week. You had PFC's or just plain buck privates driving to work at the Armed Forces Radio Service in Cadillacs and wearing whatever the equivalent was of Gucci loafers in their morning lineup. There would be a morning lineup in a lot right across from the AFRS headquarters on Santa Monica that was surrounded by a fence, and outside the fence were all the agents from William Morris and MCA waiting to give their guys assignments as soon as the morning lineup broke up. It was really hilarious. **SEE B86**.

With their new radio show for Swan Soap, the 1940s saw a resurgence of Burns and Allen's ratings, and the program continued to be a standard, with millions of devoted listeners each week. There were new characters like Herman the duck (Gracie's "son"), next door neighbor Blanche Morton (portrayed by actress Bea Benaderet) and Tootsie Sagwell (actress Elvia Allman), a spinster and friend of Gracie's, who were added to the cast. Also appearing on most of the shows were guest stars, often motion picture stars from Hollywood, on whom the storyline would evolve, usually with Gracie getting into trouble.

> George Burns and Gracie Allen continue to move with the times. The result is an offering that is as refreshing as it is pleasant. Their progressiveness had made itself notably manifest last season when they converted the patter from the slam-bang type of crossfire to humor of full stage dimensions. The sketches contain plot, an ingratiating brand of whimsey, suavely diffused hokim [sic] and overall good radio sense. The distaff side of the team is pictured as much as a zany than ever, but the characterization has been augmented with some recognizable facets of feminine impetuosity and fantasy all of which adds to the stature and appeal of this particular Dulcy. (**Variety**, October 14, 1942.)

Hank Booraem had entered show business as an actor, but he began a career in directing when he accepted a position in an advertising agency; in less than a year, he had moved to a larger company, joining its radio production department. The agency was Young and Rubicam, which now handled George and Gracie's program. It was while Booraem was on his way home to the East Coast after a sixteen-week stint as producer/director of **Screen Guild Theater** in Los Angeles that he received a wire from the agency's New York office. They wanted him to get off the train in Kansas City and return to California. There was a real problem on the Burns and Allen show. Glenhall Taylor, the show's director/producer, had gotten into an acrimonious discussion with George. In radio, even though the advertisers and the agencies had all the power, nobody could top the star. The result: Taylor was being removed from the show. Within a week Booraem, who personally preferred directing dramatic shows, was on the job with two of the world's most beloved comedians.

Vine Street between Sunset and Hollywood Boulevards was the epicenter of radio production during its heyday in Hollywood; nearly all of the major players--studios, advertising agencies, theaters, the Brown Derby restaurant--were located nearby. Just the phrase "Hollywood and Vine" evoked a glamorous image in many radio listeners' minds which has never faded; tourists from all over the world still make the pilgrimage every year to one of the most famous intersections ever designed. George kept a suite in the Hollywood Plaza Hotel at 1637 North Vine Street for the show's writers (who worked for George, not for the agency or sponsor) to use. While Booraem was with the show, writers Frank Galen, Sam Perrin, George Balzer, Paul Henning, Keith Fowler, and William (Willy Burns) were among those involved with the process of putting the show on paper. Booraem recalls the suite's two rooms, an outer room and what would be a bedroom, located on an airshaft with no view of the street, only that of a wall.

> I remember so well Burns standing at the window, looking out into that

> airshaft one time and one of the guys--I don't remember who it was (and believe me when I tell you these writers were the *best* there were)--one of the writers came up with a joke, and George never moved a muscle. He was looking out in a very contemplative fashion--looking out the window--must have been thirty seconds. He said,"Yeah. It's funny. It's funny." Not a smile; in fact, just a look of great concentration and of great concern: would the joke play? I've never forgotten that. **SEE B86.**

Reaffirming the abilities of the men who crafted the weekly scripts, Booraem remarks, "It was a roomful of talent, I can tell you...It was great fun to sit there and participate a little bit but basically listen to these extraordinary comedy minds at work."

The preparation for each week's Tuesday night broadcast was naturally on a rigid schedule, with discussions for future shows usually beginning three to four weeks ahead. Wednesdays were an off day for the director/producer. Thursdays and Fridays were reserved for meetings among the writers; Fridays and Saturdays were the days serious writing began. Sundays may or may not have seen the writers working at home. Everyone got together on Monday to pull the script together, with George's secretary typing and mimeographing the scripts. The first rehearsal with the actors started at around 2:00 P.M. on the day of the broadcast; concurrently the band rehearsed the music cues. By late afternoon the cast and crew were ready for a dress rehearsal, which inevitably included cutting and rearranging. The shows were deliberately over-written to a degree simply because at this point weaker parts could be cut more easily than lines could be added.

The sponsor and the advertising agency may have had final approval on guest stars in case someone was deemed to be unacceptable from a moral standpoint, but George knew where the script was going and whom he wanted on his show. Booraem doesn't remember anyone ever being turned down as being unsuitable from the sponsor's viewpoint.

He does, however, remember an advertiser teletyping him this simple message, "Ask George Burns to change his theme song."

> Well, that's like asking him to divorce Gracie. He'd had the theme ("The Love Nest") for years. I remember walking up Vine Street to the (Brown) Derby with George and saying "the client thinks that your theme song is getting a little old and tired, and would like to see something a little fresher, brighter." Predictably, he blew right across the road. It was really astonishing. But, I hung in there and in about three or four weeks, he said, "Hey, Hank, I've got an idea. I think we ought to change our theme song." I said, "Gee, George, have you thought this through?" He said, "Yeah, we've got a song we'd like to do." I said, "Well, I'll talk with the client about it." Just as though we'd never had the conversation four weeks before. It was

wonderful. **SEE B86.**

For whatever reason, however, "The Love Nest" was not thankfully, replaced then or really at any point during the remainder of George and Gracie's years on radio. (However, during the 1945-1949 seasons, Meredith Willson's song "You and I" was sometimes used as a theme song for portions of the **Maxwell House Coffee Time** series starring Burns and Allen.) "The Love Nest," with words by Otto Harbach and music by Louis A. Hirsch, was published in 1920 by the Victoria Publishing Corporation in New York City. The song had been written for George M. Cohan's production of **Mary**, which opened on Broadway on October 18, 1920, and ran for 220 performances. The tune proved to be so popular and so closely identified with George and Gracie that it was carried over to their television series, where it stayed for the run of the show.

In radio, vocalists may have changed because of the writers, the star, the agency, or the client, but announcers were strictly the domain of the advertisers and their agencies. Orchestra leaders were not replaced on a whim but could change for a number of reasons (George and Gracie worked with a number of impressive orchestra leaders). Radio-era character actors were generally not signed to a contract but rather hired as needed; for years they weren't even given on-air credit.

Hank Booraem recalls his part in the production process and compares directing the Burns and Allen show with others he had worked on.

> Once you were on the air with a radio show, there was no cutting. So, to that extent, you really had to know exactly what you were doing before you hit the air because, after that, there was no way out. But directing a comedy show like the Burns and Allen show was quite a different matter, actually. George and the writers knew what they wanted in terms of how to get the maximum laughter out of the situations and the gags and the one-liners that they had put into the script. So, I would be helpful in furthering that aim, but basically my job was to get the thing on the air and off the air on time, to cue in the music, see to it that everybody got to the mikes, and so forth. I worked in the control room, unlike some other directors who loved to work out on the stage and massage their egos at the same time. I threw the cues to the sound effects people, to Paul Whiteman, the musical director; I threw the cues to the actors and cued the announcer, and so on and so forth. But as far as the actual direction of the comedy was concerned, and this was true with every single one of the shows, it didn't make any difference whether it was Jack Benny or Eddie Cantor or Red Skelton, these guys knew what they were trying to do, and they knew how to get a laugh. Once in awhile you could be

> helpful by figuring out a way that a line could be rearranged or something of that sort but, generally speaking, George was doing it. **SEE B86**.

Hank sums up his own job as basically being that of a liaison between the sponsor, the agency, and the star and network.

The show was then broadcast once for the East Coast and later that evening for the West Coast (with the company having dinner between shows) in front of a live audience, something finally acknowledged by everyone as absolutely essential for a comedy show. There was no recording of any network shows at this time because Gen. David O. Sarnoff of NBC, William Paley of CBS and Ed Noble of ABC were all determined that recording would somehow destroy the networks' viability; a fear that, while they had a point, would essentially prove groundless as evidenced by the later mechanics of television. Hank Booraem was actually the one who persuaded Philco and ABC to put the first network show on record (prior to the advent of tape) with Bing Crosby, which brought the famous crooner back to radio while allowing him to avoid the weekly grind of a live broadcast.

As previously noted, George and Gracie did occasionally take the show to military camps during the war years, but "George really was a perfectionist, and he liked to do his show in the studio where he had complete control over what was going to happen." And Hank confirms that the studio audience loved the show. "It was very, very popular and very well-liked...As I recall, there was always a full audience. It was a 'hot ticket.'"

There was no "buddy buddy" atmosphere on the George Burns and Gracie Allen radio show as there were on several soap operas or dramatic shows with regular casts. Many character actors were used on the show but they weren't always recurring roles.

> Everyone came in and did their job." But "Burns had a great regard for his writers--if they were producing. If they weren't producing, he got rid of them. That didn't mean they weren't talented. It might mean that they were "written out" as far as **The Burns and Allen Show** was concerned.

Everybody on the creative staff attended the broadcasts.

> Believe me, nobody stayed home. You had to see how it was going to play. Your joke was coming up and, if it laid there...your head was in your hands. On some of the weaker comedy shows, I don't think it happened ever on the Burns and Allen show, the writers would sit under the audience mikes and laugh it up...you could recognize who they were from their continual horse laughs at *their* jokes."

Hank turns his attention to Gracie, giving us a picture of the "real" Gracie Allen.

> Gracie was a very private person, at least she seemed so to me. She was not a show biz type, amazingly enough. She was marvelous, absolutely wonderful, knew exactly what she was doing, always came in thoroughly prepared, never gave George any trouble at all...she knew that George knew what was best for them, and she did it. She would make a few suggestions on occasion and would get a few suggestions from George but, basically, it was an extraordinary team. And she didn't seem to pal around a lot with the people...I guess Bea Benaderet was a good friend of hers, for example, and Elvia Allman, and some of the other people who worked the show, but she was strangely un-show biz. George wasn't a loudmouth or blatant at all, but you had a sense of tremendous competence bordering on genius with George. He really knew what he was doing. He was a delight to work with as far as I was concerned. **SEE B86**.

Booraem, who worked on Eddie Cantor's show simultaneously with the Burns and Allen show, remembers George as "a brilliant, brilliant talent" and "if push ever came to shove, he [George] would give in."

Only two years after Gracie's presidential bid for the White House, George and his staff found yet another successful publicity stunt for Gracie. On their April 14, 1942, show the plot centers around Gracie taking piano lessons. Within weeks Gracie was prepared to present a piano concert. George and others decided to build on this and called in Felix Mills, an arranger for Walt Disney, to write the "Concerto for Index Finger" sometimes referred to as the "One Finger Piano Concerto." The orchestra would play sections of well-known melodies while Gracie sat at the piano. When she played certain keys with one finger, the orchestra would "take off" from her last note and play the selected concert music. Gracie was a hit. She played her piece on their radio show with Paul Whiteman's orchestra, and on March 16, 1943, she performed the "Concerto for Index Finger" at New York City's Carnegie Hall. According to Hank Booraem, preparation for the concert did indeed go on for months and culminated in an extraordinary event. Accompanying Gracie was Paul Whiteman and his fifty-piece orchestra, who entertained the black-tie, invitation-only audience for an hour prior to the half-hour broadcast, with more music after the radio show (**B86**). Gracie also was guest artist at the Hollywood Bowl with the San Francisco Orchestra, at Symphony Hall in Boston, Convention Hall in Philadelphia, and the Los Angeles Philharmonic Auditorium. She later performed the piece with pianist and composer José Iturbi as conductor in the 1944 MGM film **Two Girls and a Sailor** (**F35**), which was the last motion picture in which Gracie Allen appeared. Publicity pieces for this latest event would refer to Gracie as that "beloved nitwit of the networks."

Nineteen forty-four was also the year a five-times-per-week column on events of national interest "written" by Gracie began appearing in various newspapers around the country. Her name had already been connected to an earlier trademarked effort, "Topics of the Dazed." The publicity mill was still grinding away happily.

Scripts and articles were constantly being written "by" and for Burns and Allen for a multitude of projects. Whether Gracie was doing a "guest column" for Walter Winchell or George and Gracie were promoting a new film (including those in which they did not appear) or overseas broadcasts or other stars' radio shows, their writers were kept busy. George and Gracie were constantly being interviewed, and there were spots for the Safety Council, the Salvation Army and the housing shortage to be done. In addition, there were commercials and change announcements for their own radio show. The Burnses helped in the promotion of their sponsors' products, including appearing in ads in major magazines. They had to promote and perform at their personal appearances. And they participated in publicity for Paramount for current events ("Food For Thought at Breakfast"). Add to that the occasional article prepared especially for **Variety**, it was exhausting, but challenging, work being a Burns and Allen writer.

Gracie wanted to stop working in motion pictures so she could spend as much time as possible with her children. The radio show and promotions still took up some of her time, but she was so comfortable with the character of "Gracie Allen" that it seemed to be fairly easy for her to read through a radio script and then perform live on radio with little study.

Gracie tried to make her home life as normal as possible for her family. For their summer vacation in 1942 the Burnses and their children checked into a Los Angeles hotel for two weeks and pretended they were tourists--visiting Los Angeles museums and landmarks in the city they had never really seen even after six years of living in California. Having chosen their own children from an orphanage made them keenly aware of the needs of other children, and they once urged listeners to contribute to the North Carolina Health Association so that adequate medical exams could be provided to children whose parents couldn't afford them.

While those who knew Gracie acknowledged her to be a very intelligent woman, she occasionally did do some amusing things. A newspaper article of December 14, 1942, reported that Gracie had gone Christmas shopping by bus not car, as gas was being rationed for automobiles due to the war. However, she got on the wrong bus and ended up somewhere in North Hollywood. Lost, she had to phone George to come and pick her up in their car, causing him to use up their gas rationing coupons.

~~~~

After several years with Swan Soap as their radio sponsor, Burns and Allen re-signed with General Foods to take over the popular **Maxwell House Coffee Time** in September, 1945. Charlie Ruggles and Frank Morgan had briefly been associated with the show before Fanny Brice brought her "Baby Snooks" character to the show between 1940 and 1944. Joining George and Gracie were Meredith Willson and his orchestra along with with announcer Bill Goodwin. The characters of Harry and Blanche Morton continued as the Burnses' next door neighbors. More and more new radio shows were being broadcast in the 1940s, including comedy shows, bringing more competition for Burns and Allen, but as noted in 1946, "Say what you will about the lack of fresh talent in radio's bigtime comedy
~~~~

parades, the fact is that until the new laugh croppers are born, made or built, the old ones had better be kept on" (**Variety**, September 11, 1946). Their years with Maxwell House were the longest with one sponsor (1945-1949).

On February 20, 1947, George and Gracie celebrated their fifteen years on radio with guest star Al Jolson. The medium had been good to George and Gracie, and they had helped tremendously to define its popularity.

Suddenly in 1949 newspapers announced that General Foods, Burns and Allen's sponsors for the **Maxwell House Coffee Time** show, had refused to renew their radio contract. Reportedly Burns and Allen were asking for a salary of $17,500 a week. Their show was still high in the ratings. But their sponsor decided to go with a cheaper program and announced that **Father Knows Best**, starring Robert Young, would replace Burns and Allen on radio.

That same year George and Gracie returned to the London Palladium to perform for the first time in fifteen years. The team had always enjoyed great popularity in Great Britain and this visit was no exception. Their August 16 headline appearance was a sellout and the crowd loved them. They were joined by other American acts, most notably comedian Ben Blue. It was a true event, one not unnoticed by **Variety** (August 24, 1949), which said, in part, "Burns & Allen...got an ovation on entry, and immediately had the house in guffaws." Gracie played her "Concerto for Index Finger," and she and George joined Ben Blue for a re-enactment of the hilarious minuet scene from their film **College Holiday** (**F29**). Jack Benny and Jane Wyman were coaxed on stage from the audience to conclude a memorable evening for the lucky fans.

~~~~~

Since radio's inception in the 1920s NBC was the leading radio network over its competitor, CBS. While radio stars did join the CBS network from time to time, they often returned to NBC, as did Burns and Allen. But the year of 1949 saw a change. William (Bill) Paley, president of CBS, decided to try to win over the NBC stars to his network, beginning with the comedy shows. Burns and Allen were favorites of Paley's and he enjoyed comedy shows, while NBC's David O. Sarnoff disliked comedians, even though their shows had helped to make NBC the success it was with radio listeners. Paley made his decision at a time when "radio station owners were at a low point and were beginning to lose faith in radio and were still afraid of television." **SEE B407: 129**.

At the start of the 1949-1950 season, George Burns and Gracie Allen, in addition to comedians Amos 'n' Andy, Fred Allen, and their good friend Jack Benny, joined a list of NBC radio performers who switched networks and moved their shows to CBS. Block Drug Company stepped in and picked up the Burns and Allen show for one of their products, Amm-i-dent Toothpaste. This last radio season for Burns and Allen ran from September 1949 to May 1950 and was known as **The Amm-i-dent Toothpaste Show**.

The last great radio stunt for Burns and Allen was part of the Amm-i-dent show. They kicked off the "George Burns Sings" campaign on their own show, which was taped November 20, 1949, and aired on November 23 (**R771**). Gracie began a two-week blitz of other radio shows (primarily on CBS), searching for those that would allow George to fulfill his
~~~~~

dream of appearing as a singer. Her appearances on those shows, some that had live audiences and some that did not, were interspersed with mentions of her mission on some shows and the reading of telegrams about it on others. She was scheduled for a number of shows on which she may or may not have appeared. Although she was looking for a place for George to sing on Wednesday nights (the night their own show was broadcast), most of the programs she visited actually broadcast on other nights of the week.

~~~~~

In the spring of 1950, there were rumors in the entertainment business that Burns and Allen would soon be considering going into television. Within days it was announced that they would be joining CBS television in the fall of 1950. In just one season, 1949-50, radio audiences lost 20% of their audiences to television (**B407: 179**). Early television was financed by radio profits but at the same time cut into these profits. With television beginning to be successful with viewers, radio started its decline as the major broadcasting medium. This was similar to the decline of vaudeville due to the influence of motion pictures and radio in the 1920s and 1930s. Motion picture attendance was adversely affected by the advent of popular television as well, another blow to the studios that came on the heels of a forced divestiture of their theater chains. Only those studios with the foresight to join forces with the new medium rather than fight it would survive, at least until a conglomerate could come along and swallow them up anyway.

Concerning Burns and Allen's leaving radio for television, there was was a outcry that this was a capital gains arrangement. The Music Corporation of America (MCA) negotiated the CBS contract for Burns and Allen, who had been with the agency of William Morris for over twenty years. The ruling was that the CBS deal could not affect the contract with Burns and Allen.

Gracie was very apprehensive about going into television. After working for ten years in vaudeville and eighteen years in radio, she probably had thought that she was at the end of Burns and Allen's career.

Performing for radio was easy for Gracie as she simply read her scripts in front of a microphone. After playing the character "Gracie" for so many years, Gracie Allen didn't really have to work at creating a character. She wanted to retire, but George was only in his mid-fifties and knew that to continue working they both had to go into television. Even after all of the years they had worked together as a team, the public still saw Gracie as the star performer with George just playing the part as "straight man." As he had done in film and radio (whenever they had moved into a new medium) George had to convince his wife to make the move. He persuaded Gracie to do a pilot test for television (several CBS radio performers were asked to do a kinescope). Gracie's screen test was successful enough to result in her agreeing to do the television show. George felt later that Gracie was afraid of his starting work in such a competitive and new business as television because of his age (fifty-five). Although Gracie was virtually the same age, it was George who really carried on all of the business aspects of the show as well as being an important part in the development of the television show, more
~~~~~

than he had been in radio. In addition to his acting and writing on the show, television would eventually require George to work even more as a businessman. He later formed his own production company and took on the role of executive producer of the show.

George met with the CBS executives to determine what type of show Burns and Allen would be performing. They decided on the idea of a situation comedy, with themes centered around Gracie getting into trouble and involving everyone else in the cast. This was the same type of show Burns and Allen had been doing on radio for years. Presumably to draw in fans of the variety show format as well, a bit of that genre was mixed in.

Ralph Levy, a young director for CBS television, was hired as the director of the new Burns and Allen show. A pilot was made and sold to the Carnation Company, which would continue to sponsor (or cosponsor) the show for the eight years it was broadcast. Work commenced on the television show while Burns and Allen continued their radio show. They broadcast their last radio series program on May 17, 1950, (**R796**).

~~~~~

In the late summer of 1950 George and Gracie and their cast went to New York City, staying at the Algonquin Hotel near the theater district, to begin preparing for their first television show. Everyone was apprehensive--after all, Burns and Allen were firmly established in radio with eighteen years of success and now they were trying something entirely new and risky. Most of the radio stars who tried to move into television would not be successful.

At 8:00 P.M. on Thursday night, October 12, 1950, the premiere of **The George Burns and Gracie Allen Show** was broadcast live in front of a studio audience (**T1**). The performance took place at the Mansfield Theater on West 47th Street in New York City, near the Palace Theatre where vaudevillians George "Nat" Burns and Grace Allen had performed so many years before. As few television studios were available in the early days of television, shows broadcast from theaters that had to set up the television equipment as best they could. This first show received very favorable reviews from most quarters:

"One of the TV delights of the season". **Variety**.

"A first-rate show". **New York World Telegram**.

"A superb performance". **Radio Daily**.

Newspaper ads appearing in the first month of the new show claimed the **George Burns and Gracie Allen Show** as the "funniest situation comedy on anybody's channel."

One naysayer was John Crosby in his **New York Herald Tribune** column about the show's debut: "One thing I've noticed about virtually all the old radio comics, newly transferred to television. They all talk too much. George Burns even acts as narrator on his show...The only explanation I have for this strange behavior is that [he] doesn't really believe that television actually exists."

Through the years the positive comments generally outweighed the negative, however. By the next year, the **New**
~~~~~

York TV Guide (ca. December 1951) was reaffirming its admiration for George's "wonderfully good-humored manner" and his "who's-afraid-of-the-big-bad-audience nonchalance." The supporting cast, as well, received consistently good reviews.

After its debut, the Burns and Allen team worked two months in New York City, airing six shows before the cast returned to California. For the first two years the show aired every two weeks and, as in early radio, the entire country did not receive the original broadcast. The West Coast viewers, who were three time zones away, received kinescopes of the live shows two weeks later. When the coaxial cable was laid in 1951, connecting the coasts of the United States, the shipping of kinescopes became unnecessary as the entire nation could now view all shows at the time they were broadcast.

The Burns and Allen show allowed the audience a glimpse into the imaginary offstage lives of show business personalities and television stars George Burns and Gracie Allen. Art even imitated life because George's character was constantly doing something connected with their fictitious television show; Gracie seldom mentioned it. Only occasionally would Gracie allude to the fact that she contributed anything to the household income, although her friends did not hesitate to point out to George who the real star of the family was. The show let us in on their relationships with family and friends (most often their neighbors, the Mortons), and the ensuing complications that arise when, to people's surprise, the "real-life" Gracie acts just like her alter ego, a woman who takes everything quite literally. Whether the action takes place at their home at 312 Maple Drive in Beverly Hills, their suite at the St. Moritz Hotel in New York City, at the driver's license bureau or the city jail, the results are almost always the same. Everyone except Gracie is confused. She was still playing the "dumb Dora" character she had been portraying since their vaudeville days.

When the show debuted, it was part situation comedy, part variety show, with singers and dancers filling in between acts. Even before the show moved from live to film, it had dropped the variety angle and concentrated on being a sitcom. Just as in radio, the sponsor/advertising agency relationship was of paramount importance in these early years. The sponsor's products were featured liberally, and commercial spots were integrated by clever seguels within the scripts with help from the show's announcer, who wore a second hat as a member of the onscreen cast. Just as Carnation Evaporated Milk was heralded as having come "From Contented Cows," George and Gracie were called "Carnation's Contented Couple."

Stains of "Ain't Misbehavin" could be heard bridging the scenes. One of the most popular features of the show was the addition of a vaudeville-style routine at the close of each show. And Gracie, as always, would stand to George's left side, sometimes having walked onstage holding his hand. Every show would end either with "Gracie, say good night," or "Say good night, Gracie."

The one element that did not change as the show evolved was the quality of the writing, as critical to the success and longevity of a show as its execution (actually, more so) and the one thing that cannot be artificially produced, even with Hollywood's fabled wizardry. George especially knew the importance of writers and often employed the same ones as he marched from one medium into another. As brilliant as

Gracie's execution of the material was, and as effortless as George made his role seem, they were, after all, actors playing a part, memorizing words from a script. The combined talents of the writers and the actors were the primary reason for the show's appeal, then and now. It remains one of the most genuinely funny shows that ever appeared on television.

With characters and the occasional script making their way from the radio show, Burns and Allen would appear, on the surface, to be like any number of other programs trying to translate old successes into new ones. It contained some of the standard plot lines (but made unique by Gracie's spin on the situation) that populated many sitcoms of the 1950s, usually dealing with the wife trying to do something without having her husband find out. Nor was it the only show that would take on a surreal quality, having us believe that we were privy to the off-screen lives of some public people who had yet another television show that was broadcast on American television, just not the television in *our* homes. Jack Benny, after all, would soon be doing the same thing.

But all similarities to most other shows ended there. First and foremost, George and Gracie succeeded when many of their contemporaries did not. Theirs was a "talking" act, malleable to the demands of the various media. Television was kind to Burns and Allen and was a perfect showcase for their talent and appeal. As early as 1935 one writer stated they were "better on the stage than they could possibly be on the radio...the full effect of their comedy depends upon the visual image (**B321**)." There was no slapstick, which is not a criticism of that comedic form, but which can be difficult to sustain week after week. They were comfortable within themselves, and they made the audience comfortable, which is absolutely essential if an entertainer wants to be invited into viewers' living rooms week after week, year after year.

There were no irritating characters here, just warm, friendly people who shared remarkable chemistry and had charisma to burn. George wore his tolerance like a patina; Gracie was always exquisitely ladylike. They seemed like our friends and we wished they really were. Their onscreen personas were so well-honed, so familar, so pleasingly predictable, the audience didn't have to worry about being unpleasantly surprised with these two. Their characters were, in fact, far more likeable than they had been in any of their film roles. It's true they weren't really just playing themselves. But neither was there any danger of finding out that George and Gracie were anything but the nice people they appeared to be onscreen. Illusion is an essential of show business, and too much *disillusion* can be fatal to an actor's career. They didn't make that mistake.

And there is no doubt that the "Gracie" character set the stage for others like her, male and female, including modern-day actors Suzanne Somers (Chrissy Snow on **Three's Company**, ABC), Betty White (Rose Nylund on **The Golden Girls**, NBC) and the late Ted Knight (Ted Baxter on **The Mary Tyler Moore Show**, CBS). Not only do these characters make us laugh, they make us feel a little smug. "Gracie" had, in fact, become so well developed through the years that anyone in the world who loved comedy recognized Gracie Allen by her first name alone.

To be able to make the transfer from vaudeville to film to radio to television with your popularity intact--even increasing--was to be a show business phenomenon. George and

Gracie were a team whose talents complemented each other's and who were secure enough in those talents not to get in each other's way. Each was, in fact, incredibly lucky to have found the other one. Without George's brilliant offstage machinations, Gracie's dislike for the business end of show business might have mired her in professional obscurity. Likewise, Gracie's onstage persona was the perfect coattail for George in the beginning; without her, his behind-the-scenes abilities might never have found the outlet they deserved.

When George broke the fourth wall, playing directly to an audience that's traditionally "ignored" by the actors in standard theatrical staging, it was years before others in his position would emulate him (although not before it had been done successfully in the play **Our Town**). The effect was entrancing, making each member of the audience feel as if George had invited him or her into the show's inner circle, sharing privately in the fun. (Interestingly, every George Burns series that followed found him in some variation of the same position.) Occasionally, George's stammering would reappear. (Although it often seemed to just be part of the way he delivered his monologue on this and future series, it can often be detected in personal interviews as well.) Seeing him hop over part of the set to get back into the scene didn't seem at all unusual, nor did hearing Harry Von Zell urge listeners to pick up Carnation recipe leaflets so that they, too, could make 'better cake and tastier icing." The vaude-ville routines (whether they were within the storyline as a hilarious integrated skit or done as an endpiece), the running gags--Bill Goodwin's endless parade of girlfriends, Gracie's closet full of men's hats, Harry Von Zell getting fired, George's questionable vocal abilities and his magical television set--a brilliant ensemble cast, talented and prolific writers: this is the stuff of legendary television. And no other show had Gracie Allen.

~~~~~

Many of the actors employed on the series had come out of radio and had, in fact, been featured on George and Gracie's radio show from time to time. Most notable of these were Bea Benaderet and Hal March, who had been cast as the radio Mortons; both made the switch to television with George and Gracie. Bea Benaderet had years of experience working on various radio programs and had often worked with George and Gracie portraying various voices and characters. She stayed for the run of the series; March, however, soon left for other projects (which would eventually include hosting the ultrapopular quiz show **The $64,000 Question**). Interestingly, he would return later in other featured roles on the show, including the partner of his own former character!

For the first three years, in fact, the role of Harry Morton resembled a revolving door. Hal March left the show after seven episodes and was replaced by John Brown, who remained in the role for eleven episodes. When Brown left, ubiquitous character actor Fred Clark stepped in. In the show's fourth season, Larry Keating was hired to take over for the departing Clark, and he remained with the show until it went off the air. Fred Clark's interpretation certainly fleshed out the character, but Larry Keating is probably the quintessential Harry Morton. No real attempt was made to keep
~~~~~

the character the same through each of the changes in actors (even Harry's profession changed); each actor brought unique qualities to the role, which essentially changed as the actor changed. When Keating took over the role the writers accelerated the friction between Harry and George, which was in direct contrast to the relationship shared by their wives, and turned him into a walking dictionary. The one constant was the bickering that occurred between Harry and his wife, Blanche. However, it's obvious that the characters truly loved each other. They could hurl barbs at each other endlessly, but if anyone else dared to do so he or she would be making a mistake by thinking it would go unchallenged.

A number of popular character actors (including Bob Sweeney, Hal March's partner in the act, "Sweeney and March") made numerous appearances throughout the years, sometimes playing a variety of roles both before and after they were cast as a recurring character. That feeling of "family" was evident in other areas as well, since it isn't unusual to hear actual production staff members' names used as characters on the show.

Yvonne Lime, who appeared toward the end of the series as one of the janitor's daughters and was also one of the "billboard girls" who announced at the end of some shows that "George and Gracie will be back with one of their vaudeville routine," later co-starred with Ronnie Burns and Doris Packer in the series **Happy** (NBC, 1960-1961).

~~~~~

In discussing why Burns and Allen were so successful when many others had failed to make the transition from radio to television, George Burns revealed that the show was written so that the laughs were spread among the cast. This echoed what George had told interviewers in the 1930s concerning Burns and Allen working in motion pictures, with George insisting that they not be given starring roles in the films they made so that the public wouldn't tire of them by seeing Burns and Allen constantly on the screen. When that comment was made, George and Gracie gave the impression that they thought that, like most entertainers, they would not endure with the public but would decline after a period of popularity. In the early 1930s they had no idea that they would be among the very few in show business whose popularity would never cease and that they would continue as a successful comedy team until they stopped working.

In television, George and Gracie had to change the way they worked as this was a different medium than radio. In radio, George had met and worked with the writers of the show weekly. They and the advertisers and sponsors of the radio show came to realize that George knew what type of material was right for Gracie and their show. Eighteen years of success proved him to be right. But television was different. With television the audience had the potential to be on a much grander scale. And television was a visual medium, not just audio as was radio. The actors had to do more than just read from a script. Lines had to be memorized and stage movements directed for the thirty-minute show. It was unlike anything George and Gracie had done before, and it was to prove to be very demanding and stressful for the star of the team. As Gracie said, somewhat apprehensively, at the time of their television premiere in 1950, she hadn't memorized anything for
~~~~~

over twenty years. George was involved in all aspects of the show in addition to acting in it and working with his writers, Paul Henning, Sid Dorfman, Harvey Helm, and Willy Burns.

At the start of their third season, on October 9, 1952, (**T53**), **The George Burns and Gracie Allen Show** became a weekly filmed series with the Carnation Company (for Carnation Evaporated Milk) and B. F. Goodrich alternating sponsorship of the show every other week until the last season, which was co-sponsored by General Mills. George formed his own company, McCadden Productions, to distribute the show on film. The company, which was named after the street in Hollywood where Willy Burns lived, contracted for office space at the General Service Studios at 1040 North Las Palmas. Prior to this, after returning to California, the show had broadcast from CBS's television studios in Hollywood (not to be confused with Television City, which wasn't inaugurated until later that year). Now responsible for all aspects of the show and its production and distribution, McCadden Productions was spending $30,000-$35,000 a week to produce the show. As had been the case soon after Burns and Allen had started working together as a successful vaudeville team, Gracie and George each owned half the business. Paul Henning, one of the Burns and Allen writers who had worked with them since 1941, commented that if the show had had to continue live, Gracie Allen would probably have quit (**B245**). She was under a tremendous strain due to the production schedules and the amount of dialogue she had to memorize weekly. The ability to film the program helped to keep the show alive by lessening the burden on its star.

At General Service Studios, Stage One was first used for the filming of **The George Burns and Gracie Allen Show** and then the show moved to Stage Six (now renamed the "George Burns Stage"). Other early television shows were filmed at the studios, including **The Adventures of Ozzie and Harriet** and **The Lone Ranger**, as well as the Joan Davis and Ann Sothern shows. Desi Arnaz was also renting Stage Two at that studio for the filming of **I Love Lucy** with his wife, Lucille Ball.

Al Simon, associate producer for **I Love Lucy**, and cinematographer Karl Freund had developed a multiple-camera system which would allow the filming of a show from different angles and camera ranges at the same time. Producing the show on film allowed for technically better production values and the results look less dated than when viewed on kinescopes. But while **I Love Lucy** was filmed before a live audience with three cameras, the two-camera production of **Burns and Allen** was not. Two edited episodes were previewed periodically in front of live audiences of roughly one hundred fifty to two hundred people at the RCA Studios in order to record the sound of applause and laughter. **SEE B92**.

George Burns hired Al Simon as associate producer and Herb Browar, stage manager of **I Love Lucy**, to work on **The Burns and Allen Show** and put it on film. Browar would be supervisor of production. Both men would eventually team up with former **Burns and Allen** writer Paul Henning for the remarkable clutch of rural comedies that he created, produced and/or helped bring to CBS under the Filmways banner: **The Beverly Hillbillies** (1962-1971), **Petticoat Junction** (1963-1970) and **Green Acres** (1965-1971).

The show's production fit into a routine that continued week after week, and year after year. George had a routine in radio and continued it with television with some alterations. On Monday George met with his writers at his office on the studio property and Gracie sat for dress fittings. Tuesday the cast rehearsed the show and on Wednesday they filmed the show. On Thursday (Gracie's day off) and Friday, George and his writers met to plan future shows. Saturday and Sunday, George and Gracie worked on memorizing their scripts at home. Gracie always memorized the entire script and everyone's lines, even reading the commercials. Her lines were so hard to remember that she had to know all of the lines so that she could answer the questions. Then the week would begin, again following the same pattern.

Gracie's personal appearance changed during the years she worked on the television show. She always maintained her petite figure, and at one time was named the actress with the prettiest legs in the country by the American Beauty Congress. She also was on several lists as one of the best dressed women in Hollywood. For television, as in film, her dark hair needed to be lighter so she became a coppery blond. Improvements in hair, makeup and lighting techniques contributed to Gracie actually looking even younger and prettier as the series progressed than she had at its beginning.

Ronnie Burns was permanently added to the cast in 1955 after being introduced to reporters in a Beverly Hills press conference. His addition on the October 10, 1955 (**T174**) episode introduced a younger character on the show and also took some of the pressure off of his mother. Ronnie was a handsome young man, especially popular with young women, of course. Membership in his fan club soared, and thousands sent in a dollar to join, eagerly anticipating receipt of his 8x10 autographed photo and entering contests that could win them a chance to attend previews and see and talk to him. Ronnie had won a part in the 1948 film **Apartment for Peggy** at the age of twelve and eventually appeared at the Pasadena Playhouse; once he started on his parents' show, he was kept busy making guest appearances on other shows as well. That same year the show moved its story locale to New York City for a time before returning to California. When Ronnie joined the show some of the storylines began to revolve around his problems, although his mother still was involved in the solutions. But at the start of the seventh season in 1956, it was becoming obvious to some writers that Gracie Allen was playing a smaller part in the show. Not everyone liked it, either. One reviewer groused that Gracie was too domestic as a mother and not as zany.

Unknown to the public, Gracie Allen's health had started to decline in the early 1950s when she had a minor heart attack. She was diagnosed with angina but refused to quit work, even on her doctor's advice. Since she had such a private nature, she never mentioned her problems to others and attempted to carry on as before. But the strain and stress of television was beginning to take its toll on her health. As early as 1954 a rumor spread that Gracie would retire at the end of the current season.

But the show's audiences couldn't see a change on the screen, and in 1956 **The George Burns and Gracie Allen Show** was noted in the press as having the honor of being the longest-running situation comedy being broadcast. It was disappointing that the show never won an Emmy, although it was nominated four times during the eight years it was on the air. Gracie was nominated six times and went home empty-handed every Emmy night. George was never even nominated. Hindsight allows us to see how badly his talents were underrated.

But the show was popular; the two most popular shows in England in 1956 were **I Love Lucy** and **Burns and Allen**. In fact, when the series premiered in London in 1955, it handed BBC commercial television its all-time highest ratings, comparable only to radio ratings the BBC had received for the abdication of King Edward VIII in 1936 and Britain's declaration of war on Germany in 1939. Not surprisingly, George and Gracie went to England for a television appearance to promote their program's debut there. Praise was no less forthcoming in this country. John O'Hara wrote in the April 30, 1954, issue of **Collier's**, "There are some performers who never let you down...Don't know them, never met them. I just...love them." The show was even on the air in Morocco.

Not only was George busy with his show, but he and/or his company were involved with the production of other television shows, including **Life With Father** (1953) starring Leon Ames and Lurene Tuttle, **That's My Boy** (1954) with Eddie Mayehoff and the pilot for the 1955 series **Professional Father** starring Steve Dunne and Barbara Billingsley. **The People's Choice** with Jackie Cooper and a talking bassett hound named Cleo was another project that kicked off in 1955. **The Bob Cummings Show** also began broadcasting in 1955. McCadden employees worked on a pilot called **The Getter and the Holder** with Peter Lorre that same year and later produced **Panic**, a 1957 dramatic anthology. **The Many Loves of Dobie Gillis**, starring **The Bob Cummings Show**'s Dwayne Hickman, began in 1959. George had originally acquired the property for Ronnie, but the character's creator felt Ronnie was not suited for the part (**B248**). George was the executive producer for an unsold pilot called **Maggie**, starring Margaret O'Brien, Leon Ames, and Fay Baker, which CBS aired on August 29, 1960. George financed the pilot for **Mister Ed**, owned part of the show, and continued to be involved in its development after it became a series in 1961, even sitting in on "every final writer's session" (**B345**). NBC tried to get George to produce the **Fibber McGee and Molly** pilot. McCadden Productions and George did produce sitcom pilots for Carol Channing, (**The Carol Channing Show**) and George Sanders (**The Fabulous Oliver Chantry**), and McCadden produced one for Herminone Gingold (**The Hermione Gingold Show**), none of which became series. There was also a proposed series called **The Delightful Imposter**. George even worked with his buddy Jack Benny on his television show, and McCadden produced Benny's first foray into color.

~~~~~

Publicity stunts were as much a part of life for the television show as they had been for radio, although the impact might not have been quite the same. In 1954 the Associated Press announced that legendary French fashion designer Christian Dior had been offered a guest shot by George by wire, "an offer, including expenses, to come to America and appear...with a showing of his fashions which de-emphasize the bust." His remuneration? "We offered him a flat figure." On August 11, 1954, Dior "turned down" the offer with no explanation. There was also a tie-in with Bullock's Department Store in November of that year. For their August 23, 1954, episode (**T132**), in which a Western Union office is used as a setting, Willy Burns persuaded the well-known firm to distribute fifteen thousand jumbo telegrams carrying cuts of George and Gracie. Their October 11, 1954,
~~~~~

entry (**T134**) featured a salute to the Do-It-Yourself industry. Dave Willock, who appeared on the show as a carpenter, was actually their technical advisor and handled the promotion with the Delta Power Tool Company, which carried ads in **Life**, **Time**, and **Fortune** and put up display materials in 14,000 hardware stores across the country. In 1955 they kicked off the season with a train trip to New York and joined with the Santa Fe Railroad to distribute five hundred thousand heralds calling attention to the show to its passengers, and all of the trains' menus carried copy about the broadcast. The "Gracie" character was still considered by some, anyway, to be as zany as ever. U.S. Representative John H. Hay of New York declared that he considered the idea of rearranging national holidays something Gracie Allen would have dreamed up. There was even publicity about a winner on Groucho Marx's quiz show being compared to her.

The television show basically ceased production during the months of June and July, but the tireless George was on a merry-go-round and Gracie could barely put on the brakes. Contrary to what some said, George was neither an "improbable" nor a "reluctant" tycoon. Associates say that such a description was inaccurate, and his workload bears them out. McCadden Productions had gone from grossing $1.25 million in 1953 to $5 million in 1954 and was one of the top ten production companies by November of that year. The company was so busy filming pilots, series, industrials and commercials (for everyone from Carnation and B. F. Goodrich to Toni Home Permanents and U.S. Steel) they were forced temporarily to rent space at the Samuel Goldwyn Studios. McCadden was not only adding personnel to the payroll it was constantly adding new sets to **Burns and Allen**, having only started with four when the show went to film. George was offered a role in **Guys and Dolls** but had to turn it down. The **Burns and Allen Show** was clobbering its direct competition in the ratings. Although it was also successful on the whole, it only cracked the Top 25 once, according to the A. C. Nielsen Company, during the 1953-1954 season, when it registered at number twenty with a 32.4 rating compared to the number one show, **I Love Lucy**, which came in with a 58.8 (**B91**). A deal for a McCadden-produced mystery series based on stories by Craig Rice was reported in May 1954 as being closed, and it was revealed that Barbara Stanwyck was about to sign on as star. The start date for the next thirty-nine episodes of **Burns and Allen** was set for August 18, 1954. Beginning in September 1954 the show was seen throughout Canada on ten Canadian Broadcasting Company stations. A projected Burns and Allen dramatic show, a one-shot for a General Electric series, was scrapped because there was simply "no time," although George did appear later in a segment of **GE Theater** (**T399**.) CBS had plans to televise **The Mikado** with George and Gracie and Jack Benny, but it didn't materialize. The next year, 1955, saw the same frenetic pace, and there was little time to spend in the summer home the Burnses had acquired overlooking the Balboa yacht basin. George wanted to help produce a new vehicle for Jackie Gleason called **The Jack of Spades** but it was eventually deferred. The October 3, 1955, episode (**T173**) saw Burns and Allen get an eleven-point boost in the Nielsen ratings.

George and Gracie had helped sell their sponsors' products in radio; now as television stars they appeared in more commercials, including ones for Zenith Television,

Motorola, Columbia Phonographs, Stauffer Home Plan, American Airlines, McDaniel's Market, and Chevrolet. And everyone, it seemed, wanted an interview. **TV Guide** alone featured the pair on four of its covers during the show's broadcast run (the weeks of November 6, 1954, October 8, 1955, December 1, 1956, and September 28, 1957), and George and Gracie and other cast members were subjects of numerous articles for that magazine and others. And they were doing on-air promos for other stars' television and radio shows, including **Amos 'n' Andy** and **Family Party**.

Hedda Hopper reported that George and Gracie were finished with the film industry (**Los Angeles Times**, May 10, 1953), saying "we love to see movies, but not make them." Production on the television series suffered the occasional setback, as well. A fire on May 10, 1954, destroyed one of the General Service Studios' main buildings, the one that housed lumber and workshops, as well as its generator plant, which supplied power for the cameras and lighting systems. Ten fire companies responsed to the blaze, which was discovered around 7:00 P.M. The fire was contained, but arson was suspected, and the loss was estimated at between one hundred fifty and two hundred thousand dollars. In September 1954, Gracie was actually knocked unconscious for several minutes when a stuffed toy bear fell on her during a rehearsal (newspapers carrying the story declared "Gracie Allen KO'd by Bear"). A strike by the Screen Actors Guild loomed in August 1955 but it was settled quickly (**SEE B92, B420**).

By May 19, 1954, a Hollywood trade magazine was reporting that Burns and Allen might star in the film version of the Broadway hit **The Solid Gold Cadillac**, a reversal of their earlier pronouncement. George and Gracie had already turned down an offer to star in a summer-month California production of the play because of the demands of their television show (the program was going through the summer without a hiatus), but they scheduled a trip to New York City in June to discuss the film and the possibility they would coproduce it with Max Gordon and George S. Kaufman. It would be their big screen return if the details could be worked out. By June 14, 1954, George was still saying he wanted to do the film; Gracie said that television was taking enough of their time. In the end, both got their wish. George is heard as the narrator; Gracie is nowhere to be seen--or heard. **SEE F36**.

Cynthia Hobart Lindsay, wife of MCA agent Louis (Lou) Lindsay, teamed up with George in 1954 on his first book, **I Love Her, That's Why!** (**B34**), which appeared on store shelves in 1955. A writer whose articles had appeared in a number of national magazines, Lindsay's efforts were rewarded when the book, published on October 30, 1955, sold 16,000 copies at $3.50 each in its first three weeks of publication and reached number eight on **The Los Angeles Times** best-seller list in November. Before the year was out it went into its second printing. The London MCA office closed two deals for its publication in the United Kingdom, with the **London Sunday Graphic** serializing it and the E. H. Allen Company handling hardcover publication. Too busy to return to London to promote the book for its scheduled November 1, 1955, British publication date (as a tie-in to the BBC premiere of their series) George taped a message instead. George said at the time he never intended to do another book, "This is it!" Jack Benny provided the prologue: "You will find this the kind of book you can't put down. I know I won't be able to. At three cents a day from the lending library I find myself a very fast reader." The book was well written and gathered a number of good reviews, not unlike this one from the November 26-December 2, 1955, issue of **TV Guide**, "It's a funny, entertaining book, and a revealing look at what makes performers tick." Larry Wolters, in **Booklist**, December 1, 1955: 52: 144, said "It's...a beautiful love letter, one of the best since Elizabeth Barrett was writing about Robert Browning, altho the meter is different." George and his writers couldn't resist plugging the book on their show, so when the book was published, it appeared in the script with Blanche and Gracie going to a bookstore.

In 1954 George decided that the show's summer reruns should instead be called "encores." During the 1953 summer season George had tried opening each repeat episode by stepping out of his house to tell the audience that a show was being rerun. For some reason part of the audience made it known they felt they'd been fooled and George later announced, "We don't want to cheat the public." This time each repeat show would feature a "billboard" opening with the words "George Burns and Gracie Allen Encore" and contain animated cartoon characters of the couple. They would also be running several first-run shows during the summer months; this was deemed to be a smart move by newspaper television and radio editor Hal Humphrey.

Posing for photographers in July of 1954, George was accidentally hit in the right eye with a champagne cork that had popped out when heat from the lights caused the bottle to expand. Never one to miss the opportunity for a bit of good advance press, the Burns and Allen publicity mill had Gracie quoted as saying, "That George! He's just getting ready for color television." And ready he was. Their one and only color episode went into production August 18 of that year and aired on October 4 (**T133**); it was the first weekly filmed comedy to be transmitted in color by CBS. It didn't go off without a hitch, however. Someone discovered that George's cigar "looms as an extra finger on test shots," and it was suggested that the problem could be solved either by changing the shading of the cigar or the hue of his makeup.

Son Ronnie was enjoying the lifestyle of a young, handsome television actor. Working on George and Gracie's show and classes at the Pasadena Playhouse, USC and Santa Monica College had given him a taste of both the show business and academic lives, but so many options and interests made it difficult to settle on a career course. Along with his acting he had dabbled in singing; in 1958 Verve released a single of "Double Date" backed with "Kinda Cute." He did get into a bit of trouble when he was stopped for driving eightly-five miles per hour in a twenty-five miles per hour zone, and he had to perform two Saturdays of manual labor as a condition of a suspended sentence with probation.

Daughter Sandy, who had done some commercials for her parents' television show in addition to making a few acting appearances, eloped while still a teenager, marrying twenty-four-year-old Jim Wilhoite on August 8, 1953, in Las Vegas. The Burnses' first grandchild, Laura Jean (Laurie), was born in 1954 and their second, Lissa, in 1956. (Sandy's marriage eventually dissolved and on September 2, 1959, she married Ron Amateau, who had come on as the third director of her parents' show after leaving **The Bob Cummings Show** [**B248**]). Now with two grandchildren, Gracie really wanted to retire to spend more time at home. As a matter of fact, there was also a report in January 1956 that George, of all people, was contemplating retirement.

~~~~~

Suddenly on Tuesday, February 18, 1958, came the stunning announcement that Gracie Allen was going to retire at the end of the 1957-1958 season. The story of Gracie retiring eventually became the September 22, 1958, cover story of **Life** magazine (**B210**), the date coinciding with the airing of the last show of their last season on television (albeit a rerun). Gracie said that she was just tired of show business and wanted to stay at home to see her grandchildren and play her favorite game, gin rummy. In reality her doctor had finally insisted she had to quit because of her failing health. Gracie's mother had died of heart disease, and Gracie and George knew the realities of the situation. Gracie had been working nonstop for thirty-five years and the television show was the most stressful work she had ever undertaken. Friends of hers had noted the constant strain she was under in working on the show. The fact that she was a perfectionist in her work was an additional burden. George seemed to thrive on work--a very structured person, he had every hour planned out for each day. When word of her impending retirement was given to the cast and crew of the television series and they realized it was all soon going to be over, Al Simon and Herb Browar agree that the feeling among everyone was unanimous: "That's show biz. And everyone loved her." **SEE B92, B420**.

George realized that Gracie really meant it this time--she was through with show business. Although the public believed that she was fifty-one Gracie was, in fact, sixty-two years old at the time of the announcement of her retirement. (**B478**). George accepted his wife's decision, thinking that she probably would change her mind after a few months of vacation, and he apparently wasn't alone in his assessment. But as Gracie noted to interviewer Dan Jenkins in 1958, "A lot of people think I'll return to show business, but I won't" (**B274**). On June 4, 1958, the last of the two hundred and ninety-one episodes was filmed, and the curtain came down for the very last time for Burns and Allen. Rights to **The George Burns and Gracie Allen Show** were later sold to Screen Gems in a multimillion dollar deal, guaranteeing that the curtain would never quite come down on the show itself. The two hundred and thirty-nine filmed episodes were quite popular in syndication (the first fifty-two having been done live). In 1962 a reviewer was still enchanted by the show.

> It isn't a secret that the **Burns and Allen** programs now on the air are reruns...But they are so bright and fresh and gay, so much more intelligent, so much better produced than most of the current crop of comedies, that until the announcer, at the end, says something about "tonight's program," you feel that you are seeing them for the first time. (**TV Guide**, June 9-15, 1962.)
~~~~~

The Christian Broadcasting Network (now called The Family Channel) aired the series over a period of time in the mid-1980s and later showcased it with several other vintage shows during a special "Greatest Hits of the '50's and '60's Week." The show's run on CBN rated this mention by critic Jeff Jarvis in **People Weekly**: "The show holds up remarkably well over the years; it is still funny because its stars are funny." The videocassette companies have found the series, too, and the shows still receive four-star reviews. One from the WeekendPlus section of the **Chicago Sun-Times,** dated May 1, 1987: 67, reflected, "The quality of the tapes is first-rate and so is the comedy...We can only imagine what the world of comedy would be like today if Gracie were still at his side, saying good night."

~~~~~

Not ready to retire, George came back on October 21, 1958 (**T295**) with a new show, **The George Burns Show**, which had Bea Benaderet and Ronnie Burns in the cast. Everybody from the old show was there, in fact, except Gracie, and audiences missed her. The fact that Gracie was absent garnered a lot of publicity, including a **TV Guide** cover for George the week of October 25, but the audience, it seemed, wasn't ready for Burns without Allen. The show was not renewed after its year's run. For the first time in more than thirty years George was unemployed, although it was announced on April 1, 1959, that he and Milton Berle had formed a television production company. Gracie in the meantime, while unhappy that George was going through a difficult time, was enjoying the freedom that her retirement allowed her. But in 1961 she suffered another heart attack, which illustrated her declining health. George recounts that he never really realized how ill Gracie was because her medication always seemed to help her, and Ronnie Burns echoed that the doctors didn't tell his father how serious his mother's condition was because they were afraid of how he would react. There was nothing that could be done and that was the reality of the situation. Thirty years later one can only speculate what Gracie's fate might have been had today's remarkable medical procedures been available to her.

George had started to form a night club act with Carol Channing, an actress who had married Charles Lowe, Carnation's representative to **The George Burns and Gracie Allen Show**. Gracie had chosen Carol to work with George and shared with her some of her advice on acting. In 1961 George and Carole opened at Lake Tahoe in Nevada with a nervous Gracie in the audience. Gracie told friends that she was so afraid that George wouldn't be a success that she almost wished she was with him onstage. But George was successful in his first night club show and would continue to play in Las Vegas at different casinos. He regularly auditioned female singers for his annual holiday show in Las Vegas. It was reported in late 1961 that he performed six weeks yearly in Las Vegas and Lake Tahoe and that he had just returned from a joint command performance in London with Jack Benny. For the next few years he would also play the nightclub circuit with Dorothy Provine and Jane Russell. He also helped to promote young performers, such as singer Bobby Darin and multifaceted entertainer Ann-Margret, both of whom would appear in his nightclub act.
~~~~~

Reports of George's assistance and generosity to performers continued throughout his career.

In 1961 he was also supervising **Mister Ed** and writing **That's Edie**, a television pilot that he planned to produce and direct. After being away from the television cameras for five years, George decided to make another attempt in 1964. He had developed a new series for television called **Wendy and Me** in which he would play the owner of an apartment house. Two of his tenants were a pilot and his wife, Wendy (Connie Stevens), who played a character similar to "Gracie." The show was about to premiere when George was struck a shattering blow.

~~~~~

For several months, Gracie's health had been declining and she was remaining more and more at home in her second-floor bedroom during the summer of 1964. Her sisters' fates had caused her a great deal of sadness (although Hazel survived Gracie by nearly five years, Pearl had already suffered a debilitating stroke, dying in 1957, and Bessie had died in June 1964). On the evening of Thursday, August 27, 1964, Gracie became ill. George, who was at home with her, phoned Dr. Rex Kennamer, who, upon arriving, called an ambulance to rush her to Cedars of Lebanon Hospital. She was admitted at 10:25 P.M., examined and placed in a room where she died less than an hour later, at 11:15 P.M.

Gracie Allen had just reached her sixty-ninth birthday a month before. Newspapers around the country ran front-page news stories about her life, career with George, and her death. In their announcement of her death, **The Los Angeles Times** ran their largest headine, normally used only for major national and international news stories. **The Los Angeles Herald Examiner** announced "Gracie Allen Dies" above the newspaper's own title. The ambulance drivers were interviewed about the fight to save Gracie's life and how she apologized to them as "she tried to help us lift her." The Los Angeles city council adjourned in her honor on August 28. More than a thousand telegrams, perhaps as many as thirteen hundred, began pouring in.

Her funeral was held at three o'clock on Monday afternoon, August 31, 1964, at Forest Lawn Memorial Park in Glendale, California, in the Heritage Room of the Church of the Recessional. Dr. Kermit Castellanos of the All Saints Episcopal Church of Beverly Hills presided over the ceremony. Because George was Jewish, the Catholic church would not consecrate the burial of his Catholic wife, so the services were performed by an Episcopalian, not a Catholic priest. Over three hundred celebrities attended the ceremony, a number of them flying in from around the country. Two hours before the ceremony began, people began streaming in, and one thousand fans were present at the services. There was a Rosary, and the organist played "Ave Maria." Several thousand spectators were outside, one of the largest groups of mourners ever to attend the funeral of a Hollywood celebrity. At least four hundred seventeen floral tributes were received. Long-time friend George Jessel offered up a touching eulogy, saying in part, "The act is over, the bow music has faded, the billing will have to be changed--the next stage manager will have to be told 'George N. Burns, in one alone.' So be it...The hope of mankind must be in the faith that the play is never over--when the curtain falls, it rises again." A grief-
~~~~~

stricken Jack Benny offered his own eulogy of his best friend's wife, saying, "Mary and I have lost one of our two closest friends...the whole world loved Gracie...we'll never forget her, ever."

Gracie's bronze coffin, with its red roses and shell pink carnations, was shouldered by active pallbearers Jack Benny, George Jessel, Mike Connolly, Mervyn LeRoy, Edward G. Robinson and Dr. Rex Kennamer. Honorary pallbearers were Phil Berg, Bobby Darin, Fred de Cordova, Armand Deutsch, Kirk Douglas, Bill Goetz, Danny Kaye, Gene Kelly, Freddie Kohlmar, Ralph Levy, Dean Martin, Bill Orr, William Perlberg, Cesar Romero, Danny Thomas, Jack Warner, Jerry Zeitman, Milton Berle and Henry Hathaway. After the public service a private ten-minute ceremony at the Court of Freedom Mausoleum (also in Forest Lawn Memorial Park) followed. Gracie was laid to rest there in a crypt ordered by George's brother Willy. George became so overwrought that he had to be helped from the services by his son and Jack Benny. Thirty years later, people whose lives have been touched by Gracie still visit the mausoleum; according to one person who guides visitors to the site, many do not leave dry-eyed.

Gracie Allen's death marked the end of one of the longest-running comedy teams in history, one that had stayed at the top of show business for over thirty-five years. It also ended one of Hollywood's happiest marriages. George would later remark that the day Gracie died was the saddest day he ever knew. Millions of people around the world were mourning alongside George, but he had never felt so alone in his life.

~~~~~

Even in his grief George went ahead with the **Wendy and Me** show, which debuted on September 14, 1964 (**T321**), a little more than two weeks after his wife's death. As in radio, when other actresses tried to play the "Gracie" role, they discovered that they could not equal Gracie Allen's talent in portraying the character. The television show ran for only one season.

The next ten years would be ones in which George tried to find a niche for himself. He produced the television version of **No Time for Sergeants** in 1964 in conjunction with Warner Bros. The property had been a great starring vehicle for Andy Griffith when it was produced as a play in 1955 and as a film in 1958. However, the series, starring Sammy Jackson, only lasted a year on ABC. **Mona McCluskey**, produced by George and starring Juliet Prowse, lasted an even shorter time on the air after it debuted in 1965 on NBC under the United Artists banner. George later produced another pilot for United Artists starring Cliff Arquette, which aired on ABC on July 22, 1966, as part of the network's **Summer Fun** series of possible comedy shows for the upcoming season. The entry, **McNab's Lab**, went the way of the other five pilots in the series and remained unsold.

George sustained another personal and professional blow in 1966 when his beloved brother, Willy, died at the age of sixty-three on January 20, George's birthday. The strength and trust that were hallmarks of his partnership with Willy had only been surpassed by his partnership with Gracie, and now they were both gone. But show business veteran that he
~~~~~

was, he knew better than anyone that "the show must go on." And it did.

George appeared in guest spots on television shows where he was seen as one of the old-timers of show business. It is interesting to note that even in their radio show in the 1930s, George's singing and his "old" age were getting laughs even as they would fifty and sixty years later. Like his cigar smoking, it was a part of George Burns's onstage character. In real life he was a "young man" in both mind and approach to his work.

Gold Piaget watches were presented to George and his best friend, Jack Benny, in May 1972 when the New York Friars Club saluted them as "Entertainers of the Year." The six-hour toast was attended by longtime friends Cary Grant and Frank Sinatra as well as **Life** magazine, which ran two pages of photographs from the event in its May 26 issue. Sadly, George and Jack would have little time left to look back on their evening--or their lives--together.

In August 1974, George had heart bypass surgery at what was then known as Cedars of Lebanon Hospital (now Cedars-Sinai Medical Center). Despite his age and the seriousness of his condition, he bounced back and was released from the hospital on September 25. But only a short time later, Jack, too, became ill in Dallas, Texas; he was eventually diagnosed as having cancer (later revealed to be cancer of the pancreas, one of its deadliest forms). In late December of that year, just before New Year's, Jack Benny was gone. At the funeral George broke down while trying to deliver his friend's eulogy.

George often said that the ten years from Gracie's to Jack's death were the worst of his life. He had substituted for an ailing Jack in an engagement in Florida weeks after his own heart surgery. But his friend's death opened another door for George. He was about to substitute for Jack one more time.

Jack Benny had been signed to play the part of a vaudevillian in the film adaptation of Neil Simon's **The Sunshine Boys**. When he became ill, the producers were looking for a replacement and George was persuaded to audition. Irving Fein, Jack Benny's manager and publicist for many years, now was hired by George to handle his career. George was offered the part in the film, and at the age of seventy-nine a new motion picture actor was born. Playing opposite actor Walter Matthau, to whom George had once offered the part of Harry Morton on his television show, George's performance in **The Sunshine Boys** (**F37**) won him a nomination as Best Supporting Actor by the Academy of Motion Picture Arts and Sciences. Other nominees that year were Brad Dourif for **One Flew Over the Cuckoo's Nest**, Burgess Meredith for **The Day of the Locust**, Chris Sarandon for **Dog Day Afternoon**, and Jack Warden for **Shampoo**.

On March 29, 1976, George Burns became the oldest male actor (at 80 years and 69 days) to win in the supporting category (**T495**) when Linda Blair and Ben Johnson presented him with the Oscar. His acceptance speech suited him perfectly. "If you stay in this business long enough and get to be old enough you get to be new again (**B368**)." His was also the only major award that evening that did not get caught in the tidal wave called **One Flew Over the Cuckoo's Nest**, which swept the awards as no film had done since 1934's **It Happened One Night** and sank Matthau's nomination for Best Actor with a win by Jack Nicholson. George returned to the Oscar stage in 1979 with Brooke Shields to present a Best Supporting Actress to Maggie Smith for her work in **California Suite**. **SEE T527**.

His success as a film actor continued through the 1970s and 1980s with such films as **Oh God!** (**F38**) and its sequels (**F43**, **F44**). The first **Oh, God!** was reportedly produced for $2.1 million; by early 1978 it may have grossed as much as $45 million. A rumored fourth installment of **Oh, God!** never materialized, apparently due to the lack of a suitable script. There was also talk of a remake of **The Ladykillers**, but it was finally reported that plans were scotched by difficulties in sorting out the rights to the film. George's upcoming 1979 appearance in **Going in Style** (**F41**) was celebrated with a new square in the forecourt of Mann's Chinese Theatre on Hollywood Boulevard, placed adjacent to that of another comedic master, Jack Benny.

Las Vegas audiences continued to love George Burns. By 1979 he had headlined at the Sands, the Riviera, the Sahara, and the Frontier. Shows at the Sahara were particularly memorable because he had appeared there with Jack Benny and introduced the audience to young entertainers Bobby Darin and Ann-Margret.

He made an incredible number of appearances on television shows other than his own series, including talk shows, situation comedies, awards shows and specials. The Emmy nominations that eluded him during his days with Gracie finally started coming his way when he turned his attention to specials. One very *special* special, 1989's **A Conversation with George Burns** (**T643**), garnered him the Emmy in 1990. Irving Fein was the executive producer on much of George's television work via GBF Productions during his last twenty years. Veteran director Walter Miller often worked with him, and his staff writers' names often appeared in many of the credits.

George shared executive producer status with Jerry Zeitman and Irving Fein on an unsold television pilot from 1981 that ABC aired on August 3. **I Love Her Anyway** was a remake of **The George Burns and Gracie Allen Show,** with Diane Stillwell and Dean Jones as Laurie and Jerry Martin.

In 1985 series television's siren call reached his ears once more, and he agreed to lend his name and narrating abilities to **George Burns Comedy Week,** a comedy anthology that debuted on September 18, 1985 (**T358**), with funnyman Steve Martin as co-executive producer. The series folded after thirteen episodes, having been mired at the bottom of the ratings. There was talk of a television sitcom version of Burns's 1977 film **Oh, God!** (**F38**) airing in the fall of 1988 on CBS, but the series never made it to the network's lineup.

His manager undoubtedly turned down more work for George than he accepted. In fact, in 1985 **People Weekly** magazine referred to George as one of the busiest people in the world. At one time he averaged around ninety appearances a year, mostly to sold-out audiences. His personal appearances during these years included a mix of so-called meat-and-potato gigs (including colleges, fairs, and conventions), where it was estimated he received sixty thousand dollars a night, and prestige bookings (resort hotels and casinos, major halls, and one-man shows). In the late 1980s his bookings included the California Grocers Association convention in Reno, Nevada, Washington State University's Beasley Performing Arts Coliseum in Pullman, and El Camino College in Torrance, California, mixed, with engagements at Caesar's Palace in Las Vegas and

Caesar's in Atlantic City, New Jersey. His yearly contract for one-week stints at Caesar's at that time may have earned him as much as two hundred fifty thousand to three hundred thousand dollars a week (**SEE B390**).

His series of sold-out one-nighters were often punctuated by television interviews promoting his latest film. He cut back his work schedule in his last years to around four or five days a month. Each show lasted slightly less than sixty minutes. His entourage always included his manager and accompanist; his backing at a venue was usually a fifteen-piece orchestra. Since his career saw him sharing stages with everyone from Gracie Allen to Mary Hart to Pia Zadora, he could honestly say he had appeared with everyone from A to Z.

A multiyear contract with Caesar's Palace signed in the mid-1980s called for George to play at the Caesar's venues in Las Vegas, Lake Tahoe and Atlantic City. He soon re-signed with Caesar's for semiannual six-night engagements. According to Hollywood trade papers he signed with Caesar's again under a five-year contract in 1990, but there is some confusion because he reportedly signed an exclusive contract just one year later with the Riviera for two years. Regardless, he returned to Caesar's when he agreed to another three-year contract which began in 1992. Tickets that year for a George Burns live stage show ran forty-two dollars per person (forty-eight dollars per person for booth seats, if available), including taxes and gratuity.

Certainly no stranger to publicity and promotion, his commercial spokesman jobs were quite lucrative and included Brentwood (California) Savings and Loan Company, the Southern California Gas Company, with Betty White, and Southern California Edison. In Texas, he appeared in Gibraltar Savings ads. He touted a number of products in either print or electronic media, including Continental Airlines, Teacher's Scotch, Polident, IBM, Lifecall, Pollenex, LA Beer, Oldsmobile for its 90th anniversary celebration, Caesar's Man and Caesar's Woman perfumes, Ray-O-Vac, Sonassage for Conair (with O.J. Simpson), MCI, H-2-Oh!, **The Chicago Sun-Times** Wingo and Little Caesar's Pizza The National Institute on Aging used his image; he performed in conservation ads for the state of Washington, appeared in Cedars-Sinai Medical Center's $90 million endowment fund campaign, and was the American Library Association's poster boy in their "Celebrity Read" series.

George and Gracie continued to be the focus of a number of direct and oblique tributes from all quarters. George was asked to sing "Take Me Out to the Ball Game" during an All-Star game. For years he had one of the highest rankings in the "TVQs", those personal ratings of performers' likability and recognizability that many profess to loathe but that exist nonetheless. The Smithsonian Institution in Washington, D.C., requested his vaudeville trunk. Books by Dodd Darin (son of Bobby Darin and Sandra Dee), Dwayne Hickman and Ann-Margret were glowing in their praise for him; Ann-Margret spoke of him lovingly as her mentor during a 1994 televised interview with newswoman Katie Couric as well as in her 1995 appearance on **Reflections on the Silver Screen**, hosted by Professor Richard Brown on the cable television network program, American Movie Classics. Not only were streets in the Los Angeles area named for George and Gracie, but preceding that they had been similarly honored in the Streets of the Stars neighborhood at the Blue Skies Village Mobile Home Park (of which they had been shareholders) in Rancho Mirage, California, a few miles southeast of Palm Springs (**B66**). A play was published in 1979 called **Say Goodnight, Gracie**, although it was not about Burns and Allen per se.

George's anecdotes turned up in various tomes, including **The Golf Hall of Shame** and **The Little Brown Book of Anecdotes**. A collectible plate issued in 1982 for forty-five dollars rose in value within seven years to seventy dollars. By 1985 his signature on an 8x10 black and white photo fetched between twelve and fifteen dollars, although the price dropped to between four and six dollars for a signature alone (in contrast, Gracie's autograph was worth between five and eight dollars unless it was affixed to her photograph, in which case it jumped to between forty and sixty dollars). **SEE B93**. George joined more than sixty other celebrities who contributed their toothbrushes to an artist who placed them alongside portraits of his subjects. Impressionist Louise DuArt, who has spoofed both men and women, included George in her comedy special on **Showtime** in 1989 and on **Good Morning America**; Rich Little impersonated him for years. Little and his partner (now wife) Jeanette Markey included George and Gracie in their act and appeared as them on a June, 1994 program on the A&E network called **An Evening To Remember: Armed Services Hour**, commemmorating the fiftieth anniversary of D-Day and designed as a recreation of a 1940s radio show. Adolph Gottsman was hired by Ron Smith's Celebrity Lookalikes to make appearances as George Burns. There were marketing offers for T-shirts and posters; one company did offer a T-shirt with George and Gracie in a familiar pose. In 1986, an artist painted George's picture on a dinosaur bone as a gift for his ninetieth birthday. A mint condition Hollywood Walk of Fame gum card goes for three dollars. A Far Side cartoon featured a futuristic world, a la **The Jetsons**, with a marquee declaring "Appearing Tonight: George Burns." A couple in east Tennessee who have a cow named "Gracie" gave her confused paramour, a Canadian goose, the moniker of "George."

George was caricatured on the cover of **TV Guide** and in books. His and Gracie's first two **TV Guide** covers have a market value of between fifteen and thirty dollars (**B244**). In October, 1989 it was announced that singer Whitney Houston had donated lion cubs named George and Gracie to the Bronx Zoo. **Star Trek IV: The Voyage Home** (1986) prominently featured whales named George and Gracie in its storyline. George received a two-page tribute complete with photos in one of the national tabloids on the occasion of his ninetieth birthday. One of Rhea Perlman and Danny DeVito's daughters is named Gracie, and there is a production company called Gracie Films. The "Why Do Fools Fall In Love" episode of **Murphy Brown** featured an opening shot of George and Gracie. The 1990 film **Avalon** featured a scene in which **The Burns and Allen Show** is playing on television. George's 1988 Life Achievement Award at the American Comedy Awards show was saluted by full-page ads from Caesar's. George's long career was a bottomless well of tidbits for trivia buffs, including those who purchased the 1985 **Entertainment Tonight** desk calendar to see if he was prominently featured on Friday, January 20 (he was). And a television columnist for the **Los Angeles Times**, Rick Du Brow, saluted him each week by signing off with the words "Say good night, Gracie."

But George never shirked from paying his own respects to other venerated performers. No stranger to the Masquers Club, he was also a Friars Club stalwart (on both the East and West

Coasts), and he appeared at a number of Friars Club "roasts" honoring various show business veterans. He supplied radio personality Mike Palmer with material for a film-lecture on Jack Benny to celebrate the centennial of Benny's birth. When the Museum of Broadcasting (now the Museum of Television and Radio) presented a major tribute to Lucille Ball in 1985, he remarked, "she knows about directing, editing, timing...and there isn't anything that you can do, or that anybody else can do, that she can't do better." It was always difficult, however, to keep him serious for long, and he usually ended everything he said with a one-liner, such as this next sentence in his tribute to Lucy: "It must have made it awfully tough for her husband Gary on their honeymoon."

George's name cropped up almost anywhere people were talking about age, and he never suffered in comparison. One newspaper article on aging commented on the difference in aging between men and women and juxtaposed stills of George with those of actress Bette Davis (but neglected to mention that Davis had experienced a mastectomy and a stroke). George was quoted as saying that his manager, Irving Fein admonished him at the beginning of their association, "Don't tell your age." He disagreed. And it seemed to only enhance his appeal. When George was in his nineties, even columnist Ann Landers mentioned him as a possible lead in a film to be made sixty-five million years in the future!

George wrote forwards for books by friends, Jim Backus and Irving Fein, and Joan Benny; he contributed liner notes to comedy albums and dustjacket blurbs for a book by Audrey Meadows. He also found great success with his own "authoring" efforts. Many time his work was actually a collaborative effort between him and his writers. He wrote three autobiographies (**B26, B32, and B34**). Several of his books were excerpted in various magazines and tabloids, and were featured as book club selections which put him on the promotion circuit.

But critical praise for George's work reached its zenith when he turned from his spate of advice books and delved into his personal life once again. The year 1988 brought accolades for George's second love letter to Gracie, ghostwritten by David Fisher. More than thirty years after **I Love Her, That's Why!** (**B34**), its success was eclipsed by **Gracie: A Love Story** (**B22**). Dedicated "To all the fans who love Gracie," George's three hundred and nineteen page tribute to the love of his life sold nearly a quarter of a million copies in hardcover and appeared on **The New York Times** best-seller list for more than five months, including a stint in the number one slot. **All My Best Friends** (**B35**), another Fisher-penned collection of anecdotes about George's show business cronies, arrived the next year with almost four hundred thousand copies in print and graced the best-seller lists on both coasts. In 1989 the UCLA Film and Television Archive, in association with The Academy of Television Arts and Sciences Foundation, presented "George & Gracie & Jack: A Tribute to George Burns, Gracie Allen & Jack Benny" at UCLA's Melnitz Theater from August 11-September 8. The co-tribute to the longtime friends included screenings of their various films and episodes from their television shows.

Also in 1989, George and Bob Hope teamed up for the first time in their long careers and caused a media sensation. Billed as "179 Years of Comedy," (the sum of their ages, George at 93 and Bob at 86) the three-hour performance on

Sunday, October 1, at New York's Madison Square Garden began with Bob who declared, "I'm not an opening act you know." Singer Dionne Warwick came on for a thirty-minute set before George was introduced. The two veterans closed the show together, with Bob donning a wig and joining George in a Burns and Allen routine, complete with time steps and lines about Gracie's still unforgettable family. The standing ovation at the end was inevitable. Mary Campbell of the Associated Press said, "Burns...and Hope...proved their funny bones still work--though both kidded that not everything does" (**Times Leader**. October 15, 1989). David Hajdu declared, "This was simply a great show by two of the most skilled entertainers working today, who also happen to have been working 70 years ago" (**Hollywood Reporter**. October 3, 1989: 4).

The cream of the show business awards--the Oscar, the Emmy, the Grammy, the Tony--are reserved for a fortunate few. Fewer still receive awards in more than one medium. George in 1991 added a third major jewel to his awards crown when he received a Grammy for spoken word or nonmusical recording for **Gracie: A Love Story** (**D40**),to place alongside his Oscar and Emmy statuettes. He had been nominated once before for his 1979 rendition of "I Wish I Was Eighteen Again" but did not take home the prize that night, although he was scheduled to appear as a presenter or performer on the February 27, 1980, CBS telecast.

George was nearly as famous for his sayings as he will always be for "Say good night, Gracie." He had a trunk full of them and always vowed to "stay in show business until I'm the last one left." He insisted that he wouldn't die because "I can't afford to die--I'd lose a fortune, I'm booked." Or "I don't believe in dying. It's been done." And "Besides, I died in Altoona." When he made a return appearance he was delighted. "They must have liked me. Here it is (you fill in the blank) years later and I'm back again." His spin on why the audiences still came out to see him: "The young people come to see me before I die. The old people come to see me before *they* die." He thrived on "all that love that comes flowing up over the footlights from the audience." When he made his entrance to a standing ovation he declared, "If I can stand, you can stand." He went on, "It's nice to be here. It's nice to be anywhere." About his cigar: "At my age I've got to hold onto something." He admonished everyone to "Fall in love with what you do for a living," because "I'd rather have been a failure doing something I love than a success at something I hate" and "You've gotta have a reason to get outta bed every day."

He made old age fashionable: "I'm so old I'm new again." "You can't help getting older, but you don't have to get old." He hadn't a clue what he'd do if he quit working: "Retire? Retire to what?" His philosophy was that if you're in a job you have to retire from, you're in the wrong job. When his vocalizing took a turn down another road, he defended the move. "Why shouldn't I be a country singer? I'm older than most countries." How accurate were his legendary stories? "Most of what I say is true. The rest is show business." On looking back he said, "I'm not interested in anything I did yesterday. I'm only interested in what I'm going to do today." In fact, when some interviewers asked him about all the famous people he had known he concluded by saying, "You're the only person I know who's still alive."

On February 5, 1992, he was joined by Pia Zadora at California's Long Beach Terrace Theater for one night only, billed as their only Southern California appearance. The venue's 3,054 seats were priced at $20, $35, $50, and $100, but the most expensive seat in the house was on stage, an easy chair from which George delivered most of his performance. The thirty-piece orchestra was in place, as was Morty Jacobs, George's accompanist of many years. A short Burns and Allen routine was delivered at the end with Zadora's aid, followed by Carol Channing making a surprise appearance to push a cake on stage in celebration of George's recent birthday. There was no surprise, however, at his impeccable delivery. According to **Daily Variety** (February 7, 1992), the "most notable aspect of Burns' performance may have been his monologue, feigning informality while in reality more tightly constructed than a watch."

His birthdays were events and were as much celebrations of his years in show business as they were of his years on earth. In 1983 he gave himself a party and invited over two hundred of his friends to Chasen's. In 1986 Cedars-Sinai Medical Center used his ninetieth birthday to kick off the $90 million endowment fund campaign to which George contributed $1 million as its honorary chairman; the continuation of the drive a year later saw a formal affair at Los Angeles' Beverly Hilton Hotel attended by around eight hundred people who paid $500 per person for the honor of attending. A party at Bistro Gardens in Beverly Hills in 1988 featured a cake with ninety-two candles. In 1989 George celebrated his 93d birthday by presenting another $1 million gift to Cedars-Sinai Medical Center. Work and investments had made him a wealthy man.

He still lived in the house he and Gracie bought in the 1930s. He shared it with a couple from Belgium, Daniel and Arlette Dhorre, who were with him for years. The three of them shared the rest of the house with George's pet cats (in 1989 he had three). He also maintained a residence in Las Vegas, Nevada, which enabled him to avoid taking up residence in a hotel while fulfilling his personal appearance contracts in the gambling and entertainment mecca. Into his nineties, George's daily routine was as well-rehearsed as his act and was well-chronicled in the video **George Burns: His Wit and Wisdom** (**VG7**), for which he reportedly received $150,000 plus 25 per cent of the royalties (**B390**). After his morning exercise routine of indoor calisthenics and outdoor lap walking, he headed for the office he still maintained at the studio where he and Gracie filmed their television show. Two hours each day were spent there working with his writers. Harvey Berger, Fred Fox, Hal Goldman and Seaman Jacobs were with him for a number of years, working with him on his stage act and television specials. His secretary, Jack Langdon, was with him for decades. Lunch at the Hillcrest Country Club followed, then a game of bridge before he headed home for a nap. In his latter years, most of his old cronies at the Hillcrest "Comedians Round Table" (which included Jack Benny, Eddie Cantor, Al Jolson, George Jessel, Danny Kaye, Groucho Marx, et al) were gone, but George didn't dwell on the past. His grooming was always impeccable; he always had that unmistakable look of understated but expensive elegance, and catching a glimpse of him sans toupee was nearly impossible. When he was not working he went out in the evening or spent a quiet night at home. He continued to visit Gracie's crypt at Forest Lawn every month. **SEE B261**.

By the 1990s, his children Sandy and Ronnie were now nearly as old as he was when he started over in show business after Gracie's retirement. Sandy divorced Rod Amateau, married Steve Luckman and eventually became the mother of two more daughters, Brooke and Graceanne, who was born prematurely within weeks after Gracie's death. Ronnie has three sons. George now had great-grandchildren as well. Neither Ronnie nor Sandy had the sustained marriage their parents did and both managed to stay out of the spotlight for years although they did make a rare public appearance when George and Gracie were inducted into the Television Academy Hall of Fame.

George's long life was remarkably untouched by scandal except for the smuggling debacle of the late 1930s. No weekly tabloid headlines on George screamed out at shoppers from the grocery store aisles. No "daddy dearest" books issued forth from his children, and no former associate has published a tell-all tome. George's own admission of a brief unfaithfulness to Gracie during their marriage in his 1988 **Gracie: A Love Story** (**B22**) caused some ripples during the book's publicity tour but no lasting damage, perhaps in part because Gracie apparently knew of his indiscretion and forgave him. He had, in fact, revealed the same information in a **Playboy** interview (**B142**) ten years earlier, but the book received far wider press. He appeared on the cover of **Penthouse** but most of his admirers remain indulgent and apparently consider it harmless. His relationships during the past thirty years with women a fraction of his age seemed to be viewed benignly by most people and were not, in fact, publicized to the extent they once were. "I don't go out with women my age," he says. "There *are* no women my age." Cathy Carr of Dallas was his most long-term companion, but as he said on many occasions, he would never marry again.

He kidded that he had outlived the doctors who told him to quit smoking and he outlived most of the critics as well. As the calendar pages turned, critics had gotten less and less, well, critical. Hardly anyone dared or even wanted to criticize him. They may not have necessarily liked the material, but few faulted George directly. One reviewer actually verbalized it when he wrote about a video, **George Burns: His Wit and Wisdom** (**VG7**), "The tape has some flaws, especially in the hokey script, but how can you criticize George Burns? It's like criticizing God" (Richard Zacks, **City Lights**, May 7, 1989: 29). Not exactly, but apparently he had been typecast. Reportedly, even the attorney representing the Bank of America in its lawsuit against Groucho Marx's companion, Erin Fleming, hesitated before questioning defense witness Burns in February, 1983 by prefacing his queries with "I've never cross-examined God before."

And woe to those with the temerity to mock him or treat him with something less than the respect his age and stature deserve. Several years ago a segment on ABC's morning show, **Good Morning America**, featured **Spy** magazine's latest effort, **Separated at Birth 2**, which compares pictures of well-known people the magazine claims look alike. When George's picture was juxtaposed with one of Ella Fitzgerald and one of the magazine's representatives declared, "Oh, well, all old people look alike, anyway," a newspaper columnist exploded in anger in defense of both Burns and Fitzgerald. "You know what really looks alike? Garbage tabloids and scum magazines, that's what" (**Cincinnati Post**, June 22, 1990, section C: 1).

The most criticism George received in his last years came not only for the sometimes painfully repetitive stories he told when on the talk show circuit to promote a new project but because one sensed that George, the flesh and blood man, had disappeared behind his carefully cultivated image.

Perhaps as he neared the age of one hundred, he had earned the right to stick with comfortable subjects. But just as Gracie might have liked to have been thought of as a real person and not simply the character she played, it would have been refreshing to hear the voice of the "real" George Burns break through the carefully rehearsed lines; only his earlier appearances afford that occasional glimpse. Some critics felt that his autobiographical works lacked depth. George (or his writers) were so busy with the one-liners they failed to reveal the real wisdom a man of his years had no doubt gathered during his lifetime. Several years ago John Lahr, in his review of **The Third Time Around** (**B32**), stepped up to the plate and took a few carefully aimed swings.

> It's impossible to dislike a megalomaniac who confides, "By the time I found out I had no talent I was too big a star."... George Burns has been a star for so long he doesn't know how to stop being famous ...And to see a man of 82 still selling himself is at once tremendous and terrifying...This compulsion to surry favor with the public, to keep up the image, dishonors both the integrity of the performer and his accomplishments ...very little of the man and the real life of show business is conveyed. (**The New York Times Book Review**, February 10, 1980: 12.)

And reviewer David Nasaw in his critique of **All My Best Friends** (**B35**), in a 1989 edition of **The New York Times Book Review**, concluded that [George Burns]

> presents himself throughout as a simple man without much talent whose success is due entirely to luck and Gracie's talent. But Gracie has been gone for some years now and luck can only take one so far... Perhaps in his next book he'll step out side his character and let us in on some of the secrets of his success.

~~~~~

On Wednesday, July 13, 1994, George was admitted to Cedars-Sinai Medical Center in Los Angeles for observation after he slipped in his bathtub at his home in Las Vegas and hit his head. Two stitches and taking it easy for a while (which resulted in the cancellation of a scheduled appearance at Caesar's Palace) had at first seemed to be all that was required for a complete recovery, and he was released on July 22. Less than two months later, however, he was readmitted, and on September 12 he underwent surgery to drain fluid that had collected around his brain. The condition, a residual effect of his earlier fall, was discovered when his speech
~~~~~

began to be noticeably impaired. On Thursday, September 22, he was released from the hospital "in good condition" according to a Cedars-Sinai Medical Center spokesman and returned home to continue the recuperation process. And only a month later, George's last film, **Radioland Murders** (he had a cameo appearance), opened nationwide on Friday, October 21, 1994 (**F46**).

Although George's medical situation necessitated the cancellation of some engagements, he still planned to be in Las Vegas in January, 1995 to celebrate his ninety-ninth birthday. But the announcement came on December 28, 1994 that he would not be appearing in Las Vegas after all but would be celebrating quietly with friends. It was simultaneously reported that he planned to record songs from an upcoming Cy Coleman Broadway show, "sort of a precast album." Reportedly, he was back to daily bridge sessions at Hillcrest and was still drinking three martinis a day but had cut down to about three cigars daily (**Los Angeles Times**, January 20, 1995: sec. F: 2). On Saturday, February 25, 1995, he was presented with a Life Achievement award from the Screen Actors Guild by Ann-Margret in a live televised ceremony (**T747**).

For years he had been booked to play at the London Palladium for a two-week engagement on the occassion of his one hundredth birthday in 1996. As he neared the date, he announced he would also appear at Caesar's Palace in Las Vegas, making these bicontinental bookings the only birthday performances he would make. People were so anxious to be part of the milestone celebration that the Las Vegas performances were sold-out for his five shows scheduled between January 17 and 21, 1996. An August 1995 report indicated he still planned to play these dates in Las Vegas but that the possibility of subsequent appearances at Caesar's Tahoe (Stateline, Nevada) and Caesar's in Atlantic City, New Jersey, had been decided against and no further mention was made of the London Palladium appearance. Sadly, by the end of September, 1995, his dream of performing in Las Vegas to celebrate his century-long life had died. The news hit all media--print, radio and television. His manager announced that he wouldn't be playing Las Vegas in 1996 after all, saying "We just felt he was not strong enough to do an hourlong show."

The possiblity of not being able to sustain concert dates had not ruled out other activities. George still went to his office (although he stopped working with his writers, his secretary and a fan mail aide were still in evidence) and still planned to appear in yet another commercial.

The tributes continued as well. The American Movie Classics cable network included some Burns and Allen films in their salute to comedy as part of their annual film preservation project in October 1995.

On April 27, 1995, CBS announced plans for a two-hour television special, **Saluting George Burns' 100th Year**, in honor of George's one hundredth birthday to be taped in Los Angeles October 22 at the Pantages Theatre for airing during its 1995-1996 season. Proceeds from the paying audience, many of whom would also attend a dinner at the Hollywood Paladium following the taping, were to be used to help establish a Burns and Allen Research Institute at Cedars-Sinai Medical Center. However, only weeks before the scheduled event CBS informed Cedars-Sinai that taping had been postponed and they "had not yet determined a new date." The medical center then began making plans to honor him in their own way on the occasion of his upcoming birthday.

As 1995 ended and 1996 began, it became appararent to those around him that George Burns had not fully recovered from his surgery and he was becoming increasingly frail. He was unable to attend a 100th year birthday party held for him in Beverly Hills on January 16. His manager told the press that George was suffering from the flu which he caught at a Christmas party at Frank Sinatra's home. Thus, all his dreams of celebrating his 100th birthday publicly were dashed.

A month later, it was reported that George had recovered from his bout with the flu and was even going to the Hillcrest Country Club for lunch and to play bridge with his friends--keeping his daily routine as he had done for decades. However, it was not the same. Now George was too weak to walk any distance and he had to use a wheelchair. His height had been declining for years and he appeared to have shrunk to a height of five feet. Never a large man, George now seemed very small. But he attempted to carry on his life as he had before his head injury, except now he was one hundred years old.

Suddenly, on the morning of Saturday, March 9, 1996 came news reports that George Burns had passed away at his home in Beverly Hills at 10:00 A.M. He had become ill in the early morning hours and his physician was summoned but said that there was nothing that could be done. Irving Fein said that "he suffered no pain." Ronnie Burns, a nurse, and a housekeeper were at his side.

From that morning throughout the weekend all of the national media continually covered George's career and that of Burns and Allen. Fans put floral tributes on his stars on the Hollywood Walk of Fame. The neon lights in Las Vegas were dimmed in tribute. Carol Channing said that she had seen George only a few days before his death and he was excited that his latest book **One Hundred Years, One Hundred Stories** (**B513**) was on the **New York Times** best seller list. It remained there for weeks after his death. George Burns continued to entertain us even after he was gone.

His funeral was held on Tuesday, March 12, 1996 at Forest Lawn Memorial Park in Glendale, California. He was buried in the same vault as Gracie, in his toupee, with three cigars in a pocket and a ring that Gracie had given him. After Gracie's death, George had remarked that he had wished that only family members had been able to attend her funeral because of all the press and crowds. At his own funeral, his wish was granted. No press were allowed nor Hollywood acquaintances.

Few people have led such a remarkable life and career as George Burns. Indeed, the idea that there could be a possible repeat of the scope of his career in that of any future entertainer is an impossible notion. It is doubtful that we will ever see his like again.

There's an old saying "the heart soon forgets what the eyes never see." But George never forgot Gracie, and he kept a constant vigil over her memory so that no one else forgot her. He insisted that he was a failure between the ages of seven and twenty-seven and that Gracie was the one who made him a success. It disturbed him that she never got the respect she deserved for being a hard-working, highly intelligent and very gifted actress while she was alive. He once hoped that the Television Academy would give her a special citation after her retirement for her service to the industry and being a credit to her profession. It did not happen in her lifetime.

George, whose own talents were, at least by the audience, definitely overshadowed by Gracie's during their years together, came out of those shadows years ago. Whether Gracie was with him or whether he stood in the spotlight alone, entertaining people was his life. He thrived on the hard work, and he basked in its rewards and the applause. He will forever be a legend, an icon, a show business titan who conquered its every facet, and he loved every minute of it. With recordings of the Burns and Allen radio show and tapes of their television show available to today's audiences George and Gracie will be with us always. In retrospect, although Gracie could have given up show business in a heartbeat, one can imagine that the one thing George would have loved most would be to look to his left and find Gracie standing next to him and to be able to do it all over again.

~~~~~
~~~~~

VAUDEVILLE

The vaudeville team of George Burns and Gracie Allen began in the fall of 1922 at the Hill Theater in Newark, New Jersey. Information on their vaudeville appearances (year, date the booking began, length of stay, theater name and location) was gleaned from available contracts and was cross-checked against **Variety**, which listed weekly vaudeville circuits across the United States and Canada until the early 1930's, when motion pictures and radio replaced vaudeville as the popular entertainment medium desired by audiences.

When George was teamed with Billy Lorraine they worked the Pantages vaudeville circuit. The team of Burns and Allen began its vaudeville career as a "disappointment act," which meant waiting for a telephone call to replace an act which had canceled for one reason or another. Starting out with smaller booking agents (Fally Marcus) and vaudeville circuits (the Gus Sun Time), George and Gracie eventually graduated to the Loew's and B. F. Keith-Albee circuits (which itself metamorphosed into the Keith-Albee-Orpheum before it finally became the Radio-Keith-Orpheum circuit). This meant they played fewer dates since they were often booked for a week into one theatre.

In the beginning their act consisted of talking and singing and they were considered "in one," meaning they occupied the front or apron portion of the stage. Their major acts during vaudeville were "Sixty-Forty," "Lamb Chops" and "Dizzy" and gradually increased to seventeen minutes. In 1929 they began a series of successful engagements in Great Britain. They were on the closing bill for vaudeville's mecca, New York City's Palace Theater.

As vaudeville began its decline George and Gracie were able to segue into those mediums hastening the demise, film and particularly (for them) radio. In 1932 Burns and Allen's theatrical bookings began to reflect a direct linkage to their broadcasting efforts in that their personal appearances were done primarily as a promotion for their radio show.

Discrepancies were occasionally discovered during research. In those instances, the authors came to common-sense conclusions based upon their understanding of the vagaries of the business. While these listings do not include every booking of their career, they do give an insight into the arduous life of vaudeville performers who were constantly on the road, going from town to town, playing their booking and waiting for a phone call that would take them to the next date--all for little respect and very little money after expenses in the early days.

A lack of substantive as well as accurate information on theater dates they played during their separate vaudeville careers prior to their meeting prompted the authors to concentrate on the Burns and Allen vaudeville *team*.

Burns and Allen Vaudeville Engagements

1922

Date	Booking	Theater	Location
unknown	3 days	Hill	Newark, NJ
unknown	unknown	unknown	Boonton, NJ

1923

Date	Booking	Theater	Location
March 15	4 days	Myrtle	Brooklyn, NY
April 9	unknown	Fifth Avenue	New York, NY

Review: "Young chap and girl with a talking skit similar to the idea previously done by Matthews and Ayres...it will hold a spot on any of the intermediate bills." (**Variety**, April 12, 1923: 20).

Date	Booking	Theater	Location
April 16	7 days	Boston	Boston, MA
June 28	4 days	Prospect	New York, NY

Review: A show business industry trade paper reviewer noted George and Gracie's bantering (with George as the authentically sounding wisecracking rube) by saying they were better than their material and "...brighter and smarter vehicle will have to be secured eventually if they expect to advance." (**Variety**, June 28, 1923: 24).

Date	Booking	Theater	Location
August 18	2 days	Temple	Detroit, MI
October 29	7 days	Riverside	New York, NY

Review: "George Burns and Grace Allen followed, dealing out some wisecracking chatter that didn't take them far. But from this point, things picked up." (**Variety**, November 1, 1923: 33).

1924

Date	Booking	Theater	Location
March 17	7 days	Proctor's Fifth	New York, NY
April 14	7 days	Hennepin	Minneapolis, MN
April 21	7 days	Orpheum	Vancouver, CAN
April 28	7 days	Orpheum	Seattle, WA
May 5	7 days	Orpheum	Portland, OR
May 12	7 days	Hill Street	Los Angeles, CA
May 19*	7 days	Orpheum	Oakland, CA
July 7	7 days	Golden Gate	San Francisco, CA
July 14	7 days	Palace	St. Paul, MN
July 21	7 days	Orpheum	Des Moines, IA
July 28	7 days	State Lake	Chicago, IL
August 4	7 days	Palace	Milwaukee, WI
August 18	7 days	Temple	Detroit, MI
September 1	7 days	B. F. Keith's	Columbus, OH
September 15	7 days	Davis	Pittsburgh, PA
September 22	7 days	Victoria	Wheeling, WV
September 29	7 days	B. F. Keith's	Cincinnati, OH
October 6	7 days	B. F. Keith's	Dayton, OH
November 24	unknown	Earle	Philadelphia, PA
December 1	7 days	Kearse	Charleston, WV

*Full booking canceled due to Gracie's illness.

Date	Booking	Theater	Location
December 15	2 days	Peekskill	Peekskill, NY

1925

Date	Booking	Theater	Location
March 16	7 days	American Roof	New York, NY

Review: "Burns and Allen...Irish jigging suddenly cropped up after chatter and it counted neatly...couple impress us as being good troupers and with the right material ought to shove ahead." (**Variety**, March 18, 1925: 13).

Date	Booking	Theater	Location
March 30	7 days	Metropolitan	Brooklyn, NY
April 6	7 days	Gates	New York, NY
April 13	7 days	National	New York, NY
April 20	7 days	Greeley Square	New York, NY
May 4	7 days	Loew's Palace	Brooklyn, NY
May 11	7 days	Loew's	Boston, MA
May 18	7 days	Emery	Providence, RI
May 25	7 days	Lincoln Square	New York, NY
June 15	3 days	Capitol	Wilkesbarre, PA
June 18	3 days	Capitol	Scranton, PA
July 13	7 days	Grand	Atlanta, GA
July 20	7 days	Bijou	Birmingham, AL
July 27	7 days	Loew's	Memphis, TN
August 3	7 days	Crescent	New Orleans, LA
August 16	7 days	James	Columbus, OH
August 24	7 days	Miller	Milwaukee, WI
August 31	7 days	Rialto	Chicago, IL
September 7	3 days	Regent	Springfield, OH
September 10	3 days	Chateau	Chicago, IL
September 14	7 days	Loew's	London, CAN
September 21	7 days	Yonge Street	Toronto, CAN
September 28	7 days	Loew's	Montreal, CAN
October 5	7 days	State	Buffalo, NY
October 26	7 days	Grand	Atlanta, GA
November 2	7 days	Metropolitan	Brooklyn, NY
November 9	7 days	Loew's	Newark, NJ
December	unknown	unknown	Steubenville, OH
December	unknown	unknown	Ashtabula, OH

1926

Date	Booking	Theater	Location
January	unknown	unknown	Cleveland, OH
January 11	7 days	Colonial	Detroit, MI
January 18	7 days	Keith	Syracuse, NY
February 4	3 days	Palace	Jamestown, NY
February 24	4 days	Jefferson	New York, NY
March 1	3 days	Coliseum	New York, NY
March 8	3 days	National	Louisville, KY
March 11	4 days	Keith's	Dayton, OH
March 15	3 days	Ramona Park	Grand Rapids, MI
March 18	3 days	Keith's	Toledo, OH
March 21	7 days	Palace	Cleveland, OH
April 4	7 days	B. F. Keith's	Cincinnati, OH
April 25	7 days	B. F. Keith's	Indianapolis, IN
May 3	7 days	Shea's	Buffalo, NY
May 10	7 days	Shea's	Toronto, CAN
May 23	7 days	B. F. Keith's	Detroit, MI
May 30	7 days	B. F. Keith's	Rochester, NY
August 16	3 days	Regent	Paterson, NJ
August 19	3 days	Ritz	Elizabeth, NJ
August 23	7 days	Palace	New York, NY

This above-noted Palace engagement marks Burns and Allen's first appearance at vaudeville's mecca, where they performed their seventeen-minute routine, "Lamb Chops."

Date	Booking	Theater	Location
August 30	7 days	Albee	Brooklyn, NY
September 6	3 days	Jefferson	New York, NY
September 9	4 days	Tilyou	Coney Island, NY
September 13	7 days	Shea's Hippodrome	Buffalo, NY
September 20	7 days	Shea's Hippodrome	Toronto, CAN
September 27	7 days	Imperial	Montreal, CAN
October 4	3 days	Keith's	Portland, ME
October 7	4 days	B. F. Keith's	Lowell, MA
October 11	3 days	58th Street	New York, NY
October 14	4 days	125th Street	New York, NY
October 18	7 days	Riverside	Manhattan, NY
October 25	7 days	Proctor's	Newark, NJ
November 1	7 days	Keith	Philadelphia, PA

Date	Booking	Theater	Location
November 8	7 days	Maryland	Baltimore, MD
November 14	7 days	B. F. Keith's	Washington, D.C.
November 22	6 days	Norva	Norfolk, VA
November 30	2 days	Auditorium	Winston-Salem, NC
December 2	3 days	Roanoke	Roanoke, VA
December 6	3 days	New Broadway	Charlotte, VA
December 9	3 days	Plaza	Asheville, NC
December 13	3 days	Bijou	Savannah, GA
December 16	3 days	Palace	Jacksonville, FL
December 20	3 days	Victoria	Tampa, FL
December 23	2 days	La Plaza	St. Petersburg, FL
December 25	1 day	Beecham	Orlando, FL
December 26	4 days	Fairfax	Miami, FL
December 30	2 days	Kettler	W. Palm Beach, FL

1927

Date	Booking	Theater	Location
January 1	1 day	Vivian	Daytona Beach, FL
January 3	3 days	Lyric	Mobile, AL
January 6	4 days	Palace	New Orleans, LA
January 11	1 day	Saenger	Pensacola, FL
January 13	3 days	Princess	Nashville, TN
January 17	7 days	Keith	Cincinnati, OH
January 23	4 days	Keith's Rialto	Louisville, KY
January 27	3 days	Keith	Dayton, OH
January 30	7 days	Keith	Indianapolis, IN
February 6	3 days	B. F. Keith's	Columbus, OH
February 10	4 days	Palace	Canton, OH
February 14	7 days	105th Street	Cleveland, OH
February 21	3 days	Keith	Toledo, OH
February 24	4 days	Ramona Park	Grand Rapids, MI
February 28	7 days	Temple	Detroit, MI
March 13	4 days	B. F. Keith Albee	Youngstown, OH
March 17	4 days	Palace	Akron, OH
March 21	3 days	Erie	Erie, PA
March 24	3 days	B. F. Keith's	Rochester, NY
March 28	7 days	Palace	New York, NY

Review: "Burns and Allen next mopped up...The girl has developed into one of the cleverest character comediennes in vaudeville and Burns has smoothed out into an excellent feeder." (**Variety**, March 30, 1927: 26).

Date	Booking	Theater	Location
April 4	7 days	Albee	Providence, RI
April 24	7 days	Palace	Chicago, IL
May 2	6 days	Orpheum	Winnipeg, CAN
May 18	7 days	Orpheum	Vancouver, CAN
May 15	7 days	Orpheum	Seattle, WA
May 22	3 days	Heilig	Portland, OR
May 29	7 days	Orpheum	San Francisco, CA
June 5	7 days	Orpheum	Los Angeles, CA
June 18	7 days	Golden Gate	San Francisco, CA
June 25	7 days	Orpheum	Oakland, CA
July 3	7 days	Hill Street	Los Angeles, CA
July 23	7 days	Orpheum	Denver, CO
July 31	7 days	Palace	Chicago, IL
August 7	7 days	St. Louis	St. Louis, MO
August 14	7 days	Palace	Milwaukee, WI
August 21	7 days	Hennepin	Minneapolis, MN
August 28	7 days	State Lake	Chicago, IL
September 4	7 days	Orpheum	Kansas City, MO
September 11	7 days	Riviera	Chicago, IL
December 12	6 days	National	Richmond, VA
December 22	4 days	Proctor's	Yonkers, NY
December 29	4 days	State	Jersey City, NJ

1928

Date	Booking	Theater	Location
January 2	3 days	Keith	New York, NY
January 5	4 days	5th Street	New York, NY
January 16	7 days	Albee	Brooklyn, NY
January 23	3 days	Albany	Albany, NY
January 26	4 days	Proctor's	Troy, NY
January 29	4 days	B. F. Keith's	Syracuse, NY
February 2	3 days	B. F. Keith's	Rochester, NY
February 5	7 days	Shea's Hippodrome	Buffalo, NY
February 13	7 days	Shea's Hippodrome	Toronto, CAN
February 19	7 days	Imperial	Montreal, CAN
February 27	7 days	B. F. Keith's	Portland, ME
March 5	7 days	B. F. Keith's	Lowell, MA
March 12	7 days	B. F. Keith's	Boston, MA
March 19	7 days	Palace	New York, NY

Review: "Burns and Allen still doing the Al Boasberg turn, constitute a perfect vaudeville two-act. Wow material handled by top notch performers. Their easy graceful well timed way of working is a treat in these days of big pants and putty noses. They dress the act like a million bucks." (**Variety**, March 21, 1928: 45).

Date	Booking	Theater	Location
March 26	7 days	Riverside	Manhattan, NY
April 2	7 days	Davis	Pittsburgh, PA
April 22	7 days	Palace	Cincinnati, OH
April 29	7 days	B. F. Keith's	Indianapolis, IN
May 6	4 days	Rialto	Louisville, KY
May 10	3 days	Keith's	Dayton, OH
May 13	3 days	Keith's	Columbus, OH
May 17	4 days	Palace	Canton, OH
May 20	4 days	Keith's	Toledo, OH
May 24	3 days	Keith's	Grand Rapids, MI
May 27	7 days	Keith's	Detroit, MI
June 3	7 days	Palace	Cleveland, OH
June 10	4 days	Palace	Akron, OH
June 14	3 days	Keith-Albee	Youngstown, OH
June 25*	7 days	Palace	New York, NY
August 26	7 days	Orpheum	St. Louis, MO
September 3	7 days	Palace	Chicago, IL
September 10	7 days	Orpheum	Milwaukee, WI
September 17	4 days	Palace	Rockford, IL

*This date was booked but eventually cancelled.

Date	Booking	Theater	Location
September 20	3 days	New Orpheum	Madison, WI
September 23	4 days	Palace	St. Paul, MN
September 27	3 days	New Orpheum	Sioux City, IA
October 1	7 days	Hennepin	Minneapolis, MN
October 7	6 days	Orpheum	Winnipeg, CAN
October 21	6 days	Orpheum	Vancouver, CAN
October 29	7 days	Orpheum	Seattle, WA
November 5	3 days	Heilig	Portland, OR
November 12	7 days	Orpheum	San Francisco, CA
November 19	7 days	Orpheum	Los Angeles, CA
December 3	7 days	Orpheum	Oakland, CA
December 10	7 days	Golden Gate	San Francisco, CA
December 17	7 days	Hill Street	Los Angeles, CA
December 31	7 days	Orpheum	Denver, CO

1929

Date	Booking	Theater	Location
January 7	7 days	Orpheum	Omaha, NE
January 14	7 days	Main Street	Kansas City, MO
January 21	7 days	St. Louis	St. Louis, MO
January 28	7 days	Palace	Chicago, IL
February 3	4 days	Orpheum	Des Moines, IA
February 7	3 days	Capitol	Davenport, IA
February 11	3 days	Orpheum	Champaign, IL

Date	Booking	Theater	Location
February 14	3 days	New Grand	Evansville, IN
February 17	4 days	New Orpheum	Springfield, IL
February 25*	6 days	Palladium	London, ENG
March 25	6 days	Palladium	London, ENG
April 1	6 days	Empire	Leeds, ENG
April 8	6 days	Alhambra	London, ENG
April 15	6 days	Coliseum	London, ENG
April 20	6 days	Empire	Finsbury Park, ENG
April 29	6 days	Grand	Birmingham, ENG
May 6	6 days	Palladium	London, ENG
May 13	6 days	Hippodrome	Bristol, ENG
May 20	6 days	Empire	Glasgow, SCOT
May 27	2 days	Palace	Manchester, ENG
May 29	6 days	Empire	Cardiff, WALES
June 10	6 days	Coliseum	London, ENG
July 2	6 days	Moss Empire	Finsbury Park, ENG
July 8	6 days	Palladium	London, ENG
July 15	6 days	Palace	London, ENG
August 5	6 days	Holborn Empire	London, ENG
September 1	6 days	unknown	Brighton, ENG
September 8	6 days	Palladium	London, ENG
September 15	6 days	Holborn Empire	London, ENG
September 22	6 days	Empire	Birmingham, ENG
September 29	6 days	Palladium	London, ENG

*George and Gracie also had a contract for February 21, 1929 for three days to play the Palladium in South Bend, Indiana. Playing that date, however, would have made it impossible for them to reach London in time for what was referred to as their "late February" performance.

1930

January 4	unknown	Palace	New York, NY
May 21	unknown	Rivoli	New York, NY
August 9	unknown	Palace	New York, NY

1931

January 26	unknown	Golden Gate	San Francisco, CA
March 23	7 days	Palace	New York, NY

Review: In reviewing Burns and Allen's Palace routine, "Dizzy," one writer noted that the team had the ability to rise above their material more than others might but that Grace's numerous contributions to the style and tone of the act were essential to the team's success. "...What she has to sell Miss Allen sells for top value, and that (is) 100%..." George was commended as a "foil and counter-wisecracker." Burns and Allen played fourth on the bill in the next-to-closing spot, and the reviewer went on to say, "Burns & Allen can hold down that best spot anytime." (**Variety**, March 25, 1931:47).

August 5	unknown	Golden Gate	San Francisco, CA
October 31	9 wks	Palace	New York, NY

1932

January 4	4 days	Paramount	New York, NY
January 11	unknown	Civic Auditorium*	Cleveland, OH
February 15	7 days	Brooklyn	Brooklyn, NY
February 22	7 days	Capitol	New York, NY
July 4	7 days	Paramount	Los Angeles, CA
July 14	7 days	Paramount	New York, NY
August 17	7 days	Paramount	New York, NY
August 24	7 days	Paramount	Brooklyn, NY
December 9	7 days	Century	Baltimore, MD
December 29	7 days	Loew's	Jersey City, NJ

*This venue has also been known as Public Hall and the Music Hall.

1933

October 9 marked Burns and Allen's last week to work in vaudeville, their theater contract having expired. They had previously signed a film contract with Paramount to make feature films and were now appearing weekly on radio as comedians on **The White Owl Program**.

~~~~~
~~~~~

FILMOGRAPHY

George Burns and Gracie Allen

Short Films

Burns and Allen in Lamb Chops(1929)
Fit to be Tied(1930)
Pulling a Bone(1930)
The Antique Shop(1930)
Once Over, Light(1931)
100% Service(1931)
Oh, My Operation(1931)
Babbling Book(1931)
Your Hat(1931)
Hollywood on Parade A2(1932)
Hollywood on Parade B2(1932)
Patents Pending(1932)
Walking the Baby(1932)
Let's Dance(1933)
Broadway Highlights(1936)
Movietone News(1941)
Hollywood Grows Up(1954)

Feature Films

The Big Broadcast(1932)
International House(1933)
College Humor(1933)
Six of a Kind(1934)
We're Not Dressing(1934)
Many Happy Returns(1934)
Love in Bloom(1935)
Here Comes Cookie(1935)
The Big Broadcast of 1936(1935)
The Big Broadcast of 1937(1936)
College Holiday(1936)
A Damsel in Distress(1937)
College Swing(1938)
Honolulu(1939)

Gracie Allen

The Gracie Allen Murder Case(1939)
Mr. and Mrs. North(1941)
Two Girls and a Sailor(1944)

George Burns

Hollywood Fathers(1954)

The Solid Gold Cadillac(1956)
The Sunshine Boys(1975)
Oh, God!(1977)
Sgt. Pepper's Lonely Hearts Club Band(1978)
Movie Movie(1978)
Going in Style(1979)
Just You and Me, Kid(1979)
Oh God! Book II(1980)
Oh God! You Devil(1984)
18 Again!(1988)
Radioland Murders(1994)

FILMOGRAPHY

The films of Burns and Allen include short subjects and full-length features. Beginning in 1929 they starred in their first short, **Burns and Allen in Lamb Chops**; their last one, **Let's Dance**, was released in 1933. Throughout their career, the team also appeared in several newsreel and promotional films (some of those still-remaining clips are noted in the Videography portion of this work [VG74]). In 1932 they appeared in their first full-length film, **The Big Broadcast**. Burns and Allen's work in features as a team was usually as supporting players. Their last film as a team was 1939's **Honolulu**. Gracie appeared in two motion pictures without George, **Mr. and Mrs. North** and **Two Girls and a Sailor**.

George did not appear in another film until his Oscar-winning role in **The Sunshine Boys** in 1975, a role originally to be played by Jack Benny but offered to George upon Benny's death. He did, however, narrate the 1956 Judy Holliday vehicle, **The Solid Gold Cadillac**. George appeared in a number of films after **The Sunshine Boys** and he remained active in the industry until 1994, when he was ninety-eight years old.

George and Gracie's film projects as a team and separately break nicely in chronological order, so that is the way they appear here.

Short Subjects

Short subject entries include title, running time, studio, year of release, selected production credits, premise or synopsis, and reviews. All shorts star George and Gracie; additional cast credits are indicated. Each short was shot in black and white (b/w) and was released as a one-reeler. The shorts were primarily filmed in Astoria, Long Island, New York.

George Burns and Gracie Allen

F1 Burns and Allen in Lamb Chops. 10 min. b/w. The Vitaphone Corporation, Warner Bros., 1929. Dir. Murray Roth.

Premise: George and Gracie essentially perform their vaudeville stage routine in their first short, engaging in song ("Do You Believe Me?"), dance, and chatter.

F2 Fit To Be Tied. 10 min. b/w. Paramount Publix, 1930. Dir. Ray Cozine. Dialogue Dir. Max E. Hayes.

Synopsis: George is frustrated by his inability to get a department store clerk to wait on him when he comes in to buy a tie. Gracie demonstrates songs in order to induce customers to buy sheet music. George attempts to arrange a date with her. Gracie sings "I'm A Whole Lot Wilder Than I

Look." This is the first recording of George telling Gracie to say goodbye (not "good night" at this point) to the audience.

F3 Pulling a Bone. 10 min. b/w. Paramount Publix, 1930. Dir. Howard Bretherton. Dialogue Dir. Max E. Hayes.
Additional Cast: William Browning.

Premise: George enters a drugstore in an attempt to find someone who can help him dislodge a fish bone caught in his throat; Gracie works at the soda fountain.

Review: "Both Burns and Miss Allen warrant further experiment in the talkers." (**Variety**, November 12, 1930).

F4 The Antique Shop. 10 min. b/w. Paramount Publix, 1930. Dir. Ray Cozine. Dialogue Dir. Max E. Hayes. Written by George N. Burns.

Additional Cast: Chester Clute (*Pseudo Clerk*); Herschel Mayall (*Shop Owner*).

Premise: Gracie works in an antique shop. George is a customer who is trying to find an unbreakable statue.

Reviews: "...rather short but entertaining...It should provide a neat spot of amusement on almost any bill." (**Motion Picture Herald**, April 18, 1931). "Burns and Allen, from vaudeville...provide an okay subject for any program..." (**Variety**, February 18, 1931).

F5 Once Over, Light. 10 min. b/w. Paramount Publix, 1931. Dir. Howard Bretherton. Dialogue Dir. Max E. Hayes. Written by George N. Burns.

Additional Cast: Chester Clute (*Joe*).

Premise: Gracie is a manicurist at a barber shop. George is a rather cranky customer who has come in for a shave and manicure.

Review: "Slow in getting started, but winds up with a few good laughs." (**Motion Picture Herald**, 1931).

F6 100% Service. 10 min. b/w. Paramount Publix, 1931. Dir. Ray Cozine. Dialogue Dir. Max E. Hayes. Dialogue Dir. Max E. Hayes. Written by George N. Burns.

Additional Cast: Chester Clute (*Desk Clerk*).

Synopsis: George argues with the hotel desk clerk about the price of a room. He later visits the sundries counter, where Gracie works as a clerk who spends most of her time frustrating her customers by giving them incorrect change. George discovers Gracie has Hollywood ambitions and decides to test her intelligence by asking her questions.

Reviews: "Of course, it's nonsense, but that doesn't matter, since this vaudeville team puts its lines over in a really amusing style all its own." (**Motion Picture Herald**, September 5, 1931). "Gracie Allen's knack for pulling that dizzy dame character is such that...the current piece dovetails into nice enough laughter reaction to fit any program." (**Variety**, August 18, 1931: 17).

F7 Oh, My Operation. 10 min. b/w. Paramount Publix, 1931. Dir. Ray Cozine. Dialogue Dir. Max E. Hayes. Written by George N. Burns.

Premise: Gracie is a nurse at a hospital where George is her patient.

F8 Babbling Book. 10 min. b/w. Paramount Publix, 1931. Dir. Aubrey Scotto. Written by George N. Burns. (Also referred to as **The Babbling Book**).

Additional Cast: Chester Clute, Donald Meek, George Shelton.

Premise: George visits a book store and gets involved with Gracie, who is the sales clerk.

Review: "Miss Allen's line of chatter is seemingly unending, but vastly amusing." (**Motion Picture Herald**, May 7, 1932).

F9 Your Hat. 10 min. b/w. Paramount Publix, 1931. Dir. Aubrey Scotto.

Additional Cast: Chester Clute (*Salesman*).

Premise: George is the salesman who waits on Gracie when she comes into the store to buy a hat for her boyfriend.

F10 Hollywood on Parade (A-2). 6 min. b/w. Paramount Publix Corp., 1932. Prod. Louis Lewyn.

Cast: Stuart Erwin, George Burns, Gracie Allen, Bing Crosby, Olsen and Johnson, Gary Cooper (**Themselves**).

Synopsis: Stuart Erwin emcees this entry in Paramount's series of "behind-the-scenes" peeks at the stars. Bing Crosby introduces George and after trading good-natured insults they briefly discuss Burns and Allen's first film, **The Big Broadcast** (F19). Bing asks George to introduce him to Gracie so he can ask her for a date. George brings Gracie out onto the stage where she informs Bing that she is married. Comedy team Olsen and Johnsen is featured in a routine at the beach, and Gary Cooper is seen breakfasting with a chimp.

F11 Hollywood on Parade (B-2). 8 min. b/w. Paramount Publix, 1932. Prod. Louis Lewyn.

Synopsis: A three-day convention of the Motion Picture Theater Owners of America (MPTOA) held at Paramount Studios is the setting for this short emceed by Jack Haley. George and Gracie are brought on by Haley to perform a brief bit from their vaudeville days. Bing Crosby is seen briefly during George and Gracie's routine. Adolphe Menjou addresses the audience. Recent bridegroom Cary Grant speaks a few words to the gathering. Cecil B. DeMille, in the midst of filming the 1934 release of **Cleopatra**, introduces star Henry Wilcoxon and various minor players to the crowd. The president of the MPTOA plays a "stooge" to W. C. Fields.

F12 Patents Pending. 8 min. b/w. Paramount Publix, 1932. Dir. Aubrey Scotto.

Premise: Gracie's father is involved with a company that comes up with crazy inventions. George is a potential investor.

Review: "...the team can't count this...among their best efforts." (**Variety**, March 21, 1933: 16).

F13 Walking the Baby. 10 min. b/w. Paramount Publix, 1932. Dir. Aubrey Scotto. Written by George N. Burns.

Additional Cast: Chester Clute.

Premise: Gracie is a nursemaid pushing a baby stroller in the park where she meets George, a street cleaner. A flirtation ensues.

Review: "It's not of their best, stretching a few gags for ten minutes, but the now well-established ether rep of the dizzy comedy pair should carry this for some nice bookings all over." (**Variety**, July 11, 1933).

F14 Let's Dance. 10 min. b/w. Paramount Publix, 1933. Dir. Aubrey Scotto. Written by George N. Burns.

Additional Cast: Barton MacLane (*Tough Sailor*).

Synopsis: A group of sailors, including George, visit the Roseland Dance Hall. George meets a dance hall girl (Gracie) and dances with her briefly before offering her a soda. Seated, they go into one of their typical routines. The sailors receive orders to go to Shanghai, but George stays behind because he wants a date with Gracie.

F15 Broadway Highlights (Intimate News Of The Gay White Way). 10 min. b/w. Paramount, 1936. Ed. Milton Hocky, Carl Timin, and Fred Waller. Narr. Ted Husing. **SEE VG26.**

Synopsis: Four **Broadway Highlights** were produced by Paramount, each concentrating on New York City's night life and the entertainment and sports figures who peopled it. In this entry, one segment includes George and Gracie being interviewed briefly by Ted Husing after their arrival at the Hippodrome Theatre for the 1935 Broadway opening of the play **Jumbo**, produced by Billy Rose and starring Jimmy Durante with Paul Whiteman.

F16 Movietone News. Newsreel. b/w. 1941.

Synopsis: In an "On Broadway" segment, George and Gracie are seen at the premiere of the film **A Yank in the RAF**.

F17 Hollywood Grows Up. 10 min. b/w. Columbia, 1954. Dir. Ralph Staub.

Synopsis: Part of the **Screen Snapshots** series of shorts, this film includes routines by Burns and Allen and Abbott and Costello, an appearance by Larry Simms and film clips from World War II.

George Burns

F18 Hollywood Fathers. 10 min. Columbia, 1954. Dir. Ralph Staub.

Synopsis: George Burns, Joe E. Brown, and Johnny Mack Brown appear with their sons in another entry in the **Screen Snapshots** series. George is seen playing checkers with his son, Ronnie.

Feature Films

Each feature film entry includes title, running time, whether the film was shot in black and white or color, studio, year of release, Motion Picture Association of America ratings if applicable, selected production credits, cast credits, synopsis, reviews and commentary. If the film is available on videocassette and/or laserdisc, it is noted, although most are available in some form from collectors and dealers. Available soundtracks or portions thereof are also noted. A number of these features are occasionally broadcast on television, particularly those starring George from 1975 forward.

Portions of the notes for the Paramount film commentaries were obtained from the Paramount Collection at the Academy of Motion Picture Arts and Sciences.

George Burns and Gracie Allen

F19 The Big Broadcast. 87 min. b/w. Paramount, 1932.
Dir. Frank Tuttle. Screen Play by George Marion, Jr. Based on the play **Wild Waves** by William Ford Manley. Music by Ralph Rainger. Lyrics by Leo Robin. Photography by George Folsey. **SEE D82.**

Cast: Bing Crosby (*Bing Hornsby*); Stuart Erwin (*Leslie McWhinney*); Leila Hyams (*Anita Rogers*); Sharon Lynne (*Mona Lowe*); George Barbier (*Mr. Clapsaddle*); George N. Burns (*George Burns*); Grace Allen (*Reception Clerk*); Major, Sharp, and Minor (*Telephone Girls*); Ralph Robertson

(*Announcer*); Spec O'Donnell (*Office Boy*); and Kate Smith, the Boswell Sisters, Cab Calloway, the Mills Brothers, Arthur Tracy, Vincent Lopez and his Orchestra, Donald Novis, James Wallington, William Brenton, Norman Brokenshire, Don Ball (*Themselves*).

Synopsis: George's New York radio station hires Bing Hornsby (Bing Crosby) to sing on his **Grip-Tight Girdle Hour**. Bing fails to appear for three days, forcing George to put the station up for sale. The radio station is purchased by a Texan (Stuart Erwin) who promotes his new acquisition by putting on "a big broadcast," featuring several well-known radio personalities. Gracie plays one of the station's secretary-receptionists.

Review: "George (Nat) Burns with his serious-miened straighting for the dumbdoraish Gracie Allen are a sock interlude in themselves as the station manager and dumb stenog, although it evolves into more or less of a specialty routine." (**Variety**, October 18, 1932: 14).

Additional Reviews: **Film Daily**, October 15, 1932: 4; **The Films of Bing Crosby**, p. 48-49; **The Hollywood Reporter**, October 1, 1932: 3; **Motion Picture Herald**, October 8, 1932: 91; **The New Outlook**, November 1932: 161: 46; **The New Yorker**, October 22, 1932: 8: 57; **The New York Times**, October 15, 1932: 13: 1; **Rob Wagner's Script**, October 22, 1932: 8: 8.

Commentary: The most notable musical feature is the inclusion of Crosby's theme song, "When the Blue of the Night Meets the Gold of the Day." To advertise the film, theater owners could order, among other things, an 8x10 still for a dime and window cards for seven cents each. The Paramount publicity department suggested to theater owners that fans submit humorous sayings appropriate as "Gracie-isms", with the winner receiving movie tickets as a prize. The film was also "not to be presented as a revue or vaudeville show." The studio wanted to market it as a "strong romantic, humorous story in which giant radio personalities appear" although the names of the radio stars were to be given "adequate, but secondary, display." Also see B85.

F20 International House. 70 min. b/w. Paramount, 1933.
Dir. Edward Sutherland. Assoc. Prod. Albert Lewis. Screen Play by Francis Martin and Walter DeLeon. From a story by Neil Brant and Louis E. Heifetz. Music and Lyrics by Ralph Rainger and Leo Robin. Photography by Ernest Haller. Available on videocassette and laserdisc. **SEE VG69.**

Cast: Peggy Hopkins Joyce (*Peggy Hopkins Joyce*); W. C. Fields (*Professor Quail*); Stuart Erwin (*Tommy Nash*); Sari Maritza (*Carol Fortescue*); George Burns (*Doctor Burns*); Gracie Allen (*Nurse Allen*); Bela Lugosi (*General Petronovich*); Edmund Breese (*Doctor Wong*); Lumsden Hare (*Sir Mortimer Fortescue*); Franklin Pangborn (*Hotel Manager*); Harrison Greene (*Herr Von Baden*); Sterling Holloway (*Dancer*); Lona André (*Female Chorister*); and Rudy Vallee, Colonel Stoopnagle and Budd, Cab Calloway, Baby Rose Marie (*Themselves*).

Synopsis: Advertised as "The **Grand Hotel** of Comedy," this film features a motley cast of characters converging on a hotel in Wu Hu, China, for the unveiling of Dr. Wong's (Edmund Breese) new invention, the radioscope (i.e. television), which allows pictures to be transmitted around the world and viewed on a screen. To demonstrate his invention, he intercepts signals from a bicycle race and performances by various entertainers. Businessmen from around the world are arriving to bid on the rights. In various sub-plots, Professor Quail (W. C. Fields) is traveling to Wu Hu in an autogyro. Tommy Nash (Stuart Erwin), representing an American company desiring the rights to the invention, has travelled by car overnight to the city with Peggy Hopkins Joyce as a passenger. Upon his arrival at the hotel, he meets his fiancée, Miss Fortescue (Sari Maritza). Their relationship has become strained due to his becoming ill several times just prior to their wedding which has prevented their marriage from taking place. This, coupled with the circumstances of his arrival, causes friction with Miss Fortescue. In a supreme case of bad timing, Nash is diagnosed by Dr. Burns, the hotel physician, as having the measles. He is placed in quarantine in the hotel by Dr. Burns, assisted by his nurse, Miss Allen. General Petronovich (Bela Lugosi) takes advantage of the situation by having the entire hotel quarantined, preventing any other potential bidders from arriving at the hotel to participate in the bidding process.

Reviews: "Although the writing is uneven, a great deal of it is funny, and it is of particular help to Mr. Fields and to Burns and Allen." (**The New York Times**, May 27, 1933: 11: 5). "For B. and A. it's a walk, their assignment being plain and fancy cross-fire with their regular stage routine split into four or five brief sections." (**Variety**, May 30, 1933: 15).

Additional Reviews: **Film Daily**, May 27, 1933: 3; **The Films of W. C. Fields**, p. 80-82; **The Hollywood Reporter**, May 8, 1933: 2; **Motion Picture Herald**, May 20, 1933: 33; **The Nation**, June 21, 1933: 136: 708; **The New Yorker**, June 3, 1933: 9: 58; **Rob Wagner's Script**, May 27, 1933: 9: 9; **Time**, June 5, 1933: 21: 20; **Vanity Fair**, July 1933: 40: 59; **W. C. Fields: A Life on Film**, p. 109-115.

Commentary: Peggy Hopkins Joyce and Burns and Allen were the first to be cast and Cary Grant was among those considered for parts from the list of contract players. Theatergoers could win tickets to the film by participating in various methods of "exploitation" (an industry term) dreamed up by Paramount's publicity department: drawing Gracie's missing brother, doing impersonations of Burns and Allen, and filling in a Burns and Allen comic strip. The film faced difficulties from industry censor Joseph Breen (the man who picked up the gauntlet from Will H. Hays), who suggested to the studio that it withdraw its application for approval because, in his words, it "is filled with gross vulgarities in both action and dialogue." As if that weren't enough, an earthquake (albeit minor) rocked the area during filming. Sweden considered the film unsuitable for distribution, not due to vulgarity, but because the story was considered "too artificial and absurd." Franklin Pangborn is credited on-screen as "Franklyn Pangborn." Also see B148, B275, B499.

F21 College Humor. 80 min. b/w. Paramount, 1933.
Dir. Wesley Ruggles. Associate Prod. William LeBaron. Screen Play by Claude Binyon and Frank Butler. From a story by Dean Fales. Music and Lyrics by Arthur Johnston and Sam Coslow. Photography by Leo Tover.

Cast: Bing Crosby (*Professor Danvers*); Jack Oakie (*Barney Shirrel*); Richard Arlen (*Mondrake*); Mary Carlisle (*Barbara Shirrel*); George Burns (*George, a Caterer*); Gracie Allen (*Gracie, a Caterer*); Mary Kornman (*Amber*); Howard H. Jones (*Football Coach - USC*); Joseph Sauers (*Tex Roust*); Lona André (*Ginger*).

Synopsis: A popular professor, Frederick Danvers (Bing Crosby) chaperons a fraternity dance where Burns and Allen are the caterers. The professor is also the third side of a love triangle involving a female co-ed and her football star boyfriend, whose jealousy throws his game off so much the girl's own brother becomes the school's newest gridiron sensation. George and Gracie perform a short Scottish song and dance routine. This musical comedy is similar to an earlier motion picture, **Sweetie**. Crosby sings "Alma Mater," Colleen of Killarney," "The Old Ox Road," "I'm A Bachelor Of the Art Of Ha-Cha-Cha," "Learn to Croon," "Moonstruck," and "Play Ball."

Reviews: "Burns and Allen, hilarious clowns, have too little catering to do..." (**The New York Times**, June 23, 1933: 15: 4). "(These musical pictures) are intended to delight rural cinemaddicts whose tastes in diversion have been shaped by wireless. Thus, **College Humor** contains George Burns and Gracie Allen." (**Time**, July 3, 1933: 22: 30). "Combination of Bing Crosby, Richard Arlen, Burns and Allen, and Jack Oakie ought to attract." (**Variety**, June 27, 1933: 14).

Additional Reviews: **Film Daily**, June 14, 1933: 6; **The Films of Bing Crosby**, p. 50-52; **The Hollywood Reporter**, June 6, 1933: 11; **Motion Picture Herald**, June 17, 1933: 34; **The New Outlook**, August 1933: 162: 44; **Newsweek**, July 1, 1933: 1: 31.

Commentary: Cary Grant and Carole Lombard were among the available contract players who were to be considered for any remaining parts, but obviously were not cast. Director Wesley Ruggles, brother of beloved character actor Charles (Charlie) Ruggles, gathered a number of impressive credits on his directing resumé in the 1930's, including **Cimarron** (1931), **No Man of Her Own** (1932), **I'm No Angel** (1933), **The Gilded Lily** (1935) and **Sing You Sinners** (1938). Also see B85.

F22 Six of a Kind. 62 min. b/w. Paramount, 1934.
Dir. Leo McCarey. Assoc. Prod. Douglas MacLean. Screen Play by Walter DeLeon and Harry Ruskin. Based on a story by Keene Thompson and Douglas MacLean. Music by Ralph Rainger. Photography by Henry Sharp. Ed. LeRoy Stone.

Cast: Charles Ruggles (*J. Pinkham Whinney*); Mary Boland (*Flora Whinney*); W. C. Fields (*Sheriff John Hoxley*); George Burns (*George Edward*); Gracie Allen (*Gracie Devore*); Alison Skipworth (*Mrs. K. Rumford*); Bradley Page (*Ferguson*); Grace Bradley (*Goldie*); William J. Kelly (*Gillette*); Phil Tead (*Newspaper Office Clerk*).

Synopsis: A bank clerk and his wife (Charles Ruggles and Mary Boland) are planning to take a second honeymoon trip to California and, to save on expenses, place an ad in the newspaper for a couple to travel with them. They do find a couple, George and Gracie (and Gracie's dog, Rang Tang Tang), but the trip detours into trouble when a fellow employee of the bank clerk places $50,000 in stolen money into the innocent man's luggage. The thief intends to retrieve the money during the trip but, with Gracie along, the couple does not follow their planned itinerary. The trip is beset with problems and, when the weary travelers arrive at a small town in Nevada, they discover that Phinney is Sheriff Hoxley's (W. C. Fields) and the bank officials' leading suspect in the bank robbery.

Reviews: "Gracie Allen, as is to be expected, never by any chance does the correct thing." (**The New York Times**, March 10, 1934: 18: 3). "They (Burns and Allen) succeed so admirably in being pests that their departure five minutes before the picture ends is a genuine relief." (**Variety**, March 13, 1934).

Commentary: Charlie Ruggles and Mary Boland were already established as popular Paramount co-stars when cast in this film. Used primarily as comic relief in their three previous Paramount features, George and Gracie's appearance in **Six of a Kind** marks their first full-length roles on screen. A merchandising tie-in with White Owl Cigars was suggested by Paramount publicists. It was also suggested that department stores stock bins full of grab bags (collections of "goofy" things, if possible) to be sold for a dollar apiece to customers lured by Gracie's words, "Maybe you'll find my brother in with these things!" Miriam Hopkins, Ida Lupino and Myrna Loy were among those considered for parts in the film as were Richard Arlen, Herbert Marshall and George Raft. "Contrasts of 1934," a stage show starring Jack Haley, entertained the film's audience in New York, probably at Paramount's Time Square Theater since the film was being shown there and at Brooklyn's Paramount Theater simultaneously. Also see B275.

F23 We're Not Dressing. 77 min. b/w. Paramount, 1934.
Dir. Norman Taurog. Assoc. Prod. Benjamin Glazer. Screen Play by Horace Jackson, Francis Martin and George Marion, Jr. Based on stories by Walton Hall Smith and Benjamin Glazer. From J. M. Barrie's play **The Admirable Crichton**. Lyrics and Music by Mack Gordon and Harry Revel. Photography by Charles Lang. Ed. Stuart Heisler. Available on videocassette. **SEE VG77.**

Cast: Bing Crosby (*Stephen Jones*); Carole Lombard (*Doris Worthington*); George Burns (*George Martin*); Gracie Allen (*Gracie Martin*); Ethel Merman (*Edith*); Leon Errol (*Hubert*); Raymond Milland (*Prince Michael*); Jay Henry (*Prince Alexander*).

Synopsis: A wealthy young woman (Carole Lombard), several of her decadent friends (including the Ethel Merman and Raymond Milland characters), and a sailor (Bing Crosby) survive the wreck of the woman's yacht and swim ashore to what appears to be an uninhabited island. Forced to depend upon the sailor for food and shelter, the willful heiress eventually admits her love for him. George and Gracie, on a botanical expedition on another part of the island, eventually aid the castaways prior to their rescue. This musical also features the song "It's Just A New Spanish Custom," sung by Leon Errol and Ethel Merman with the others, "Goodnight, Lovely Little Lady," "I'll Sing About the Birds and the Bees," "It's a Lie," "Let's Play House," "Love Thy Neighbor," "May I?", "My Gigolo," "Once In A Blue Moon," "Riding 'Round in the Rain," and "She Reminds Me of You," sung by Bing Crosby.

Reviews: "The Burns and Allen team assuredly serves this film valiantly." (**The New York Times**, April 26, 1934: 27: 2). "She (Carole Lombard) is eclipsed in the femme division both by Miss Allen and Miss Merman...It's Burns and Allen who really rate the second honors to Crosby, the unofficial star." (**Variety**, May 1, 1934).

Commentary: Director Norman Taurog cut an Ethel Merman song, "It's The Animal In Me" from this film but later inserted it into another Burns and Allen film he directed, **The Big Broadcast of 1936** (F27). One of the publicity contests was for fans to guess what ten articles Gracie Allen would take with her if she "planned" to be shipwrecked on an uninhabited island. Location shooting was done on Catalina Island off the coast of southern California. Also see B85.

F24 Many Happy Returns. 60 min. b/w. Paramount, 1934.
Dir. Norman McLeod. Assoc. Prod. William LeBaron. Screen Play by J. P. McEvoy and Claude Binyon. Adaptation by Keene Thompson and Ray Harris. Based upon a story by Lady Mary Cameron. Lyrics and Music by Sam Coslow and Arthur Johnston. Photography by Henry Sharp. Ed. Richard Currier.

Cast: Guy Lombardo (*Guy Lombardo*); The Royal Canadians (*Themselves*); George Burns (*Burns*); Gracie Allen (*Gracie*); George Barbier (*Horatio Allen*); Joan Marsh (*Florence Allen*); Ray Milland (*Ted Lambert*); Egon Brecher (*Dr. Otto von Strudel*); Stanley Fields (*Joe*); John Kelly (*Mike*); William Demarest (*Brinker*); Johnny Arthur (*Davies*); Franklin Pangborn (*Secretary*); Morgan Wallace (*Nathan Silas*); Kenneth Thomson (*Director*); Veloz and Yolanda (*Dancers*); Larry Adler (*Harmonica Player*); Taylor and Rutledge (*Dancers*).

Synopsis: Gracie's father (George Barbier) nearly has an apoplectic fit when he returns from a trip and finds that Gracie has tried to turn his department store into a bird sanctuary and has torn up Guy Lombardo's radio contract (which Mr. Allen also owns) so Lombardo can go to Hollywood to be in a picture. A psychoanalyst says Gracie's problems will be solved if she is paired with Burns (the radio station announcer billed as "the voice of romance") and, although Burns is not interested in Gracie, he is interested in the $10 per mile Gracie's father is willing to pay him if he will marry her and take her from New York to Los Angeles for their honeymoon. Gracie's sister, Florence (Joan Marsh), is also on her way to Hollywood, having won an appearance as the Mystery Girl in the same film Lombardo is appearing in, **Murder While The Band Plays**. Songs include "The Sweetest Music This Side of Heaven," "Good Bye, Good Luck and Fare Thee Well," "Bogeyman," and "When You Whisper I Love You."

Reviews: "Situations that in other hands might even bring ridicule fit Gracie Allen like a new glove and she romps through with the ease of a cinema veteran..." (**Daily Variety**, April 27, 1934). Another reviewer felt that Gracie's character, while receiving much of the film's attention, would be better utilized in a minor role as opposed to that of a lead character since George and Gracie "appear to exhaust themselves...This film's activities seem just a wee bit too much for the Burns and Allen team to shoulder." (**The New York Times**, June 17, 1934: sec. IX, 3: 2). "'Many Happy Returns' is primarily an excuse for bringing a radio-celebrated vaudeville cross-fire team, Burns and Allen, and a dance orchestra, also radio-celebrated, Guy Lombardo's Royal Canadians to the screen." (**Variety**, June 12, 1934).

Commentary: Continuing their best-known "bit" into their feature film career, George tells Gracie to "say good night" to the train porter. The title of this script was once known as **Slightly Married** but was not registered at the suggestion of the Hays Office. (To respond to the public outcry against scandal-ridden Hollywood in the late 1920's, the Motion Picture Producers and Distributors of America, Inc. was formed and eventually adopted voluntary self-censorship in the form of a Production Code, which was overseen by the MPPDA's original president, Will H. Hays [hence the name, the Hays Office]. In 1934 the MPPDA was forced to adopt a more formal, mandatory code when some producers began pushing the envelope with films containing more sex and violence than many audience members were willing to accept, and Joseph I. Breen was named to head the new Production Code Administration. The MPPDA eventually became known as the Motion Picture Association of America [MPAA] which has been helmed by Jack Valenti for nearly three decades; today's film ratings system was inaugurated in 1968 and has undergone some revision since then). **SEE B417.** The final script was also not as romantic for George and Gracie as it was first written at the beginning of 1934. Australia and some Canadian provinces were among those who only approved the film's distribution if the "hip wiggling" was deleted. Ohio asked that all "honeymoon dialogue" be eliminated, New York, Massachusetts, and Kansas approved the film "without eliminations." In order to publicize the "romantic" side of the story, however, theater owners were encouraged to pay for the wedding licenses of the first five or ten couples who made plans to marry the week of the film's showing and registered their intent in Gracie's name at the box office. Buster Crabbe, William Frawley, Baby LeRoy, Gail Patrick, and Ida Lupino were among the available contract players Paramount could have cast in the film. Some of the film's music, while credited to Guy Lombardo, was actually performed by the Duke Ellington Orchestra. According to a published interview in **The New York Times** (May 6, 1934) this film marked the first time George did not pen his and Gracie's portion of the script. Also see B275, B386.

F25 Love in Bloom. 75 min. b/w. Paramount, 1935.
Dir. Elliott Nugent. Prod. Benjamin Glazer. Original Screen Play by Frank R. Adams. Adaptation by J. P. McEvoy and Keene Thompson. Additional Dialogue by John P. Medbury. Lyrics and Music by Mack Gordon and Harry Revel. Photography by Leo Tover. Ed. William Shea.

Cast: George Burns (*George Downey*); Gracie Allen (*Gracie Downey*); Joe Morrison (*Larry Deane*); Dixie Lee (*Violet Downey*); J. C. Nugent (*Col. "Dad" Downey*); Lee Kohlmar (*Pop*); Richard Carle (*Sheriff*).

Synopsis: George and Gracie are employees of his father's (J. C. Nugent) carnival, "Dixie De Luxe Shows," a life from which George's sister, Violet (Dixie Lee), escapes by going to the city, where she meets and falls in love with a talented but as-yet unsuccessful songwriter, Larry Deane (Joe Morrison). Their eventual happiness is delayed by her father's trickery. Gracie sings "Lookie, Lookie, Lookie, Here Comes Cookie" in this film but not in their next one, which carries the title **Here Comes Cookie** (F26). "My Heart is an Open Book," "Got Me Doin' Things," and "Let Me Sing You to Sleep With a Love Song" round out the musical numbers.

Reviews: "Mr. Burns and Miss Allen do their best to beat the ebbing tide of the story..." (**The New York Times**, April 20, 1935: 16: 2). "Radio pair may save their latest celluloid effort but it won't help their future on the screen." (**Variety**, April 24, 1935: 13).

Additional Reviews: **Film Daily**, April 20, 1935: 4; **The Hollywood Reporter**, February 26, 1935: 3; **Motion Picture Herald**, March 9, 1935: 48.

Commentary: This film was originally titled **The Big Broadcast of 1934** and then changed to **Win or Lose** before it was released with the title **Love in Bloom**. Despite its title, it does not contain the familiar Jack Benny theme song by the same name. The writer who receives additional dialogue credit, John P. Medbury, was also writing for George and Gracie's radio show at this time. The Singer's Midgets headlined the stage show when the film premiered at New York's Roxy Theater. Also see B275.

F26 Here Comes Cookie. 65 minutes. b/w. Paramount, 1935.
Dir. Norman McLeod. Prod. William LeBaron. Story by Sam Mintz and Don Hartman. Screen Play by Don Hartman. Music and Lyrics by Richard Whiting and Leo Robin. Photography by Gilbert Warrenton.

Cast: George Burns (*George Burns*); Gracie Allen (*Gracie Allen*); George Barbier (*Harrison Allen*); Betty Furness (*Phyllis Allen*); Andrew Tombes (*Botts*); Rafael Storm (*Ramon del Ramos*); James Burke (*Broken-nose Reilly*); Lee Kohlmar (*Mr. Flugsnort*); Milla Davenport (*Mrs. Flugsnort*); Jack Powell (*Jack*); Irving Bacon (*Thompson*); Frank Darien (*Clyde*); Del Henderson (*Lloyd*); Harry Holman (*Stuffy*); Jack Duffy (*Wilbur*); Jack Powell (*Drummer*); and vaudeville acts The Buccaneers, Big Boy Williams, Cal Norris and Monkey, Jack Cavanaugh and Partner, Jester and Mole, Johnson and Dove, Moro and Yaconelli, Pascale Perry and Partner, Seymour and Corncob, Six Olympics, Seymour and Corncob, The Six Candreva Bros. (*Themselves*).

Synopsis: Gracie's father (George Barbier), fearing his other daughter is being romanced only because she comes from a wealthy family, gives all of his money to Gracie for sixty days while he leaves town, believing that his action will cause the suitor to think the Allens have lost all their money. Gracie sings "Vamp of the Pampas."

Reviews: "Providing a field day for the Burns and Allen team, it clips Miss Allen from the lunatic fringe and sews her onto the border of absolute idiocy." (**The New York Times**, October 12, 1935: 12: 2). "It's not a picture to cop critical raves for individual performances but the starred duo do reveal anew their practiced vaudeville-taught sense of timing." (**Variety**, October 16, 1935).

Additional Reviews: **Daily Variety**, August 14, 1935; **The Hollywood Reporter**, August 14, 1935; **Motion Picture Daily**, August 15, 1935; **Motion Picture Herald**, August 24, 1935.

Commentary: This film was originally titled **Soup to Nuts.** In England, where the British Censor Board invariably deleted the word "gigolo" from any approval it gave, it was released as **The Plot Thickens**. One **Sun** reviewer noted that the camera was "giving Gracie a better break at last." Unfortunately, better lighting and camera angles couldn't save the film from its shortcomings. **Here Comes Cookie** made its New York premiere at the Paramount Theater on a double bill with **Wings Over Ethiopia**. According to **The New York Times** review previously cited, **Wings Over Ethiopia** had been filmed the previous year as a "travelogue and exploitation medium for a new Swiss-African airline." Ironically, during the interim period between the film's lensing and release, the African empire became a battleground, and the film took on greater proportions than anyone could have foreseen. It tended to overshadow its companion on the marquee, as evidenced by the reviewer's remarks, "...its timeliness, its natural interest and excellent photography make it well worth seeing--even at the risk of running into the Burns and Allen epic." Also see B275.

F27 The Big Broadcast of 1936. 97 min. b/w. Paramount, 1935.
Dir. Norman Taurog. Prod. Benjamin Glazer. Screen Play by Walter DeLeon, Francis Martin and Ralph Spence. Music and Lyrics by Ralph Rainger, Richard Whiting, Leo Robin, Dorothy Parker, Mack Gordon, Harry Revel and Ray Noble. Photography by Leo Tover. Ed. Ellsworth Hoagland. Dance Ensembles Staged by LeRoy Prinz.

Cast: Jack Oakie (*Spud*); George Burns (*George*); Gracie Allen (*Gracie*); Lyda Roberti (*Countess*); Henry Wadsworth (*Smiley*); Wendy Barrie (*Sue*); C. Henry Gordon (*Gordonio*); Akim Tamiroff (*Boris*); Fayard Nicholas (*Dash*); Harold Nicholas (*Dot*); Benny Baker (*Herman*); and Bing Crosby, Amos and Andy, Ethel Merman, Sir Guy Standing, David Holt, Gail Patrick, Bill Robinson, Ina Ray Hutton and Her Melodiers, Vienna Boys Choir, Ray Noble and His Band, Mary Boland, Charlie Ruggles (*Themselves*).

Synopsis: George and Gracie try to sell her uncle's new invention, "The Radio Eye" (similar to a television but a bit more fanciful) to a nearly-broke radio station operator (Jack Oakie) who eventually realizes that the device could be the winning entry in a broadcast competition. In order to get the money he needs to purchase it, the man tries wooing a young heiress (Lydia Roberti), who has other ideas and spirits him away to an island while he still has possession of the gadget and where another jealous suitor awaits them. Then it's George and Gracie to the rescue of their contraption and a rollicking conclusion.

Reviews: "In star name and feature personality values alone, this picture should occasion a showman's holiday." (**Motion Picture Herald**, September 21, 1935: 41). "Situations are their new forte, and Burns and Allen now can not only carry a story, but walk away with it." (**Variety**, September 18, 1935: 35).

Additional Reviews: **Canadian Magazine**, November 1935: 84: 40; **Film Daily**, September 14, 1935: 7; **The Hollywood Reporter**, September 10, 1935: 3; **The New Yorker**, September 21, 1935: 11: 59-60; **The New York Times**, September 16, 1935: 15: 2; **Newsweek**, September 21, 1935: 6: 17; **Rob Wagner's Script**, September 21, 1935: 14: 10; **Time**, September 23, 1935: 26: 45.

Commentary: Originally scheduled to be **The Big Broadcast of 1935**, filming of the musical numbers took more time than had been originally anticipated, hence the title change. Ironically, a song not originally part of the script, Ethel Merman's rendition of "It's The Animal In Me," which was filmed for then cut from **We're Not Dressing** (F23), won choreographer LeRoy Prinz an Oscar nomination after its insertion into this film. Also see B275

F28 The Big Broadcast of 1937. 102 min. b/w. Paramount, 1936.
Dir. Mitchell Leisen. Prod. Lewis E. Gensler. Screen Play by Walter DeLeon and Francis Martin. Based on a story by Erwin Gelsey, Arthur Kober and Barry Trivers. Music and Lyrics by Ralph Rainger and Leo Robin. Photography by Theodor Sparkuhl. Ed. Stuart Heisler. Dance Ensembles Staged by LeRoy Prinz.

Cast: Jack Benny (*Jack Carson*); George Burns (*Mr. Platt*); Gracie Allen (*Mrs. Platt*); Bob Burns (*Bob Black*); Martha Raye (*Patsy*); Shirley Ross (*Gwen Holmes*); Ray Milland (*Bob Miller*); Frank Forest (*Frank Rossman*); Benny Fields (*Benny Fields*); Sam Hearn (*Schlepperman*); Larry Adler (*Larry Adler*); Virginia Weidler (*Flower Girl*); David Holt (*Train Bearer*); Billie Lee (*Train Bearer*); Louis DaPron (*Louis DaPron*); Eleanore Whitney (*Eleanore Whitney*); Don Hulbert (*Page Boy*); Irving Bacon (*Property Man*); and Leopold Stokowski and His Symphony Orchestra and Benny Goodman and His Band (*Themselves*).

Synopsis: In the first of Burns and Allen's and Jack Benny's two co-starring film roles (the other one being the upcoming **College Holiday**), Benny is a radio station director for the National Network Radio Company who must contend with Platt Golf Ball program sponsors George and Gracie. An agent (Ray Milland) suggests the station hire a "romantic singer." The singer (Frank Forest) later becomes incensed when he hears a small-town female radio host (Shirley Ross) sing along with his record and make disparaging remarks about his singing. He tells his agent to "get her off the air" but, instead, the agent signs her as a client and she becomes a great success. The Benny, Milland, and Ross characters later become involved in a love triangle which results in a wedding. The majority of the story takes place around the radio station, with the Bob Burns' character arriving for an audition and walking in on several programs. A number of popular New York night spots, including Lindy's and El Morocco, receive some nice publicity. Musical numbers include "Night in Manhattan," Benny Fields singing "Love in Your Eyes," "Vote for Mr. Rhythm" by Martha Raye, "I'm Talking Through My Heart" and "You Came to My Rescue" by Shirley Ross, and "La Bomba" sung by Frank Forest.

Reviews: "Miss Allen and the long-suffering Mr. Burns are again Lunacy and Sanity Incarnate, with Lunacy triumphing." (**The New York Times**, October 22, 1936: 31: 1). "(Gracie Allen) clicks from the outset..." (**Variety**, October 28, 1936: 14).

Additional Reviews: **Commonweal**, November 20, 1936: 25: 104; **Esquire**, January 1937: 7: 109; **Film Daily**, October 6, 1936: 12; **Hollywood Director**, p. 100-104; **The Hollywood Reporter**, October 2, 1936: 3; **Hollywood Spectator**, October 10, 1936: 11: 17+; **Motion Picture Daily**, October 3, 1936; **Motion Picture Herald**, October 10, 1936: 52-53; **The New Masses**, November 3, 1936: 21: 29; **The New Republic**, October 28, 1936: 88: 351; **The New Statesman and Nation**, November 7, 1936: 12: 710; **New York Herald-Tribune**, October 22, 1936; **The New York Times**, October 22, 1936: 13: 1, October 29, 1936: 31: 3; **Rob Wagner's Script**, October 17, 1936: 16: 10; **Stage**, December 1936: 14: 14; **Time**, October 19, 1936: 28: 67.

Commentary: Only the names of Jack Benny and/or Burns and Allen were allowed to precede Bob Burns' name in the credits. Once again, censor Joseph Breen objected to various portions of the script, including an "effeminate man trying to get a radio job." Breen also called the dance number, "La Bomba," "very suggestive," and did not want various "girls' anatomy parts" showing. Even the name "Mr. Pratt" was considered suggestive. (George and Gracie's last name in the film was changed to "Platt"). In a letter to Paramount's John Hammell on May 2, 1936, Breen asks the studio to omit, among other things, references to the "traveling saleslady" and said there "should be no showing...of nationally advertised products specifically mentioned by name." Future costuming legend Edith Head was already working for Paramount, where she eventually became chief costume designer, a position she held for nearly thirty years. Also see B79, B275.

F29 College Holiday. 88 min. b/w. Paramount, 1936.
Dir. Frank Tuttle. Prod. Harlan Thompson. Screen Play by J. P. McEvoy, Harlan Ware and Henry Myers, Jay Gorney. Songs by Ralph Rainger, Leo Robin, Burton Lane and Ralph Freed. Photography by Theodor Sparkuhl and William C. Mellor. Ed. LeRoy Stone. Dances Staged by LeRoy Prinz.

Cast: Jack Benny (*J. Davis Bowster*); George Burns (*George Hymen*); Gracie Allen (*Calliope Dove*); Mary Boland (*Carola Gaye*); Martha Raye (*Daisy Schloggenheimer*); Ben Blue (*Electrician*); Marsha Hunt (*Sylvia Smith*); Leif Erikson (*Dick Winters*); Eleanore Whitney (*Eleanore Wayne*); Johnny Downs (*Johnny Jones*); Etienne Girardot (*Prof. Hercules Dove*); Olympe Bradna (*Felice L'Hommedieu*); Louis DaPron (*Barry Taylor*); Jed Prouty (*Sheriff*); Margaret Seddon (*Mrs. Schloggenheimer*); Nick Lukats (*Wisconsin*); Spec O'Donnell (*Lafayette*); Jack Chapin (*Colgate*); The California Collegians (*Themselves*).

Synopsis: A college student (Marsha Hunt) is summoned home due to her father's illness brought on by the near-bankruptcy of his California hotel, Casa del Mar. The holder of the mortgage (Mary Boland) is on her way to the hotel with Professor Hercules Dove (Etienne Girardot) to begin conducting eugenics experiments. They need participants and meet J. Davis Bowster (Jack Benny) on their way to the hotel. He suggests they hire college students as hotel "entertainers" when, in fact, they will become part of the experiment. It now becomes Benny's job to prevent any romantic entanglements among the unwitting participants. Professor Dove's daughter, Gracie, also arrives with her companion, George, to take part in the experiment and to find "the perfect man." The hotel is actually saved after the college students put on the "intercollegiate Minstrel Show." One of the film's few highlights is George and Gracie dancing a minuet with Ben Blue as part of the show. Jack Benny makes an appearance at the end to explain that none of this is "real" and he hopes the audience enjoyed the film. Songs include "I Adore You," "The Sweetheart Waltz," "Who's That Knocking at My Heart?" "A Rhyme for Love," and "So What?" The Rainger-Robin tune, "Love in Bloom," which is as identified with Jack Benny as "The Love Nest" is with George and Gracie, provides Benny with some funny moments as he tries to play it amidst numerous interruptions.

Review: "It's even too silly for Gracie Allen to handle effectively and there's nothing sillier than that." (**Variety**, December 30, 1936: 10).

Additional Reviews: **Film Daily**, December 19, 1936: 3; **The Hollywood Reporter**, December 16, 1936: 3; **Motion Picture Daily**, December 17, 1936; **Motion Picture Herald**, December 26, 1936: 54; **The New Statesman and Nation**, January 23, 1937: 13: 119; **The New Yorker**, January 2, 1937: 12: 50; **New York Herald-Tribune**, December 24, 1936; **The New York Times**, December 24, 1936: 21: 2; **Rob Wagner's Script**, January 2, 1937: 16: 13; **The Spectator**, January 23, 1937: 158: 122; **Time**, January 4, 1937: 29: 22.

Commentary: College pictures became something of a fixture at Paramount due to the studio's success with several scripts. This film, however, was not considered a hit. Gracie's character was originally named "Aphrodisia," which was changed at the insistence of the Hays Office. The eugenic mating references were "very dangerous from the standpoint of the Production Code," undoubtedly due to the sexual concerns. (The concept, while not new, was being used for race improvement for social control in Nazi Germany). However, by September 30, 1936 Joseph Breen reports to Mr. Hays that the script changes make him believe the finished picture will be acceptable. Burns and Allen were not to receive star billing on the screen without first obtaining their written consent. Spec O'Donnell is credited on-screen as "Speck O'Donnell."

F30 A Damsel in Distress. 101 min. b/w. RKO, 1937.
Dir. George Stevens. Prod. Pandro S. Berman. Screen Play by P. G. Wodehouse, Ernest Pagano, and S. K. Lauren. From the story by P. G. Wodehouse and play by P. G. Wodehouse and Ian Hay. Music by George Gershwin. Lyrics by Ira Gershwin. Photography by Joseph H. August. Ed. Henry Berman. Dance Direction by Hermes Pan. Available on videocassette and laserdisc. **SEE VG51, D2, D3, D4, D14, D210, D218.**

Cast: Fred Astaire (*Jerry*); George Burns (*George*); Gracie Allen (*Gracie*); Joan Fontaine (*Lady Alyce*); Reginald Gardiner (*Keggs*); Ray Noble (*Reggie*); Constance Collier (*Lady Caroline*); Montagu Love (*Lord Marshmorton*); Harry Watson (*Albert*); Jan Duggan (*Miss Ruggles*).

Synopsis: A wager made among members of an English aristocrat's household staff causes an American performer (Fred Astaire) to become embroiled in a case of mistaken identity involving the nobleman's daughter (Joan Fontaine). Wrongly believing the young woman has fallen in love with him and needs his help to escape her overprotective family, he finds himself falling in love with her only to discover she's in love with someone else. George is Astaire's publicity-hungry press agent, and Gracie is George's secretary. Songs include "A Foggy Day In London Town", "Ah Che A Voi Perdoni Iddio" (from Flotow's "Marta"), I Can't Be Bothered Now," "Nice Work If You Can Get It," "Put Me to the Test," "Sing of Spring," "The Jolly Tar and Milkmaid," and "Things Are Looking Up."

Review: "Burns and Allen blend excellently, and their comedy is a standout, besides which they manage two difficult terp routines with their co-star in no small way." (**Variety**, November 24, 1937: 16).

Additional Reviews: **Commonweal**, December 3, 1937: 27: 160; **Film Daily**, November 20, 1937: 7; **The Fred Astaire and Ginger Rogers Book**, p. 134-135; **The Hollywood Musical**, p. 120-121; **The Hollywood Reporter**, November 18, 1937: 3; **Life**, November 29, 1937: 3: 74-75; **Motion Picture Herald**, November 27, 1937: 52+; **The Nation**, December 18, 1937: 145: 697; **The New Masses**, November 30, 1937: 25: 27; **The New Yorker**, November 27, 1937: 13: 73; **The New York Times**, November 25, 1937: 37: 1; **Newsweek**, December 10, 1937: 10: 33; **Rob Wagner's Script**, December 25, 1937: 18: 5; **Scholastic**, December 11, 1937: 31: 19; **The Spectator**, April 15, 1938: 160: 671; **Starring Fred Astaire**, p. 163-171; **Time**, December 6, 1937: 30: 49; **World Film News**, May-June 1938: 3: 83.

Commentary: RKO went to Paramount to borrow Burns and Allen for this film. Hermes Pan won an Academy Award for choreographing the fun-house sequence in which George and Gracie dance with Astaire and she sings "Stiff Upper Lip." Astaire was also involved with the choreography of the film, although uncredited. Special effects were handled by Vernon L. Walker. Most professional reviewers were impressed with George and Gracie's performances, even if they weren't charmed by the film overall. It's usually considered Astaire's first box-office failure, but one must take into account the times and the fact that audiences were not yet terribly interested in seeing Astaire without Ginger Rogers. In fact, as far as George and Gracie's roles are concerned, this is a much better vehicle for them than many of their earlier films. The truly interesting comments came from preview audiences in cities like Oakland and Pomona, California. When asked which players they liked well enough to want to see their future pictures, Burns and Allen were usually among the favorites. Although one audience member claimed never to have liked Burns and Allen, the majority were pleasantly surprised at the versatility of the duo. One viewer made a helpful suggestion: "George Burns good, needs better parts." George adopted the whiskbroom number used in the film from a vaudeville team, Evans and Evans. Co-star Ray Noble began his long association with George and Gracie as orchestra leader of their radio show in the spring of 1937. Composer George Gershwin died unexpectedly during the filming due to a brain hemorrhage. Also see B178, B217, B367, B466.

F31 College Swing. 86 min. b/w. Paramount, 1938.
Dir. Raoul Walsh. Prod. Lewis E. Gensler. Screen Play by Walter DeLeon and Francis Martin. Based on an Adaptation by Frederick Hazlitt Brennan of an idea by Ted Lesser. Original Songs by Frank Loesser, Hoagy Carmichael, Manning Sherwin and Burton Lane. Photography by Victor Milner. Ed. LeRoy Stone. Dances Staged by LeRoy Prinz. Available on videocassette. **SEE VG48, D6.**

Cast: George Burns (*George Jonas*); Gracie Allen (*Gracie Alden*); Martha Raye (*Mabel*); Bob Hope (*Bud Brady*); Edward Everett Horton (*Hubert Dash*); Florence George (*Ginna Ashburn*); Ben Blue (*Ben Volt*); Betty Grable (*Betty*); Jackie Coogan (*Jackie*); John Payne (*Martin Bates*); Cecil Cunningham (*Dean Sleet*); Robert Cummings (*Radio Announcer*); Skinnay Ennis (*Skinnay*); and The Slate Brothers, Bob Mitchell, St. Brendan's Choristers

(*Themselves*). Jerry Colonna also appears, although he is not billed on-screen.

Synopsis: A female Alden has not been able to graduate from their family-owned college in two hundred years. If Gracie does not pass her exams, her grandfather's money will be used permanently by the school and she will lose her inheritance. Bud Brady (Bob Hope), who teaches at the college, approaches Gracie about tutoring her for her exam, although he is more interested in Gracie's money than he is her mind. Alumnus Hubert Dash (Edward Everett Horton), who has a "woman phobia," agrees to administer the test but sends his assistant, George Jonas (George Burns), in his place. She does pass (accidentally), inherits the college, and hires vaudeville performers to teach classes. Songs include "College Swing," "How'ja Like to Love Me?", "I Fall In Love With You Every Day," "Moments Like This," "The Old School Bell," "What a Rhumba Does to Romance," and "What Did Romeo Say To Juliet?". Gracie sings "You're A Natural" and dances an Irish jig.

Review: "It might be a good thing...if some enterprising company...would just stop trying to keep up plot appearances in musicals of this type, and advertise them frankly as variety shows...And the rest is Gracie, of the firm which really ought to change its billing to Allen and Burns." (**The New York Times**, April 28, 1938: 27: 2).

Additional Reviews: **Film Daily**, April 28, 1938: 4; **The Hollywood Reporter**, April 12, 1938: 3; **Motion Picture Herald**, April 16, 1938: 33; **Rob Wagner's Script**, April 30, 1938: 19: 8; **Variety**, April 27, 1938: 22.

Commentary: This film was released in Great Britain as **Swing, Teacher, Swing** and was George and Gracie's last Paramount project as a team. A number of state and national organizations generally panned the effort, many of them noting the film's strong beginning that could not be sustained. The American Legion Auxiliary proclaimed that it had "a definite tendency to vulgarity," the California Congress of Parents and Teachers declared its social values "censurable," the California Council of Federated Church Women lamented it as a "waste of time," and the Women's University Club stated that the film was "entertaining only in proportion to one's liking for the broad humor of...specialized comedians..."

F32 Honolulu. 83 min. b/w. MGM, 1939.
Dir. Edward Buzzell. Prod. Jack Cummings. Original Story and Screen Play by Herbert Fields and Frank Partos. Music by Harry Warren. Lyrics by Gus Kahn. Incidental Music by Franz Waxman. Photography by Ray June. Film Ed. Conrad A. Nervig. Dance Direction by Bobby Connelly and Sammy Lee. Available on videocassette. **SEE VG67, D7.**

Cast: Eleanor Powell (*Dorothy March*); Robert Young (*Brooks Mason/George Smith*); George Burns (*Joe Duffy*); Gracie Allen (*Millie De Grasse*); Rita Johnson (*Cecilia Grayson*); Clarence Kolb (*Mr. Horace Grayson*); Jo Ann Sayers (*Nurse*); Ann Morriss (*Gale Brewster*); Willie Fung (*Wong*); Cliff Clark (*1st Detective*); Edward Gargan (*2nd Detective*); Eddie Anderson (*Washington*); Sig Rumann (*Psychiatrist*); Ruth Hussey (*Eve*); Kealoha Holt (*Native Dancing Girl*); Edgar Dearing (*Jailer*); and Andy Iona's Islanders, The King's Men (*Themselves*).

Synopsis: It's "the Prince and the Pauper," told this time with a tropical twist. Screen star (and heartthrob) Brooks Mason (Robert Young) can't get away from his adoring fans (or his personal manager, Joe Duffy, played by George Burns) long enough to take a much-needed rest until he meets his lookalike, a pineapple plantation owner from Hawaii named George Smith (also played by Robert Young). After convincing Smith to trade places with him, Mason leaves for Hawaii by ship and meets Dorothy and Millie (Eleanor Powell and Gracie Allen), singers/dancers who have a job waiting for them at a Honolulu hotel. Mason falls in love with Dorothy but must deal with life as Smith once he reaches the islands, a life which includes an eager fiancee and a charge of embezzlement leveled at him by her father. Songs include "This Night Will Be My Souvenir" and "Hymn To The Sun." "Hawaiian Medley" features Andy Iona's Islanders. "The Leader Doesn't Like Music" is performed by the King's Men with Gracie, who also sings the title song.

Reviews: "Burns is grand as the Hollywood star's manager...Gracie Allen supplies the comedy..." (**Film Daily**, February 3, 1939: 12). "The heroine and dream princess of the pic is none other than Gracie Allen." (**The Hollywood Reporter**, January 27, 1939: 3). "...the comedy by Burns and Allen would hardly excite the laughter even of those strangely susceptible people who attend radio broadcasts." (**The New York Times**, February 23, 1939: 19: 2).

Additional Reviews: **Commonweal**, February 24, 1939: 29: 497; **Hollywood Spectator**, February 4, 1939: 13: 12; **Motion Picture Daily**, February 1, 1939; **Motion Picture Herald**, February 4, 1939: 56; **The New Yorker**, February 25, 1939: 15: 58; **Rob Wagner's Script**, February 18, 1939: 21: 16; **Scholastic**, February 25, 1939: 34: 34; **Time**, February 20, 1939: 33: 68; **Variety**, February 1, 1939: 13.

Commentary: The script for **Honolulu** was first titled **Lucky Star**. George and Gracie had been borrowed from Paramount by MGM for the film. Lounging pajamas, references to Bellevue Hospital, native costumes and the male star being seen in his underwear were among the problems the censors had with early scripts. The censors probably carefully scrutinized a scene in which Gracie appeared as Mae West in a "come as your favorite movie star" costume party held onboard ship. Art director Cedric Gibbons, recording director Douglas Shearer and costume designer Adrian, three of MGM's most celebrated behind-the-scenes names, shared onscreen credit with those already mentioned. **The New York Times** continued its decidedly underwhelmed impression of the film when it published these remarks in its Sunday, February 26, 1939 issue, having first declared it "...one of those things having a musical comedy plot and not deserving the exemption of musical comedy...Mr. Burns's mind obviously was on other matters and Miss Allen's, as usual, was not anywhere..."

Gracie Allen

F33 The Gracie Allen Murder Case. 74 min. b/w. Paramount, 1939.
Dir. Alfred E. Green. Prod. George Arthur. Screen Play by Nat Perrin. Based on the novel by S. S. Van Dine. Music and Lyrics by Matty Malneck and Frank Loesser. Photography by Charles Lang, Jr. Ed. Paul Weatherwax. **SEE D6, D8, D11, D16.**

Cast: Warren William (*Philo Vance*); Ellen Drew (*Ann Wilson*); Kent Taylor (*Bill Brown*); Jed Prouty (*Uncle Ambrose*); Jerome Cowan (*Daniel Mirche*); Donald MacBride (*Dist. Attorney Markham*); H. B. Warner (*Richard Lawrence*); William Demarest (*Sergeant Heath*); Judith Barrett (*Dixie Del Marr*); Horace MacMahon (*Gus, The Waiter*); Al Shaw and Sam Lee (*Two Thugs*); Gracie Allen (*Gracie Allen*).

Synopsis: Gracie attends the annual picnic for the Vogue Perfume Company, owned by her uncle. While at the picnic someone driving by throws out a lighted cigarette and a matchbook cover with the name of a nightclub, the Diamond Slipper Cafe, on it. The cigarette burns a hole in Gracie's dress. With Gracie is Bill Brown (Kent Taylor), a perfume mixer for the company, who recognizes the cigarette blend. Near the picnic area is a prison from which a convict has escaped. After his escape he telephones the owner of the Diamond Slipper Cafe and asks him to pick him up. When he doesn't show up at the appointed place the owner of the club confides in one of the club's show girls (Judith Barrett), who suspects that the escapee is dead. Gracie and Bill later pay a visit to the club and, before they leave, circumstances and incriminating evidence point to Bill as the murderer. Famed detective Philo Vance (Warren William) joins the investigation on Bill's behalf, and Gracie inadvertently helps in the solving of the crime. Gracie sings "Snug As A Bug In A Rug."

Reviews: "Divorced, and happily divorced, from George Burns and her too depressingly familiar radio routines, Gracie Allen should be a vision of sheer delight to Gracie Allen addicts... (**The New York Times**, June 8, 1939: 31: 3). "It's Gracie Allen at her best..." (**Variety**, May 17, 1939: 12).

Additional Reviews: **Commonweal**, June 9, 1939: 30: 189; **Film Daily**, May 17, 1939: 5; **The Hollywood Reporter**, May 13, 1939: 3; **Motion Picture Herald**, May 20, 1939: 43; **Newsweek**, May 29, 1939: 13: 28; **The New Yorker**, June 10,

1939: 15: 75; **New York Herald-Tribune**, June 8, 1939; **Photoplay**, July 1939: 53: 62; **Rob Wagner's Script**, July 15, 1939: 21: 18; **Stage**, June 1939: 16: 34-35; **Time**, June 12, 1939: 33: 78.

Commentary: Gracie was the first actress to have her name as part of the title of a non-biographical film and the first actress to have a novel title include her name. Gracie's name was to be in the largest type, which would be seventy-five percent of the title type. Warren William was not the only actor to portray the *Philo Vance* character, although he did appear in only one other entry, **The Dragon Murder Case**. William Powell played in four of the fourteen Philo Vance films (which were released between 1929 and 1947), more than any other actor. The author of the novel on which the film was based, S. S. Van Dine, died before the picture was released but had already enjoyed great success with the Philo Vance book and film series. The character was transferred to radio on July 5, 1945, as a summer replacement for Bob Burns and was revived in 1948 for over one hundred episodes starring Jackson Beck before its final telecast on July 4, 1950. Regardless of the audience's familiarity with the character and his line of work, censors still admonished Paramount to "take care with showing of dead body...plant (the idea) in one or two scenes, then merely suggest the presence of the body in those which follow." Parker Brothers released a board game by the same title on May 2, 1939. Also see B75, B179, B208, B383, B474.

F34 Mr. and Mrs. North. 67 min. b/w. MGM, 1941.
Dir. Robert B. Sinclair. Prod. Irving Asher. Screen Play by S. K. Lauren. Based on the play Mr. and Mrs. North by Owen Davis (produced on the New York stage by Alfred DeLiagre, Jr.) and on the stories by Richard and Frances Lockridge. Photography by Harry Stradling. Ed. Ralph Winters.

Cast: Gracie Allen (*Pamela North*); William Post, Jr. (*Gerald P. North*); Paul Kelly (*Lt. Weigand*); Rose Hobart (*Carol Brent*); Virginia Grey (*Jane Wilson*); Tom Conway (*Louis Berex*); Felix Bressart (*Arthur Talbot*); Porter Hall (*George Reyler*); Millard Mitchell (*Mullins*); Lucien Littlefield (*Barnes*); Inez Cooper (*Mabel Harris*); Keye Luke (*Kumi*); Jerome Cowan (*Ben Wilson*); Stuart Crawford (*Stuart Blanton*); Fortunio Bonanova (*Buono*).

Synopsis: Mr. and Mrs. North (William Post, Jr. and Gracie Allen) arrive at their apartment after a several day absence apart and find a dead body in one of their closets. Trying to solve the crime, the Norths gather a number of their friends together in order to find a plausible suspect. Another murder is committed before the first one is solved.

Reviews: "The story baffles synopsis." (**Motion Picture Daily**, December 17, 1941). "It was an inspired notion...to hand over the role of Mrs. North to Gracie Allen..." (**The New Yorker**, January 24, 1942).

Additional Reviews: **The Hollywood Reporter**, December 17, 1941; **The New York Times**, November 2, 1941: sec. IX, 5: 3, January 22, 1942: 13: 2; **Variety**, December 17, 1941.

Commentary: Millard Mitchell recreates his role from the play. Once a radio show, **Mr. and Mrs. North** became a television series in the early 1950's, starring Richard Denning and Barbara Britton. Also see B2.

F35 Two Girls and a Sailor. 124 min. b/w. MGM, 1944.
Dir. Richard Thorpe. Prod. Joe Pasternak. Original Screen Play by Richard Connell and Gladys Lehman. Photography by Robert Surtees. Ed. George Boemler. Dance Dir. Sammy Lee. Available on videocassette and laserdisc. **SEE VG1, D15.**

Cast: June Allyson (*Patsy Deyo*); Gloria DeHaven (*Jean Deyo*); Van Johnson (*John Dyckman Brown III*); Tom Drake (*Frank Miller*); Henry Stephenson (*John Dyckman Brown I*); Henry O'Neill (*John Dyckman Brown II*); Ben Blue (*Ben*); Carlos Ramirez (*Carlos*); Frank Sully (*Private Adams*); Donald Meek (*Mr. Nizby*); Jimmy Durante (*Billy Kipp*); Frank Jenks (*Dick Deyo*); and Albert Coates, José Iturbi, Amparo Novarro, Virginia O'Brien, The Wilde Twins, Harry James and his Music Makers with Helen Forrest, Xavier Cugat and his Orchestra with Lina Romay (*Themselves*). Gracie Allen is credited as the "Concerto Number" and Lena Horne as a "Specialty."

Synopsis: Gracie has a cameo (playing the "Concerto for Index Finger," one of her most famous publicity stunts from radio) in this story of two sisters (June Allyson and Gloria DeHaven) who team up in a song and dance act and find love as they entertain the troops and spearhead a movement to establish a soldiers' canteen.

Review: "If this sort of story were performed for its own sake, it would play only to ushers and to those who scrape chicle from the undersides of theater seats." (**Time**, June 19, 1944). "...specialties include...a rather clever comical one-finger piano concerto by Gracie Allen..." (**Variety**, April 26, 1944).

Additional Reviews: **Los Angeles Examiner**, June 22, 1944; **The New York Times**, June 15, 1944: 16: 1.

Commentary: "Inka Dinka Doo" found its way into the film via the man who had made it famous, Jimmy Durante. A number of other personalities appear uncredited onscreen including Ava Gardner, Buster Keaton, Don Loper, Gigi Perreau, Doodles Weaver, and Joe Yule. Irene is credited as costume supervisor. Also see B2, B11.

George Burns

F36 The Solid Gold Cadillac. 99 min. b/w and color. Columbia, 1956. Dir. Richard Quine. Prod. Fred Kohlmar. Screen Play by Abe Burrows. Based on the play by George S. Kaufman and Howard Teichmann (produced on the stage by Max Gordon). Music by Cyril J. Mockridge. Photography by Charles Lang. Ed. Charles Nelson.

Cast: Judy Holliday (*Laura Partridge*); Paul Douglas (*Edward L. McKeever*); Fred Clark (*Clifford Snell*); John Williams (*John T. Blessington*); Hiram Sherman (*Harry Harkness*); Neva Patterson (*Amelia Shotgraven*); Ralph Dumke (*Warren Gillie*); Ray Collins (*Alfred Metcalfe*); Arthur O'Connell (*Jenkins*); Richard Deacon (*Williams*); Marilyn Hanold (*Miss L'Arriere*); Anne Loos (*Blessington's Secretary*); Audrey Swanson (*Snell's Secretary*); Larry Hudson (*Chauffeur*); Sandra White (*Receptionist*); Harry Antrim (*Sen. Simkins*); Madge Blake (*Lady Commentator*); George Burns (*Narrator*).

Synopsis: George Burns narrates this story of Laura Partridge (Judy Holliday), a young woman who attends a stockholders' meeting of a company in which she owns ten shares. Laura asks so many questions the current company management begins to fear she will somehow cause a glitch in their ongoing plans to engage the company in questionable business practices. When the Board realizes they will not easily appease Miss Partridge, they offer her a job as Director of Stockholder Relations, an empty title for a basically non-existent job, although Laura does not realize that at the time. Tired of waiting for the stockholders to write to her, she begins to write letters to them and forges a relationship with people around the country. When a company employee, Amelia Shotgraven (Neva Patterson), is fired she tells Laura about some of the Board's shenanigans. Laura soon finds out that the conglomerate put one of its own companies out of business, and she decides to go into action. The Board, upset because the company isn't being rewarded any defense contracts, sends Laura to Washington, D.C. to talk to the founder, Mr. McKeever (Paul Douglas), who sold his stock in the company to avoid accusations of favoritism when he started working for the Department of Defense. Ignoring the reason she was sent to Washington, Laura asks McKeever to return to the company he founded and to put it back on the right track. They eventually do join forces, gain a landslide victory over the Board with proxy votes from the small shareholders and are married. Laura's wedding present from the stockholders? A solid gold Cadillac.

Reviews: "...as though she (Miss Holliday) had no predecessor, she is knocking the role completely dead." (**The New York Times**, October 25, 1956: 40: 3.) "Film has a narration by George Burns, although it serves no particular purpose as far as the comedy is concerned." (**Variety**, August 15, 1956).

Commentary: **The Solid Gold Cadillac** was adapted to film after the two act Kaufman-Teichmann comedy opened on Broadway November 5, 1953 at the Belasco Theatre for a run of 526 performances. George's role was handled in the theatrical version (and pre-recorded) by Fred Allen (who died in 1956); Miss Holliday's by Josephine Hull in her Broadway swan song. The difference in the actresses' physical appearances was obvious but each left an indelible mark on the role. As mentioned in the biographical portion of this book George and Gracie had been offered roles in a West Coast summer production of the play but had to turn it down due to a heavy workload on their television series. Industry buzz for a time was that they might star in the film version or co-produce it. Judy Holliday, an enormously talented comedienne whose life and career were tragically cut short by cancer, often played parts that shared a number of the "Gracie" character traits. However, seeing Miss Holliday in the film makes it difficult to imagine anyone else in the role. She and actor Paul Douglas were no strangers to each other, having appeared together in the Broadway production of Garson Kanin's **Born Yesterday**. She reprised her role of *Billie Dawn* in the 1950 film version of the play and won the Oscar as Best Actress. A **George Burns and Gracie Allen Show** alum, the ubiquitous Fred Clark, played one of the company's less than upright executives. The picture opened at the Victoria Theater in New York City and was reviewed for **The New York Times** by the venerable Bosley Crowther. The final scene in the film shows off the car in all its Technicolor glory. Jean Louis earned an Oscar for costuming. The film was finally released on videotape by Columbia Tristar Home Video (70893) in late 1995 under their "Columbia Classics" line, a treat for fans since it is seldom shown on television.

F37 The Sunshine Boys. 111 min. color. MGM, 1975. PG.
Dir. Herbert Ross. Prod. Ray Stark. Screen Play by Neil Simon (based on his play). Photography by David M. Walsh. Ed. Margaret Booth, John F. Burnett. Available on videocassette and laserdisc. **SEE VG22.**

Cast: Walter Matthau (*Willy Clark*); George Burns (*Al Lewis*); Richard Benjamin (*Ben Clark*); Lee Meredith (*Nurse in Sketch*); Carol Arthur (*Doris*); Rosetta LeNoire (*Nurse*); F. Murray Abraham (*Mechanic*); Howard Hesseman (*Commercial Director*); Jim Cranna (*T.V. Director*); Ron Rifkin (*T.V. Floor Manager*); Jennifer Lee (*Helen*); Fritz Feld (*Man at Audition*); Jack Bernardi (*Man at Audition*); Garn Stephens (*Stage Manager*); Santos Morales (*Desk Clerk*); Archie Hahn (*Assistant at Audition*); Sid Gould (*Patient*); Tom Spratley (*Card Player*); Rashel Novikoff (*Woman in Hotel*); Sammy Smith (*Man on Street*); Dan Resin (*Mr. Ferranti*); Milt Kogan (*Doctor*); Bob Goldstein (*Waiter*); Walter Stocker (*NBC Executive*); Duchess Dale (*Ben's Secretary*); Bill Reddick (*Announcer*); Eddie Villery (*Delivery Boy*); Gary K. Steven (*Boy*). Phyllis Diller and Steve Allen make cameo appearances.

Synopsis: The comedy team of Lewis & Clark (George Burns and Walter Matthau), also known as "The Sunshine Boys," (which broke up after forty-three years when Al Lewis retired in the middle of the act on **The Ed Sullivan Show**) can make $10,000 for an appearance on a television variety show special about the history of comedy, but only if Willy Clark's agent-nephew (Richard Benjamin) can convince them to work together again. His biggest obstacle is their "artistic differences." They both hate each other. Ben finally persuades them to do the show, which, considering the events to follow and the ironic ending, was the easy part.

Reviews: "...Burns, after a 36-year absence from movies, couldn't be better as his (Matthau's) birdlike, gentle and long-suffering foe-friend." (**The Miami Herald**, December 20, 1975, sec. C: 5). "Burns gives an astonishingly legitimate performance. (**The New York Times**, November 9, 1975: sec. II, 17: 1). "Burns...provides in his standout performance the right complementing aspects to the pair's love-hate relationship..." (**Variety**, October 29, 1975).

Additional Reviews: **The New York Times**, November 7, 1975: 28: 1; **Palm Beach Post-Times**, January 18, 1976: sec. G: 2; **SR**, November 15, 1975: 31.

Commentary: This was George's first on-screen film appearance since 1939 and obviously his most impressive up to this point. It was also the second film in a row in which he played a role brought to life on Broadway by another actor. Finally given the opportunity to play someone other than himself (and without a cigar), he gave his all to the project, even memorizing the entire script before production started (B342, B368). His efforts garnered him an Oscar for Best Supporting Actor in a role originally scheduled to be played by his best friend, Jack Benny, who died before filming began. There has been at least one published report that the film project had been planned with George and Jack Benny in mind from the beginning (B342), with George cast in what became Walter Matthau's role, although most reports indicate that George stepped in only after Benny's death. Columnist Joyce Haber reported that the final casting decision before Benny's death was made only after a number of actors had been considered, including Milton Berle, Phil Silvers, Red Skelton, Art Carney and Jack Albertson, and that Bob Hope had bid against Ray Stark for the film rights as a vehicle for himself and Bing Crosby. (**Los Angeles Times**, August 24, 1975, Calendar: 31). The film opens with a shot of the ultimate goal of all vaudeville performers (including Burns and Allen), B. F. Keith's Palace Theatre, and the opening credits are superimposed over a montage of vaudeville scenes. The story is at least loosely based on the lives of the vaudeville team, Smith and Dale. Neil Simon's two act play, **The Sunshine Boys**, opened on Broadway on December 20, 1972 at the Broadhurst Theatre and ran for 538 performances with Jack Albertson as *Willy* and Sam Levene playing *Al*, with the roles later taken over by Jack Gilford and Lou Jacobi. Mr. Simon later adapted his script for a one-hour television pilot starring Red Buttons as *Willy* and Lionel Stander as *Al* for NBC, where it aired on June 9, 1977. It was not picked up as a series. The film, however, broke the all-time attendance record for a single day at Radio City Music Hall (B68) when it bowed as that year's Christmas holiday release (B368), but by 1978 George was reported as saying "I thought 'Sunshine Boys' would make a fortune, but the people in small towns didn't dig it." (**Los Angeles Times**, February 1, 1978: sec. IV, 9). Make-up artist Dick Smith did a masterful job in helping Matthau, no stranger to playing characters older than himself, create *Willy Clark*. Walter Stocker was incorrectly credited as an NBC executive; it should have been ABC. It was announced in the January 21-28, 1995 issue of **TV Guide** that CBS plans to broadcast a made-for-television adaptation of **The Sunshine Boys** starring Peter Falk and Woody Allen; it was later noted that the film would air May 21, 1996. Also see B118, B144, B192, B198, B222, B342, B378, B387, B440, B505.

F38 Oh, God! 104 min. color Warner Brothers, 1977. PG.
Dir. Carl Reiner. Prod. Jerry Weintraub. Screen Play by Larry Gelbart. Based on the novel by Avery Corman. Music by Jack Elliott. Photography by Victor Kemper. Ed. Bud Molin. Available on videocassette and laserdisc. **SEE VG16.**

Cast: John Denver (*Jerry Landers*); George Burns (*God*); Teri Garr (*Bobbie Landers*); Donald Pleasence (*Dr. Harmon*); Ralph Bellamy (*Sam Raven*); William Daniels (*George Summers*); Barnard Hughes (*Judge Baker*); Paul Sorvino (*Rev. Willie Williams*); Barry Sullivan (*Priest*); Dinah Shore (*Dinah*); Jeff Corey (*Rabbi*); George Furth (*Briggs*); David Ogden Stiers (*Mr. McCarthy*); Titos Vandis (*Greek Bishop*); Moosie Drier (*Adam*); Rachel Longaker (*Becky*); Jerry Dunphy (*Newscaster*); Mario Machado (*TV Reporter*); Connie Sawyer (*Mrs. Green*); Jane Lambert (*Mrs. Levin*); Kres Mersky (*Check-out Girl*); Byron Paul (*TV Engineer*); Hector Morales (*Waiter*); Wonderful Smith (*Court Clerk*); Murphy Dunne (*Stenographer*); Boyd Bodwell (*Religious Fanatic*); Zane Buzby (*Girl*); Dennis Kort (*Norman*); Bob McClurg (*Mechanic*); Celeste Cartier (*2nd Check-out Girl*); Carl Reiner (*Dinah's Guest*).

Synopsis: Jerry Landers (John Denver) leads quite a normal life as an up and coming assistant manager of a grocery store living with his wife (Teri Garr) and two children in the suburbs. He's a good man, but not a religious one, until he receives a summons to meet God (George Burns), Who says there are "too many non-believers" and asks Jerry to spread the word that they have spoken and that He exists.

Reviews: "If **Oh, God!** achieves anything, it shows some of the unusual problems people would have with the incarnation." (**Christianity Today**, December 30, 1977: 23-24). "The only problem is that the moments that Burns is on the screen are so special that the other segments seem a little lacking." (**The Cleveland Plain Dealer**, October 8, 1977). "...I can imagine that a good many churchgoers will resent this image of a cab-driving Jehovah..." (**The Hollywood Reporter**, October 3, 1977: 3). "...Burns proves all over again that he is one of the most appealing of all new movie presences." (**Los Angeles Herald Examiner**, October 7, 1977). "...film belongs all to Burns and Denver, who fit together on the screen as well as Burns did with Walter Matthau in 'The Sunshine Boys.'"

(**Variety**, October 5, 1977: 28). "...forgive me Gracie, Jack, and Groucho, but George Burns is no deity...Without Walter Matthau and up against John Denver's impersonation of Pat Boone, Burns is more like wet bread pudding." (**The Village Voice**, October 17, 1977: 53). "...Burns' impeccable--and legendary--timing...is a quality as essential to working miracles as it is to telling jokes." (**Time**, October 31, 1977, 110: 90).

Additional Reviews: **BFI/Monthly Film Bulletin**, November 1977: 44: 236; **Christian Century**, November 23, 1977: 94: 1095; **Christianity Today**, December 30, 1977: 22: 23-24; **Films and Filming**, December 1977: 24: 32; **Independent Film Journal**, November 25, 1977; **Los Angeles Times**, October 7, 1977: sec. IV, 1; **Maclean's**, November 14, 1977: 90: 88; **Motion Picture Herald Product Digest**, October 19, 1977: 38; **New Statesman**, April 28, 1978: 95: 577; **The New York Times**, October 8, 1977: 13: 1; **Senior Scholastic**, November 17, 1977: 110: 32.

Commentary: The late Ralph Bellamy once recalled this incident during the shooting of the film: "He (George) had a very long scene with the Judge as he sat in the witness box. It was not only long, it was tricky. The Judge didn't say a word. I think it was George's 80th birthday. They had a teleprompter and cue cards set up for him; he didn't use either. He came into the studio at about ten, did the scene in one take and another for protection and we all left for an early lunch." Also see B47, B440.

F39 Sgt. Pepper's Lonely Hearts Club Band. 111 min. color. Universal, 1978. PG. Dir. Michael Schultz. Prod. Robert Stigwood. Exec. Prod. Dee Anthony. Screen Play by Henry Edwards. Music and Lyrics by John Lennon and Paul McCartney. Music and Lyrics for "Here Comes The Sun" by George Harrison. Photography by Owen Roizman. Ed. Christopher Holmes. Choreography by Patricia Birch. Available on videocassette and laserdisc. **SEE VG20, D70.**

Cast: Peter Frampton (*Billy Shears*); Barry Gibb (*Mark Henderson*); Robin Gibb (*Dave Henderson*); Maurice Gibb (*Bob Henderson*); Frankie Howerd (*Mean Mr. Mustard*); Paul Nicholas (*Dougie Shears*); Donald Pleasence (*B. D. Brockhurst*); Sandy Farina (*Strawberry Fields*); Dianne Steinberg (*Lucy*); Steve Martin (*Dr. Maxwell Edison*); Aerosmith (*Future Villain*); Alice Cooper (*Father Sun*); Earth, Wind & Fire (*Benefit Performers*); Billy Preston (*Sgt. Pepper*); Stargard (*The Diamonds*); George Burns (*Mr. Kite*); Carel Struycken (*The Brute*); Patti Jerome (*Saralinda Shears*); Max Showalter (*Ernest Shears*); John Wheeler (*Mr. Fields*); Jay W. MacIntosh (*Mrs. Fields*); Eleanor Zee (*Mrs. Henderson*); Scott Manners (*Young Sgt. Pepper*); Woodrow Chamblis (*Old Sgt. Pepper*); Pat Cranshaw (*Western Union Messenger*); Teri Lynn Wood (*Bonnie*); Tracy Justrich (*Tippy*); Anna Rodzianko (*Computerette*); Rose Aragon (*Computerette*); Stanley Coles, Stanley Sheldon, Bob Mayo (*the Young Lonely Hearts Club Band*); Hank Worden, Morgan Farley, Delos V. Smith (*the Old Lonely Hearts Club Band*).

Synopsis: George Burns narrates and appears in several scenes as mayor of Heartland, home town to the original Sgt. Pepper and his Lonely Hearts Club Band, famed for the music it makes with instruments that have the power to make dreams come true. When Sgt. Pepper dies, he bequeaths his legacy to his grandson who, twenty years later, forms a new Lonely Hearts Club Band, which becomes the target of a sinister takeover attempt. George sings "Fixing A Hole" and joins Maurice Gibb, Peter Frampton, and the rest of the Bee Gees on "Being For The Benefit of Mr. Kite."

Review: "Suffice it to say that showmanly-cast George Burns, supplying enough voiceover exposition for a documentary, is testimony to the writing achievement." (**Variety**, July 19, 1978).

Additional Review: **The New York Times**, June 21, 1978: sec. III, 16: 1.

Commentary: In addition to the above-noted cast, dozens of well-known entertainers appeared as themselves in the finale: among them were artists as diverse as Peter Allen, Keith Carradine, Carol Channing, Donovan, José Feliciano, Leif Garrett, Heart, Nona Hendryx, Etta James, Mark Lindsay, Nils Lofgren, Jackie Lomax, Curtis Mayfield, Peter Noone, Robert Palmer, Wilson Pickett, Anita Pointer, Bonnie Raitt, Helen Reddy, Minnie Riperton, Chita Rivera, Johnny Rivers, Monte Rock III, Sha-Na-Na, Del Shannon, Seals & Croft, Connie Stevens, Tina Turner, Frankie Valli, Gwen Verdon, Grover Washington, Jr., Hank Williams, Jr., Margaret Whiting, Johnny Winter and

Wolfman Jack. Mostly music and pantomime, with practically no dialogue except for George's narration and a tenuous plot, this film would be considered essentially a very extended-play music video if it were made today. A book about the making of the film was published in 1995.

F40 Movie Movie. 107 min. b/w and color. Warner Bros., 1978. PG.
Dir./Prod. Stanley Donen. Exec. Prod. Martin Starger. Screen Play by Larry Gelbart and Sheldon Keller. Music by Ralph Burns and Buster Davis. Songs and Lyrics by Larry Gelbart and Sheldon Keller. Photography for "Dynamite Hands" by Charles Rosher, Jr. Photography for "Baxter's Beauties of 1933" by Bruce Surtees. Ed. George Hively. Choreography by Michael Kidd. Available on videocassette. **SEE VG15.**

Cast of "Dynamite Hands": George C. Scott (*Gloves Malloy*); Trish Van Devere (*Betsy McGuire*); Red Buttons (*Peanuts*); Eli Wallach (*Vince Marlowe*); Harry Hamlin (*Joey Popchik*); Ann Reinking (*Troubles Moran*); Jocelyn Brando (*Mama Popchik*); Michael Kidd (*Pop Popchik*); Kathleen Beller (*Angie Popchik*); Barry Bostwick (*Johnny Danko*); Art Carney (*Dr. Blaine*); Clay Hodges (*Sailor Lawson*); George P. Wilbur (*Tony Norton*); Peter T. Stader (*Barney Keegle*); George P. Wilbur (*Tony Norton*).

Cast of "Baxter's Beauties of 1933": George C. Scott (*Spats Baxter*); Barbara Harris (*Trixie Lane*); Barry Bostwick (*Dick Cummings*); Trish Van Devere (*Isobel Stuart*); Red Buttons (*Jinks Murphy*); Eli Wallach (*Pop*); Rebecca York (*Kitty*); Art Carney (*Dr. Bowers*); Maidie Norman (*Gussie*); Jocelyn Brando (*Mrs. Updike*); Charles Lane (*Pennington*); Barney Martin (*Motorcycle Cop*).

Synopsis: George's part is again limited to a voice-over in this double spoof of boxing movies and musicals. The first part, "Dynamite Hands," filmed in black and white, tells the story of a young man (Harry Hamlin) who drops out of law school and enters the boxing ring to earn enough money to pay for an operation that will keep his sister (Kathleen Beller) from going blind. When he refuses to throw a fight, the consequences force him to return to law school to see that justice is served. "Baxter's Beauties of 1933" attempts to recreate the old Busby Berkeley style of musical and retells the classic tale of a young girl who goes out as a member of the chorus line and comes back the star. The film comes complete with a trailer of "coming attractions."

Review: "'Movie Movie' is awful awful...Donen tacked on, after the pic was shot, a prolog by George Burns telling the audience that, yes, 'Movie Movie' is intended as fun. Too bad Burns didn't stick around for the rest of the film." (**Variety**, November 15, 1978: 18).

Additional Reviews: **BFI/Monthly Film Bulletin**, April 1979: 46: 75; **Films in Review**, March 1979: 30: 181; **The Hollywood Reporter**, November 15, 1978: 4; **Motion Picture Herald Product Digest**, November 29, 1978: 49; **The Nation**, January 6, 1979: 228: 27; **Newsweek**, November 27, 1978: 92: 93-94; **The New Yorker**, December 4, 1978: 54: 192-195; **The New York Times**, November 22, 1978: sec. III, 9; **The New York Times**, December 3, 1978: sec. II, 13: 4; **Stanley Donen**, p. 220-227; **Time**, December 11, 1978: 112: 109-110.

Commentary: George sandwiched this brief offscreen part between other roles that certainly were far better showcases for his abilities. Perhaps he was drawn to the project because of the reputation of the talented Gelbart, a comic genius on the other side of the camera, probably best known to audiences for his work on the television series, **M*A*S*H** (CBS, 1972-1983). **The Motion Picture Guide** (B346) indicates that viewers would be well-advised to be familiar with the films **Body and Soul** and **42nd Street** to better appreciate what **Movie Movie** attempted to accomplish.

F41 Going in Style. 96 min. color Warner Bros., 1979. PG.
Dir. Martin Brest. Prod. Tony Bill, Fred T. Gallo. Exec. Prod. Leonard Gaines. Screen Play by Martin Brest. Based on a story by Edward Cannon. Music Composed and Conducted by Michael Small. Photography by Billy Williams. Ed. Robert Swink, C. Timothy O'Meara. Available on videocassette. **SEE VG10.**

Cast: George Burns (*Joe*); Art Carney (*Al*); Lee Strasberg (*Willie*); Charles Hallahan (*Pete*); Pamela Payton Wright (*Kathy*); Siobhan Keegan (*Colleen*); Brian Neville (*Kevin*); Constantine Hartofolis (*Boy in Park*); Mary Testa (*Teller*); Jean Shevlin (*Mrs. Fein*); James Manis (*Hot Dog Vendor*); Margot Stevenson (*Store Cashier*); Tito Goya (*Gypsy Cab Driver*); William Pabst (*Bank Guard*); Christopher Wynkoop (*Bank Manager*); John McComb (*Businessman in Bank*); Melvin Jurdem (*Businessman in Bank*); Joseph Sullivan (*Moon*); Bob Maroff (*Cab Driver*); Vivian Edwards (*Bellhop*); Barbara Ann Miller (*Waitress*); Betty Bunch (*Restaurant Cashier*); Karen Montgomery (*Hooker*); Catherine L. Billich (*Casino Cashier*); Robert L. Zay (*Salesman*); Anthony D. Call (*FBI Agent in Charge*); Raf Baldwin (*Stunt Driver*); Jim Tipton, Ron Gagliano, Victor Masi, Raymond Kernodle, Richard Teng, Patrick Donoho (*Crap Dealers*); William Larson, Reathel Bean, Alan Brooks (*FBI Agents*); Mark Margolis, Pedro E. Ocampo, Sr., Toni Di Benedetto (*Prison Guards*); Paul Smith, Bruce Charles (*Radio Announcers*).

Synopsis: Joe, Al, and Willie (George Burns, Art Carney, and Lee Strasberg) are three old cronies sharing an apartment in New York City, leading a routine existence in which the major excitement is receiving and cashing their social security checks. Tired of spending most of his days sitting in the park, Joe notices an armored car delivery being made at a bank and gets an idea so exciting he can't sleep. If the idea works, he figures they'll be in great shape; if not, they'll get three years (maybe) of free room and board and have thirty-six social security checks waiting for each of them. He broaches the subject to his roommates at breakfast the next morning; within a few days, with guns "borrowed" from Al's nephew (Charles Hallahan) and in Groucho Marx disguises, the three set out in purposeful style to rob a bank.

Reviews: "...though the cast is headed by three fine actors, two of whom, Mr. Burns and Mr. Carney, are also extremely funny men, it never elicits any emotional response more profound than curiosity." (**The New York Times**, December 25, 1979: 17: 4). "Once again, George Burns turns in a good performance in a tailored role." (**Variety**, December 19, 1979).

Commentary: The film opened during the Christmas holiday season. One of its most poignant scenes is one in which Joe (George) takes down a box of pictures from a closet, sits down, and cries as he slowly looks through them. The pictures used for the scene were of George and Gracie. George celebrated the upcoming release of the film by placing his prints in the forecourt of Mann's Chinese Theatre. Also see B134, B177, B512.

F42 Just You and Me, Kid. 95 min. color. Columbia, 1979. PG.
Dir. Leonard Stern. Prod. Jerome M. Zeitman, Irving Fein. Screen Play by Oliver Hailey and Leonard Stern. Story by Tom Lazarus. Music Composed and Conducted by Jack Elliott. Photography by David Walsh. Ed. John W. Holmes. Photography by David Walsh.

Cast: George Burns (*Bill*); Brooke Shields (*Kate*); Lorraine Gary (*Shirl*); Ray Bolger (*Tom*); Leon Ames (*Manduke the Magnificent*); Carl Ballantine (*Reinhoff the Remarkable*); Keye Luke (*Dr. Device*); John Schuck (*Stan*); Nicolas Coster (*Harris*); Andrea Howard (*Sue*); William Russ (*Demesta*); Christopher Knight (*Roy*); Julie Cobb (*Dr. Nancy Faulkner*); Peter Brandon (*Mr. Woodrow*); Jacque Lynn Colton (*Edna*); Robert Doran (*The Box Boy*); Burl Ives (*Max*).

Synopsis: Bill (George Burns), an ex-vaudevillian whose alarm clock wakes him every morning to the sound of applause, befriends a young girl (Brooke Shields) running away from an unsavory acquaintance who tried to involve her in a drug deal. His efforts to hide her complicate his own life, especially when the neighbors report the girl's presence to his daughter (Lorraine Gary), who is already concerned about her father's financial generosity to old show business pals and is considering asking the court to appoint her as conservator of his affairs.

Reviews: "...by teaming him (George Burns) with Miss Shields the film effectively bogs him down." (**The New York Times**, July 27, 1979: sec. III, 6: 1). "No one else can come close to Burns in doing what he does best. But even the venerable performer can't pick up a deflated concept and run with it when there's nowhere to go." (**Variety**, July 18, 1979).

Commentary: One of the working titles for the film was **Uncle Bill and the Queen of Hollywood**. Actress Jodie Foster was mentioned in early 1978 as a possible co-star in the role ultimately played by Brooke Shields. Also see B329.

F43 Oh, God! Book II. 94 min. color. Warner Bros., 1980. PG.
Dir./Prod. Gilbert Cates. Screen Play by Josh Greenfeld, Hal Goldman, Fred S. Fox, Seaman Jacobs and Melissa Miller. Story by Josh Greenfeld. Music by Charles Fox. Photography by Ralph Woolsey. Ed. Peter E. Berger. Available on videocassette. **SEE VG17.**

Cast: George Burns (*God*); Suzanne Pleshette (*Paula*); David Birney (*Don*); Louanne (*Tracy*); John Louie (*Shingo*); Conrad Janis (*Mr. Benson*); Anthony Holland (*Dr. Jerome Newell*); Hugh Downs (*Newscaster*); Joyce Brothers (*Joyce Brothers*); Wilfrid Hyde-White (*Judge Miller*); Marian Mercer (*Harriet*); Bebe Drake Massey (*Dr. Young*); Mari Gorman (*Miss Hudson*); Vernon Weddle (*Superintendent Hodges*); Alma Beltran (*Rosa*); Denise Galik (*Joan*); Tad Horino (*Mr. Yamamoto*); Mitsu Yashima (*Mrs. Yamamoto*); Jessica Rains (*Helen*); Sunshine Parker (*Derelict*); Deborah Allison (*1st Girl in Lounge*); Terry Bolo (*2nd Girl in Lounge*); Albert Rosen (*Priest*); Edie McClurg (*Mr. Benson's Secretary*); Ruth Silveira (*Dr. Newell's Nurse*); Ted White (*Motorcycle Policeman*); Bob Terhune (*Motorcycle Policeman*); Jerry Brutsche (*GOD's Stunt Double*); Bobby Porter (*Tracy's Stunt Double*); Lisa Robertson (*Medical Technician*); Rodney Allen Rippy (*Charlie*); Ricky Segall (*Randy*); Justin Randy (*Harold*); Erin Ramsey (*Lisa*); Elizabeth Bryant (*Lizzi*); G. Lewis Cates (*1st Child*); David Yanez (*2nd Child*); Suzanne Chandonae (*3rd Child*); Howard Duff (*Dr. Whitley*); Hans Conried (*Dr. Barnes*); Susan Krebs (*Woman Psychiatrist*); Edmund Stoiber (*Psychiatrist 1*); James Kirkwood (*Psychiatrist 2*); Robin Braxton (*Psychiatrist 3*); Andre Philippe (*Psychiatrist 4*); Henri Polic II (*Psychiatrist 5*); Richard Reicheg (*Psychiatrist 6*).

Synopsis: Deciding that the earth's problems lie with its people, God (George Burns) makes another visit and calls this time upon a little girl (Louanne) to help Him remind people that He's "still around." Hearing her explain a farfetched film plot to her father (David Birney) by telling him, "It's kind of like believing in God. Sometimes you just have to believe in things you can't see," He tells her that He needs the children on His side and that she can help. Inspired by her father's work in advertising, she suggests to God that He needs to come up with a slogan, something that will "make Him a household word." Slogan in hand, she is given her next assignment--spread the message.

Review: "The great George Burns seemingly can do no wrong (even if most of his pictures do go wrong) and he's as lovable as ever in the tailor-made role of God." (**The Film Journal**, October 1980). "...this...sequel...needs more George Burns...whether or not there'll be a cry for 'Book III' remains to be seen." (**The Hollywood Reporter**, September 30, 1980: 2). "...(a) knock-off, featuring a super-subdued Burns (he just reads his lines and walks through quietly)..." **The Los Angeles Herald Examiner**, October 3, 1980). "Burns is fine once again, a master of the throwaway line and well-suited to tone down the religious philosophy in the script." (**Variety**, October 1, 1980: 20).

Additional Reviews: **Boxoffice**, October 1980; **Los Angeles Times**, October 3, 1980: sec. VI, 1; **Motion Picture Herald Product Digest**, October 8, 1980: 34; **The New York Times**, October 3, 1980: sec. III, 8: 4.

Commentary: According to **Daily Variety** (January 28, 1980: 14), Warner Bros. paid an additional insurance premium (amount undisclosed) to cover the movie in the event something happened to George during its filming. A few weeks into their ten-week shooting schedule producer/director Gil Cates is quoted as praising George's stamina, professionalism and cooperative attitude. But George reportedly had his own ground rules. "'Listen, Gil, I walk slow. I talk slow. I smoke my cigar slow. If you want the scene to move faster, rush someone else.'" The film was referred to at one time as **Oh God! Oh God!** George's staff writers were among those given screen play credit. **Book II**'s success quotient in the trilogy *may* be gauged by the fact that the other two films were eventually released not only on videocassette but on laserdisc; this one has made it to videocassette only thus far. If the original **Oh, God!** was the cream of the crop, this one is skim milk.

F44 Oh, God! You Devil. 96 min. color. Warner Bros., 1984. PG.
Dir. Paul Bogart. Prod. Robert M. Sherman. Executive Prod. Irving Fein. Written by Andrew Bergman. Music by David Shire. Photography by King Baggot. Ed. Randy Roberts, Andy Zall. Available on videocassette and laserdisc. **SEE VG18.**

Cast: George Burns (*God/Harry O. Tophet/The Devil*); Ted Wass (*Bobby Shelton*); Ron Silver (*Gary Frantz*); Roxanne Hart (*Wendy Shelton*); Eugene Roche (*Charlie Gray*); Robert Desiderio (*Billy Wayne*); James Cromwell (*Priest*); Robert Picardo (*Joe Ortiz*); John Doolittle (*Arthur Shelton*); Jane Dulo (*Widow*); Martin Garner (*Shamus*); Arthur Malet (*Houseman*); Susan Peretz (*Louise*); Jason Wingreen (*Hotel Manager*); Julie Lloyd (*Bea Shelton*); Ian Giatti (*Young Bobby*); Janet Brandt (*Mrs. K*); Belita Moreno (*Mrs. Vega*); Danny Ponce (*Joey Vega*); Danny Mora (*Bellhop*); Steve Dunaway (*Waiter*); Mitchell Group (*Cap*); Anthony Sgueglia (*Bodyguard*); Cynthia Tarr (*Receptionist*); Christie Mellor (*Groupie*); Tracy Bogart (*Woman in Restaurant*); Crawford Binion (*Man in Restaurant*); Arnold Johnson (*Preacher*); Patricia Springer (*Reporter*); Buddy Powell (*Stage Manager*); Jim Hodge (*Doctor*); Brandy Gold (*Bobby's Daughter*); Henry Reiss, Joseph Samperi, Donald Cadette (*the Wedding Trio*); Kent De Marche, Trey Thompson, Charles Button, Dave Morgan, John Wolff, Jack Kelly (*Billy's Band*); Dom Angelo, Red McIlvaine, Betty Bunch, Roger Rhu (*the Poker Players*); Chere Bryson, George Fisher, Ted Grossman, Tom Rosales, Jr., Victoria Vanderkloot (*the Stunt Players*).

Synopsis: Bobby Shelton (Ted Wass), a young singer/songwriter who was saved from death by his father's prayer as a boy, sells his soul to the Devil twenty-four years later for a chance to make it in the music business as "Billy Wayne." His success is everything he was promised, but the price is higher than he anticipated: he still remembers being "Bobby" and the wife who thinks another man is her husband. He finally finds God in Las Vegas, but he's doomed to commit suicide unless God can win his soul back from the Devil by bluffing His way through a card game.

Review: "It's amazing to watch the performance(s) of a man who was already three months old when a film was first shown publicly in this country." (**New Republic**, December 24, 1984: 25). "George Burns has got a hit in 'Oh, God! You Devil,' which is at least 20 times better than 1980's 'Oh, God! Book II' and a match for the 1977 original..." (**The Hollywood Reporter**, November 1, 1984). "After two turns as an amusing Supreme Being, George Burns proves to be an equally diverting demon..." (**Variety**, November 7, 1984: 16).

Additional Reviews: **The Hollywood Reporter**, November 7, 1984: 3; **L.A. Weekly**, November 9, 1984; **Los Angeles Times**, November 9, 1984: Calendar, 1; **The New York Times**, November 9, 1984: Calendar, 15; **Newsday**, November 9, 1984: III, 7; **New York Post**, November 9, 1984: 19; **Saturday Review**, January-February 1985: 82; **Time**, December 3, 1984: 79; **The Washington Post**, November 9, 1984: F, 8; **The Washington Post**, November 9, 1984: Weekend, 27.

Commentary: The blasphemous title fronts a film that does nothing to dispel the feeling that good ideas shouldn't be milked dry; the success of the original was diluted by not just one but two comparatively pale sequels. The real God must have been relieved that the writer at least let Him come out on top again. Also see B122.

F45 18 Again! 100 min. color. New World Pictures, 1988. PG.
Dir. Paul Flaherty. Prod. Walter Coblenz. Exec. Prod. Irving Fein, Michael Jaffe. Co-Prods. Jonathan Prince, Josh Goldstein. Written by Josh Goldstein and Jonathan Prince. Music by Billy Goldenberg. "I Wish I Was 18 Again" written by Sonny Throckmorton. Additional Music by Gus Edwards and Edward Madden, Stan Lee, Chuck Wagon and Leonard Phillips. Photography by Stephen M. Katz. Ed. Danford B. Greene. Choreography by Larry S. Blum. Available on videocassette and laserdisc. **SEE VG4.**

Cast: George Burns (*Jack Watson*); Charlie Schlatter (*David Watson*); Tony Roberts (*Arnie Watson*); Anita Morris (*Madelyn*); Miriam Flynn (*Betty Watson*); Jennifer Runyon (*Robin*); Red Buttons (*Charlie*); George Di Cenzo (*Coach*); Bernard Fox (*Horton*); Kenneth Tigar (*Professor Swivet*); Anthony Starke (*Russ*); Pauly Shore (*Barrett*); Emory Bass (*Art Teacher*); Joshua Devane (*J. P.*); Benny Baker (*Red*); Hal Smith (*Irv*); Lance Slaughter

(*Mikey*); Earl Boen (*Robin's Dad*); Toni Sawyer (*Robin's Mom*); Stephanie Baldwin (*Robin's Sister*); Nancy Fox (*Waitress*); Leeza Vinnichenko (*Woman at Party*); Kimberlin Brown (*Receptionist*); Kevin Haley (*Team Member*); Mark Kamiyama (*Team Member*); Karl Wiedergott (*Team Member*); Mark Kramer (*Track Team Starter*); Edwina Moore (*First Nurse*); Kate Benton (*Third Nurse*); Pat Crawford Brown (*Old Lady*); Nicholas Cascone (*Frat Member*); Darren Powell (*Frat Member*); Michael J. Shea (*First Orderly*); Freddie Dawson (*Second Orderly*); Jim Jackman (*First Asylum Orderly*); Michael Rider (*Second Asylum Orderly*); Parker Whitman (*Doctor*); Connie Gauthier (*Artist's Model*); Cathy Scott (*Runner*); Michael Fallon (*Bewildered Art Student*).

Synopsis: It's the night of Jack Watson's (George Burns) eighty-first birthday party, and his wish as he blows out the candles is to be eighteen again. Later that night, his and his grandson's (Charlie Schlatter) spirits accidentally exchange bodies after he loses control of the car in which they are riding. While Jack, in David's body, is having the time of his life re-defining David's life, the real David is barely hanging onto life in Jack's body. It's not until David's parents (Tony Roberts and Miriam Flynn) make the painful decision to turn off the life support system that another collision results in another exchange, altering all of their lives forever. George sings "I Wish I Was Eighteen Again," the title song of his 1980 album. **SEE D45.**

Reviews: "...(George Burns) maintains his status as a true comedy treasure..." (**Boxoffice**, June 1988). "The twinkle in George Burns' eyes...should light up the boxoffice..." (**The Hollywood Reporter**, April 4, 1988). "...it's not likely to make fans of either 18- or 81-year-olds." (**Los Angeles Times**, April 8, 1988).

Additional Reviews: **The Los Angeles Herald Examiner**, April 8, 1988: 4; **The New York Times**, April 8, 1988: sec. III, 12: 1.

Commentary: The usual speculation about the cost of insuring the film with George as its star circulated as its August 1987 shooting schedule approached. A studio representative predicted there would be no problems, however, and George apparently had none during the filming. Also see B122, B197.

F46 Radioland Murders. 112 min. color. Universal, 1994. PG.
Dir. Mel Smith. Prods. Rick McCallum, Fred Roos. Exec. Prod. George Lucas. Screenplay by Willard Huyck and Gloria Katz, Jeff Reno and Ron Osborn. Story by George Lucas. Music Supervision by Joel McNeely. Choreography by Brad and Jennifer Moranz. No Director of Photography (other than 2nd Unit) or Film Editor credits per se are listed that would seem to be the equivalent of those in other films in this section.

Cast: Brian Benben (*Roger*); Mary Stuart Masterson (*Penny*); Ned Beatty (*General Whalen*); George Burns (*Milt Lackey*); Scott Michael Campbell (*Billy*); Brion James (*Bernie King*); Michael Lerner (*Lieutenant Cross*); Michael McKean (*Rick Rochester*); Jeffrey Tambor (*Walt Wahlen Junior*); Stephen Tobolowsky (*Max Applewhite*) Christopher Lloyd (*Zoltan*); Larry Miller (*Katzenback*); Anita Morris (*Claudette*); Corbin Bernsen (*Dexter Morris*); Rosemary Clooney (*Anna*); Bobcat Goldthwait (*Wild Writer*); Robert Walden (*Tommy*); Dylan Baker (*Jasper*); Billy Barty (*Himself*); Tracy Byrd (*Himself*); Candy Clark (*Billy's Mom*); Anne De Salvo (*Female Writer*); Jennifer Dundas (*Deirdre*); Bo Hopkins (*Billy's Father*); Robert Klein (*Father Writer*); Harvey Korman (*Jules Cogley*); Joey Lawrence (*Frankie Marshall*); Peter MacNicol (*Son Writer*); Harold Bergman (*Affiliate*); Rita Butler (*Affiliate's Wife*); Dave Hager (*Laughing Man*); Kim Head (*Waitress*); Scott Hilley (*Drunk Affiliate*); Ed Lillard (*Loud Affiliate*); Leighann Lord (*Morgana*); Joann Luzzatto (*P.A.*); Eric Paisley (*Enthusiastic Affiliate*); Anthony Pender (*Revolving Stage Operator*); Jeffrey Pillars (*Nerdy Stagehand*); Steve Rassin (*Page*); Pam Stone (*Dottie*); Leslie Truman (*Woman in Audience*); Norm Woodel (*Announcer*) with various radio performers, dancers and cops.

Synopsis: The story takes place in 1939 on the evening of the debut of a new radio network at its Chicago-based flagship station, WBN. Chaos first reigns in the form of unfinished scripts flying around against the ominous background sounds of sponsors threatening to pull the plug. It quickly turns into a multiple murder mystery, with all fingers pointing one by one to head writer Roger Henderson (Brian Benben). His wife, Penny (Mary Stuart Masterson), also works at the station as the owner's secretary, and has announced she's filing for divorce because she thinks he's been having an affair with Claudette (Anita Morris). While Roger fights to clear his name and save his marriage, it's left up to Penny to get the show on the air and, eventually, help Brian track down the real murderer.

Reviews: "Executive producer George Lucas' affection for radio was obvious in **American Graffiti**, and his desire to make **Radioland Murders**...dates back more than two decades...**Radioland Murders** is a great-looking mess, sadly not worth Mr. Lucas' long wait." (**The Dallas Morning News**, October 21, 1994: C: 1). "...A parade of usually reliable talent stumbles behind him (Benben)--hypnotized, perhaps, by the fact that George Lucas...came up with the story..." (**Entertainment Weekly**, November 4, 1994: 51).

Additional Reviews: **Premiere**, October 1994: 114; **Time**, October 24, 1994: 74.

Commentary: George's role was strictly that of a cameo, although he did have a double, played by Ralph Corley. Strangely enough, one of the funniest bits comes at the end in a reference to *television*. Head of Lucasfilm Ltd. George Lucas utilized state-of-the-art technology to set up communication capability between his headquarters in San Rafael, California and the shoot location at Carolco Studios in Wilmington, North Carolina. The art deco sets and special effects are impressive, of course, but the film gives practically nothing to fans of vintage radio, who might have been happier with a bit more realism. There's quite a lot delivered, however, for those film buffs who ever wondered what it would be like if the Three Stooges ever met up with the Keystone Kops. Music from the era is used to full advantage with songs like "Love Is On The Air Tonight," "What'll I Do," "Crazy People," "I'll Be Glad When You're Dead (You Rascal You)," "In The Mood," "That Old Black Magic" and "Flight Of The Bumble Bee." The inclusion of "Crazy People" perhaps was merely coincidental, but it had been used as George and Gracie's theme song during their 1934-1935 radio season. The film was given two "thumbs down" by critics Siskel & Ebert; average to below average reviews seem to be the norm, although the newspaper ads for the film do manage to contain some glowing excerpts. It grossed $800,000 during its first weekend of release, a $990 per-screen average. Actress Anita Morris (*Claudette*), who had co-starred with George in **18 Again!** (**F45**), died before the film was released, and it is dedicated to her memory.

~~~~~
~~~~~

RADIO SERIES

Guy Lombardo and His Orchestra, with George Burns and Gracie Allen

The Robert Burns Panatela Program. 30 min.

February 22, 1932 to May 16, 1932	CBS	Monday	10:00 P.M.
May 25, 1932 to December 28, 1932	CBS	Wednesday	9:00 P.M.
January 4, 1933 to May 17, 1933	CBS	Wednesday	9:30 P.M.

The White Owl Program. 30 min.

May 24, 1933 to June 13, 1934	CBS	Wednesday	9:30 P.M.

The George Burns and Gracie Allen Show

The Adventures of Gracie. (Also known as The Vintage White Owl Program). 30 min.

September 19, 1934 to September 25, 1935	CBS	Wednesday	9:30 P.M.

Campbell's Tomato Juice Program. 30 min.

October 2, 1935 to March 24, 1937	CBS	Wednesday	8:30 P.M.

The Grape-Nuts Program. 30 min.

April 12, 1937 to August 1, 1938	NBC	Monday	8:00 P.M.

The Chesterfield Program. 30 min.

September 30, 1938 to June 23, 1939	CBS	Friday	8:30 P.M.

The Hinds Honey and Almond Cream Program. 30 min.

October 4, 1939 to April 24, 1940	CBS	Wednesday	7:30 P.M.
May 1, 1940 to June 26, 1940	CBS	Wednesday	6:30 P.M.

The Hormel Program. 30 min.

July 1, 1940 to March 24, 1941	NBC	Monday	7:30 P.M.

The Swan Soap Show. 30 min.

October 7, 1941 to June 30, 1942	NBC	Tuesday	7:30 P.M.
October 6, 1942 to December 26, 1944	CBS	Tuesday	9:00 P.M.
January 1, 1945 to June 25, 1945	CBS	Monday	8:30 P.M.

Maxwell House Coffee Time. 30 min.

September 20, 1945 to May 30, 1946	NBC	Thursday	8:00 P.M.
September 5, 1946 to June 23, 1949	NBC	Thursday	8:30 P.M.

The Amm-i-dent Toothpaste Show. 30 min.

September 21, 1949 to May 17, 1950	CBS	Wednesday	10:00 P.M.

RADIO

George and Gracie starred on radio from 1932 until 1950 (after a short series of successful guest appearances) in a thirty-minute show that, although it technically carried a variety of names, eventually became best known as simply **The George Burns and Gracie Allen Show**. Sponsors were very closely identified with radio programs, as they would be during the early years of television, and it was not unusual for sponsors, networks, broadcast days, time slots, and even a show's title to occasionally change. It should be noted that radio shows were often known by the sponsor's product name and would run for a number of years featuring various performers. **The Maxwell House Coffee Time** (1945-1949) is a good example of this practice. Burns and Allen were the fourth stars to be associated with the show.

The information in **Radio Series** deals with each incarnation of their radio program and includes program title, sponsor, product, agency, network, broadcast day, time slot (Eastern Standard Time), scriptwriters, announcer, orchestra name or orchestra leader name, vocalist, actors, theme songs, premise, series notes and/or additional notes and broadcast date. City and state or other place of origination as they change, major stand-up routine topics or episode synopses, comments and occasional reviews form the balance of this section. Program changes (including those for announcer, orchestra leader and vocalist) are noted as they occur. Songs sung by Gracie and/or by George are indicated by the words "Featured song" within the synopsis unless they are otherwise woven into the text. Parodies of well-known plays and films are also noted, although occasionally, one of Gracie's "new plays" was not actually performed on air but was simply used as a topic of discussion. In the 1940's, the show began to include guest stars and special guests, and these are noted, either by incorporating them into the synopsis or so indicating at the end of the synopsis. Their broadcast originated at different times from the CBS stations WABC in New York City and KNX and KHJ (a Don Lee station) in Hollywood. Their NBC affiliations were WEAF (NBC Blue) and WJZ (NBC Red) in New York City and KFI in Hollywood. As can be seen from the synopses, they also broadcast their show from various other cities in the country, usually to coincide with personal appearances.

The evolution of the show is obvious in both style and premise. The early Burns and Allen radio shows consisted primarily of stand-up comedy. They were on radio for nearly a year before the shows began to revolve around a structured plotline. Their radio career was half over before they appeared as husband and wife in any of their series. The latter years of the show formed the basis for the television show which followed.

Appearances made by George and Gracie on other radio shows are listed in the **Radio Guest Appearances** section of this chapter. They are listed in chronological order, and the information includes program title and network (when known) as well as a synopsis. Gracie skipping from show to show to promote three of their publicity stunts--the search for her "missing" brother, her campaign for the Presidency and finding a singing job for George--is best understood by a study of the guest appearance section. If an appearance involved their breaking out of their familiar persona or if they were not on as a team, that is also noted. The length of the radio shows on which they made guest appearances varied--fifteen minutes, half hour, one hour, and up. Programs for which the date is unknown are listed at the end of the guest appearances section. Because George and Gracie were so inextricably linked during their radio years, and because many of George's appearances after Gracie's death include clips of Gracie's work, the authors have chosen not to break the appearances down into separate listings.

Various radio station retrospectives, personality tributes, radio history, compilation programs, etc. have been produced throughout the years. If an appearance by George and/or Gracie, either live or (more likely) via an earlier recording, could be *confirmed*, it is included here.

It should be noted that, although several companies offer the Burns and Allen radio shows on audio cassettes, it is a curiously small amount of product compared to the number of shows actually produced.

Fifty-six half hour shows from **The Burns and Allen Show** (primarily during its sponsorship by Maxwell House Coffee), as well as one of their holiday episodes in a package with eleven selections from other series and programs, are currently syndicated by Charles Michelson, Inc. and are heard on various stations throughout the country.

Radio Series (1932-1950)

George Burns contributed to the writing and production process throughout his and Gracie's entire radio career. Those who participated in the production process at various times throughout the eighteen years George and Gracie were on the airwaves are as follows:

Producers: Hendrik Booraem, Jr., William Burns, Dave Elton, Glenhall Taylor.
Directors: Hendrik Booraem, Jr., William Burns, Ed Gardner, Al Kaye, Glenhall Taylor, Ned Tollinger, Herschell Williams.
Scriptwriters: Harmon J. Alexander, George Balzer, Hal Block, Ray Bradbury, Bill Brooks, William Burns, Carroll Carroll, Harry Conn, Eugene (Gene) Conrad, Sid Dorfman, Keith Fowler, Frank Galen, Ed Gardner, Henry (Hank) Garson, Helen Gould Harvey, Harvey Helm, Paul Henning, Larry Cline, Don Langan, John P. Medbury, Sam Perrin, Artie Phillips, Aaron J. Ruben, Stanley Shapiro (writers did not necessarily contribute to full seasons of shows).

George Burns and Gracie Allen

1. The Robert Burns Panatela Program. 1932-1933. CBS. 30 min.

Sponsor: The General Cigar Company.
Product: Robert Burns Panatela Cigars.
Agency: J. Walter Thompson.
Network: CBS.
Broadcast Day: Monday.
Time Slot: 10:00-10:30 P.M. (Eastern Standard Time).
Scriptwriters: Carroll Carroll, Harry Conn, John P. Medbury, William Burns. Harvey Helm joined the staff when Harry Conn left to work for Jack Benny.
Announcer: Santos Ortega, Frank Knight.
Orchestra: Guy Lombardo and His Royal Canadians.
Vocalist: Phil Regan.
Opening Theme Song: "Comin' Through The Rye."
Closing Theme Song: "Auld Lang Syne."
Premise: George and Gracie co-star with Guy Lombardo and His Royal Canadians (billed as "The Ace Dance Orchestra of the Air"). The orchestra included the following Lombardo brothers: Carmen as vocalist and on lead saxophone, Lebert on lead trumpet, Victor on baritone saxophone and Guy as orchestra leader. The Royal Canadians were featured in some musical numbers, then continued to play music in the background during George and Gracie's comedy routines. In this first series, Gracie and George play single friends. The shows are comprised of short routines which incorporate rhymes, the Lombardos' music, and the advertiser's commercials (the General Cigar Company was earning profits of $800 million a year) intertwined with Burns and Allen, who were being introduced as "two royal comedians." George and Gracie and Guy Lombardo and His Royal Canadians

were often broadcasting from two different cities when the Lombardos were making personal appearances.

Episode Synopses

R1 February 22, 1932 (New York, NY)
George and Gracie begin as regular members of Guy Lombardo's radio program for Robert Burns Panatelas. Routines: fan letters sent by Gracie to listeners from last week's show (in which George and Gracie made a guest appearance) who have sent in their names and addresses; Gracie's name; Gracie tying strings onto her fingers to keep from forgetting things; the band; golfer Bobby Jones; the kidnap (actually arrest) of her father; banks and cashing checks.

R2 February 29, 1932
Routines: fan mail has given Gracie a cold; a card trick Gracie learned from her brother; George tries to teach Gracie how to be a straight man so he can be the comedian; George's suit; Gracie's family; Gracie proposes a contest where the winners send her money.

R3 March 7, 1932
Routines: Gracie attempts to announce the program; the progress of last week's contest; Gracie's family having a warped sense of humor; reincarnation; discussion of the four Lombardo brothers; counting sheep; Gracie's brothers playing baseball for the State Prison and County Jail; Gracie's father being in prison; putting suspense into the program.

R4 March 14, 1932
Routines: the idea of having a more suspenseful show continues briefly; one of the show's listeners calls in to request louder music and no talking; Gracie is writing a song with her brother; Gracie has hidden her family in the instruments so they can watch the broadcast; kissing; betting on horses.

R5 March 21, 1932
Routines: the fan mail has increased to one letter; Gracie tries to interest George in a new game, Guess It (if you can't, you win); Gracie's brother is taking up the violin and wants Guy Lombardo to help him; Gracie compliments Guy on his instrument--the baton; everyone tries to top the others as to who plays instruments the longest; boats carved out of wood; plays on words.

R6 March 28, 1932
Routines: another word game; Gracie's intelligence; George selling dogs; plays on words; Gracie thinks it is difficult to talk to some people; Gracie is going to open a chain of department stores.

R7 April 4, 1932
Routines: Guy wants to tell a joke while Gracie is outside; this week their fan mail is a postcard; poetry; wearing glasses; everyone exchanges performing duties; boats; Gracie "flubs" the announcements. George sings "Just Picture a Penthouse."

R8 April 11, 1932
Routines: Gracie talks about her and her family's nightly dreams; a word game; Gracie's garden and what she's not going to plant.

R9 April 18, 1932
Routines: Gracie is late for the broadcast because of a cab ride; Gracie wrote a song after being inspired by a visit to the zoo; George teaches Gracie the musical scale.

R10 April 25, 1932
Routines: Gracie is happy; there is constant patter with a host of subjects.

R11 May 2, 1932
Gracie has filled the studio with packages, all containing inventions; she decides her best invention is an invention for inventing inventions.

R12 May 9, 1932

Tonight's running gag: Gracie is going into politics and decides to run for Governess of the State of Coma. She introduces her campaign cheer and gives her campaign speech.

R13 May 16, 1932 (Guy is in Boston, MA)
Gracie's political campaign continues.

The show moves to Wednesday at 9:00-9:30 P.M.

R14 May 25, 1932 (Buffalo, NY)
Gracie is no longer running for Governess of the State of Coma; she tells about her father's fish farm in Kansas and plays a cigar store clerk trying to sell the sponsor's products.

R15 June 1, 1932 (Detroit, MI)
Gracie talks about her problems with the train from Buffalo, the train conductor and her brother and her twin sisters; Gracie offers to drive George home after the broadcast; George and Gracie do a song and dance with patter.

R16 June 8, 1932 (Indianapolis, IN)
Gracie is happy because her brother is "making" money; George asks her about her schooling; and Gracie talks about her "crazy" other brother (who's really just normal).

R17 June 15, 1932 (St. Louis, MO)
Gracie talks about her dream, her birthday, and her grandfather; George phones his sister while Gracie and Guy play a game; word games; Gracie confuses George's car problems with the budget; and Gracie explains what is wrong with the country.

R18 June 22, 1932 (Hollywood, CA)
George and Gracie are in Hollywood working on **The Big Broadcast** (F19). This episode begins with George trying to determine if Gracie will be a success in motion pictures and becomes a potpourri of straight lines, jokes, and word games.

R19 June 29, 1932
Gracie talks about her uncle, who is in the canning business, then receives a telegram from her brother, who has inherited their uncle's business and has made Gracie a silent partner; George and Gracie are going to her house for dinner after the show until she explains her cooking methods to him.

R20 July 6, 1932 (Guy is in New York, NY)
Gracie takes a phone call; Gracie talks about her family and the old woman they won in a raffle who lives in their house; Gracie wants to play a game with George called "eliminations" (she mentions six or seven things, and the subject left over is the one she will talk about); her father has taken over a newspaper business, and Gracie wants to start a paper.

R21 July 13, 1932
George and Gracie discuss the Olympic Games to be held in Los Angeles; George tells Gracie to stop dancing; swimming pool routine; kissing routine with man offstage.

R22 July 20, 1932 (New York, NY)
George and Gracie have just returned from Hollywood; George accuses Gracie of baby talk; Gracie has to move to another apartment because she didn't pay her rent.

R23 July 27, 1932
Gracie's uncle has tried to rob a police station, and her brother went over there to look for a job after he saw a "murderer wanted" poster; George suggests that Gracie write an autobiography and call it **Popular Ignorance**; Gracie talks about manufacturing a man like Frankenstein and has written a poem.

R24 August 3, 1932
George and Gracie are playing bridge when the station announcer reminds them that they are on the air; Gracie announces the show; Gracie wants to open her own theater and writes a play.

R25 August 10, 1932
Gracie has returned from the dentist; she introduces Helen, the girl at the information desk, to George; Helen asks Gracie to work at the switchboard for five minutes; Gracie returns from getting a soda in the middle of the broadcast and announces she had an automobile accident.

R26 August 17, 1932
George comments to Gracie that it sure is a big surprise to see her on time for a change; Gracie is worried because a Hollywood movie studio wants her to sign a contract, but without her brother; they have been back in New York for a month, but Gracie still thinks she is in Hollywood; George asks Gracie how many accidents are in her family. The song, "Oh, Holding the Bag" is performed on tonight's telecast.

R27 August 24, 1932
Gracie is upset and not herself today; she received a letter from home, and her family is having a wonderful time; she talks about her uncle's family and her father's chicken business; all of her family are in the circus except her mother; her cousin is a ventriloquist.

R28 August 31, 1932
Gracie is happy because she has solved a problem; she talks about her family and how they have not paid their rent for two years; Gracie took a taxi home last night and was followed by a gunman; she makes up impossible riddles (example: if an airplane left Los Angeles with fourteen people, how many people got off in Denver?); she does a handkerchief trick with cards.

R29 September 7, 1932 (Chicago, IL; Guy is in New York, NY)
George comments about the nice ovation they have received in Chicago; Gracie thinks that she is on her vacation; George goes to a baseball game; Gracie talks about her mother; George wants her *not* to talk about her brother; Gracie has gone with her brother to the dentist, where he is going to open an orangeade stand.

R30 September 14, 1932 (Chicago, IL; Guy is in New York, NY)
Gracie talks about her family, even after George requests she not speak for the rest of the evening.

R31 September 21, 1932 (Chicago, IL; Guy is in New York, NY)
George and Gracie are staying at the Edgewater Beach Hotel; Gracie talks about giving a party.

R32 September 28, 1932 (New York, NY)
Back in New York from Chicago, Gracie starts the show by saying hello to the boys in the band; Gracie has brought her brother's dog back with her on the train; she bought Guy a gift of eyeglasses, which he cannot use; Gracie could not sleep last night; she and her brother are going into the advertising business and tells Guy that her idea is to make everybody in the world want their product.

R33 October 5, 1932
Talk about mustard; Gracie looks for her dog; Gracie is gifted with a monkey.

R34 October 12, 1932
Gracie is reading out loud (she is reading **Telephone Directory** by Bell) but tells George that it has too many characters in the plot; later, she tries to sell George a watch and talks about politics and campaigning for a man named Herbert J. Roosevelt.

R35 October 19, 1932 (Boston, MA; Guy is in New York, NY)
Gracie's family has been robbed five times this week; she mentions she has more than one brother; they play golf on a pitch and putt course in Boston.

R36 October 26, 1932 (New York, NY)
George tells Gracie "I just can't wait until we have television so people can see how silly you are." They perform the black stocking and the appendectomy scar on Gracie's father's neck routines.

R37 November 2, 1932

Gracie ate a goldfish thinking she could then swim like one; George calls a doctor for her but he faints, and they have to call another doctor to treat Gracie.

R38 November 9, 1932 (Philadelphia, PA)
Gracie is giving George a headache; Gracie's family had a fight last night; Gracie tells the story of election night at the Allens'; George and Gracie go on a boat ride where George meets his friend Henry.

R39 November 16, 1932 (Washington, DC)
A guide asks if George and Gracie want to go through the White House, then asks Gracie for a kiss; they visit the Smithsonian and the Treasury; Gracie receives a telegram that mentions her sister has had a new baby; baby routine.

R40 November 23, 1932 (New York, NY)
The boys in the band ask Gracie about her trip; she has brought them gifts; baby routine; they visit the Empire State Building.

R41 November 30, 1932
Gracie talks about her family; George and Gracie go to the Brown-Colgate game and talk about football.

R42 December 7, 1932
Gracie is upset because her mother has given her two quarters, and she doesn't know which one is for cabbage and which is for lettuce; she talks about her family; Guy talks to George about the troubling day he has had; Gracie's uncle died and left her $30,000; her brother bought some land for her.

R43 December 14, 1932 (Baltimore, MD)
George and Gracie talk about a party they went to last night and take a trip to the U.S. Naval Academy.

R44 December 21, 1932 (New York, NY)
George and Gracie are late for the broadcast; the announcer picks their conversation up on the street, where they talk about Christmas presents.

R45 December 28, 1932
They talk about Christmas and go to a prize fight at Madison Square Garden. Later, they perform a routine about buying a piece of a turkey.

The show's time slot changes to 9:30-10:00 P.M.

The program now begins to rely less on routines and more upon plot. Initiating the change is what would become Burns and Allen's most famous publicity stunt and one of the most well-known in the history of radio--the search for Gracie's missing brother.

R46 January 4, 1933
New Year's Eve Party. Gracie gets a phone call from her mother saying her brother is missing; Gracie goes to a crystal gazer for help in locating her brother. The narrator asks the audience for cooperation in the manhunt. They are asked "to communicate any knowledge they may have to Miss Gracie Allen at any of the stations."

R47 January 11, 1933
George and Gracie look for her missing brother. She makes a phone call from a drug store. Herman (her police dog) is along. Detective Dittenfest is hired to shadow George and Gracie. George and Gracie perform a brother and ironing board routine.

R48 January 18, 1933
Rajah Zenda, a phrenologist, has been sent to help find her brother. George and Gracie perform their "Dizzy" routine. Frank Buck announces he is leaving for India in two weeks to make a new picture entitled **Wild Cargo**. He believes that he can be of service to Gracie since he believes her brother is missing in the jungles of India.

R49 January 25, 1933
Gracie gets ten telegrams, and three tell where her missing brother is. Riddles occupy a portion of the broadcast. She gets a phone call from

Mrs. Dittenfest and hears that her brother is hiding on the farm. Herman the dog appears.

R50 February 1, 1933 (Chicago, IL)
George and Gracie have gone to Chicago to look for her missing brother. They get a tour of the grounds of the Chicago World's Fair although the fair has not yet opened.

R51 February 8, 1933 (Hollywood, CA)
Gracie continues to search for her brother. The show includes a hunting skit with her grandfather and uncle; Gracie calls on director Raymond Black.

R52 February 15, 1933
Gracie receives a telegram from some people that says they are holding her brother prisoner and want a $10,000 reward for him, dead or alive. George and Gracie perform an early to bed routine. Gracie owes the car company money.

R53 February 22, 1933
Tonight is the fourth anniversary program for Guy Lombardo. For a gift, Gracie has written a book, **Smart Sayings by Gracie Allen To Comin' Through the Rye** (B16). Gracie thinks her brother is coming home because of the bank holiday (Washington's birthday).

R54 March 1, 1933
Still looking for her brother, Gracie asks George why he doesn't propose to her. They talk about sports. Gracie writes in her diary and plans a trip on money she will get from Paramount, even though she has no job. A mustached man sees Gracie about taking a trip to England, Paris and Scotland for $1,500. Tonight's program includes a promotion for Gracie book, **Smart Sayings** (B16), which is "illustrated with cartoons and photos of George, Gracie, Guy and the band" and is offered free of charge to listeners who write to Robert Burns Cigars in New York City.

R55 March 8, 1933
They try to find her brother in Hollywood. Gracie wants to go into the clothing business. They tour Los Angeles.

R56 March 15, 1933
Gracie is going in for higher learning and has written to Albert Einstein about the fifth dimension. A man, Croveny (a name that appears throughout various film and radio broadcasts and in various guises) represents a company that will let people make their own jigsaw puzzles.

R57 March 22, 1933
Gracie has received a $1,000 check from her brother, but his signature is missing. Gracie talks about Joan of Arc and is writing a Hollywood column for the newspaper.

R58 March 29, 1933
Gracie talks about her aunt and uncle's beauty parlor. George and Gracie perform the manicurist routine from their short, **Once Over, Light** (F5). A real estate man wants to sell them a home. Gracie does the routine about her niece growing three feet.

R59 April 5, 1933
Gracie talks about her nephew and his farm and drives George around in her automobile.

R60 April 12, 1933
Gracie brings Herman the dog to the studio. She and George have been in Hollywood for nine weeks. George has fallen down the stairs. Gracie has been talking to Prince ZoSo Boo the Palmist while in a trance.

R61 April 19, 1933
Gracie receives a telegram that someone is holding her missing brother for a $10,000 ransom and tells George to remember that they are partners. She talks about her family and complains of a headache.

R62 April 26, 1933 (New York, NY; Guy is in Atlanta, GA)

George and Gracie have returned to New York after three months in Hollywood where they made two feature films for Paramount, **International House** (F20) and **College Humor** (F21). Gracie is at a store.

R63 May 3, 1933
William Williams, a newspaper man, wants an interview and asks Gracie how she liked Hollywood. George and Gracie are taking up Hollywood's latest fad, bicycle riding. Her brother is still missing.

R64 May 10, 1933 (Guy is in Philadelphia, PA)
Gracie's Shakespeare club is going to present two plays. At the rehearsal, Gracie plays Juliet, from William Shakespeare's **Romeo and Juliet**.

R65 May 17, 1933
Tonight's show revolves around Gracie's missing brother, her friend getting married, and George being dressed up for a wedding.

This is the last show for Robert Burns Panatela Cigars.

2. The White Owl Program. 1933-1934. CBS. 30 min.

Sponsor: The General Cigar Company.
Product: White Owl Cigars.
Agency: J. Walter Thompson.
Network: CBS.
Broadcast Day: Wednesday.
Time slot: 9:30-10:00 P.M. (Eastern Standard Time).
Scriptwriters: Carroll Carroll, Harvey Helm, John P. Medbury, William Burns.
Announcer: Santos Ortega, Frank Wright.
Orchestra: Guy Lombardo and His Royal Canadians.
Vocalist: Phil Regan.
Opening Theme Song: "Comin' Through The Rye."
Closing Theme Song: "Auld Lang Syne."
Premise: There is no change.

R66 May 24, 1933 (Chicago, IL)
This is George, Gracie and Guy's first broadcast for White Owl Cigars. Gracie brings presents to the band and drives George to the World's Fair, where they are involved in an accident.

R67 May 31, 1933
George and Gracie are still at the World's Fair; Gracie is looking for a little gold ring.

R68 June 7, 1933
Gracie speaks on the "Progress of the Present Administration" and has also been practicing five days for a dance marathon. Featured song: "Merry Widow Waltz."

R69 June 14, 1933 (New York, NY)
Gracie has an hour to kill before she meets her sister, so asks George to marry her. Useless inventions are discussed. Gracie's family is going into the Coney Island business.

R70 June 21, 1933
Gracie tells George about the party he missed at her house the previous evening. Gracie's family has changed its collective mind about the Coney Island business and has decided to go into the hotel business.

R71 June 28, 1933
Gracie is getting out of the hotel business and is going to work in her uncle's antique store. She can't stop whistling because her mother gave her birdseed instead of breakfast food. George and Gracie perform the window washer routine.

R72 July 5, 1933 (Atlantic City, NJ)
Gracie may have spent too much time out in the sun--she's talking to herself. George and Gracie are on the Boardwalk.

R73 July 12, 1933 (New York, NY)
Gracie takes her driving test, hits someone, is sued for criminal negligence and acts as her own legal counsel.

R74 July 19, 1933
George and Gracie catch a bus to go out. Gracie "treats" George to a baseball game where he tries to explain the rules to her.

R75 July 26, 1933
Gracie is working at the General Information Bureau, fielding telephone calls and greeting people who have questions. Gracie is going on vacation, and she and George visit a department store, where she gets stuck in a revolving door, thinking it's a fan.

R76 August 2, 1933 (Washington, D.C.)
George and Gracie visit the Senate Building. Gracie wonders if the country has a national anthem, which segues into a conversation concerning her answer for solving the job shortage.

R77 August 9, 1933 (New York, NY)
George and Gracie look for her missing brother in a trunk in the attic, but find what appears to be a treasure map instead; while searching for the treasure on what they believe to be a deserted island, they become stranded with Herman the dog (Herman did not become the name of her pet duck until several years later) and an ostrich named Lily. Featured song: "The Irish Jig."

R78 August 16, 1933
George and Gracie discover they were never on an island at all but on the side of a hill. A fur smuggler offers them a ride, and the entire group is stopped by a policeman, who thinks George is a gang leader.

R79 August 23, 1933 (Guy is broadcasting from Long Island, NY)
George and Gracie are on their way to the police station, but the charges are eventually dropped, and Gracie is credited with the capture of the gang of smugglers and given a $50,000 reward.

R80 August 30, 1933 (Toledo, OH; Guy is still on Long Island, NY)
Gracie wants to use her reward money to start the Gracie Allen Shakespearian Repertory Dramatic Club and is upset when she can't get Shakespeare on the telephone to make changes to the play, **Julius Caesar**.

R81 September 6, 1933 (Chicago, IL)
George and Gracie are putting on the play **Julius Caesar**. Gracie is playing Marc Antony. A man criticizes Gracie's acting. She talks about her blue hat. George says he has known her for two years. In two weeks she has made $100,000 on the play. Several newspapermen want to interview Gracie.

R82 September 13, 1933 (New York, NY; Guy is in Chicago, IL)
Gracie has bought ten cars with her $100,000 and plans to go into business as the Baby Blue Taxi Company. She and George don disguises to spy on the way her drivers are treating the customers but later sells the company for $200,000.

R83 September 20, 1933
Gracie is on the roof of her new Park Avenue penthouse and thinks a ghost is stalking her servants.

R84 September 27, 1933
Gracie pushes the button in room 13, and the room begins to sink. She and George go into an apartment where there is a party.

R85 October 4, 1933
No broadcast. This half hour given to President Roosevelt.

R86 October 11, 1933
Gracie has a new business, the Gracie Allen Realty Company.

R87 October 18, 1933
Gracie has made $270,000 and purchases a memorial park; a mysterious stranger takes Gracie to Cincinnati, OH.

R88 October 25, 1933 (Cincinnati, OH; Guy is in Detroit, MI)
After six days of looking George finds Gracie and tries to save her from kidnappers, who are accused of taking her money.

R89 November 1, 1933 (Kansas City, MO; Guy is in Cleveland, OH)
George has again lost Gracie but later finds her working behind a store counter; a crook has taken her money.

R90 November 8, 1933 (Hollywood, CA; Guy is in Baltimore, MD)
George and Gracie are in Hollywood making another feature picture. Detective Dittenfest is trying to get Gracie's money back.

R91 November 15, 1933 (Guy is in Washington, D.C.)
George is in jail, accused of stealing Gracie's money.

R92 November 22, 1933
Gracie and George are on a farm. The case against George was thrown out of court.

R93 November 29, 1933 (Guy is in New York, NY)
Gracie goes out to buy a Thanksgiving turkey, meets Chico Marx, and invites him to dinner.

R94 December 6, 1933 (Guy is in Boston, MA)
Gracie talks about her family; her uncle is ill, and she and George go to the hospital to visit him.

R95 December 13, 1933
George and Gracie are on their way to a football game at Wrigley Field.

R96 December 20, 1933 (Guy is in St. Louis, MO)
George and Gracie are in the makeup room at Paramount Studios, where they are making **Six of a Kind** (F22). They watch Bert Wheeler and Robert Woolsey making a film at RKO Studios.

R97 December 27, 1933
Guy Lombardo and his brothers are in Los Angeles for New Year's with George and Gracie. Most of tonight's conversation centers around Christmas gifts.

R98 January 3, 1934
Gracie is missing. She had received a $1,200 diamond bracelet but was exchanging it for a fur coat. Gracie has moved into a bungalow where George meets with trouble when he comes across Jack Frost, the North Wind and a snowman.

R99 January 10, 1934
Gracie is meeting with Prince Ozatz, a crystal gazer.

R100 January 17, 1934
Gracie and George talk about their lines for their next picture with Bing Crosby, **We're Not Dressing** (F23).

R101 January 24, 1934
Gracie is looking for a job and finds one as a cashier for a barber shop.

R102 January 31, 1934
Guy Lombardo is still with George and Gracie in Los Angeles and is trying to buy a present for his brother Victor's baby. Gracie's brother is still missing. Gracie is having their picture made by a street hawker on Hollywood Boulevard.

R103 February 7, 1934
George and Gracie are in an automobile approaching the Mexican border, and they go through customs. Her brother is still missing. At the gambling casino at Caliente, George lends Gracie one dollar and she wins $46,000. Gracie wants him to take half back and gives him fifty cents.

R104 February 14, 1934
Guy Lombardo is sending George and Gracie a wire for Valentine's Day when they show up at the same telegraph office. Gracie is in a candy shop buying sweets for Valentine's Day. Featured song: "Grass Shack."

R105 February 21, 1934
George and Gracie are having a picnic in Griffith Park where she has brought a phonograph player along with recordings of her relatives. She and George talk about rhymes. Gracie is very happy and tells George if he asks her to be his wife, she'd--well, she's not *that* happy.

R106 February 28, 1934
George and Gracie are at the Wilmington pier waiting to board a boat to Catalina Island. Gracie tells George that they have been going around together for five years and it means nothing. George looks good but hasn't any money but she's crazy about him.

R107 March 7, 1934
Gracie is going to sell insurance policies to George and Guy.

R108 March 14, 1934
Gracie is looking for her brother in a shack. She finds workmen who are making cold cream, mascara, and flavored lipsticks and has hired detectives to watch her vanishing cream.

R109 March 21, 1934
Gracie gets a job at the newspaper office of the **Daily Tabloid**. Featured song: "He Raised His Hat, I Raised My Eyes."

R110 March 28, 1934
George and Gracie visit a grocery store and Gracie offers to substitute for the clerk when he receives a call from the hospital telling him he's a father.

R111 April 4, 1934
Gracie recites a song that she and her missing brother wrote. She decides to change her name but changes movie stars' names instead. Later, she misunderstands a girl's remarks and thinks everyone thinks George is nuts.

R112 April 11, 1934 (Guy is in San Francisco, CA)
Gracie's talk about her family includes her brother's fractured skull and arm, her nephew's trip to Brooklyn and her grandfather eating spaghetti.

R113 April 18, 1934
Gracie decides to sell the magazines she bought for a sick friend after she realizes she can't find the friend's house but George is the one who is arrested for peddling without a license.

R114 April 25, 1934 (Guy is in Galveston, TX)
Gracie is packing for New York; once on the train, she tells George she forgot his overcoat, which has his cigars, money and the train tickets inside.

R115 May 2, 1934
George and Gracie are on an uninhabited island rehearsing for their film, **We're Not Dressing** (F23), and explore the area; later, the remainder of the cast and crew arrive and the director attempts to explain a scene to Gracie. In reality the "uninhabited" island that provided the film's location was Catalina Island off the coast of California.

R116 May 9, 1934 (New York, NY; Guy is in New Orleans, LA)
Gracie invites George home to meet her family, but no one is home (they're at the airport because Gracie's brother has fallen out of an airplane again), so Gracie shows George home movies instead.

R117 May 16, 1934
Gracie enters Herman in a dog show; Herman wins first place so Gracie enters him in a dog race.

R118 May 23, 1934 (Guy is in Columbus, OH)
Gracie is upset about being left at home to do the spring housecleaning while her family is in Kansas City, Missouri; Gracie explains her gardening methods to George.

R119 May 30, 1934 (Guy is in Pittsburgh, PA)
George and Gracie attempt to collect a debt that's been owed to her grandfather for twenty years; the woman who owes the twelve dollars turns over her boarding house to Gracie in lieu of the cash.

R120 June 6, 1934
George and Gracie are on the set of their new film, **Many Happy Returns** (F24). The cast is instructed by the director to rehearse a scene in his absence but Gracie passes out the wrong scripts.

R121 June 13, 1934
George and Gracie are going to Europe for the summer and say good-bye to Guy Lombardo, who is getting a new sponsor and show. Featured song: "Auld Lang Syne." **SEE B443.**

3. The Adventures of Gracie. 1934-1935. CBS. 30 min.

Sponsor: The General Cigar Company.
Product: White Owl Cigars.
Agency: J. Walter Thompson.
Network: CBS.
Broadcast Day: Wednesday.
Time Slot: 9:30-10:00 P.M. (Eastern Standard Time).
Scriptwriters: Carroll Carroll, Harvey Helm, John P. Medbury, Eugene (Gene) Conrad, William Burns.
Announcer: Bill Goodwin.
Orchestra Leader: Robert Emmett (Bobby) Dolan.
Vocalists: The Picken Sisters; an octet, the White Owl Buccaneers.
Theme Song: "Crazy People."
Premise: Gracie's escapades take her to various locations, with George and the audience along for the ride. George and Gracie's comedic turns are interspersed with musical numbers featuring the orchestra and the vocalists.
Series Notes: The program is later referred to as **The Vintage White Owl Program**. A **New York Times** article published on October 23, 1934 stated that by frequently using the "fade-in" and "fade-out" methods George brought the motion picture technique to the microphone in this series. He and Gracie were also described as "strongly opposed" to a studio audience, finding them distracting and not a proper gauge of how the show is going over. "Moreover, no matter how hard a comedian tries, there is a natural tendency to play up to the studio visitors, and this is not fair to the far greater unseen audience."

R122 September 19, 1934 (New York, NY)
Burns and Allen's first radio series without Guy Lombardo find them picking the itinerary for their European vacation at the travel bureau. In Venice Gracie falls off the gondola into the water; in Moscow they visit a tea room, and in London they are going to the Palladium Theatre to make a personal appearance. Featured song: "I Know How To Use The English Language."

<u>Review</u>: "Burns and Allen are still dealing jokes and the jokes were the best and only really effective part of this program." (**Variety**, September 25, 1934: 40).

R123 September 26, 1934
George and Gracie are aboard a ship bound for the United States. Featured song: "Yankee Doodle Blues."

R124 October 3, 1934
George and Gracie talk about being back in the United States. She is looking for an apartment and decides to have a housewarming to which the guests are asked to bring furniture. Gracie sings a song she heard in Budapest, "Oda Vodjak Mug Ayert." **This broadcast is the date of their first coast-to-coast hookup.**

R125 October 10, 1934
Gracie is horseback riding at the Central Park livery stables, and her horse runs away. She and her dog Herman go to the zoo. Gracie says the stork brought her twenty years ago. George and Gracie are guests of honor at the Central Park Casino that night. Featured song: "Everything's Been Done Before."

R126 October 17, 1934
George and Gracie are serving as jurors and Gracie keeps the jury deliberating for days.

R127 October 24, 1934
Miss Mary Kelly is ill and Gracie and George (whom Gracie has been referring to as "Georgie Porgie") go to visit her. Mary is a teacher and is worried about losing her job so Gracie takes over her class. Featured song: "It Was A Blind Date." The role of Mary Kelly was played by actress Mary Kelly, a friend of George and Gracie's for a number of years and a former girlfriend of Jack Benny's. She appeared in a number of episodes over a period of time.

R128 October 31, 1934 (Philadelphia, PA)
The president of Armstrong Airline Company, Mr. Vanderlip, is giving a dinner and his wife wants Gracie to pose for publicity pictures with their new airplane, the Skyhawk. At the flying field George and Gracie accidentally take off in the plane and break the world endurance record of twenty-eight days in the air.

R129 November 7, 1934 (New York, NY)
A busload of entertainers are going to perform an annual vaudeville show at the state prison. Gracie sings "Lover, I Do," and George joins in the second chorus.

R130 November 14, 1934
George and Gracie are on the train to California to begin work on **Win or Lose**, which will be retitled **Love in Bloom** (F25). Gracie shows George a telegram from Paramount Pictures telling them not to leave New York until they hear from the studio. Featured song: "So Long, Mary."

R131 November 21, 1934
George and Gracie try to rent a car to take them to a football game; a convoluted series of events results in George becoming the game's announcer.

R132 November 28, 1934
Gracie and George go to McGuire's Turkey Ranch to buy a Christmas turkey; Gracie buys extra turkeys and goes door-to-door trying to give them away to wealthy families. Later, when George takes her home, she realizes she doesn't know where she lives because she moved two years ago. Featured song: "When Love Comes Swingin' Along."

R133 December 5, 1934 (Hollywood, CA)
Gracie and George are at Lake Arrowhead where one of the guests gets lost in the mountains so a rescue party is formed. Gracie is engaged to six different men ("Sometimes I think Cupid must have shot me with a machine gun."). Featured song: "Hands Across The Table."

R134 December 12, 1934
A case of mistaken identity leads Gracie into becoming involved with a production of **Uncle Tom's Cabin**. Featured song: "Oh, the Object of My Affection."

R135 December 19, 1934
George and Gracie visit Hawaii. Featured song: "King Ka May Ha May Ha."

R136 December 26, 1934
Gracie's brother has had a Christmas party and asks George and Gracie to distribute the leftovers--the men who haven't gone home yet. George helps Gracie exchange Christmas gifts and Gracie gives a party for department store Santa Clauses. This is the last show with a prologue. Featured song: "Pop Goes Your Heart."

R137 January 2, 1935
Gracie enters a float in the Tournament of Roses parade and wins first prize for an ingenious entry.

R138 January 9, 1935
George and Gracie get lost in the woods while trying to find a picnic spot and stumble onto a golf course, where a case of mistaken identity causes them to be entered into a tournament.

R139 January 16, 1935
George and Gracie perform stand up routines. Featured song: "As Long As I'm With You." This is the first time the show was broadcast with a studio audience, taking place at the Figueroa Playhouse in Los Angeles.

R140 January 23, 1935
George and Gracie perform stand up routines and talk about Gracie's new subdivision. Gracie mentions her dog Herman. Featured song: "Take A Number From One To Ten."

R141 January 30, 1935
George and Gracie perform stand up, take a taxi to the railroad station to meet her brother and talk about going to the Brown Derby Restaurant. Featured song: "Love Is Just Around The Corner."

R142 February 6, 1935
The team does more stand up routines, and Gracie drives a sightseeing bus in Hollywood.

R143 February 13, 1935
George and Gracie perform stand up routines, George has a tooth pulled, and Gracie sings "Lookie, Lookie, Lookie, Here Comes Cookie" to promote their latest film, **Love in Bloom** (F25), in which Gracie also sings the song.

R144 February 20, 1935
Stand up routines sandwich a segment in which Gracie accompanies George to the barbershop. Gracie sings "You've Got Me Doin' Things," another song from the film, **Love in Bloom.** **SEE F25.**

R145 February 27, 1935
Two stand up routines precede George visiting the office of Gracie's newspaper, **The Daily Anemic**. Featured song: "Don't Be Afraid To Tell Your Mother."

R146 March 6, 1935
Stand up; Gracie takes George to a hat shop to buy him a hat. Featured song: "What's The Reason I'm Not Pleasin' You."

R147 March 13, 1935
George and Gracie visit the Museum of Natural History and perform stand up. Featured song: "Lookie, Lookie, Lookie, Here Comes Cookie."

R148 March 20, 1935
Stand up; Gracie goes to the bank for a loan. Featured song: "Whose Honey Are You?"

R149 March 27, 1935
Stand up; George insists Gracie go to the doctor for her cold. Featured song: "Do Me A Favor."

R150 April 3, 1935
Stand up; Gracie's uncle asks her to run his stock brokerage office which they call "Flim Flam and Scram." Featured song: "She's a Latin From Manhattan."

R151 April 10, 1935
Stand up. This is the last show for orchestra leader Bobby Dolan. Featured song: "Oda Vodjak Mug Ayert."

R152 April 17, 1935
Stand up; Gracie visits an auction in mid-broadcast and breaks a $2,000 mirror; a new recurring character, Dr. Smearbach, makes an appearance when he volunteers to be Gracie's psychoanalyst. Ferde Grofe joins the show as the new orchestra leader. Featured song: "I'm Just An Ordinary Human."

R153 April 24, 1935
The first stand up spot features Gracie's family; Gracie is tired from spring housecleaning; Dr. Smearbach makes another "house call." Bill Goodwin, who now refers to the show as **The Vintage White Owl Program** brings on Ernie Young, a film makeup artist in Hollywood, who gives a testimonial for White Owl Cigars (Mr. Young says the Depression caused him to look for a more economical cigar). Featured song: "Lady In Red."

R154 May 1, 1935
Stand up; Dr. Smearbach returns. The orchestra plays a special arrangement of "The Continental" in honor of George and Gracie's European tour from several months earlier. Eddie Borden, a vaudevillian who has come to

Hollywood to do films, does the cigar testimonial this week. Featured song: "Love Is The Thing."

R155 May 8, 1935
Stand up; "Rockabye Baby" is performed as it might be done by John Barrymore, Gertrude Stein, Louis Armstrong and Maggie Allen (Gracie's mother); Dr. Smearbach visits. Dr. Moore, a Los Angeles physician, offers a testimonial for White Owl Cigars. Featured song: "Love And A Dime."

R156 May 15, 1935
Gracie talks about her Uncles Bonehead and Deadpuss and her brother Imbe getting a job; burglars have broken into Gracie's house and stolen everything but soap and towels; a telephone man is trying to put a phone in Gracie's apartment. Featured song: "Hate to Talk About Myself."

R157 May 22, 1935
Gracie talks about her brothers and Norman Van Hoven, her old sweetheart, and Dr. Smearbach visits. Gracie sings "Du Bist Mine Kleine Puppshen," with the studio audience joining in the third chorus.

R158 May 29, 1935
Gracie talks about her family; Dr. Smearbach comes to call; Gracie meets Ferde Grofe's wife; Horace Fenesvessy wants to get into broadcasting; there is a court room scene. Ferde has prepared a medley of "Crazy People," You're Driving Me Crazy," "Crazy Words for Broadcast" and "Where Were You On the Night of June the Third?".

R159 June 5, 1935
Dr. Smearbach returns; Gracie has wrecked Ferde's car; she has a new secretary; Gracie criticizes the orchestra; an architect brings some blueprints to Gracie. Featured song: "And Then Some."

R160 June 12, 1935
Gracie is drawing a picture for her "nephoo's" birthday; a man comes into the studio for tickets; Gracie wants to hear herself on the radio; there is some question as to whether George likes Gracie's new secretary; Gracie wants to make an appointment with the New York millionaire, Mortimer J. Van Patten, so her burglar brother can rob his house. Featured song: "I Want to be in Pictures."

R161 June 19, 1935
Dr. Smearbach; pie/cheese routine; Matzo Bara Kudie, a Japanese chauffeur, is looking for Gracie because he wants a job. Gracie and the octet sing "Latin from Manhattan."

R162 June 26, 1935
George and Gracie are playing a game called "lies"; Gracie says she has got to get more attention on the program--she has found out she is royalty and has green blood in her veins (Irish royalty); a fan appears with her boyfriend; Dr. Smearbach and Matzo visit; patter. Featured song: "His Majesty The Baby."

R163 July 3, 1935
Matzo is arrested for running over a street cleaner; Gracie talks about her family; Dr. Smearbach comes by; Gracie says that she is going to make up jokes. Gracie and George sing "Yankee Doodle Blues" with the octet.

R164 July 10, 1935
Gracie has changed her name to Dolly Johnson and George's to Sam Jones; she talks about her little blue hat; there is a message for Burns and Allen; Horace wants a favor; a man is looking for Gracie's grandfather; Dr. Smearbach comes to the studio. Featured song: "Lady in Red."

R165 July 17, 1935
Gracie has a new boyfriend who works at a service station. She blows George a kiss over the radio wires. Gracie talks about her granddaddy and her sister Hazel's forthcoming marriage. Gracie wants to be a telephone operator like her sister. Gladys Zell is introduced as Bill Goodwin's sweetheart. George and Gracie perform their "Pants On Backwards" routine. Featured song: "Coney Island."

R166 July 24, 1935
Stand up. Featured song: "You're An Eyeful of Heaven."

R167 July 31, 1935
Two stand up spots are capped by George and Gracie leaving California (the film season is over) and returning to New York by train. This year they were cast members of the films **Love in Bloom** (F25), **Here Comes Cookie** (F26) and **The Big Broadcast of 1936** (F27). Featured song: "It's The Animal In Me."

R168 August 7, 1935
George and Gracie had gotten as far as Tucson and were called back to Hollywood to shoot a few more scenes for **Here Comes Cookie** (F26) (Gracie thinks they are in New York). She has written a play and bought it from herself for five dollars. This is the last program with Bill Goodwin. Tonight's song is "That's What You Think."

R169 August 14, 1935 (New York, NY)
Bill Brenton joins the program as the new announcer. Reporters ask for the "lowdown" on Hollywood; Ferde's upset at being the butt of George's jokes; and Gracie's family has been evicted. Featured song: "Vamp Of The Pampas."

R170 August 21, 1935
The introduction features George in the control room and the announcer giving instructions to the audience and explaining the importance of laughter. Stand up; Mrs. Grofe visits. Featured song: "I Want To Learn To Speak Hawaiian."

R171 August 28, 1935
Stand up; Bill Brenton isn't feeling well. Featured song: "I Wish I Were Aladdin."

R172 September 4, 1935
Stand up; Dr. Snodgrass, another psychoanalyst, visits Bill, then Gracie. Featured song: "From The Top Of Your Head."

R173 September 11, 1935
Stand up. Joseph Rizzuto, a sales manager, tells how his doctor advised him to switch to White Owl Cigars. Featured song: "I'd Love To Take Orders From You."

R174 September 18, 1935
Stand up. Featured song: "Now You've Got Me Doin' It!"

R175 September 25, 1935
Stand up; a farewell to White Owl and General Cigar. Gracie orders bouquets for herself and pretends they've come from other people. An announcement is made that, beginning next Wednesday, they will be on another program over the same network. This is the last show with Ferde Grofe and Bill Brenton. Featured song: "I'm On A See-Saw."

4. Campbell's Tomato Juice Program. 1935-1937. CBS. 30 min.

Sponsor: Campbell Soup Company.
Product: Campbell Tomato Juice and Soups.
Network: CBS.
Broadcast Day: Wednesday.
Time Slot: 8:30-9:00 P.M. (Eastern Standard Time).
Scriptwriters: Carroll Carroll, Harvey Helm, John P. Medbury, William Burns.
Announcer: Ted Husing.
Orchestra Leader: Jacques (Jack) Renard.
Vocalist: Milton Watson.
Theme Song: "Campbells Are Coming."
Premise: "Mother Juice Rhymes" and play parodies are an integral part of this series of broadcasts. On quite a few occasions, Gracie mentions her "little blue hat," another phrase that will become closely connected to the show. Gracie's character starts falling in love with the program's vocalists. This "character trait" will ultimately cause a slip in the ratings of their later series as the audience, knowing that George and Gracie were a happily married couple in real life, became less willing to accept her fictitious flirtations.

Series Notes: For the duration of this series, the primary product emphasis switches back and forth from tomato juice to chicken soup, both products of the Campbell Soup Company.

R176 October 2, 1935
In their first show for Campbell's, George and Gracie meet the new cast and talk about Gracie's family; Gracie makes up a poem about Campbell's Tomato Juice. Featured song: "No Other One."

R177 October 9, 1935
George says, "We are on a new program, and we ought to do something new," so, of course, Gracie talks about her family; Ted Husing has kidded a girl about giving her a tryout on radio. Featured song: "I've Got A Feelin' You're Foolin'."

R178 October 16, 1935
Gracie talks about her family and George and Gracie talk about their appearance on the radio show, **Hollywood Hotel** (R822). Featured song: "The Milky Way."

R179 October 23, 1935
George has a fever and doesn't feel well; Ted Husing tells George that Jack Renard is mad at Gracie because she has been talking about his weight; Ted and George tell Jack to go to the gym and get some reducing records; Gracie has written herself a love note; and she and Milton Watson get into an argument. Featured song: "I Fell Asleep At The Football Game."

R180 October 30, 1935
A radio listener has been sending Gracie fruit; Gracie answers George's question and tells him she has three brothers, is kissing all the men in the band, and has made up games called "Tomato Juice"; Gracie is making Milton Watson angry (he is not romantically inclined toward her) and she wants to neck with Ted Husing. Featured song: "Sugar Plum."

R181 November 6, 1935
Gracie's brother wants Jack Renard to give him a job in the band; Gracie orders flowers, candy and theatre tickets from Milton Watson and sends him the bill; Ted Husing has written a book, **Mistakes While Broadcasting**. Featured song: "A Picture of Me Without You."

R182 November 13, 1935
Gracie wants Milton Watson to kiss her; she calls him "Miltie Wiltie," and he hates it; Gracie fell down and dirtied her dress but didn't have time to change it before the broadcast. Featured song: "Please Put On Your Wraps."

R183 November 20, 1935
Gracie talks about her sister and Jack Renard's sick friend; riddles; Gracie's brother is another topic of conversation; Milton Watson tells George he is in love; Gracie and her brother have made up a new language; Ted Husing has a girl he wants to try out on radio, but her husband shows up and is not happy. Gracie and George sing "Jack Robinson."

R184 November 27, 1935 (Cleveland, OH)
George and Gracie are at the Automobile Show and have an audience of 12,000 people; Gracie is hit while in Milton Watson's car; she has made up a game about the auto show. Featured song: "Top Of Your Head."

R185 December 4, 1935 (New York, NY)
George and Gracie talk about Thanksgiving last week at Gracie's and the dog show; Milton Watson met a girl in Cleveland and Gracie is upset; she talks about her brother. Featured song: "Twenty-Four Hours A Day."

R186 December 11, 1935
Gracie is now a member of the backwards club and says the opposite of what she wants to say; she wants to know why George always gets angry before she asks a question; a Mother Juice Rhyme; Gracie tells a girl looking for Milton Watson that she and "Miltie" are going to be married (her way of keeping it a secret); a doctor has been sent over by Campbell's to see what is wrong with Ted Husing. Featured song: "How'd Ya Like To Be A Little Birdie?"

R187 December 18, 1935
Gracie's sister and brother-in-law take medicine and go to the hospital for people who don't want to; Gracie wants to go ice skating; someone (Gracie) has stolen Milton Watson's photograph from his dressing room. George and Gracie sing "I Know How To Use The English Language."

R188 December 25, 1935
The Christmas show includes the songs "Lookie, Lookie, Lookie, Here Comes Cookie," "The Broken Record," a poem ("Twas The Nuts Before Christmas), and a play, **The Christmas Caramel**.

R189 January 1, 1936 (Minneapolis, MN)
Clellan Card announces tonight's show. Stand up; Ted Husing calls from New York; a Mother Juice Rhyme. Featured song: "I Feel Like A Feather In The Breeze."

R190 January 8, 1936 (Chicago, IL)
Truman Bradley is tonight's announcer. Stand up; a Mother Juice Rhyme. Gracie sings "Sugar Plum" with a little help from George.

R191 January 15, 1936 (New York, NY)
Ted Husing returns as the announcer. Stand up; a Paramount talent scout is considering Milton Watson for a part in a film; Gracie tries to help him by acting out the *Sadie Thompson* role in **Rain**, but only Jack Renard is chosen (he'll be the stand-in for a load of hay). Gracie mentions running for political office, Governess of the State of Coma. Tonight's show also features Jack Kling. Featured song: "How Do I Rate With You?" **SEE D175.**

R192 January 22, 1936 (Boston, MA)
Bill O'Connell from Boston takes Ted Husing's place tonight as the announcer. Stand up about things "Bostonian"; the cast acts out the story of John Alden, Miles Standish, and Priscilla; Jack Renard renews old Boston acquaintances when he's served with two subpoenas. Featured song: "I'm Building Up To An Awful Let-Down."

R193 January 29, 1936 (New York, NY)
George and Gracie talk about the orchestra and Jack Renard; Milton Watson brings in his vocal coach; Gracie brings in a dentist for George. Featured song: "Wake Up And Sing."

R194 February 5, 1936
George and Gracie celebrate their fourth anniversary in radio; Gracie says goodbye to Milton Watson; George and Gracie try to catch the train; Jack Renard and Milton are going with them. This is Ted Husing's last show. Featured song: "What's The Name Of That Song?" This is the last show broadcast from New York.

R195 February 12, 1936 (Hollywood, CA)
Stand up. Announcer Ken Niles joins the show. "Lookie, Lookie, Lookie, Here Comes Cookie" becomes the show's new theme show. Featured song: "Goody."

R196 February 19, 1936
Director Norman Taurog is listening to the broadcast, so the cast performs **Shanghai Gesture** to help Milton Watson, who is hoping to get a screen test. Featured song: "Kissing My Baby Good-night."

R197 February 26, 1936
Stand up; Gracie's family is discussed; Milton Watson's snobbish girlfriend visits, and Gracie is not pleased; later, he is "framed" for theft by his girlfriend and a man he thinks is a cop. Gracie faints and wakes up in time to do the program's sign off. Featured song: "You Hit The Spot."

R198 March 4, 1936
George and Gracie talk about horse racing; Gracie is planning to throw a party for the servants of Hollywood stars but doesn't tell Jack Renard or his wife that she's giving the party at their house. Gracie sings "I'm Dreamin' Crazy Dreams" and kisses a stranger, who does the program's sign off.

R199 March 11, 1936

A new recurring segment, a parody of Aesop's Fables, is introduced; Gracie has joined a poetry club and wants to dramatize **Hiawatha** so the cast obliges. Featured song: "Laughing Irish Eyes."

R200 March 18, 1936 (San Francisco, CA)
A prologue features three women discussing Gracie as a youngster; Gracie is happy to be back in her home town; Milton Watson tricks Gracie into getting rid of a girl for him; tonight's fable is the one about the fox, the crow and cheese; George tells Gracie about the new San Francisco Bay Bridge. Featured song: "I'm Building Up To An Awful Let-Down."

R201 March 25, 1936
The story of Christopher Columbus discovering America is dramatized; tonight's fable is about the dog and his reflection; Gracie recites a poem. Featured song: "Us On A Bus."

R202 April 1, 1936 (Hollywood, CA)
The tortoise and hare fable is retold; Gracie talks about her brother's wedding; Gracie gets Milton Watson in trouble when she thinks an income tax agent is a theatrical booking agent. Featured song: "I Feel So Spanish Tonight."

R203 April 8, 1936
Tonight's fable is about the golden goose; Gracie puts her Easter hat on George, brings rabbits to the studio and charges a mink to Mrs. Renard's account. Gracie sings, for the first time, a song written especially for her by Eddie Moran and Sammy Stept, "It's Double Talk For I Love You."

R204 April 15, 1936
"Dramatizations" become a staple of the show and continue for several months. **The Burning of Rome** is dramatized tonight. The fable about the grasshopper and ant receives the Gracie Allen treatment; Gracie explains Roman history to George. Featured song: "Meet The Future President."

R205 April 22, 1936
Gracie talks about the sleep habits of the men in her family; a representative from the musicians' union visits Jack Renard to get him to pay his dues; a Mother Juice Rhyme; Gracie decides to start a union for housewives. Featured song: "It's Been So Long."

R206 April 29, 1936
Membership in the Housewives' Union is growing; Gracie asks George to interpret a dream; Gracie recites another Mother Juice Rhyme; a letter from comedian Ed Wynn arrives. Featured song: "It's You I'm Talkin' About."

R207 May 6, 1936
Gracie talks about her family; her nephew's teacher visits the broadcast; the cast dramatizes **The Private Life of Mrs. Paul Revere**. Featured song: "A Little Robin Told Me So."

R208 May 13, 1936
Gracie talks about her aunt and recites a Mother Juice Rhyme; Jack Renard is having a life insurance examination; a process server arrives to see Gracie, Jack and Milton Watson about an auto accident they were involved in. George and Gracie are awarded **Radio Guide Weekly**'s medal "For Outstanding Merit"; Ken Niles reads a telegram from Curtis Mitchell, editor of the magazine. Featured song: "Too Good To Be True."

R209 May 20, 1936
Gracie tells George about an experience she had today, then tries to tell him a joke; Jack Renard wants to get into pictures; the Housewives' Union is having a parade; Gracie gets Jack into trouble with his wife.

R210 May 27, 1936
Gracie's dressmaker brings her a dress like Joan Crawford's; another famous event in history, the story of Adam and Eve, is dramatized. Featured song: "Telegram Song."

R211 June 3, 1936
Once again it's Gracie's night as she describes a fight her brother got into, buys a book of new slang expressions, is jealous of Milton Watson's

new girlfriend, explains the object of the Housewives' Union and sings "And Still No Luck With You."

R212 June 10, 1936
Gracie wants to be a roving reporter, so she has Milton Watson and Ken Niles bring people up from the audience for her to interview; Gracie has realized that she's president of the Housewives' Union but can't be a housewife without a husband, so she's hired a fortune teller to visit Milton and convince him to marry her. Featured song: "Meet The Family."

R213 June 17, 1936
Gracie can only talk backward; inspired by her brother's graduation, she awards diplomas to the cast; the life of Mrs. Robinson Crusoe is dramatized. Featured song: "Do You Or Don't You Love Me?"

R214 June 24, 1936
Tonight the Housewives' Union holds its convention to nominate its candidate for the November election; the film **The Big Broadcast of 1937** (F28) is a topic of discussion. Featured song: "Cross Patch."

R215 July 1, 1936
Gracie invites the audience to come up and entertain the cast. She has written a poem to say goodbye to Milton Watson, who is leaving the program for Broadway, and for Jack Renard, who is preparing to tour the country with his band. Featured song: "Is It True What They Say About Dixie?"

R216 July 8, 1936
Eddy Duchin and Jimmy Newell are introduced as the new orchestra leader and new vocalist, respectively. Upon meeting Jimmy Gracie declares that Milton Watson meant nothing to her. A new spot, "I Always Say" (described by George as Gracie's "foolosophy"), is introduced. This is also the name given to the cartoon based on the "Gracie" character which is distributed by King Features and printed in newspapers across the country for a number of months. Featured song: "I'll Never Let You Go."

R217 July 15, 1936
In their opening stand up routine, George and Gracie talk about the Brown Derby Restaurant; Gracie's aunt has been in an accident; tonight's dramatization is **The Private Life of Napoleon's Wife, Josephine**; "I Always Say" concerns a congressman. Featured song: "Gotta Dance My Way To Heaven In Your Arms."

R218 July 22, 1936
Gracie's daddy has robbed a bank; Jimmy Newell can't rest because his house is still being finished; George and Gracie talk about her nephew; Dr. Brockenfurst, Eddy Duchin's old music teacher from Vienna, arrives; Gracie has another "I Always Say." Featured song: "Why Do I Lie To Myself About You?"

R219 July 29, 1936
Tonight's routines: George asks Gracie a riddle and if her nurse dropped her when she was a baby; Jimmy Newell and Eddy Duchin trade compliments; fan mail; two song pluggers interrupt the program; Gracie talks about her father; Gracie explains the art of songwriting to Jimmy; the subject of tonight's "I Always Say" is war. Featured song: "Swing Me High, Swing Me Low."

R220 August 5, 1936
Gracie celebrates Jimmy Newell and Eddy Duchin being on the show for five weeks by giving George's watch to Eddy and his wallet to Jimmy and throwing a party for them; in Eddy and Jimmy's honor Gracie has dramatized the private lives of the wives of Henry the Eighth; the "I Always Say" topic is the wolf at the door. Featured song: "It Ain't Rite."

R221 August 12, 1936
Gracie talks about her school days; a friend, Elvia, introduces her son, Rollo, who has decided to go into radio as a singer; Gracie has made up a new game called "Mouthies"; Rollo is missing; "I Always Say" centers on pessimists, optimists and doughnuts. Featured song: "The Girl In The Garden."

R222 August 19, 1936

Gracie is going to be a bridesmaid at her friend's wedding; Rollo stops by the studio; Gracie has another "Mouthie" and another "I Always Say." Featured song: "You Turned The Tables On Me."

R223 August 26, 1936
Gracie questions George about the way he opens the program every week; George tries to explain the phrase "I bring the ducks" to Gracie; Jimmy Newell is late for the program; tonight's play is **The Private Life of Sir Walter Raleigh**; and tonight's "I Always Say" subjects are parting, sadness and baldheadedness. Eddy Duchin is leaving the program to play some dates in the East. Featured song: "Bye Baby."

R224 September 2, 1936
Henry King is introduced by George as the new band leader. (King, who was in San Francisco six days a week, only came to Hollywood for the show's broadcasts). Every time George tries to introduce Henry to Gracie she changes the subject; everyone tells how he got his start in show business; Jimmy Newell wants to take Henry out and show him Hollywood. Featured song: "This Is A Fine Romance."

R225 September 9, 1936
Ken Niles needs a $50 loan to pay for a C.O.D.; Jimmy Newell's snooty new girlfriend comes to the studio; the topic of tonight's "I Always Say" is fountain pens. Featured song: "Ta Hu Wa Ha Wai."

R226 September 16, 1936
Dick Powell and Frances Langford substitute for George and Gracie this week due to Gracie's illness. The program ends with a "telegram" from Gracie.

R227 September 23, 1936
George and Gracie thank Frances Langford and Dick Powell for filling in for them last week; Gracie has a new game called "Answer Answer...Who's Got The Question?"; **The Private Life of Mrs. Jesse James** is dramatized. Featured song: "Sing Baby Sing."

R228 September 30, 1936
Ken Niles spends the entire half hour trying to tell a joke but Gracie keeps interrupting him; a man applies for the position of Henry King's valet; Gracie gives the valet instructions. Featured song: "Talking Through My Heart."

R229 October 7, 1936
Henry King introduces Jolly Joe Klotzman, "The World's Greatest Comedian," who has been writing jokes for him and wants to write the Burns and Allen program; tonight's "I Always Say" is about brains and good looks. Featured song: "Coney Island."

R230 October 14, 1936
Gracie talks about the male drinkers in her family and is upset with Henry King because he wouldn't give her brother a job in his band; tonight's play spoofs **Lucretia Borgia**. Featured song: "You Do The Darndest Things Baby."

R231 October 21, 1936
The cast talks again about **The Big Broadcast of 1937** (F28), and Gracie talks about her family; a woman is suing Jimmy Newell for $150,000 for breach of promise; raining pitchforks is the subject of Gracie's "Mouthie"; tonight George asks Gracie to say good night to everybody. Featured song: "Tea On The Terrace."

R232 October 28, 1936
This is the first show in which George acts the part of Master of Ceremonies. Stand up routines include Gracie's family and football; the cast honors the city of Brooklyn; and Jack Benny is the subject of "I Always Say." Featured song: "Sing Baby Sing."

R233 November 4, 1936
Yesterday's Presidential election is tonight's topic of conversation; Ken Niles and Jimmy Newell have to pay off election bets; Jimmy's girlfriend visits.

R234 November 11, 1936

Gracie asks for autographs for her brother, who is learning to be a forger; they talk about Armistice Day, have breakfast at Gracie's house and dramatize Gracie's play, **William Tell**. Featured song: "De-Lovely."

R235 November 18, 1936
The city of Chicago is honored; Gracie talks about a pussy cat born in October (an "Octopussy"); telegrams arrive from Chicago; the Blue Law is discussed; Jimmy Newell has met twin sisters from Chicago. This is the last show for Jimmy Newell, who is leaving to make a film.

R236 November 25, 1936
Tony Martin joins as the program's vocalist. Gracie thinks Jimmy Newell walked out on her; Gracie says Tony will be judged by his kissing, not his singing, because he's the romantic type; Gracie kisses Henry King, Ken Niles and George; she has written a play about the pilgrims titled **The Landing of the Indians**. Featured song: "With Plenty of Money and You."

R237 December 2, 1936
Henry King and Ken Niles talk about Ken's mustache; Tony Martin is late; Gracie and Tony act out a love scene. Featured song: "Now That Summer Is Gone."

R238 December 9, 1936
New Orleans is chosen as the city of honor; Tony Martin has a date with Alice Faye, and Gracie tries to bribe him by hinting she may take him off the program--she hires and fires the singers. Gracie ends the show with the line "Goodnight, everybody". Featured song: "My Sugar Takes Me With A Grain of Salt."

R239 December 16, 1936
Gracie kisses George and pretends she is kissing Tony Martin; they play a game which uses letters of the alphabet and dramatize the life of Pancho Villa. Featured song: "When Reuben Swings The Cuban." Although the Mexican embassy in Washington, D.C. reportedly "professed ignorance of the incident," a January 26, 1937 newspaper article stated that "some one" in the Mexican embassy protested against this broadcast because of its reference to Pancho Villa, claiming it "insulted" the Mexican government. A CBS executive in Washington referred the matter to the network's commercial editor, Gilson Gray, who in turn forwarded the complaint to Burns and Allen to "handle as they saw fit." Gray stated that he understood George and Gracie "had arranged to send a personal apology to the embassy." Whether they did or not is unknown.

R240 December 23, 1936
Gracie flirts with Tony; she decides to do her Christmas shopping after Christmas so she will know what her friends wanted as presents; the cast performs **A Christmas Carol**. Featured song: "I Love You From Coast to Coast." **SEE D223, D288.**

R241 December 30, 1936 (New York, NY)
George and Gracie are back in New York (for a ten day vacation) after being away for a year; a reporter wants to interview Gracie since he has heard she is going to marry Tony Martin; actors from the Friars Club come up to visit; George and Gracie have been working on the films **The Big Broadcast of 1937** (F28) and **College Holiday** (F29). Featured song: "De Lovely."

R242 January 6, 1937
Gracie has a new resolution; the group is leaving for Hollywood tomorrow; Gracie is going to give New Yorkers her recipe for Hollywood sweetie pie; they do a play on actors' names and food and engage in backward talk. Featured song: "Plenty of Money and You."

R243 January 13, 1937 (Hollywood, CA)
After spending ten days in New York, Gracie is too tired to answer anyone's questions; they honor the city of Los Angeles tonight; Gracie fires George and Henry King. Featured song: "Never Should Have Told You."

R244 January 20, 1937
Henry King has just been married; George wants Gracie and Tony Martin to make up; Gracie gives out parts for her play, **Samson and Delilah**. Featured song: "Love And Learn."

R245 January 27, 1937
Gracie has had badges printed for the cast so the audience that does not have radio will know who everyone is; Gracie wishes Tony Martin would take her home after the broadcast. Featured song: "Nephew From Nice."

R246 February 3, 1937
The cast re-writes and performs a war play based on the radio program **Hollywood Hotel** with Gracie in a dual role. Featured song: "Ridin' High."

R247 February 10, 1937
The sound man keeps missing his cues; a gentleman formerly with the BBC drops in to have a "go" at the American wireless system. It's announced that the Hearst Radio Editors Poll of 1936 has resulted in Gracie being chosen as the year's most popular comedienne and that Burns and Allen are the year's most popular radio team.

R248 February 17, 1937
On George and Gracie's fifth anniversary of being on the air, they reminisce about their start on radio and about looking for Gracie's brother on other programs. Lynn Hayes and Dave Webber are credited with recreating the voices of Eddie Cantor, Rudy Vallee, Walter Winchell, Fred Allen, Joe Penner, Singing Sam and Ben Bernie. Gracie introduces Pinky Tomlin's new song, "The Love Bug Will Bite You If You Don't Look Out."

R249 February 24, 1937
Gracie tells George about her brother's invention to keep people from running into telephone poles; Henry King celebrates his eight week wedding anniversary; **The Three Musketeers Who'd Gladly Swing For Wine, (And) Women, (And) Henry King** is performed by the Gracie Allen Shock Company. Featured song: "Gee But You're Swell."

R250 March 3, 1937
Gracie pays homage to the "city" of Alaska and sings "You Can't Take It With You."

R251 March 10, 1937
The cast is in unusually good spirits, and Gracie thinks it's the flu; she sings a few numbers (1-17) then sends herself a telegram in honor of a new holiday, "Yourself Day," and gets a phone call from her parents; George tries to tell the audience about **Dulcy**, a play he and Gracie are scheduled to appear in on the Lux Radio Theater in late March (R838); Henry King wants to buy his wife jewelry for her birthday, and Tony Martin offers some pieces he has for sale. Featured song: "Strongest Weakness."

R252 March 17, 1937
The stand up routines include talk about things Irish in honor of St. Patrick's Day; the Gracie Allen Shock Company's most recent production is **The Private Life of Ponce de Leon**. Featured song: "Laughing Irish Eyes."

R253 March 24, 1937
George and Gracie say farewell to the Campbell show and to the cast. Henry King is going to the Palmer House in Chicago for an indefinite engagement, and Ken Niles is staying on as the announcer for the new **Campbell's Tomato Juice Program** which will feature Ken Murray, Oswald, Shirley Ross and the Lud Gluskin Orchestra; Gracie says she "doesn't mind" losing Henry, Ken, Campbell's Tomato Juice or CBS, but she does mind losing Tony Martin (actually, he eventually goes to the new program with them); they receive a telegram from the sponsor along with an engraved silver tray; it's announced that Burns and Allen will begin a new program for Grape-Nuts two weeks from Monday on another network; the program includes a promotional spot for their appearance in **Dulcy** next Monday on the **Lux Radio Theater** (R838). Featured song: "Let's Call The Whole Thing Off."

5. The Grape-Nuts Program. 1937-1938. NBC Red. 30 min.

Sponsor: General Foods Corporation.
Product: Grape-Nuts Cereal.
Agency: Young and Rubicam, Inc.
Network: NBC Red. (Eastern Standard Time).
Broadcast Day: Monday.
Time Slot: 8:00-8:30 P.M.
Production: Everard Meade.

Scriptwriters: John P. Medbury, William Burns.
Announcer: Ronald Drake.
Orchestra Leader: Ray Noble.
Vocalist: Dick Foran.
Premise: Very little structural changes are noticeable in this new show. Gracie is still chasing the unattached men in the cast, and the announcer, orchestra leader, and vocalist remain highly-developed and prominent members of that cast. A new feature is inaugurated, "Grape Mome-Nuts from History," and George and Gracie are referred to by the announcer as "those two Grape-*Nuts*, George Burns and Gracie Allen."
Additional Notes: Ray Noble came to America in 1934 after a number of band recordings he made in his native England became hits stateside, requiring him to make personal appearances here. Glenn Miller put together a band for Noble, who was also a notable songwriter. In fact, he wrote his band's theme song, "The Very Thought of You." The group became the featured entertainment at New York City's famed Rainbow Room for a little more than two seasons before Noble left New York for Hollywood and the life of a musical director in radio. He had a definite persona, "both vague and charming," but, like Gracie, it was an act, and he was an astute businessman. He did leave the country for a time, but eventually returned to Santa Barbara, where he died in 1977. **SEE B421.**

R254 April 12, 1937 (Hollywood, CA)
Gracie meets all the new members of their show for Grape-Nuts and confuses Foran, Noble and Drake with King, Martin and Niles from the previous series; George and Gracie receive telegrams from various radio personalities, including Jack Benny, Al Jolson and Eddie Cantor. Featured song: "Cause My Baby Says It's So."

Review: "In the case of Burns and Allen General Foods has acquired an act which is as much a staple article in radio as it was two to three years ago." (**Variety**, April 14, 1937: 38).

R255 April 19, 1937
George tells Gracie to say hello; Gracie has a poem, "Grape Nutsery Rhyme"; they're going to perform a play, **Pretty Predicament of Poor Picadilly Pete** or **Lady Windamere Trying To Choose Between Three Lovers**. Gracie sings "I'm Bubbling Over" from the Twentieth Century-Fox Film **Wake Up And Live**.

R256 April 26, 1937
Gracie's brother thinks he's a ghost; her mother phones; Gracie wants Dick Foran to give her a kiss then tries to get him to marry her. Gracie sings "Let's Call the Whole Thing Off" from the 1937 RKO picture **Shall We Dance?**

R257 May 3, 1937
George asks Gracie to say hello to everybody; Ronald Drake has a new suit, and Gracie reminds Dick Foran that they are engaged; Gracie does an ad for Jell-O; one of Ray Noble's friends visits the studio. Featured song: "I'm Hatin' This Waitin' Around."

R258 May 10, 1937
Dick Foran is complaining to George about Gracie saying they're engaged; George makes a suggestion on how to discourage her but Gracie overhears them talking; George tries to tell a story and Gracie keeps interrupting him; Ray Noble's friend's wife annoys George. Featured song: "Wake Up and Live."

R259 May 17, 1937
Gracie wants to open the program differently; she's mad at Dick Foran; they get a phone call that Ray Noble's friends have been in an auto accident. Featured song: "While You're Dancing The Espagnole."

R260 May 24, 1937
Gracie's brother says hello; Gracie wants Dick Foran to marry her.

R261 May 31, 1937
Gracie talks to Ray Noble's friend, who is coming to the studio, but cannot understand a word he says. Featured song: "Way Out West."

R262 June 7, 1937

Herman the dog makes an appearance; Dick Foran invites George and Gracie over to a wienie roast at his ranch; Dick will be leaving the program for a few weeks while he does a picture for Warner Bros.; Gracie's dog bites and everyone encourages her to get him a muzzle. Featured song: "Little Old Fashioned Lady."

R263 June 14, 1937
Tony Martin returns to the cast as the featured vocalist after a three month absence. George tries to get Gracie to say "hello, everybody"; Tony gives Gracie a kiss but she doesn't remember him; Gracie talks about her daddy; she has written a poem in honor of Tony Martin; Mr. Finnigan of **Radio Guide** has come to interview Tony.

R264 June 21, 1937
Tony Martin is going to the Louis-Braddock fight and everyone bets on the match; Gracie answers the phone and it's her mother telling her that her nephew has a new job as assistant to an ostrich; Tony's singing teacher comes by to give voice lessons; Gracie asks her mother if she liked the show; a man comes to take out the phone.

R265 June 28, 1937
Tony Martin sings a Ray Noble composition, "The Very Thought of You"; "Grape Mome-Nuts From History" is the first installment of **A Certain Night In The Private Life Of The Wife Of Robin Hood**. Featured song: "Pancho's Widow."

R266 July 5, 1937
Stand up routines feature Gracie and the elevator man, Independence Day, out-of-work (for the summer) radio actors looking for work on the Burns and Allen show and part two of **Robin Hood**. Guest star Charles (Charlie) Winninger appears to promote his radio show for Maxwell House. George sings "Ain't Misbehavin'."

R267 July 12, 1937
An executive from Paramount, who has confused George and Gracie with John Barrymore and Elaine Barrie) is coming over to discuss purchasing the rights to **Robin Hood**.

R268 July 19, 1937
Stand up routines include Gracie's claims to have been practicing to be a ventriloquist, her brother and nudist camps; Tony Martin is in trouble with the brother of the waitress who works across the street from the studio; Gracie asks Tony to introduce them to Alice Faye; and tonight is the conclusion of **Robin Hood**.

R269 July 26, 1937
The cast talks about the new RKO film, **A Damsel in Distress** (F30), in which George, Gracie and Ray Noble appear with Fred Astaire; the film's director compliments everyone in the cast except George; Gracie has decided to change her name to "Ginger" Allen in honor of Astaire's former dance partner; Gracie is producing a new musical, **The Robin Hood Follies of 1937**, and has hired **Damsel**'s dance director (Hermes Pan) to take the reins of her production; it's Gracie's birthday (in real life) and everyone sings "Happy Birthday" to her. Special guest: Hermes Pan.

R270 August 2, 1937
Gracie is still only answering to the name "Ginger"; Ronald Drake, disappointed not to have been in **A Damsel in Distress** (F30) has disappeared; the songwriters Gracie hired for her musical drop by; Gracie rehearses another love scene.

R271 August 9, 1937
Gracie talks about her father; Tony Martin plugs Paramount Pictures; the songwriters return; Gracie tells a wild tale in the life of her brother and has hired a Frenchman to produce her musical. One of the program's commercials explains the history of Grape-Nuts.

R272 August 16, 1937
Ronald Drake is still unhappy he was left out of the cast of George and Gracie's latest film; a modiste arrives to take costume measurements for Gracie's new musical; Gracie describes her brother's new musical instrument to Ray Noble; Gracie does an imitation of Jack Benny; the French producer drops by. Featured song: "Happy Birthday To Love."

R273 August 23, 1937
Stand up routines include Gracie going out after the broadcast and comparisons being made between Tony Martin and Franchot Tone; Fanny and Annie, chorus girls, come by to inquire about jobs in **The Robin Hood Follies of 1937**. Featured song: "Have You Got Any Castles, Baby?"

R274 August 30, 1937
Stand up; Gracie abandons **The Robin Hood Follies of 1937** since she found out she couldn't get the real Robin Hood to play the part but has an idea for a new musical, **Miss Gracie Goes To Town**, a ballet to be performed underwater. Featured song: "Vieni."

R275 September 6, 1937
This Labor Day broadcast includes Ronald Drake having a screen test at Twentieth Century-Fox; Tony Martin has married Alice Faye; Gracie talks to a banker about a $50,000 loan for her new musical and explains the "Animal Interlude" portion of **Miss Gracie Goes To Town**. Featured song: "I Want It Sweet Like You."

R276 September 13, 1937
Gracie talks about her nephew; Tony Martin talks about his marriage to Alice Faye; Gracie gives out her recipe for duck and explains "The Glamorous Garden Spectacle" portion of **Miss Gracie Goes To Town**. Featured song: "How'd Ya Learn How."

R277 September 20, 1937
Stand up; Tony Martin wants a raise now that he's married and has responsibilities; Gracie thinks banks should hold theater nights and get even with theaters; she's having trouble with "The Ballet of Birds" portion of her play.

R278 September 27, 1937
Stand up; Tony Martin calls Alice; Gracie talks to Alice and finds out she's expecting a "visitor"; Gracie needs four comedians for her play; her nephew's school teacher comes by to tell Gracie about the problems she is having with the child; **Miss Gracie Goes To Town** concludes with "Fruit and Vegetable Extravaganza." Featured song: "Stop! You're Breaking My Heart."

R279 October 4, 1937
The last broadcast before George and Gracie's New York vacation is played against the backdrop of trying to get packed and a rush to catch the train, complicated by the fact that Gracie has sold their tickets to her brother for thirty dollars in stage money. Ronald Drake is leaving the program, but Ray Noble and Tony Martin will stay on with the show's substitutes for the next four weeks. Ronald announces two new programs being sponsored by General Foods, **Believe It Or Not** and a show for Log Cabin Syrup starring Jack Haley. Featured song: "I Want To See Some More Of Samoa."

R280 October 11, 1937
Bob Burns and His Bazooka substitute.

R281 October 18, 1937
Phil Baker with Beetle and Bottle substitute.

R282 October 25, 1937
Eddie Cantor substitutes.

R283 November 1, 1937
Al Jolson and Ruby Keeler substitute.

R284 November 8, 1937
George and Gracie return from vacation; Tony Martin has grown a moustache for a new film; George wonders if there is any news about his **A Damsel in Distress** (F30) reviews and introduces John Conte, who has become the new announcer during their vacation; John asks Gracie what impressed her the most during her trip to New York; George finds out Al Jolson doubled everyone's salary while he was gone and, when George tells them they can't have it, they retaliate by refusing to talk to him; Gracie receives a phone call from her mother; George wanted to bring back gifts to everyone and had given the money to Gracie; George and Gracie thank those who filled in for them during their absence. Gracie sings "Stiff Upper Lip" from **A Damsel in Distress** (F30).

R285 November 15, 1937
Tony Martin, Ray Noble, and John Conte went to the preview of **A Damsel in Distress** (F30); Tony and John compliment George's acting so he will give them a raise; George asks an audience member to decide if the boys should be given a raise; Gracie wants John to take her out; the boys do go out--on strike. Gracie sings "Nice Work If You Can Get It" from **A Damsel in Distress** (F30).

R286 November 22, 1937
George and Gracie talk about Thanksgiving, a concept lost on Englishman Ray Noble, so George tries to explain it to him; Tony Martin tries in vain to tell George that someone has stolen George's overcoat but George refuses to listen because he thinks Tony is still trying to ask for a raise; Gracie pleads with the audience to buy more Grape-Nuts so John Conte can get a raise, buy a car and take her out; Gracie has written a play in honor of Thanksgiving, **Who Picked The Feathers Off The Plymouth Rock?** Featured song: "Rosalie."

R287 November 29, 1937
Gracie talks about superstition (and how her father invented it) and advises Tony Martin on how to get a raise; when she receives a telegram from her daddy she gives him a birthday party over the radio. Featured song: "Bob White."

R288 December 6, 1937
George announces their new film, **College Swing** (F31); Tony Martin still wants a raise; Gracie asks John Conte to rehearse her love scene from the film; Gracie's mother calls; an inmate from an insane asylum has escaped; the asylum keeper takes Tony with him. Featured song: "My Fine Feathered Friend."

R289 December 13, 1937
An upset Tony Martin returns from three days in the asylum and all (except Gracie) agree not to mention it; Gracie has written a play, **Big Moments From The Private Life Of Queen Elizabeth**. Featured song: "You Can't Stop Me From Dreaming."

R290 December 20, 1937
Gracie reveals her mother's recipe for plum pudding; Dr. Smearbach, who treated Tony Martin in the asylum, visits; George and Gracie wish everyone a Merry Christmas. Featured song: "Why Do Hawaiians Sing Aloha?"

R291 December 27, 1937
Gracie thanks George for the Christmas present he didn't give her so he knows how happy she *would* have been; Gracie gave John Conte George's watch for Christmas; Tony Martin is embarrassed about the ribbing he's been receiving from his friends about being in the asylum so Gracie tries not to mention the word "asylum"; Gracie has written another play, **Murdered In A Phone Booth** or **Your Party Has Been Disconnected**, which begins a new recurring segment as Gracie "writes" more murder mysteries.

R292 January 3, 1938
George and Gracie are interviewed by Radio Guide on what they consider to be the ten most important events of 1937; Gracie's new mystery is **Murdered On A Street Car**; routines include Clark Gable and the Rose Bowl Game. Featured song: "I'm Like A Fish Out of Water."

R293 January 10, 1938
Gracie plugs their new film, **College Swing** (F31), mentioning everyone but George; Tony Martin hires a secretary to answer his fan mail and Gracie tries to remember where she has seen him before; Gracie's new murder mystery is **Slay It With Music** or **Death Begins At Eight Dollars and Forty Cents** and she has brought in a professional screamer to help out; George and Gracie are in a hurry to see **A Damsel in Distress** (F30) at the Pantages Theater. Featured song: "Bei Mir Bist Du Schön."

R294 January 17, 1938
George tries to explain expressions and customs to Gracie; Tony Martin extolls the virtues of his health club and encourages George to become a member; Gracie receives a phone call from her mother; Gracie has changed the title of her play to **The Case of the Empty Watch** or **Give 'Em The Works**, which includes a "musical" number, "The Fantasy of the Cities," an elaborate routine of puns drawn from names of cities, towns and states.

John Conte asks the audience to send ten cents to President Roosevelt to help fight infantile paralysis (the campaign known as The March of Dimes). Featured song: "I Double Dare You."

R295 January 24, 1938
John Conte and Tony Martin talk about being at the race track on Sunday; Gracie has a system for picking losers and credits herself for the Dale Carnegie system; she also has a new pet, a parrot named Rufus; the new murder mystery is **A Killing On The Stock Exchange** or **It's A Wise Stock That Knows Its Own Par**. Featured song: "Ten Pretty Girls."

R296 January 31, 1938
Gracie brings her pet to the broadcast; Boy Scout Week is saluted; Gracie explains the problems of a classic poem to Tony Martin. Featured song: "Sweet Stranger."

R297 February 7, 1938
Gracie tries to interest a disinterested George in a riddle; Ray Noble tries to improve the program; Gracie addresses "The Women of America"; tonight's murder mystery is **Death In The Dog Pound** or **Well, Dog Gone!**; John Conte reads a wire from Ralph Starr Butler, the vice president in charge of advertising for General Foods, who congratulates George and Gracie on their selection by the radio editors of Hearst newspapers as the leading comedy team of the air and Gracie as radio's leading comedienne. Featured song: "Things Are Looking Up."

R298 February 14, 1938
George and Gracie talk about Valentine's Day; Gracie's parrot is causing problems in the lobby; the broadcast studio's Information Desk girl has a crush on George; Gracie tells how her daddy won a poll and sends herself a valentine from John Conte. Gracie introduces the song "You're A Natural" from **College Swing** (F31).

Review: "We discovered that Miss Allen was up to genuinely comic antics and had abandoned that wanting a kiss routine..." (**New York Post**, February 15, 1938).

R299 February 21, 1938
George explains the importance of George Washington's birthday to Gracie and thinks everyone should pay homage tonight by telling the truth; Gracie's mother sends a census taker (who becomes a recurring character for several broadcasts) to see Gracie; Gracie's new play is **Murdered In A Lunch Wagon** or **Cold Cuts A La Carte**. Featured song: "Shenanigans."

R300 February 28, 1938
Gracie has purchased a portable x-ray machine; she invites Tony Martin to join her club; Gracie sings "How'd Ja Like To Love Me?" from **College Swing** (F31). John Conte announces that two new General Foods programs, **Lum and Abner** for Postum coffee and another starring commentator Boake Carter for Huskies will begin this week.

R301 March 7, 1938
Gracie announces that she's going to become a commentator and is inspired to write a series of new plays centering on women. Her first attempt: **Mrs. Little Caesar**. Gracie sings "What A Rhumba Does To Romance" from **College Swing** (F31). John Conte gives the recipe for hot Grape-Nuts.

R302 March 14, 1938
Gracie thinks there should be more holidays; her new play is **Mrs. Wells Fargo**. Featured song: "You're An Education."

R303 March 21, 1938
Gracie is working for the Los Angeles Chamber of Commerce; her play is **Mrs. Captains Corsages** (as opposed to "Courageous"). Featured song: "Ti-Pi-Tin." After this show was broadcast the author of "Ti-Pi-Tin" (Maria Grever) sent George and Gracie a telegram thanking them for the "wonderful interpretation of her song."

R304 March 28, 1938
Gracie's family is having problems with the house they bought through the mail; the orchestra plays "George & Gracie Swing"; Ray Noble is leaving for vacation and it's announced that Jan Garber will fill in; Gracie salutes their orchestra leader with **The Life of Raymond Noble**, a tribute

interspersed with events in American history; Tony Martin tries to explain throughout the program why he's late again. Featured song: "Ten Pretty Girls."

R305 April 4, 1938
George introduces the new orchestra leader, Jan Garber. The show celebrates its first anniversary for Grape-Nuts; Gracie's new play is **Mrs Good Earth**. George and John Conte do the closing commercial for Grape-Nuts, and John thanks the audience for its loyalty to the program sponsor's product. Featured song: "Sissy."

R306 April 11, 1938
Gracie is making up new laws; Jan Garber talks about his mottos in life; the census taker is still making appearances; Gracie has a new publication, **Gracie Allen's Microphoney Magazine**; Gracie and John Conte work in a spot for Grape-Nuts in which she makes him repeat the words "deliciously nutritious" four times because she likes to watch his Adam's apple move up and down. Featured song: "Couldn't Be Cuter."

R307 April 18, 1938
George and Gracie talk about yesterday having been Easter Sunday including how her family waited for the Easter Bunny to come down the chimney; Tony Martin "accidentally" left on a boat to Honolulu while seeing his wife off on a trip so Frank Parker (who is usually on **Hollywood Hotel**) will be filling in as the program's vocalist; George and Gracie perform the routine in which her brother is held up by two men; Gracie has made arrangements for everyone to go (right now) to the premiere of **College Swing** (F31) at the Paramount Theater, but the entire experience is a disaster; a telegram arrives from Tony. By special request, Gracie gives an encore performance of "Ti-Pi-Tin."

R308 April 25, 1938
Gracie thinks everybody should have a side line and that people involved in the film industry should have side lines that fit their names (for example, "Carole Lumber" and "All-Day Zukors); Gracie's play is **Mrs. Marco Polo**. Featured song: "Where Have We Met Before."

R309 May 2, 1938
Gracie talks about May Day and tries to make John Conte jealous; Frank Parker's life is dramatized in honor of Tony Martin returning next week; a waiter to whom Frank owes forty cents is looking for him. "Josephine" is the song. Guest star: Benny Rubin.

R310 May 9, 1938
Gracie wants to surprise Tony Martin when he arrives at the studio; Tony now "speaks" Hawaiian; Gracie has a telephone conversation with her mother about Grape-Nuts; Tony tries to show some home movies from his vacation. Gracie introduces the song "Hold On To Your Heart (Here We Go Again!)" to the radio audience.

R311 May 16, 1938
Gracie announces she has something to say; Tony Martin brought Gracie a ukelele from Hawaii and she tries to tune it up by playing "My Dog Has Fleas"; George throws the instrument out the window but it's returned by a passerby; Tony brings Alice's first cake to the studio and Gracie sings it a lullaby; **Mrs. Twentieth Century Limited** is performed. Featured song: "Crooner's Lullaby."

R312 May 23, 1938
Gracie has finally learned a song on the ukelele and offers to teach John Conte how to play but discovers it's missing again; Tony Martin's new friends from Honolulu, the Van Eatons, stop by for a visit; an Inspector arrives to investigate the theft of the ukelele. John Conte introduces a new product, Grape-Nuts Flakes. Featured song: "Says My Heart."

R313 May 30, 1938
Gracie brings a copy of **Time** magazine to the studio and provides a running commentary on the pictures and items; Tony Martin has purchased a new camera and dark room; the Van Eatons return; the Inspector returns to find the watch he lost last week while searching for the ukelele. Featured song: "Alexander's Ragtime Band."

R314 June 6, 1938

Gracie has been learning proper etiquette in anticipation of her attendance at a formal dinner party that evening. George offers to rehearse with her to calm her nerves. Featured song: "Natch'rally."

R315 June 13, 1938
Gracie's niece, Jeannie, is graduating from grammar school this evening and the principal asks Gracie to give out the diplomas and make a speech; Tony Martin is testing against Tyrone Power for a role in the film **Carmen**. Featured song: "Who Do You Think I Saw Last Night?"

R316 June 20, 1938
Talk turns to dreams and Gracie's family; Gracie tells about dreaming of Clark Gable and her dream club; Jan Garber's wife pays a visit. Featured song: "The Cute Little Hat Check Girl."

R317 June 27, 1938
George and Gracie talk about the surprise birthday party she gave for Mary Livingstone; this is Jan Garber's last broadcast because he is going on an extended tour so Gracie dramatizes **The Life of Jan Garber**; it's announced that Glen Gray and his Casa Loma Orchestra will be with them next week. In a repeat performance by special request, Gracie sings "Where Have We Met Before?"

R318 July 4, 1938
George introduces Glen Gray and the Casa Loma Orchestra, which includes two vocalists, Pee-Wee Hunt and Kenny Sargent, who want to hear all about Alice Faye from Tony Martin; Gracie does her new play, **Daughter of the Sheik** or **Til the Sands in the Spinach Grow Cold**, in honor of Glen joining the program on the Fourth of July. Featured song: "What Do You Hear From The Mob In Scotland?"

R319 July 11, 1938
Tony Martin hired a singing teacher on Gracie's recommendation; at the request of her mother Gracie interviews Glen Gray and his vocalists. Featured song: "When They Played The Polka."

R320 July 18, 1938
Gracie has changed the map of the United States over the weekend; Tony Martin is angry at the film director; George tries to tell about his experiences as part of a quartet but Gracie keeps interrupting him about a dinner party her sister Hazel is giving for her boyfriend; Tony receives some assistance in rehearsing the film script rewrites. The boy who delivers the script to Tony Martin asks George if he's worried about what he's going to do when television comes in (which undoubtedly would have seemed very futuristic to 1938 radio audiences). Featured song: "We'll Get A Bang Out Of Life."

R321 July 25, 1938
Gracie asks George to propose to Hazel so her boyfriend will get jealous; a reluctant George finally agrees but, as he had feared, she accepts his proposal and when George refuses to marry her she sues him for breach of promise. It's announced that Tony Martin will be going out on the road with a band. Gracie sings a repeat of "Why'd Ya Make Me Fall in Love?"

R322 August 1, 1938
This is the last show for Grape-Nuts. George and Gracie prepare to leave for eight weeks to go to Honolulu and Gracie is buying her souvenirs before she goes; a telegram is received from Tony Martin, who is in Fond u Lac, Wisconsin; Gracie bids farewell to the boys and tunes up her ukelele. It's announced that Bob Ripley will be taking over this spot and that their new program will begin on September 30th in New York for Chesterfield. George, Gracie, and John Conte say good-bye for Grape-Nuts. Featured song: "What Do You Hear From The Mob in Scotland?"

6. The Chesterfield Program. 1938-1939. CBS. 30 min.

Sponsor: Liggett and Myers Tobacco Company.
Product: Chesterfield Cigarettes.
Network: CBS.
Broadcast Day: Friday.
Time Slot: 8:30-9:00 P.M. (Eastern Standard Time).

Scriptwriters: Harvey Helm, John P. Medbury, William Burns, Bill Brooks, Don Langan.
Announcer: Paul Douglas.
Orchestra Leader: Ray Noble.
Vocalist: Frank Parker.
Premise: George and Gracie are now being introduced as "ches two fools," Gracie will begin "writing" musicals, and George begins to compliment Gracie on her singing.

R323 September 30, 1938 (New York, NY)
It's their first show for Chesterfield, and Gracie can't understand why the cast looks so familiar--did they meet during her Hawaiian vacation? Ray Noble wonders what kind of humor is expected of him and tells jokes throughout the show, which will become a recurring theme; Gracie's family is glad to see her back; Frank Parker's date sends in a substitute. Gracie sings "I'm Going To Lock My Heart and Throw Away the Key," but begins to mix her singing with patter.

R324 October 7, 1938
Gracie describes how she's resting in New York; Frank Parker has another date and, once again, a substitute shows up; Gracie meets a gentleman who's been admiring her surrealistic paintings in the Julien Levy Gallery; Paul Douglas attempts to tell how Chesterfields are made. Featured song: "When A Prince Of A Fella Meets A Cinderella." **SEE D223.**

R325 October 14, 1938
The cast prepares to leave for Hollywood after tonight's broadcast; it's Frank Parker's last show for Chesterfield in New York and the last one for this sponsor to be produced in New York. Gracie has let a stranger take their suitcases and George's money and railroad tickets; Frank is worried because he has been going out with a woman he didn't know was married and he's afraid she might leave her husband for him. Featured song: "Natch'rally."

R326 October 21, 1938 (Hollywood, CA)
Tony Martin rejoins the program. Gracie thinks Hollywood has changed; Tony has a business deal that is going to make him wealthy and he is willing to let George in on it for $300,000; Gracie's family is having trouble at home. She and George perform the sister with the black feet routine.

R327 October 28, 1938
George tries to tell everyone he is giving a Halloween party on Monday; Gracie is going to a football game on Saturday; Tony Martin has a new business deal; George is tired of Ray Noble's jokes. Featured song: "F.D.R. Jones."

R328 November 4, 1938
Gracie wants to do a musical but George tells her the sponsor won't allow it (until she tells him she's written a song especially for him); the musical, **Three Loves Has Gracie and Two To Go**, takes place on an ocean liner going to Catalina Island with George, Tony Martin, Ray Noble and Paul Douglas playing chorus girls. George and Gracie sing "De-Lovely" (with George doing the honors on the word "it's").

R329 November 11, 1938
This is the Armistice Day broadcast and Tony Martin and his business partner are putting a new movie camera on the market; Gracie has met a man who offers them $10,000 plus expenses to broadcast from the San Francisco World's Fair for one week. Paul Douglas does a spot for Community Chest Welfare Funds. Featured song: "Why Doesn't Somebody Tell Me These Things?"

R330 November 18, 1938
Gracie is terribly excited because she found a copy of the S. S. Van Dine book, **The Gracie Allen Murder Case** (B482), at the bookshop and decides to write her own book, **Homicide by the Fireside** or **Death Comes Down the Chimney and Catches the Flu**. Featured song: "Let This Be A Warning To You Baby."

R331 November 25, 1938

Gracie tells George about the Thanksgiving dinner her family had; George is discouraged since a play he wrote, **The Buccaneer of Broadway**, has been rejected by the Hollywood Play Producer's Corporation; George doesn't want to act it out but Gracie talks him into it. In a role reversal, Gracie tells George to say good night. Featured song: "What Have You Got That Gets Me?"

R332 December 2, 1938
George declares they're not at a broadcast studio but a bargain basement when he discovers that, while Gracie was at his house waiting for him, she sold seven of his suits to someone for fifty cents each, Paul Douglas has tickets for Saturday's football game and is trying to sell them and Tony Martin is selling Christmas cards; a man wanting to use the pencil sharpener keeps interrupting the show; and Emily Post calls Gracie for advice. Gracie introduces the song "Your Eyes Are Bigger Than Your Heart."

R333 December 9, 1938
Gracie's new musical is **Jitterbugs of the Jungle** or **Hunting Gigolos with Bow and Arrow** and again promises George he can sing. This is Tony Martin's last show. Featured song: "You Must Have Been A Beautiful Baby."

R334 December 16, 1938
Tonight is Frank Parker's first broadcast for Chesterfield in Hollywood. Gracie tells George that Earl Carroll wants them to star in a musical comedy on Broadway this winter; Frank Parker says he is returning to the program because he and Tony Martin flipped a coin and Frank lost; and a woman keeps interrupting the program to tune her guitar. The niece who's grown three feet gag is included in tonight's show. Featured song: "Little Brown Gal." Tonight's episode was carefully scrutinized, at least by the media, for evidence of strain caused by George's recent indictments for jewelry smuggling.

R335 December 23, 1938
George is throwing a party on Christmas Eve and wants everyone to come; Gracie reads aloud parts of her new book, **Little Rollo's First Christmas**; someone is looking for Frank Parker; Gracie wishes everyone Merry Christmas. Featured song: "Ferdinand The Bull."

R336 December 30, 1938
George has decided not to get excited anymore when things go wrong; Paul Douglas is trying to get George a ticket to the Rose Bowl game; Frank Parker hires someone to play his girlfriend; Gracie is working on her diary and has a New Year's poem. Featured song: "You're Gonna See A Lot Of Me."

R337 January 6, 1939
Gracie does both her and George's parts--no one knows or seems to care where George is--and everyone offers to team up with Gracie. George finally arrives at the studio, tells them he was stuck in traffic and heard the broadcast then offers to let them try to replace him in the act. Gracie presents "The Outstanding Highlights of 1938" and sings "Honolulu."

R338 January 13, 1939
There is talk about Friday the 13th; it is announced that one of the sponsor's executives from San Francisco is coming to the broadcast; a man and his son come to the show thinking they're appearing on **Professor Quiz** and are mistaken for the sponsor representative.

R339 January 20, 1939
Gracie tells about the tar and feather wedding she and her sister, Bessie, attended; in honor of George's birthday, and in spite of all the kidding given him about his age, Gracie has written a play, **George of Troy** or **The Greeks Had A Worm For It**, but George puts a stop to it by singing "Ain't Misbehavin'." Gracie repeats, by request, "You Must Have Been A Beautiful Baby."

R340 January 27, 1939
Gracie's family has decided to make up questions for a quiz show but they don't know the answers; Paul Douglas has been on a fishing trip to Mexico; Gracie is going to dramatize the life of their sound man. Featured song: "Romance Runs In The Family."

R341 February 3, 1939
George announces that MGM is previewing their new film, **Honolulu** (F32), at Grauman's Chinese Theatre and that they can all attend but he soon regrets it; Gracie has a new boyfriend, Freddie. Featured song: "You're A Sweet Little Headache."

R342 February 10, 1939
The cast talks about **Honolulu** (F32); Gracie has written a melodrama, **West Los Angeles**, and has more to say about her boyfriend.

R343 February 17, 1939
Gracie announces that things are going to be "different" tonight; Frank Parker tries to impress the barbershop manicurist by pretending to be something he's not; Freddie re-enters the conversation. Featured song: "Gotta Get Some Shut-Eye."

R344 February 24, 1939
Gracie attended the Motion Picture Academy Award Dinner last night and can't understand why she didn't win for **The Gracie Allen Murder Case** (F33) until George explains that it's not finished yet; Frank is still pursuing the manicurist; Gracie decides to write the screenplay that's going to win an Academy Award next year. Gracie sings "What Makes The World Go 'Round?" from **Honolulu** (F32).

R345 March 3, 1939
Gracie decides to "go dramatic" since her performance with Melvyn Douglas on the Screen Guild show (R847). Featured song: "Could Be."

R346 March 10, 1939
Gracie overheard two Paramount executives say that George was going to direct a picture; the rest of the cast is hoping for a raise. Gracie repeats the song "Romance Runs In The Family."

R347 March 17, 1939
It's St. Patrick's Day and Gracie invites everyone over to her house for dinner; Frank Parker asks George's opinion of his fan mail picture proofs and sings "Danny Boy"; Gracie saw one of the Paramount executives again and told him "George's" idea for producing a picture; in honor of the American Legion's twentieth anniversary Gracie invites everyone on a world tour to find a location for their next convention and announces next week's play. Gracie introduces a song from **The Gracie Allen Murder Case** (F33), "Snug As a Bug In A Rug."

R348 March 24, 1939
Tonight's play is **King Henry the Eighth**. Featured song: "All Hail The King."

R349 March 31, 1939
The script for this week's broadcast isn't finished but George and the writers can't complete it because Gracie keeps interrupting; Gracie gets a call from President Roosevelt and invites him over for a fireside chat; Gracie reviews a new book she's just written, **Romance in a Drug Store**. Featured song: "Step Up And Shake My Hand."

R350 April 7, 1939
Gracie is going to be in the Easter Parade on Sunday; George receives a fan letter; Frank Parker's uncle is coming to the broadcast; Gracie reads chapter two of **Romance In A Drug Store**. Featured song: "Are There Any More At Home Like You?"

R351 April 14, 1939
George is acknowledged as the boss of the show; Gracie wants to use chocolate lipstick because chocolate is Paul Douglas' favorite flavor; George has a new spring suit; Frank Parker comes in and he is in love; Uncle Jerome has come to see Gracie; she is interested in Paul and she tells him she can give him a raise if he sells more Chesterfields; Gracie talks about Clark Gable and Carole Lombard getting married; Ray, a pilot, is flying the cast to Kansas City; they land on the Harvard campus in Cambridge, hurry onboard a river boat bound for Memphis and the Ozark mountains then go back to the studio. Featured song: "Class Will Tell."

R352 April 21, 1939

The cast performs the musical, **The Ride of Paul Revere**, with Gracie playing Mrs. Revere, a woman who doesn't believe her husband made the ride at all and makes him retrace his steps looking for someone who remembers him but the only one who remembers him is a talking horse (rather prophetic considering George's future involvement with another talking horse, Mister Ed). Everyone sings "Horse and Buggy Ride." Gracie again sings "Snug As A Bug In A Rug" from **The Gracie Allen Murder Case** (F33).

R353 April 28, 1939
George and Gracie are on their way to the Santa Fe Station heading for New York but Gracie may have given their train tickets to a man in front of the studio who wanted tickets to the radio broadcast. Tonight's episode received a rare bad review in **Variety**.

R354 May 5, 1939 (New York, NY)
The duo is in New York for the World's Fair which opened five days ago; Gracie wants to make the program "New Yorky"; she talks about her aunt and uncle's anniversary; the Friars Club is giving a stag dinner for George; Gracie introduces the studio employees to George; she's met a man who takes her sightseeing. By request Gracie repeats "Snug As A Bug In A Rug." Gracie only spoke the lyrics instead of singing them because Ray Noble's band made a mistake and played a different song.

R355 May 12, 1939
Gracie takes a walk through the park; Frank Parker is getting married; Ray Noble finds a script used on another radio broadcast and finds out the other show has been stealing Burns & Allen's material; Gracie gets a letter from her sister, Bessie. Tonight's song is "Ain't Cha Comin' Out?"

R356 May 19, 1939
Gracie is going to give a lecture on what every tourist should know about New York; she gives directions to the World's Fair and opens the Gracie Allen Go Where You Want To Go, Do What You Want To Do Travel Bureau; she has written a love story, **Romance in a Grocery Store**.

R357 May 26, 1939
Gracie assigns the cast its parts for the musical comedy, **The Private Life of John Smith and Pocahontas** or **Me Sleepy in Teepee and Get Heepie Jeepie**; everyone sings "Pocahontas."

R358 June 2, 1939
Gracie receives a letter from her sister, Bessie, who has just previewed **The Gracie Allen Murder Case** (F33) in Hollywood; Frank Parker is anxious to pick out a wedding ring; Gracie is in the studio next door doing a television broadcast; the cast dramatizes **The Life of Mr. Douglas**. Featured song: "Ya Had It Comin' To Ya."

R359 June 9, 1939
Gracie has gone to a baseball game with a man but refuses to reveal his identity to George; Ray Noble asks George if he would be interested in helping a poor family he ran across in the play **Tobacco Road**; Frank Parker walked into a door and came away with a black eye, so he says; guests are taken on a sightseeing trip to the automat, Gimbel's basement, Michigan, Montana and Nevada. Featured song: "Class Will Tell."

R360 June 16, 1939
The cast performs a radio version of **The Gracie Allen Murder Case** which bears no resemblance to the movie (F33) and discusses Gracie's performance on **Information Please** (R850) scheduled for the following week; Gracie attempts to prepare for her appearance by asking herself questions. Featured song: "Quote and Unquote."

R361 June 23, 1939
This is the last show for Chesterfield. Gracie tells what happened on **Information Please** (R850); Gracie notes that this is their last broadcast of the season and she thinks everyone on the show should make a speech of appreciation to the listeners; George gives a summary of their season: 208 "thank you's", 412 "quiets", 392 "oh, keep stills", 250 "oh, yeahs", 175 "oh, nuts"; everyone keeps interrupting George before he can make his thank you speech.

7. **The Hinds Honey and Almond Cream Program.** **1939-1940. CBS. 30 min.**

Sponsor: Lehn and Fink Products Company.
Product: Hinds Honey and Almond Cream.
Network: CBS.
Broadcast Day: Wednesday.
Time Slot: 7:30-8:00 P.M. (Eastern Standard Time)
Scriptwriters: John P. Medbury, Hal Block, William Burns.
Announcer: Truman Bradley.
Orchestra Leader: Ray Noble.
Vocalist: Frank Parker.
Actors: Elliott Lewis, Hal Rorke, Ted Allen, Pauline Swanson, Gene Coughlan, Al Span (sound effects).
Premise: The style of the show remains basically the same, but the sponsor will reap the rewards of a new publicity stunt, Gracie's campaign for the Presidency.
Series Notes: Mary Kelly, George and Gracie's friend since vaudeville days, joins the cast as "Bubbles." Her weight was often the subject of ridicule, something which seems quite out of character for the kind-hearted Gracie. Burns and Allen wanted a new theme song so Ray Noble wrote a little melody which had four "cuckoo" calls. There were so many requests for copies of the song and lyrics that Noble considered lengthening the song and writing more lyrics due to public requests.
Additional Notes: Hinds Honey and Almond Cream was a "face, hands, skin and complexion" lotion that was first manufactured in Portland, Maine by a family-owned company. Lehn and Fink sponsored the very first American network radio variety program, **Hall of Fame** (NBC, 1934).

R362 October 4, 1939 (Hollywood, CA)
This is the first show for Hinds Honey and Almond Cream, and Gracie plans big things for this year; "Bubbles" is introduced as Gracie's 300 pound girlfriend who is worrying about her blind date while stuck in a phone booth; Gracie talks about driving back to Hollywood from New York after their last broadcast in New York; Gracie winds up joining Bubbles and her blind date. Gracie Allen was rolled up in bandages during this broadcast due to a case of poison ivy. Featured song: "Don't Look Now."

R363 October 11, 1939
Gracie has purchased a new dress; Ray Noble is planning next year's vacation; Gracie receives a note from another dress shop; tonight's big topic is the changing of Thanksgiving Day (President Roosevelt changed the date to the last Thursday in November); Bubbles and Gracie hear a tale in French. Featured song: "It's Me Again."

R364 October 18, 1939
Gracie has run over a policeman; Frank Parker calls one of his girl-friends; Ray Noble is saving stamps; Bubbles talks about shopping, and Gracie talks about her singing teacher; she and Bubbles have written a book, **Gracie's Ditty Dictionary**, which tells people what songs they should sing; someone is looking for Frank. Featured song: "If I Only Had a Brain."

R365 October 25, 1939
The talk is about Gracie's appearance last Sunday on the **Screen Guild Theater** (R851) in an Irish play with James Cagney; Frank Parker is in love; Gracie went to a party with Pat O'Brien at Jimmy Cagney's home; the cast acts out the first part of **Calling Dr. Killjoy**. Featured song: "Especially for You."

R366 November 1, 1939
Ray Noble's wife doesn't believe that he was late getting home due to rehearsal; Tuesday is election day; Gracie mentions her little blue hat; Bubbles phones; the cast does the second installment of **Calling Dr. Killjoy**. Featured song: "All In Favor Say Aye."

R367 November 8, 1939
Gracie talks about the 1939 film, **Mr. Smith Goes To Washington**; Ray Noble is annoyed at the manager of the Beverly Wilshire Hotel; the niece of the show's sponsor is coming in by train and they go to meet her at Union Station. Featured song: "Scatterbrain."

R368 November 15, 1939

George has witnessed a bank robbery; Ray Noble talks about food; someone inquires if a tall man left behind a dead body; they talk about the USC-Stanford football game; Bubbles and Gracie talk about the opera; tonight's murder mystery is **Knife Blades In The Sunset, Who Shot The Shots That Sent Schultz Shooting Down The Shoot The Chutes?** Featured song: "Put That Down in Writing."

R369 November 22, 1939
This Thanksgiving episode revolves around Frank Parker eloping to Yuma in a station wagon. Featured song: "You're the Greatest Discovery Since 1492."

R370 November 29, 1939
George wants to get laughs; Gracie has bought a new car; Bubbles has a job as a telephone operator; tonight's play is **Hotel For Men**.

R371 December 6, 1939
Gracie has a boy friend; she bought George a Christmas present, and he tries to find out what it is; Bubbles has gone to an astrologer looking for a husband; a man comes in opening and closing windows; on Wednesday night at a literary talk Gracie will review her new book, **When Iris Eyes Are Smilax** or **What Did Lily Of The Valley Say When Sweet William Found A Bachelor Button On Her Patio?**, written by Gracie Elm and dedicated to George Bulbs; Gracie tells George that she is selling her book, **The Romance In A Garden**.

R372 December 13, 1939
Gracie found a lost wallet with $700 inside and receives a reward from the owner; an impresario, Mrs. Van Dusen, thinks Frank Parker's future is in the field of opera; they perform **Small Town**; Bubbles has a new diet and a reducing column, "Flabby Days Are Here Again"; Hymie, the window opener and closer, appears again. Featured song: "Night Before Christmas."

R373 December 20, 1939
Gracie wants to get a reservation for New Year's Eve; Mrs. Van Dusen has gotten Frank Parker a part in Carmen; George invites Gracie to go to the Beverly Wilshire Hotel on Christmas Eve where Bubbles is the telephone operator; while George is trying to get their reservations, another radio show, **Pot Of Gold**, has been trying to reach him. There was a real show at this time named **Pot o' Gold** which was on another network.

R374 December 27, 1939
George and Gracie have an adventuresome day at a department store while shopping for a shirt for George before they attend a Hollywood premiere. Featured song: "Ma."

R375 January 3, 1940
Gracie talks about a New Year's Eve party she attended; George was there and saw her flirting with Herbert Marshall; Gracie has written a "prison play." Featured song: "Scatter-Brain Again."

R376 January 10, 1940
Gracie invites everyone over to meet her latest flame, who thinks George, Frank Parker, Ray Noble and Truman Bradley are Gracie's employees. "The Answer is Love." Guest star: Herbert Marshall.

R377 January 17, 1940
Gracie talks about items she read in the paper, is not seeing Herbert Marshall anymore and decides to redecorate her house. The cast performs a new play. Featured song: "Baby Face."

R378 January 24, 1940
Gracie is happy because it's Leap Year but she's not asking George to marry her; Gracie helps her nephew; tonight's play is "The Census Taker"; Bubbles has a new husband. Featured song: "I Happen to be in Love."

R379 January 31, 1940
A portable typewriter is delivered to Gracie at her home; she wants to call her new play **Destry Rides Again** in honor of the movie. Featured song: "Way Back in 1939 A.D."

R380 February 7, 1940

Gracie talks about her uncle and aunt; Gracie can't make up her mind what to do after the broadcast--knit a sweater or run for President; Bubbles has signed a motion picture contract with Universal Studios to play an Indian squaw but Gracie is also selling magazines to help Bubbles work her way through college. The February 7, 1940 broadcast is the first in which Gracie mentions running for President, one of the most famous publicity stunts ever created for radio. It was certainly one of the top four engineered for the team of Burns and Allen, the other three being the earlier search for Gracie's "missing" brother, her upcoming "Concerto for Index Finger," and, in the late 1940's, Gracie trying to get George a singing spot on other radio programs.

R381 February 14, 1940
The boys (Truman Bradley, Ray Noble and Frank Parker) have sent candy to Gracie for Valentine's Day; George has picked up Gracie on the way to the studio. His car needs gas and, while at the gas station waiting for change, people mistake him and Gracie for employees. Featured song: "Mm Mm Mm, Would You Like to Take A Walk?"

R382 February 21, 1940
The cast has received a letter from Darryl F. Zanuck saying a Mr. Brown is coming over to the show to see if they want to be in a new Twentieth Century-Fox motion picture; Bubbles brings in a telegram from Senator Robert Kenny from California that asks Gracie why she doesn't run for President; Gracie concludes that, since she's being forced into it, she will *have* to run. Featured song: "Confucius Say."

R383 February 28, 1940
Tonight is the first complete "Presidential" broadcast: "Vote for Gracie" banners are out, and billboards are up with "Put Gracie in the White House." George didn't realize that Gracie was serious about running for President. Her slogan is "It's in the Bag," her mascot is the kangaroo and her party is the Surprise Party. She announces her platform and Cabinet members. Featured song: "Chula Chihuahua."

R384 March 6, 1940
Gracie tells about campaigning on **Baby Snooks** (R856), **The Jell-O Program** (R858), **Bob Hope** (R860) and **Fibber McGee & Molly** (R861) radio programs during the past week, announces that her convention will be held in Omaha, Nebraska and introduces her campaign song, "Vote For Gracie."

R385 March 13, 1940
Gracie has returned from Washington, D.C., where she was the honored guest at the Women's National Press Club's Annual Dinner; she talks about the speech she gave and mentions that her convention will be held in May; and she sings her campaign song again because George sings a chorus in it.

R386 March 20, 1940
"Gracie Allen for President" clubs are being formed around the country and Gracie mentions endorsements from Springfield High School and Multnomah College in Oregon and Lowell House at Harvard University; Portland Hoffa is named as her campaign manager. Listeners can write to Hinds Honey & Almond Hand Cream and receive a copy of her campaign song.

R387 March 27, 1940
The dates of the Surprise Party convention will be May 15-18; Gracie mentions other endorsements from colleges around the United States and announces that, if elected President, she will appoint Frank Parker as Postmaster General and Ray Noble as Secretary of the Navy. Featured song: "Vote For Gracie."

R388 April 3, 1940
Gracie is limited to $3 million for her campaign fund; she threw out the first ball of the Pacific Coast season at the Hollywood Ball Park; the special Union Pacific train is going to take their party from Los Angeles to Omaha, where there will be a torch light parade with 25,000 men in whiskers for convention week; a man-in-the-street interview is conducted. Featured song: "The Pizzicato Polka."

R389 April 10, 1940
Gracie received 63 votes last Tuesday in Wisconsin's state primary; she receives a phone call from George Jessel; the kangaroo is ill; Ray Noble and Gracie sing "Ain't Misbehavin'."

R390 April 17, 1940
Charlie McCarthy and George Jessel telephone Gracie; she admires George's new serge suit; Gracie talks about her campaign and that women and men will be wearing old-time style dress for the week in Omaha; George asks if she got the plane tickets for Dallas, where they will be on Friday for the Variety Club; Gracie gives the speech she will make in Dallas. Featured song: "When the Sweet Potato Piper Plays."

R391 April 24, 1940
Gracie talks about her speech in Dallas; Dr. Smearbach is interested in Gracie's campaign and wants to test her I.Q. Featured song: "I Can't Love You Anymore."

The show's time slot changes to 6:30-7:00 P.M.

R392 May 1, 1940
Ray Noble gives George and Gracie presents (George's gift is dissolving suspenders); an Indian tries to sell George a blanket. Featured song: "You Little Heartbreaker You."

R393 May 8, 1940
George and Gracie are planning to leave for the National Convention in Omaha immediately after the broadcast but Gracie has given their train tickets away (again!) and has been told she can't take the kangaroo on the train. Featured song: "April Played the Fiddle."

R394 May 15, 1940 (Omaha, Nebraska)
The broadcast is taking place from the Ak-Sar-Ben Coliseum in front of an audience of 15,000; George introduces the cast; last night in Omaha, the Indian village chief, White Buffalo Hide, made George and Gracie honorary members of his tribe; Gracie's new name is Princess Malasho (pronounced "Ma La Jo"); they talk about meeting Mayor Butler and Gracie's visit the day before at Creighton University; Gracie gives a one-woman angle on running the government; George thanks Mayor Butler for being so nice and joining in the fun; Gracie tells the Mayor "I've got something for you," and gives him a kiss. Featured song: "Vote For Gracie." The Coliseum's name, "Ak-Sar-Ben," is "Nebraska" spelled backwards. 1995's Ak-Sar-Ben is a race track.

R395 May 22, 1940 (Hollywood, CA)
They are back home and mention there were over 100,000 people who met Gracie on the street and in the various stations where they stopped on their way to the convention; she is made Honorary Mayor of Boy's Town; Raymond D. McGrath gives the nominating speech and Gracie gives her acceptance speech; a man invites Gracie and the cast to broadcast from the San Francisco World's Fair next week but wants to get rid of George as "he's no good"; everyone talks crazy to George to make him think he's crazy; George ends up unconscious in a hospital; the doctor tells Gracie that the only way to save George is to take him to San Francisco with the rest of the cast. Featured song: "I Can't Love You Anymore."

R396 May 29, 1940 (San Francisco, CA)
The cast is at Treasure Island inside the San Francisco World's Fair-grounds; someone is coming over to help Gracie in her campaign; they discuss Gracie's third grade teacher and a friend; an announcement to make donations to the Red Cross is made in closing. Featured song: "Tennessee Fish Fry."

R397 June 5, 1940 (Hollywood, CA)
They talk about the World's Fair, Gracie's father and her brother; tonight's play is from RKO's 1940 version of **Swiss Family Robinson**; Gracie's friend from San Francisco arrives. "You Little Heartbreaker You" is tonight's song.

R398 June 12, 1940
The second installment of **Swiss Family Robinson** is performed; Gracie's book, **How To Become President** (B7), is going on sale.

R399 June 19, 1940
Everyone except George spends the weekend at a dude ranch; the play, **One Million B.C.**, is performed.

R400 June 26, 1940
This is George and Gracie's last show for Hinds. On Saturday night they participated in a radio benefit for war relief (R863) and Gracie did a "love scene" with Edward G. Robinson; George mentions that next Monday they will be on a different network for a new sponsor; they reminisce with the cast; Gracie has "found" a new singer for the show and a new announcer. Truman Bradley will be leaving the show for the summer to do a picture. Featured songs: "Vote for Gracie" and "Row, Row, Row."

8. The Hormel Program. 1940-1941. NBC. 30 min.

Sponsor: George A. Hormel Packing Company.
Product: Spam.
Network: NBC.
Broadcast Day: Monday.
Time Slot: 7:30-8:00 P.M. (Eastern Standard Time).
Scriptwriters: Harvey Helm, John P. Medbury, Hal Block, Artie Phillips, William Burns.
Announcer: John "Bud" Heistand.
Orchestra Leader: Artie Shaw.
Vocalist: Smoothies Three.
Premise: The most obvious difference in the shows for this new sponsor is the proliferation of guest stars. Señor Irving Lee, a guitarist described as a "Latin word-bungler," plays a recurring role.
Series Notes: The first show of the season marked the combining of the NBC Red and Blue networks coast to coast. This resulted in the Hormel program becoming part of the most powerful network of any commercial show on the air at the time with a sixty station hookup across the United States.
Additional Notes: Orchestra leader Artie Shaw, who formed numerous bands during his career, had his first big hit with an old Cole Porter composition, "Begin the Beguine." Considered an "intellectual snob" by some, including his own musicians, he disliked the business end of the music business. He also disliked talk about his private life, which included marriages and divorces with two of Hollywood's biggest stars, Lana Turner and Ava Gardner. After leaving the music business, he successfully pursued a number of other careers in his lifelong quest to "find something new." **See B421.**

R401 July 1, 1940 (Hollywood, CA)
In their first show for Spam, a Hormel product, George and Gracie talk about other comedians at NBC and meet new cast members, including Señor Lee, the guitar player from South America; Jack Benny has sent them four dozen roses (well, actually, a package of seeds for four dozen roses).

R402 July 8, 1940
Gracie talks about her brother and a trip she made to Catalina and invites everyone to her grandfather's 92nd birthday party.

R403 July 15, 1940
Gracie and Bud Heistand are going to the Cocoanut Grove after the broadcast; she and George talk about the party they went to at Norman Taurog's house; George has trouble with Señor Lee; Mr. Taurog is looking for a boy actor and Gracie has a famous Hollywood makeup artist come over to make George look young; Bud and George engage in a "heart to heart talk"; Gracie talks about the gossip she picks up at the beauty shop. Special guest: makeup artist Ern Westmore (a member of Hollywood's fabled makeup artist dynasty).

R404 July 22, 1940
The talk tonight is about last week's presidential convention with Roosevelt and Wilkie; they enact **The Life of Rosie O'Connor** (an "oomph" girl of the 1890's).

R405 July 29, 1940
Gracie talks about the hot weather, Señor Lee and kiddie parties; later, talk turns to a party and Georgie Jessel's young wife; the curfew officer arrests George because now he looks like a kid. Featured song: "One More Chance."

R406 August 5, 1940

Bud Heistand and Gracie have a date at the Hollywood Bowl; a Hollywood producer is looking for a comedian for his next movie and is coming to see George; George instructs everyone how to act when the producer arrives and Gracie tells everyone to help George but a dark horse candidate gets the job instead. Special guest: film producer Joe Pasternak.

R407 August 12, 1940
George reminisces about vaudeville and when he first met Gracie; the play is **Gold Rush Maisie**.

R408 August 19, 1940
George is late for the broadcast; Elsie Tralafas claims George promised to make her his new partner.

R409 August 26, 1940
Elsie Tralafas is suing George for $100,000 for breach of promise; her boyfriend is suing him for $200,000 for alienation of affections.

R410 September 2, 1940
The setting is the courthouse as Gracie wins the trial for George.

R411 September 9, 1940
Gracie tries to get the court costs fixed.

R412 September 16, 1940
The sponsor wants a guest star. Guest star: Lynn Hayes.

R413 September 23, 1940
George does a guest column for Ed Sullivan and a gangster threatens him so he pretends to be Gracie's Aunt Clara.

R414 September 30, 1940
The gangster proposes to "Aunt Clara."

R415 October 7, 1940
The "gangster" was hired by George as a gag.

R416 October 14, 1940
George and Gracie were seen last night at a revue at the El Capitan Theater, where Jack Benny was Master of Ceremonies; Bud Heistand complains that they didn't mention the sponsor's product; Gracie talks about her new dress and has bought a car; George is worried that Gracie is crazier than ever so he asks a professor to give her a scientific test and the man tries to hypnotize Gracie.

R417 October 21, 1940
Everyone is still worried about Gracie; Professor Thorndike has observed her all week and wants George to agree with Gracie and cater to her.

R418 October 28, 1940
George has a date with Fifi, a dancer from the Follies Bergere, and tries to get out of the broadcast.

R419 November 4, 1940
It's Election Eve and Gracie is voting for Clark Gable; the saga of "Fifi of the Follies Bergere" continues.

R420 November 11, 1940
Gracie has written the music to a musical comedy, **The Lives Of King Henry's Wives** or **When Things Get Dull, He Sharpens His Knives**; Gracie tells George they have another mouth to feed--her mother's.

R421 November 18, 1940
Gracie's grandfather is ill so the broadcast is done from Gracie's home.

R422 November 25, 1940
The cast rehearses for next week's show.

R423 December 2, 1940
The sponsor is scheduled to come for a visit.

R424 December 9, 1940

George and Gracie talk about their Navy show broadcast from San Diego (R863) and the Tijuana Fiesta.

R425 December 16, 1940
Gracie has ordered a new Christmas hat and written a new play, **The Los Angeles Sun**; Noel Coward calls her for advice; Gracie and the Smoothies sing "Goodbye."

R426 December 23, 1940
The play from last week was to continue but Gracie left the scripts in a taxi.

R427 December 30, 1940
Christmas and New Year's plans are discussed along with the Rose Bowl game.

R428 January 6, 1941
Gracie signs George's name to a check at Ciro's; Brother Willie sends a letter. Guest star: Eddie Cantor.

R429 January 13, 1941
Gracie is interested in the society pages; Brother Willie's second letter arrives. Guest star: Cobina Wright, Jr.

R430 January 20, 1941
Brother Willie's third letter is in the mail. Guest star: Cobina Wright, Jr.

R431 January 27, 1941
The cast goes to Cobina's party; Gracie receives another letter from Brother Willie. Guest stars: Cobina Wright, Sr. and Cobina Wright, Jr.

R432 February 3, 1941 (Chicago, IL)
Jimmy Wallington is the new announcer. George and Gracie talk about being in Chicago six years ago for the fair; they stopped off to entertain at Fort Sheridan; Gracie talks about her brother in the Army; Gracie complains that she couldn't sleep on the train; Artie Shaw wants to meet a girl who has left a message for him. Special guest: Chicago's Mayor Kelly. **SEE D171.**

R433 February 10, 1941 (New York, NY)
Gracie talks about New York and her stay at the Waldorf Astoria; they can't agree on a title for her play. **SEE D224.**

R434 February 17, 1941
Gracie has written a new book, **The Knight In Armor** or **Tin Pants Alley**. **SEE D225.**

R435 February 24, 1941
Gracie thinks she and Artie Shaw were made for each other. Guest star: Beatrice Fairfax.

R436 March 3, 1941
Gracie is in love with Artie and thinks they are engaged. Part of the March 3, 1941 broadcast did not air due to the station, WEAF, going off the air temporarily.

R437 March 10, 1941
Gracie gives Artie a ring from a box of Cracker Jacks.

R438 March 17, 1941
George tries to break up Gracie and Artie.

R439 March 24, 1941
George and Gracie are on their way by train to her sister Bessie's wedding; Gracie has an article in **Coronet**; vacation begins next week; George has been offered a part in the play **I'll Love You Tuesday**; Artie wants more room on the train for his clarinet. This is the last show for Hormel. Featured song: "Sugar Pie." **SEE D225.**

9. **The Swan Soap Show. 1941-1945. NBC, CBS. 30 min.**

Sponsor: Lever Brothers Company.

Product: Swan Soap.
Network: NBC, later CBS.
Broadcast Day: Tuesday (Thursday in Chicago, IL).
Time Slot: 7:30-8:00 P.M. (Eastern Standard Time); 9:30 P.M. in Chicago, IL.
Producer: Glenhall Taylor, Hendrik Booraem, Jr., Dave Elton.
Director: Glenhall Taylor, Hendrik Booraem, Jr.
Scriptwriters: Paul Henning, Harvey Helm, Sam Perrin, Frank Galen, Keith Fowler, George Balzer, William Burns.
Announcer: Bill Goodwin.
Orchestra Leader: Paul "Pops" Whiteman.
Vocalist: Jimmy Cash, The Swantets.
Actors: Edith Evanson, Dick Ryan, Mel Blanc, Bea Benaderet, Hans Conried, Elvia Allman, Clarence "Ducky" Nash, Richard Haydn, Hal March.
Theme Song: "The Love Nest."
Premise: The ratings slump evidenced by their long "vacation" precipitated two major changes: there is a change in sponsors and George and Gracie are, for the first time in radio, portrayed as a married couple. The show is rapidly becoming a full-blown situation comedy with succinct plots that will eventually help transfer Burns and Allen to television. Guest stars are used to full advantage.
Series Notes: Bill Goodwin introduces a familiar catch phrase in this series, "Well, I Swan, it's George and Gracie!" Gracie welcomes the audience into their "home" each week with the words "Well, hello. Come right in. Oh, George! We've got company!" Their theme song, "The Love Nest," would continue its association with the team for the remainder of their careers. The song was written in 1920 by Otto Harbach and Louis A. Hirsch and was first heard in the musical, **Mary**, by Janet Velle and Jack McGowan.

The series was aired over 103 NBC stations on Tuesdays and on over thirty-one CBS and Mutual stations by transcription other evenings (the program would eventually switch from NBC to CBS). Three hundred eighty-five audience members were admitted to each CBS broadcast from Studio B of Radio City in Hollywood. The audience was seated twenty minutes prior to the start of show and were entertained by the band, followed by introductions and gags by George.

Señor Irving Lee is held over from the previous series. *Hilda the Cook* and her boyfriend *Olaf Sven* (Edith Evanson and Dick Ryan) play continuing roles on this new show. Clarence Nash, the voice of *Herman the Duck*, Gracie's pet, was the originator of the "Donald Duck" voice characterization. Bea Benaderet appears as *Blanche Morton* with Hal March as *Harry Morton*, George and Gracie's neighbors. Mel Blanc is *The Happy Postman*, Elvia Allman is *Tootsie Sagwell*, and Gale Gordon is *Mr. Judson*. Most of these actors had previously appeared on the show in various non-recurring character roles.

At some point during the run of this series the Lever Bros. account was taken over by Young & Rubicam. Ned Tollinger assumed directing duties and scripters included Hank Garson and Aaron Ruben. Represented by the William Morris Agency, George and Gracie's package deal commanded $7,500 per week.

During their stint for Swan Soap, George and Gracie's third publicity stunt is born, the "Concerto for Index Finger."
Additional Notes: Paul "Pops" Whiteman, who took on George Gershwin's "Rhapsody in Blue" as his own theme song, was already a legendary band leader by the time he joined George and Gracie's radio show, having achieved national acclaim as early as 1918. Called the "King of Jazz," he was instrumental in the early careers of many musical giants, including the Dorsey brothers (Jimmy and Tommy), Bing Crosby and Johnny Mercer. He once resisted recording his music in order to avoid competing with his own live shows and later, with his own live radio shows (he helmed around a dozen). Ironically, he later briefly became a disc jockey with yet another network radio show. He died in 1967. **See B421, B487.**

R440 October 7, 1941 (Hollywood, CA)
In their debut show for Swan Soap Gracie "discovers" singer Jimmy Cash in a grocery store. In reality, Gracie was shopping at a market in the Los Angeles area and heard Cash singing and mentioned to George that they might consider him for the show as a singer. Cash continued to work at his "real job" while singing on the radio show.

R441 October 14, 1941
Jimmy Cash is signed to a contract.

R442 October 21, 1941
George is being examined for an insurance policy. **SEE D275.**

R443 October 28, 1941
Gladys Hall is coming to interview the cast for a magazine article.

R444 November 4, 1941
George tells Gracie that MGM wants her to make a picture called **Mr. and Mrs. North** (F34); Gracie finds a gold locket Paul Whiteman purchased for his wife and incorrectly assumes that George bought it for her.

R445 November 11, 1941
George and Gracie go duck hunting and Gracie finds a baby duck, which she adopts and eventually names Herman.

R446 November 18, 1941
Gracie's high school friend, Keith Fowler, writes that he's coming for a visit and Gracie keeps George wondering what happened on "that rainy afternoon" she spent with Keith when they were in school. Keith Fowler was the name of one of the show's writers. **SEE D203, D235.**

R447 November 25, 1941
Gracie interviews cooks. Guest star: Melvyn Douglas.

R448 December 2, 1941
The search for a cook continues and an interior decorator is scheduled to arrive. **SEE B168.**

R449 December 9, 1941
George and Gracie go Christmas shopping at the May Company.

R450 December 16, 1941
Gracie and George are trying to mail a package at the post office. Gracie promotes the buying of Defense Savings Bonds. **SEE D275.**

R451 December 23, 1941
Gracie has a dream about going to the North Pole with Herman on a Magic Carpet. Featured song: "Oh Ducky, You Get Your Christmas Wish." Guest star: Edna May Oliver. **SEE D162, D185, D195, D215, D242.**

R452 December 30, 1941
People have dropped in at George and Gracie's on New Year's Eve and won't go home; Gracie talks about **Mr. and Mrs. North** (F34).

R453 January 6, 1942
Herman the Duck is missing. Guest star: Basil Rathbone.

R454 January 13, 1942
Gracie tells Herman about **Mr. and Mrs. North** (F34); she and George attended the film's opening last night; they talk about saving paper for the war effort and Gracie decides to collect tin. The Volunteers of America are mentioned as an organization that runs these various collections for the government.

R455 January 20, 1942
George and Gracie go on a second honeymoon.

R456 January 27, 1942
Gracie reads the newspaper to Herman; the Ladies Club of Beverly Hills, for which Gracie is vice president, secretary and treasurer, is meeting; when Gracie discovers that $65 is missing she decides to organize a raffle, for which George unknowingly donates the prize.

R457 February 3, 1942
Herman is sick. Guest star: Lionel Barrymore.

R458 February 10, 1942
Tootsie Sagwell makes the first appearance of many as Gracie's plain and plainly man-crazy friend.

R459 February 17, 1942

Gracie thinks George is run down and needs to go to Palm Springs to rest; Gracie has lost her key ring but, as usual, that doesn't mean quite the same to Gracie as it does to most people.

R460 February 24, 1942
Gracie goes to a movie with her friend, Blanche Morton, while George hosts a poker party. (The popular character of *Blanche* [and her husband, *Harry*] will eventually be transferred to television when Burns and Allen switch mediums).

R461 March 3, 1942
Gracie witnesses a car accident.

R462 March 10, 1942
Married friends of George and Gracie quarrel.

R463 March 17, 1942
Gracie asks George to dig a Victory Garden. Listeners could receive ten gladioli bulbs if they sent ten cents and two Swan Soap wrappers to the Gracie Allen Garden Club in Los Angeles.

R464 March 24, 1942
George has hurt his back digging the Victory Garden.

R465 March 31, 1942 (Camp Haan in Riverside, CA)
Tootsie Sagwell meets a lieutenant but can't get him to propose so Gracie offers her some advice. An announcement was made at the end of show that the programs are shortwaved to the armed forces everywhere.

R466 April 7, 1942 (Hollywood, CA)
Gracie decides to try working at men's jobs and becomes a barber, a repairman, a gas station attendant and a taxi driver.

R467 April 14, 1942
Gracie takes piano lessons. Tonight's episode plants the seeds that will eventually bloom into Burns and Allen's third great publicity stunt on radio.

R468 April 21, 1942
Gracie's piano lessons continue with a different teacher.

R469 April 28, 1942 (San Francisco, CA)
Gracie wants to visit her family in San Francisco but finds out they have gone to Los Angeles to live with her while they try to sell their house. Burns and Allen broadcast from the new radio studios in San Francisco for this show.

R470 May 5, 1942
Gracie thinks she's ready to give a piano concert and decides to have her hands insured.

R471 May 12, 1942
Gracie's piano lessons find George locked in his room to avoid the noise; Gracie has a club meeting at their house.

R472 May 19, 1942
Gracie still plans to give a piano concert.

R473 May 26, 1942
Gracie gives her concert at the Beverly Hills Playhouse.

R474 June 2, 1942
A baby is found on George and Gracie's doorstep.

R475 June 9, 1942 (Naval Training Station in San Diego, CA)
Gracie attempts to cook a meal for a visiting Naval officer.

R476 June 16, 1942
Gracie tries to decide on what to buy George for Father's Day and settles on a picture of Herman the Duck.

R477 June 23, 1942

The Beverly Hills Uplift Society meets at George and Gracie's but Gracie is not amused at the evening's entertainment because one of the potential club members flirts with George.

R478 June 30, 1942
Tootsie Sagwell is delighted that George and Gracie have rented out their house to a bachelor for the summer while they vacation in New York City. Guest stars: Tommy Riggs and Betty Lou.

The show moves to CBS at 9:00-9:30 P.M.

R479 October 6, 1942
George and Gracie reminisce about their courtship. "Six Hits and a Miss" are the guest singers.

Review: "George Burns and Gracie Allen continue to move with the times...Result is an offering that is as refreshing as it is pleasant." (**Variety**, October 14, 1942: 32).

R480 October 13, 1942
Gracie tries methods from a booklet published by the Successful Marriage Institute.

R481 October 20, 1942
The Beverly Hills Uplift Society has its first meeting of the new season.

R482 October 27, 1942
George rents an office and Gracie interviews secretaries.

R483 November 3, 1942
Tootsie Sagwell meets the MGM studio plumber.

R484 November 10, 1942
George thinks Gracie is expecting a baby.

R485 November 17, 1942
Gracie invites the Mortons to Thanksgiving dinner; the turkey and Herman are in love.

R486 November 24, 1942
Ida Cantor becomes a member of the Beverly Hills Uplift Society. Guest star: Eddie Cantor.

R487 December 1, 1942
Gracie and Tootsie Sagwell fix George's car.

R488 December 8, 1942
Gas rationing is causing people to stay home and get friendly with their neighbors.

R489 December 15, 1942
Gracie tries to get Tootsie Sagwell a date. Guest star: Herbert Marshall.

R490 December 22, 1942
Gracie tells Herman the Duck about Christmas. Guest star: Akim Tamiroff.

R491 December 29, 1942
Gracie plays matchmaker for the postman. Guest star: Rita Hayworth.

R492 January 5, 1943
The Beverly Hills Uplift Society performs **Dr. Jekyll and Mr. Hyde**.

R493 January 12, 1943
George is reading the latest installment of **Cowboy Love Tales**; the Christmas bills arrive; and Gracie buys an 89-volume set of almanacs.

R494 January 19, 1943
Is today George and Gracie's anniversary? Guest star: Brian Donlevy.

R495 January 26, 1943
George may be descended from royalty.

R496 February 2, 1943
The search for a new cook begins again.

R497 February 9, 1943
The members of the Beverly Hills Uplift Society elect a new president. Guest star: Charles Laughton.

R498 February 16, 1943
Tootsie Sagwell thinks Bill Goodwin will marry her if she looks like a movie star. Guest star: Veronica Lake.

R499 February 23, 1943
George receives a letter from a woman with marriage on her mind. Guest star: Bob Burns.

R500 March 2, 1943 (New York, NY)
George and Gracie are in New York for Gracie's concert at Carnegie Hall. Guest star: Madeleine Carroll.

R501 March 9, 1943
Everyone is trying to convince Gracie she shouldn't play at Carnegie Hall. Guest stars: Deems Taylor and José Iturbi.

R502 March 16, 1943
Although George has promised Gracie he'll do anything if she won't do it, Gracie performs her "Concerto for Index Finger" at Carnegie Hall with Paul Whiteman; Tootsie Sagwell has a real boyfriend at last.

R503 March 23, 1943
George tries to get Gracie to give up the Beverly Hills Uplift Society.

R504 March 30, 1943
Gracie plans a large-scale Victory Garden.

R505 April 6, 1943
Tootsie Sagwell has joined a Lonely Hearts Club.

R506 April 13, 1943
Gracie thinks George should be a lawyer. Claudette Colbert appears to promote the sale of war bonds.

R507 April 20, 1943
Gracie needs fifty dollars for a new Easter outfit.

R508 April 27, 1943 (March Field in Riverside, CA)
Gracie tries to get Tootsie Sagwell a date with a serviceman.

R509 May 4, 1943
Gracie wants to become a dramatic actress.

R510 May 11, 1943
Gracie mistakenly uses breakfast food as silver polish and tries to get a refund.

R511 May 18, 1943
The star of Gracie's favorite radio program, **The Sunshine Man**, asks George and Gracie to substitute for him as the happiest married couple in the world. To assist in the war effort, Gracie asks the audience to save at least a tablespoon of waste fat every day and take it to the butcher to help make bombs and bullets.

R512 May 25, 1943
George runs for the school board.

R513 June 1, 1943
Gracie appears in traffic court.

R514 June 8, 1943
Gracie and Tootsie Sagwell apply for jobs at a millionaire playboy's mansion as maid and cook.

R515 June 15, 1943

In an effort to put more glamour into the crusade to encourage people to save more waste fat for the war effort Gracie recruits George for her "Kitchen Fat Caravan" and promises George that, if he'll help her campaign, he can sing "Ain't Misbehavin'" at every house they visit.

R516 June 22, 1943
Gracie tries to find a husband for Tootsie Sagwell by purchasing a love potion.

R517 June 29, 1943
Gracie pretends to have amnesia. Felix Mills and his orchestra replace Paul Whiteman.

R518 August 31, 1943
George enters a singing contest after he and Gracie return from entertaining at Army camps. Guest star: Frank Sinatra. This week's script won honorable mention for Most Outstanding Script, Comedy from **Radio Life** magazine.

R519 September 7, 1943
When Gracie learns there's a three-to-one man shortage she's afraid there are two more women somewhere in the world who belong to George. At first she wishes she were single again but changes her mind. **SEE D99, D120.**

R520 September 14, 1943
George's laundry has been mixed up with Brian Donlevy's and Gracie goes to his house to make the exchange because she wants to convince Brian to be the leading man in her new dramatic play. There is an ad at the end of the show asking listeners to save waste kitchen fat for the war effort. **SEE D85, D249.**

R521 September 21, 1943
Tootsie Sagwell is determined to marry a man she saw at a war bond rally. Guest star: Ray Milland.

R522 September 28, 1943
Bill Goodwin falls in love. Guest star: Ann Sheridan.

R523 October 5, 1943
Gracie's new next door neighbor's feelings about the untrustworthiness of men causes Gracie to become suspicious of George.

R524 October 12, 1943
George and Gracie invite a friend to dinner. Guest star: Eddie Cantor, replacing the previously scheduled Monty Woolley.

R525 October 19, 1943
Gracie's old school chum visits. Guest star: Pat O'Brien.

R526 October 26, 1943
Tootsie enters the Queen of the Fleet beauty contest and encounters some stiff competition. Guest star: Hedy Lamarr.

R527 November 2, 1943
Gracie meets Jack Benny at the beauty shop and attempts to blackmail him into allowing George sing on his show. George sings "Ain't Misbehavin'," which is his "theme" song throughout much of their radio career. **SEE D79, D147, D193.**

R528 November 9, 1943
Tonight's episode includes another war drive, this time for waste paper, but can George part with his newly-found collection of **Cowboy Love Tales**? Some sources indicate Jack Benny guested on tonight's episode. **SEE D85, D103.**

R529 November 16, 1943
The new next-door neighbor is a sitting duck for Tootsie Sagwell. Guest star: Walter Pidgeon.

R530 November 23, 1943
Gracie is sued over an article she wrote for a gossip magazine. Guest star: Loretta Young.

R531 November 30, 1943
Gracie sees a movie and develops a crush on the star. Guest star: Charles Boyer. **SEE B190.**

R532 December 7, 1943 (Naval Air Station, Terminal Island, CA)
An actress researches a new role as a scatter-brained wife by talking to Gracie. Guest star: Ida Lupino.

R533 December 14, 1943 (Hollywood, CA)
Tootsie Sagwell falls in love again. Guest star: Kay Kyser.

R534 December 21, 1943
Charles Laughton plays Santa Claus. He and Elsa Lanchester guest star.

R535 December 28, 1943
John Garfield tries to prove to Gracie that he's a tough guy.

R536 January 4, 1944
Gracie gets lessons on how to keep a man. Guest star: Paulette Goddard.

R537 January 11, 1944
No broadcast. The time slot is used for a speech by President Roosevelt.

R538 January 18, 1944
A pupil enrolls in Gracie's culture school. Guest star: William Bendix.

R539 January 25, 1944
Gracie advertises her culture school with a fake testimonial. Guest star: Paul Henreid.

R540 February 1, 1944
George and Gracie have an overnight guest. Guest star: William Powell.

R541 February 8, 1944
Gracie thinks Adolphe Menjou and Verree Teasdale are breaking up.

R542 February 15, 1944
George is disturbed in his office by a dancer going through his paces on the floor above him. Guest star: Fred Astaire. **SEE D139, D148, D168, D255.**

R543 February 22, 1944
Gracie tries to get George a singing role in a new film. Guest star: Cecil B. DeMille.

R544 February 29, 1944
Gracie campaigns for George to get a role as a leading man. Guest star: Dorothy Lamour.

R545 March 7, 1944
George plays poker. Guest star: Alan Ladd.

R546 March 14, 1944
Gracie tries to get Paul Lukas to appear in her new play.

R547 March 21, 1944
With husband Orson Welles out of town, Rita Hayworth is afraid to stay at home alone and asks George and Gracie to spend the night. Gracie starts thinking that George can be a genius like Orson. **SEE D139, D149, D234, D255.**

R548 March 28, 1944
The Beverly Hills Uplift Society has an auction. Guest star: Brian Aherne.

R549 April 4, 1944 (Ontario Army Air Field, CA)
Does a certain redhead intend to elope with George? Gracie thinks so. Guest star: Lucille Ball.

R550 April 11, 1944 (Hollywood, CA)
Tootsie Sagwell sets her sights on an old flame. Guest star: Herbert Marshall. **SEE B190.**

R551 April 18, 1944
Barbara Stanwyck misses husband Robert Taylor, who is in the military, so Gracie tries to cheer her up. Gracie tries to get George to help her with the household cleaning.

R552 April 25, 1944
George is running for Second Assistant Substitute City Councilman from the Third District. Guest star: Frank Morgan.

R553 May 2, 1944
Gracie thinks George will get more votes if people think a movie queen is in love with him. Guest star: Lana Turner.

R554 May 9, 1944
The race for the council seat continues as George and Gracie conduct a door-to-door campaign and Ray Milland suggests that George take his views to the voters via the radio; unfortunately the station is owned by his opponent, Gordon Cates. Jimmy Cash sings "It Had To Be You" in a salute to Eddie Cantor on his 35th anniversary in show business. An appeal was made for single women and non-farm housewives with no young children to get into "war work." It was announced that if viewers send in 10¢ to Gracie Allen at Box 84, New York City 8, New York, they will receive a painting of more than 20 babies on a ship, printed on 12" x 15" heavy art paper, done in storybook style and containing no advertising.

R555 May 16, 1944
Can George sing his way into office? Guest star: Lawrence Tibbett.

R556 May 23, 1944
A failed political career behind him, George may decide to become a producer. Guest star: George Jessel.

R557 May 30, 1944
Gracie tries to help Tootsie by substituting a movie star's pictures for hers. Guest star: Betty Grable.

R558 June 6, 1944
George prepares to leave for Kansas City when he thinks he's been chosen as that city's favorite singer. Guest star: Dinah Shore. **SEE D86, D103, D119, D129.**

R559 June 13, 1944 (Municipal Auditorium in Kansas City, MO
George and Gracie are in town for the Kansas City War Bond Rally for the Fifth War Loan Drive. In a continuation of last week's episode the truth comes out when it's announced that Kansas City's favorite singer is someone else but George still gets to sing when Gracie blackmails the man in charge. George "Sugar Throat Burns" sings "I Can't Give You Anything But Love, Baby" with Dinah Shore. Guest star: Dinah Shore. **SEE D86, D104, D119, D129, D193, D249.**

R560 August 15, 1944 (Hollywood, CA)
Bill Goodwin welcomes George and Gracie back to the air. Felix Mills replaces Paul Whiteman. Gracie became a reporter over the summer and wrote a series of columns from both political conventions; George doesn't understand how Gracie could have been chosen for such a task; Gracie has offended the landlord with her columns, and George is afraid he won't renew their lease.

Review: "...one of the more consistent chuckle providers...just signed 5 year contract last spring with Swan covering network radio appearances." (**Variety**, August 23, 1944: 30).

R561 August 22, 1944
Another redhead, who doesn't know Gracie is married, develops a crush on her when he sees her entertaining at the "Canteen" in Hollywood. Gracie performs her "Concerto for Index Finger." In real life, Gracie has colored her naturally black hair to red. Guest star: Van Johnson.

Review: "Resuming after a brief hot weather layoff the Burns and Allen troupe, intact as to cast and musical trimmings, is depending on the reliable formula...which has served to establish the stanza as one of the more consistent chuckle providers along the spectrum." (**Variety**, August 23, 1944: 30).

R562 August 29, 1944
Gracie and Blanche Morton buy several items at an auction and then, realizing they don't have the money to pay for them, try to get the cash from their husbands.

R563 September 5, 1944
Gracie prepares to write a column for Consolidated News Features.

R564 September 12, 1944
Is George a better singer than Bing Crosby? Guest star: Louella Parsons.

R565 September 19, 1944
George and Gracie are expecting guests for dinner.

R566 September 26, 1944
George is in a bad mood and Gracie asks him to be a handyman and fix the plumbing in the kitchen sink.

R567 October 3, 1944
Bill Goodwin falls for a golddigger and Gracie tries to save him from his fate. **SEE D234.**

R568 October 10, 1944
Joe Bagley has a piece of land for sale and Gracie wants to buy it in order to build a house. **SEE D203.**

R569 October 17, 1944
George thinks he dented the fender on the car. **SEE D159.**

R570 October 24, 1944
Gracie's success as a columnist inspires her to write a book but she wants to "suffer" for her craft.

R571 October 31, 1944
Gracie tries to make George jealous. Guest star: Van Johnson.

R572 November 7, 1944
No show due to Election Day.

R573 November 14, 1944 (Symphony Hall in Boston, MA)
Gracie and George are in Boston for the United War Fund Rally. Gracie wants George to sing at the rally and calls Arthur Fiedler, director of the Boston Pops Orchestra. George duets with James Melton. **SEE D178.**

R574 November 21, 1944 (New York, NY)
Gracie and George are in New York for a war bond tour, searching desperately for a hotel room, since Gracie wouldn't let George wire ahead. Finally settled into Franchot Tone's temporarily unoccupied room without Mr. Tone's knowledge, Gracie begins to confuse being asleep with being awake and thinks that George is Franchot and vice versa. Gracie opens tonight's show with a plea for recruits to the U.S. Merchant Marine, saying that they need 8,000 men per month, "with or without sea experience."

R575 November 28, 1944 (Convention Hall, Philadelphia, PA)
Gracie thinks she has been invited to Philadelphia to perform her "Concerto for Index Finger." Guest star: José Iturbi.

R576 December 5, 1944
George's plans to play golf are interrupted when he has to explain the game to Gracie.

R577 December 12, 1944
Gracie tries to prevent Frank Sinatra from singing at the bond show; she thinks George should do the singing instead.

R578 December 19, 1944
There are five shopping days 'til Christmas and everyone is hinting for a present from George; Gracie suggests she and George not exchange gifts this year but those plays go awry and they nearly drive a department store clerk crazy.

R579 December 26, 1944

When the sponsor announces a change to Monday nights Gracie decides to make a change of her own--to dramatic actress. This is Jimmy Cash and Bill Goodwin's last show.

The show moves to Monday nights at 8:30-9:00 P.M.

R580 January 1, 1945
Harry Von Zell becomes the show's announcer. George has written a comedy script and one of Hollywood's most beloved leading men wants a chance to do comedy but Gracie makes a dramatic switch with a script of her own. The show has a new opening: "Swan, the white floating soap that's pure as fine castiles, brings you George Burns and Gracie Allen." Guest star: Charles Boyer.

R581 January 8, 1945
Shirley Temple wants a part in a Selznick picture in which she would play a young girl opposite an older man and decides to practice with George.

R582 January 15, 1945
Gracie makes George sit through an Alan Ladd movie three times then goes to Alan's house to make George jealous. Guest star: Alan Ladd. It's announced that every baby born in 1945 can get a cake of Swan Soap free. Gracie notes that paper is needed for the overseas war effort ("Paper Packs a Punch"). **SEE D233.**

R583 January 22, 1945
The Beverly Hills Uplift Society is meeting at the Burnses' home where they talk about Tootsie Sagwell whom they have sent to finishing school to help her get married. **SEE D233.**

R584 January 29, 1945
George and Gracie re-live their wedding day.

R585 February 5, 1945
Gracie's Uncle John arrives for a visit.

R586 February 12, 1945
George runs for scoutmaster.

R587 February 19, 1945
George's political nemesis, Gordon Cates, rents the house next door.

R588 February 26, 1945
George tries to get Gordon Cates to move.

R589 March 5, 1944
Gracie and Uncle John visit a burlesque theater.

R590 March 12, 1945
George's problems with Gordon Cates multiply.

R591 March 19, 1945
George discovers Gordon Cates can out-sing him, too.

R592 March 26, 1945
The feud between George and Gordon ends and Gracie tries to start it up again because, when George was jealous of Gordon, he was paying a lot more attention to her.

R593 April 2, 1945
George goes rabbit hunting.

R594 April 9, 1945
It's national "Clean Out Your Closet Week," and everyone is asked to send clothes to citizens of the allied nations who have suffered the effects of the war.

R595 April 16, 1945
No broadcast due to the death of President Roosevelt.

R596 April 23, 1945
George and Gracie try to get a loan to buy a lot for a new house.

R597 April 30, 1945
George and Gracie hire a new housekeeper.

R598 May 7, 1945
George and Gracie's starstruck maid demands a visit from a movie star. Guest star: Turhan Bey.

R599 May 14, 1945
Gracie thinks she and George aren't legally married and makes George court her again.

R600 May 21, 1945
George finds out their marriage is legal and so does Gracie but she doesn't tell George so he pretends that, now that he's "single," he's been drafted.

R601 May 28, 1945
George is the prize at a war bonds booth.

R602 June 4, 1945
Everyone tries to discourage Harry Von Zell from getting married.

R603 June 11, 1945
There's a mouse in the house.

R604 June 18, 1945
People mistake George for Gracie's father on Father's Day so Gracie tries to make him young again. **SEE D87, D104, D127.**

R605 June 25, 1945
George and Gracie prepare to leave for a camp and hospital tour to entertain troops. The announcement is made that the "government wants the public to continue home canning." In closing, Gracie notes that this marks the end of four years with the Swan program and George says that it has been four of the happiest years they have ever known. They announce that viewers can send a dime to Swan Soap and get a color picture of a baby playing. This time slot is to be taken over by comedienne Joan Davis. **SEE D87, D100, D127.**

10. Maxwell House Coffee Time. 1945-1949. NBC. 30 min.

Sponsor: General Foods Corporation.
Product: Maxwell House Coffee.
Agency: Benton and Bowles.
Network: NBC.
Broadcast Day: Thursday.
Time Slot: 8:00-8:30 P.M. (EST).
Director: Al Kaye.
Scriptwriters: Paul Henning, Keith Fowler, Frank Galen, William Burns.
Announcer: Bill Goodwin.
Orchestra Leader: Meredith Willson and the Maxwell House Orchestra.
Vocalists: The Les Paul Trio.
Actors: Bea Benaderet, Mel Blanc, Hal March, Elvia Allman, Verna Felton, Margaret Brayton, Hans Conried, Gale Gordon, Elliott Lewis, Dawn Bender, Tommy Bernard, Doris Singleton, Mary Lee Robb, Richard Crenna, Ernest (Ernie) Whitman, Barbara Eiler, Joseph Kearns, Eric Snowden, Lois Corbett, Lou Merrill, Frank Nelson, Jerry Hausner, Virgil Rimer, Jim Backus, Sandra Gould, Lurene Tuttle, Wally Maher, Sheldon Leonard, Irene Tedrow, Dick Ryan, Harry Luden, Bobby Jellison, Tony Barrett, Frank Gerstle, Pat McGeehan, Gerald Mohr, Joan Banks, Marvin Miller, Henry Blair, Robert Bence, Isabel Randolph, Sarah Berner, Ollie O'Toole, Will Wright, Cathy Lewis, Paula Winslowe, Anna Whitfield, Veola Vonn, Bill Demling, Leora Thatcher.
Theme Song: "The Love Nest."
Premise: There are no major changes from the previous series. However, there is a greater use of featured performers as continuing characters in a role.
Additional Notes: Meredith Willson went on to become most well-known as the composer of the music for **The Music Man** and **The Unsinkable Molly Brown**, both of which went from stage to film. **See B216.**

R606 September 20, 1945
Maxwell House Coffee Time was already a well-established program prior to George and Gracie stepping in as its stars. Meredith Willson moves in as George and Gracie's new neighbor.

R607 September 27, 1945
George gives a surprise party for Gracie.

R608 October 4, 1945
George send Gracie to buy a jeep but she returns with what she thinks are one hundred pair of nylons.

R609 October 11, 1945
George and Gracie find a secret door in their new house.

R610 October 18, 1945
Gracie gives Meredith Willson tips on getting dates.

R611 October 25, 1945
Gracie decides to redecorate the living room.

R612 November 1, 1945
Gracie pretends to be Bill Goodwin's wife so he'll have a better chance getting cast as a husband in a movie. **SEE D126, D141, D183, D187, D217.**

R613 November 8, 1945
George gets the lead part in a new motion picture and "goes Hollywood." Dick Joy is tonight's announcer. Guest star George Jessel and Gracie sing "My Mother's Eyes." **SEE D96, D141, D187, D192, D217.**

R614 November 15, 1945
George tests to sing in a new Betty Grable picture. Guest star: Mischa Auer.

R615 November 22, 1945
George enrolls in college and receives some money from a relative. **SEE D130, D278.**

R616 November 29, 1945
Jack Benny joins George at college (Beverly Hills Tech), where they compete for "most popular man on campus," which includes a talent contest. Jack plays his violin and George sings. **SEE D88, D100, D109, D112, D130, D144, D190, D278.**

R617 December 6, 1945
Look magazine wants to interview George on the same day he's trying to avoid an insurance salesman.

R618 December 13, 1945
Gracie hopes her new gown will give her the advantage over Dinah Shore on next week's show.

R619 December 20, 1945
George and Gracie team up with the **Birdseye Open House** starring Dinah Shore for a special one-hour show. A misunderstanding arises over an item in a gossip column that mentions a man named "George." Guest stars: Dinah Shore and George Montgomery, the Bobby Dolan Orchestra and the Ken Lane Singers. Harry Von Zell also appears.

R620 December 27, 1945
Can George and Gracie's happy marriage be an inspiration to the postman and his wife?

R621 January 3, 1946
The housing shortage caused by the return of veterans causes orchestra leader and radio star Kay Kyser to move in with George and Gracie and turn his house over to a veteran.

R622 January 10, 1946
The Beverly Hills Uplift Society is in debt.

R623 January 17, 1946

George is forced out of the radio show by the Beverly Hills Uplift Society.

R624 January 24, 1946
George is hoping that Meredith Willson will move. Guest star: Kay Kyser.

R625 January 31, 1946
George "pretends" to be hypnotized into acting like Charles Boyer.

R626 February 7, 1946
George and Gracie are finalists in a search for Hollywood's ideal married couple.

R627 February 14, 1946
The show's sponsor comes to dinner. Special guest: Charles Mortimer.

R628 February 21, 1946
George receives a letter from someone named Harry who needs help for a big job in Washington and thinks it came from President Truman. (President Truman requested a copy of the script of this show).

R629 February 28, 1946
George is disappointed. The letter was from Harry Morton.

R630 March 7, 1946
Meredith Willson thinks George and Gracie should buy a chicken ranch.

R631 March 14, 1946
Gracie opens a matrimonial bureau. **SEE D153.**

R632 March 21, 1946
George enters a wrestling match.

R633 March 28, 1946
George and Gracie go on a double date with Meredith Willson and his prospective new girlfriend.

R634 April 4, 1946
The month's bills have come in and Gracie tries to hide them from George. **SEE D154, D255.**

R635 April 11, 1946
Gracie tries to join a literary society; George would rather read **Cowboy Love Tales**. **SEE D79, D128, D150, D305.**

R636 April 18, 1946
George's fascination with **Cowboy Love Tales** inspires Gracie to try to turn George into a singing cowboy.

R637 April 25, 1946
George accepts the lead in the Beverly Hills Uplift Society play until the ladies decide Charles Boyer would be better suited for the part. Special guest: NBC vice-president Sydney Strotz.

R638 May 2, 1946
George and Gracie again join with the **Birdseye Open House** starring Dinah Shore for a one-hour show. Charles Boyer accepts a part in the Beverly Hills Uplift Society's play. Guest stars: Charles Boyer and Frances Langford (Dinah Shore was to appear but developed a case of laryngitis).

R639 May 9, 1946
Gracie hires Harpo Marx as a reporter.

R640 May 16, 1946
George and Gracie's new neighbors are newlyweds, which gives Gracie ideas.

R641 May 23, 1946
Gracie gives advice to the new bride. Guest star: Sharon Douglas.

R642 May 30, 1946
Who will take over the show for the summer while George and Gracie are on vacation? Guest star: Ben Gage.

The show's time slot changes to 8:30-9:00 P.M.

R643 September 5, 1946
Gracie thinks George has an allergy.

Review: "...they were...a pair of sure footed troopers who had control of every moment." (**Variety**, September 11, 1946: 34).

R644 September 12, 1946
Gracie brings home a burglar. Guest star: Dewey Robinson.

R645 September 19, 1946
George thinks everyone has forgotten his birthday and may wish they had when he hears about Gracie's gift; she's volunteered him for a trip to outer space--and he's been accepted!

R646 September 26, 1946
George and Gracie become quiz show contests. Guest star: Kay Kyser.

R647 October 3, 1946
Gracie plays matchmaker to Meredith Willson and one of Eddie Cantor's daughters.

R648 October 10, 1946
Gracie is upset when George would rather listen to the World Series on the radio than have an outing with her.

R649 October 17, 1946
Gracie thinks MGM should give Clark Gable's part in **The Hucksters**, a film to be released in 1947, to George.

R650 October 24, 1946
The Beverly Hills Uplift Society tries to convince George that Gracie is right about **The Hucksters** part. **SEE D88, D110, D250.**

R651 October 31, 1946
Jack Carson thinks he should have the Gable role. Guest star: Jack Carson. Similar to R750. **SEE D89, D110.**

R652 November 7, 1946
Gracie tries to get Frank Sinatra out of town so he won't get the part in **The Hucksters**. **SEE D294.**

R653 November 14, 1946
Gracie enlists Louella Parsons' aid in getting George the lead in the film.

R654 November 21, 1946
The two "contenders" for the role meet. Guest star: Clark Gable.

R655 November 28, 1946
Gracie tries to earn some extra money to buy George's Christmas present.

R656 December 5, 1946
Still trying to earn Christmas money, Gracie answers a newspaper ad for a "problem explainer."

R657 December 12, 1946
Gracie's next attempt, babysitting, hits a snag when George mistakenly sells a baby for $200.

R658 December 17, 1946
The Christmas countdown continues. Will Gracie be successful as a department store clerk?

R659 December 26, 1946
George receives a smoking jacket as a Christmas gift but it's actually a bribe. Guest star: Eddie Cantor.

R660 January 2, 1947
Gracie and Blanche Morton are tired of the way their husbands treat them and decide to form a Housewives Association. **SEE D295.**

R661 January 9, 1947
Gracie's Christmas bills arrive and she has to find a way to pay them.

R662 January 16, 1947
Angry over George's poker playing Gracie hears him talking about the "kitty" and thinks he may really have been out chasing women.

R663 January 23, 1947
Gracie tries to play matchmaker for her cousin, Nellie, and Bill Goodwin.

R664 January 30, 1947
Gracie tries to enlist Beatrice Lillie's aid in making Nellie more sophisticated.

R665 February 6, 1947
Is Sonny Tufts the ideal mate for Nellie?

R666 February 13, 1947
Or is Cary Grant better suited?

R667 February 20, 1947
George and Gracie reminisce about their fifteen years in radio by recalling when they worked with Al Jolson, who thought Gracie was a ventriloquist and George her dummy. George and Al sing "April Showers." Guest star: Al Jolson. **SEE D89, D109, D113, D181, D191, D227, D270.**

R668 February 27, 1947
After getting months of past due bills, George wants Gracie to run the house like a business. A salesman tries to sell Gracie the True Tone Victaphone. There is an ad at the end of the show for young women to become nurses. **SEE D90, D102.**

R669 March 6, 1947
Gracie imagines herself to be a detective like the one on one of her favorite radio shows.

R670 March 13, 1947
Gracie overhears two exterminators' conversation and thinks they're coming to kill George.

R671 March 20, 1947
Gracie buys a dog for protection but it hates George.

R672 March 27, 1947
Gracie's dog has a screen test for a role in a Charles Boyer film.

R673 April 3, 1947
Gracie wants George to give her money for an Easter hat.

R674 April 10, 1947
Gracie tries to sell the house.

R675 April 17, 1947
Gracie sells the house.

R676 April 24, 1947
George and Gracie move in with Bill Goodwin, then with Meredith Willson.

R677 May 1, 1947
An apartment is available but there's one catch. George has to be the janitor.

R678 May 8, 1947
George goes to live in the YMCA while Gracie moves into the YWCA. **SEE D155, D255.**

R679 May 15, 1947
Four weeks after Gracie sold their home she and George have been able to buy it back and are moving in; Gracie is contrite. **SEE D128, D151.**

R680 May 22, 1947
The Beverly Hills Uplift Society's latest project: getting Congress to appropriate funds for the purchase of hats.

R681 May 29, 1947
George and Gracie try to agree on a vacation destination. **The Frances Langford Show** will be their summer replacement for the next thirteen weeks.

R682 September 4, 1947
Tobe Reed joins the cast to share announcing duties with Bill Goodwin. George and Gracie talk about their vacation and the new longer dress styles.

R683 September 11, 1947
Gracie buys a dress without George's permission, returns it, and George re-buys it.

R684 September 18, 1947
The battle over long versus short dresses rages on. Guest stars: Edith Head, Howard Greer and Orry Kelly.

R685 September 25, 1947
Gracie tries to convince a man to invest in a play about her family.

R686 October 2, 1947
Gracie writes a play about her family, **I Remember Mama's Life With Father In Tights**, and asks William Powell to appear in it.

R687 October 9, 1947
While Cary Grant is out of town Gracie gets a job as his secretary and moves into his house. When she refuses to come home George moves in, too.

R688 October 16, 1947
Cary Grant returns home and Gracie must keep him and George from running into each other.

R689 October 23, 1947
George and Gracie buy chickens to lay eggs and discover they have only roosters.

R690 October 30, 1947
Cary Grant takes George's place as Gracie's husband.

R691 November 6, 1947
Gracie is expecting a pig to arrive from Cousin Nellie but her Cousin Henry shows up instead. Guest star: Arnold Stang.

R692 November 13, 1947
Gracie wants Cary Grant to speak to her Beverly Hills Uplift Society using the theme "Women, Are They Here to Stay?"

R693 November 20, 1947
The royal wedding in Great Britain is approaching and Gracie dreams she is Princess Elizabeth.

R694 November 27, 1947
George is "awarded" the French Legion of Honor Medal for "bravery in singing." Guest star: Jean Sablon.

R695 December 4, 1947
Gracie thinks George will be the country's top singer if she can get Bing Crosby to retire. Guest star: Bing Crosby. **SEE D90, D96, D114, D177, D181, D189, D192, D203, D227, D232, D270.**

R696 December 11, 1947
If shy Meredith Willson can be hypnotized into being a "wolf" Gracie figures it should work with George, too.

R697 December 18, 1947
George tries to find out what Gracie wants for Christmas. They decide not to give each other presents but both end up at the same department store to select each other gifts.

R698 December 25, 1947
"Gracie" tries to find a way for George to sing at their Christmas dinner. Jane Wyman substitutes for an ailing Gracie Allen.

R699 January 1, 1948
George continues in his efforts to get the Beverly Hills Uplift Society to break up. **SEE D115.**

R700 January 8, 1948
Jack Benny and George dream of being a concert violinist and a world-famous singer so Gracie suggests a gypsy concert. Guest star: Jack Benny. **SEE D91, D102, D105, D143, D194.**

R701 January 15, 1948
Gracie thinks George has defrauded the government and is going to be sentenced to Alcatraz. There is an announcement about supporting teachers and school systems.

R702 January 22, 1948
Gracie and a friend recall their early years in San Francisco. Guest star: Walter O'Keefe. **SEE D91, D105, D115, D164.**

R703 January 29, 1948
Gracie thinks she and George should take separate vacations.

R704 February 5, 1948
In order to get a fur coat for Gracie George decides to go rabbit hunting. **SEE D167.**

R705 February 12, 1948
Kay Kyser and his wife have a new baby and are looking for a nurse when Kay meets Gracie at the soda fountain, who volunteers George for the job. Mr. Judson, a friend from Texas, arrives.

R706 February 19, 1948
Gracie goes to the doctor to have a dream interpreted but tells him one of George's instead. Mr. Judson tries to sell George some cattle.

R707 February 26, 1948
Gracie is going to New Orleans for the Fete de Chapeau Festival. She plans to buy several new hats while there but George refuses to give her the money.

R708 March 4, 1948
A friend of George and Gracie's has a problem: he thinks he's Bing Crosby. Guest star: Eddie Cantor.

R709 March 11, 1948
Inspired by a visit to the Freedom Train and a speaker who encouraged people to become more involved in the governmental process, Gracie tries to fulfill her civic duty by writing letters (and lots of them) to Congress. Gracie hints to George that their anniversary is coming up and George tries to buy her lingerie. She also hires two child actors to pose as her children, thinking it will "hold" George. Harry Lubin and his orchestra appear. Featured song: "Oh How We Danced On the Night We Were Wed."

R710 March 18, 1948
Gracie tries to find a hair restorer for George.

R711 March 25, 1948
It's a twist on the usual Easter theme when Gracie wants to buy George an outfit.

R712 April 1, 1948
Has George's voice made him a lady killer?

R713 April 8, 1948
Gracie doesn't believe George when he says he went to a lecture on fossils.

R714 April 15, 1948
George thinks Gracie is going to replace him with their neighbor, Joe Bagley, and go on television.

R715 April 22, 1948

Joe Bagley tricks George into *not* giving Gracie a bouquet of roses, and George plots revenge. Normally radio shows at this time were performed twice, once for the West Coast and several hours later for the East Coast. The April 22, 1948 broadcast, however, was different. An announcement was made at the show's opening that "Due to an attack of laryngitis, Gracie Allen is unable to appear in person at this time. This broadcast is a transcription of an earlier broadcast." In that earlier broadcast, Gracie's voice problems are apparent. **SEE D92, D146.**

R716 April 29, 1948
George and Gracie finally receive their priority slip and can buy a new car but Gracie comes home with a 1918 Stutz Bearcat.

R717 May 6, 1948
George, Gracie and Joe Bagley try to find a husband for Mr. Judson's sister, unaware she's trying to find the one who left twenty years ago. **SEE D156, D255.**

R718 May 13, 1948
George's mother-in-law arrives for a visit; Gracie can't resist a door-to-door salesman. **SEE D79, D152, D212.**

R719 May 20, 1948
Gracie's mother doesn't think George can take care of things around the house and she refuses to leave until he can prove that he's a handyman. **SEE D157, D255, D284.**

R720 May 27, 1948
Gracie buys a piece of land that turns out to be in a swamp.

R721 June 3, 1948
Joe Bagley leads George into the doghouse again over a poker game that was raided.

R722 June 10, 1948
It's vacation time and, once more, George and Gracie can't agree on where to go.

R723 September 30, 1948
Harry Lubin is the new orchestra leader. One of the new neighbors gets the mistaken impression that George is going to leave Gracie and ask her to elope with him. At the same time Gracie tries to help teenagers Harold and Emily elope. George sings "Sweet Sue." **SEE D83, D140, D177, D197.**

R724 October 7, 1948
George fears Gracie has become a kleptomaniac.

R725 October 14, 1948
George and Gracie take a second honeymoon even though George lost the Ideal Husband contest.

R726 October 21, 1948
George wants to join the Crestline Country Club but is turned down because he's in show business so Gracie tries to help him qualify.

R727 October 28, 1948
Gracie can't get money from George for a new dress so she opens up their house as a hotel.

R728 November 4, 1948
Gracie's fictional story about a wife-beating husband appears in a magazine and everyone thinks George was the inspiration.

R729 November 11, 1948
George tries to surprise Gracie on their wedding anniversary with a gift of lingerie but Gracie thinks he bought it for someone else. Tonight's song is "Oh, How We Danced on the Night We Were Wed."

R730 November 18, 1948
George and Gracie try to advise quarreling lovers by each claiming to be the boss at home. **SEE D169.**

R731 November 25, 1948

It's Thanksgiving and the turkey swallows a ring George was keeping as best man for a friend's wedding.

R732 December 2, 1948
George pretends to be the butler when Gracie's school friend comes to visit.

R733 December 9, 1948
Gracie insists she's going to give George a Christmas gift she's making herself but George is worried when he sees what she's using to make it.

R734 December 16, 1948
George and Gracie move into Jack Benny's house while he's away and drive the neighbors crazy. Guest stars: Ronald Colman and Benita Hume.

R735 December 23, 1948
George encourages the Beverly Hills Uplift Society to enter a Christmas carol contest.

R736 December 30, 1948
George and Gracie have their New Year's Eve party one night early. Guest star: Meredith Willson.

R737 January 6, 1949
After seeing how romantic Gregory Peck is on the screen Gracie wants George to be more romantic so George arranges for Gracie to have dinner at Mr. Peck's home. **SEE D169.**

R738 January 13, 1949
Gracie and Blanche receive mink coats.

R739 January 20, 1949
Gracie wants Bill Goodwin to get married and he ends up fighting with Cesar Romero over the same girl. **SEE D131, D196, D201, D203, D222.**

R740 January 27, 1949
As a gift to George Gracie asks Gene Kelly to play George in a movie and re-enact George's marriage proposal.

R741 February 3, 1949
Gracie sells the house again when she hears warnings from the Safety Council about the dangers of home accidents.

R742 February 10, 1949
George and "Sam Spade" are in jail thanks to a misunderstanding on Gracie's part. Guest star: Howard Duff.

R743 February 17, 1949
James and Pamela Mason have moved to Beverly Hills and Gracie wants to meet them so, knowing that the Masons are cat lovers, she tells them that George has a cat collection. **SEE D92, D114, D135, D136, D137, D143, D194, D204.**

R744 February 24, 1949
A handwriting expert concludes that George should be a doctor. **SEE D93, D101, D122, D135, D163, D166, D196, D204, D222, D250, D286.**

R745 March 3, 1949
Gracie wrecks the car. Guest star: Richard Widmark.

R746 March 10, 1949
The Girl Scouts celebrate an anniversary and Gracie becomes a troop leader.

R747 March 17, 1949
George is sick with a cold and gets a "grandmotherly" type babysitter while Gracie attends a Beverly Hills Uplift Society pageant. Guest star: Marlene Dietrich. **SEE D180.**

R748 March 24, 1949
Gracie tries to keep an Oscar nominee calm. Guest star: Jane Wyman.

Miss Wyman, nominated as part of an impressive list of actresses in celebrated roles, *did* win the Academy Award in 1949 for Best Actress for her role in 1948's **Johnny Belinda**. **SEE D93, D122, D140.**

R749 March 31, 1949
Gracie reminisces about the time Jack Benny and George proposed to her and how it led to Jack becoming a cheapskate. **SEE D94, D101, D106, D134, D160.**

R750 April 7, 1949
Gracie tries to get George a part in Mr. Judson's new movie based on Napoleon. Similar to R651. Guest star: Robert Montgomery.

R751 April 14, 1949
Blanche and Gracie want to rearrange their furniture.

R752 April 21, 1949
George and Gracie try to help a friend who is lonely because her husband is working too hard. Guest star: Eddie Cantor. The National Safety Council's campaign against home accidents and their theme, "Don't be a Gracie Allen," culminated with Gracie being elected national president of the "Don't be a Gracie" club. Housewives were asked to check their homes for safety, at least thirty-five cities had home chapters and several future broadcasts contain ads for the club, encouraging people to write to Gracie at the "Hollywood Plaza Hotel, Hollywood 28, California."

R753 April 28, 1949
George inadvertently wins prizes for ladyfingers and needlework at a county fair.

R754 May 5, 1949
George's fear of TV causes him to consider becoming a cowboy. Guest star: William Boyd.

R755 May 12, 1949
George fears his lack of sex appeal will cause him to be a failure on television. Guest star: Marie McDonald. **SEE D167.**

R756 May 19, 1949
Gracie decides to adopt Mickey Rooney. "Don't Be A Gracie Club" is announced as supported by the National Safety Council to help prevent home accidents. Guest star: Mickey Rooney. **SEE D97, D113, D117, D125, D135, D137, D138, D166, D191, D197, D198, D199, D204, D208, D276.**

R757 May 26, 1949
An old friend of Gracie's has become a member of the international crowd.

R758 June 2, 1949
Gracie pretends to be a magician. Guest star: Chester Morris.

R759 June 9, 1949
Gracie joins the Women's Movement.

R760 June 16, 1949
Gracie confuses Emily Vanderlip's boyfriend with an older man. Guest star: Rudy Vallee. **SEE D83, D132.**

R761 June 23, 1949
George and Gracie prepare for a trip to England. This is the last show for Maxwell House Coffee. Guest star: Robert Young.

10. The Amm-i-Dent Toothpaste Show. 1949-1950. CBS. 30 min.

Sponsor: Block Drug Company.
Product: Amm-i-dent Toothpaste.
Network: CBS.
Broadcast Day: Wednesday.
Time Slot: 10:00-10:30 P.M. (Eastern Standard Time).
Producer/Director: William Burns.
Scriptwriters: Paul Henning, Harvey Helm, Sid Dorfman, Larry Klein, Stanley Shapiro.
Announcer: Bill Goodwin, Tobe Reed.

Orchestra Leader: Harry Lubin.
Actors: Bea Benaderet, Howard McNear, Hal March, Marvin Miller, Joan Rae, Wally Maher, Hans Conried, Mary Jane Croft, Joseph Kearns, Ollie O'Toole, Sheldon Leonard, Jane Morgan, Jerry Hausner, Jay Novello, Lois Corbett, Ken Christy, Dave Light, Gerald Mohr, Veola Vonn, Shirley Mitchell, Gerald Borum.
Theme Song: "The Love Nest."
Premise: This last sponsor change for their radio show before they moved to television prompted no major changes in the show's style. Their fourth and last publicity stunt, Gracie making guest appearances on other shows while she tries to find someone who will allow George to utilize his vocal abilities, was launched during this series.

R762 September 21, 1949
The first show for Amm-i-dent of their final radio series finds the Burnses returning from Europe. Gracie's Uncle John comes for a visit but George thinks he's the new sponsor.

R763 September 28, 1949
Gracie had hoped their visit to Paris would make George become more romantic. **SEE D131, D763.**

R764 October 5, 1949
Gracie thinks George should replace Ezio Pinza in **South Pacific**.

R765 October 12, 1949
George and Gracie can't figure out why today's date is circled in red on the calendar.

R766 October 19, 1949
George has a ticket to a major football game until Gracie gets involved.

R767 October 26, 1949
Gracie plays matchmaker for her Uncle John.

R768 November 2, 1949
George hopes to be appointed head of the Beverly Hills Park Board.

R769 November 9, 1949
Gracie learns about the barter system.

R770 November 16, 1949
Gracie thinks George has lost all of their money playing poker.

R771 November 23, 1949
Blanche Morton and Gracie argue at Thanksgiving dinner over who's the better singer, Bing Crosby or George. This episode kicks off George and Gracie's last major publicity stunt on radio, the "George Burns Sings" campaign.

R772 November 30, 1949
Gracie interrupts other radio shows asking for a singing spot for George.

R773 December 7, 1949
George finally makes his singing debut. Guest stars: The Andrews Sisters.

R774 December 14, 1949
George is depressed over his debut so Gracie throws a party and asks him to sing.

R775 December 21, 1949
Gracie goes shopping for a Christmas tree and George goes caroling.

R776 December 28, 1949
Disappointed that the Mortons can't attend the Friars Club New Year's Eve masquerade ball with her and George because they're not members, Gracie makes an appeal to the club's abbot. Guest star: George Jessel.

R777 January 4, 1950
Gracie visits a museum and decides to become a painter. **SEE D95.**

R778 January 11, 1950

Gracie goes to MGM to talk to producer Joe Pasternak about getting a friend's daughter a movie contract.

R779 January 18, 1950
Gracie tries to change her life by not worrying anymore.

R780 January 25, 1950
George has written a speech for a Friars Club dinner and wants to rehearse it but Gracie interrupts him to tell him about a dream she had. Guest star: Ronald Reagan. President Reagan shared a memory of Gracie in a **Los Angeles Herald Examiner** article from February 26, 1988. He related that, during an appearance he made on a Burns and Allen broadcast, Gracie's entire radio script fell from the rack to the floor. According to the former President she froze at first but averted disaster by automatically going into one of her and George's old vaudeville routines. **SEE D77, D296.**

R781 February 1, 1950
Gracie attempts to discover how Al Jolson maintains such a vigorous lifestyle.

R782 February 8, 1950
George is writing a song; she is talking about the Fete de Chapeau Festival; the car fender is dented again and Gracie thinks she did it and has just forgotten about it. George and Gracie sing "Do You Believe Me?", the song they sang in their first film short in 1929, **Burns and Allen in Lamb Chops**. **SEE F1**.

R783 February 15, 1950
George tries to get his song recorded; a theatrical agent wants Gracie and George to star in the play **Dulcy**. An announcement is made about heart disease and the 1950 campaign to raise funds.

R784 February 22, 1950
The Burnses and Mortons go to the horse races at Santa Anita and George has words with Sam the Tailor. Tonight's song is "Ain't Misbehavin." Judge Roger Alton Fox of Los Angeles gives the 1949 Award of Merit to George and Gracie on behalf of the National Safety Council and thanks George and Gracie for giving their time and talent (without remuneration) to promoting safety. **SEE D144.**

R785 March 1, 1950
Gracie tries to help their tax man in filing their return. **SEE D79, D95, D132, D134, D161, D164, D305.**

R786 March 8, 1950
Gracie wants to re-decorate the house. Guest star: William Haines.

R787 March 15, 1950
George and Gracie receive an offer to do a television show.

R788 March 22, 1950
George prepares for an appearance in the Friars Frolic.

R789 March 29, 1950
A friend of George and Gracie's is scheduled to appear on Jack Benny's show but Benny doesn't want to pay him. Guest star: Al Jolson.

R790 April 5, 1950
George and Gracie prepare to leave for a trip to Palm Springs.

R791 April 12, 1950
The Burnses talk about their trip to Palm Springs.

R792 April 19, 1950
George and Gracie are interviewed by **Pageant**.

R793 April 26, 1950
It's time for Gracie to renew her driver's license.

R794 May 3, 1950
George gets the wrong impression when a famous singer asks him for a song. Guest star: Dinah Shore.

R795 May 10, 1950
George and Harry Morton go to a baseball game while Gracie and Blanche go to the movies but Gracie has the baseball tickets with her.

R796 May 17, 1950
George and Gracie toast their eighteen years on radio and prepare to move **The Burns and Allen Show** to television.

Radio Guest Appearances (1929-1995)

George Burns and Gracie Allen Individually and as a Team

R797 Vaudeville. BBC (British Broadcasting Company), London. June 10, 1929.
This is Burns and Allen's first radio broadcast. Beginning at 8:41 P.M., their performance consists of thirteen minutes of their vaudeville routine, "Lamb Chops," written by Al Boasberg, and the singing of the song "I Do."

R798 Vaudeville. BBC, London. June 17, 1929.
For their second radio broadcast the team is billed as "The Famous American Comedy Duo" on a summer vaudeville program with four other acts. They will broadcast a total of fifteen weeks of shows for the BBC. **SEE B385.**

R799 Vaudeville. BBC, London. June 28, 1929.
Burns and Allen perform another comedy spot for British radio.

R800 Vaudeville. BBC, London. July 2, 1929.
George and Gracie continue their series of guest appearances on this program from Great Britain.

R801 Burns and Allen. Daventry Experimental, 5GB. July 3, 1929.
Burns and Allen, the "American Musical Comedy Duo," present sixteen minutes of "Songs and Patter" on this experimental BBC radio station (erected in 1926) which was located seventy-five miles from London. Some sections of the show are broadcast from Birmingham, England.

R802 Vaudeville. BBC. September 30, 1930.
Burns and Allen return to England for the second year. They are the second performers on this seventy-minute broadcast and are billed as the "Famous American Musical Comedy Duo." **SEE B385.**

R803 RKO's Theatre of the Air. NBC. January 2, 1931.
Still under contract with Radio-Keith-Orpheum for vaudeville appearances, George and Gracie appear on this variety program featuring Phil Cook.

R804 Chase & Sanborn Hour. NBC. November 15, 1931.
Eddie Cantor invites Gracie to appear on his musical variety show where she acts the part of a newspaper reporter who interviews Cantor. **SEE B114, B494.**

R805 Fleischmann Yeast Hour. With Rudy Vallee. NBC. January 28, 1932.
Burns and Allen are guests on Rudy Vallee's popular variety show. The show's announcer has been advised to be brief due to the unusual amount of dialogue necessary in using Burns and Allen to advantage. Someone has a temporary crush on Gracie, who has confused the announcer, the vocalist and Rudy Vallee. George and Gracie perform a take-off on their old vaudeville routine, "Dizzy," and sing "I Love Her I Do."

R806 The Robert Burns Panatela Program. With Guy Lombardo. CBS. February 15, 1932.
Burns and Allen appear in two one-minute spots as the guest comedians on this musical show. By the following week (R1), they begin making regular appearances.

R807 Meet the Artist. CBS. April 12, 1932.

On this fifteen-minute interview program, George and Gracie tell about their early years, family, etc. Gracie mentions that she first came East "twelve years ago."

R808 **Chase & Sanborn Hour**. With Eddie Cantor. NBC. April 24, 1932. George and Gracie fill in for the ailing scheduled guest, Harry Richman. Part of tonight's routine includes a spoof of Paul Revere's ride. Broadcast from NBC's Times Square Studio in New York City, the show is being heard on the Pacific coast for the first time.

R809 **The Big Broadcast** radio preview. ca. 1932. George and Gracie promote their first feature film, **The Big Broadcast** (F19).

R810 **Fleischmann Yeast Hour**. With Rudy Vallee. NBC. January 5, 1933. Burns and Allen are guests on this popular variety program. The song "Crazy People" is played as their opening song. This is the program that went to an audio blackout when Vallee, using the wrong script, asked Gracie about her missing brother, to the network's chagrin.

R811 **Chase & Sanborn Hour**. With Eddie Cantor. NBC. January 8, 1933. Gracie appears without George and does a bit about her brother and teaches Cantor "the language of flowers."

R812 **Canada Dry Program**. With Jack Benny. CBS. January 8, 1933. Eddie Cantor calls Jack to warn him about Gracie breaking into programs looking for her brother. Jack is determined she won't, but Gracie does anyway. She also gives Mary Livingstone a recipe for cabbage layer cake.

R813 **Tydol Jubilee**. CBS. January 11, 1933. George appears to coax Gracie off the show, where she is looking for her missing brother.

R814 **Singin' Sam**. CBS. January 11, 1933. George and Gracie interrupt singer Harry Frankel's musical show to talk about Gracie's missing brother and he tries to be helpful.

R815 **Meet the Artist**. CBS. May 31, 1933. Burns and Allen are guests for the second time on this interview program.

R816 **Alice in Wonderland**. KFI (NBC), Los Angeles. November 16, 1933. Burns and Allen are part of a promotion for the new Paramount film version of the classic children's tale.

R817 **New Year's Columbia Stars**. KHJ (CBS), Los Angeles. December 31, 1933.
George asks Gracie about her New Year's resolutions on this New Year's Eve broadcast.

R818 **Columbia Radio Playhouse Dedication**. Special. KHJ (CBS), Los Angeles. February 3, 1934.
Burns and Allen are guests on this show celebrating the dedication of the Columbia Radio Playhouse. George and Gracie perform their "pants on backwards" routine.

R819 **Burns and Allen (Special Broadcast)**. CBS. June 23, 1934. George and Gracie broadcast from aboard the Italian line ship, the S.S. Rex. Also onboard are Jack Pearl (Baron Munchausen), with whom George does a routine, and his wife. Gracie talks about her "little blue hat." **SEE VG74.**

R820 **Burns and Allen (Special Broadcast)**. WGBI (CBS), Scranton. October 4, 1934.
Burns and Allen are appearing locally at the Capitol Theatre in Scranton, Pennsylvania on Thursday, Friday and Saturday.

R821 **Burns and Allen (Special Broadcast)**. CBS. October 29, 1934. George and Gracie are appearing at the Earle Theatre in Philadelphia, Pennsylvania, where they had earlier played in November 1924. The radio show is titled "Lesser's Court Room Trial" and the story line has Gracie preparing to go to court in an attempt to collect damages for a recent automobile accident.

R822 Hollywood Hotel. CBS. October 11, 1935.
Burns and Allen appear on this show with guests Irene Dunne and Robert Taylor.

R823 Hollywood Movie Parade. ca. 1935.
George and Gracie broadcast a preview of the 1935 film, **Love in Bloom. SEE F25.**

R824 Predictions For 1936. CBS. January 4, 1936.
George and Gracie are appearing at the Chicago Theatre in Chicago, Illinois, for one week and are part of this show which forecasts predictable events of the new year. The broadcast is introduced in New York City by J. V. Connolly, the president of King Features. News experts throughout the world take part in the broadcast. Appearing on stage with Burns and Allen are dancer and comedian Ben Blue, magician Cardini, orchestra leader Jacques Renard and vocalist Milton Watson.

R825 Burns and Allen (Special Broadcast). With Colonel J. C. Flippen. WHN. January 28, 1936.
George and Gracie appear on this special broadcast of an amateur program from New York.

R826 A & P Gypsies. CBS. February 3, 1936.
Burns and Allen appear on this special broadcast for The Great Atlantic and Pacific Tea Company, a grocery chain.

R827 Herald-Express Interview. CBS. March 3, 1936.
Burns and Allen are interviewed in Hollywood by Jimmy Vandiveer for the Los Angeles newspaper to discuss their personal appearance at the Paramount Theater on March 5. Gracie sings "From The Tip of Your Toes."

R828 Hollywood Hotel. CBS. March 6, 1936.
George and Gracie guest host this Campbell Tomato Juice program for regular host Dick Powell, who is ill with laryngitis. "Lookie, Lookie, Lookie, Here Comes Cookie" is the theme song played as their introduction.

R829 Hollywood Hotel. CBS. March 20, 1936.
Burns and Allen continue as guest hosts while Dick Powell recovers from his illness. There was also a report of them guesting on the show on March 27, 1936 with Victor McLaglen to celebrate Dick Powell's return after his illness.

R830 Hollywood Hotel. CBS. April 3, 1936.
Burns and Allen return as guest hosts.

R831 Opening of Mayflower Doughnut Shop. KNX (CBS), Los Angeles. Special. September 3, 1936.
George and Gracie appear with Ken Niles at the opening of this Hollywood establishment.

R832 Hollywood Hotel. CBS. September 18, 1936.
Appearing on columnist Louella Parson's show, George and Gracie act in a sketch with Dick Powell and Frances Langford.

R833 Hollywood Hotel. CBS. September 25, 1936.
Burns and Allen substitute for Master of Ceremonies, Dick Powell. Tonight's show includes an interview with Louella Parsons.

R834 The Big Broadcast of 1937 radio preview. ca. 1936.
George and Gracie promote another of their feature films (F28).

R835 College Holiday radio preview. ca. 1936.
George and Gracie promote their latest feature film (F29).

R836 Hollywood Hotel. CBS. February 26, 1937.
Master of Ceremonies Fred MacMurray welcomes George and Gracie.

R837 Hollywood Hotel. CBS. March 12, 1937.
Burns and Allen are again guests on this show which features Barbara Stanwyck, Hal Roach and Joel McCrea.

R838 Lux Radio Theater. CBS. March 29, 1937.

George and Gracie join Elsa Maxwell, Hedda Hopper, and others for this radio production of the stage play **Dulcy**, written by George S. Kaufman and Marc Connolly. The one-hour comedy is broadcast from the Music Box Theater in Hollywood. **SEE D213, B141.**

R839 The Jell-O Program. With Jack Benny. NBC. April 11, 1937.
Gracie appears to promote the start of her and George's new show for Grape-Nuts beginning April 12, 1937 (T254). (Grape-Nuts and Jell-O were and are, of course, produced by the same company, the General Foods Corporation). **SEE D80, D261.**

R840 Artists & Models. NBC. June 1937.
George and Gracie do a radio promo for this new Paramount film, which stars Jack Benny and Ida Lupino.

R841 Starlit Roof. NBC. September 28, 1937.
Burns and Allen guest on this Packard variety show and trade quips with comedian Charlie Butterworth.

R842 Town Hall Tonight. NBC. September 29, 1937.
George and Gracie are guests on Fred Allen's comedy show.

R843 Hollywood Hotel. CBS. November 5, 1937.
Burns and Allen are featured in audio scenes from their new film, **A Damsel in Distress** (F30), with Fred Astaire and Joan Fontaine.

R844 The Jell-O Program. With Jack Benny. NBC. November 11, 1937.
Gracie and George appear on their old friend's show for General Foods.

R845 Dale Armstrong. NBC. February 8, 1938.
Radio editor Dale Armstrong of the **Los Angeles Times** interviews Burns and Allen.

R846 March of Dimes. With Eddie Cantor. CBS. January 22, 1939.
The guests include President Franklin D. Roosevelt and Burns and Allen. Cantor was instrumental in the initiation of the March of Dimes campaign designed to stamp out infantile paralysis (polio), an affliction suffered by the President.

R847 Screen Guild Theater. CBS. February 26, 1939.
Burns and Allen, actor Melvyn Douglas, and singer Shirley Ross are guests on this Gulf Oil Company revue show benefitting the Motion Picture Relief Fund. Master of Ceremonies George Murphy presents the cast in **The Shining Hour** in which George plays *David Linden* and Gracie plays a famous dancer, *Olivia Reilly*. **SEE D292.**

R848 Lifebuoy Program. CBS. March 7, 1939.
The Burnses are guests on this show hosted by Al Jolson. Gracie dramatizes **The Life of Al Jolson**. Martha Raye also appears.

R849 Christian German Refugee Benefit. CBS. June 15, 1939.
Burns and Allen perform on this show broadcast from Madison Square Garden in New York City.

R850 Information Please. NBC. June 20, 1939.
Gracie appears on this quiz show courtesy of Chesterfield. She answers questions in the following categories: fictional characters who flew without benefit of modern inventions (answering three out of five correctly); recent news events; famous warnings; babies; double talk; current movie titles (answering three out of four correctly); and old-time song lyrics. Other topics are U.S. relations with the Far East; Republicans who have served two full terms as President since the Civil War; birds; and islands that figure in international affairs of the day. Her answers prompt the Master of Ceremonies to ask, "Gracie, when are you going to step back into character and get some of these wrong, anyway?" **SEE D9, B141.**

R851 Screen Guild Theater. CBS. October 22, 1939.
George introduces Gracie, who appears in a rare dramatic performance, in the title role of **Sheela**. This playlet was specially written by Sidney Cook and Hartman Renaud about the Irish uprising of 1916. Also appearing in the cast is James Cagney. Roger Pryor is the host of the show, which

is sponsored by Gulf. The program was instrumental in raising money for the Motion Picture Relief Fund. **SEE B141.**

R852 American Red Cross Roll Call. CBS. November 11, 1939.
Burns and Allen are guests on this annual show to earn money for the American Red Cross.

R853 Salvation Army Party. December 16, 1939.
Lum and Abner invite George and Gracie to the show, but Gracie thinks they are on the Hinds program.

R854 March of Dimes. CBS. January 20, 1940.
George and Gracie are guests on this annual fund raiser.

R855 Finnish Relief. CBS. February 17, 1940.
George and Gracie appear on a benefit show for the people of Finland.

R856 Good News of 1940 (Baby Snooks). NBC. February 29, 1940.
Gracie appears on this show for Maxwell House Coffee to talk about her Presidential campaign. Fanny Brice starred as "Baby Snooks" in this version of **Maxwell House Coffee Time** prior to Burns and Allen becoming the show's stars in 1945.

R857 Rudy Vallee Alumni Program. NBC. March 1, 1940.
Burns and Allen certainly belong on this particular Vallee program since their appearance on his show in 1932 (R805) led to their first radio show contract on **The Robert Burns Panatela Program.**

R858 The Jell-O Program. With Jack Benny. NBC. March 3, 1940.
Gracie breaks into her husband's best friend's comedy show and starts talking about her Presidential campaign.

R859 Dr. IQ. NBC. March 4, 1940.
Gracie briefly appears on this quiz show talking about her Presidential campaign.

R860 Bob Hope. NBC. March 5, 1940.
Gracie shows up on this comedy variety program to plug her campaign for President.

R861 Fibber McGee & Molly. NBC. March 5, 1940.
Gracie appears suddenly to talk about her Presidential campaign. This is the first episode in which the famous closet routine is used by McGee when he opens the door and the listener hears the noise as the objects from the closet endlessly fall out onto the floor. **SEE D1, D5, D243.**

R862 Texaco Star Theater. NBC. March 6, 1940.
Gracie appears with Gladys George in **The Third Degree. SEE D13.**

R863 Radio Benefit for War Relief. NBC. June 22, 1940.
This war benefit for the American Red Cross was held on Stage Six of the Warner Bros. Sunset Studios in Hollywood. Mickey Rooney, Orson Welles, Fanny Brice, Pat O'Brien, Lum and Abner, Blondie & Dagwood, James Cagney, Mary Martin, Shirley Temple, Paul Muni, Bing Crosby, Gene Autry, Charles Laughton, Don Ameche, Edward G. Robinson and others appear along with George and Gracie. The inclusion of a network name would indicate this was broadcast and not merely done as a personal appearance.

R864 It Happened in Hollywood. NBC. June 28, 1940.
Gracie is a guest on this fifteen-minute daytime musical show (which is going off the air) sponsored by Hormel. She is there to promote the new Burns and Allen show which will debut for Hormel on July 1 (R401).

R865 American Red Cross Broadcast. NBC. June 29, 1940.
Gracie appears without George to give a serious speech on her decision to withdraw from her mock Presidential campaign. She announces the donation of the proceeds of her book, **How to Become President** (B7), to the American Red Cross.

R866 Gracie Allen Adopts the Navy. NBC. December 3, 1940.
Burns and Allen appear at the U.S. Naval Training Station in San Diego, CA.

R867 British Relief Show. NBC. December 25, 1940.
Burns and Allen are guests on this ninety-minute show, **Christmas Greetings to Great Britain**, with Basil Rathbone, Brian Aherne and Adolphe Menjou.

R868 Time to Smile. With Eddie Cantor. NBC. January 1, 1941.
Burns and Allen guest star with Dinah Shore and Margaret Hamilton. Gracie wants to produce a picture for Eddie.

R869 Eddie Cantor Presents The March of Dimes. NBC. January 25, 1941.
Burns and Allen join Cantor and a host of other stars (including Dinah Shore, Fanny Brice, Rudy Vallee, James Cagney, Humphrey Bogart and Bob Hope) at the KNX auditorium studio in Hollywood in this hour-long appeal for contributions to fight infantile paralysis.

R870 Burns and Allen. NBC. February 14, 1941.
George and Gracie appear on a show broadcast from Toronto, Canada.

R871 All Star Broadcast. NBC. February 15, 1941.
Burns and Allen are among the radio stars on this broadcast.

R872 U.S.O. Program. NBC. June 30, 1941.
Burns and Allen join others in support of the United Service Organization.

R873 Millions for Defense. CBS. July 16, 1941.
Burns and Allen appear on this program sponsored by the Treasury Department, one of the first shows to promote the sale of savings bonds. In the show George tries to buy a ten cent defense saving stamp; Gracie is the clerk.

R874 NBC 15th Anniversary Program. NBC. November 15, 1941.
In this program to celebrate the uniting of NBC's Red and Blue networks, Gracie talks about the radio stars she has seen and appears as "your Hollywood reporter" with "exclusive" Hollywood gossip.

R875 Tribute to Movie and Radio Guide Magazine. NBC. ca. 1941.
Burns and Allen appear on this show in honor of the popular trade magazine.

R876 Naval Training Station. NBC. January 24, 1942.
Burns and Allen are on this Navy broadcast from a Naval Training Station in California. It's another enlistment program for manning new ships.

R877 United China Relief. April 11, 1942.
Gracie tries to bring George closer to his "son" (*Herman the Duck*) and asks for money for China.

R878 Command Performance. Armed Forces Radio Service (AFRS). April 23, 1942.
Burns and Allen appear on this Hollywood Victory Committee show with Master of Ceremonies Pat O'Brien and other guests Sammy Kaye, Maxie Rosenbloom and Frank Morgan. Stars appeared on request from American soldiers serving abroad during World War II. The broadcasts were transmitted via shortwave to eighteen international stations.

R879 American Women's Voluntary Service Show. May 13, 1942.
Gracie, as chairman of the organization, is on the show without George.

R880 Time to Smile. With Eddie Cantor. NBC. May 27, 1942.
Gracie appears without George in this musical comedy show broadcast from Camp Elliot in San Diego.

R881 Treasury Star Parade. Syndicated. June 25, 1942.
George and Gracie make an appeal for the War Bond 10% Club (giving ten percent of one's income to buy war bonds and stamps) on this United States Government variety show.

R882 Victory Parade. NBC. June 28, 1942.
Lionel Barrymore hosts this show designed to win support for the troops during World War II in the fourth program of this summer series. George and Gracie have returned from Gracie's cousin's wedding and Gracie is inspired.

R883 War Bond Campaign. July 28, 1942.

Gracie appears on this broadcast of the New York Victory Rally held July 28 and 29 at the Public Library in New York City.

R884 Stage Door Canteen. CBS. July 30, 1942.
George and Gracie join Helen Hayes on the premiere of this program, broadcast from a New York theater. Gracie is inspired to open a Stage Door Canteen with her ladies' club members as hostesses. Many celebrities like Burns and Allen appeared on this entertainment show during World War II.

R885 Star-Spangled Vaudeville of 1942. NBC. August 2, 1942.
George listens as Gracie talks about diamonds and shopping for her friends. The show's Master of Ceremonies is Walter O'Keefe.

R886 Command Performance. AFRS. September 3, 1942.
Burns and Allen are again selected by servicemen to appear on this program. Gracie talks about her brother, who is in the army but classified as 4F.

R887 Over Here. November 28, 1942.
Gracie has moved the pins around on George's war map, and he's angry. George explain the various war fronts to Gracie.

R888 Mileage Rationing Show. December 1, 1942.
George and Gracie appear with Jack Benny, Eddie Cantor and Dinah Shore. The storyline is about Jack car pooling.

R889 Time to Smile. With Eddie Cantor. NBC. December 2, 1942.
Gracie makes a solo appearance to discuss rationing.

R890 Soldiers with Wings. AFRS. December 6, 1942.
Burns and Allen appear on this variety broadcast from the Army Air Forces West Coast Training Center in Santa Ana, California with Virginia O'Brien. Gracie has written a play, **The Pilot Was Glued to His Seat** or **Who Put the Mucilage on the Fusilage?**

R891 Mail Call. AFRS. December 30, 1942.
George and Gracie appear on this show, which answers letters and requests from American soldiers abroad during the second World War. The program is being broadcast from the CBS Vine Street Playhouse and co-stars Mary Martin. Gracie is writing letters to *all* the soldiers and sailors.

R892 The March of Dimes. With Eddie Cantor. NBC. January 23, 1943.
Gracie's ladies' club is trying to come up with money-making ideas for the March of Dimes.

R893 Command Performance. AFRS. February 6, 1943.
Gracie tries to balance her checkbook.

R894 Lux Radio Theater. CBS. February 15, 1943.
In **Are Husbands Necessary?** George and Gracie play *Jim* and *Jane Cugat*, a "normal, everyday man and wife...well, his wife is either above or below (normal), it's hard to tell."

R895 Bob Burns. NBC. February 18, 1943.
Burns and Allen guest on this comedy variety program.

R896 The Grape-Nuts Program. With Jack Benny. NBC. March 7, 1943.
George and Gracie substitute for Jack, who has a cold, but Gracie is reluctant to do so. Since she's been practicing for her piano concert, she only wants to appear on musical programs, not comedies, and she fears her appearance on the show will ruin the image she's cultivating. The program is broadcast from New York. Bill Goodwin and Paul Whiteman join George and Gracie as do some of Jack's cast members. **SEE D263, D264.**

R897 Open House for Paul Whiteman. NBC. April 10, 1943.
Gracie appears on this show with orchestra leader Paul Whiteman to perform her "Concerto for Index Finger." She is also made an honorary member of the musicians' union, Local 47.

R898 Command Performance. AFRS. April 24, 1943.
Gracie appears without George, joining Ann Sheridan and José Iturbi, with whom she discusses music.

R899 Take It or Leave It. CBS. May 23, 1943.
Gracie is a guest on this quiz program.

R900 Time to Smile. With Eddie Cantor. NBC. June 9, 1943.
Burns and Allen guest on Cantor's musical variety show, dropping by to celebrate his and his wife's 29th wedding anniversary.

R901 Paul Whiteman Presents. NBC. June 13, 1943.
Burns and Allen appear on this **Chase & Sanborn Hour** program with their band leader/host on the second airing of his summer replacement show for Edgar Bergen and Charlie McCarthy. Gracie is having a dinner party and is trying to explain the seating arrangements, etc., to George.

R902 A Cruiser for Los Angeles. NBC. June 30, 1943.
Guests for this wartime show include Burns and Allen, Bing Crosby, Cecil B. DeMille, Kathryn Grayson, Betty Hutton, Edward G. Robinson, Dinah Shore and Rudy Vallee.

R903 Paul Whiteman Presents. CBS. August 8, 1943.
George and Gracie again guest on this summer replacement program for Chase & Sanborn. Gracie tries to play matchmaker to Dinah Shore and Bill Goodwin.

R904 Mail Call. AFRS. August 19, 1943.
Burns and Allen appear in celebration of the program's first birthday. William Powell hosts, and José Iturbi and Amparo Navarro join George and Gracie on tonight's show. As a gift to the soldiers Gracie has written the story of her life.

R905 Cavalcade for Victory. NBC. September 8, 1943.
This show was the first to open the "Third War Bond Loan Drive" held across the United States to raise money to support the government in the second World War. Several radio and screen actors, like Burns and Allen, participated in these fund raisers.

R906 Mail Call. AFRS. November 17, 1943.
George and Gracie join Doris Day, Dorothy Lamour and Fred MacMurray. Gracie interrupts Lamour's introduction to build up George's singing abilities.

R907 The Elgin Holiday Program Show. NBC. November 25, 1943.
Burns and Allen appear on this Thanksgiving variety program. George is looking forward to a cozy Thanksgiving dinner with Gracie but she's made other plans.

Review: "...George Burns and Gracie Allen did a funny, though slightly long, sketch about a guest army for turkey dinner." (**Variety**, December 1, 1943).

R908 G.I. Journal. AFRS. ca. 1944.
George and Gracie appear in this broadcast for the U.S. armed forces along with Robert Young and Mel Blanc. **SEE D236, D237.**

R909 Radio Hall of Fame. ABC. January 2, 1944.
Burns and Allen are among the guests on this one-hour variety program which features outstanding radio performers. George and Gracie reminisce about their wedding, and Gracie admires George's physique. Music is by Paul Whiteman. The show is sponsored by Philco.

R910 Jubilee. AFRS. February 14, 1944.
George and Gracie are guests on this program for the Afro-American armed forces. George tries to explain jive to Gracie.

R911 Command Performance. AFRS. April 1, 1944.
Program #158 includes appearances by George and Gracie, Sir Aubrey Smith and Dame Mae Whitty.

R912 Maxwell House Coffee Time (Baby Snooks). NBC. April 6, 1944.
Burns and Allen are guests on this comedy variety show with Fanny Brice and Meredith Willson. By September 1945 (R606) **Maxwell House Coffee Time** will be their own program.

R913 Soldiers with Wings. AFRS. May 3, 1944.

George and Gracie try to decide what they will do to entertain the soldiers. **Soldiers with Wings** is referred to as the "official voice of the Army Air Forces."

R914 Your All-Time Hit Parade. NBC. May 26, 1944.
Although George and Gracie only plan to *listen* to the show, Gracie starts complimenting George on *his* singing, and he does bits of "Ain't Misbehavin'."

R915 The Bakers of America Salute the Armed Forces. NBC. June 4, 1944.
Burns and Allen appear on this **Standard Brands Show** sponsored by Chase & Sanborn to honor the United States Armed Forces. George and Gracie discuss tonight's show, which is starring Bob Hope, Bing Crosby, Judy Garland, and Edgar Bergen; Gracie's voice fades into Bergen's spot.

R916 Town Tattler. July 1944.
This show from Chicago, Illinois features Gracie in Chicago as a newspaper reporter to cover the Democratic Convention as she did the Republican Convention. Host "Nate" Gross interviews George and Gracie.

R917 Mail Call. AFRS. August 23, 1944.
Gracie thinks George is a better singer than tonight's host, Nelson Eddy.

R918 Your All-Time Hit Parade. NBC. September 3, 1944.
To Tommy Dorsey's chagrin Gracie announces that George will be singing tonight.

R919 Birdseye Open House. NBC. October 19, 1944.
Gracie tries to talk Dinah Shore into allowing George to sing on the show and pushes announcer Harry Von Zell into trying to become the star of the show so that *he* will have the clout to get George a singing spot.

R920 Radio Hall of Fame. ABC. November 19, 1944.
George and Gracie appear with baseball announcer Red Barber and actor Louis Jourdan. Gracie announces that George has left her.

R921 The Frank Sinatra Show. CBS. December 11, 1944.
Gracie's ladies' club has chosen Sinatra to sing at their Christmas party.

R922 Mail Call. AFRS. December 20, 1944.
Lucille Ball hosts. Gracie's afraid she's losing George to Lucy so she tries to make him jealous.

R923 The Elgin Christmas Show. CBS. December 25, 1944.
This holiday show features Bob Hope, Bing Crosby, Jack Benny and Burns and Allen. Gracie is afraid George will "show up" the others. Car pooling is still "in." Don Ameche is the Master of Ceremonies.

R924 Time to Smile. With Eddie Cantor. NBC. January 17, 1945.
This show is being broadcast in honor of Cantor's 53rd birthday (January 31st) with Burns and Allen and others as guests.

R925 Command Performance. AFRS. January 18, 1945.
George and Gracie appear as the Master and Mistress of Ceremonies and discuss the life of a single man versus the life of married man.

R926 Time to Smile. With Eddie Cantor. NBC. January 31, 1945.
Eddie's wife, Ida, says Eddie is depressed about his birthday and asks George and Gracie to cheer him up. **SEE D214.**

R927 How to Listen to the Radio. CBS. February 12, 1945.
The Burnses appear with Robert Benchley. CBS has asked their "official critic" to tell Burns and Allen what's wrong with their program and, although he says nothing is wrong, Gracie thinks it should be more like a daytime serial (George has indicated the real Gracie was a big fan of the genre).

R928 Dick Haymes Show. NBC. February 27, 1945.
Burns and Allen guest on this musical variety show hosted by vocalist Dick Haymes and featuring Helen Forrest.

R929 Mail Call. AFRS. March 21, 1945.

Gracie conspires with neighbor Rita Hayworth about their husbands. Tonight's show also features Frank Morgan, Eddie Cantor, Harpo Marx and Bea Benaderet (out of character) as *Clara Bagley*.

R930 **NBC Parade of Stars**. NBC. October 8, 1945.
Gracie asks Dinah Shore's advice: she wants George to sing but she doesn't want to upset Rudy Vallee.

R931 **Danny Kaye Show**. CBS. October 19, 1945.
George and Gracie are substitute hosts for Danny Kaye on this Pabst Blue Ribbon show. Gracie wants a new hat and she and George have problems with Danny's car.

R932 **The Ginny Simms Show**. CBS. November 2, 1945.
Singer Ginny Simms plays hostess to George and Gracie who are "appearing through the courtesy of Maxwell House Coffee." Gracie thinks George needs a vacation.

R933 **Sister Kenny**. Transcription. November 7, 1945.
Burns and Allen record a radio spot for the Australian nurse's medical work in polio therapy.

R934 **Request Performance**. CBS. January 13, 1946.
Tonight's show also stars Dennis Morgan and Jane Powell and is produced by the Masquers' Club of Hollywood. Gracie continues her one-woman crusade to extol the virtues of George's vocal abilities when she writes five hundred letters to the program requesting to hear him sing. She also expresses disbelief that Warner Bros. let Dennis Morgan sing the lead in **The Desert Song** with George available. After all, "what has (he) got that you haven't got, or couldn't get, or didn't used to have, or wouldn't like to have now, or wouldn't know what to do with if you had it?" Sandra Moore of Great Falls, Montana has requested Gracie do a dramatic scene. Jane suggests one from **Stella Dallas**, so Gracie tries it out on an unsuspecting George.

R935 **Kay Kyser's Kollege of Musical Knowledge**. NBC. February 6, 1946.
Burns and Allen are guests on this musical quiz show (also known as **Kay Kyser's College of Musical Knowledge**) as it starts its ninth year on the air. Gracie says *Harry Morton* won a prize on a quiz show, and he's the stupidest man she ever met, so she wants George to prove that he's just as smart and asks him to drop by the show. George tries to answer questions but Gracie and Kay get wrapped up in other things.

R936 **Radio Hall of Fame**. ABC. March 10, 1946.
Broadcast from the Earl Carroll Theater in Hollywood, Gracie tells Paul Whiteman how George courted her by mail (actually, he sent letters and poems asking her for money), and she tells George how glad she is she married him. Gracie also talks to Hedda Hopper about her hat contest.

R937 **Truth or Consequences**. ABC. March 23, 1946.
George appears on this quiz program hosted by Ralph Edwards.

R938 **Mail Call**. AFRS. April 3, 1946.
Tonight's show with George and Gracie is hosted by Virginia O'Brien and George Murphy.

R939 **Louella Parsons**. ABC. July 21, 1946.
Gracie "refuses" to be interviewed by the Hearst newspaper gossip columnist from Hollywood, citing "professional competition." George also appears.

R940 **Eddie Cantor Show**. NBC. September 26, 1946.
George and Gracie get the mistaken idea that Eddie has gone broke and gone into the laundry business, so they decide to help him out. Jim Backus appears as *Hubert Updyke*.

R941 **American Veterans Committee Salutes Al Jolson**. October 1, 1946.
Gracie thinks the committee should pay homage to George instead of to Al Jolson.

R942 **Command Performance**. AFRS. October 8, 1946.

George and Gracie join Gloria DeHaven on tonight's show. Gracie is trying to do a crossword puzzle but George just wants to read the newspaper. He also gets confused as to who is coming for Gracie's ladies' club meeting.

R943 NBC Parade of Stars. NBC. October 13, 1946.
Burns and Allen are introduced by Kay Kyser on this two-hour program. George and Gracie are celebrating fifteen years on radio and Gracie tells Kay the secret of staying happily married. Stars of other NBC shows also appear.

R944 Hollywood Star Time. CBS. December 7, 1946.
Herbert Marshall hosts the program. Burns and Allen again perform in the play, **Dulcy**, with Gracie as the scatterbrained wife, *Dulcy Smith*, and George as *Gordon*, her long-suffering husband. Also appearing in the cast are Barney Phillips, Sharon Douglas, Howard McNear, Arthur Q. Bryan, Norman Field and Hans Conried. George and Gracie had previously appeared in the play on the **Lux Radio Theater** on March 29, 1937 (R838).

R945 Eddie Cantor Show. NBC. January 2, 1947.
Guests include Burns and Allen, Abbott and Costello and George Jessel, with Margaret Whiting and the Fairchild Orchestra.

R946 The Lucky Strike Program. Starring Jack Benny. NBC. January 12, 1947.
Burns and Allen are the sole guests on tonight's show. **SEE D262.**

R947 Philco Radio Time. ABC. January 15, 1947.
George appears on Bing Crosby's show with Skitch Henderson, Al Jolson and the Trotter Orchestra.

R948 The Jack Carson Show. NBC. January 15, 1947.
George and Jack Carson vie to substitute for Frank Sinatra in a film.

R949 Here's to Veterans. NBC. February 9, 1947.
George and Gracie appear together on this fifteen minute program.

R950 Guest Star. Syndicated. March 14, 1947.
Gracie's ladies' club is determined to sell a million dollars' worth of government bonds and it's announced that anyone who buys a bond gets a date with George, but Gracie soon regrets the offer. Doris Singleton and Verna Felton also appear. This show is also known as the **U.S. Savings Bonds Treasury Show**. **SEE D257.**

R951 Take it or Leave It. CBS. March 16, 1947.
George and Gracie again appear on this quiz program sponsored by Eversharp. George asks host Phil Baker to let Gracie win and gives him $64 to give her as her prize (Gracie had wanted a new Easter outfit, and George doesn't want to seem to be a "soft touch"). But the plans go awry. This program eventually became **$64 Question**, the forerunner of television's popular **The $64,000 Question** starring **Burns and Allen** radio and television alum, Hal March.

R952 Kay Kyser's New Kollege of Music and Knowledge. NBC. March 19, 1947.
Gracie says George has "gone Hollywood" since being voted one of the ten best-dressed men in America so she asks Kay to get him to be his old self again. Jane Russell also appears.

R953 Tony Martin Show. CBS. April 13, 1947.
Gracie implores George not to sing on tonight's episode of **Texaco Star Theater** because Texaco might be so impressed with George's singing they'll put Tony (George and Gracie's own former vocalist) to work in a filling station. **SEE D304.**

R954 Songs By Sinatra. CBS. May 14, 1947.
Gracie demonstrates various types of swoons and talks to co-star Jane Morgan about the birds and bees and how to handle men. George duets with Sinatra on "Why Shouldn't It Happen To Us?" **SEE D220.**

R955 Tony Martin Show. CBS. May 25, 1947.
Gracie wants George to sing but George is unhappy about what happened the last time they appeared on Tony's show (R953). Tony still refuses to let

him sing and, to get even, Gracie decides to show off George's acting abilities.

R956 Guest Star. Syndicated. July 6, 1947.
Burns and Allen are featured on this show sponsored by the Treasury Department to promote the sale of savings bonds. **SEE D257.**

R957 Front & Center. NBC. August 17, 1947.
Dorothy Lamour's show for the U.S. Army Recruitment Service has Burns and Allen and Ronald Reagan as guests with the Henry Russell Orchestra. Gracie thinks George should be Dorothy's leading man in another one of her South Sea island pictures.

R958 Philco Radio Time. With Bing Crosby. ABC. January 14, 1948.
Tired of being introduced as "the man behind the woman," and saying that Gracie is everything and he's nothing, George has decided to make a name for himself as a vocalist and appears on tonight's show without Gracie. He asks Bing to be on the flip side of a record he has made and Bing encourages him to do his own radio show, **Hour of Love**, as "Sugar Throat Burns." George and Bing duet on "It Might As Well Be Spring." This show was recorded November 28, 1947.

R959 Philco Radio Time. With Bing Crosby. ABC. January 21, 1948.
The advertisement for this show notes that George had broken up the show last week (R958) with his jokes so they have brought him back for another week with Gracie, billed as "Radio's Merriest Mr. and Mrs." Gracie shows up to try to talk Bing into being on a record with George. This show was recorded November 30, 1947.

R960 Eddie Cantor Show. NBC. January 29, 1948.
Gracie is giving a birthday party for her brother but Eddie thinks the party is for him. Gracie shows George a new card game.

R961 Treasury Bandstand. CBS. March 11, 1948.
George and Gracie go door-to-door selling security bonds and singing.

R962 Camp Fire Girls Salute. Mutual. March 15, 1948.
Gracie is upset because George won't let her join the Camp Fire Girls. Dennis Day, Joan Leslie and Frances Langford also appear. Eddie Cantor is Master of Ceremonies and Harry Von Zell is the announcer.

R963 Guest Star. Syndicated. May 9, 1948.
Program #59 finds George and Gracie joined by their own regular cast members Bea Benaderet, Mel Blanc and Verna Felton. **SEE D257.**

R964 Command Performance. AFRS. June 1, 1948.
George appears without Gracie to emcee the show, anxious to showcase his talents and "call the shots."

R965 Louella Parsons. ABC. June 6, 1948.
Gracie fills in for Louella, who's on vacation. Gracie actually reads the news on this fifteen minute show and interviews actor Victor Mature. George stops by.

R966 Louella Parsons. ABC. June 13, 1948.
Gracie returns with George for a second appearance, this time with guest star Turhan Bey, whom Gracie tries to get interested in her sister, Hazel.

R967 Red Feather Salute. NBC. October 10, 1948.
Gracie tries to get money out of George for the sponsor, Community Chest of America, and has no trouble because he says it's a fine service. Bea Benaderet also appears to detail the organization's work.

R968 Sparkle Time. ABC. October 13, 1948.
Burns and Allen are featured in this show hosted by Meredith Willson. George has insulted *Blanche Morton* and *Clara Bagley*, and Gracie enlists Meredith's aid in getting George to apologize to *Blanche* and going to dinner at her house.

R969 Kraft Music Hall. With Al Jolson. NBC. November 4, 1948.
Burns and Allen join series regular Oscar Levant. Gracie tries to get George to show off his voice, telling him tonight is his "big chance." **SEE D266, D307.**

R970 **Wrigley's Christmas Festival**. CBS. December 25, 1948.
Among the guests on this two-hour holiday show joining host Gene Autry are Burns and Allen, Eddie Anderson, the Andrews Sisters, Lionel Barrymore, Pat Buttram, Bing Crosby, Dan Dailey, Hedda Hopper, Frank Nelson and Sweeney and March. Gracie decides George will become "the new cowboy singing star" since he's tried to make it other ways and people don't seem to want him. The program was also sent over the Armed Forces Radio Service.

R971 **Hollywood Star Theater**. NBC. January 15, 1949.
George and Gracie introduce actor Booth Colman as a "star of tomorrow" in the playlet, **Death Watch**, in this show sponsored by Anacin. Also in the cast are Jack Webb and Virginia Gregg. George and Gracie are interviewed in a short segment after the playlet.

R972 **American Cancer Society**. Mutual. January 25, 1949.
Gordon MacRae hosts this show, which also features Jerry Colonna, Peggy Lee and Jane Wyman. Gracie thinks George is in love with Jane.

R973 **Eddie Cantor Show**. NBC. February 18, 1949.
Burns and Allen appear with Dinah Shore and Billie Burke. Eddie thinks he's on his last legs, so Gracie tries to cheer him up by comparing him to George.

R974 **Rupert Lucas**. March 10, 1949.
Burns and Allen are interviewed by the Canadian-born Lucas. Much of the talk centers on his native country.

R975 **Tobe Reed Show**. ABC. March 30, 1949.
George appears with George Jessel in a show recorded on Friday, March 18 to promote the April 16th Friars Frolic at the Shrine Auditorium in Los Angeles. The Frolic, which will salute the Friars' first abbot, George M. Cohan, is a benefit for the Motion Picture Relief Fund Home and Hospital and will run three hours.

R976 **Twenty Questions**. Mutual. May 11, 1949.
Limited to asking twenty questions, a panel tries to identify George and Gracie.

R977 **The Garry Moore Show**. CBS. November 24, 1949.
George and Gracie have kicked off their last major publicity stunt, the "George Burns Sings" campaign, on their own show (which aired last night [R771]). Now Gracie begins a spate of guest appearances on other shows in her quest to find someone who will let George make a guest appearance as a singer. Gracie tells Garry that he could kill two birds with one stone by allowing George to sing on his show because she wants George to sing, and he (Garry) needs a sponsor (Gracie's illogical logic at work again).

R978 **Club 15**. CBS. November 24, 1949.
During Gracie's first appearance on the show to plead George's case, star Dick Haymes suggests he sing on the Crosby show instead.

R979 **Hallmark Playhouse**. CBS. November 24, 1949.
Gracie asks the show to do a musical starring "Sugar Throat Burns" next week.

R980 **Leave It To Joan**. CBS. November 25, 1949.
Gracie asks Joan Davis to get George a job singing in the music section of the department store where Joan is employed.

R981 **Young Love**. CBS. November 25, 1949.
Gracie asks the cast to put George in a college production of a musical comedy and to call it "The Mask and Wig Production" (she says George could play either part).

R982 **The Adventures of Phillip Marlowe**. CBS. November 26, 1949.
Two scripts were written for this episode. In the one that was apparently used, Marlowe asks Gracie how she got into his apartment. She tells him the key didn't fit so she walked in.

R983 **Louella Parsons**. ABC. November 27, 1949.
Louella tells Gracie she would give her her right arm...but please don't ask her to let George sing on her show.

R984 Escape. CBS. November 29, 1949.
Three scripts were written for this show. The one that may have been used is one in which Gracie tells the star that "When he (George) sings, everybody will be looking for escape!"

R985 Life With Luigi. CBS. November 29, 1949.
Gracie, explaining to star Bob Stevenson why he should hire George to sing on his show, "it could be as big for you as when you wrote **Treasure Island**."

R986 Dr. Christian. CBS. November 30, 1949.
Gracie asks Dr. Christian (Jean Hersholt) to temporarily deaden Bing Crosby's vocal cords, referring to him as a "famous singer who's jealous of George's voice."

R987 Bing Crosby. CBS. November 30, 1949.
Gracie interrupts Bing and Al Jolson as they prepare to close the show. She tells them they're the second and third greatest singers in the world after George but that Bing is afraid of competition. She goes on to say that she understands, since he's got a family to support.

R988 Art Linkletter's House Party. CBS. November 30, 1949.
Gracie offers up George as the "Mystery Voice."

R989 Lum and Abner. CBS. November 30, 1949.
Lum suggests to Gracie that George sing opera instead because his voice "is just too good for our program."

R990 Curt Massey. CBS. December 1, 1949.
Gracie tells Curt, "If you let him sing on this show, all his fans will listen in," to which Massey replies, "You will?"

R991 Suspense. CBS. December 1, 1949.
Gracie interrupts the show during a commercial for Auto-Lite Spark Plugs the night James Stewart is the guest star. When told the show is booked for the next eighty years, Gracie asks, "How about the week after that?"

R992 My Favorite Husband. CBS. December 2, 1949.
Gracie interrupts star Lucille Ball as she is doing a Middle Ages commercial for Jell-O Pudding. Ball tells Gracie to look her up in eight hundred years. Gracie replies, "Keep on that same dress so I'll know you."

R993 Pursuit. CBS. December 2, 1949.
Gracie tells star Ted de Corsia that George could wear kilts so he wouldn't be "out of place" and that he could sing between two murders.

R994 Gene Autry's Melody Ranch. CBS. December 3, 1949.
Gracie insists George is convincing as a singer of western songs like "Bury Me Out On The Lone Prairie."

R995 Carnation Contented Hour. CBS. December 4, 1949.
Gracie continues her search for a program that will allow George to sing. Tonight she goes to singer Jo Stafford for help.

R996 Club 15. CBS. December 5, 1949.
Gracie makes another appearance on George's behalf and reminds the co-stars of the show, the Andrews Sisters, that they are coming over next Wednesday to sing on her and George's show. **See R773**.

R997 Saturday At The Shamrock. ABC. July 1, 1950.
George and Gracie appear on this coast-to-coast broadcast emanating from the Houston, Texas Shamrock Hotel and perform a routine about Gracie at the exchange counter of a department store.

R998 Saturday At The Shamrock. ABC. July 8, 1950.
George and Gracie wind up their stay in Texas with another appearance on the show. This time, Gracie is trying to get a Texas temporary driver's license. George and Gracie received shares in an oil company from hotel owner Glenn H. McCarthy. Once America's largest hotel, The Shamrock would be gone by 1987.

R999 Jack Quigg's Hollywood. Associated Press News. February 18, 1951.
George and Gracie are the subject of tonight's broadcast.

R1000 This Is San Francisco. April 13, 1951.
Gracie appears on this Friday, 8:00 A.M. broadcast from San Francisco to tell host Jim Grady what she will do with the Golden Gate Bridge, now that she's bought it. She's in town to appeal for contributions to the Saints and Sinners Milk Fund.

R1001 Bill Weaver Show. April 13, 1951.
Gracie gives an interview on this 2:00 P.M. San Francisco broadcast to talk about the local television show for the Saints and Sinners Milk Fund. Gracie has "bought" the Golden Gate Bridge and says she will be collecting the tolls. Those who pledge ten dollars or more will receive a special police pass and Gracie's personal souvenir check. George and Gracie will be at the bridge between 10:00 A.M. and 12:00 noon (apparently the next day) to shake hands.

R1002 Hedda Hopper. NBC. May 13, 1951.
George and Gracie prepare to have Hedda come to their home for an interview about working in radio and television.

R1003 Frances Scully. ABC. June 1951.
Burns and Allen are interviewed on this show from Hollywood as a promotion for their television show. They discuss the differences between radio and television and are portrayed as (sponsor) "Carnation's own contented couple."

R1004 Interview with Howard Greer. June 9, 1951.
This interview conducted with Gracie and clothing designer Greer reveals that Gracie, known as the "Best Dressed Actress in Radio," will wear his designs on television.

R1005 The Lucky Strike Program. CBS. January 20, 1952.
George appears without Gracie on Jack Benny's show and sings "Jack's Song." **SEE D50, D51, D53.**

R1006 The Lucky Strike Program. CBS. March 2, 1952.
George again appears without Gracie, this time with Danny Kaye, Groucho Marx and Frank Sinatra. They sing "When You say 'I Beg Your Pardon,' Then I'll Come Back to You." **SEE D23, D49, D52.**

R1007 Bob Hope Show. NBC. March 25, 1952.
Gracie appears without George.

R1008 This is Cinerama. April 29, 1953.
Both George and Gracie are guests on this interview program.

R1009 National Dairy Show. NBC. June 1953.
Introduced by Bob Hope, George and Gracie engage in a standup routine about cows and Gracie's brother on a farm on this show for the National Dairy Industry.

R1010 Bob Hope Show. NBC. ca. June 1954 or 1955.
George and Gracie guest on Bob's show when it was sponsored by American Dairy. A fifteen minute transcription was broadcast over the Armed Forces Radio Service.

R1011 Amos 'n' Andy Music Hall. CBS. September 24, 1954.
George makes a singing appearance on this program that was broadcast five times a week from 1954 until November, 1960.

R1012 June Dairy Month Radio Show. NBC. June 1955.
George and Gracie appear on another edition of the program, again emceed by Bob Hope.

R1013 Walter O'Keefe Almanac. KHJ (CBS). Los Angeles. November 25, 1962.
George is interviewed on O'Keefe's premiere show and talks about Hollywood, Jack Benny, Gracie and the various mediums in which he and Gracie appeared, including vaudeville and radio.

R1014 Monitor. NBC. 1964.
A tribute to George for his 68th birthday includes verbal bouquets from fellow comedians.

R1015 The Big Broadcast of 1965. KNX (CBS). Los Angeles. November 25, 1965.
George is interviewed on the Hollywood radio station along with Edgar Bergon, Bing Crosby, Charles Correll (*Andy* of **Amos 'n' Andy**) and Novis Goff (*Abner* of **Lum and Abner**).

R1016 KFI's 50th Anniversary. KFI (NBC). Los Angeles. April 17, 1972.
A history of the Hollywood radio station, narrated by Ralph Edwards, includes reminiscences by George Burns of the **Burns and Allen** radio show. George wishes the radio station (which once broadcast his and Gracie's radio show) a musical "happy fiftieth anniversary" and offers to sing at listeners' parties, after which he and Gracie are heard in a clip from their Swan Soap program which was originally broadcast on November 18, 1941 (R446). Next, George briefly traces the beginnings of the team of Burns and Allen, and they are heard in an excerpt from a 1941 appearance on **Time to Smile** starring Eddie Cantor (R868). George tells how he used to lift jokes from humor magazines before he could afford writers and introduces a clip which features him and Gracie in a routine they performed "more than twenty years ago," as they discuss her cousin, composer and conductor Mozart Allen. George and Gracie also talk about her uncle, Quentin Allen. (The Mozart and Quentin Allen routines are ostensibly from radio, but sound remarkably like ones from their television show, episodes T261 and T263). George goes on to talk about a time the studio lights went out during a radio broadcast and, since they couldn't read their scripts, he and Gracie went into their vaudeville act to fill airtime until the lights came back on. George then introduces a routine from one of their radio broadcasts in which Gracie tells George about the gifts she has purchased for her brother, who's going into the Army. George's ending congratulatory words to KFI are preceded by a few orchestral bars of his and Gracie's theme song, "The Love Nest."

R1017 Ray Briem Talk Show. KABC. Los Angeles. September 3, 1976.
George appears on this long-running West Coast-based interview program. (Briem, who retired from radio in 1994 after nearly fifty years, hosted KABC's all-night show for twenty-seven years).

R1018 The Golden Days of Radio. KGIL. Los Angeles. November 28, 1976.
George is interviewed by Frank Bresee on the latter's Los Angeles, CA based program featuring important members of radio's vintage years. Interviewed shortly after winning the Academy Award for his role in **The Sunshine Boys** (F37), George talks about the growing sophistication of audiences, the practice of sweetening laugh tracks and his upcoming film for Warner Bros. with John Denver, **Oh, God!** (F38). "...God would sing better than I do; I wouldn't do that to Him...Anything I do right now is a miracle anyway, so that's why they cast me for God."

R1019 Johnny Carson Salutes 50 Years of NBC Comedy. November 21, 1982.
In part two of this multi-part tribute special, excerpts from **Burns and Allen** are included.

R1020 Golden Age of Comedy. n.d.
George narrates this two-hour special which features the work of Burns and Allen, Jack Benny, Eddie Cantor and Red Skelton.

R1021 Flying Red Horse Tavern. CBS. n.d.
This was a musical variety show sponsored by Mobil which ran from October 4, 1935 to September 25, 1936 and on which George and Gracie made a joint appearance.

R1022 Colonel Stoopnagle and Budd. n.d.
George and Gracie appear together in this comedy program starring Frederick Chase Taylor and Wilbur Budd Hulick. In one of its time slots the series ran as a summer replacement show on CBS for Burns and Allen from July 6, 1943 to August 24, 1943.

R1023 Anchors Aweigh. n.d.
Burns and Allen are the first to appear on this program from the Naval Base in San Diego.

R1024 Music You Can't Forget. n.d.
The program, a fifteen minute show with Carol Channing, features a solo performance by George.

R1025 Chase & Sanborn Hour. With Edgar Bergen and Charlie McCarthy. NBC. n.d.
George and Gracie visit the most popular real dummy on radio and the man who pulls his strings on this long-running (1937-1948) and beloved show.

R1026 G.I. Journal. AFRS. n.d.
This program was broadcast to America's armed forces between 1944-1946. There is evidence that George and Gracie made at least two appearances on the show. **SEE D236.**

R1027 Lucille Ball and Desi Arnaz Testimonial Dinner. CBS. 1958.
This tribute reportedly was scheduled to be broadcast over CBS radio.

R1028 The Golden Days of Radio. Program #2702. Armed Forces Radio and Television Service (AFRTS). 1995.
Frank Bresee salutes George's 99th birthday with an encore of his earlier interview (R1018), adding audio clips of Burns and Allen appearances from other sources, including one of George and Gracie's earliest records (1933) and KFI radio's 50th anniversary program (R1016). George's 1963 television appearance on **The Tonight Show** (T415) during the then East Coast-based show's visit to the West Coast concludes the tribute. George and Johnny Carson discuss Gracie as well as Jack Benny, who had appeared on the show the previous evening. They also talk about George's career, and George demonstrates his habit of stringing together a number of obscure songs but never finishing them. "I love to sing and I love to smoke. And the people that hear me sing say they'd rather hear me smoke."

~~~~~
~~~~~

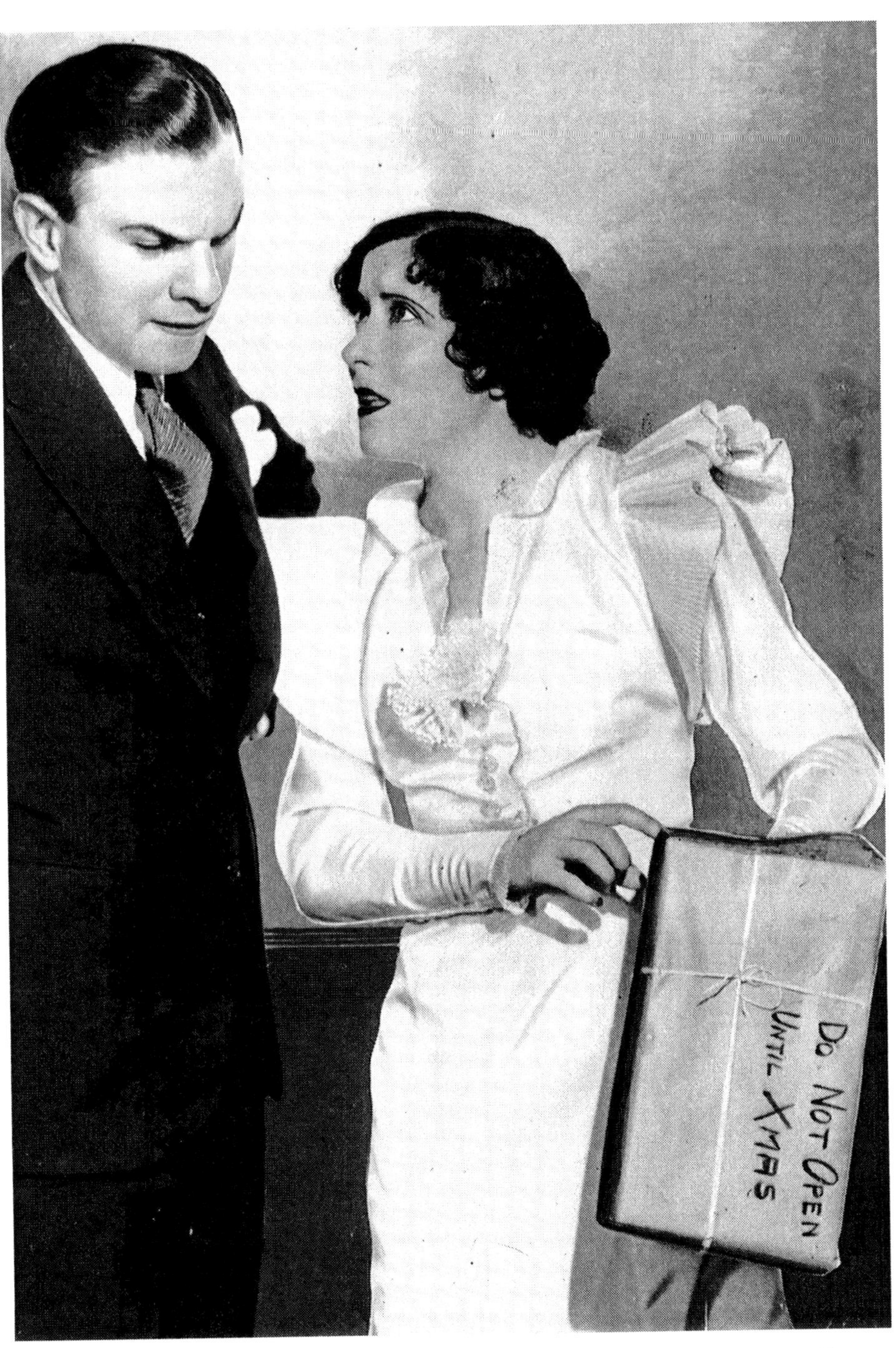

A 1935 publicity photo with Gracie in her role of always trying to explain things to George. (Photo courtesy of the San Francisco Public Library)

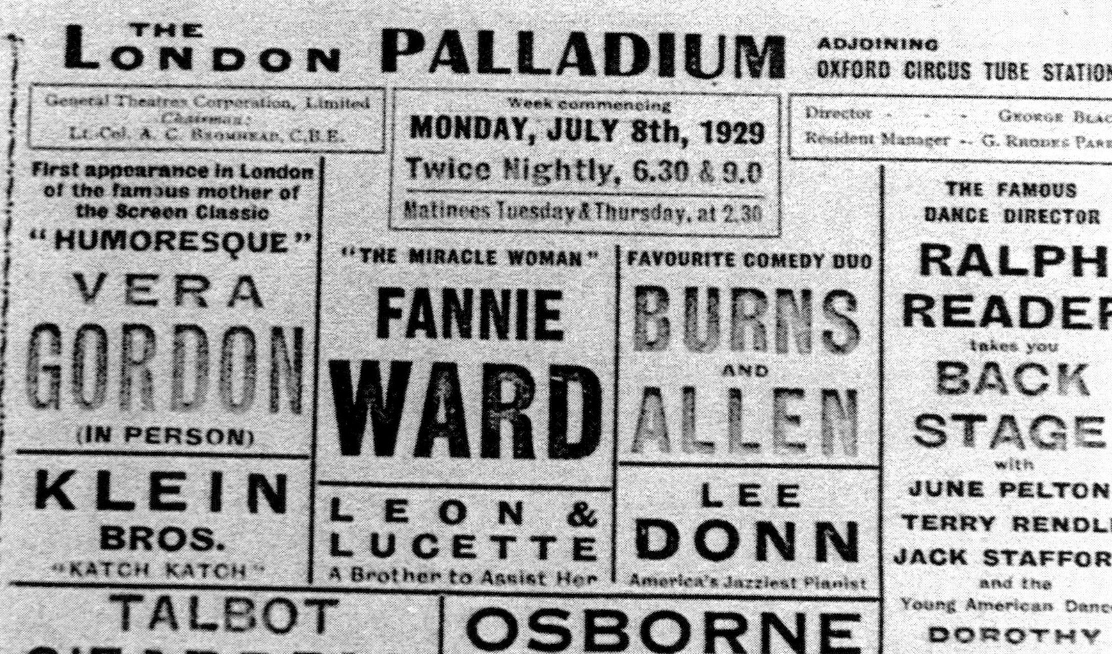

The playbill from Burns and Allen's 1929 appearance at the London Palladium. (Photo courtesy of the London Palladium)

A Burns and Allen vaudeville publicity photo from around 1929, when they were performing their routine, "Lamb Chop." (Photo by Wiese Studio. Courtesy of USC Cinema-Television Library and Archives of Performing Arts)

Broadcasting from San Francisco's Golden Gate International Exposition, June 1940. (Photo courtesy of the San Francisco Public Library)

TELEVISION

George Burns and Gracie Allen starred in one television series together, **The George Burns and Gracie Allen Show** (also known as **The Burns and Allen Show** or simply **Burns and Allen**) from 1950-1958. Subsequent to Gracie's retirement, George appeared in another series, **The George Burns Show** (1958-1959). After Gracie's death, George teamed up with Connie Stevens from 1964-1965 for **Wendy and Me** and twenty years later (1985) hosted **George Burns Comedy Week.** The **Television Series** portion of this chapter is devoted to these series.

Series are divided between George and Gracie together and George alone. Information listed for each series may include any of the following pertinent information, depending upon the series: the program title, running time, series notes, sponsor, product, advertising agency, network, broadcast day, time slot (Eastern Standard Time), announcer, production notes, and premise. The original air date, syndication title, and episode synopses are also included, as are subjects of the vaudeville routines that ended a number of episodes of **The Burns and Allen Show.** As in radio, scripts were occasionally recycled, and those are indicated by a "similar to" reference. Only one re-run date of a **The Burns and Allen Show** episode is included, and the reason for its inclusion is explained in the synopsis. Pre-emptions during the run of each series are also noted and are assigned their own "T" designation. Full cast, supporting cast and production credits for **The George Burns and Gracie Allen Show** are quite lengthy and appear prior to the first season listings. The production credits are written as they appeared onscreen unless members of the production staff for the show pointed out a discrepancy. Since **The Burns and Allen Show** was in production for multiple seasons, the producer/director/scriptwriter credits are included in the umbrella format that precedes each season's synopses and can be used as a quick reference to the program's pertinent information. **The George Burns Show** and **Wendy and Me** cast and production credits are as they appeared onscreen. Directing and writing credits for **George Burns Comedy Week** will be found at the end of each episode synopsis, and production information is part series, part episodic. Featured players (not to be confused with the supporting cast) in **The George Burns and Gracie Allen Show** were given audio credit at the end of an episode when it was telecast and are shown here in alphabetical order if they were not a regular or semi-regular cast member. If an actor appeared outside a role he or she was normally associated with, that is also indicated. Guest stars and special guests are noted as well. Featured players (again, not to be confused with the supporting cast) for **The George Burns Show** and **Wendy and Me** are listed with the actors' names in alphabetical order. Guest stars, co-stars, and supporting players for **George Burns Comedy Week** are listed with the actor's name and the role played. Portions of reviews (primarily for season premieres) are reprinted here to spotlight certain pertinent observations.

Television Guest Appearances chronicles many of their appearances on other shows (primarily in the U.S. although their appearances have never been limited to this country and including those in which either one or both may not have appeared in person but, rather, via archival footage) and George's guest appearances, specials and movies made for television after Gracie's retirement and death. The guest appearances have not been separated out into "his" and "her" categories because so many of George's appearances, even after Gracie's death, include clips of Gracie's work. Black and white film predominated, of course, until the mid-1960's, when color film became the medium of choice. Videotape eventually usurped film on many programs, especially comedy, since it seems to present its subjects in a much more intimate way.

Information for George and Gracie's guest appearances includes the program name, episode title, network or syndication information, the original air date in chronological order, a description of the show if warranted or known and an occasional review. The abbreviation "n.d." indicates the air date is unknown. Syndication dates can vary from market to market. Some programs one would assume they would be included on (for example, a July 23, 1983 episode of Showtime's **Laughing Matters** concentrating on comedy teams and **Sitcom Moms**, a 1989 Nickelodeon special) have not yet lent themselves to verification. Reports of George's appearance on **Celebrity Billiards** (with Minnesota Fats) has, likewise, not yet been proven, nor has an appearance on **I've Got A Secret**. He also may have appeared on various televised awards for which he was nominated (Emmys, his first Grammy and the Golden Globes).

For the most part, talk shows such as **The Tonight Show** are listed without further description. It should be noted that, although they may not be listed every year, shows such as **Entertainment Tonight** and **Showbiz Today** (and their weekend editions) always included George in their celebrity birthday salutes. The Cable News Network (CNN) frequently included news bits about George during their regular programming. Appearances on **Entertainment Tonight** and CNN programming are representative.

A number of news programs commented on events in their lives such as Gracie's retirement and subsequent death as well as George's 1974 heart bypass operation and 1994 illness and surgery and his death in 1996; however, because of their ubiquitous nature, they are not included.

Throughout both sections, the authors have inserted bits of information that we hope will contribute to the reader's enjoyment of the text or understanding of the era in which the show was produced.

Television Series (1950-1985)

George Burns and Gracie Allen

1. **The George Burns and Gracie Allen Show. 1950-1958. CBS. 30 min. b/w.**

Series Notes: This thirty-minute situation comedy was sponsored by the Carnation Company (Erwin, Wasey & Co., Ltd.) for its first two seasons and co-sponsored by the B. F. Goodrich Company (BBD&O) during the next five with General Mills via Dancer, Fitzgerald, Sample picking up part of the costs during the eighth season. It was broadcast on CBS from October 12, 1950, until September 22, 1958 (the last first-run episode aired on September 15, 1958). The series began as a bi-weekly show (performed live at the Mansfield Theater in New York City and later at the CBS Studios in Hollywood) and featured guest singers and dancers in the early episodes. Airing on alternating Thursdays at 8:00 P.M. (sharing the time slot with, variously, **Starlight Theatre**, **The Garry Moore Show** and **Star of the Family** starring Mary Healy and Peter Lind Hayes), it became a weekly Thursday night show on October 9, 1952, and moved to Mondays at 8:00 P.M. on March 30, 1953, where it remained a weekly schedule entry until it ceased production due to Gracie's retirement from show business. Two hundred and ninety-one episodes were produced, although only two hundred and thirty-nine episodes, those that were produced on film, are in syndication. Readers will notice two hundred ninety-four entries for **The Burns and Allen Show**, but that includes pre-emptions, as explained in the introduction to this section. Of the filmed episodes, one was shot in color; the others in black and white. There were fifty-two live shows with the remainder of the shows filmed at the General Service Studios in Hollywood. Preview audiences provided the reactions heard on the soundtracks of the filmed episodes.

The program's main theme song was "The Love Nest" (by Otto Harbach and Louis A. Hirsch).

TELEVISION SERIES

Series One. **The George Burns and Gracie Allen Show**. CBS. 30 min.

October 12, 1950 to August 30, 1951	Thursday	8:00 P.M.
September 13, 1951 to September 25, 1952	Thursday	8:00 P.M.
October 9, 1952 to March 26, 1953	Thursday	8:00 P.M.
March 30, 1953 to August 17, 1953	Monday	8:00 P.M.
October 5, 1953 to August 23, 1954	Monday	8:00 P.M.
October 4, 1954 to July 4, 1955	Monday	8:00 P.M.
October 3, 1955 to September 24, 1956	Monday	8:00 P.M.
October 1, 1956 to July 1, 1957	Monday	8:00 P.M.
September 30, 1957 to September 15, 1958	Monday	8:00 P.M.

Series Two. **The George Burns Show**. NBC. 30 min.

October 21, 1958 to April 14, 1959	Tuesday	9:00 P.M.

Series Three. **Wendy and Me**. ABC. 30 min.

September 14, 1964 to May 24, 1965	Monday	9:00 P.M.

Series Four. **George Burns Comedy Week**. CBS. 30 min.

September 18, 1985 to December 25, 1985	Wednesday	9:30 P.M.

The Burns and Allen Show became a McCadden Corporation (later San-Ron Corporation) Production when it went to film and was eventually sold to Screen Gems and syndicated by Columbia Pictures.

Cast: George Burns (*George Burns*); Gracie Allen (*Gracie Allen*); Bea Benaderet (*Blanche Morton - next-door neighbor and Gracie's best friend*); John Brown (*Harry Morton #2 - next-door neighbor and Blanche's husband*); Ronnie Burns (*Ronnie Burns - George and Gracie's son*); Fred Clark (*Harry Morton #3*); Bill Goodwin (*Bill Goodwin - Announcer*); Larry Keating (*Harry Morton #4*); Hal March (*Harry Morton #1*); and Harry Von Zell (*Harry Von Zell - Announcer*).

George and Gracie's daughter, Sandra (Sandy), appeared in a number of episodes, either in person or as a voice on the telephone, but did not play a truly recurring character. Ronald (Ronnie) Burns also appeared in various roles before eventually playing himself.

Supporting Cast: Darlene Albert (*June Jantzen*); Elvia Allman (*Jane - Gracie's wardrobe woman*); Judi Boutin (later known as Judi Meredith) (*Bonnie Sue McAfee - Ronnie's girlfriend and Brian's sister*); Peter Brocco (*Peter - waiter at St. Moritz Hotel*); King Donovan (*Roger - Blanche's brother*); Ralph Dumke (*Mr. McAfee - Bonnie Sue and Brian's father*); Robert Easton (*Brian McAfee - Ronnie's friend*); Bobby Ellis (*Ralph Grainger - Ronnie's friend*); James Flavin (*Detective Sawyer*); Irene Hervey/Verna Hillie (*Clara Bagley - neighbor*); Mary Ellen Kaye (*Joan Jantzen*); Yvonne Lime (*Joy Jantzen*); Jackie Loughery (*Joyce*); Hal March (*Casey - Harry Morton's partner*); Kathy Marlowe (*Kathy - Ronnie's friend*); Howard McNear (*Mr. Jantzen - the plumber*); Lou Merrill/Grandon Rhodes/Stanley Takkie (*Chester Vanderlip - neighbor, banker, and Lucille's husband*); Doris Packer (*Mrs. Millicent Sohmers*); Kay Reihl/Sarah Selby) (*Lucille Vanderlip - Chester's wife*); Rolfe Sedan (*Mr. Beasely - the postman*); Sarah Selby (*Mamie Kelly*); Hart Spraeger (*Jim Boardman*); Phil Tead (*Mr. Larkin - the postman in earlier episodes*); Jody Warner (*Jean Jantzen*); and Frank Wilcox (*Mr. Boardman*).

Production Credits: *Producer/Directors:* Ralph Levy (first, second, and third seasons); Frederick (Fred) de Cordova (fourth, fifth, and sixth seasons); Rod Amateau (seventh and eighth seasons). *Scriptwriters:* William (Willy) Burns, Sid Dorfman, Keith Fowler, Jesse Goldstein, Harvey Helm, Paul Henning, Norman Paul, Nate Monaster. *Assistant Directors:* Joseph Depew; Leonard Shapiro; Robert G. Vreeland. *Associate Producer:* Al Simon. *Supervisor of Production:* Herbert Browar. *Art Direction:* Lou Crebber; Frank Durlauf; Edward Ilou; George Van Marter. *Assistant to the Producer:* Richard (Dick) Fisher; George King. *Casting:* Ruth Burch; Kerwin Coughlin; Bobby Friar. *Chief Electrician:* William D. King. *Costumer:* Jane Vogt. *Director of Photography:* Philip Tannura; James Van Trees. *Editor:* Stanley Frazen; Larry Heath. *Editorial Associate:* Bill Garst; Lynn McCallon; Jerry Shepard. *Film Editor:* Willard Nico. *Grip:* Jimmy Lloyd. *Hair Stylist:* Bertha (Bert) French. *Makeup:* Gene Roemer. *Musical Director:* Lud Gluskin; Mahlon Merrick; Leith Stevens; Harry Sosnik; (Wilbur Hatch conducted the music for the August 2, 1951 episode). *Original Set Design (live shows):* Robert T. Lee. *Paint Department:* John Fisher. *Production Assistant:* William A. Porter. *Property Master:* Joe Thompson; Nat Thurlow. *Assistant Prop Man:* Steve Ferry; Nat Thurlow. *Script Supervisor:* Phyllis Taft. *Second Assistant Director:* George King. *Secretary to Mr. Burns:* Jeri Boggio; Jack Langdon. *Set Decorator:* Claude Carpenter; Anthony C. Montenaro (Mr. Montenaro was actually the head of the prop department for General Service Studios and dressed the extra sets). *Sets:* Frank Durlauf; Steven Goosson. *Scenic Design:* Chris Choate; Harry R. Klemm. *Sound:* R. W. Glass; Richard H. Olson; Earl Spicer. *Sound Editor:* Larry Heath; William Martin. *Supervising Editor:* Stanley Frazen; Larry Heath. *Supervising Film Editor:* Larry Heath. *Stagehand:* Frank Osborne. *Superintendent of Construction:* Don Wells. *Writers' Secretary:* Tommy Clapp.

Additional Credits: John McNeil is also given credit as a set decorator in a press clipping. Miss Allen's gowns were furnished throughout the years by various designers: De De Johnson of California, Howard Greer, Don Loper, Marjorie Michael, and Maxwell Shieff. Mr. Burns' (and Ronnie Burns') wardrobe was by Tavelman's - Los Angeles (and, later, Beverly Hills). Home furnishings were by Brown-Saltman California. Furs were furnished by Edwards and Crow.

First Season: 1950-1951

Sponsor: The Carnation Company.
Product: Carnation Evaporated Milk.
Agency: Erwin, Wasey & Co., Ltd.
Network: CBS.
Broadcast Day: Thursday (bi-weekly).
Time Slot: 8:00-8:30 p.m. (Eastern Standard Time).
Producer/Director: Ralph Levy.
Scriptwriters: Paul Henning, Sid Dorfman, Harvey Helm, William Burns.
Announcer: Bill Goodwin.
Production Notes: These were live shows, originally filmed in New York City at a theater location and later moving to film and television studios in Hollywood. None of these shows are in syndication, although a few kinescopes are available.

Episode Synopses

T1 October 12, 1950 New York, NY
George introduces himself ("I'm George Burns, Gracie Allen's husband") and explains what it means to be a straightman; an encyclopedia salesman has an encounter with Gracie; George tries to trick Gracie and Blanche with a new card game (Kleebob) so he and Harry can avoid going to the movies with their wives and attend the fights instead. Featuring Henry Jones, the quintet the Skylarks, and Maurine Zollman. George joins the Skylarks on "April Showers." At show's end, Gracie receives a huge bouquet of carnations and declares that they are thrilled to be on television and with the Carnation Company (even if she can't figure out how they get milk from carnations). Hal March appears as Harry Morton. **SEE VG33, VG41, VG63, B40.**

Review: "Carnation Milk fell heir to one of the TV delights of the season when the Burns and Allen show debuted on CBS last Thursday..." (**Variety**, October 18, 1950).

T2 October 26, 1950
Inspiration strikes after Gracie spends some time at an art museum and she decides that the world could use another great artist--her. Featuring dancers (Bob) Fosse and Niles, Billy M. Green and Truman Smith. Similar to T154.

T3 November 9, 1950
The tax assessor arrives to appraise the Burnses' furniture. Gracie, afraid she's put a "dent" into her and George's plans to attend a football game with the Mortons, asks Bill Goodwin for assistance. George and Gracie close the show, which George says is running short, with one of their vaudeville routines in which they both try to talk at once. Featuring Marilyn Clark, vocalist Ellen Hanley, Ronald Kane and Bob Sweeney. **SEE VG27, VG34, VG42, VG60.**

T4 November 23, 1950
It's Thanksgiving and Blanche can count her blessings--Harry's new secretary is a man. Gracie invites everyone to dinner and shows them a card game (the same one used in their film **International House** [F20]). Gracie Allen makes one of her few stage mistakes when she steps out of camera range at the end of the show and George has to bring her back so they can finish their routine. Featuring Richard Dana, Camilla DeWitt, Bob Fosse and Harrison Muller. **SEE VG76.**

T5 December 7, 1950
Gracie explains to Harry why she is returning George's Christmas presents before he sees them, which becomes perfectly clear to Harry after he sees one of the gifts; Mr. Vanderlip pays a call on George and asks him to keep Gracie out of the bank. George and Gracie's ending routine isn't seen or heard due to broadcasting errors. Featuring Bill Foster, Jean Mahoney and Bert Thorn. **SEE VG35, VG42.**

T6 December 21, 1950
In their first Christmas show, Gracie purchases a tree, which she and George decorate while enjoying carolers; they exchange presents; and Gracie reminisces about Christmas as a child. The music is "Contented." Featuring Kathleen Comegys and Leslie Littomy.

T7 December 28, 1950 Hollywood, CA
Gracie hires an instructor to give George and Harry Morton dance lessons but they don't prove to be eager pupils until they mistake the instructor's assistant for the instructor. This episode, the first one produced in Hollywood, was an additional telecast and was shown in New York City one week later on January 4, 1951, via kinescope.

Review: "The show is still a prime example of how best to transfer a top radio show into TV." (**Variety**, January 10, 1951).

All of the remaining shows were produced in Hollywood.

T8 January 4, 1951
Gracie throws a party but has one problem: she doesn't know why she's giving it. John Brown takes over the role of Harry Morton. Guest star: Jack Benny. **SEE VG43.**

T9 January 18, 1951
George and Harry Morton try to "duck" out of a trip to Palm Springs. Featuring Leo Fields.

T10 February 1, 1951
Softhearted Gracie gives refuge to a dog whose antics aren't making him very popular with other people in the Burnses' neighborhood, including George.

T11 February 15, 1951
Blanche is furious when she discovers Harry hasn't been bringing home his entire paycheck but George has the answer he hopes will send Blanche back home to Harry and out of his and Gracie's guest room. Featuring Felix Instadt and Arthur Stebbins.

T12 March 1, 1951
The local baker wants George to speak at a banquet, Gracie meets with the income tax man and George explains California's community property law to Gracie. Featuring Frank Jackée and Joseph Kearns. **SEE VG36.**

T13 March 15, 1951
The Vanderlips invite George and Gracie to a party but Gracie doesn't want to go without Blanche and Harry; Bill Goodwin wants George to sign a note so he can buy a car. Featuring Jay Novello.

T14 March 29, 1951
A gangster learns a lesson in crime and punishment when he tries to bully Gracie into testifying for him in court.

T15 April 12, 1951
George has a cold and, when Gracie goes to the market to get him a steak, she wrecks the car; meanwhile, George is starving because friends keep bringing him food but eat it before he can.

T16 April 26, 1951
Emily Vanderlip spends the weekend with George and Gracie while her parents are out of town. Her boyfriend Chuck comes to pick up Emily for a date and they show the Burnses some new dance steps. After they leave, George and Gracie dance to the records. Featuring Bill Foster and Jean Mahoney. **SEE VG27, VG31, VG39, VG41.**

T17 May 10, 1951
The neighborhood just isn't big enough for George's singing *and* new neighbors; Bill Goodwin's nephew saves George from drowning.

T18 May 24, 1951
Everyone's looking forward to the Vanderlips' masquerade party but Chester Vanderlip can't mask his displeasure when he sees what his wife wants him to wear. Fred Clark assumes the role of Harry Morton.

T19 June 7, 1951
An old friend from Gracie's school days, Mamie Kelly, comes for a visit and overstays her welcome with George. Sarah Selby, who later assumes the role of Lucille Vanderlip, plays Mamie.

T20 June 21, 1951
The fur flies when Harry Morton tries to get out of going to visit his mother-in-law.

T21 July 5, 1951
An exterminator pays a visit to the Burnses and kills George's plans for spending time away from the Mortons.

T22 July 19, 1951
How do you keep a gangster from moving into Beverly Hills? Introduce him to Gracie, of course.

T23 August 2, 1951
Gracie and Blanche become vegetarians but can they get George and Harry to swallow a new diet? An autographed Carnation cookbook, **The Cook's Handbook**, is being offered for thirty-five cents to anyone writing to Gracie Allen. Featuring Butch Cavell and Alan Mowbray. **SEE VG43, VG60.**

T24 August 16, 1951
Mamie Kelly and her three daughters make a return visit to the Burnses' home. Featuring Sarah Selby.

T25 August 30, 1951
Gracie orders new appliances from a wholesaler, but George refuses to accept the delivery. Featuring Harry Von Zell.

Second Season: 1951-1952

Sponsor: The Carnation Company.
Product: Carnation Evaporated Milk.
Agency: Erwin, Wasey & Co., Ltd.
Network: CBS.
Broadcast Day: Thursday.
Time Slot: 8:00-8:30 P.M. (Eastern Standard Time).
Producer/Director: Ralph Levy.
Scriptwriters: Paul Henning, Sid Dorfman, Harvey Helm, William Burns.
Announcer: Harry Von Zell.

T26 September 13, 1951
Gracie repays a woman's kindness by throwing the woman's daughter a lavish wedding. Featuring Steve Dunn, Maurice Marsac, Shepard Menken, Noreen Michaels and June Whitley. Harry Von Zell begins his first full season on the show. George makes the announcement of him permanently replacing Bill Goodwin by interrupting the action on stage to say that Bill left to go to New York to star in his own show. Gracie is given a bouquet of carnations at show's end to celebrate the beginning of their second year with the Carnation Company. Similar to T135. **SEE VG25, VG32, VG43, VG60.**

T27 September 27, 1951
As Blanche's best friend, Gracie sees nothing abnormal about taking her place at a visit to a psychiatrist. Similar to T115.

T28 October 11, 1951
The Beverly Hills Uplift Society has been locked out of its clubhouse because Gracie, the club treasurer, used the rent money to buy a wall safe. Out of desperation George finally gives the club money for their rent and they repay him with kisses. The Carnation cookbook is still being advertised and Gracie says she's autographing them as fast as she can. This is the first time the show is broadcast coast to coast via the new coaxial cable connection. Featuring Mary Adams, Florence Bates, Cecily Brown, Margie List, Joyce McCluskey and Hope Sansbury. **SEE VG37, VG41.**

T29 October 25, 1951
Gracie is arrested when she tries to sell some extra tickets to a football game. At the end of the show Gracie appeals for blood to be given to the Red Cross for the Armed Forces. Featuring Bob Sweeney.

T30 November 8, 1951
George's surprise birthday party holds one more surprise that George wishes he could return--a bill from the Mocambo for twenty-six people! Featuring Veola Vonn.

T31 November 22, 1951
George and Gracie invite some friends over to share their Thanksgiving dinner and Gracie fears one of the guests has become the subject of ridicule. Featuring Hal March as Casey.

T32 December 6, 1951
Gracie and Blanche resort to trickery to obtain new dresses for a concert the Munetti String Ensemble is presenting for the Beverly Hills Uplift Society.

T33 December 20, 1951
Mamie Kelly and her three daughters arrive to spend Christmas with the Burnses. Gracie's attempts to recount a classic holiday tale includes twists that even Charles Dickens never thought of. Featuring Jeri James, Melinda Plowman, Kathleen O'Malley and Jill Oppenheim. **SEE VG46, VG50, VG58, VG62.**

T34 January 3, 1952
Gracie's desire to have a place for home-canned foods turns into a bigger project than George had envisioned. Featuring Damian O'Flynn, Steve Pendleton, Benny Rubin and Bob Sweeney.

T35 January 17, 1952
The campaign for presidency of the Beverly Hills Uplift Society finds Blanche locked in a heated battle with her opponent and her own husband, who doesn't want her to run for office. Featuring Florence Bates and Joseph Kearns.

T36 January 31, 1952
George and Harry Morton prepare themselves for what they assume is going to be a boring evening at the Vanderlips'. Featuring Bob Sweeney.

T37 February 14, 1952
Gracie attempts to keep George from discovering that she has put another dent in their car.

T38 February 28, 1952
Blanche tries to persuade Harry to let her go to Palm Springs with George and Gracie. Mary Livingstone Benny's dog, Suzette, makes an appearance.

T39 March 13, 1952
Gracie reports her lost engagement ring to the police. Featuring Jerry Hausner, Ida Moore and Steve Pendleton.

T40 March 27, 1952
George and Gracie prepare for an evening at Romanoff's; Gracie tries to help her wardrobe woman's brother out of a messy situation; and someone has an even messier suggestion on how George can improve his television show. Featuring Bob Sweeney and Veola Vonn.

T41 April 10, 1952
George and Gracie are interviewed for a film about show business. A projection shot was used to show the Burnses shopping downtown. Featuring Jan Arvan, Skeets Gallagher and Theodore Von Eltz.

T42 April 24, 1952
Gracie and Mary Livingstone intercede when an argument between George and his best friend threatens to end their relationship. Featuring Bob Johnson and Theodore Von Eltz. Guest star: Jack Benny.

T43 May 8, 1952
Gracie tries to get George out of the house so she can redecorate. Featuring Steve Pendleton.

T44 May 22, 1952
Gracie's friend, Mamie Kelly, and her husband are considering a move to Los Angeles from San Francisco, so Mamie arrives with their three young daughters to visit "Aunt" Gracie and "Uncle" George, but they're only a few of the distractions George must endure while trying to write a speech. Harry Von Zell announces that George and Gracie received Sylvania's Pioneer Award this week for their work in radio and television. Featuring Jeri James, Jill Oppenheim, Melinda Plowman, Sarah Selby and Pierre Watkin. **SEE VG38, VG42.**

T45 June 5, 1952
Gracie puts into motion a plan that will allow a fortune teller's prediction to come true: that she will be married twice. Featuring Lee Miller, Steve Pendleton and Walter Woolfe King. **SEE VG49.**

T46 June 19, 1952
Harry Morton and Harry Von Zell invest money in a musical comedy and, when the writers ask George to invest five thousand dollars, he agrees--if they will give him the starring role. Featuring Hal March, Lee Miller and Buddy Pepper.

T47 July 3, 1952
It could only happen to Gracie: she confuses a desk with a person, which results in Blanche thinking Gracie is having an affair with Harry Morton. Featuring Barbara Pepper.

T48 July 17, 1952
Gracie secures a recording contract for George by promising someone more than she can deliver. Harry Von Zell is ill and is replaced in tonight's show by Hy Averback. Bea Benaderet also plays the switchboard operator. Featuring Walter Woolfe King and Kathleen O'Malley.

T49 July 31, 1952
Gracie not only believes George's latest excuse for not spending time with the Mortons, she also believes they must be broke and, when a telephone call to a finance company doesn't net her the desired results, she rents out their spare bedroom. Featuring Butch Cavell, Ed Clark, Bob Sweeney and Kay Wiley.

T50 August 14, 1952
George is arrested when Gracie innocently buys a stolen racehorse. Featuring Chuck Alford, Frankie Darron, Alan Reed and Mickey Young.

T51 August 28, 1952
Gracie, as usual, takes it literally when George tells her he ran into Georgie Jessel at the club. Featuring Dick Crockett, Joseph Kearns and Arthur Stebbins.

T52 September 25, 1952
It's redecorating time again and Gracie persuades George to go to Las Vegas for two weeks so she can get him out of the house. Featuring Joseph Kearns and Donald Lawton.

This is the last of the fifty-two live shows.

Third Season: 1952-1953

Co-Sponsors: The Carnation Company, B. F. Goodrich.
Products: Carnation Evaporated Milk, automobile tires and other rubber made products.
Agency: Erwin, Wasey & Co., Ltd.; BBD&O.
Network: CBS.
Broadcast Day: Thursday.
Time Slot: 8:00-8:30 P.M. (Eastern Standard Time).
Producer/Director: Ralph Levy.
Scriptwriters: Sid Dorfman, Jesse Goldstein, Harvey Helm, Nate Monaster, William Burns, Paul Henning. Mr. Henning left during the 1952 season to become a television producer, beginning with **The Bob Cummings Show**.

The show becomes a weekly filmed series.

T53 October 9, 1952
"Wardrobe Woman Wins Free Trip to Hawaii"
Gracie's wardrobe woman has won a fabulous trip, and Gracie is afraid Jane will be spending her vacation alone unless Gracie can convince Harry Von Zell to accompany her, somehow not realizing that Jane is already married. Featuring James Flavin with Hal March as the head of a marriage bureau.

<u>Reviews</u>: "Miss Allen has no peer at her particular brand of nitwitticisms, and her spouse is excellent with his offkey vocalizing and asides on his wife's flightiness." (**Daily Variety**, October 10, 1952). "After two years

on live TV, Burns and Allen have switched to film and, for once, there's no noticeable difference in the quality of the show." (**Variety**, October 15, 1952).

T54 October 16, 1952
"Gracie Giving Party for Atomic Scientist"
Gracie's dinner party has run amok--George is upset about the cost, the hired help quits, the new butler eats all the food, the guest of honor walks out and the other guests never arrive because Gracie forgot to mail the invitations.

T55 October 23, 1952
"George Sneezing--Gracie Thinks He's Insane"
How do you get a doctor to make a diagnosis of your husband's medical affliction without letting your husband know? If you're Gracie you take George's place at the examination.

T56 October 30, 1952
"Gracie Buying Boat for George"
Everyone but George seems to think he needs a hobby and everyone but George seems to think that buying a boat would provide the perfect hobby. Featuring Bob Sweeney.

T57 November 6, 1952
"Gracie Having George's Portrait Painted"
Gracie hires an artist to paint a portrait of George for his birthday but she wants the painting to be a surprise and makes the artist hide in the closet to do his work. Featuring Rex Evans, Joseph Kearns and Leon Tyler.

T58 November 13, 1952
"Gracie and Blanche Hire Two Gigolos to Take Them Out"
When George and Harry show little interest in taking Gracie and Blanche out the girls resort to Plan B. Featuring Gilbert (Gil) Frye and Gerald Mohr. Special guest: Charlie Morrison, owner of Hollywood's Mocambo Club, who plays himself.

T59 November 20, 1952
"Sampter Clayton Ballet--Selling Tickets"
Eager to convince her disinterested husband to become a ballet sponsor, Gracie resorts to some fancy footwork of her own. Featuring Dick Darcy, Joseph Kearns, Mary Lavalle and Lee Miller.

T60 November 27, 1952
"Skating Pearsons Comes to Visit"
George and Gracie are asked to intercede when their friends' son is determined to go into show business and his parents are just as determined he not follow in their footsteps. Featuring Verna Felton, Skeets Gallagher and Barbara Pepper.

T61 December 4, 1952
"Gracie Selling Swamp So Harry Will Buy TV Set"
Gracie tries to help Blanche get a television by trying to help Harry sell some of his less-than-prime real estate. Featuring Rex Evans and Bob Sweeney.

T62 December 11, 1952
"Silky Thompson: Gracie Writes My Life with George Burns"
Gracie's article for **Look** magazine causes problems for George; in it, she claims he beat up a gangster who had robbed a bank so he could back George in a show. This article did appear in **Look** but was not written by Gracie and is not serious in content. Featuring Gordon Barnes and Charles Evans. Guest star: Sheldon Leonard. **SEE VG28, VG64.**

T63 December 18, 1952
"Gracie Thinks George Is Going to Commit Suicide"
Gracie is already confused over something she thinks is a suicide note so George decides to use her confusion to his advantage. Featuring John Call and Maurice Marsac.

T64 December 25, 1952
"Von Zell Dates Married Woman--Jealous Husband"

Harry Von Zell has unknowingly been dating a married woman but the sparks really fly when her husband finds out and goes after the wrong man--Harry Morton. Featuring Jan Arvan, Chuckie Bradley and Hugh Sanders.

T65 January 1, 1953
"Uncle Clyde Comes to Visit: Renting Room"
George tries to rent out their spare bedroom before Gracie's Uncle Clyde arrives for a visit. Ronnie and Sandra Burns are introduced in the Burnses' living room setting up a projector to watch a show; they also do the closing routine in place of George and Gracie. Featuring Charles Lane and Howard McNear.

T66 January 8, 1953
"Gracie Thinks Harry Morton Is in Love with Her"
In order to have some privacy while making a telephone call about an anniversary gift for Blanche, Harry Morton has to get Gracie to leave the room--so he tells her he's in love with her; a novelty salesman tries to sell Gracie on the idea of marketing the aprons she wears on the show. Featuring Marvin Miller. **SEE VG56.**

T67 January 15, 1953
"Gracie Trying to Keep Mortons from Moving Away"
Harry Morton is determined to trade his house and Gracie, who doesn't want to lose Blanche as her neighbor, is even more determined to stop a new tenant from moving in. Ed Sullivan phones and asked Burns and Allen to appear on his **Toast of the Town** television show next week. Featuring Gail Bonney and Lester Matthews. **SEE VG56.**

T68 January 22, 1953
"Gracie Thinks She's Not Married to George"
George's marriage *and* his career may go up in smoke if he can't find someone to convince Gracie that she and George are really married; Gracie moves in with the Mortons while George tries to find the witness to their wedding. Featuring Fay Baker and Paul Powers. Guest star: Jack Benny. **SEE VG28, VG56, VG64.**

T69 January 29, 1953
"Tax Refund"
Gracie invites the mayor of Los Angeles to dinner in order to return their tax refund--all two dollars and thirty-eight cents. Featuring John Crawford and Lurene Tuttle. Special guest: Los Angeles Mayor Fletcher Bowron.

T70 February 5, 1953
"Cigarette Girl--Georgie Jessel--Teddy Bear"
George gets first-hand experience about the power of the press when he has to try to convince Gracie that an item she read in a newspaper gossip column is not what it appears to be.

T71 February 12, 1953
"Gracie on Train--Murder"
Gracie, returning home from San Francisco on a train, confuses her dining car companions and they decide to convince Gracie that one of them is going home to kill his wife. Featuring John Bosher, James Flavin, Ray Hite, Bob Johnson and Robert Roy.

Review: "...up to its usual high-grade zany level...Gracie ran off with the chief honors, as usual...But couldn't Georgie find a more respectable place to read his **Variety** than in jail?" (**Variety**, February 18, 1953).

T72 February 19, 1953
"Blanche Wants New Car: Gracie Gets Von Zell a Wife"
Gracie plans to buy cars for herself and Blanche with the three thousand dollars she thinks Harry Von Zell is going to pay her for finding him a wife and three children. Gracie's article in the **Woman's Home Companion** is mentioned. Featuring Chuck Alford, John Crawford, Verna Felton and Dick Reeves.

T73 February 26, 1953
"Gracie Gives a Swamp Party"
Gracie always takes people's remarks literally so when Harry Morton mentions that if he just had the right party, he could sell some swamp property, how better to help a friend than to give a swamp party?

Featuring Phil Arnold, Nestor Paiva, George Pembroke, Beverly Simmons, Edith Simmons and Jack Wright.

T74 March 5, 1953
"George and Gracie Hear a Burglar: Up All Night"
Detective Sawyer reluctantly responds to a report of a burglar in Beverly Hills called in by the bane of his existence, Mrs. George Burns. Featuring William Henry.

T75 March 12, 1953
"Gracie Buying a Ranch for George"
George and Gracie have spent the weekend at Fred Astaire's ranch and when George jokingly mentions it's his life's ambition to get up every morning at four o'clock Gracie goes shopping again, this time for a ranch. Featuring Ed Cassidy and Hal March as Dr. Brown.

T76 March 19, 1953
"Gracie Gets George in the Army"
Is it possible that, when Uncle Sam said, "I Want You for the U.S. Army," he really meant to point his finger at George and Harry Morton? Probably not, but that doesn't stop Gracie from getting George enlisted when she becomes concerned about his physical fitness (Harry becoming enlisted was just an accident!). Featuring Dick Erdman, Gil Fletcher, Don Ganett, Bert Moorhouse, Rolfe Sedan as Dr. Mangrum and Paula Winslow.

T77 March 26, 1953
"Gracie Reports Car Stolen"
George's writers are meeting in Palm Springs but Gracie is determined to keep George from leaving town to join them because she thinks he's been jinxed. Featuring Isabel Jewel, Peter Leeds and Gloria Mendelson.

The show moves to Monday nights at 8:00 P.M.

T78 March 30, 1953
"Gracie Pretends To Be College Boy's Mother"
A young man working his way through college as George and Gracie's yard boy is embarrassed when his girlfriend sees him, so he pretends to live there, with Gracie posing as his mother when his parents come to visit. The young college boy is named Ronnie and his girlfriend Sandy, the actual names of George and Gracie's children. George smokes a cigarette on the show rather than his usual prop cigar. Featuring David Blair and Ruta Kilmonis with Grandon Rhodes and Kay Reihl as Mr. and Mrs. Cummings. Similar to T270.

T79 April 6, 1953
"Misunderstanding Over Buying Mountain Cabin"
Blanche and Harry are upset when they think George is buying a mountain cabin from someone other than Harry. Featuring Don Gibson and Lester Matthews.

T80 April 13, 1953
"Blanche Secretly Buys a Fur Stole"
George finds a fur stole in the house and reluctantly begins to believe Gracie may have lied to him when she said it belongs to Blanche. Featuring Herbert Robinson.

T81 April 20, 1953
"Gracie Takes Spanish Lessons"
George further complicates Gracie's efforts to help her Spanish teacher extend his visa when he pretends to be an illegal alien to an audience of one--an immigration official. Featuring Bob Sweeney.

T82 April 27, 1953
"Gracie and Cleaning Woman: Vanderlips"
Gracie thinks Mr. Vanderlip gave his cleaning woman a diamond bracelet and a fur on his wife's birthday. Featuring Cecily Brown and Verna Felton.

T83 May 4, 1953
"Von Zell's Girl Friend Between Trains"
Gracie poses as "Mabel Von Zell" when Harry's college girlfriend stops by for a visit between trains. Featuring Ann Doran.

T84 May 11, 1953
"George Lecturing at U.C.L.A."
George receives what he thinks is an invitation to be part of a lecture series on television at UCLA. During a rare poignant moment, he loses his self-confidence when he hears his friends laughing at the idea, so Gracie seeks the help of a personality consultant. George and Gracie promote Car Safety Month. Featuring Rex Evans, Hal Taggart, Buck Young and Carlton Young.

T85 May 18, 1953
"Gracie and Harry Morton: Missing Person Bureau"
Gracie thinks Harry Morton has been kidnapped when he doesn't come home for lunch so she reports him to the missing person bureau and contacts his insurance company. Featuring Bob Bray, Don Brody and Joseph Kearns.

T86 July 6, 1953
"Surprise Party for Mortons: Sanitarium Routine"
While at the Mortons' home hiding Blanche's birthday presents to Harry Gracie receives a telephone call intended for Blanche and thinks that George is going to be the guest of honor at a surprise party. Featuring Dick Bowman, Frank Gerstle and Myron Healey. **SEE VG75.**

T87 July 13, 1953
"Perry and Pete, Gracie's Cousins, Sneak Thieves"
Gracie finds two burglars in the house and fixes them something to eat; George thinks they are her cousins and invites them to be houseguests but they soon turn out to be thieves robbing the neighborhood and hiding their booty in the Burnses' garage. Featuring Dick Erdman, Peter Leeds and George Pembroke.

T88 July 20, 1953
"Gracie Doing a Picture Without George"
Gracie is determined not to stand in George's way when she thinks he's been offered a part in a Broadway show without her so she tries to make him believe she's been offered a role in a film that doesn't include *him*. Featuring Lester Dorr.

T89 July 27, 1953
"Gracie Trying to Get George to Go on Trip East"
George avoids taking a cross-country trip with the Mortons so he can spend his vacation at home and then must contend with all the people Gracie invited over to use their pool while they were gone. Featuring Dick Elliott, Clarence Straight and Kay Wiley.

T90 August 3, 1953
"Gracie Sees a Hold-Up: Johnny Velvet"
A bank robber and his accomplice attempt to kidnap George to keep the only witness, Gracie, from testifying in court. Featuring Ben Welden. Guest stars: Sheldon Leonard and Ronald Reagan.

T91 August 10, 1953
"Gracie and George Locked Out of Their House"
After a late evening spent with the Mortons Gracie accidentally locks herself and George out of their house and must later explain to the locksmith's suspicious wife why the check Gracie gave him was so large. Similar to T288.

T92 August 17, 1953
"Gracie at Department Store"
Gracie trips and falls in the McCadden Department Store and tears her stockings. The store's insurance adjuster wants to settle out of court with Gracie but she keeps refusing the money--she thinks that she has to pay the company rather than the company paying her. The store's doctor goes to the Burnses' home to examine Gracie and he is convinced after the examination that she hurt her head when she fell. Featuring Jan Arvan, Lester Matthews and Grandon Rhodes as Dr. Wilburn. Similar to T264. **SEE VG41.**

Fourth Season: 1953-1954

Co-Sponsors: The Carnation Company, B. F. Goodrich.

Products: Carnation Evaporated Milk, automobile tires and other rubber made products.
Agency: Erwin, Wasey & Co., Ltd.; BBD&O.
Network: CBS.
Broadcast Day: Monday.
Time Slot: 8:00-8:30 P.M. (Eastern Standard Time).
Producer/Director: Frederick (Fred) de Cordova.
Scriptwriters: Sid Dorfman, Harvey Helm, William Burns, Keith Fowler.

T93 October 5, 1953
"Morton Buys Iron Deer: Gracie Thinks George Needs Glasses" George can't see Harry Morton spending two hundred dollars on an iron deer, so Gracie thinks he's losing his eyesight. Larry Keating joins the cast as Harry Morton. Featuring Joseph Kearns and Pierre Watkin.

Review: "It's still among the brightest TVers to be seen...Larry Keating, a newcomer to the cast, scored as her (Bea Benaderet's) husband." (**Variety**, October 7, 1953).

T94 October 12, 1953
"Gracie Helps Mortons Get C.P.A. Account"
Blanche makes the mistake of telling Gracie that Harry is trying to sign up a new account with a gentleman who seems to prefer his associates to be playboys. Featuring Paul Harvey and Howard McNear.

T95 October 19, 1953
"Gracie Gets a Jury Summons"
The Mortons, Harry Von Zell and the postman attempt to convince a judge that having Gracie serve on a jury would be an injustice to the judicial system. Featuring Lester Matthews and Will Wright.

T96 October 26, 1953
"George Teaches Gracie Not To Be Careless"
George, hoping to teach Gracie a lesson in responsibility, hides her wristwatch at the Mortons', where Gracie finds it and fears Blanche has become a kleptomaniac. The show includes a public service announcement for the National Safety Council.

T97 November 2, 1953
"George and Harry Morton Mad at Each Other"
Harry Morton and George are feuding because Gracie misunderstood remarks she heard both of them make about someone else. Sandra Burns appears with her mother in a commercial. Featuring Walter Woolfe King.

T98 November 9, 1953
"Gracie Getting a Business Manager, Roger"
A prospective business manager comes down from San Francisco for a visit, but everyone confuses him with a tramp who's doing odd jobs in the neighborhood. The "Roger" in this episode is not to be confused with the recurring character of Blanche Morton's brother, "Roger." Featuring Joseph Kearns and Johnson White.

T99 November 16, 1953
"Raccoon Coat Story"
Thinking it's one of George's old vaudeville costumes, Gracie gives away Harry Morton's cherished raccoon coat to the gardener for his wife to make into coats for their children. Featuring Lester Matthews, Syd Saylor and Chip Taylor.

T100 November 23, 1953
"Gracie Thinks Harry Von Zell Is Broke"
Gracie thinks Harry Von Zell is broke and enlists the aid of the State Welfare Board; George gives Gracie a refresher course on California's community property law. Featuring Jan Arvan, John Gallaudet and Dana Ryan.

T101 November 30, 1953
"Gracie Going to San Francisco"
George sings the blues when Gracie's confusion over a visit with her mother threatens to spoil his plans for an evening with friends. Featuring Verna Felton and Leon Tyler.

T102 December 7, 1953

"Gracie Trades Home for Mountain Cabin"
Thinking George is retiring from show business, Gracie trades their Beverly Hills home for a one-room mountain cabin. Featuring Mabel Albertson, Frank Wilcox and Will Wright. Jack Benny plays himself as a voice on the telephone with Sandra Burns as the operator.

T103 December 14, 1953
"George and Gracie Going to Rose-Marie Premiere"
George is given tickets to a movie premiere but is left holding the (popcorn) bag when he and Gracie accidentally give away all of the tickets to their friends. Featuring Fay Baker, Ruth Brady, Ray Roche and Kay Wiley.

T104 December 21, 1953
"Jane (Wardrobe Woman) and Her Problem"
Gracie thinks if she makes more money than George she'll be able to solve her wardrobe woman's problems with *her* husband. Featuring Peter Leeds.

T105 December 28, 1953
"Gracie's Anniversary Present"
Gracie misunderstands when she hears George ordering a plane over the phone; she assumes he's buying her an airplane for their anniversary. Featuring Dan Tobin and the voice of Sandra Burns.

T106 January 4, 1954
"Uncle Harvey's Invention"
Gracie's Uncle Harvey sends her a formula he promises will make plants grow and, when it looks like the Allen family black sheep has finally come up with a winner, everyone hopes to hit pay dirt by investing in it. Featuring Sandra Burns.

T107 January 11, 1954
"George Reading Play To Be Done in London"
A theatrical producer from London may regret making a trip to Beverly Hills.

T108 January 18, 1954
"Gracie Helps Mechanic with Girl Friend"
Gracie agrees to help persuade an auto mechanic's starstruck girlfriend that being married to an actor is a terrible life but accidentally tells it to a newspaper writer instead who prints the story in the afternoon edition.

T109 January 25, 1954
"Gracie Discovers George's Secret Weakness"
Harry Von Zell shows Gracie a newspaper item quoting a judge as saying one out of five husbands has a secret vice so Gracie decides to find out what George's is.

T110 February 1, 1954
"Gracie Has to Sell George's Car by Five O'Clock"
A fire inspector's order to dispose of some flammable material sitting too near the car confuses Gracie and, when she tries to sell the car to a used car salesman, he thinks it's stolen. A public service announcement for Fire Prevention Week is included in tonight's show. Featuring Tyler McVey, Ralph Montgomery, Lyle Talbot and Anthony Warde.

T111 February 8, 1954
"Gracie Wins a Television Set"
Gracie is convinced she won a television set after correctly answering a telephone quiz show question even though she looked up the answer after she hung up the phone! Featuring Harry Antrim, Robert Hutton and Roy Rowan.

T112 February 15, 1954
"No Fan Mail for George"
Blanche writes a fan letter to George as a favor to Gracie, signing it "Violet McGonigle," and all is letter perfect until Harry Morton thinks his wife has developed a crush on George and the real Violet McGonigle's jealous husband comes looking for George. Featuring Barbara Pepper.

T113 February 22, 1954
"George and Gracie Going to Opera Carmen"

Mr. Vanderlip invites the Burnses and the Mortons to the opera but George would rather go to a 3-D movie. Featuring Isabel Randolph and Olan Soulé.

T114 March 1, 1954
"Harry Morton Is Missing"
Harry Morton is missing and Harry Von Zell hires a detective to find him, but the case becomes more open than shut when Gracie pretends to be Blanche, and the detective sees Harry Morton having lunch with a blonde--whom he doesn't realize is the real Mrs. Morton. Featuring Anthony Warde and Frank Wilcox.

T115 March 8, 1954
"Gracie Goes to Psychiatrist for Blanche's Dream"
Blanche makes an appointment with a psychiatrist to discuss a persistent nightmare but Gracie goes in her place and the doctor tells Harry Morton his wife is a very sick woman. Featuring Sandra Burns and Frank Wilcox. Similar to T27.

T116 March 15, 1954
"Gracie's Old Boy Friend, Dan Conroy, Comes to Town"
Perhaps George can't compete with Dan's athletic abilities but, by the conclusion of the show, you have to wonder if Dan could compete with George's abilities to cope with Gracie.

T117 March 22, 1954
"Gracie Tries to Get George in College"
Gracie thinks George wants to be a college man and tries to enroll him; George goes to jail after his business manager tries to get one of Gracie's traffic tickets fixed. Featuring Douglass Dumbrille, Jack Lomas, Lester Matthews, Mitchell Powell, Anthony Warde and Howard Wendell.

T118 March 29, 1954
"Columbia Pictures Doing Burns and Allen Story"
Columbia Pictures wants to make the Burns and Allen story but the project never sees the light of the silver screen after Gracie "discovers" George has a wife and four sons in San Diego and calls off the picture to keep the whole world from finding out. Featuring Fay Baker, Herb Ellis, John Gallaudet, Nestor Paiva, Margie Pickner and Dan Tobin. Sandra Burns provides the secretary's voice on the telephone. **SEE VG43.**

T119 April 5, 1954
"An Elephant Sits on Gracie's Fender"
Gracie's car fender has a dent in it, and Gracie tells George an elephant sat on it, but he thinks she's not telling the truth. Featuring Douglas Fowley, Bill Kennedy, Ralph Montgomery and George E. Stone.

T120 April 12, 1954
"George Gets Black Eye from Open Door"
Gracie thinks that George and a member of their television show's production staff have gotten into a fight.

T121 April 19, 1954
"Dolores De Marco, George's Ex-Vaudeville Partner"
Gracie hopes the reappearance of a woman from George's past doesn't bring the curtain down on their marriage. Featuring John Hoyt, Adrienne Martin, Penny Parker, Diane Robinson and Lyle Talbot.

T122 April 26, 1954
"Vanderlip Buys Black Negligee for His Wife"
Gracie intervenes when she assumes Mr. Vanderlip is buying a negligee for a woman who is not his wife. Featuring Richard Deems, Mary Ellen Kaye, Joel Marston and Herb Vigran. The part of Lucille Vanderlip is played by Kay Reihl, not Sarah Selby as announced in the credits.

T123 May 3, 1954
"Gracie and George Have a Mystery Anniversary"
Gracie throws a party but can't answer the question everyone keeps asking, "what are we celebrating?" Featuring Kathryn Card, Rex Evans, Lois January, Helen Mahon, Lee Miller, Alan Ray, Judith Rutherford and Lyle Talbot.

T124 May 10, 1954
"George Resting for Insurance Examination"

Twenty-four hours can seem like a very long time in the Burns and Allen household when you're trying to rest in order to pass an insurance exam. At the end of the show George and Gracie do an ad for U.S. Savings Bonds. Featuring Mitch Call, Allen Dexter, Pauline Drake, Jack Lomas, Doris Packer, Russell Trent and Howard Wendell.

T125 July 5, 1954
"Harry Morton Has Only a Week To Live"
Blanche and Gracie are in tears. They each think the other one is going to be a widow within a week.

T126 July 12, 1954
"Gracie Buys Old Movies To Sell to Television"
Gracie puts thousands of dollars into something she thinks is a "reel" deal, selling old films to television, but the transaction infuriates their friends because George had already advised them against doing the same, saying it wasn't a good business investment.

T127 July 19, 1954
"Emily Vanderlip's Elopement"
Gracie thinks Emily Vanderlip is going to elope. Featuring Richard Bauman and Mildred (Millie) Doff.

T128 July 26, 1954
"Gracie Runs for City Council"
Gracie runs for the Beverly Hills City Council. Featuring Douglas Fowley, Joseph Graham, Isabel Randolph, Marion Ross and Martha Wentworth.

T129 August 2, 1954
"Burnses and Mortons Choosing Movie To Attend"
Trying to find a movie that no one has seen grows more difficult as the crowd in George and Gracie's living room grows larger. Featuring Raymond Greenleaf, Billy Griffith, Jack Lomas, Helen Mahon, Bill O'Brien, Phil Tead and Lyle Talbot.

T130 August 9, 1954
"Gracie Buys a Toaster Wholesale"
Gracie re-invents the phrase "I can get it for you wholesale" when she goes shopping for a toaster and buys a truckload of new appliances for herself and Blanche. Featuring Ronnie Burns, Robert Foulk, Joseph Kearns, George E. Stone and James Todd.

T131 August 16, 1954
"Mortons Exchange Houses with the Gibsons from New York"
It seemed simple enough when Blanche and Harry took Gracie's suggestion to swap houses with Harry Von Zell's friends while staying in New York but a classic mix-up finds the Mortons in their own home, Von Zell and his friends in the Burnses' home and George and Gracie sleeping in their car. Featuring Mabel Albertson, Ross Elliott and Don Sheldon.

T132 August 23, 1954
"George Teaches Gracie Not To Start Rumors"
Blanche misunderstands Gracie (for a change) and starts a rumor that George won money gambling in Las Vegas. Featuring Sandra Burns, Douglass Dumbrille, Adrienne Martin and Doris Packer.

Fifth Season: 1954-1955

Co-Sponsors: The Carnation Company, B. F. Goodrich.
Products: Carnation Evaporated Milk, automobile tires and other rubber made products.
Agency: Erwin, Wasey & Co., Ltd.; BBD&O.
Network: CBS.
Broadcast Day: Monday.
Time Slot: 8:00-8:30 P.M. (Eastern Standard Time).
Producer/Director: Frederick (Fred) de Cordova.
Scriptwriters: Sid Dorfman, Harvey Helm, William Burns, Keith Fowler.

T133 October 4, 1954
"George Invites Critics to Watch First Show of Season"
It's the first show of the new season for their "other" television program and, to ensure good notices, George invites the TV editors of **Variety** and

The Hollywood Reporter over to the house to watch it, unaware that Gracie has invited every stranger she met in three stores and on the bus. Gracie takes over the "say goodnight" tag. **This episode was the only one filmed in color**. Featuring Don Curtis, King Donovan, Ross Elliott, William Forrest, Paul Guest and Irene Tedrow.

Review: "It's generally okay entertainment, although the trade paper critic theme was overdone for anywhere outside the Bel Air Circuit." (**Daily Variety**, October 6, 1954).

T134 October 11, 1954
"Gracie Goes to the Do It Yourself Show"
Gracie has her heart set on having a dresser made by George's own two hands but he's more comfortable holding a cigar than a saw and hammer. Featuring John Alvin, Robert Foulk, Frank Scannell, Clarence Straight and Dave Willock.

T135 October 18, 1954
"Gracie Gives Wedding in Payment of a Favor"
Gracie returns a favor by throwing a wedding for the woman's daughter. Ronnie Burns appears as the groom in his debut speaking part in the show and is introduced at the close of the show. He was nineteen years old. The show was filmed September 15, 1954. Featuring Gail Bonney, Eugene Borden, Tris Coffin, Emlen Davies, Mavis Davenport, Hal K. Dawson, Gloria Donovan, Estelle Etterre, Sally Frazer, Pitt Herbert, Maurice Marsac, William McLean, Howard Negley and Helen Spring. Similar to T26.

T136 October 25, 1954
"Gracie Gives a Baby Shower for Virginia Beasely"
Gracie plans to give the postman's daughter a baby shower at the Brown Derby; George hires someone to decorate their home for the shower on the same evening. Featuring Richard Deacon, Mary Lawrence, Forrest Lewis, Betty Lynn and Doris Packer.

T137 November 1, 1954
"Auto License Bureau: George Becomes an Author"
Gracie gets her driver's license renewed; George begins writing his autobiography and, although the two Harry's (Morton and Von Zell) think that he is too "low brow" to write a book, they both want to be included in it. There is an ad for "Party Sweets", recipes which are mailed if one writes to Gracie Allen. Featuring Ken Christy, John Gallaudet, Louise Larimore and Dayton Lummis. **SEE VG42.**

T138 November 8, 1954
"George Trying To Keep Doctor's Appointment"
George becomes keyed up when his attempts to drive to the doctor's office are thwarted by well-meaning friends. Featuring Fay Baker, Robert Carson, Jill Jarman, Jack Lomas, George Meader, Mary Newton, Walter Reed and Eve Whitney.

T139 November 15, 1954
"Gracie Thinks She and George Are Moving to New York"
Gracie plants the idea in George's head that he was a witness to an armed robbery, hoping the ensuing commotion will circumvent a move to New York. Featuring Paul Avery, Jay Douglas, Garry Marshall and Mike Ross. Special guest: Portland Mason, the six-year old daughter of James and Pamela Mason. No one in producer-director Garry Marshall's office is aware of him appearing as a child actor in **The George Burns and Gracie Allen Show** as *Joey Bagley* and age-wise it appears highly unlikely. Mr. Marshall was on vacation at the time of the inquiry and unavailable for comment.

T140 November 22, 1954
"Shoplifter and the Missing Ruby Clip"
Gracie thinks Lucille Vanderlip has stolen a piece of costume jewelry from a department store.

T141 November 29, 1954
"Gracie Saves Blanche's Marriage"
Gracie is convinced the Mortons' marriage is headed for the rocks when Blanche bumps into a handsome stranger in the market only moments after she receives a tantalizing prediction about her future. Featuring Margaret Brayton, William Boyett, Mimi Doyle, Adrienne Marden, Frances Mercer, John Warburton and Jean Willes.

T142 December 6, 1954
"Burnses and Mortons Going To Hear Antonelli Concert"
George hopes everyone gets so interested in trying to solve a jigsaw puzzle that they'll want to stay home instead of attending a string quartet recital. Featuring Vivi Janniss, Myra Marsh, Doris Packer, Dorothy Patrick and Helen Towne.

T143 December 13, 1954
"George Gets Call From Unknown Visitor About Him"
Has Gracie bungled a telephone message that could have had an important impact on George's career?

T144 December 20, 1954
"Harry Morton's Alumni Banquet"
Convincing George to be the MC at Harry's alumni banquet should be as simple as ABC but, when Gracie gets involved, someone needs to untangle the confusion PDQ.

T145 December 27, 1954
"Gracie Thinks Bob Cummings Is in Love with Her"
Gracie jumps to the wrong conclusion when she overhears Bob Cummings reciting lines from a play to George. Guest star: Bob Cummings.

T146 January 3, 1955
"George's Mother-in-Law Trouble"
Harry Von Zell fears Gracie will get a divorce if George doesn't let her mother come for a visit. Featuring Bill Chambers, Bill Kennedy, Mary Treen and Herb Vigran.

T147 January 10, 1955
"George and the Glendale Eagle Publicity Stunt"
Gracie helps to arrange a publicity stunt for George but for some reason he has no desire to be at the airport at six A.M. to shake hands with "The Glendale Eagle." This is one of the few episodes which films George and Gracie in their bedroom.

T148 January 17, 1955
"No Seats for Friars Club Dinner"
The Friars Club tribute for George and Gracie is a sellout, and even more so when Gracie invites the Mortons and the Bagleys, who can only get in if they pose as waiters and cigarette girls. Featuring Mimi Doyle, Doug Evans, Lester Matthews, Russell Trent and Michael Whalen.

T149 January 24, 1955
"Blanche and Clara Bagley Leave Their Husbands"
Blanche and Clara fight with each other, then with their husbands, then move in with Gracie and George, who has to put up his own fight to get them to move back home. Featuring Mabel Albertson and Michael Whalen.

T150 January 31, 1955
"Gracie Gets a Valet for George"
George has no intention of keeping the valet Gracie hired so she has to find a way to get him to quit. Featuring Michael Emmet, Olaf Hytten, Shirley Mitchell and Doris Packer as Mrs. James Randolph Pringle III.

T151 February 7, 1955
"Vanderlip Leaves His Parakeet with George"
Gracie thinks George gave her a parakeet for their anniversary and sets it free (seeing it peeking through the bars reminds her of her Uncle Harvey), then finds out George was only watching it as a favor to Mr. Vanderlip. Featuring Madge Blake, Nan Boardman, Byron Foulger, Garry Marshall and George E. Stone.

T152 February 14, 1955
"Blanche's Brother, Roger the Moocher, Visits"
Blanche Morton's charming but work-shy brother arrives from Seattle and alienates everyone except Blanche and Gracie, who finds him a job, inadvertently sending him back home to Seattle. Featuring Frank Ferguson and Jean Willes.

T153 February 21, 1955
"George and the Missing Five Dollars and Missing Baby Pictures"

George has to find baby pictures to include in his new book but, before he finds them, realizes he's also missing five dollars. While George turns everything upside down to find the pictures, Gracie, the Mortons and Harry Von Zell think he's looking for the money and try to cure him of his "money neurosis." This script was reprinted in George's book **I Love Her, That's Why!** (B34). Featuring Ross Elliott, Syd Saylor and Frank Wilcox as Dr. Bellamy.

T154 February 28, 1955
"Gracie Becomes a Portrait Artist After Museum Visit"
Gracie's visit to an art gallery inspires her to become a painter. Featuring Bill Baldwin, Ruth Brady, Lillian Bronson, Alexander Campbell, William Schallert and Dan Tobin. Similar to T2.

T155 March 7, 1955
"George and the Fourteen-Karat Gold Trombone"
An acquaintance of George's borrows fifty dollars from him, leaving an old trombone as collateral, which Gracie has Harry Von Zell give away before she hears it's solid gold and worth ten thousand dollars. Featuring Benny Fields, Douglas Fowley, John Hoyt and Fred Sherman.

T156 March 14, 1955
"The Romance of Harry Morton and Countess Braganni"
Blanche is furious, then heartbroken, when she thinks Harry has changed his image in order to impress a European countess who has bought the house next door. Featuring Pamela Duncan and Anna Lee.

T157 March 21, 1955
"The Mistaken Marriage of Emily Vanderlip and Roger"
Emily Vanderlip confides to Roger that she's getting married but Gracie only hears part of the conversation and assumes Roger is the man Emily's planning to wed. Featuring Mildred (Millie) Doff.

T158 March 28, 1955
"Gracie Adopts Great Dane Dog"
George thinks Gracie is hiding her Uncle Harvey in the guest room but begins to get suspicious when he hears barking noises coming from behind the door. Featuring Garry Marshall.

T159 April 4, 1955
"Gracie Tries to Select George's Next Wife"
Gracie intercepts a phony telegram sent to help George avoid a yachting trip and mistakenly believes she only has a short time to live. Featuring Joan Banks, Sandra Burns, Ann Doran and James Todd.

T160 April 11, 1955
"Gracie Gets a Ticket Fixed by the Judge"
Judge Russell nearly hangs up his robes when Gracie, who thinks he fixed a traffic ticket for her, tries to get one fixed for Blanche, who didn't get a ticket in the first place. Featuring Douglass Dumbrille, Jack Lomas, Mitchell Powell and Anthony Warde.

T161 April 18, 1955
"Gracie Hires a Safe Cracker for Her Wall Safe"
Gracie surprises George with a wall safe, then surprises him even more when she locks the combination inside the safe. Featuring Robert Carson, Alan Dexter, Ross Elliott and Will Wright.

T162 April 25, 1955
"Gracie Consults Dr. Kirby's Problem Clinic"
Gracie hopes her appearance on a television show, **Dr. Kirby's Problem Clinic**, will help her high school chum, who fears she may be a bigamist, but complications arise when George and Gracie's friends think *Gracie* is the bigamist. Featuring Jane Buchanan, Lucille Curtis, Frank Ferguson, William Forrest and Dan Tobin.

T163 May 2, 1955
"Gracie Wants the House Painted"
George and Gracie can't agree whether they should paint their house white or coral. The result: a two-tone house. Featuring Irving Bacon, Yvonne Lime and William Schallert.

T164 May 9, 1955

"Gracie Plays Talent Scout for Imitator"
George gets the wrong impression when a young man enlists the Burnses' help to get into show business. Featuring Louis Jean Heydt, Eddie Ryder and Barry Truex.

T165 May 16, 1955
"Gracie and George Try for a Day at the Beach"
George's plans for an important business meeting at an associate's beach house are capsized when Gracie packs a lunch and invites their friends. Featuring John Alvin, Kathryn Card, Vivi Janniss, Ronald Keith, Pierre Watkin and Jean Willes. Ending routine is Gracie talking about the Allen family at the beach.

T166 May 23, 1955
"The Uranium Caper"
Gracie and Blanche overhear George pitching a story line to one of his writers and think he's discovered a huge uranium deposit. Featuring Michael Emmet and Paul Harvey.

T167 May 30, 1955
"Blanche and Brother Roger Move in with Burnses"
It's George, for a change, who jumps to the wrong conclusion when he overhears Gracie's conversation with a divorce lawyer. Featuring Walter Woolfe King. Ending routine is about Gracie going to an auction.

T168 June 6, 1955
"Gracie Believes George Has a Criminal Record"
Gracie assumes the worst when she sees a picture of George with a former vaudeville partner when George and the man were billed as the "Jolly Jailbirds." Featuring Robert Brubaker, Kathryn Card, Frank Gerstle, Jack Lomas and Ray Teal. Ending routine is about getting a driver's license.

T169 June 13, 1955
"Gracie Gets an Extension Visa for Jeanette Duval"
Gracie proves her friendship knows no boundaries when she tries to help a young French woman stay in the United States. Ending routine is about Gracie's Uncle Harvey.

T170 June 20, 1955
"Gracie Tries to Cure Roger of Amnesia"
Harry Morton persuades a sawmill in Utah to offer Blanche's brother a job but Roger develops amnesia when a piece of George and Gracie's kitchen ceiling "accidentally" falls on his head moments before his scheduled departure. Ending routine is about Gracie's older sister Hazel's eyesight.

T171 June 27, 1955
"Lucille Vanderlip Gives a Barbecue Party"
This time it's George who's confused when he thinks Gracie is giving a barbecue against his wishes, and it turns into an expensive mistake. Ronald Burns plays a tourist who asks the bus driver questions about Gracie Allen. Featuring Tom Brown Henry, Hugh Sanders and Herb Vigran. Ending routine is about Gracie's Aunt Clara moving into a new house and the housewarming.

T172 July 4, 1955
"Burnses and Mortons Going to Hawaii"
Harry Morton insists he and Blanche can't afford a trip to Honolulu--until her brother arrives for a visit. Ending routine is about Gracie buying shoes in a shoe store.

Sixth Season: 1955-1956

Co-Sponsors: The Carnation Company, B. F. Goodrich.
Products: Carnation Evaporated Milk, automobile tires and other rubber made products.
Agency: Erwin, Wasey & Co., Ltd.; BBD&O.
Network: CBS.
Broadcast Day: Monday.
Time Slot: 8:00-8:30 P.M. (Eastern Standard Time).
Producer/Director: Frederick (Fred) de Cordova.

Scriptwriters: Harvey Helm, William Burns, Keith Fowler, Norman Paul. *Production Notes:* This year the series switches locales. The Burnses' new address is Apartment 2215 of the St. Moritz Hotel in New York City.

T173 October 3, 1955
"Burnses Going to New York"
George and Gracie are on their way by train to New York City to do some television shows, and George agrees with Harry Von Zell that it would be a great publicity gimmick if Gracie were to have her picture taken with a famous scientist traveling incognito on the same train. George and Von Zell don't realize, however, that the man they think is the scientist is actually a salesman. The passenger Gracie has struck up an acquaintance with (whom George thinks is a cardsharp) is the real scientist. Blanche laughs at Harry's idea that frozen yogurt will ever catch on. Featuring John Alvin, Robert S. Carson, Damian O'Flynn, Roy Glenn, Paul Harvey, and Jim Hayward. Ending routine is the one about the bus that Burns and Allen performed at vaudeville's Palace Theatre.

Review: "On last night's seasonal launching B & A entrained for NY...The takeoff had all the speed and motion of the Super Chief rolling across the Great Plains...And it was George, normally the straightman, who boffed 'em with his gags." (**Daily Variety**, October 4, 1955).

T174 October 10, 1955
"Ronnie Arrives"
The show, which has undergone a change in locale, undergoes an even bigger transformation when we meet George and Gracie's son in "real" life and in "reel" life--Ronnie, an aspiring dramatic actor. Ronnie performs a scene from **Picnic** in tonight's episode, a recreation of his actual onstage performance at California's Pasadena Playhouse. Featuring Paula Hill. Ending routine is about hunting.

Review: "Burns & Allen can always retire and let son Ronny (sic) bring in the bread & butter, though at the rate they're going...their rocking chair has not yet been built." (**Variety**, October 12, 1955).

T175 October 17, 1955
"Ronnie Meets Sabrina"
Ronnie decides to date an older woman to prepare for a role in a play and later sets his sights on an older woman. Featuring Judi Boutin as Velma and Paula Hill. Ending routine is about Gracie's explorer uncle, Otis.

T176 October 24, 1955
"Changing Names"
Ronnie fears that he'll never be considered a serious actor with the last name of "Burns" and changes his name to Cobb Cochran. George is working on his book with a female editor and Ronnie thinks his father is interested in her. Ending routine is about Gracie's cousin's wedding.

T177 October 31, 1955
"Harry Morton's Cocktail Party"
George's book **I Love Her, That's Why!** (B34), has gone on sale; Blanche is mortified to discover that a man from the book store she wrongly accused of being a masher is not only coming to dinner but is an important client of her husband's. Featuring Kathleen Freeman, Russell Hicks and Barbara Knudsen. Ending routine is about Gracie's Uncle Harvey trying to get employment.

T178 November 7, 1955
"The Musical Version"
The success of George's book prompts the possibility of a Broadway musical until the investors learn that George wants to play himself or, at the very least, provide the singing voice; Ronnie is rehearsing a play. George and Gracie perform a song and dance routine to the title song, written by Al Hoffman and Dick Manning. George also sings "In the Heart of a Cherry." Featuring Judi Boutin as Velma, Charles Bagby, Robert S. Carson, Charles Evans and Lewis Martin. Special guests: Loomis & Palmer, songwriter Mack Gordon. Ending routine is about Gracie's father and a photographer. **SEE B34, D258.**

Review: "...All in all, an innocuous show, but revealing the technique of how to make a plug palatable--on a show that's always in there with the high audiences, because everyone loves 'em, that's why." (**Variety**, November 9, 1955).

T179 November 14, 1955
"Ronnie Moves to Village"
Ronnie makes the move that many young actors feel compelled to make, the one to Greenwich Village. Gracie feels that Ronnie is suffering so she goes dressed as a beatnik to check up on where he is living. She poses as the art model, Mona Lisa. Featuring Frank Wilcox and Bud Wolf. Ending routine is about Gracie's Aunt Clara and her multiple husbands.

T180 November 21, 1955
"Gracie Helps Lola"
Never one to merely wait around when someone needs her, Gracie tries to tip the scales in favor of young love. Featuring Barbara Knudsen. Ending routine is about Aunt Clara.

T181 November 28, 1955
"Anniversary Party"
It's George and Gracie's twenty-sixth anniversary but the party is nearly ruined when Gracie attempts to help the Boardmans, a couple whose marriage is threatened by jealousy. Gracie then discovers that George isn't jealous of *her*, which upsets her. American Flyer train display by A. C. Gilbert. Featuring Fay Baker and Gail Bonney. Ending routine is about Gracie shopping.

T182 December 5, 1955
"George Becomes a Dictator"
George tries to do all the right things to give Ronnie's career a boost but, as far as Ronnie is concerned, he's doing all the wrong things. Featuring Judi Boutin as the actress. Ending routine is about sightseeing.

T183 December 12, 1955
"Ronnie's Elopement"
Gracie thinks Ronnie is planning to elope with the hotel's cigarette girl. Featuring Isabel Withers and James Flavin. Ending routine is about interesting people at the doctor's office.

T184 December 19, 1955
"Company For Christmas"
It's going to be a black Christmas at the Mortons'. Blanche has invited the one person Harry detests to spend the holidays with them and then discovers that Harry has also invited someone--the one person *she* detests. Instead of saying her usual "good night" Gracie wishes everyone a "Merry Christmas." Featuring Douglass Dumbrille and Michael Emmet. Ending routine is about the Allen family's Christmas.

T185 December 26, 1955
"Gracie Pawns Her Ring"
A friend of Ronnie's hopes to get his play produced and Gracie steps in with the financing when George turns him down. Ending routine is about an insurance company.

T186 January 2, 1956
"Appearances Are Deceiving"
Blanche and Gracie try to convince the father of an aspiring actress that things are not what they seem when he misinterprets his daughter's actions with Ronnie. Featuring Lisa Gaye and John Hoyt. Ending routine is about Gracie mailing a birthday cake to her sister Hazel.

T187 January 9, 1956
"Let's Dance"
Gracie wouldn't be having so much difficulty living up to her promises when she sold tickets to Ronnie's school dance if she hadn't kept making the same promise to everyone--a date with the hotel's cigarette-counter girl. The timbre of Gracie's voice takes on a noticeable change in this episode. Featuring William Better and Tom Brown Henry. Ending routine is about Gracie's uncle Otis' farm.

T188 January 16, 1956
"George Goes Skiing"

George tries to become more of a buddy to Ronnie but it's all downhill once they hit the ski slopes. George is gone two days from home and Gracie doesn't know that he has gone to learn how to ski (George left her a note but she doesn't find it until after he gets back). Ending routine is about the drugstore.

T189 January 23, 1956
"Ronnie Gets An Agent"
Ronnie discovers there really is no business like show business when he receives a visit from a prospective agent the same night of an important dinner party. Featuring Lois Collier, Richard Danworth, Jack Devlin, Nancy Hadley, Pat Moran, Ray Saunders and Lyle Talbot. Special guest: Jack Benny as part of an acrobatic team. Ending routine is about fishing.

T190 January 30, 1956
"Politeness Never Pays"
Ronnie and his date go skating and talk about how discourteous George is; Gracie takes drastic measures in order to get George to pay more attention to her. Featuring Russell Hicks and Maurice Marsac. Ending routine is about the musical Allen family.

T191 February 6, 1956
"Alice Gets Married"
Harry Von Zell fears an old flame's impending visit means his days as a bachelor are about to go up in smoke. Ending routine is about a pet shop.

T192 February 13, 1956
"George Needs Glasses"
Convinced that George needs glasses when he pretends not to see the results of her latest shopping expedition, Gracie persuades all their friends to wear glasses so George won't feel self-conscious about wearing them. Featuring Raymond Bailey. Ending routine is about the athletic Allen family.

T193 February 20, 1956
"The Indian Potentate"
Gracie's curiosity is piqued by a reclusive hotel guest. Featuring Donald Randolph. Ending routine is once again about Aunt Clara's husbands.

T194 February 27, 1956
"The Ladies Club"
Harry Morton has ulterior motives for not wanting Gracie to be accepted for membership in an exclusive club. Ending routine is about studying nature.

T195 March 5, 1956
"Cyrano de Bergerac"
Ronnie turns to a famous actor's recording of **Cyrano** to provide inspiration for his own interpretation of the role. Guest voice: Jose Ferrer. Ending routine is about a fortune teller.

T196 March 12, 1956
"The Stolen Plants"
Gracie innocently takes two jonquil bulbs from Central Park, then turns herself in to the police when Harry Morton says she's actually guilty of stealing. Featuring Dabbs Greer, John Gallaudet, Howard McNear and Billy Wayne. Ending routine is about New York City's Grand Central Station.

T197 March 19, 1956
"The English Playwright"
Gracie resorts to a trick any red-blooded American stage mother would be proud of--pretending to be a widow in order to persuade a writer to cast Ronnie in his play. Featuring Paul Cavanaugh. Ending routine is about Gracie's mother.

T198 March 26, 1956
"A Week-End on Long Island"
The Mortons have been invited to Oyster Bay for the weekend; Gracie thinks she is also invited and arranges a surprise party for one of Ronnie's drama teachers. Ending routine is about the zoo.

T199 April 2, 1956
"The Newlyweds"

Emily Vanderlip tries to hide her newly-changed marital status (she secretly married) from Gracie and George helps her. Featuring Morris Ankrum, Robert Carson, Elinor Donahue and Bobby Ellis as Frank Foster. Ending routine is about the Easter parade.

T200 April 9, 1956
"Night of Vaudeville"
George and Gracie bring back the memories of vaudeville when he directs and she emcees a variety show starring the students in Ronnie's acting school. Featuring Tom Brown Henry, Judy Clark as "Sophie Tucker," Jay Wheeler as "Eddie Cantor," Don Zeena and Bill Lloyd as "Doyle and Dixon" and Ronnie Burns and Diane Jurgens as "Burns and Allen."

T201 April 16, 1956
"Burlesk"
George and Gracie are disturbed when they discover that Ronnie has found a job in a burlesque theater. Featuring Jack Albertson and Sylvia Lewis. Ending routine is about travel.

T202 April 23, 1956
"The Right People"
Gracie is delighted when she believes Ronnie is getting married but the girl's mother is worried that her family's blue blood will be diluted by "those vaudevillians." Featuring Carolyn Craig and Hayden Rorke. Ending routine is about the library.

T203 April 30, 1956
"The Magic Act"
Mistakenly believing George has turned down a solo movie role because he doesn't want to break up the act, Gracie finds a new partner. Featuring Donald Kerr, Damian O'Flynn and Harry Mendoza. Ending routine is about Gracie's artist aunt, Bridget.

T204 May 7, 1956
"The Paris Creation"
George insists that Gracie not make any changes to her new evening gown but to let the dressmaker do it and Gracie happily agrees--the man lives in Paris! Featuring Adele August, Jacqueline Beer, Marla English, Steven Garrett, Donald Lawton and Benny Rubin. Ending routine is about an auto show. Jacqueline Beer is a former Miss France.

T205 May 14, 1956
"Back from Paris"
Gracie plans to open a dress shop with merchandise she brought home from Paris. Ending routine is about Gracie's participation in a backyard circus, which she did when she was a child in San Francisco.

T206 May 21, 1956
"The 24 Dresses"
Gracie has twenty-five Paris creations (twenty-four dresses and one French model) but George refuses to give her the one thousand American-made dollars she needs to go into the dress shop business. Ending routine is about flowers.

T207 May 28, 1956
"Ronnie Is Lovesick"
Ronnie is actually only preparing for a screen test but Gracie thinks that he has decided to join the Foreign Legion in order to be closer to his girlfriend, who has returned to France. Featuring Kathleen Case and Walter Woolfe King. Ending routine is about a beauty show.

T208 June 4, 1956
"The Night Out"
For once Gracie comes to a logical conclusion when George doesn't come home one night and his topcoat arrives the next morning via a nightclub hatcheck girl but, as usual, she's wrong. Ending routine is about the Allen family graduation.

T209 June 11, 1956
"The Triple Surprise Party"
It's no surprise when confusion reigns at a Burns/Morton party: is it for Harry Morton's birthday, for Ronnie or for Harry Von Zell? Ending routine is about Gracie's Uncle Harvey.

T210 September 10, 1956
"Questions & Answers"
Harry Morton fears Blanche will resign from a literary club, causing him to lose valuable business contacts, if Gracie doesn't pass the test necessary for membership. Featuring Helen Spring and Katharine Warren. Ending routine is about the beach.

T211 September 17, 1956
"Mrs. Sohmers Needs a Psychologist"
The strain of trying to understand Gracie's non sequiturs drives Mrs. Sohmers to visit a psychologist twenty-one times in three weeks. Featuring Dabbs Greer. Ending routine is about rodeo cowboys.

T212 September 24, 1956
"Switchboard Operators"
Blanche and Gracie foil Harry Morton's attempts to use the telephone by taking over the hotel switchboard and it's quickly apparent that neither one missed her calling by not becoming a telephone operator. Ending routine is about astrology and superstition.

Seventh Season: 1956-1957

Co-Sponsors: The Carnation Company, B. F. Goodrich.
Products: Carnation Evaporated Milk, automobile tires and other rubber made products.
Agency: Erwin, Wasey & Co., Ltd.; BBD&O.
Network: CBS.
Broadcast Day: Monday.
Time Slot: 8:00-8:30 P.M. (Eastern Standard Time).
Producer/Director: Rod Amateau.
Scriptwriters: Harvey Helm, William Burns, Keith Fowler, Norman Paul.

T213 October 1, 1956
"Return To California"
The Burnses, Mortons, and Von Zell return home unexpectedly from New York and find that Ronnie has turned their homes into college dormitories for his friends from USC. The show contains advertisements for the **Cook Book for Kids**. Ending routine is about Gracie's relative, Pioneer Allen.

Review: "If there was any noticeable change, it was in the scarcity of Gracie's participation, and that's not good." (**Daily Variety**, October 3, 1956).

T214 October 8, 1956
"The Shakespearean Paper"
Gracie re-writes a paper Ronnie has prepared for class in an attempt to influence his professor into giving him a better grade. Special guest: historian Dr. Frank C. Baxter of the University of Southern California. Ending routine is about Gracie's relatives involvement in politics.

T215 October 15, 1956
"The Woman In The Car"
Gracie inadvertently causes marital problems for Harry Morton when she borrows his and Blanche's car. Ending routine is about home remedies.

T216 October 22, 1956
"The Interview"
A reporter from **TV Guide** has his journalistic skills tested when he's assigned to do a piece on George and Gracie at home. Featuring John Hoyt. Guest star: Francis X. Bushman. Ending routine is about Halloween.

T217 October 29, 1956
"The Initiation"
Ronnie undergoes a fraternity initiation; Gracie thinks Blanche is moving to Pasadena. Featuring Alan Reed, Jr. and Herbert Rudley. Ending routine is about Gracie's trip to Western Union where she goes to send her mother a wire.

T218 November 5, 1956
"Ronnie's Bashful"
Gracie misunderstands Ronnie's reluctance to attend a college dance (his girlfriend can't go) and asks his friends to find him a date. Featuring

Connie Dugovic, Lisa Gaye and Mary Lawrence. Ending routine is about Gracie's Uncle Ben and a country fair.

T219 November 12, 1956
"The Big Stamp Robbery"
Harry Morton is ready to cancel someone's life when he discovers a valuable stamp missing from his collection. Ending routine is about Gracie's uncle Fred and his winter resort.

T220 November 19, 1956
"George's Gray Suit"
Gracie has to pretend George's favorite gray suit was stolen after she mails it to Blanche's brother without George's permission. Ending routine is about Gracie's relative, "Scoop Allen," a newspaperman.

T221 November 26, 1956
"Von Zell's Raises"
George turns down Harry Von Zell's request for a raise until Gracie tells him that Harry needs the money so he can get married, something not on the confirmed bachelor's agenda. Featuring Connie Dugovic, Mary Lawrence and Claude Stroud. Ending routine is about Gracie's relative, Daniel Allen, frontier trailblazer and pathfinder.

T222 December 3, 1956
"The Refrigerator Salesman"
Ronnie, working in a department store to earn extra money for Christmas, has been transferred from electric shavers to refrigerators but George doesn't know that when he places an order for several of them as gifts. Featuring Donald Lawton. Ending routine is about Gracie's Uncle Waldo and the French Foreign Legion.

T223 December 10, 1956
"The Girl Behind The Perfume Counter"
Ronnie's in love--again--but Gracie thinks he's fallen for an older woman and schemes with Harry Von Zell to break them up. Featuring Eleanor Audley, John Eldridge, Adele Jergens and Susan Luckey. Ending routine is about a volunteer fire brigade.

T224 December 17, 1956
"Ronnie Quits College Because His Father Is Broke"
Gracie fibs to Ronnie in an attempt to persuade him to finish college but her well-meaning plan backfires. Featuring John Eldridge, Susan Luckey, and Frank Wilcox as Professor Clinton. Ending routine is about a ferryboat pilot.

T225 December 24, 1956
"Christmas In Jail"
In jail at Christmas, George recounts the circumstances leading up to his predicament which began when he bought Gracie a Christmas present. Featuring Ray Bennett, Paul Birch, Frank Mills, John Stephenson and George E. Stone. Ending routine is about the Allens and Christmas Eve. **SEE VG29.**

T226 December 31, 1956
"The Costume Party"
George, Harry Morton and Harry Von Zell toss a party for Mr. Vanderlip to encourage him to invest in a real estate deal but throw him out when he comes dressed in a costume they think is being worn by Blanche's brother, Roger. Featuring Gloria Marshall and Jean Willes. Ending routine is about Gracie's relative who drives a cab.

T227 January 7, 1957
"Gracie and the Bullfighter"
Gracie learns the fickle nature of youth when she tells George they should get more involved in Ronnie's hobbies. Featuring Peggy Gordon and Paula Victor. Ending routine is about Gracie's cousin, Nelson, a Canadian Northwest Mountie.

T228 January 14, 1957
"The Ugly Duckling"
Gracie, Blanche, and George play fairy godmother to one of Ronnie's classmates so she can go to the prom. Featuring Cynthia Baxter and Lyle Fox. Ending routine is about Gracie's family.

T229 January 21, 1957
"The Aptitude Test"
Ronnie explains to Gracie that a man who acts miserable and grouchy may actually need a career change so Gracie decides George should take an aptitude test. Featuring Hayden Rorke. Ending routine is about Gracie's relative Casey Allen, who was a railroad engineer.

T230 January 28, 1957
"Going To Palm Springs"
Gracie tries to persuade George to accompany Ronnie when he decides to go to Palm Springs for a few days. Featuring Cynthia Baxter, Sandra Burns and Harry Cheshire. Ending routine is about Gracie's cousin Philo, a private detective.

T231 February 4, 1957
"The Matrimonial Bureau"
Gracie visits a matrimonial bureau to find a wife for Ronnie but comes away instead with a new wife for George--and a new husband for herself! Featuring Harry Antrim, Eleanor Audley, Nesdon Booth, Carolyn Kearney and Roy Roberts. Ending routine is about Gracie's relative Wyatt Allen, a town marshal.

T232 February 11, 1957
"The Fortune Teller"
Gracie goes on a spending spree when a gypsy predicts that a fortune is in George's future. Featuring Kay Stewart and Jean Willes. Ending routine is about a veterinarian.

T233 February 18, 1957
"Fighting For Happiness"
Deciding that marriages must be strengthened by fighting, Gracie attempts to start one with George; Harry Von Zell is trying to get a part in a film. Featuring Robert S. Carson, Marian Collier and Jody McCrea. Ending routine is about Gracie's relative Doc Allen, a medicine man.

T234 February 25, 1957
"The Termites"
Gracie tries to convince George they have termites so she can get him out of the house long enough to have their bedroom redecorated. Featuring Frank Wilcox as Michael Rockford. Ending routine is about Burglar Robin Allen.

T235 March 4, 1957
"The $15,000 Error"
Gracie thinks the bill for redecorating their bedroom came to fifteen thousand dollars and begins proceedings to mortgage the house in order to pay it. Featuring Sidney Smith, the voice of Sandra Burns and Frank Wilcox as Michael Rockford. Ending routine is about movie director Cecil B. Allen.

T236 March 11, 1957
"The Ring"
Gracie gives Ronnie her engagement ring to give to his girlfriend then asks Blanche to come up with a plausible excuse to give to George for its disappearance. Ending routine is about a cruise hostess.

T237 March 18, 1957
"The Plumber's Helper"
Ronnie's problems with his fiancee are quadrupled when Gracie agrees to "babysit" the plumber's four beautiful daughters. Featuring Sandra Burns. Guest star: Mary Livingstone. Ending routine is about Gracie's relative Edward R. Allen, a news analyst.

T238 March 25, 1957
"Going To Houston"
The Burnses and Blanche trek to Texas, hoping to persuade Brian McAfee's father to let him finish college. Judi Boutin makes her first appearance as Bonnie Sue. Ending routine is about poet Henry Wadsworth Allen.

T239 April 1, 1957
"The Stray Dog"
The hotel Gracie checks into in Houston has a strict "no pets" policy but she still manages to get involved with a French poodle. Featuring S. John

Launer, Lewis Martin and Donald Power. Ending routine is about Gracie's relative, inventor Thomas A. Allen.

T240 April 8, 1957
"Ronnie Gets A Movie Role"
Gracie tries to keep George from discovering that Ronnie has been cast in a film because the role interferes with his school work. Ending routine is about bowling.

T241 April 15, 1957
"The Plumber's Union"
Gracie attempts to find Mr. Jantzen a wife by advertising in the personal ad section of the newspaper. Featuring Lois Collier. Ending routine is about Gracie's barnstorming relative, Wilbur Orville Allen.

T242 April 22, 1957
"Harry's Homecoming"
Tired of hearing Blanche and Gracie complain about their unromantic husbands, George tries to teach them a lesson by persuading Harry Morton to disguise himself as a Frenchman well-schooled in the art of romance. Featuring Sandy Harrison and Steve Reeves. Ending routine is about Gracie's deep-sea diving relative Doodle Allen.

T243 April 29, 1957
"The Publicity Romance"
It's only a publicity stunt but Ronnie has a hard time making his girlfriend believe that when she hears about a romance he's having with a movie starlet. Featuring Francis DeSales, Lita Milan and John Sorrentino. Ending routine is about strong man Atlas Allen.

T244 May 6, 1957
"The Texan Lady Macbeth"
Brian McAfee asks Gracie to talk his sister out of going into show business. Featuring Sandy Burns. Ending routine is about animal tamer Clyde Allen.

T245 May 13, 1957
"Ronnie's Boat"
George questions the wisdom in Ronnie's purchase of a cabin cruiser. Featuring Forrest Lewis and Hugh Sanders. Ending routine is about construction engineer Boulder Allen.

T246 May 20, 1957
"A Trip To Tahiti"
Ronnie and Ralph hope to recreate the Kon-Tiki's voyage to Tahiti in their twenty-four foot cabin cruiser but change their minds when they realize the fun they'll be leaving behind--the Jantzen girls. Featuring John Gallaudet. Ending routine is about a process server.

T247 May 27, 1957
"The Home Graduation"
Thinking that Brian McAfee is still not going to graduate from college, even though he's been in school for nine years, Gracie concocts a plan to make his father think he has. Featuring Ralph Dumke and Frank Wilcox as Professor Clinton. Ending routine is about a lifeguard.

T248 June 3, 1957
"Blanche's Mother Arrives"
Gracie offers refuge to Blanche's mother when her scheduled arrival unhappily coincides with the cancellation of Harry Morton's out-of-town trip. Bea Benaderet plays both Blanche and Blanche's mother in this episode. Ending routine is about a camp counselor.

T249 June 10, 1957
"A Marital Mix-Up"
The Cupid's arrow meant for Mr. Jantzen takes a detour around Harry Von Zell. Featuring Jean Willes. Guest star: Bob Cummings. Ending routine is about Gracie's Uncle Ole, mountain climber.

T250 June 17, 1957
"The Wading Pool At Acapulco"

George and Harry Von Zell take Ronnie and Ralph's place at lifeguard tryouts for a Mexican hotel. Featuring Fran Bennett and Barbara Darrow. Ending routine is about C.F. Allen, postmaster.

T251 June 24, 1957
"A Pain In The Back"
Blanche and Gracie try to talk Harry and George into spending more time together and George has to come up with a plausible reason why they can't. Featuring Bob Hall. Ending routine is about the Allen family's annual picnic.

T252 July 1, 1957
"Ronnie's Twenty-One"
Ronnie confronts the first dilemma of his now-officially adult life: turning down a beautiful young French girl's marriage proposal. Ending routine is about a butler.

Eighth Season: 1957-1958

Co-Sponsors: The Carnation Company, General Mills.
Products: Carnation Evaporated Milk, cereal products.
Agency: Erwin, Wasey & Co., Ltd., Dancer, Fitzgerald, Sample.
Network: CBS.
Broadcast Day: Monday.
Time Slot: 8:00-8:30 P.M. (Eastern Standard Time).
Producer/Director: Rod Amateau.
Scriptwriters: Harvey Helm, William Burns, Keith Fowler, Norman Paul.

T253 September 30, 1957
"The General"
The course of true love takes a sharp turn to the left when Gracie tries to help one of Ronnie's friends, a newlywed who has to find the courage to tell his father he's now ineligible for West Point; George pokes fun at the glut of TV westerns. Featuring William Bakewell, Mason Alan Dinehart, Douglass Dumbrille, and Gail Land. Ending routine is about Gracie's great grand-uncle, Hickok Allen, Pony Express rider. Gracie is dressed in western clothes for this routine.

Review: "Burns & Allen found their formula a long time ago and they've maintained a high comedic level intertwined with slick production values." (**Variety**, October 2, 1957).

T254 October 7, 1957
"Too Much Pot Roast"
Gracie hopes that Ronnie will become bored with girls and turn his attentions to his studies if she introduces even more beautiful women into his life. Featuring four real-life beauty pageant contestants: Joan Adams (Miss Nevada); Marianne Gabe (Miss Illinois); Inger Jonsson (Miss Sweden); and Lisa Simone (Miss France). Ending routine is about novelist Balzac Allen.

T255 October 14, 1957
"The Texan Italian"
Italian actresses are the new Hollywood rage and Ronnie's girlfriend, Bonnie Sue McAfee, is upset to realize that, as an actress from Texas, she is only being cast in bit parts, so Gracie turns her into "Tina Cacciatore." Actress Judi Boutin, who plays Bonnie Sue, is now known as Judi Meredith. Featuring Booth Colman. Ending routine is about Rush Allen, the bus driver.

T256 October 21, 1957
"An English Tea"
Gracie succeeds in making a good impression on a cultured guest. Featuring Isobel Elsom, Joe Flynn, Pamela Light and Carl Sax. Ending routine is about Gracie's Cousin Noah, zookeeper.

T257 October 28, 1957
"September and May"
Gracie comes to the rescue when one of Mr. Jantzen's daughters fears he's becoming romantically involved with a woman considerably younger than he. Featuring Rosemary Ace and Paula Winslowe. Ending routine is about Gracie's Southern uncle Beauregard.

T258 November 4, 1957
"The Star Maker"
Brian McAfee is back for his tenth year of school and worried that he's not going to pass an important exam so Gracie asks the class egghead to help out. Featuring Hooper Dunbar. Ending routine is about a press agent.

T259 November 11, 1957
"The African Hunter"
Gracie invites a big-game hunter to dinner on the same night Ronnie overcomes his hesitancy to ask a new girlfriend over. Featuring Phil Arnold, Edward Ashley, Eileen Janssen and Carl Sax. Ending routine is about Uncle Freud Allen, psychiatrist.

T260 November 18, 1957
"One Little Fight"
Blanche and Gracie try to convince Ronnie and Ralph that best friends shouldn't fight by staging one of their own. Ending routine is about Uncle Death Valley Allen.

T261 November 25, 1957
"With or Without Glasses"
How will Gracie convince one of Ronnie's classmates to wear his glasses again after she told him he was movie-star handsome without them? Featuring Hooper Dunbar, Sue George, Lewis Martin and Howard Wendell. Ending routine is about Mozart Allen, famous composer and conductor.

T262 December 2, 1957
"A Box of Cigars"
Gracie tries to help Ronnie and Ralph influence voters in a homecoming queen election. Featuring Valerie Allen and Irving Bacon. Ending routine continues from previous show about Mozart Allen.

T263 December 9, 1957
"Misery Loves Company"
Ralph has girl trouble and Gracie decides she has the perfect solution to his problem. Featuring Valerie Allen, Jolene Brand, Barbara Darrow and Michael Mason. Ending routine is about Uncle Quentin Allen, prison warden.

T264 December 16, 1957
"A Hole In The Carpet"
Gracie thinks she has to pay a department store for damages when she falls down after tripping on a hole in the carpet but the store personnel are convinced she's suffered a head injury and fear she'll sue them. Featuring Harry Cheshire, Addison Richards and Hugh Sanders. Ending routine is about Nurse Florence Allen. Similar to T92.

T265 December 23, 1957
"How To Wrap A Mink"
Blanche and Gracie have visions of "furry little things" dancing in their heads as they anticipate what gifts their husbands might be planning to give them for Christmas. Featuring John Stephenson. Ending routine is about a bird lover.

T266 December 30, 1957
"Invitation To The Party"
The Mortons receive an invitation meant for George and Gracie. Featuring Eleanor Audley and Gilbert (Gil) Frye. Ending routine is about another Allen relative, a sculptor.

T267 January 6, 1958
"The Stolen Car"
Hoping to ensure Ronnie a job on the school's newspaper as an ace reporter, Gracie tries to arrange for him to find her "stolen" car so that he'll have an exclusive story. Featuring Barbara Darrow and Arlene Field. Ending routine is about one of Gracie's amorous relatives.

T268 January 13, 1958
"Ronnie Finds A Friend An Apartment"
Gracie misinterprets the remarks made by the neighbor of one of Ronnie's friends. Ending routine is about a soldier.

T269 January 20, 1958
"McAfee and the Manicurist"
Bonnie Sue tries to convince her father that the young woman he's interested in isn't his type. Featuring Jeanne Taslof and Trudi Zizkind. Ending routine is about a plantation owner.

T270 January 27, 1958
"Too Many Fathers"
Gracie pretends to be the mother of one of Ronnie's friends in an attempt to impress his new girlfriend's wealthy parents. Featuring Sheila Bromley, Steve Terrell, Ned Weaver and Susan Whitney. Ending routine is about a taxi dancer. Similar to T78.

T271 February 3, 1958
Pre-empted for the "Lucy Wins a Race Horse" episode of **The Lucy-Desi Comedy Hour.**

T272 February 10, 1958
"The Accident"
Gracie has a difficult time deciding whose side she is on when she and Harry Morton are involved in a traffic accident with a young woman who catches Ronnie's eye. Featuring Willis Bouchey and Maye Loizeau. Ending routine is about a poll taker.

T273 February 17, 1958
"The Japanese Texan"
Bonnie Sue wants George to arrange an audition for her for a role in a Japanese film. Featuring Charles Meredith and Chiya Tota. Ending routine is about Gracie's uncle, Judge Roy Allen.

T274 February 24, 1958
"Hypnotizing Gracie"
A hypnotist delivers on his promise to make Gracie a new woman. The episode concludes next week. Featuring Lee Belser, Jack Raine and Hal Sherman. Ending routine is about Gracie not doing jokes. **SEE B471.**

T275 March 3, 1958
"Gracie Is Brilliant"
In a continuation of last week's show George, preferring the "old" Gracie, knows he must find the hypnotist and ask him to change Gracie back into a lovably loony lady before their career in show business is destroyed. Featuring Stephen Ferry, Jack Raine, John Stephenson and Jeanne Taslof. Ending routine is about Uncle Barnum Allen. **SEE B471.**

T276 March 10, 1958
"Ronnie's Fan Club"
Ronnie accidentally makes a date over the telephone with a young fan who wants to be the president of his fan club, thinking he's reached her older sister instead. Featuring Myrna Fahey, Steven (Stevie) Firstman and Anna Maria Nanasi. Ending routine is about a diplomat.

T277 March 17, 1958
"Frozen Passion"
Ronnie asks Gracie to help Bonnie Sue's acting career. Featuring Raymond Bailey and Herbert Heyes. Ending routine is about a horticulturist.

T278 March 24, 1958
Pre-empted for "The Australian Outback" episode of **High Adventure with Lowell Thomas**.

T279 March 31, 1958
"High Blood Pressure"
George gets teed off when his plans to play golf are shafted by a series of interruptions from family, friends and an insurance company doctor who is trying to give Mr. Jantzen a physical and thinks George is Mr. Jantzen. Featuring Valerie Allen, Don Dillaway and Peg Hillias. Ending routine is about Gracie's fortune hunting relative, Rhinestone Lil.

T280 April 7, 1958
"Softening The Professor"
Gracie comes to Ronnie and Ralph's rescue when she fears there will be serious repercussions from their cutting class. Featuring Irene Hervey

(as the professor's wife) and Lewis Morton. Ending routine is about sharpshooter Annie Allen.

T281 April 14, 1958
"The Publicity Marriage"
Gracie tries to discourage Ronnie's fourteen-year-old fan club president from her continued infatuation with him. Featuring Myrna Fahey, Steven (Stevie) Firstman and Anna Maria Nanasi. Ending routine is about a motorcycle cop.

T282 April 21, 1958
"Blanche Gets A Jury Notice"
Harry Morton's enthusiasm over the prospect of Blanche serving a lengthy jury duty arouses the judge's suspicions, so he turns Blanche down in favor of the next name on the list--Gracie Allen. Featuring Valerie Allen, Harry Cheshire and Douglass Dumbrille. Ending routine is about an Allen relative who is a lecturer and traveler.

T283 April 28, 1958
"Gracie And The Jury"
Gracie serves on the jury in a counterfeiting trial and accidentally gives the evidence to Blanche and asks her to buy a hat with it but Harry Von Zell runs the errand instead and is promptly arrested. Featuring Ralph Clanton, Douglass Dumbrille, John Harmon, John Stephenson and Phil Tead. Ending routine is about a forest ranger.

T284 May 5, 1958
"Ronnie Makes A Record"
The son of "Old Sugar Throat" Burns lands a recording contract. This is another "imitation of real life" episode. The recording of "She's Kind of Cute" is heard. Featuring David Lewis and Lyle Talbot. Ending routine is about Uncle Ben Allen, the farmer.

T285 May 12, 1958
"Ronnie's Royalty Check"
Gracie fears that Ronnie will spend his first royalty check on a girl who Gracie thinks is interested only in Ronnie's money. Featuring Lisa Davis. Ending routine is about a lifeguard.

T286 May 19, 1958
"A Visit From Charles Vidor"
Gracie tries to influence a famous director into casting Bonnie Sue in his new film; George is more interested in getting himself cast as the master of ceremonies at an industry dinner the director is helping to organize. Special guest: Charles Vidor. Ending routine is about a jewel thief.

T287 May 26, 1958
"Ronnie Goes Into The Army"
Gracie tries to prepare Ronnie and herself for the rigors of military life in the event he's drafted. Featuring Steve Mitchell, William Schallert and Ned Weaver. Ending routine is about a woman.

T288 June 2, 1958
"Locked Out"
George is afraid he has missed an important call from a British broadcasting executive and returns home to await another call from the gentleman, only to discover that he and Gracie are locked out of the house. Featuring Rex Evans, Jackie Loughery as Vicki Donovan, Lomax Study and Jack Weston. Ending routine is about moving. Similar to T91.

T289 June 9, 1958
"A Week In New York"
Ronnie plans a party for Bonnie Sue when he hears Gracie is planning a trip to New York. Featuring Barbara Stuart. Ending routine is about Cousin Hilton Allen, resort owner.

T290 June 16, 1958
"The June Wedding"
George and Gracie offer to let newlywed friends of Ronnie's spend part of their honeymoon in their home when the young couple's hotel reservations get mixed up. Featuring Angela Austin, Mike Mason and Barbara Stuart. Ending routine is about the manager of an amusement park.

T291 June 23, 1958
"The Summer School"
Ronnie's plans for the summer are thwarted by George, who feels Ronnie's grades warrant attending summer school instead. Featuring Jackie Loughery as Vicki Donovan and Howard Wendell. Ending routine is about Aunt Clara, baseball team manager.

T292 September 8, 1958
"The Grammar School Dance"
Ronnie has to escort his fan club president to her prom, which causes problems between him and his girlfriend. Featuring Norm Alden, Yvonne Lime as Patricia and Anna Maria Nanasi. Ending routine is about a sailor.

T293 September 15, 1958
"The Exchange Student"
Ronnie is afraid that Bonnie Sue will exchange him for the young French student who is visiting the Burnses' home. Featuring Daniele Aubry. Ending routine is about Uncle Robinson Allen on a desert island. **This is the last first-run episode of the series. SEE B210.**

T294 September 22, 1958
Re-run of T283 ("Gracie and the Jury") and the last show of the series before it goes into syndication. It is being replaced the following week by a new western, **The Texan**, starring Rory Calhoun.

George Burns

2. The George Burns Show. 1958-1959. NBC. 30 min. b/w.

Series Notes: George's first television series after Gracie's retirement was another half hour situation comedy, sponsored by the Colgate-Palmolive Company (McCann-Erickson). But it was NBC, not CBS, who carried the twenty-five black and white episodes (seven were live, the rest were filmed) of this one-season series between October 21, 1958, and April 14, 1959, airing it on Tuesdays at 9:00 P.M. The series was produced in Hollywood by Banda Productions.

Cast: George Burns (*George Burns*); Bea Benaderet (*Blanche Morton - George's secretary*); Ronnie Burns (*Ronnie Burns - George's son*); Larry Keating (*Harry Morton - George's accountant and Blanche's husband*); Judi Meredith (*Judi Meredith - show business hopeful and Ronnie's girl friend*); and Harry Von Zell (*Harry Von Zell - announcer and friend*).

Supporting Cast: Charles Bagby (*Sid*); Lisa Davis (*Miss Jenkins*); and Barbara Stuart (*Lily*).

Production Credits: *Producer/Director:* Rod Amateau, Bob Henry. Mr. Amateau retained producer status but shared directing duties with Mr. Henry in later live episodes. *Scriptwriters:* Norman Paul, Keith Fowler, Harvey Helm (not the full season), William (Willy) Burns. *Art Director:* John Shrum. *Associate Director:* Roy Montgomery. *Camera:* James Van Trees. *Editor:* Larry Heath. *Lighting:* John Freschi. *Musical Director:* Jeff Alexander with the Jeff Alexander Orchestra. *Production Supervisor:* George King. *Technical Director:* William F. Wallace. *Unit Manager:* John Hinsey. *Wardrobe:* Lisa Werner.

Sponsor: Colgate-Palmolive.
Product: Health and beauty aids, detergent and cleaning products.
Agency: McCann-Erickson.
Network: NBC.
Broadcast Day: Tuesday.
Time Slot: 9:00-9:30 P.M. (Eastern Standard Time).
Premise: **The George Burns Show** retained the core cast from **The Burns and Allen Show** minus Gracie but cast them in slightly different roles that revolved around George as a former comedian now working as a theatrical producer. In later episodes, when the format changed for several episodes to include guest stars presented in live musical variety showcases, the original cast was primarily utilized in sketches.

Episode Synopses

T295 October 21, 1958
"George and the Private Eye"
George isn't ready to join Gracie in retirement so he decides to become a producer. His first project is a private detective series but the script is so bad he has to find a way to get out of the deal. Featuring Jack Albertson, Joby Baker, Nicky Blair, Francis DeSales, John Duke, Gil Garfield, Robert Emmett Keane, Steve Mitchell, Pat Murtagh and John Stephenson. Special guests: Jack Benny and Bob Cummings. **SEE B273.**

Review: "There were a few laughs, to be sure, but not enough for a strong teeoff for Burns as a 'single.'" (**Variety**, October 29, 1958).

T296 October 28, 1958
"Jack Benny Comes Over"
Everyone thinks George is planning to revive the comedy team with a new partner--Ronnie's girlfriend, Judi--and Ronnie asks his father's best friend to talk him out of it. Featuring Joseph Kearns. Guest star: Jack Benny.

T297 November 4, 1958
No show tonight; preempted for general election returns.

T298 November 11, 1958
"The French Revue"
George tries to trick Blanche into quitting her job as his secretary. Featuring Chana Eden and Charity Grace.

T299 November 18, 1958
"A Walk-On for George" (also known as "Bill Goetz Guests")
A film producer offers Ronnie a part in a picture as an "all-American boy" but, when Ronnie thinks George is being forced to appear in the film with him without billing, he tries to get out of the project by posing as a beatnik. Featuring Norm Alden and Peggy Knudsen. Special guest: William Goetz.

T300 November 25, 1958
"The 18 Year Old Novelist"
George hopes to get a young novelist to sell him the rights to her book.

T301 December 2, 1958
"Tony Martin Visits"
Judi wants to fill in for Blanche as George's secretary and George wants to be the replacement for a vocalist who may not be able to perform as scheduled at the Cocoanut Grove. Featuring Jack Albertson and Lillian Bronson. Guest star: Tony Martin.

T302 December 9, 1958
"George's Eviction"
George doesn't know whether he's coming or going when he begins having problems with the landlord and his friends are no help. This episode was originally scheduled for airing on November 25, 1958. Featuring Charles Carmen, Douglass Dumbrille, Lewis Martin and Jerry Summers.

T303 December 16, 1958
"Eddie Fisher Guests"
George tries to prove to a dubious Eddie Fisher that his vocal talent is genuine by appearing on a locally-televised amateur show, **Stairway to Stardom**. George pantomimes a Fisher recording of "Oh, My Papa," duets with Eddie on "I'd Love To Call You Rose, Dear," and does a bit of tap dancing with guests The Dunhills. Fisher sings "Hello, Young Lovers." Featuring Laurie Wilhoite (one of George and Gracie's granddaughters). This is the first of the live shows and follows George's own appearance on Fisher's show the previous week. **SEE T395.**

Review: "Unshackled from the rigid format of his film segment, Burns and a relaxed cast pranced right through a delightful half-hour that had pace, zest and high humor." (**Variety**, December 18, 1958).

T304 December 23, 1958
"La Vie en Rose" (also known as "A Wife For Christmas")

George has booked a French singer into a night club and, when it looks like she may not be able to fulfill the contract because she needs to temporarily leave the country, George first tries to convince Harry Von Zell to marry her; failing that, he decides to fill in for her himself. Featuring Chantal Noel and Benny Rubin.

T305 December 30, 1958
"Dale Robertson Guests"
The star of **Tales of Wells Fargo** offers Ronnie a role in a western, performs "The Riddle" and duets with George on "Pony Boy." This is a live show. Guest stars: Dale Robertson and The Lennon Sisters.

T306 January 6, 1959
"George Signs Carol Channing"
George can get Ronnie and Judi booked into a nightclub under one condition: the club needs a top female act and George has twenty-four hours to find one. Featuring Frank Wilcox. Guest star: Carol Channing.

T307 January 13, 1959
"Anna Maria Alberghetti Guests"
George accompanies Anna Maria to a movie premiere.
Anna Maria sings "Day In--Day Out" and duets with George on "Some of These Days." This is a live show. Guest stars: Anna Maria Alberghetti and The Henry Rose Trio.

T308 January 20, 1959
"George on Juke Box Jury"
Blanche and Harry Von Zell are surprised that George's album seems to be selling so well so George decides to submit one of his records to **Juke Box Jury**. Special guests: Bob Cummings, Jr. (son of Bob Cummings), Kathleen Heflin (daughter of Van Heflin), Deena Kaye (daughter of Danny Kaye), Gary Lewis (son of Jerry Lewis) and Peter Potter (host of the radio (later television) show, **Juke Box Jury**.

T309 January 27, 1959
"Rosemary Clooney Guests"
Rosemary is scheduled to appear on George's show but is having problems finding a babysitter, so George asks Ronnie and Judi to fill in so the show can be done from Rosemary's house. Rosemary sings "April In Paris" and duets with George on "Slow Boat To China." Bob Cummings has a cameo in celebration of the fifth anniversary of his own television show, which George's production company produces in real life. This is a live show. Guest stars: Rosemary Clooney, Bob Cummings and The Collins Kids.

T310 February 3, 1959
"Carol Channing Guests"
It's **T.V. Court** when Carol thinks George dented the fender on her new car. Songs include George singing "Augustus J. McCann Was A Henpecked Married Man"; Carol does an impersonation of Tallulah Bankhead, sings "Bye, Bye, Baby" and duets with George on "Down By The Sheltering Palms." This is a live show. Guest star: Carol Channing. **SEE VG9.**

T311 February 10, 1959
"Xavier Cugat and Abbe Lane Guest"
Abbe makes the men forget their poker game when she appears in a new dress. Abbe sings "Taking A Chance On Love" and duets with George on "Lady In Red." This is a live show. Guest stars: Xavier Cugat, Abbe Lane and The Bob DeVoye Trio.

T312 February 17, 1959
"Howard Duff Guests"
George and Howard play twin brothers in a wagon train headed west. All sing "California, Here I Come." This is a live show. Guest stars: Howard Duff, Arthur Murray, The George Garabidian Troubadours and the Mellow Men.

T313 February 24, 1959
"Ronnie Takes an Apartment"
Ronnie moves into his own apartment and Judi decides they should get married right away. Jill Corey sings "Big Daddy" and duets with George on "Last Night On The Back Porch." Featuring Raymond Greenleaf. Guest stars: Jill Corey and the dancing Steiner Brothers.

T314 March 3, 1959
"Jimmie Rodgers Moves in with Ronnie"
George has to get rid of the three girls who followed Jimmie when he moved in with Ronnie. Guest stars: Jimmie Rodgers and The Gardner Sisters.

T315 March 10, 1959
"The Landlord's Daughter"
The landlord's daughter has show business aspirations which goes against her father's wishes; when other tenants in the building continue to complain about the noises coming from George's office, he has to promise to tell her she has no talent in order to avoid eviction. Featuring Douglass Dumbrille and Mary Moore.

T316 March 17, 1959
"Orchid Room" (also known as "The Contract To Sing")
George books himself into a hole-in-the-wall club to protect Ronnie and Judy from appearing there. Featuring Howard Wendell.

T317 March 24, 1959
"George's Trial"
The owner of the Orchid Room tries to break his contract with George.

T318 March 31, 1959
"Breaking Up the Team"
Ronnie decides to quit "Burns and Meredith" because he thinks Judi has all the talent and he might be standing in the way of her success. Featuring Dick Humphrey and Hayden Rorke.

T319 April 7, 1959
"The Monster Trend"
George holds auditions in his office for a horror movie he's decided to produce.

T320 April 14, 1959
"George Invests in a Record Company"
George is promised a recording contract if he'll invest $10,000 in the company and everyone else puts money into it because they think the company has signed Frank Sinatra. This is the last show of the series. It is being replaced in this time slot by the return of **The Californians**.

3. Wendy and Me. 1964-1965. ABC. 30 min. b/w.

Series Notes: This ABC situation comedy was broadcast from September 14, 1964 through September 6, 1965 (the last first-run episode aired on May 24, 1965) and was basically an attempt to recapture the zany spirit of the still-missed Gracie and the chemistry that she and George had shared. Once again, George was the narrator; the focus of the series, however, was on the character of Wendy and George did not give himself as much on-screen time as he had in his two previous series. He did, however, insert monologues between scenes and introduced each breakaway for a commercial with the words "do it." Beginning production in 1964, the first episode was, ironically, aired just two weeks after Gracie's death. Thirty-four black and white episodes were produced on film and occupied the Monday night 9:00-9:30 P.M. time slot. The series, which lasted for one season, was produced in Hollywood by Warner Bros. Pictures in association with Natwil Productions, Inc. (later syndicated by Worldvision). Jack Webb was responsible for entering Warner Bros. Television into this co-production deal when he became head of television production for the studio.

Cast: Connie Stevens (*Wendy Conway*); Ron Harper (*Jeff Conway - Wendy's husband, a pilot*); James Callahan (*Danny Adams - Jeff's best friend and co-pilot*); Shary Marshall (*Linda Harris - Mr. Norton's secretary*); J. Pat O'Malley (*Mr. Bundy - apartment building superintendent*); Bartlett Robinson (*Willard Norton - General Manager of the airline*); Bonnie Jones (*Edna Rogers - a friend of Danny's*); and George Burns (*George Burns also known as "Me" - owner of an apartment building*).

Production Credits: *Executive Producer*: Wm. T. Orr. *Producer:* George Burns. *Director:* Richard Crenna (pilot); Gene Reynolds. *Scriptwriters:* William (Willy) Burns, Robert O'Brien (co-writer on pilot), Elon Packard, Norman Paul. *Art Director:* Perry Ferguson; Art Loel; Carl Macauley; George Renne. *Assistant Director:* Phil Rawlins; Victor Vallejo.

Associate Producer: Herman (Herm) Saunders. *Director of Photography:* Louis Jennings; Jack Marquette. *Film Editor:* George R. Rohrs; Noel L. Scott; Bill Wiard. *Makeup Supervisor:* Gordon Bau. *Music:* George Duning. *Music Editor:* Erma L. Levin. *Set Decorator:* Theodore Driscoll; William L. Kuehl. *Sound:* Samuel F. Goode; Stanley Jones; Francis E. Stahl. *Supervising Hair Stylist:* Jean Burt Reilly.

Additional Credits: Connie Stevens' wardrobe is designed and furnished by Trés Gay. Wardrobe for George Burns is furnished by Tavelman's of Beverly Hills.

Product: El Producto Cigars.
Network: ABC.
Broadcast Day: Monday.
Time Slot: 9:00-9:30 P.M. (Eastern Standard Time).
Theme Song: Written by Ervin Drake.
Premise: George has purchased the Sunset de Ville apartment building at 4820 Highland and maintains an apartment (#104) there in order to rehearse his singing act. The primary action, however, revolves around the daily antics of his tenant in apartment 217, Wendy Conway, a former airline stewardess now married to a pilot.

Episode Synopses

T321 September 14, 1964 "Wendy and Me" (pilot episode)
In order to keep Danny's blood pressure at a level that will enable him to pass his airline physical, Wendy suggests that Jeff take his place when a beautiful out-of-town visitor arrives, expecting Danny to take her out. Featuring John Hubbard, Diane McBain, Jackie Russell, and George Winters.

Reviews: "**Wendy and Me** premiere distressing disappointment owing to a largely clumsy format. Appeared to be attempt to capture **Burns and Allen Show**...failed...George Burns very comfortable. Connie Stevens simply lacks any semblance of Gracie Allen's wit." (**Evening Outlook**, September 15, 1964). "George says 'the show is our monument to Gracie'." (**The Hollywood Reporter**, Mike Connolly, September 16, 1964: 2). "...giving her (Connie Stevens) the benefit of a couple of long doubts, she is at least in the tradition of the late, great Gracie Allen..." (**TV Guide**, December 12-18, 1964: 25).

T322 September 21, 1964
"Wendy"s Anniversary For?"
Wendy wants Jeff to propose to her again to commemorate their first wedding anniversary. Featuring Ann McCrea, Rolfe Sedan, Amzie Strickland and Marlo Thomas.

T323 September 28, 1964
"Swing Low, Aunt Harriet"
Two airline stewardesses from Japan make plans to visit Wendy for the weekend. Featuring Sheila Bromley, Beverly Hills, Caroline Kiddo and Moko Mokusho.

T324 October 5, 1964
"Wendy's Secret Wedding"
Wendy plans a wedding for a friend. Featuring Ken Berry, Jonathan Hole, Erin O'Donnell and Elizabeth Shaw.

T325 October 12, 1964
"George Burns While Rome Fiddles"
Wearing a black wig, Wendy takes another stewardess's place aboard a flight bound for Rome without the knowledge of her husband, who's piloting the plane. Featuring Bruno Della Santina, Don Orlando, Penny Santon, Mary Jane Saunders, Darlene Tompkins, A. G. Vitanza and Lana Wood. Jack Benny is seen in a montage of clips.

T326 October 19, 1964
"Jeff, The Senior Citizen"
The phrase "you haven't changed at all" doesn't quite seem to fit when guests arrive for a dinner intended to reunite some of Jeff's friends from college. Featuring Frank Ferguson, Harry Harvey, Sr., Pat Priest and Howard Wendell.

T327 October 26, 1964
"It Takes Two To Tangle"
Wendy has another visitor--a child who's on her way to becoming a product of a broken home. Featuring Eileen Baral, George Ives, Burt Metcalfe and Sue Randall.

T328 November 2, 1964
"Wendy's Private Eye"
Doubtful about Jeff's faithfulness, Wendy hires a detective to follow him, but the gumshoe mistakes Jeff for Danny. Featuring Stanley Adams, Betty Connor, Karen Jensen and Eileen O'Neill.

T329 November 9, 1964
"Room At The Bottom"
Mr. Norton is coming to dinner but Mr. Bundy seems to have taken over the Conway apartment. Featuring Colleen O'Sullivan.

T330 November 16, 1964
"Danny, The Married Bachelor"
Danny asks Wendy to pretend to be his wife when he hears that an old girlfriend is due to arrive for a visit with her big brother in tow. Featuring Med Flory and John Marlowe.

T331 November 23, 1964
"Wendy, The Waitress"
Ever-helpful Wendy offers to fill in for a waitress who can't leave work to attend her sister's wedding. Featuring John Hubbard and Nancy Rennick.

T332 November 30, 1964
"Belle Of The Malt Shop"
Danny gets confused over which of Mr. Norton's daughters has arrived for a visit and prepares to become the boss's son-in-law, not realizing this daughter is only twelve years old. Featuring Illana Dowling, Robert Gothie and Donald Losby.

T333 December 7, 1964
"East Is East And West Is Wendy"
Wendy tries to help Jeff land the plum assignment of piloting a potentate to Washington, DC. Featuring John Abbott, John Alvin, Jan Arvan, Brenda Benet, Francis DeSales and John Holland.

T334 December 14, 1964
"Four Of A Kind"
It's a simple enough tale when Wendy agrees to look after a friend's sheep dog, but her problems multiply when the dog wanders off.

T335 December 21, 1964
"Wendy, The Woman In The Gray Flannel Suit"
Wendy tries to help Edna get a job as a secretary. Featuring Pamela Bartholomew, William Bramley, Dorian Brown, Kaye Farrington, Marianne Gaba and John Hoyt.

T336 December 28, 1964
"Five Minutes To Show Time"
Will George agree to act as master of ceremonies as a favor to Wendy and Jeff? (Would Georgie Jessel deliver a eulogy?) Featuring Don Gazzaniga, Robert Hunter and Leonard Weinrub.

T337 January 4, 1965
Preempted for the State of the Union address by President Johnson.

T338 January 11, 1965
"A Bouquet For Mr. Bundy"
Mr. Bundy catches a wedding bouquet thrown out the window by Danny so Wendy tries to find him a wife. Featuring Dabbs Greer, Marrisa Mathes and James Millhollin.

T339 January 18, 1965
"The Wendy Mob"
Wendy didn't bank on the trouble she gets into when she bumps into a robber's parked getaway car. Featuring Richard Bakalyan and Stacy Harris.

T340 January 25, 1965

"Who's In The Guest Room Tonight?"
Mr. Norton's older daughter is spending the weekend with the Conways while her parents go to San Francisco and Wendy fears she's planning to elope with Danny. Featuring Robyn Grace, Steve Harmon, Jennifer Stuart and Sandra Warner.

T341 February 1, 1965
"Wendy Sails In The Sunset"
Mr. Norton loans Jeff and Wendy his boat for the weekend, but a trip Jeff had hoped would be a second honeymoon turns into a cruise for fourteen. Featuring Robyn Grace, Robert Hunter, Harry Lauter, Dorothy Neumann, Marlis Torre and Raquel Welch.

T342 February 8, 1965
"Tea Leaves For Two"
A fortune teller casts a cloud over Wendy's marriage. Featuring Tara Ashton, Ann McCrea, Naomi Stevens and Julie Van Zandt.

T343 February 15, 1965
"Happiness Is A Thing Called Misery"
Wendy wonders how her marriage can be a happy one if she and Jeff never argue. Featuring Russ Conway, Nicolas Coster, Charles Lane, Margaret Mason and Ann McCrea.

T344 February 22, 1965
"Jeff Takes A Turn For The Nurse"
Jeff is sick with worry when he misunderstands a message concerning Wendy and why she's at the hospital. Featuring Virginia Gregg, Jon Lormer and Ann McCrea.

T345 March 1, 1965
"How Not To Succeed In Stealing"
A necklace turns into a string of troubles for Wendy. Featuring Brenda Benet and Lori Martin.

T346 March 8, 1965
"Wendy Gives Uncle The Brush"
How will Wendy explain those extra splashes of paint on the portrait of Jeff's uncle? Featuring Rachel Roman and Walter Sande.

T347 March 15, 1965
"Tacos, Enchiladas And Wendy" was to have aired tonight but didn't until May 24, 1965 (T357). What actually did appear in tonight's time slot is unknown.

T348 March 22, 1965
"Wendy Is Stranger Than Fiction"
A writer moves into the building and, of course, Wendy wants to help him with his "writer's block". Featuring Woodrow Parfrey. The writer's name, William Norman Packard, is an inside joke. The show's writers are *William* Burns, *Norman* Paul, and Elon *Packard*.

T349 March 29, 1965
"Let's Go Where The Wild Geisha Goes"
Wendy and Mr. Bundy prepare to accompany Jeff on a trip to Japan. Featuring Pat Li and Yuki Shimoda.

T350 April 5, 1965
"You Can Fight City Hall"
Wendy might have better luck paying a parking ticket rather than let Danny help her get it "taken care of." Featuring Lloyd Babitt, Barbara Dodd, Frank Ferguson, Melody Patterson and Richard X. Slattery.

T351 April 12, 1965
"Wendy Lends A Helping Voice"
Wendy offers refuge to singing twins. The Earl Twins appear as themselves and sing "I May Be Wrong." Connie Stevens joins Jane Earl in a duet on "Ain't We Got Fun?" Featuring Sid Clute.

T352 April 19, 1965
"Wendy's Instant Intellect"
Wendy discovers you can't always go by the book if you want to join a literary club. Featuring Jane Morgan, Doris Packer and Darlene Patterson.

T353 April 26, 1965
"Danny's Double Life"
Everyone knows Danny's a real ladies' man, but does he really need two apartments? Featuring Michele Carey, Natalie Masters, Herb Vigran and Anne Whitfield.

T354 May 3, 1965
Pre-empted for a special, **Melina Mercouri's Greece**.

T355 May 10, 1965
"Wendy's Five Thousand Dollar Chair"
Wendy's plans to become a cost-conscious consumer fall to earth with a loud thud, just like she does when the pricey chair underneath her gives way. Featuring Michele Carey, Jean Carson and Herb Ellis.

T356 May 17, 1965
"Call Me Or I'll Call You"
Wendy feels disconnected from Jeff when she doesn't receive a phone call from him after his plane arrives in Seattle. Featuring Floy Dean and Robert Hogan.

T357 May 24, 1965
"Tacos, Enchiladas And Wendy"
A planned vacation in paradise takes a detour. This episode was postponed from March 15, 1965. Featuring Pitt Herbert, Monty Margetts and Vito Scotti.

The series goes into weekly re-runs from May 31, 1965, through September 6, 1965, and will be replaced the following week by the debut of **A Man Called Shenandoah**, starring Robert Horton.

4. George Burns Comedy Week. 1985. CBS. 30 min. color.

Series Notes: This series was George's first comedy anthology; all episodes were, naturally, comedic in spirit and were broadcast on Wednesdays from 9:30-10:00 P.M. (in a return, after twenty-seven years, to CBS). The program, consisting of thirteen filmed episodes, began September 18, 1985 and ended on December 25, 1985. It did spawn a short-lived spinoff, **Leo & Liz in Beverly Hills** starring Harvey Korman and Valerie Perrine, that aired on CBS April-June, 1986. The program was produced in Hollywood by 40 Share Productions, Inc. in association with Universal Television.

Cast: George Burns, who hosts/narrates each episode, is the only regular cast member; however, he does not appear in any of the shows per se. There is no series supporting cast.

Production Credits: *Executive Producers:* Steve Martin and Carl Gottlieb. *Producers:* George E. Crosby and Paul Perlove. *Associate Producer:* William Cairncross; Deborah Hwang. *Executive Story Editor:* Pamela Pettler. *Art Director:* Leon Ericksen; Francis J. Pezza. *Casting:* Don Pemrick. *Conductor:* Charles Fox. *Costume Supervisor:* Charles DeMuth; Dorothy Baca. *Creative Consultant:* Earl Pomerantz. *Director of Photography:* Ronald W. Browne. *Editor:* Janice Hampton. *Executive Story Editor:* Pamela Pettler. *Film Editor:* Larry Heath. *First Assistant Director:* Barbara Bass. *Music:* Charles Fox; David Frank. *Music Editor:* Mary Morlas. *Production Executive:* Marcia Zwilling. *Set Decorator:* Michele Guiol. *Sound:* Thomas E. Allen, Sr. *Sound Editor:* Phil Haberman. *Sound Mixer:* Pat Somerset. *Press Representatives:* Dan Bagott (Hollywood) and Bob Higgins (New York). *Second Assistant Director:* Warren R. Turner. *Story Editor:* David Axlerod. *Theme:* Claude Debussy. *Unit Production Manager:* Mitchell L. Gamson.

Additional Credits: Color by Technicolor. Titles & Optical Effects by Universal Title.

Network: CBS.
Broadcast Day: Wednesday.
Time Slot: 9:30-10:00 P.M. (Eastern Standard Time).
Premise: Every week a different story written, directed, and acted by some of Hollywood's biggest comedic talent is presented, sandwiched between George's opening and closing monologues.

Episode Synopses

T358 September 18, 1985
"The Dynamite Girl"
A young woman unjustly confined to a sanitarium while her family attempts to declare her incompetent wanders away just in time to defuse a potentially explosive situation. *Director:* Peter Bonerz. *Writer:* Carl Gottlieb. *Story:* Steve Martin and Carl Gottlieb. Starring Tim Matheson (*Jake Wellman*); Catherine O'Hara (*Sally Hayes*); Richard Libertini (*Dr. Wyman*); Macon McCalman (*Lester Shankman*); Luis Avalos (*Dr. Lyman*); Julie Payne (*Loretta Hayes*); Redmond Gleeson (*Sgt. Hanlon*); and Ruth Buzzi (*Juliette*). Co-starring John O'Leary (*Dr. Engle*); Mina Kolb (*Doris Shankman*); Robert Clotworthy (*Philip Hayes*); Dominick Brascia (*Orderly*); Keone Young (*Young Customer*); Sam Chew Jr. (*Commissioner #1*); Byron Morrow (*Commissioner #2*); Ann Weldon (*Commissioner #3*); Charles Walker (*Second Policeman*); Lee Ryan (*First Policeman*); and Dan Barrows (*Store Manager*). With Will Gill Jr. (*Detective*) and Carol Androsky (*Nurse Receptionist*).

Review: "Burns is clearly on hand as a peg to try to get viewers to watch every week..." (**Variety**, September 25, 1985).

T359 September 25, 1985
"Home For Dinner"
A New Yorker who has moved to Florida goes on a fishing trip with his neighbors; the only "catch" is that his newly-found friends go fishing with guns. *Director:* Carl Gottlieb. *Writers:* Larry Levin and Jonathan Day. Guest stars: Eugene Levy (*Robert Galvin*); Anne Lockhart (*Susan Galvin*); Fred Willard (*Fred Mangan*); Joe Flaherty (*Jerry*); Greg Morris (*Lee*); Frank Bonner (*Stu*); Dan Calfa (*Weitlin*); Jonathan Ward (*Bobby Galvin*); Jeanette O'Connor (*Lorraine*); and Susan Powell (*Alice*).

T360 October 2, 1985
"Death Benefits"
A salesman gives new meaning to the term "life insurance." *Director:* Neal Israel. *Writers:* Neal Israel and Amy Heckerling. Starring Joe Piscopo (*Lou Kerwin*); Deborah Harmon (*Adele Kerwin*); Gary Riley (*Irwin Kerwin*); Robert Klein (*Jay*); Ian Abercrombie (*Doctor*); Arthur Rosenberg (*Jay's Lawyer*); William Boyett (*Judge*); Richard Partlow (*Dr. Hirsh*); and Robert Lussier (*Lou's Lawyer*).

T361 October 9, 1985
"The Smiths"
Lack of funding for a witness-protection program creates some strange bedfellows. *Director:* Phil Robinson. *Writers:* James Berg and Stan Zimmerman. Starring Martin Mull (*Donald*); Tess Harper (*Janet*); Ken Stovitz (*Buddy*); Gigi Vorgan (*Sally*); Candy Azzara (*Iris*); Jeffrey Alan Chandler (*Dick*); Jon Cedar (*Head agent*); and Floyd Levine (*Dolan*).

T362 October 16, 1985
"The Couch"
A couple hopes a costly antique will be the key to acceptance when their daughter marries into a wealthy family. This episode provided the spinoff for the series **Leo & Liz In Beverly Hills**. *Director:* Steve Martin. *Writer:* Ed Scharlach. *Story:* Steve Martin and Carl Gottlieb. Starring Harvey Korman (*Leo*); Valerie Perrine (*Liz*); Carrie Fisher (*Mitzi*); Parker Whitman (*Mr. Winthrop*); Marlena Giovi (*Mrs. Winthrop*); Fritz Feld (*Caterer*); Michael Ensign (*Minister*); Ken Olfson (*Florist*); Bronson Pinchot (*Richardson*); Jack Heller (*Auctioneer*); Jay Robinson (*Felber*); Susan Powell (*Wife*); and Michael McManus (*Fedderson*).

T363 October 23, 1985
"Disaster At Buzz Creek"
A relatively minor flood takes on new proportions when townspeople try to find a way to qualify for disaster relief. *Director:* John Landis. *Writer:* Andy Breckman. Starring Don Rickles (*Mayor Dubin*); Don Knotts (*Rooter*); Fannie Flagg (*Mrs. Shawn*); Lana Clarkson (*Priscilla Twang*); Stephen Collins (*Investigator*); Jack Blessing (*Eli*); Paul Barselou (*Minister*); and Paul Brinegar (*Silas*).

T364 October 30, 1985
"The Assignment"
An "Indiana Jones" type hero tackles one of his toughest jobs in the wilds of Africa. *Director:* Phil Robinson. *Writer:* Bruce Jay Friedman.

Starring Elliott Gould (*Flick*); Telly Savalas (*Fleeger*); Diane Salinger (*Jeanette*); Severn Darden (*Le Blanc*); James Avery (*Chief*); Freddye Chapman (*Waitress*); Michael Ansara (*Supervisor/Warden*); and Brian Thompson (*Gibbens*).

T365 November 6, 1985
"Dream, Dream, Dream"
An inanimate object comes to life and changes the life of the man whose obsession has become reality. *Director:* John Fox. *Writer:* David Simon. Starring Patrick Duffy (*Gordon Kramer*); Colleen Camp (*Kay*); Geena Davis (*Angelica/Sandi/Woman*); Anthony Holland (*Pendleton*); Raymond Singer (*Kilburn*); Charles Fleischer (*Dr. Bernard*); and Eve Brenner (*Aunt Clara*).

T366 November 13, 1985
"Boris And Ivan In Las Vegas"
Soviet cosmonauts make an unscheduled landing in the Nevada desert but must wait to be rescued. *Director:* Carl Gottlieb. *Writer:* Paul Perlove. *Story:* Carl Gottlieb. Starring Bronson Pinchot (*Boris*); Dave Thomas (*Ivan*); Candy Clark (*Kelly*); Vladimir Skomarovsky (*Lapachov*); Howard Witt (*Colonel Dexter*); Waldemar Kalinowski (*Vladimir*); Kimberly Ross (*Race Groupie*); Jim Doughan (*Bellhop*); and Michael Rider (*Sergeant*).

T367 November 20, 1985
Pre-empted for **Lost In London**, a movie made for television.

T368 November 27, 1985
"The Honeybunnies"
A "serious" writer discovers that his work is not being taken seriously at all--until he creates a cartoon. This episode airs at a special time from 8:30-9:00 p.m. and was originally to have been broadcast November 6, 1985. *Director:* Peter Bonerz. *Writers:* David Cohen and Roger Schulman. Starring Howard Hesseman (*Andy Pace*); Laraine Newman (*Leeza*); David L. Lander (*Willard*); Sandy Baron (*Bushmiller*); Casey Kasem (*Don Crowley*); Nicole Rosselli (*Heather*); and Al Pugliese (*Al*).

T369 December 4, 1985
"The Funniest Guy In The World"
A financier offers a small fortune to the person who can bring some laughter into his life. *Director:* John Korty. *Writer:* Pamela Pettler. Starring Jack Gilford (*Winslow*); Victoria Tennant (*Maggie*); Paul Reiser (*Jack*); and Peter Macpherson (*Phelps*).

T370 December 11, 1985
"Christmas Carol II: The Sequel"
Too much of a good thing results in a second ghostly visit for Ebenezer Scrooge. *Director:* Carl Gottlieb. *Writers:* Carl Gottlieb and David Axlerod. Based on characters created by Charles Dickens. Starring James Whitmore (*Scrooge*); Roddy McDowall (*Bob Cratchit*); Samantha Eggar (*Mrs. Cratchit*); Ed Begley, Jr. (*Tiny Tim, Sr.*); and James Widdoes (*Frederick*). Also starring Conrad Janis (*The Baker*); Carolyn Seymour (*Mrs. Buffit*); Paul Benedict (*Marley's Ghost*); and Severn Darden (*The Spirit of Christmas Present*). Co-starring Larry Hankin (*Mr. Sneavil*); Shawn Southwick (*The Spirit of Christmas Past*); Dean Dittman (*Portly Man*); Bernard Kuby (*Publican*); Stuart Rogers (*Urchin*); and Jerry Supiran (*Tiny Tim, Jr.*) With Hy Pyke (*Cabbie*); Martin Clark *The Spirit of Christmas Yet-to-Come*); and Signy Coleman (*Carol/Alice*).

T371 December 18, 1985
Preempted for the special, **Kenny And Dolly: A Christmas To Remember**.

T372 December 25, 1985
"Kidnappers Of The Rich And Famous"
Kidnappers find that an indifferent victim definitely makes their job more difficult. This is the last show of the series. **George Burns Comedy Week** shared the hour between 9:00-10:00 P.M. with the Flip Wilson series, **Charlie & Co**. By the next season, CBS moved **Magnum, P.I.** into the time slot. *Director:* Alan Myerson. *Writer:* Pamela Pettler. *Story:* Merrill Markoe. Starring Peter Bonerz (*Charlie*); Michael McKean (*Joey*); Candy Azzara (*Katharine*); Florence Halop (*Mrs. Shapiro*); Anna Mathias (*Housewife*); John-Michael Williams (*Man*); and Julia Jennings (*Woman*).

Television Guest Appearances (1952-1995)

George Burns and Gracie Allen as a Team and Separately

T373 The Jack Benny Program. "Gracie Bit." CBS. March 9, 1952. George and Gracie guest in this episode in which Jack impersonates Gracie, who has gone to Denver for a sandwich. Gracie finally appears but she mistakes Jack (still in costume and makeup as Gracie) for a woman she thinks George is seeing. **SEE T377.**

T374 The Olympics Fund Telethon. NBC-CBS. June 21-22, 1952. Burns and Allen join dozens of other entertainers, including co-hosts Bob Hope and Bing Crosby (with Dorothy Lamour and Martin & Lewis) in this fourteen and a half hour marathon broadcast over two networks. Pledges ran slightly over one million dollars for the Helsinki-bound athletes. This was Crosby's first foray into television.

T375 Stars In The Eye: Dedication of CBS Television City. CBS. November 11, 1952.
George and Gracie join other stars and network and political dignitaries as "CBS Presents The T.V. City Inaugural Show" for the dedication of Television City, CBS' new thirty-five million dollar facility in Hollywood, the first plant opened exclusively for television production. The program was produced and directed by Ralph Levy, who was holding the same position on George and Gracie's television show at this time. Among those in attendance were Amos 'n' Andy, Eddie "Rochester" Anderson, Eve Arden, Desi Arnaz, Jack Benny, Los Angeles Mayor Fletcher Bowron, Art Linkletter and Alan Young. Gracie was the honorary escort to California Governor Earl Warren and sang "When I Say I Beg Your Pardon." This date is correct per the UCLA archives; other sources (including the script) give it as November 15, 1952. **SEE VG73.**

T376 The Jack Benny Program. CBS. March 21, 1954.
Jack reminisces about the time that he, George and Bing Crosby performed as the vaudeville song and dance team of Goldie, Fields and Glide (the actual name of one of George's vaudeville teams). Bob Hope makes a cameo appearance. **SEE VG12, VG13, VG14.**

T377 The Jack Benny Program. "The Burns and Allen Show." CBS. April 11, 1954.
In a recycled plot from 1952, Gracie is again impersonated by Jack when she doesn't show up for her guest spot with George. This gag proved to be so popular that George and Jack recreated it at numerous charity dinners. **SEE T373.**

T378 What's My Line? CBS. June 6, 1954.
George and Gracie (reportedly appearing without makeup) attempt to stump the panel on this long-running game show by answering their questions with one knock for "no" and two knocks for "yes" (which was the opposite of how they had been instructed by host John Charles Daley). When they were asked to start answering the panel's questions vocally Gracie chimed in "Don't answer, George!" which, of course, gave them away immediately. Steve Allen, a regular panelist, was present this night, just a few months before he left to start **The Tonight Show. SEE T571.**

T379 BBC television appearance to promote premiere of **The George Burns and Gracie Allen Show** in Great Britain. ca. 1955.
In addition to this scheduled appearance, George and Gracie later announced plans to return to London in the spring of 1956 to appear on another television show to plug their series. Specifics of such an appearance are unknown at this time.

T380 Toast of the Town. Hosted by Ed Sullivan. CBS. January 30, 1955. George joins Jack Benny as a guest on this half hour salute to radio's 35th anniversary.

T381 This Is Your Life. Hosted by Ralph Edwards. NBC. September 28, 1955.
George is featured as the surprise guest on the season opener of this testimonial program whose unsuspecting honorees are brought back to the

television studio to listen to their life stories. Guests who appear to honor George on the show include Jack Benny, Sid Gary, George Jessel, Billy Lorraine, the Peewee Quartet, Jackie Cooper, who is starring in a new television series, **The People's Choice**, produced by George's production company and of course, Gracie, who tells of their early romance and how she chose the "one with the gold tooth." George's book, **I Love Her, That's Why!** (B34), receives some publicity. On the distaff side, Ralph Edwards notes that a library at a Boys Club in Hollywood will be named in Gracie's honor as a way of thanking her for her efforts on behalf of their organization. There was a report at the time that many people wished Gracie had been the subject of the show that night and that, in fact, she was suspicious she might be the honoree instead of George and refused to leave the Hollywood Knickerbocker Hotel until the last possible minute.

Review: "That Burns was 'taken in' was reflected in his apparent surprise and it didn't look like a prop emotion." (**Variety**, October 5, 1955).

T382 **The Bob Cummings Show**. "Hawaii Calls." CBS. October 27, 1955.
George appears in this show in which Bob becomes jealous when he learns that Jack Carson is dating his girlfriend. (**The Bob Cummings Show** became known as **Love That Bob** when it entered syndication).

T383 **Shower of Stars**. Hosted by William Lundigan. "Auto Show." Also known as "The Jack Benny Show." CBS. November 3, 1955.
Gracie is one of the guests on this live musical revue sponsored by the Chrysler Corporation. Other guests are Jack Benny, Gary Crosby, Joan Druckenmiller, Frankie Laine, Marilyn Maxwell and The Sportsmen. Skits include Gracie making a flower planter out of Jack Benny's famous Maxwell automobile.

Review: "Gracie Allen spun some of her vacuous whimsy and made the scene with Benny a comedy high spot." (**Daily Variety**, November 4, 1955).

T384 **Shower of Stars**. Hosted by William Lundigan. "Quentin Reynolds Writing Story of Jack's Life." CBS. January 19, 1956.
In this edition of the musical variety program George sings "I Love Her, That's Why" and dances with Shirley MacLaine. The show also features Jack Benny, singers Mary Costa and Oreste, Quentin Reynolds, Eddie "Rochester" Anderson and, in cameos, Frank Sinatra and Red Skelton. The storyline revolves upon the premise that writer Reynolds is penning Benny's biography.

Review: "Burns caught a few chuckles and a rousing plug for his book but he, too, has been much funnier on his own show." (**Daily Variety**, January 20, 1956).

T385 **Climax**. Hosted by William Lundigan. "The Louella Parsons Story." CBS. March 8, 1956. Based on Parsons' book, **The Gay Illiterate.**
George and Gracie are included in this dramatic anthology of Gracie's friend, Hollywood columnist Louella Parsons. The plot features flashbacks in which celebrities are interviewed by phone.

T386 **The Jack Benny Program**. "George Burns, Spike Jones Show." CBS. October 7, 1956.
George appears in this episode with Spike Jones.

T387 **The Ed Sullivan Show**. CBS. ca. 1957.
George and Gracie make an appearance on this variety show. It has been published that George made a total of four appearances on the program through the years (perhaps including **Toast of the Town**, the program's earlier name, although the other dates are unknown at this time). **SEE T680.**

T388 **The Jackie Gleason Show**. CBS. ca. 1957.
George and Gracie appear on Gleason's comedy/variety show.

T389 **The Bob Cummings Show**. "Bob Meets The Mortons." CBS. March 21, 1957.
George and Gracie appear in this episode when photographer Bob Cummings gets involved with both the Burnses and their next door neighbors, *Blanche* and *Harry Morton*, as they all try to "fix" Bob up with his secretary, *Schultzy*.

T390 The Jack Paar Show. NBC. ca. 1958.
George appears on this variety talk show (a forerunner of **The Tonight Show**).

T391 The George Gobel Show. NBC. ca. 1958.
George is one of Gobel's guests on his comedy variety show.

T392 The George Jessel Show. KCOP, Hollywood. September 1958.
George and Miss Canada appear in this Tuesday night debut of a twice-weekly program broadcast (with plans to syndicate) hosted by George Jessel.

T393 The Jack Benny Program. CBS. November 16, 1958.
George and Jack compare notes on the lives of their television alter-egos.

T394 The Bob Cummings Show. "Bob Butters Beck--Beck Butters Better." CBS. December 2, 1958.
George teaches Bob how to be a rock and roll impresario. **SEE VG24.**

T395 The Eddie Fisher Show. NBC. December 9, 1958.
George guests on this live musical variety show, where he's introduced in a familiar position--leaning against the proscenium ala **The George Burns and Gracie Allen Show**. During the program George reflects on vaudeville, his meeting with Gracie, and tells Eddie he needs a partner.

T396 The Bob Cummings Show. "Bob Helps Martha." NBC. May 26, 1959.
Bob tries to fix up *Schultzy*'s friend, Martha, with George Burns' friend, Harry Von Zell.

T397 The Bob Cummings Show. "Bob Helps Von Zell." NBC. June 2, 1959.
In a continuation of last week's storyline Bob and George try to prevent a Latin model from interfering with Martha and Harry Von Zell's romance.

T398 Lincoln-Mercury Startime. "George Burns in The Big Time." NBC. November 17, 1959.
Jack Benny, Eddie Cantor, Bobby Darin, George Jessel and The Kingston Trio join George in a look at the various types of entertainment that made up vaudeville in George's very first television special. George sings "Don't Take Me Home" and "Red Rose Rag" and does a song-and-sand-dance to "I Ain't Got Nobody" with Darin.

Reviews: "George Burns did fine in the big aura of his first tv special. But the rest of his show didn't." (**Daily Variety**, November 19, 1959). "It came off a pretty lacklustre affair, more sentiment than entertainment." (**Variety**, November 25, 1959).

T399 General Electric Theater. "Platinum on the Rocks." CBS. November 29, 1959.
George plays an ex-vaudeville comedian who is a modern day Robin Hood. Co-starring Fred Beir, Kay Elhardt and Milton Frome. **SEE T408.**

T400 The Jack Benny Program. "The George Burns Show." CBS. December 27, 1959.
George appears on his best friend's show in an episode that takes the same name as that of his new series without Gracie.

T401 The Dinah Shore Chevy Show. NBC. ca. 1960.
George is a guest on Dinah's musical variety show, along with Dwayne Hickman, performing a monologue and engaging in a skit with Dinah.

T402 Ford Startime. NBC. June 7, 1960.
George hosts this variety special sponsored by the Ford Motor Company. Guests are Jack Benny, Polly Bergen, Bobby Darin, Betty Grable and the Hermes Pan Dancers. George sings "Doin' The Grizzly Bear," "Lily of the Valley," and "Red Rose Rag."

Review: "Actually, Burns, in his own way and style, is an accomplished vocalist..." (**Variety**, June 15, 1960).

T403 Eleanor Roosevelt's Diamond Jubilee Plus One. NBC. October 7, 1960.
Mrs. Eleanor Roosevelt makes a brief appearance in this special, produced as an appeal to raise funds for the Eleanor Roosevelt Cancer Foundation.

The program segments feature Jack Benny, George Burns, Carol Channing, Nat King Cole, Jimmy Durante, Bob Hope, Mahalia Jackson and Mary Martin, with cast members from the Broadway production of **The Sound of Music.** Lucille Ball, General Omar Bradley, Dr. Tom Dooley, Irene Dunne, Senator John F. Kennedy, Paul Newman, Vice President Richard M. Nixon, Simone Signoret, Joanne Woodward and others also appear.

Review: "It wasn't lavish, because there was a minimum of production, but it was enjoyable, because there was a maximum of talent." (**Variety**, October 12, 1960).

T404 The Jack Benny Program. "The 'Nightbeat' Takeoff." CBS. October 16, 1960.
George appears with Tony Curtis, Robert Wagner and Mike Wallace in this first weekly Benny show in which Jack is worried he may not have the strength to do a television show every week. **Nightbeat** was an interview show with Mike Wallace, who already had a reputation for toughness.

T405 Open End. Moderated by David Susskind. NBC. December 6, 1960.
George is a guest on David Susskind's talk show, joining Joey Bishop, Jimmy Durante, Buddy Hackett and Groucho Marx. Normally syndicated, this is a special network entry.

Review: "...within the framework of the given questions, the program never got off the ground." (**Variety**, December 14, 1960).

T406 The Garry Moore Show. CBS. ca. 1961.
George is a guest on Moore's variety show, introduced as "Sugar Throat" Burns, a singer who "learned twelve songs in 1914 and..has refused to learn any new ones since."

T407 The Jack Benny Program. "Variety Show." CBS. April 2, 1961.
George introduces his "discovery," singer/dancer/actress Ann-Margret, and performs a routine with Jack, who also claims to have "discovered" her. In real life, Burns is given the credit of "introducing" her to bigtime show business.

T408 Comedy Spotlight. CBS. ca. Summer 1961.
Included in this anthology series is a rebroadcast of **General Electric Theater's** "Platinum on the Rocks." **SEE T399.**

T409 The DuPont Show of the Week. "Laughter USA." NBC. September 17, 1961.
George appears in the first show of the series, which explores the history of American humor and features many comedians and film clips. George hosts and narrates the one-hour film, which includes a clip of him and Gracie performing their routine, "Backyard Circus."

T410 The Dinah Shore Show. NBC. December 29, 1961.
Among Dinah's guest stars on her musical variety show are George Burns, Nat "King" Cole and Ginger Rogers.

T411 The Jack Paar Show. NBC. ca. 1962.
George makes another appearance on this variety show.

T412 Perry Como's Kraft Music Hall. NBC. January 31, 1962.
George appears on Como's version of Kraft's variety show that was successfully transplanted from radio, albeit some nine years later, but where it had enjoyed an impressive sixteen-year run.

T413 Mister Ed. "George Burns Meets Mister Ed." CBS. February 18, 1962.
Roger Addison has read a newspaper article that says George Burns is willing to pay $25,000 for a novelty act to be performed in Las Vegas and Mister Ed's owner, Wilbur Post, decides there aren't too many things more novel than a talking horse. He goes to George's office to try and sell him the act but, unfortunately, Mister Ed refuses to cooperate. Larry Keating, who plays *Roger Addison*, is a former cast member of **The George Burns and Gracie Allen Show** and **The George Burns Show**; George's production company produces **Mister Ed**. The episode is also known as "Ed Finally Talks." **SEE B345, T755.**

T414 The Jack Paar Show. NBC. March 29, 1962.

George guests again without Gracie who has, of course, retired from show business; this time, it's to say "good night" to Paar, who is leaving the show.

T415 The Tonight Show. NBC. ca. 1963.
George makes an appearance the night after his best friend, Jack Benny, had been on the show. The program is making a visit to the West Coast from its usual home in New York City. **SEE R1028.**

T416 The Jack Paar Show. NBC. ca. 1963.
George makes yet another appearance on this variety show.

T417 The Jack Benny Program. "Jack Is Kidnapped." CBS. March 12, 1963.
George appears with Merry Anders in this episode about bank robbers.

T418 Bob Hope Birthday Special. NBC. May 29, 1963.
George joins Lucille Ball, Milton Berle, Bing Crosby, Jimmy Durante and Frank Sinatra in a birthday salute to Bob Hope.

T419 The Perry Como Special. NBC. October 3, 1963.
George, June Allyson, Cyd Charisse, the Ray Charles Singers and Allan Sherman engage in comedy and music with Perry Como.

T420 Sing Along With Mitch. NBC. ca. 1964.
George appears on this musical variety show hosted by Mitch Miller.

T421 The Jack Benny Program. "How Jack Met George Burns." CBS. January 7, 1964.
George beats Jack in a game of golf, which infuriates Jack and leads George to reminisce about their first meeting. In relating the story to Jack's secretary, George begins by saying that he and Jack were working together in Chicago and Jack insisted that they start splitting their money evenly because "he's as good as George." George calls him ungrateful and declares he could do the act with anybody, even the landlady's daughter. It's an idea that Jack scoffs at until he visits the theater backstage and hears the voice of the landlady's daughter. The episode ends with a song and Jack chasing George offstage with a hook. Gracie's voice is heard (as the landlady's daughter), but she does not appear on the show.

T422 The Hollywood Palace. ABC. March 21, 1964.
George makes the first of several appearances as guest and host on this lavish variety show broadcast live from Hollywood's ABC Palace Theater. Tonight's host is Nat "King" Cole.

T423 The Hollywood Palace. ABC. March 28, 1964.
George is host to Mel Brooks, juggler Rudy Cardenas, the Dunhills, Sergio Franchi, The Lennon Sisters, Patti Page, Carl Reiner and Mac Ronay.

T424 The Tonight Show Starring Johnny Carson. NBC. ca. 1965.

T425 The Hollywood Palace. ABC. February 13, 1965.
George hosts Rich Little, Wayne Newton and Connie Stevens.

T426 The Hollywood Palace. ABC. May 15, 1965.
George is host to Mel Brooks, Metropolitan Opera star Mary Costa, highwire act the Flying Zacchinis (who perform outside the theater), Jack Jones, Carl Reiner, juggling act Cully Richards & Co. and the singing group, the Young Americans.

Review: "The comic grace of George Burns wears well over the years." (**Variety**, May 19, 1965).

T427 An Evening With Carol Channing. CBS. February 18, 1966.
George and David McCallum join Carol on her first variety special.

T428 The Tonight Show Starring Johnny Carson. NBC. March 17, 1966.

T429 Wayne & Shuster Take an Affectionate Look at...George Burns. CBS. July 19, 1966.
In this documentary program (a summer replacement series), the Canadian comedians Johnny Wayne and Frank Shuster profile George Burns' career.

Review: "Best of show featured vintage footage with Burns doing a soft shoe, singing a couple of his zany songs and playing straight man--with throw-away lines--to the late Gracie Allen." (**Variety**, July 20, 1966).

T430 The Lucy Show. "Lucy and George Burns." CBS. September 12, 1966. George meets Lucy while at the bank to review some documents and invites her to be his new partner. He and Lucy perform a vaudeville routine, including a soft shoe routine to "Some Of These Days." Jack Benny is heard on the telephone as George's agent.

T431 The Hollywood Palace. ABC. September 17, 1966.
In the season opener, Bing Crosby hosts guests George Burns (who sings), Sid Caeser, Lola Falana, the Mamas & Papas and the Rodins, a male and female aerialist duo who perform their act in a Hollywood parking lot near the theater from which the program emanates. **SEE T715.**

Review: "George Burns, for all his wit, is also a singer whose mission is to perpetuate obscure songs." (**Variety**, September 21, 1966).

T432 The Tonight Show Starring Johnny Carson. NBC. September 28, 1966.

T433 The Smothers Brothers Comedy Hour. CBS. February 19, 1967.
George guests with Jack Benny. A clip from this show appears in the HBO special on Benny, **Comedy In Bloom** (T713), but indicates that their appearance was in 1968.

T434 The Tonight Show Starring Johnny Carson. NBC. March 9, 1967.

T435 The Hollywood Palace. ABC. March 18, 1967.
George is host to Lainie Kazan, The King Family and Enzo Stuarti. **SEE T721.**

T436 The Tonight Show Starring Johnny Carson. NBC. October 2, 1967.

T437 The Kraft Music Hall. "Tin Pan Alley Today." NBC. October 11, 1967.
George hosts this edition of the musical variety show, which features Nancy Ames, Dick Cavett, Sergio Mendes and Brasil '66 and Dionne Warwick.

T438 The Dean Martin Show. NBC. January 18, 1968.
George performs with Dean in the early years of his long-running comedy variety show.

T439 Carol Channing and 101 Men. ABC. February 29, 1968.
George Burns guests on long-time friend Channing's special, joining Eddy Arnold and Walter Matthau.

T440 Jack Benny's Carnival Nights. NBC. March 20, 1968.
George makes a cameo appearance (along with Don Drysdale, Bob Hope, Dean Martin, The Smothers Brothers and Danny Thomas) in a highly-rated Jack Benny special that stars Lucille Ball, vaudevillian Ben Blue, Johnny Carson and Paul Revere and the Raiders.

T441 The Tonight Show Starring Johnny Carson. NBC. July 18, 1968.

T442 That's Life. ABC. September 24, 1968.
George delivers a monologue on the first episode of this comedy variety series which stars Robert Morse and E. J. Peaker. Maureen Arthur, The Association, Tony Randall, The Turtles, the Elliot Lawrence Orchestra and the United States Air Force Academy Chorale also perform.

T443 The Dean Martin Show. NBC. ca. 1969.

T444 The Jackie Gleason Show. CBS. ca. 1969.
George is a guest on "The Great One's" variety show.

T445 Chrysler Presents The Bob Hope Special. NBC. February 17, 1969.
Vaudeville is re-interpreted by host Bob Hope, George, Bing Crosby, Lisa Miller, Martha Raye and Diana Ross and The Supremes. A few members of the **Laugh-In** cast were also present as were Jack Benny and Johnny Carson.

Review: "And the great underwritten comedic skills of George Burns were refreshingly apparent in an old Burns & Allen turn as reborn via young comedienne Lisa Miller (who very wisely strove for Gracie's timing while eschewing the ding-dong projection)." (**Variety**, February 19, 1969).

T446 The Tonight Show Starring Johnny Carson. NBC. February 27, 1969.

T447 This is Tom Jones. ABC. April 14, 1969.
George is a guest on this musical variety show starring Welsh singer Tom Jones.

T448 The Brass are Coming. NBC. October 29, 1969.
Herb Alpert and the Tijuana Brass host the show with guests George Burns and Petula Clark.

T449 The Tonight Show Starring Johnny Carson. NBC. November 23, 1969.

T450 Jack Benny's New Look. NBC. December 3, 1969.
Jack Benny gets into the spirit of the 1960's with guests George Burns, Eddie "Rochester" Anderson, Gregory Peck, Gary Puckett and the Union Gap and Nancy Sinatra. Lucille Ball makes an appearance, and Frank Nelson (a longtime Benny sidekick) has a cameo. Peck joins Burns and Benny in a vaudeville routine, a surprisingly (to some) effective bit. **SEE T743.**

T451 George Burns Sings. WPIX, New York. ca. 1969 or 1970.
This half hour program was the brainchild of former Burns and Allen radio show producer/director Hendrik Booraem, Jr.

T452 The David Frost Show. Syndicated. n.d.
George guests with The Mills Brothers.

T453 The Kraft Music Hall: The Friars Club Roasts Jack Benny. NBC. January 21, 1970.
George joins Vice President Spiro Agnew, Milton Berle, Johnny Carson, Dennis Day, Phil Harris, Alan King and Ed Sullivan on the dais when the Friars toast and roast Jack Benny.

T454 The Hollywood Palace. ABC. February 7, 1970.
The final original entry in ABC's answer to **The Ed Sullivan Show** airs tonight with its most frequent host, Bing Crosby. George appears in a clip package with all the major stars who performed on the program during its run. Discount Video Tapes, Inc. of Burbank, CA used to offer a video of this particular episode but it is no longer available. **SEE VG11.**

T455 The Bob Hope Show. NBC. November 16, 1970.
Bob Hope hosts another vaudeville tribute with George, Lucille Ball, Tom Jones and Danny Thomas.

T456 Here's Lucy. "Lucy and Jack Benny's Biography." CBS. November 23, 1970.
George appears in a cameo in an episode based on Lucy going to Jack Benny's home to type his memoirs.

T457 The Tonight Show Starring Johnny Carson. NBC. February 17, 1971.

T458 Everything You Always Wanted to Know About Jack Benny but Were Afraid to Ask. NBC. March 10, 1971.
George, Lucille Ball, Phil Harris, Bob Hope, author Dr. David Reuben, Dionne Warwick and John Wayne guest in this special built around biographical sketches from Jack's career, including how Jack and George first met.

T459 The Osmond Brothers Show. CBS. March 23, 1971.
The five Osmond brothers play host to George and Tina Cole in a one-hour variety special.

T460 The Tonight Show Starring Johnny Carson. NBC. May 19, 1971.

T461 The Tonight Show Starring Johnny Carson. NBC. August 2, 1971.

T462 Bobby Darin: The Darin Invasion. Syndicated. October 1971.
Darin's only television special before his premature death featured guest stars George Burns and Linda Ronstadt. **SEE VG21.**

T463 The Tonight Show Starring Johnny Carson. NBC. November 12, 1971.

T464 The Tonight Show Starring Johnny Carson. NBC. February 21, 1972.

T465 Playhouse New York. "The 1940's--The Great Radio Comedians." WNET. May 12, 1972.
This retrospective on the lost art of radio comedy features films, sound, and photos of the great radio comedians is co-hosted by George Burns, Jack Benny and Edgar Bergen and Charlie McCarthy. George retraces the comedic art of Gracie Allen.

T466 The Tonight Show Starring Johnny Carson. NBC. June 29, 1972.

T467 The Ken Berry "Wow" Show. ABC. July 22, 1972.
George guests on the second show of Berry's summer replacement series, joining Chad Everett and Lyle Waggoner.

T468 The Tonight Show 10th Anniversary. NBC. September 30, 1972.
The show, which is being broadcast over two nights (September 29 and 30), features guests from past shows, including George.

T469 The Midnight Special. NBC. ca. 1973.
George is guest host on this popular music program.

T470 Jack Benny's First Farewell Special. NBC. January 18, 1973.
Jack Benny announces his "retirement" from show business and Johnny Carson, Bob Hope, and Ronald Reagan, Flip Wilson, Joey Heatherton, Isaac Hayes and Lee Trevino appear to help him reminisce. George arrives to present Jack with a special gift.

T471 The Tonight Show Starring Johnny Carson. NBC. February 13, 1973.

T472 Ann-Margret--When You're Smiling. NBC. April 4, 1973.
A portion of Ann-Margret's night club act is transferred to television. George and Bob Hope are guest stars.

T473 The Tonight Show Starring Johnny Carson. NBC. July 2, 1973.

T474 The Tonight Show Starring Johnny Carson. NBC. October 16, 1973.

T475 The Many Faces of Comedy. ABC. December 4, 1973.
Alan King plays host to George and other comedic experts Milton Berle, Godfrey Cambridge, Nancy Dussault, Totie Fields, Don Knotts, Steve Landesberg, Rich Little, Howard Morris, Danny Thomas and Henny Youngman as they explore the humor of yesterday and today.

T476 The Tonight Show Starring Johnny Carson. NBC. December 28, 1973.

T477 Hi-Ho, Steverino: A 25th Anniversary Salute to Steve Allen. ABC. ca. 1974.
George appears on this tribute to the multi-talented Steve Allen.

T478 One More Time. CBS. January 10, 1974.
George, Patti Andrews, Pearl Bailey, Pat Boone, Carol Channing, George Gobel, The Jackson Five, The Mills Brothers, The Pointer Sisters, Tiny Tim and others represent the past and present in comedy and music.

T479 Jack Benny's Second Farewell Special. NBC. January 24, 1974.
Jack tries one more time to "retire." In addition to George, who appears in a skit with Jack portraying Roman statues with "pigeon trouble," the guest stars are Johnny Carson, Redd Foxx and Dinah Shore with cameos by **Dragnet** stars Jack Webb and Harry Morgan.

T480 The Tonight Show Starring Johnny Carson. NBC. June 7, 1974.

T481 The Tonight Show Starring Johnny Carson. NBC. November 13, 1974.
SEE D41.

T482 The Today Show. NBC. ca. 1975.
Barbara Walters interviews George on the early morning news show.

T483 The Smothers Brothers Comedy Hour. NBC. January 13, 1975.
George is one of the guests on this comedy variety show.

T484 Televised ceremony presenting George with the Will Rogers

Humanitarian Award from the American Academy of Humor. ABC. January 25, 1975.

T485 Entertainment Hall of Fame Awards. NBC. February 22, 1975. Gene Kelly plays host to George Burns, Richard Chamberlain, Roy Clark, Bette Davis, Sandy Dennis and Peter Falk.

T486 The Tonight Show Starring Johnny Carson. NBC. September 2, 1975.

T487 The Rich Little Show. NBC. September 3, 1975.
George guests on this comedy special with Glen Campbell, Sandy Duncan and Peter Marshall.

T488 The Adventures of Ellery Queen. "The Adventure of Veronica's Veils." NBC. November 13, 1975.
George plays the part of a burlesque house owner who has died and appears at his own funeral on videotape telling the audience that he has been murdered. Jim Hutton plays the series title role; co-starring on tonight's episode are Julie Adams, Jack Carter, William Demarest, Don Porter and Barbara Rhoades.

T489 Saturday Night Live With Howard Cosell. ABC. November 1975.
George appears on this variety show with sports announcer and personality Howard Cosell.

T490 The Merv Griffin Show. Syndicated. ca. 1976.

T491 The Mike Douglas Show. Syndicated. ca. 1976.

T492 The Tonight Show Starring Johnny Carson. NBC. January 1, 1976.

T493 The Entertainer of the Year Awards. CBS. January 11, 1976.
George receives an award for his role in **The Sunshine Boys** (F37). The special was taped December 21, 1975 at Caesars Palace in Las Vegas.

T494 Joys! NBC. March 5, 1976.
Thirty guests, all comedians, at a Bob Hope party disappear and the police and private detectives solve the mystery. George is one of the guests.

T495 The 48th Annual Academy Awards. ABC. March 29, 1976.
George receives the Best Supporting Actor Oscar from Linda Blair and Ben Johnson for his work in the 1975 film, **The Sunshine Boys** (F37).

T496 The Tonight Show Starring Johnny Carson. NBC. July 1, 1976.

T497 NBC's First 50 Years On the Air: Part II. NBC. October 24, 1976.
This "big event" is a 270-minute retrospective on the history of NBC. George Burns reportedly appears in two parts of the show. **SEE T498.**

T498 NBC's First 50 Years On the Air: Part IV. NBC. November 21, 1976.
Gracie's voice, as well as George's, may have been heard on tonight's installment. The audio version of this (D216) indicates this was Part III rather than Part IV. **SEE T497.**

T499 The Tonight Show Starring Johnny Carson. NBC. November 30, 1976.

T500 The George Burns Special. CBS. December 1, 1976.
George is joined by Johnny Carson, Madeline Kahn, Walter Matthau, The Osmond Brothers and Chita Rivera in this variety show, taped in November 1976. Madeline Kahn plays the part of Gracie in a Burns and Allen routine. Due to a network audio problem the first seven minutes of the show were broadcast without sound.

Review: "Gracie Allen's unique talent can best be understood when someone else tries to do her material." (**Variety**, December 8, 1976).

T501 The Muppet Show. Syndicated. ca. 1977.
Billed as the "king" of comedy, George makes a special guest appearance during the puppets' second year on television. **SEE VG19.**

T502 The Entertainer of the Year Awards. CBS. January 16, 1977.
George appears as a presenter on this seventh annual show.

T503 **The Tonight Show Starring Johnny Carson**. NBC. February 21, 1977.

T504 **People's Command Performance**. CBS. April 7, 1977.
George co-hosts the show with Bernadette Peters. Performers appear courtesy of a public opinion survey (not to be confused with the **People's Choice Awards**).

T505 **When TV Was Young: Part I**. CBS. April 28, 1977.
Short films of early television comedy shows, including **The George Burns and Gracie Allen Show**, are aired.

T506 **NBC: The First Fifty Years: A Closer Look**. NBC. October 23, 1977.
Narrated by Orson Welles, with George Burns, Chevy Chase, Dan Haggerty, Burt Reynolds and Don Rickles, this 150-minute show looks at the history of NBC.

T507 **The Tonight Show Starring Johnny Carson**. NBC. November 14, 1977.

T508 **The George Burns One-Man Show**. CBS. November 23, 1977.
George is joined by Ann-Margret, Johnny Carson, Bob Hope, Gladys Knight and the Pips and The Captain and Tennille as George contemplates his mortality. This special was nominated for an Emmy as Outstanding Special--Comedy-Variety or Music but lost to one hosted by Bette Midler.

Review: "There is a metronome built into the head of every great comic that makes comedic gold out of base material, and few do it better than George Burns." (**Variety**, November 30, 1977).

T509 **Circus of the Stars**. CBS. December 5, 1977.
George appears in this occasional series of specials which features entertainers in the role of circus performers. He did not appear as a ringmaster; the exact nature of his participation as a performer is unknown at this time.

T510 **Alice**. "Oh, George Burns." CBS. January 1, 1978.
George pays a visit to Mel's Diner and movie fan *Vera* (Beth Howland) thinks she's seeing God. This episode has also been referred to as "Ladies and Gentlemen, Presenting Burns and Alice" and "Vera Meets George Burns."

T511 **Texaco Presents the Bob Hope All-Star Comedy Tribute to the Palace Theatre**. NBC. January 8, 1978.
George returns to his roots in this 90-minute salute to vaudeville, hosted by Bob Hope, which also stars Sammy Davis Jr., Eydie Gorme, Carol Lawrence and Steve Lawrence.

T512 **Dean Martin Celebrity Roast**. NBC. February 7, 1978.
Frank Sinatra is "roasted" by his fellow entertainers, including George. The program was taped at the MGM Grand Hotel in Las Vegas, NV.

T513 **The Goldie Hawn Special**. CBS. March 1, 1978.
Goldie hosts George along with Shaun Cassidy, The Harlem Globetrotters, John Ritter and the Patrica Birch Dancers.

T514 **Hollywood Out-Takes**. NBC. March 26, 1978.
In a prelude to tonight's Oscar telecast, George joins columnist Marilyn Beck in co-hosting a collection of previously unseen clips from this year's Academy Award-nominated films.

T515 **Celebration of 50 Years: CBS On the Air**. CBS. March 26, 1978.
George co-hosts one of the segments when CBS, over a span of seven nights (March 26 to April 1) and nine and one-half hours, pays tribute to its five decades of radio and television. Walter Cronkite and Mary Tyler Moore host the entire special with a number of other celebrities acting as co-hosts.

T516 **The National Collegiate Cheerleading Championships**. CBS. April 24, 1978.
George appears with Phyllis George, Bruce Jenner, Gene Kelly, Cheryl Ladd and Lou Rawls on this ninety minute variety show special.

T517 **Stars Salute Israel at Thirty**. NBC. May 8, 1978.
George may have had a cameo in this special.

T518 **Dean Martin Celebrity Roast**. NBC. May 10, 1978.
George appears to roast James Stewart. The program was taped at the MGM Grand Hotel in Las Vegas, NV.

T519 **Dean Martin Celebrity Roast**. NBC. May 17, 1978.
George appears at the Las Vegas, Nevada MGM Grand Hotel as tonight's guest of honor.

T520 **Happy Birthday, Bob**. NBC. May 29, 1978.
This three hour gala performance in honor of Bob Hope and his work with the USO features President Gerald Ford, Lynn Anderson, Pearl Bailey, Lucille Ball, George and other entertainers. The program was taped at The Kennedy Center for Performing Arts in Washington, D.C.

T521 **The Comedy Company**. CBS. July 21, 1978.
George appears as himself in a serio-comic film about the personal and professional struggles of comedic hopefuls and the nightclub in which they hone their craft. Jack Albertson, Michael Brandon, Herbert Edelman, Howard Hesseman, Lawrence-Hilton Jacobs, Susan Sullivan, Joyce Van Patten and Abe Vigoda co-star.

T522 **The Dick Cavett Show**. PBS. ca. 1979.
SEE B329.

T523 **The Today Show**. NBC. ca. 1979.
George is interviewed by Gene Shalit. **SEE T702.**

T524 **The Other Broadway**. Syndicated. January 1979.
In this London special which he co-hosts with Abbe Lane, George performs some of his monologues. This show was actually taped in 1975.

T525 **The Tonight Show Starring Johnny Carson**. NBC. January 19, 1979.

T526 **George Burns' 100th Birthday Party**. CBS. January 22, 1979.
Party guests Milton Berle, Debbie Boone, Pat Boone, Johnny Carson, Bob Hope, George Jessel, Dean Martin, Steve Martin, Gregory Peck, Helen Reddy, Don Rickles and James and Gloria Stewart join guest stars Goldie Hawn and Andy Gibb in helping the birthday boy celebrate the 100th anniversary of the day of his birth--17 years early--since he plans to be playing the London Palladium that evening. George and Goldie duet on "Some of These Days" and George brings the festivities to a close with "The Party's Over." The program's producer/director was Stan Harris, who shared producing duties with Irving Fein on George's Emmy-nominated 1977 special, **The George Burns One-Man Show** (T508).

T527 **The 51st Annual Academy Awards**. ABC. April 9, 1979.
George joins Brooke Shields in presenting the Oscar for Best Supporting Actress to Maggie Smith for her work in 1978's **California Suite**.

T528 **The Barbara Walters Special**. ABC. May 29, 1979.
George is interviewed by Barbara Walters about his life and career both with and without Gracie. George ends the interview by saying "Say good night, Barbara." **SEE VG5, T619, T723, T742, T745, B489.**

T529 **The Bob Hope Show**. NBC. December 7, 1979.
George is a guest on one of Bob Hope's specials.

T530 **The Tonight Show Starring Johnny Carson**. NBC. January 3, 1980.
George is among the guests on this late night show.

T531 **10th Annual Entertainer of the Year Awards Show**. CBS. January 23, 1980.
In a variety special taped at Caesar's Palace in Las Vegas, George hosts the presentation of awards as selected by the American Guild of Variety Artists (AGVA), the world's largest theatrical union. Recipients of the AGVA awards receive a "Georgie" named for entertainer George M. Cohan. George performs "I Wish I Was Eighteen Again." Among the winners: Billy Joel, Donna Summer, Mitzi Gaynor, Wayland Flowers & Madame, The Village People, Doc Severinsen, Kenny Rogers, Gilda Radner, Robin Williams and Benji. Comedian Red Skelton received the Golden Award for his lifetime of providing entertainment to the American public.

T532 **Miss World Beauty Contest**. February 1980.

George makes an appearance on this pageant special.

T533 Ann-Margret - Hollywood Movie Girls. ABC. May 3, 1980.
Ann-Margret is joined by mentor George Burns in her first special for ABC. Dom DeLuise, Danny DeVito, Dean-Paul Martin, Roger Moore and Bill Saluga lend their talents as well in this musical variety tribute to Hollywood hopefuls, past and present. Costumes were by Bob Mackie.

T534 The Tonight Show Starring Johnny Carson. NBC. October 2, 1980.

T535 George Burns in Nashville??? NBC. November 13, 1980.
Following the release of his country album, "I Wish I Was Eighteen Again," (D27) George taped his first country music special at the Opryland/Grand Ole Opry complex in Nashville, Tennessee with guests Roy Acuff, Larry Gatlin and The Gatlin Brothers, Loretta Lynn, Minnie Pearl and Ben Smathers and the Stoney Mountain Cloggers. George sings six songs from his album, including the title cut, "Old Bones" and "A Real Good Cigar," joins Loretta Lynn for a song "Do You Believe Me?," joins Minnie Pearl in a comedy routine about her never-ending romantic problems and shows the Grand Ole Opry dancers what a New York boy from Beverly Hills can do. The special was originally intended for airing on November 15, 1980 and was rebroadcast on April 13, 1981. **SEE B403.**

Review: "...an object lesson in how to hold an audience by underplaying, illustrated by a master of the art." (**Variety**, November 19, 1980).

T536 30 Years of TV Comedy's Greatest Hits. NBC. November 25, 1980.
Beatrice Arthur, Jane Curtin, Howard Hesseman, Carl Reiner and Dick Van Dyke host a two-hour special that, among other things, looks back at memorable moments from shows in various comedy categories representing all three major networks. The program features clips of over one hundred stars in approximately forty shows, including **Burns and Allen**. In another segment of the program, Gracie is among those chosen to receive a special "tribute to comedy greats." Taping took place at the Hollywood Palladium on November 20, 1980.

T537 Bob Hope's 30th Anniversary TV Special. January 18, 1981.
George joins Ann-Margret, Lucille Ball, Milton Berle, Sammy Davis Jr., Douglas Fairbanks Jr., Eydie Gorme, Steve Lawrence, Marie Osmond, Brooke Shields, Danny Thomas, Tanya Tucker and Robert Urich in a two-hour show celebrating Bob Hope's three decades in television.

T538 American Bandstand. ABC. January 27, 1981.
George appears on this popular music dance show hosted by Dick Clark.

T539 A Love Letter to Jack Benny. NBC. February 5, 1981.
The late Jack Benny (who died in 1974) is remembered by his best friend, George Burns, and others, including Johnny Carson and Bob Hope. The two-hour special utilizes clips from Benny's own television series and specials. **SEE B413.**

T540 Two of a Kind: George Burns and John Denver. ABC. March 30, 1981.
George teams up with his **Oh, God!** (F38) co-star John Denver in this musical variety special. **SEE VG23.**

T541 Live From Studio 8H: 100 Years of America's Popular Music. NBC. April 27, 1981.
George hosts Steve Lawrence and Eydie Gorme, Gregory Hines, Henry Mancini and Sarah Vaughn as they take viewers on a tuneful trip through a century of America's favorite musical genres in this third entry in the Emmy-winning series of specials. George's musical contributions include joining Steve and Eydie in "Alexander's Ragtime Band" and "Don't Get Around Much Anymore" with Hines as well as soloing on "This Is the Army" and "Old Bones." Paul Simon had been scheduled to appear but was not able to. First Lady Nancy Reagan provided taped remarks. Composer Irving Berlin (at 92, older than George) contributed new lyrics to his "Say It with Music" for the telecast's finale. Studio 8H was the origination point of **Let's Dance**, an NBC radio program credited with giving swing music nationwide attention. The program was an Armstrong Circle Theatre presentation (not to be confused with the original dramatic anthology series by that name that ran from 1950-1963; Armstrong apparently revived the name).

T542 Academy of Country Music Awards. NBC. April 30, 1981.
George receives the association's Social Achievement Award for his work in country music in 1980. The live broadcast was held at the Shrine Auditorium in downtown Los Angeles and was hosted by Larry Gatlin, Don Meredith and Tammy Wynette.

T543 The Tonight Show Starring Johnny Carson. NBC. November 13, 1981.

T544 George Burns' Early, Early, Early Christmas Special. NBC. November 16, 1981.
Guests Ann-Margret, Hans Conried, the Hawkins Family, Bob Hope, and The Playboy Playmates (who sing "I Ain't Got Nobody") are showcased in this variety hour. The special, taped at NBC's Burbank, California studios on June 27 and 28, 1981 includes a duet by George and Ann-Margret, a medley with George and the Hawkins Family, George and Bob Hope in a sketch about entertaining the troops and a "Scrooge" bit with George and Hans Conried. **SEE B354.**

T545 Showbiz Today. CNN. November 23, 1981.
Harry Von Zell's obituary notice includes a film clip from **The George Burns and Gracie Allen Show.** He appeared on the television show as an actor and as its announcer from 1951 to 1958 and had also appeared with Burns and Allen during their days in radio.

T546 George Burns in Concert. HBO. December 20, 1981.
This is a taped concert of George's stage act performed at the Hamilton Place Theatre in Toronto, Ontario, Canada.

T547 Night of 100 Stars. ABC. March 8, 1982.
George appears in the first extravaganza of its kind to raise money for the Actors Fund, televised from New York City's Radio City Music Hall (pre-taped in front of an audience of approximately six thousand people who had paid between fifty and one thousand dollars per ticket).

T548 Bob Hope Laughs with the Movie Awards. NBC. March 28, 1982.
George, Andy Gibb, Ann Jillian, and Lee Marvin guest in a parody of the most recent Academy Award-nominated films.

T549 The Tonight Show Starring Johnny Carson. NBC. August 13, 1982.

T550 Two of a Kind. CBS. October 9, 1982.
In what is billed as his television dramatic debut, George plays the part of a widower, Ross "Boppy" Minor, in this made-for-tv movie. Placed in a nursing home by his son (Cliff Robertson) after the death of his wife, "Boppy" regains his will to live with the help of his mentally handicapped grandson (Robby Benson). Barbara Barrie, Dirk Blocker, Ronny Cox, Karla DeVito, Geri Jewell, Frances Lee McCain and Peggy McCay co-star. Songwriters James Di Pasquale and Dory Previn received an Emmy for the movie's original song, "We'll Win the World."

T551 Showbiz Today. CNN. November 4, 1982.
George receives the Jack Benny Award for Excellence in Entertainment at UCLA. A filmed segment includes a clip of George with Gracie doing the soft shoe.

T552 The Tonight Show Starring Johnny Carson. NBC. November 5, 1982.

T553 George Burns and Other Sex Symbols. NBC. November 8, 1982.
Guesting as the "other sex symbols" are Linda Evans, Bernadette Peters, who sings "Wake Up & Live" and joins George in a routine from his days with Gracie and John Schneider. George sings "As Time Goes By," "Frog Kissin'" and "Young at Heart."

Review: "...the miracle is that George Burns...can still call on the precision timing that made him one of the master straightmen of all time." (**Variety**, November 17, 1982).

T554 The Fourth Annual TV Guide Special. January 1983.

T555 Bob Hope's Road to Hollywood. NBC. March 2, 1983.
Bob Hope's career in films is traced and applauded by guests Lucille Ball, George Burns, Rosemary Clooney, Rhonda Fleming, Dorothy Lamour, Virginia

Mayo, Dina Merrill, Martha Raye, Jane Russell and Jill St. John in this two-hour special.

T556 The Kids from Fame. NBC. March 3, 1983.
George hosts a London appearance by several of the stars from the prime-time series **Fame**, including Debbie Allen and Lori Singer.

T557 Grandpa, Will You Run With Me? NBC. April 3, 1983.
Producer Ken Ehrlich attempts to bridge the generation gap between the very old and the very young using film instead of concrete and steel in his hour-long special hosted by George Burns. The sense of appreciation and enjoyment each feels for the other is reflected in personal reminiscences, scenes and variety performances by Jack Albertson, Lloyd Bridges, Scatman Crothers, Quinn Cummings, Mac Davis, Erik Estrada, Andy Gibb, Dorothy Hamill, Nancy Marchand, Martin Mull and Kenny Rogers.

T558 The Tonight Show Starring Johnny Carson. NBC. May 11, 1983.

T559 Parade of Stars. ABC. May 22, 1983.
This show, "Performed without intermission for one night only as a benefit for the Actors' Fund of America," written and produced by Hildy Parks and presented by Alexander H. Cohen, recaptures the magic of vaudeville at its mecca, New York's Palace Theatre, in a tribute for its seventieth anniversary. Appearing as himself, George receives a standing ovation upon his introduction and speaks of his years with Gracie and their work in vaudeville. A multitude of other actors, dancers and singers play themselves or impersonate other great Palace stars and variety acts. The show was pre-taped.

T560 Happy Birthday, Bob! NBC. May 23, 1983.
George joins President and Mrs. Reagan, Lucille Ball, Christie Brinkley, Lynda Carter, Kathryn Crosby, Phyllis Diller, Dolores Hope, Ann Jillian, Loretta Lynn, Barbara Mandrell, Dudley Moore, George C. Scott, Tom Selleck, Brooke Shields, Cheryl Tiegs and Flip Wilson in wishing Bob Hope a happy 80th birthday during a three-hour show.

T561 The Tonight Show Starring Johnny Carson. NBC. September 16, 1983.

T562 George Burns Celebrates 80 Years in Show Business. NBC. September 19, 1983.
John Forsythe hosts a stellar cast (Ann-Margret, Milton Berle, Red Buttons, Johnny Carson, Jack Carter, Carol Channing, Phyllis Diller, Larry Gatlin and The Gatlin Brothers, Billy Graham, Shecky Greene, Buddy Hackett, Bob Hope, Bernadette Peters, Don Rickles, Kenny Rogers, James Stewart, Danny Thomas, Fred Travalena and Dionne Warwick) as they salute George for his long career in show business. George made his entrance to a standing ovation during the song "I Wish I Was Eighteen Again." He was nominated for an Emmy for Outstanding Individual Performance in a Variety or Music Program for this ninety-minute special but lost to Cloris Leachman for the **Screen Actors Guild 50th Anniversary Celebration.** **SEE B162.**

T563 George Burns: An Hour of Jokes and Songs. HBO. January 22, 1984.
George's night club act (for which he has writing credit) is again adapted for television.

T564 Bob Hope in Who Makes the World Laugh, Part 2. NBC. April 4, 1984.
In this sequel to an April 20, 1983 special George joins Bob, Lucille Ball and Mickey Rooney in acknowledging the contributions of American comedians.

T565 The Funniest Joke I Ever Heard. ABC. May 21, 1984.
George and other celebrities (Anthony Geary, John Hillerman, Dom DeLuise, Jack Lemmon, Rich Little, Barbara Mandrell, Brooke Shields, and James Stewart) as well as non-celebrities tell their favorite jokes in this program hosted by Heather Thomas and Robert Urich.

T566 The Tonight Show Starring Johnny Carson. NBC. September 14, 1984.

T567 George Burns' 'How to Live to be 100' Special. NBC. September 17, 1984.
Guests Catherine Bach, Dr. Joyce Brothers, Diahann Carroll, Bob Hope, Morty Jacobs, Arte Johnson, the Los Angeles Rams Cheerleaders, Todd Susman

and others join George in a comedy-variety special based upon his book, **How to Live to be 100--or More** (B24). Offering tips on longevity garners George and Catherine Bach this week's cover of **TV Guide** (B37).

Review: "...this comedy-variety hour starring the 88-year-old top banana was a lackluster, old-hat affair...It was mostly a familiar comedic road being traveled once again." (**Variety**, September 26, 1984).

T568 Phil Donahue. Syndicated. October 24, 1984.
George makes an appearance to promote his new film, **Oh God! You Devil** (F44), as well as his new book, **Dr. Burns' Prescription for Happiness** (B19). Included in the show is an audio from the Burns and Allen radio show as well as of his hit country song, "I Wish I Was Eighteen Again." George talks about his and Gracie's careers, including the time he turned down Frank Sinatra's offer to join the Burns and Allen radio show for $250 a week but took a group called The Smoothies instead.

T569 The Tonight Show Starring Johnny Carson. NBC. November 7, 1984.

T570 Comedy Tonight. Syndicated. ca. 1985 or 1986.
George appears on a series hosted by New York's Bill Boggs that mixes the new crop of comedians with more seasoned performers.

T571 TV's Funniest Game Show Moments #2. ABC. January 15, 1985.
William Shatner hosts this hour-long special produced by Mark Goodson Television Productions featuring game show hosts looking back at memorable footage from their shows. In a segment co-hosted by Steve Allen, George and Gracie are seen in a clip from their appearance on **What's My Line?** in June, 1954. **SEE T378.**

T572 Night of 100 Stars II. ABC. March 10, 1985.
George, as star #81, explains how medicine shows evolved into vaudeville, which introduces a segment featuring The McGuire Sisters, Doug Henning, Roby Gasser's Sea Lions, ventriloquist Ronn Lucas, Robert Klein, and The Manhattan Transfer.

T573 CNN. August 23, 1985.
A segment on the aging of America features a short clip of George and other celebrities.

T574 CNN. September 16, 1985.
George and Gracie are included in a story about the renewed popularity of old-time radio.

T575 Bob Hope Buys NBC? NBC. September 17, 1985.
George appears in a cameo on this Bob Hope special which has Bob's friends trying to help him buy NBC by raising funds via a telethon. Other guests include Milton Berle, Lynda Carter, Dick Cavett, Mr. T and Danny Thomas with a number of other celebrities making cameo appearances.

T576 The Tonight Show Starring Johnny Carson. NBC. October 16, 1985.

T577 CNN. October 28, 1985.
In a quick (nine second) bit furnished by KTLA of Los Angeles, George vows to say in show business until he's the "last one left."

T578 The Start of Something Big. Syndicated. October 31, 1985.
Steve Allen hosts this series which explains how people and things become famous, using Allen's own well-known composition as its title and theme song. Guests on this episode include George Burns, Phyllis Diller, Larry Manetti and Sheryl Lee Ralph.

T579 Entertainment Tonight. Syndicated. November 1985.
Tim Conway hosts a "Masters of Comedy" segment that includes clips of George and Gracie from **The Big Broadcast** (F19), **International House** (F20) and their television series.

T580 Larry King Live. CNN. November 7, 1985.
George shares tonight's guest spot with Judy Carne.

T581 Kraft Salutes George Burns' 90th Birthday--A Very Special Special. CBS. January 17, 1986.

Ann-Margret, Diahann Carroll, Billy Crystal, John Denver and Walter Matthau join host John Forsythe in an hour of accolades (via comedy, music, and anecdotes about George's long and varied career) as his 90th birthday approaches. The impressive list of pre-taped cameo appearances was headed by President Ronald Reagan and included Phylicia Ayers-Allen, Steve Allen, Milton Berle, Red Buttons, Johnny Carson, Carol Channing, Chevy Chase, Bill Cosby, Cary Grant, Bob Hope, Jack Lemmon, Rich Little, Joe Piscopo, Don Rickles, Joan Rivers, Kenny Rogers, Brook Shields, Frank Sinatra, James Stewart and Danny Thomas. The program, fully sponsored by Kraft through its advertising agency, J. Walter Thompson U.S.A., Inc., was written by Hal Goldman and produced by Irving Fein and Walter Miller for GBF Productions, Inc. The musical director was Peter Matz. A black tie audience attended the taping on January 11 at Los Angeles' Beverly Theater. **SEE B251.**

Review: "Highlight of the hour was the footage from past Burns performances, with and without Gracie Allen...The remarkable career of a remarkable man was best understood in the context of these performances over the years." (**Variety**, January 29, 1986).

T582 **Bugs Bunny/Loony Tunes All-Star 50th Anniversary**. CBS. January 14, 1986.
George joins other stars from popular music, screen, stage and television in saluting Warner Bros.' fifty-year contribution to the art of animation. This special was a continuation of a celebration that began several months earlier at New York's Museum of Modern Art. It was also a "Read More About It" book project with The Library of Congress and captioned for the deaf and hearing impaired.

T583 CNN. January 20, 1986.
George's 90th birthday is commemorate with scenes from the 1984 release, **Oh, God! You Devil** (F44) and stills of George with Gracie.

T584 CNN. March 24, 1986.
George is among the stars seen arriving at Irving "Swifty" Lazar's annual post-Oscar party at the Spago restaurant in Los Angeles.

T585 CNN. April 10, 1986.
A street outside the Cedars-Sinai Hospital in Beverly Hills is named in George's honor.

T586 CNN. May 2, 1986.
A profile of the declining **Playboy** empire includes a shot of George singing in one of the clubs.

T587 **NBC 60th Anniversary Celebration**. NBC. May 12, 1986.
George is seen in a clip from **The Tonight Show** and he and Gracie are heard in a Bob Hope-hosted segment saluting NBC radio when they purportedly were guests on the **Chase & Sanborn Hour** with Edgar Bergen and Charlie McCarthy, using shaving cream to decorate a birthday cake. It's an appearance that has, strangely, not lent itself to verification of a broadcast date, although Gracie was *scheduled* to make another appearance with Bergen on his *CBS* show in 1949 and George and Gracie did appear with Bergen on an NBC presentation called **The Bakers of America Salute the Armed Forces** (R915) which was sponsored by Chase & Sanborn; it's possible that this latter show actually provided the clip for this special.

T588 CNN. May 28, 1986.
George talks about signing a multi-year contract with Caesar's Palace in Las Vegas; another segment features him onstage on the American Association of Retired Persons convention.

T589 **Our World**. ABC. November 6, 1986.
This short-lived (competing with **The Cosby Show**) documentary series hosted by Linda Ellerbee and Ray Gandolph was an interesting, but not costly, experiment in packaging archival footage with commentary. Tonight's episode focused on 1954, including popular television programming. Scenes from **The George Burns and Gracie Allen Show** are featured. **SEE D263.**

T590 CNN. January 20, 1987.
George talks about his plans for his 91st birthday.

T591 CNN. January 25, 1987.

George's 91st birthday is noted with scenes from his party with guests Bob Hope, Steve Lawrence, Walter Matthau and James Stewart, photos of him and Gracie, a clip from **The George Burns and Gracie Allen Show**, stills from the 1975 film **The Sunshine Boys** (F37), George receiving one of his Hollywood Walk of Fame stars and George performing on stage.

T592 **Our World**. ABC. May 21, 1987.
Radio in 1937 is a topic of this episode and features popular entertainers George Burns and Gracie Allen. The documentary series is hosted by Linda Ellerbee and Ray Gandolph. **SEE D262.**

T593 CNN. January 17, 1988.
In a press conference George talks about his upcoming 92nd birthday, a new movie, a new book in progress and smoking; after the press conference, he signs autographs and is driven away in a limousine.

T594 CNN. January 20, 1988.
Carol Channing, Carl Reiner and Danny Thomas help George celebrate his 92nd birthday with a huge birthday cake.

T595 CNN. January 21, 1988.
In a look back at "Hollywood Happenings" for the week, George is seen at his 92nd birthday party.

T596 **Disney's Magic in the Magic Kingdom**. NBC. February 12, 1988.
George hosts a show for Walt Disney Productions featuring magic acts and is joined by comedy actor/magic aficionado Harry Anderson. World-famous illusionists Siegfried & Roy attempt to make the nearly eight stories high Sleeping Beauty Castle at Disneyland disappear. This special replaced the originally scheduled **Disney's DTV 'Doggone' Valentine Special** and was apparently encored on the Disney Channel on May 23, 1991.

T597 CNN. March 2, 1988.
Clips from George's new film **18 Again!** (F45) are featured.

T598 **America's Tribute to Bob Hope**. NBC. March 5, 1988.
In a show taped January 2 at the opening of The Bob Hope Cultural Center in Palm Desert, California George joins other old friends in honoring a fellow entertainer while simultaneously celebrating dance, drama and music. Hope receives the first annual "America's Hope Award," given to an American "who exemplifies the spirit of America," by President Ronald Reagan.

T599 CNN. March 24, 1988.
George is profiled to promote his latest film, **18 Again!** (F45). Included are clips of him with Gracie from their television show.

T600 CNN. March 31, 1988.
A profile of George promoting **18 Again!** (F45) includes clips of him and Gracie from their television series.

T601 CNN. March 31, 1988.
The University of Hartford in Hartford, Connecticut bestows an honorary doctorate upon George.

T602 CNN. April 1, 1988.
The "East Coast Happenings" segment features George receiving his honorary doctorate.

T603 CNN. April 12, 1988.
George is among the celebrities seen arriving at the Spago restaurant for Hollywood's traditional post-Academy Awards celebration.

T604 CNN. April 26, 1988.
A "fountain of youth" segment includes George, as well as other celebrities and experts on the subject.

T605 **Happy Birthday, Bob - 50 Stars Salute Your 50 Years with NBC**. NBC. May 1988.

T606 CNN. May 2, 1988.

Clips from Bob Hope's latest television special (which celebrates his 85th birthday and marks a half-century affiliation with NBC) includes a brief shot of George onstage.

T607 CNN. May 13, 1988.
George is seen as a guest at Bob Hope's 85th birthday party.

T608 American Comedy Awards. ABC. May 17, 1988.
George receives the special "Life Achievement Award" from Chevy Chase. **SEE T609, T610.**

T609 CNN. May 17, 1988.
George is shown receiving his award during the "American Comedy Awards" followed by a standing ovation. **SEE T608.**

T610 CNN. May 18, 1988.
George appears in a backstage clip from yesterday's **American Comedy Awards** show. **SEE T608.**

T611 60 Minutes. CBS. November 6, 1988.
In a segment hosted by Ed Bradley, George is seen rehearsing with his music director and Susan Anton at Caesar's Palace in Las Vegas. Next, he and Gracie perform an old vaudeville routine, and Gracie exhibits her off-center thought processes in a scene from one of their early television shows. George recounts the story of how he once cheated on Gracie, and the camera goes with him when he pays one of his regular visits to Gracie at Forest Lawn cemetery, where Gracie is buried. ("We're going to be on **60 Minutes**. We're working together again."), telling Ed Bradley that, when he dies, "...I'm going to change the billing. It's going to be Gracie Allen and George Burns." A clip is shown from the 1975 film **The Sunshine Boys** (F37), George and Ed visit George's old neighborhood on New York's Lower East Side, and the piece ends with George performing today's act, in which he recites a bit of his philosophy ("You can't help getting older, but you don't have to get old") and ends with the song "Young At Heart." **SEE T690.**

T612 The Today Show. NBC. November 14-15, 1988.
George appears in a two-part interview.

T613 Entertainment Tonight. Syndicated. November 15, 1988.

T614 Phil Donahue. Syndicated. November 16, 1988.
George's appearance to promote his new book, **Gracie: A Love Story** (B22), includes clips from **The George Burns and Gracie Allen Show**. He also sings "Young At Heart."

T615 CNN. November 17, 1988.
The "New York Happenings" segment finds George autographing his latest book; in another portion of the show he is seen giving a thank-you speech for receiving the American Image Award for lifetime achievement; in a photo opportunity, George kisses Eva Gabor, smokes his cigar, tells jokes and poses with singer Peggy Lee.

T616 Larry King Live. CNN. November 17, 1988.
Guest host Bernard Kalb interviews George.

T617 CNN. November 19, 1988.
In a review of the latest New York events George is seen at the podium at the American Image Awards as he receives the lifetime achievement award.

T618 The Tonight Show Starring Johnny Carson. NBC. November 23, 1988.

T619 The 50th Barbara Walters Special. ABC. November 29, 1988.
Highlights from twelve years' of interviews, including one with George from May 29, 1979 are stitched together in this milestone entry. See **VG5, T528.**

T620 CNN. December 4, 1988.
George is seen with Roger Stevens, Chairman of the Board of Trustees of The Kennedy Center, and the other honorees from the **11th Annual Kennedy Center Honors** ceremony, which is to be held on today's date and taped for broadcast on December 30, 1988. **SEE T623.**

T621 CBS This Morning. CBS. December 5, 1988.
George is interviewed about the Kennedy Center award. **SEE T623.**

T622 Good Morning, America. ABC. December 5, 1988.
Entertainment Editor Joel Siegel had interviewed George on December 3 concerning the Kennedy Center Honors as well as the honor of being "the oldest author ever of a number one bestselling book, **Gracie: A Love Story** (B22), and presents that interview here, mixed with clips of the December 4th gala as well as the State Department reception which was held on December 3rd. **SEE T623.**

T623 The 11th Annual Kennedy Center Honors: A Celebration of the Performing Arts. CBS. December 30, 1988.
Hosted by Walter Cronkite, the Kennedy Center Honors, which are for "individuals who throughout their lifetimes have contributed significantly to American culture through the performing arts," pay tribute to George Burns, Alvin Ailey, Myrna Loy, Alexander Schneider and Roger L. Stevens. John Denver introduces a film that traces George's life and career, ending with a clip of George on stage singing "Young At Heart." Bob Hope takes some playful jabs at George and President Ronald Reagan and then, on a serious note, says, "And, George, I think you know that sitting right up there in that box with you tonight, her heart filled with pride, is Gracie Allen...thanks for the laughs and for the memories." Tommy Tune and Ann Reinking end the segment with a dance salute to vaudeville. The program was taped December 4, 1988 in Washington, D.C. as a black-tie benefit. In making the August 4 announcement of the honorees, Chairman Ralph P. Davidson declared George to be "one of the nation's great entertainers." The irony of George being honored at the same ceremony as Myrna Loy was not unnoticed since George had recently revealed in **Gracie: A Love Story** (B22) that Loy was one of the few Hollywood actresses whom Gracie did not like. **SEE T620, T621, T622, VG70.**

T624 The Joan Rivers Show. Syndicated. ca. 1989.
George appears during the winter holiday season to promote his latest book, **All My Best Friends** (B35). During his interview, which was interspersed with clips of him and Gracie, he declares that he doesn't get stage fright, talks about his sold-out London Palladium 100th birthday engagement and says that Gracie died in 1962 (it was actually 1964). This show was rerun on May 27, 1991.

T625 CNN. January 8, 1989.
The latest awards ceremony for the Television Academy Hall of Fame (which includes George and Gracie) is featured. **SEE T629.**

T626 CNN. January 9, 1989.
Another clip featuring George and Gracie from the January 8 ceremony honoring the newest inductees into the Television Academy Hall of Fame is included in today's show. **SEE T629.**

T627 CNN. January 20, 1989.
Six and one-half minutes of today's show are devoted to George's 93rd birthday.

T628 Bob Hope's All-Star Super Bowl Party. NBC. January 21, 1989.
George, billed as "the world's oldest living football player," joins Bob Hope, Sammy Davis Jr., Shelley Long, singer Tiffany and quarterbacks Boomer Esiason and Joe Montana as Super Bowl XXIII draws near.

T629 The Fifth Annual Television Academy Hall of Fame. Fox. January 23, 1989.
Steve Lawrence and Eydie Gorme provide a musical tribute to Burns and Allen when George and Gracie are inducted into the Television Academy Hall of Fame along with Jack Benny, Chet Huntley and David Brinkley, Red Skelton, David Susskind and David L. Wolper in this special taped January 8th and hosted by Johnny Carson, Bob Hope and Burt Lancaster. George and Gracie's rarely seen grown children were also present. The honor will be symbolized by bas-relief sculptures placed in the Hall of Fame Plaza at the Academy of Television Arts and Sciences in North Hollywood, California. **SEE T625, T626.**

T630 The Pat Sajak Show. CBS. February 6, 1989.
George makes his only appearance on this short-lived late-night talk show, joining John Goodman, fight promoter Don King and boxer Mike Tyson.

T631 CNN. February 13, 1989.
George attends a celebrity fundraiser for the Cedars-Sinai Hospital in Los Angeles.

T632 **Hollywood Insider**. USA. February 25, 1989.
George is featured in a segment of this cable interview show.

T633 CNN. April 26, 1989.
Reactions to the death of Lucille Ball include George talking about his admiration for her. Also in the show is Miss Ball's obituary by Dennis Michael, again including a shot of George.

T634 CNN. April 27, 1989.
A montage tribute to Lucille Ball includes George.

T635 **Diet America Challenge**. CBS. April 28, 1989.
George's exercise video, **George Burns, His Wit and Wisdom** (VG7) is among those noted in this special hosted by Cheryl Tiegs, which examines how America's preoccupation with diet and fitness have affected ordinary people as well as celebrities.

T636 **Magical World of Disney: The Disney-MGM Studios Theme Park Grand Opening**. NBC. April 30, 1989.
George is among a galaxy of stars and world leaders who celebrate the historic joining of two magical names in show business as the new Florida complex officially opens for business. **SEE T637.**

T637 CNN. May 1, 1989.
A story on the opening of the Disney-MGM Studios Theme Park includes George on stage and George and Bob Hope putting their hand prints into wet cement, along with Mickey and Minnie Mouse and Roger Rabbit. **SEE T636.**

T638 CNN. May 11, 1989.
George's exercise video (VG7) is featured.

T639 **Entertainment Tonight**. Syndicated. July 20, 1989.

T640 **George Burns**. Showtime. August 1987. (out of order; had been '89)
Paris' Lido and Moulin Rouge help provide the backdrop for the production numbers; George provides the comic touch in this one-hour special.

T641 CNN. August 17, 1989.
George and Bob Hope hold a press conference to announce their upcoming joint appearance at New York's Madison Square Garden.

T642 CNN. August 18, 1989.
In the "Showbits" segment George and Bob Hope are seen at their recent press conference.

T643 **A Conversation with George Burns**. Disney. August 27, 1989.
George takes the stage at Walt Disney World in Florida and answers questions from the audience in this program and featured during the Disney Channel's Fall Preview Weekend. George won an Emmy for Outstanding Performance in Informational Programming for this special, which included film and television clips and anecdotes. Occasionally the Disney channel reruns the show as it did on December 2, 1990, September 14, 1994 and, most recently, on January 21, 1995.

T644 **Bob Hope's Love Affair with Lucy**. NBC. September 23, 1989.
George, who made two guest appearances with Lucille Ball after Gracie's death (T430, T456), joins Bob Hope, Kirk Cameron, Danny Thomas, Betty White and others to share stories about the legendary redhead. Hope appeared opposite Miss Ball (who died in April 1989) in many films and television shows and offers a retrospective of their work in this ninety-minute special.

T645 CNN. October 1, 1989.
George and Bob Hope's joint stage appearance at New York City's Madison Square Garden is featured; the segment includes a clip of George with Gracie.

T646 **Entertainment Tonight**. Syndicated. November 2, 1989.
George attends comic Sid Caesar's opening in New York City.

T647 CNN. November 2, 1989.
George's attendance at comedian Sid Caesar's New York show is featured.

T648 **Entertainment Tonight**. Syndicated. November 2, 1989.
George's appearance at Sid Caesar's live show in New York City is covered.

T649 **Good Morning America**. ABC. November 3 and 6, 1989.
This two-part interview with George conducted by Charles Gibson centers Friday on George's book, **All My Best Friends** (B35) and continues via tape on the following Monday, when they speak about age, George's "feud" with Groucho Marx, Milton Berle, the famous group of comedians who used to lunch together at the Hillcrest Country Club, early years in George's career and "George Burns, the philosopher." George talks about being booked at the London Palladium for two weeks when he turns one hundred years old. Charles Gibson ends by mentioning that George was honored by the Museum of Broadcasting in New York in a tribute held Sunday, November 5th, 1989, an event emceed by Marlo Thomas.

T650 **Phil Donahue**. Syndicated. November 6, 1989.
George appears in a promotion for his new book, **All My Best Friends** (B35). Carol Channing and Alan King appear on stage with George and they all answer questions from their host and the studio audience. Carol mentions that having Gracie's approval to work with George (after Gracie's retirement) was "like being knighted in St. James' court." Alan says he took the idea of using a cigar on stage from George after seeing a performance by Burns and Allen when he was eight years old. George and Carol sing a duet on Sophie Tucker's signature song, "Some of These Days."

T651 **Entertainment Tonight**. Syndicated. November 6, 1989.
George's tribute from the Museum of Broadcasting is noted.

T652 **Larry King Live**. CNN. November 10, 1989.
George discusses, among other things, being a "sex symbol." **SEE T756**.

T653 **The Tonight Show Starring Johnny Carson**. NBC. November 10, 1989.

T654 **Entertainment Tonight**. Syndicated. November 20, 1989.
Coverage of the Friars Club award for Bob Hope includes footage of George.

T655 **Showbiz Today**. November 24, 1989.
A profile of George designed to promote his latest book, **All My Best Friends** (B35), includes clips of **The George Burns and Gracie Allen Show**.

T656 **Fifty Years of Television: A Golden Celebration**. CBS. November 26, 1989.
George is among those who appear in this CBS special documentary hosted by Walter Cronkite, Kermit the Frog, Miss Piggy, Carl Reiner and Jane Seymour which examines the evolution of television programming since it began at the 1939 World's Fair. The show was part of "America's Homecoming on CBS," the name given by the network to its block of family entertainment during 1989's Thanksgiving week.

T657 **The Arsenio Hall Show**. Fox. January 2, 1990.
George talks about his "groupies."

T658 **The Byron Allen Show**. Syndicated. January 12, 1990.
In an appearance to promote his book, **All My Best Friends** (B35), George comments to Byron: "Here we are...Burns and Allen. You don't look like Gracie. You're too tall."

T659 **Entertainment This Weekend**. Syndicated. January 21, 1990.
George's most recent birthday is mentioned.

T660 **Entertainment Tonight**. Syndicated. January 22, 1990.
George's recently celebrated birthday (his 94th) is mentioned as well as his involvement in a music video for the eye disease, retinitis pigmentosa. **SEE VG6**.

T661 **Mary Hart Presents: Love in the Public Eye**. Syndicated. March 23, 1990.
George speaks briefly about **Gracie: A Love Story** (B22) and his marriage to Gracie in this special hosted by Mary Hart from **Entertainment Tonight**, saying that Gracie married him because he made her laugh. Other guests

offer comments on the effect of trying to maintain a marriage while living in publicity's spotlight (including Tom and Roseanne Arnold in their first national interview as a married couple). The program also gives the results of a Gallup poll of Americans concerning various germane subjects, including if they feel the press "goes overboard," if they always believe what they hear about celebrities and if they feel they have a right to know about the private lives of public figures.

T662 Conversation with Dinah. TNN. July 11, 1990.
George reminisces with Dinah about how he got his name, his show business beginnings, Gracie and their start on radio, Jack Benny, the Hillcrest Country Club Round Table, golfing, sings "The Grizzly Bear" and finishes with his version of "Young At Heart." A clip from his and Gracie's television show is also shown as well as some family photos of Burns and Allen and their children. The Nashville Network normally runs these programs more than one time, so dates may vary.

T663 Bob Hope's 'Don't Shoot, It's Only Me'. NBC. September 15, 1990.
In this special based on the book of the same title, George joins Bob in a throwback to vaudeville with a classic Burns and Allen routine and sand dance. Other guests include Milton Berle, Henry Kissinger, Frances Langford, Gloria Loring, President Ronald Reagan, Connie Stevens and Danny Thomas. Bob's wife, Dolores, also appears, and the special features footage from Bob's appearances with more American Presidents and stars.

T664 Arts & Entertainment Revue. A&E. September 21, 1990.
A segment of the program focusing on new home videos includes **Burns and Allen** television shows available from the Columbia/CBS Video Library. **SEE VG55.**

T665 CBS News Sunday Morning. CBS. October 28, 1990.
George and Gracie are included via a brief clip in a network remembrance of CBS chairman William S. Paley following his death. Another tribute to the broadcasting giant was produced by CBS News and aired on the network on October 31, 1990 in prime time.

T666 Entertainment Tonight. Syndicated. November 19, 1990.
George is seen in a clip as the California Friars Club salutes Danny Thomas.

T667 Entertainment Tonight. Syndicated. December 4, 1990.
George is featured in a clip as he sings "Ain't Misbehavin'" in a tribute to Frank Sinatra. **SEE T669.**

T668 Crook and Chase. TNN. December 5, 1990.
George is featured in an interview on The Nashville Network program (he did not appear in person) and is rerun the next day.

T669 Sinatra at 75: The Best is Yet to Come. CBS. December 16, 1990.
George joins Harry Connick, Jr., Ella Fitzgerald, Helen Forrest, Eydie Gorme, Jack Jones, Steve Lawrence, Peggy Lee, Sophia Loren, Paul Newman, Helen O'Connell, Tom Selleck, Jo Stafford, Barbra Streisand, The Manhattan Transfer, Bruce Willis and guest of honor Sinatra. Clips and stills are featured from radio and big-band years, television specials, movies, with Elvis Presley and Frank recording with Quincy Jones. **SEE T667.**

T670 Entertainment Tonight. Syndicated. January 8, 1991.
The program includes a promotional spot for George's upcoming television special to celebrate his ninety-fifth birthday. **SEE T676.**

T671 Entertainment Tonight. Syndicated. January 8, 1991.
George appears in a promotion of his upcoming 95th birthday special.

T672 The Today Show. NBC. January 18, 1991.

T673 Entertainment Tonight. Syndicated. January 21, 1991.
George celebrates his 95th birthday in Las Vegas.

T674 E! Entertainment Television. January 29, 1991.

T675 Entertainment Tonight. Syndicated. January 29, 1991.

T676 George Burns' 95th Birthday Party. CBS. February 1, 1991. Ann-Margret, Milton Berle, Red Buttons, Sid Caesar, Whitney Houston, Richard Lewis, Carl Reiner, Kenny Rogers, Rita Rudner, Bob Saget and Ben Vereen were scheduled to perform in a mix of music and comedy routines in this birthday salute to George, who contributed songs and monologues. Clips from the past showcase performances of George and Gracie, Jack Benny and a scene from the 1937 film, **A Damsel in Distress** (F30). The special was taped on January 6 at Television City in Hollywood. Reiner directed George's 1977 film **Oh, God!** (F38) and Rogers has included George in his photography collections. **SEE T670.**

Reviews: "Clips of Jack Benny in drag hoofing with Burns; of Burns, Gracie Allen and Fred Astaire dancing in **Damsel In Distress** and of other bits with Allen almost make the show worth watching." (**Daily Variety**, February 1, 1991). "...**George Burns' 95th Birthday Party** is one terrific celebration." (**The Hollywood Reporter**, February 1, 1991).

T677 Instant Recall. Syndicated. February 4, 1991. George comments on Groucho Marx in a segment devoted to slapstick comedy in film.

T678 Entertainment Tonight. Syndicated. February 6, 1991. George is seen in a clip that is part of a remembrance of the late Danny Thomas.

T679 Night Flight. Syndicated. February 16, 1991. In a clip from a USO broadcast (the original date is unknown, but it was during the Eisenhower presidency) George is seen in a chorus line with Jack Benny and James Stewart.

T680 The Very Best of 'The Ed Sullivan Show'. CBS. February 17, 1991. George and Gracie are seen in a clip from their appearance on **The Ed Sullivan Show** (probably in 1957 [T387]). The special is hosted by Carol Burnett and was the second-highest rated of the season in that genre according to **TV Guide** (behind the Academy Awards).

T681 The 33rd Annual Grammy Awards. February 20, 1991. George wins a Grammy Award for the audio recording (D40) of his book, **Gracie: A Love Story** (B22), although the award was not presented in person.

T682 Entertainment Tonight. Syndicated. March 1, 1991. George is among those who will take part in the upcoming Easter Seal Telethon. **SEE T683.**

T683 Easter Seal Telethon. Syndicated. March 2/3, 1991. George makes a midnight appeal to "give to Easter Seals." **SEE T682.**

T684 The 63rd Annual Academy Awards. ABC. March 25, 1991. In a segment introduced by Bob Hope, George and other stars reminisce about the first movie they ever saw.

T685 Memories...Then and Now. Syndicated. March 31, 1991. George is seen in the "Flash" segment doing exercises featured in his video. **SEE VG7.**

T686 Hollywood Insider. USA. April 14, 1991. A smoking ban in the card room of the Hillcrest Country Club in Los Angeles results in a letter to the organization's Board of Directors from George (seen in stills only; he was later excused from the rule).

T687 Entertainment Tonight. Syndicated. June 3, 1991. George appears at the National Bookseller's Convention in New York City to promote his new book, **Wisdom of the 90's** (B36).

T688 Entertainment Tonight. Syndicated. July 15, 1991. George is seen celebrating Milton Berle's 83rd birthday.

T689 Entertainment Tonight. Syndicated. October 4, 1991. The "Coming Attractions" segment includes a promo for the **60 Minutes** special airing the same evening. **SEE T690.**

T690 60 Minutes: The Entertainers. CBS. October 4, 1991.

This two-hour collection of clips culled from interviews the program has done over the years with show business personalities includes a portion of Ed Bradley's interview with George from 1988 in which George discusses his marriage to Gracie. **SEE T611, T689.**

T691 Entertainment Tonight. Syndicated. October 21, 1991.
The Jack Benny retrospective hosted by the Museum of Television and Radio is featured; George is seen in a clip from a television special, **Jack Benny's New Look** in which he, Benny, and Gregory Peck perform as a song-and-dance team. **SEE T450.**

T692 Funny Women of Television. NBC. October 24, 1991.
This show attempts to chronicle the development of the role of women comedians in television. Gracie Allen (introduced by Mary Tyler Moore) is shown in a short television clip from **The Burns and Allen Show** and is included in the older (stage and radio) age when women comedians were not individuals and played silly women who had to be controlled by males. Given Gracie's eight successful years in a television series and her numerous Emmy nominations, she is given curiously short shrift. Presented by the Museum of Television and Radio, the ninety-minute program was taped October 11, 1991 in Los Angeles, California.

T693 The Today Show. NBC. November 7, 1991.

T694 Regis & Kathie Lee. Syndicated. November 7, 1991.
George continues on the promotion trail for his book, **Wisdom of the 90's** (B36).

T695 Entertainment Tonight. Syndicated. November 11, 1991.
George is seen at a book signing of **Wisdom of the 90's** (B36).

T696 The Tonight Show Starring Johnny Carson. NBC. November 14, 1991.

T697 Entertainment Tonight. Syndicated. November 19, 1991.
George turns down the script to a fourth **Oh, God!** film because he "didn't like it."

T698 Entertainment Tonight. Syndicated. November 26, 1991.
It's announced that the December 3rd issue of **Playboy** will feature George on the cover.

T699 Entertainment Tonight. Syndicated. December 26, 1991.
George, Quincy Jones, and George Schlatter promote their upcoming television special, **The Meaning of Life** (T700), hosted by George and executive-produced by Jones and Schlatter with David Salzman.

T700 The Meaning of Life. CBS. December 27, 1991.
Hosted by George (who reminisces about Gracie) and executive-produced by George Schlatter, Quincy Jones, and David Salzman, the program asks an age-old question and the famous and not-so-famous attempt to answer it in this program, which is based upon the book, **The Meaning of Life: Reflections in Words and Pictures on Why We Are Here**, published by **Life** magazine. Contemplations by Erma Bombeck, Art Buchwald, Jimmy Connors, George Foreman, Alex Haley, Hammer, Quincy Jones, Dudley Moore, Paul Rodriguez, Marlo Thomas, Lily Tomlin, Betty White and Oprah Winfrey and songs by Garth Brooks, Natalie Cole and Kenny Rogers are interwoven with stories of ordinary people overcoming extraordinary obstacles as well as remarks by "average" Americans. **SEE T699.**

Reviews: "George Burns hosts ably..." (**Daily Variety**, December 27, 1991: 7). "Despite its good intentions, this special just isn't very special." (**The Hollywood Reporter**, December 27, 1991: 5).

T701 Entertainment Tonight. Syndicated. January 2, 1992.
George's caricature from Vincent Sardi, Jr.'s new book, **Off The Wall At Sardi's**, is featured.

T702 Today at 40. NBC. January 14, 1992.
George is seen in a 1979 **Today Show** interview with Gene Shalit, talking about a $1.25 cigar in this retrospective produced to celebrate the morning talk show's birthday. **SEE T523.**

T703 Entertainment Tonight. Syndicated. January 20, 1992.

George's 96th birthday is noted in the regular celebrity birthday segment.

T704 Entertainment Tonight. Syndicated. March 3, 1992.
George is seen congratulating Walter Matthau upon his receiving the first Screen Actors Guild Jack Oakie Award.

T705 The 64th Annual Academy Awards. ABC. March 30, 1992.
George is seen in character in a scene from **Oh, God!** (F38) in the opening segment of tonight's show, a montage of scenes that have made moviegoers laugh throughout the years.

T706 Entertainment Tonight. Syndicated. April 6, 1992.
George is honored by the United Jewish Fund for his aid to Russian Jews.

T707 19th Annual Daytime Emmy Awards. NBC. June 23, 1992.
George appears via a clip stating, "I'd date women my age if there *were* any women my age."

T708 The Arsenio Hall Show. Fox. August 17, 1992.
George appears with Bobby Vinton and discusses their joint recording (**D13**) as well as Gracie and the Peewee Quartet. He has also re-signed with Caesar's Palace and has done a video for Vinton's live show.

T709 Good Morning America. ABC. August 24, 1992.
George and Bobby Vinton appear to discuss their joint recording project. **SEE D18.**

T710 Crook and Chase. TNN. August 27, 1992.
In a segment shot in George's office at the old General Service Studios, he and singer Bobby Vinton discuss their recording of "As Time Goes By." **SEE D18.**

T711 The 44th Annual Emmy Awards. Fox. August 30, 1992.
In a bumper for how "TV watches TV," George is shown in a clip from **The George Burns and Gracie Allen Show** when he tunes in to his special television set and notes how cute Gracie is on TV.

T712 Entertainment Tonight. Syndicated. October 5, 1992.
George is seen in an excerpt from tonight's HBO special on Jack Benny. **SEE T713.**

T713 Jack Benny: Comedy In Bloom. HBO. October 5, 1992.
Narrated by comedian Tom Smothers, this special contains clips from Benny's radio and television shows, television specials and films as well as his guest appearances on other shows. There is only a brief shot of Gracie, but George appears rather prominently to reminisce about his old friend, as do Jack's daughter, Joan, entertainers Ann-Margret, Carol Burnett, Johnny Carson, Bob Hope and Dinah Shore. Benny's manager (now George's), Irving Fein, also shares his thoughts (he was also the program's executive producer) as do Fred de Cordova and writers Sam Perrin, George Balzer and Hal Goldman. One of the highlights is a portion of the "Gracie bit" that Jack and George perfected over the years with Benny impersonating Gracie in a Burns and Allen routine. This program was eventually made available to PBS stations and aired in at least one market on December 20, 1994. **SEE T433, T712.**

T714 Entertainment Tonight. Syndicated. October 9, 1992.
George receives an award from the National Institute on Aging, for whom he has done a public service announcement and is shown with singer Bobby Vinton.

T715 Best of The Hollywood Palace. ABC. November 25, 1992.
ABC dips into its archives to pull out clips from the 1964-1970 variety series in this one-hour retrospective hosted by Suzanne Somers. George is seen from the guest appearance he made on September 17, 1966 (T431) telling how he has tried to combine the singing styles of Dean Martin, Bing Crosby and Sammy Davis, Jr.

T716 Entertainment Tonight. Syndicated. January 28, 1993.
George's upcoming guest appearance on **Golden Palace** is featured (T717). George compares the character of Betty White to Gracie Allen; the cast sings "Happy Birthday" in honor of his 97th birthday.

T717 Golden Palace. NBC. February 12, 1993.
George appears as an old friend of *Sophia*'s (Estelle Getty) at a comedy competition. **SEE T716.**

T718 Inside The Comedy Mind. COM. February 17, 1993.

T719 CBS This Morning. CBS. February 18, 1993.
George guests with the girls from **Golden Palace** (Estelle Getty, Rue McClanahan and Betty White), a program on which he recently appeared.

T720 Legends of Comedy. Disney. March 14, 1993.
Lucille Ball, Jack Benny, Milton Berle, Jackie Gleason, Burns and Allen and Red Skelton are among those profiled in the last segment of a special series on comedians; this entry looks at those who were successful on television after coming up through the ranks of radio and film. This series of fifty-five minute programs is occasionally rerun, as it was on April 3, 1993 and January 25, 1995.

T721 More of the Best of The Hollywood Palace. ABC. May 11, 1993.
Suzanne Somers returns to host this second retrospective of the popular variety show. The special includes a clip from George's last stint as host of the series made on March 18, 1967 (T435) in which he says that he and the producers compromised about his singing (so he'll sing his jokes) and that singers need applause, but he'll be back anyway.

T722 Entertainment Tonight. Syndicated. May 12, 1993.
George is seen in a video-only preview of tonight's Barbara Walters special, **What Is This Thing Called Love? See T723.**

T723 Barbara Walters Special: What Is This Thing Called Love? ABC. May 12, 1993.
George Burns offers up comments on the subject of love via a clip from a previous Walters special. **SEE VG5, T528, T722.**

T724 Bob Hope Special: A 90th Birthday Celebration. NBC. May 14, 1993.
Only two comedians are vying with George Burns to have the longest-running career in show business (Bob Hope and Milton Berle) and George pays tribute to the former tonight in this three-hour special saluting Hope's "first ninety years" that looks at the career of the comedian who will turn 90 on May 29. Other guests include Lucie Arnaz, Johnny Carson, Angela Lansbury, Betty White, President Clinton and all five living former Presidents. This show won an Emmy for variety, music, or comedy special.

T725 20/20 15th Anniversary Special. ABC. May 25, 1993.
George is seen in the television ads for the program but was not seen in the footage actually aired in this retrospective of the newsmagazine.

T726 Good Morning America. ABC. August 5, 1993.
George and John Candy are interviewed about Canada's Montreal International Comedy Festival '93 awards that will include a tribute to Burns. **SEE T727.**

T727 Montreal International Comedy Festival '93. Showtime. August 7, 1993.
John Candy hosts the eleventh annual festival; George appears to accept a tribute by the attendees. **SEE T726.**

T728 The Statler Brothers Show. TNN. August 28, 1993.
George and Gracie are seen in a clip from their television show in the "Yesteryear" segment.

T729 Entertainment Tonight. Syndicated. August 30, 1993.
George is seen in a group shot of those attending last night's taping of the Comedy Hall of Fame awards, at which he was honored. **SEE T732.**

T730 60 Minutes...25 Years. CBS. November 14, 1993.
The venerable show celebrates its silver anniversary with two hours worth of clips from past shows, including an interview with George. **SEE T611.**

T731 Entertainment Tonight. Syndicated. November 24, 1993.
Backstage at tonight's Comedy Hall of Fame awards show George (one of the honorees) is seen with his date, actress Sharon Stone. **SEE T732.**

T732 The First Annual Comedy Hall of Fame. NBC. November 24, 1993. Paul Reiser and Sharon Stone help pay tribute to George as one of the inductees into the Comedy Hall of Fame for the Museum of Television and Radio and the UCLA Television Archives. Other honorees are Milton Berle, Carol Burnett, Walter Matthau, Red Skelton and Jonathan Winters. Included are clips from **The George Burns and Gracie Allen Show**. The two-hour special hosted by John Ritter was taped August 29 at the Beverly Hilton hotel in Los Angeles, California. **SEE T729, T731.**

T733 This Is Your Life. NBC. November 26, 1993. This special, hosted by Pat Sajak, recalls the popular television series; George and Jack Benny are seen in the opening. George was the subject of one of the original episodes, which aired on September 28, 1955. **SEE T381.**

T734 One On One: Classic Television Interviews. CBS. November 29, 1993. The Museum of Television and Radio presents a selection of interviews with Presidents and celebrities, hosted by Bob Costas. George is seen from his 1988 **60 Minutes** interview with Ed Bradley. **SEE T611.**

T735 TV Guide's 40th Anniversary. Fox. December 20, 1993. In a brief appearance from his office with a picture of Gracie behind him, George offers a tip of the hat to the popular magazine with the words, "Happy 40th anniversary, **TV Guide**. Ten years from now I'll congratulate you again."

T736 Legend To Legend Night. NBC. December 28, 1993. Katie Couric hosts this two-hour tribute as show business and sports "legends" pay homage to other "legends." George, feted by Bob Newhart, sings "Old Bones." Other honorees include Muhammad Ali, Tony Bennett, Gene Kelly and James Stewart.

T737 Entertainment Tonight. Syndicated. March 3, 1994. A report on the March 2nd death of actress Anita Morris, who co-starred in George's 1988 film, **18 Again!** (F45) (and the upcoming **Radioland Murders** [F46]), includes scenes from her first film with George.

T738 Songs Sung For The Oppressed. WPIX, New York. April 10, 1994. George appears with Tony Randall in the American television debut of Ukrainian singer Masha Itkina, a show described as a celebration of the 135th birthday of the A & P supermarket chain. Masha, as she is being introduced in the United States, performs primarily in Yiddish and Hebrew and is a film actress and well-known singer in Russia.

T739 Entertainment Tonight. Syndicated. May 2, 1994. George's upcoming guest appearance on **Phenom** (T740) is noted.

T740 Phenom. ABC. May 3, 1994. One of the members of the Doolan family fantasizes herself as a talk show host to a very special guest, George Burns. **SEE T739.**

T741 Bob Hope's Birthday Memories. NBC. May 14, 1994. George is on the roster of celebrities who make a brief flashback appearance on a special celebrating Hope's 91st birthday (fifteen days early), joining in-person guests Bea Arthur, Angie Dickinson, Phyllis Diller, John Forsythe, Sugar Ray Leonard, Leslie Nielsen, John Ritter, Betty White, Jonathan Winters and Hope's wife, Dolores.

T742 Barbara Walters Special: Happy Hour. ABC. May 23, 1994. A few veterans were chosen but the spotlight is on the more recently established comedians as Walters explores, among other things, the sources of comedy in clips of interviews (some never before seen) selected from previous shows. George tries to teach her comedy and how to "work the elevator." **SEE VG5, T528.**

T743 Biography. A&E. July 1994. A program tracing the career of Gregory Peck includes a clip of him, George and Jack Benny from the 1969 Jack Benny special, **Jack Benny's New Look**. Years later, Mr. Peck recalls the experience as "...the most fun I ever had performing." The show was rerun in 1995. **SEE T450.**

T744 Entertainment Tonight. Syndicated. July 1994. George is pictured with singer Vanessa Williams.

T745 Barbara Walters - Interviews of a Lifetime. Lifetime. December 16, 1994.
Walters has put together a series of one-hour programs for the Lifetime cable network containing past interviews from her ABC specials coupled with new introductory and closing remarks. George is seen in his 1979 interview with Walters; the other half is with singer/actress Diana Ross. The program was re-run February 6 and March 26, 1995. **SEE VG3, T520.**

T746 Entertainment Tonight. Syndicated. January 20, 1995.
George's 99th birthday is included in the celebrity birthday segment.

T747 Screen Actors Guild Awards. NBC. February 25, 1995.
George makes an increasingly rare television appearance on this, the first annual film and television acting awards show presented by the sixty-three year old union and the only awards voted on solely by its 78,000 members. The statuette given to recipients is called "The Actor." George is present to pick up the Guild's thirty-third Life Achievement award from his friend and protégée, entertainer Ann-Margret. Television and film clips from George (and Gracie's) career preceded the award, which George received at his table after a standing ovation from the audience. His remarks were quite brief, principally that he was "...going to do something very difficult...sit down." Although the Life Achievement award has been presented for thirty-two years, this is also the first time the ceremony has been televised. The special was broadcast live from Universal Studios in Los Angeles, California.

T748 The 67th Annual Academy Awards. ABC. March 27, 1995.
George and Gracie are included in the clips used to illustrate the theme of tonight's Oscar telecast, comedy.

T749 Entertainment Tonight. Syndicated. n.d.
George discusses his appearances as God in films that show religion in a comic light, including 1984's **Oh, God! You Devil** (F44).

T750 Entertainment Tonight. Syndicated. n.d.
In a show broadcast on a Saturday, George appears in a promo for the upcoming Monday show concerning Hollywood's latest controversy, the resurgence of cigar smoking among celebrities.

T751 Interview with James Brady. n.d.
Writer Brady, columnist for **Parade Magazine**, a Sunday newspaper supplement, had this to say about the experience of interviewing George on television, "...the wisecracks and the cues came too fast for me to stay with him."

T752 The Golden Years of Television. Syndicated. n.d.
The Burns and Allen Show was included in this package of vintage television series run on various stations around the country. **SEE VG59.**

T753 Eddie Cantor Comedy Theatre. Syndicated. n.d.
George and Gracie apparently appeared on this mid-1950's program in an episode that celebrated Cantor's 65th birthday and honored his long show business career and performed a routine about the Allen family's annual backyard circus.

T754 The Max Bygraves Show. n.d.
George made an appearance on this program emanating from London.

T755 Ultimate TV Trivia Challenge. ABC. May 11, 1995.
George is featured in a clip from his 1962 appearance on **Mister Ed** (T413) in this potpourri of questions and answers about television. Question: how did they make Mister Ed talk? Answer: fishing line.

T756 Larry King Live 10th Anniversary. CNN. June 4, 1995.
This one-hour retrospective features clips culled from shows that have aired over the past ten years, including one with George from November 1989. **SEE T652.**

T757 Fifty Years of Funny Females. ABC. June 29, 1995.
Clips of famous females in comedy are set up by host Annie Potts, including one featuring Gracie with George in a scene from one of their television shows in which Gracie recounts a trip she made to the doctor's office with her neighbor, Clara Bagley.

DISCOGRAPHY

All entries are phonodisc unless otherwise indicated, although the bulk of the Burns and Allen product consists of audiocassette tape recordings of their radio shows. Distributor, product number and year of release are included. The titles of radio shows are those used by the distributors for ease in identifying, locating and ordering only. The authors have cross-referenced those shows in which the distributors appear to be accurate in their program descriptions and broadcast dates and then information could be confirmed. The reader is advised to go to this book's radio section for additional accurate dates and should keep in mind the practice of occasional recycling of scripts.

Gracie Allen

D1 **Comedy II**. Audiocassette. Radio Yesteryear, 14, 1988.
Gracie Allen makes a guest appearance on the **Fibber McGee & Molly Show** (R861). Three other radio shows are included in this collection: **The Jack Benny Show, Can You Top This?** and **The Danny Kaye Show**.

D2 **Crazy for Gershwin: Original Versions of Gershwin's Songs. Recordings from 1922-1941**. Compact Disc. Memoir, CDMOIR 502, 1993.
A collection of over twenty songs written by George Gershwin, with lyrics by Ira Gershwin, make up this collection which features numerous artists. Gracie Allen sings "Stiff Upper Lip" from the musical, **A Damsel in Distress** (F30), accompanied by the Ray Noble Orchestra.

D3 **A Damsel in Distress**. Scarce Rarities, 0598, 1980.

D4 **A Damsel in Distress/Follow the Fleet**. Scarce Rarities Productions, 5505, n.d.
This incomplete soundtrack of **A Damsel in Distress** (F30) includes Gracie Allen in "Stiff Upper Lip" and also includes music from a non-Burns and Allen vehicle, 1936's **Follow the Fleet**, which starred Fred Astaire and Ginger Rogers. **SEE D218.**

D5 **Fibber McGee & Molly**. Audiocassette. Radiola, MR-1055, 1975.
Gracie Allen walked in on the March 5, 1940 show mentioning her Presidential campaign (R861). The December 9, 1941 show, **I Can Get It For You Wholesale**, is also included.

D6 **Frank Loesser in Hollywood, 1937-1955**. JJA Records, 19762, 1976.
Gracie sings "You're a Natural" from **College Swing** (F31) and "Snug as a Bug in a Rug" from **The Gracie Allen Murder Case** (F33) in this two record anthology.

D7 **Hollywood is on the Air**. Radiola, MX AAB-1215/8, n.d. Radiola, 17-18, 1978; Audiocassette. 2CMR-1718, 1988.

This two record/cassette anthology features recordings of twenty-five movie trailers promoting musical films from 1934 to 1942 includes the motion picture **Honolulu** (F32), in which Gracie sings and dances with Eleanor Powell.

D8 Hollywood Party. Pelican, 130, 1974.
Gracie sings "Snug as a Bug in a Rug" from the motion picture **The Gracie Allen Murder Case** (F33) on this anthology LP.

D9 Information Please. Audiocassette. Echoes of the Past, 154, n.d. The tape contains the July 5, 1938 and June 20, 1939 shows from this quiz show sponsored by Canada Dry. Gracie Allen was a guest on the June show where she surprised her guest panelists and the audience with the number of her correct answers. **SEE R850.**

D10 The 1930's Movie Musicals of Harry Revel. JJA, 19813, 1981.
This two record anthology includes Gracie Allen in the featured talent.

D11 Personalities on Parade: Vol. 2. Canada, PP-2 (PNS94), 1988.
Gracie Allen sings "Snug as a Bug in a Rug" (recorded March 14, 1939) from the motion picture **The Gracie Allen Murder Case** (F33). Other popular songs are sung by Ethel Merman, Maurice Chevalier, Claudette Colbert, Eddie Cantor, Al Jolson, Gus Van and Joe Schenck. Also featured is the complete November 9, 1931 broadcast of the Cremo cigar program with Bing Crosby. This record was released in a limited edition of 750 copies.

D12 Sensational Sirens of the Silver Screen. Compact Disc. Vintage Jazz Classics, VJC 1010-1, 1991.
This is an anthology LP.

D13 Texaco Star Theater. Audiocassette. Radio Spirits, 1046, 1992.
Gracie appeared on the March 6, 1940 musical variety show (hosted by John Barrymore) with Gladys George in **The Third Degree** (R862). Side two has another show with guest John Garfield.

D14 Those Sensational Swinging Sirens of the Silver Screen. Compact Disc. Vintage Jazz Classics, VJC 1002-2, 1990.
A collection of twenty popular and motion picture songs sung by the female vocalists who made them famous. Gracie Allen sings "Stiff Upper Lip" from **A Damsel in Distress** (F30).

D15 Two Girls and a Sailor. Hollywood Soundstage, HS-2307, 1975.
This is a recording from the motion picture of the same name (F35) in which Gracie Allen performs her "Concerto for Index Finger." The record company is sometimes also noted as "Sound/Stage."

D16 You're So Indiff'rent: Fox Trot. Bluebird, B-10215, 1939; Rust, 1978.
A jazz record recorded by Artie Shaw and his orchestra in New York on March 12, 1939. Helen Forest and Tony Pastor are the vocalists. "Snug as a Bug in a Rug" from the motion picture **The Gracie Allen Murder Case** (F33) is featured in an excerpt from motion picture music.

George Burns

D17 The Arizona Whiz/A Real Good Cigar. 45 rpm. Mercury, 57021, 1980. **SEE D45, D68.**

D18 As Time Goes By. Compact Disc. Curb Records/CEMA, D2-77544, 1992. George Burns and Bobby Vinton contribute songs about age. George sings the new song "Gracie" which is about his late wife. Other songs are "I Know What it is to be Young (But You Don't Know What It Is To Be Old," "As Time Goes By," "Young at Heart," "Good Old Bad Old Days," "I Believe (I'm In Love With You)," "Let the Heartaches Begin," "You've Changed," "How Old Do You Get" and "The Only Way to Go."

D19 Benny and Burns Testimonial Dinner. Friars, 1972.
This is the recording of the Friars Club dinner which honored both Jack Benny and George Burns at the Americana Hotel in New York City on May 13, 1972. The evening earned some $195,000 for charity.

D20 Benny Fields and His Minstrel Men. Colpix, 501, 1965.
George Burns sings "Lily of the Valley," "I'll Buy the Ring" and a chorus medley in this recording of popular songs. Other featured artists are singer Benny Fields and comedians Milton Berle, Jack Benny and Phil Silvers. This was also released in stereo as **The Minstrel Men**. **SEE D62.**

D21 Bing Crosby & Friends. Murray Hill, 894637, 1984.
George is included in this four record anthology.

D22 Bing Crosby & Friends. World Record Club, SH-279, 1978.
A United Kingdom release.

D23 Canned Laughter. Audiocassette. The Mind's Eye, 1985.
Two Jack Benny radio shows, the March 2, 1952 show with George Burns, Groucho Marx, Danny Kaye and Frank Sinatra (R1006), and the March 28, 1948 broadcast featuring the famous skit "Your Money or Your Life" are part of a group of recordings uniquely packaged in a tin can, hence the name.

D24 Dean Martin Testimonial Dinner. Friars, 1959.
George was one of the speakers at this Friars Club roast for Dean Martin on November 8, 1959.

D25 Don't Take Me Home/La Vie en Rose/Red Rose Rag/Some of These Days. EP. Colpix, 129, 1959.

D26 Dr. Burns' Prescription for Happiness. Audiocassette. Nightingale-Conant Corp., 1985.
An audio recording narrated by actor Red Buttons of excerpts from George Burns' book by the same name (B19).

D27 An Evening with George Burns. Pride, PRD-00011, 1974; DJM Records (Great Britain), DJMD 8004; Audiocassette. Dove/Newman, 58010, 1985; Dove, 10680, 1992.
A recording of George Burns' June 16, 1974 show at the Shubert Theater in Los Angeles, California with an introduction by Jack Benny. George sings "Red Rose Rag," ("When the Evening Sun is Sinking") "To Make Sweet Georgia Mine," "Pack Up Your Sins," "My Gal is a High Born Lady," "Grizzly Bear," "I'm Going to Take the Train Back Home," "Sweetheart Number One, Two..." and "Where Did You Get That Girl?" "I Aim to Please" was sung by the Sylvers Family. Other songs include "Yankee Doodle Blues" and "Monkey Rag." The Mike Curb Congregation sings "Joy to the World," "In the Mood," "This is America," "It All Depends on You," "You Made Me Love You" and "Don't Take Me Home." The recording of this live performance was released as a double record set and sold at one time for $25 per copy.

D28 Forgotten Eyes. 1990.
George participated in the recording of this single to benefit research to find a cure for the eye disease, retinitis pigmentosa. **SEE VG6.**

D29 Frank Sinatra Duets. Compact Disc. P. J. International, 001, 1986.

D30 Friars Club Heart Benefit. Friars, 1957.
George was one of the speakers at this dinner on February 14, 1957.

D31 Gary Cooper Testimonial Dinner. Friars, 2507, 1961.
George Burns was one of the guest presenters at this dinner for actor Gary Cooper at the Friars Club on November 8, 1961.

D32 George Burns: A Comedian Reminisces. Vital History Cassettes, No. 1. CBS News Audio Resource Library, 11751, 1975.
In this November 25, 1975 interview with reporter Mike Wallace, George Burns talks about his life and career in show business before and after teaming with his late wife, Gracie Allen.

D33 George Burns in Nashville. Mercury, SRM-6001; 1981. Audiocassette. MCR-4-1-6001; 8 track. MC-8-1-600, 1980.
George sings the following: "Here's To the Man In the Moon," "Just Send Me One," "It's Good to See You Smiling Again," "Inflatable Dream," "Jody and the Kid," "Using Things and Loving People," "Willie, Won't You Sing a Song With Me," "Ain't Misbehavin'," "The Good Old, Bad Old Days" and "Here's To My Friends."

D34 **George Burns Sings**. Buddah, BDS-5025, 1969. Reissued as **A Musical Trip With George Burns**. Buddah, BDS-1527, also 8 track and Audiocassette, 1972; Compact Disc. Special Music Co., SCD-4934, 1989.
Neil Bogart, head of Buddah Records, asked Lewis Merenstein to produce this record album with George Burns. George sings "In the Beginning," "With A Little Help From My Friends," "Mr. Bojangles," "King of the Road," "59th Street Bridge Song," "I Kissed Her On the Back Porch," "Satisfaction," "Ain't Misbehavin'," "Your Mother Should Know," "I'll Buy the Ring," "It All Depends on You," "You Made Me Love You," "1941," "Grizzly Bear," "Old Folks" and "The Sun Shines on My Street." **SEE D64.**

D35 **George Burns Sings**. Colpix 129; Nixa 4400 (Great Britain), n.d.
George sings "Don't Take Me Home," "La Vie En Rose," "Red Rose Rag" and "Some of These Days" on this British recording of four songs taken from the album by the same name.

D36 **George Jessel Testimonial Dinner**. Friars, 1948.
George Burns is featured on this recording from the April 4, 1948 Friars Club roast for Jessel. Ronald Reagan was also a guest speaker.

D37 **G.I. Jive-Hollywood Stars Go To War**. Compact Disc. Vintage Jazz Classics, VJC 1048, 1993.

D38 **The Golden Age of Radio: Starring Bing Crosby**. United Artists, UAK-30115, 1982.
This is an anthology LP.

D39 **Golden Hits 1968**. Classic Sound, Inc. (CSI), 10068, 1968.
George Burns sings "Mr Bojangles" in a recording of various artists singing songs from the year 1968.

D40 **Gracie: A Love Story**. Audiocassette. Simon & Schuster Audioworks, 68928-2, 1989; Metacom, M801, 1992.
George records his memories which are based on his book (B32) about his and Gracie's life and career together. This recording won a 1991 Grammy Award.

D41 **Here's Johnny: Magic Moments from the Tonight Show**. Casablanca, CAB1-1296, 1974.
Highlights of music, song and comedy performances from the long-running late night NBC television show hosted by Johnny Carson includes "Free for All," a skit with Jerry Lewis, Joey Bishop and George Burns recorded in November 1974 (T481).

D42 **How to Live to be a Hundred**. Compleat, 112, 1989.
This is a shortened version of a recording of George's book by the same name (B24).

D43 **How to Live to be 100--or More**. Audiocassette. Nightingale-Conant Corp., 1985.
Comedian/actor Red Buttons reads from George Burns' book in which the author gives his advice on how to live to age 100--or more (B24).

D44 **I Know What It Is to Be Young, But You Don't Know What It Is Like To Be Old**. 45 rpm. Curb Records, 1992.
A single from Bobby Vinton's and George's compact disc recording titled **As Time Goes By** (D18).

D45 **I Wish I Was Eighteen Again**. Mercury, SRM-5025, 1980. Audiocassette. Mercury, MCR4 1-5025, 1980.
George sings "The Arizona Whiz," "Old Bones," "The Baby Song," "The Only Way to Go," "Forgive Her A Little (And Love Her a Lot)," "I Wish I Was Eighteen Again," "Old Dogs, Children and Watermelon Wine," "A Real Good Cigar," "One of the Mysteries of Life" and "Nickels and Dimes."

D46 **I Wish I Was Eighteen Again/One of the Mysteries of Life**. 45 rpm. Mercury, 57011, 1979.
SEE D45, D67.

D47 **It's Good To See You Smiling Again/Using Things and Loving People**. 45 rpm. Mercury, 57039, 1980.
SEE D71.

D48 Jack Benny. Audiotape. KXL, 1974.
At a 1974 benefit performance in Portland, Oregon, Jack Benny talks about his career, current events and George Burns.

D49 Jack Benny Program. Audiocassette. BRC, 1813, n.d.
Jack's March 2, 1952 and March 9, 1952 radio shows are featured. George appeared on the March 2 show. **SEE R1006.**

D50 The Jack Benny Program. Audiocassette. BRC, 1811, 1988.
Two radio shows featuring the "Palm Springs Murder Mystery," broadcast December 9, 1951 and "George Burns Sings Jack's Song," a January 20, 1952 broadcast (R1005).

D51 The Jack Benny Program. Audiocassette. Echoes of the Past, 56, n.d.
George Burns was a guest on the January 20, 1952 show featured on this tape. **SEE R1005.**

D52 The Jack Benny Program. Audiocassette. Hello Again, Radio, 692, n.d.
Jack's March 2, 1952 and December 11, 1938 radio shows are featured. George appeared on the March show. **SEE R1006.**

D53 The Jack Benny Program. Audiocassette. Radio Spirits, 130, n.d.
Two episodes from Jack's radio show are featured: "Jack's Life Story" from November 4, 1951 and "George Burns Sings Jack's Song" from January 20, 1952 are featured (R1005).

D54 Jack Benny Testimonial Dinner. Friars, 1951.
George Burns was one of the guest speakers for this November 9, 1951 Friars Club dinner honoring Jack Benny's twenty years in radio.

D55 Jack Benny's Minstrel Men. Colpix, CP-503, 1964.

D56 Just Send Me One/Willie, Won't You Sing a Song With Me. 45 rpm. Mercury, 57045, 1981.
SEE D73.

D57 Kings of Comedy. Longines Symphonette Society, SYS 5282, 1970.
George Burns narrates this recording which asks the question "guess who these comedians are?" Featured are Abbott and Costello, Will Rogers, Jackie Gleason, Jack Benny, Smith and Dale, Al Jolson and Groucho Marx.

D58 Lucille Ball and Desi Arnaz Testimonial Dinner. Friars, 1958.
George spoke at this November 23, 1958 Friars Club roast for Lucy and Desi, who never had the chance to speak at their own dinner due to the fact that the last speaker, Harry Einstein (Parkyakarkus) died immediately upon returning to his seat on the dais. This dinner was reportedly broadcast on CBS radio (R1027).

D59 Make Room For Danny. Audiocassette. Audio Renaissance Tapes, 1992.
George makes a special guest appearance on this audio version of Danny Thomas' autobiography (written with Bill Davidson), joining others in reading the words and relating anecdotes about Thomas. All artist fees and sale proceeds of the project were donated to Thomas' favorite charity, St. Jude Children's Hospital in Memphis, Tennessee.

D60 Man of the Year. Audiocassette. Nostalgia Lane, 1982.

D61 Mervyn LeRoy Testimonial Dinner. Friars, 1961.
George was one of the guest speakers for the Friars Club roast for film producer and director LeRoy on October 22, 1961.

D62 The Minstrel Men. Colpix, CP-434 (stereo), 1963.
SEE D20.

D63 Mr. Bojangles/Old Folks. 45 rpm. Buddah 338, 1973.
SEE D66.

D64 A Musical Trip with George Burns. Buddah, BDS-1527, 1972; Compact Disc. Special Music Co., SCD-4934, 1989.
SEE D34.

D65 My Favorite Story. 20th Century Fox Records, TFM 3106, 1963.

Humorous stories and monologues by some of America's greatest performers, including George Burns.

D66 **Old Folks/Mr. Bojangles.**
SEE D63.

D67 **One of the Mysteries of Life/I Wish I Was Eighteen Again.**
SEE D45, D46.

D68 **A Real Good Cigar/The Arizona Whiz.**
SEE D17, D45.

D69 **Salute to the Hollywood Canteen.** Stanyan, 2SR-10066, 1972.

D70 **Sgt. Pepper's Lonely Hearts Club Band.** RSO Records, 2-4100, 1978.
This motion picture soundtrack (F35) includes George Burns singing "Fixing a Hole" and joining Peter Frampton and the Bee Gees on "Being for the Benefit of Mr. Kite." A book titled **With A Little Help From My Friends: The Making Of Sgt. Pepper**, published in 1995, was written by record producer George Martin with William Pearson and details the 700+ hours that went into the making of the album.

D71 **Using Things and Loving People/It's Good To See You Smiling Again.**
SEE D47.

D72 **Whatever Happened to Randolph Scott/Young At Heart.** 45 rpm. Mercury, 76149, 1981.
SEE D75, D76.

D73 **Willie, Won't You Sing a Song With Me/Just Send Me One.**
SEE D56.

D74 **Wisdom of the Nineties.** Harper Audio, CPN 2264, 1991.
Actor Harvey Korman reads excerpts from George's book of the same name.
SEE B36.

D75 **Young at Heart.** Mercury, SRM 1-4061; Audiocassette. MCR4-1-4061, 1982; Compact Disc. PolyGram, 314-532 478-2, 1996.
Among the songs George sings are "Young at Heart," "Kids," "The Old Fashioned Way," "You're Nobody 'Til Somebody Loves You," "As Time Goes By," "Whatever Happened to Randolph Scott?" "Ain't Misbehavin'," and "I Wish I Were Eighteen Again."

D76 **Young at Heart/Whatever Happened to Randolph Scott.**
SEE D72, D75.

George Burns and Gracie Allen

D77 **Abbott & Costello Show, The Fred Allen Show, Burns & Allen.** Audiocassette. Nostalgia Lane, NLC-50, 1970.
The three featured radio shows include Burns and Allen's show with guest Ronald Reagan. Possibly from R780.

D78 **All Star Comedy Shows.** Audiocassette. Great American Audio, 45016, 1993.
Several shows from the radio comedy genre including Burns and Allen.

D79 **The Best of Burns and Allen.** Audiocassette. Metacom, J603, BB603, 1985.
From the **Golden Age of Radio** series comes a collection of four Burns and Allen's programs, "Beauty Parlor" (R527), "Literary Club" (R635), "Door to Door Salesman Skit" (R718) and "H & R Blockhead" (R785).

D80 **The Best of Old Time Radio.** Audiocassette. Radio Yesteryear, 1991.
Featured are two Jack Benny radio shows from April 4, 1937 and April 11, 1937, the latter featuring guests George Burns and Gracie Allen (R839).

D81 **The Best of Old Time Radio Greatest Comedies.** Audiocassette. Nostalgia Lane, NLC 5002, 5003, 5006, 5021, 5024, 5028, 1980; Great American Gift Co., 1989.

A collection of six radio broadcasts and their stars. Included in the set are the shows of Burns and Allen, Jack Benny, Fibber McGee & Molly, Groucho Marx, Amos 'n' Andy and W. C. Fields.

D82 **The Big Broadcast of 1932**. Soundtrak, 101, 1974; Sunbeam Records, 1974; Audiocassette. Sandy Hook Records, SH 2007, 1978.
Songs and excerpts from the motion picture soundtrack of **The Big Broadcast** (F19) includes skits by Burns and Allen ("Take a Letter" and "Moneymaking Brother") and songs by other cast members: the Boswell Sisters, Cab Calloway, the Mills Brothers, Kate Smith, Bing Crosby, the Vincent Lopez Orchestra and Donald Novis. Once other **Big Broadcast** films were produced, this first one is often referred to as **The Big Broadcast of 1932** to distinguish it from its successors.

D83 **Burns and Allen**. Audiocassette. Armstrong Radio Service, 1979.
Two Burns and Allen radio programs originally broadcast on September 30, 1948 (R723) and June 16, 1949 (R760) are featured.

D84 **Burns and Allen**. Audiocassette. BRC, 1542, 1987.
Two Burns and Allen radio shows from the early 1940's are featured.

D85 **Burns and Allen**. Audiocassette. BRC, 1543, 1987.
The September 14, 1943 (R520) and November 9, 1943 (R528) Burns and Allen radio shows are featured.

D86 **Burns and Allen**. Audiocassette. BRC, 1544, 1987.
Two episodes from George and Gracie's radio show are featured: "George is Depressed" from June 6, 1944 (R558) and the Fifth War Bond Drive show with guest star Dinah Shore, June 13, 1944 (R559).

D87 **Burns and Allen**. Audiocassette. BRC, 1545, 1987.
Two episodes from George and Gracie's radio show are featured: "Making George Younger" from June 18, 1945 (R604) and "Preparing for a Troop Entertainment Tour" from June 25, 1945 (R605).

D88 **Burns and Allen**. Audiocassette. BRC, 1546, 1987.
Two episodes from George and Gracie's radio show are featured: Jack Benny and George going to college from November 29, 1945 (R616) and the October 24, 1946 show (R650).

D89 **Burns and Allen**. Audiocassette. BRC, 1547, 1987.
Two episodes from George and Gracie's radio show are featured: one with guest star Jack Carson from October 31, 1946 (R651) and with guest star Al Jolson from February 20, 1947 (R667).

D90 **Burns and Allen**. Audiocassette. BRC, 1548, 1987.
Two episodes from George and Gracie's radio show are featured: "Gracie, Business Executive" from February 27, 1947 (R668) and the December 4, 1947 show with guest star Bing Crosby (R695).

D91 **Burns and Allen**. Audiocassette. BRC, 1549, 1987.
Two episodes from George and Gracie's radio show are featured: Jack Benny is the guest star on January 8, 1948 (R700) and Walter O'Keefe guests on the January 22, 1948 show (R702).

D92 **Burns and Allen**. Audiocassette. BRC, 1550, 1987.
Two episodes from George and Gracie's radio show are featured: "No Flowers for Gracie" (referred to by some distributors as "Gracie Has Laryngitis) from April 22, 1948 (R715) and a show with guest stars James and Pamela Mason from February 17, 1949 (R743).

D93 **Burns and Allen**. Audiocassette. BRC, 1551, 1987.
Two episodes from George and Gracie's radio show are featured: "George, a Doctor?" from February 24, 1949 (R744) and the March 24, 1949 show with guest star Jane Wyman (R748).

D94 **Burns and Allen**. Audiocassette. BRC, 1552, 1987.
Two episodes from George and Gracie's radio show are featured: "Gracie is Courted by George" and the March 31, 1949 show with guest star Jack Benny (R749).

D95 **Burns and Allen**. Audiocassette. BRC, 1553, 1987.

Two episodes of the Burns and Allen radio show are featured: one broadcast from March 1, 1950 (R785), the other from January 4, 1950 (R777).

D96 Burns and Allen. Audiocassette. BWP Radio, 397, 1987.
Two episodes from George and Gracie's radio show are featured: the December 4, 1947 broadcast (R695) with guest star Bing Crosby and "George Goes Hollywood" (R613) from November 8, 1945.

D97 Burns and Allen. Audiocassette. BWP Radio, 399, 1980.
Two episodes from George and Gracie's radio show are featured: one with guest star Mickey Rooney (R756) and the other centering on the Burnses' new neighbors.

D98 Burns and Allen. Audiocassette. Center for Cassette Studies, 38745, 1977.
A Burns and Allen show "from the good old days of radio" is featured.

D99 Burns and Allen. Audiocassette. Echoes of the Past, 20, n.d.
Two Burns and Allen radio broadcasts from 1943 include the September 7 program (R519).

D100 Burns and Allen. Audiocassette. Echoes of the Past, 21, n.d.
Two Burns and Allen radio broadcasts from 1945 include one from November 29 (R616) and the June 25 (R605) show.

D101 Burns and Allen. Audiocassette. Echoes of the Past, 22, n.d.
Two Burns and Allen radio broadcasts from 1949 include one from February 24 (R744) and the March 31 (R749) show.

D102 Burns and Allen. Audiocassette. Echoes of the Past, 23, n.d.
This tape contains the February 27, 1947 (R668) and January 8, 1948 (R700) Burns and Allen radio broadcasts.

D103 Burns and Allen. Audiocassette. Echoes of the Past, 24, n.d.
Two episodes of the Burns and Allen radio show are featured: one from November 9, 1943 (R528), the other from June 6, 1944 (R558).

D104 Burns and Allen. Audiocassette. Echoes of the Past, 25, n.d.
The June 13, 1944 (R559) and June 18, 1945 (R604) radio broadcasts are featured.

D105 Burns and Allen. Audiocassette. Great American Gift Co., 2636, 1987.
The January 8, 1948 (R700) and January 22, 1948 (R702) radio broadcasts are featured.

D106 Burns and Allen. Audiocassette. Great American Gift Co., 2639, 1987.
Two radio broadcasts, including one from March 31, 1949 with guest star Jack Benny (R749), are featured.

D107 Burns and Allen. Audiocassette. Great American Gift Co., 2640, 1987.
Contains two Burns and Allen shows.

D108 Burns and Allen. Audiocassette. Great American Gift Co., 5010, 1987.
Two episodes from George and Gracie's radio show are featured.

D109 Burns and Allen. Audiocassette. Great American Gift Co., 5011, 1987.
The November 29, 1945 (R616) and February 20, 1947 (R667) Burns and Allen radio shows are featured.

D110 Burns and Allen. Audiocassette. Great American Gift Co., 5012, 1987.
The October 24, 1946 (R650) and October 31, 1946 (R651) Burns and Allen radio shows are featured.

D111 Burns and Allen. Audiocassette. Great American Gift Co., 5421, 1987.
Four broadcasts from the Burns and Allen radio show are featured.

D112 Burns and Allen. Audiocassette. The Hall Closet, 113, n.d. Two shows from the 1940's include George and Gracie's November 29, 1945 (R616) radio show.

D113 Burns and Allen. Audiocassette. The Hall Closet, 199, n.d. The February 20, 1947 (R667) and May 19, 1949 (R756) Burns and Allen radio shows are featured.

D114 Burns and Allen. Audiocassette. Hello Again, Radio, 156, n.d. The December 4, 1947 (R695) and February 17, 1949 (R743) Burns and Allen radio shows are featured.

D115 Burns and Allen. Audiocassette. Hello Again, Radio, 160, n.d. The January 1, 1948 (R699) and January 22, 1948 (R702) Burns and Allen radio shows are featured.

D116 Burns and Allen. Audiocassette. Hello Again, Radio, 898, n.d. Two episodes of George and Gracie's radio show are featured.

D117 Burns and Allen. Audiocassette. Hello Again, Radio, 899, n.d. Two episodes of George and Gracie's radio show are featured, including one with guest star Mickey Rooney (R756).

D118 Burns and Allen. Audiocassette. Hello Again, Radio, 900, n.d. Two episodes of George and Gracie's radio show are featured.

D119 Burns and Allen. Audiocassette. Hello Again, Radio, 951, n.d. The June 6, 1944 (R558) and June 13, 1944 (R559) Burns and Allen radio shows are featured.

D120 Burns and Allen. Audiocassette. Hello Again, Radio, 952, n.d. Two episodes of George and Gracie's radio show are featured, including the September 7, 1943 broadcast (R519).

D121 Burns and Allen. Audiocassette. Hello Again, Radio, 953, n.d. Two episodes of George and Gracie's radio show are featured.

D122 Burns and Allen. Audiocassette. Hello Again, Radio, 956, n.d. The February 24, 1949 (R744) and March 24, 1949 (R748) broadcasts of George and Gracie's radio show are featured.

D123 Burns and Allen. Audiocassette. Hello Again, Radio, 957, n.d. Two episodes of George and Gracie's radio show are featured.

D124 Burns and Allen. Audiocassette. Hello Again, Radio, 958, n.d. Two Burns and Allen shows are featured.

D125 Burns and Allen. Audiocassette. Jim Harmon, C16, n.d. Mickey Rooney (R756) and Bing Crosby guest star on two different Burns and Allen radio shows.

D126 Burns and Allen. Audiocassette. Jim Harmon, C53, n.d. Two episodes of George and Gracie's radio show are featured, including one from November 1, 1945 (R612).

D127 Burns and Allen. Audiocassette. Metacom, BB409, 1985. Back-to-back episodes of George and Gracie's radio show are featured: those from June 18, 1945 (R604) and June 25, 1945 (R605).

D128 Burns and Allen. Audiocassette. Metacom, GS 462, 1990. Two episodes from the Burns and Allen radio show are featured, "The Literary Club" (R635) and "Gracie Repents" (R679).

D129 Burns and Allen. Audiocassette. Metacom, J035, 1985. Two episodes from the Burns and Allen radio show are featured: "Kansas City Calamity: Part 1" from June 6, 1944 (R558) and "Kansas City Calamity: Part 2" from June 13, 1944 with guest star Dinah Shore (R559).

D130 Burns and Allen. Audiocassette. Metacom, J036, 1985. Two episodes from the Burns and Allen radio show are featured: "George Inherits $5,000" from November 22, 1945 (R615) and "Jack Joins George At College" from November 29, 1945 with guest star Jack Benny (R616).

D131 **Burns and Allen**. Audiocassette. Metacom, J038, 1985, 1993.
Two episodes from George and Gracie's radio show are featured: one from September 28, 1949 (R763), the other from January 20, 1949 (R739).

D132 **Burns and Allen**. Audiocassette. Metacom, J914, 1985, 1992.
Two episodes from the Burns and Allen radio show are featured: "Teenage Daughter" from June 16, 1949 (R760) and "H & R Blockhead" from March 1, 1950 (R785).

D133 **Burns and Allen**. Audiocassette. Metacom, J950, 1985.
Two Burns and Allen shows are featured.

D134 **Burns and Allen**. Audiocassette. Metacom, RC302, 1990.
Two episodes from the Burns and Allen radio show are featured: "H & R Blockhead" (R785) and "The Cheapskate" (R749).

D135 **Burns and Allen**. Audiocassette. The Mind's Eye, 1985.
Three episodes from the Burns and Allen radio show are featured: May 19, 1949 (R756), February 17, 1949 (R743) and February 24, 1949 (R744).

D136 **Burns and Allen**. Audiocassette. The Mind's Eye, 1985.
James and Pamela Mason (R743) and Jack Benny guest star on two different Burns and Allen radio shows.

D137 **Burns and Allen**. Audiocassette. The Mind's Eye, 508-7, 289-4, 1985; Jabberwocky, 1982.
Four separate radio broadcasts packed in a can (marketed as **Canned Laughter**) with guest stars Mickey Rooney (R756), Jack Benny, James and Pamela Mason (R743) and the regular Burns and Allen cast are featured. **SEE D204.**

D138 **Burns and Allen**. Audiocassette. The Mind's Eye, 340-9, 1992.
The May 19, 1949 radio show with guest star Mickey Rooney (R756) is featured.

D139 **Burns and Allen**. Audiocassette. Murray Hill, 59095, n.d.
The February 15, 1944 (R542) and March 21, 1944 (R547) Burns and Allen radio shows are featured.

D140 **Burns and Allen**. Audiocassette. Nostalgia Central, 394, 1987.
The September 30, 1948 (R723) and March 24, 1949 (R748) Burns and Allen radio shows are featured.

D141 **Burns and Allen**. Nostalgia Lane, NLR-1002, 1978.
Two original radio broadcasts from the **Maxwell House Coffee Time** starring George and Gracie from November 1, 1945 (R612) and November 8, 1945 (R613) are featured.

D142 **Burns and Allen**. Nostalgia Lane, PBO 157.

D143 **Burns and Allen**. Audiocassette. Old Time Radio, 497, 1988.
Broadcasts of the Burns and Allen radio show from January 8, 1948 with guest star Jack Benny (R700) and February 17, 1949 with guest stars James and Pamela Mason (R743) are featured.

D144 **Burns and Allen**. Audiocassette. Old Time Radio, 521, 1979.
Broadcasts of the Burns and Allen radio show from November 29, 1945 (R616) and February 22, 1950 (R784) are featured.

D145 **Burns and Allen**. Audiocassette. Radio Reruns, R23, 1980.
Gracie tries to help a friend by breaking up his romance in this episode from their radio show titled "George and Gracie Play Counter-Cupid."

D146 **Burns and Allen**. Audiocassette. Radio Reruns, R129, 1980.
Gracie loses her voice in this episode of their radio show titled "Gracie Has Laryngitis" (R715). This is also referred to by at least one distributor as "No Flowers for Gracie."

D147 **Burns and Allen**. Audiocassette. Radio Reruns, R130, 1977, 1980.
This recording of their November 2, 1943 radio show features Gracie catching guest star Jack Benny in the beauty parlor (R527).

D148 **Burns and Allen**. Audiocassette. Radio Reruns, R262, 1980.

This is a recording from George and Gracie's February 15, 1944 broadcast in which guest star Fred Astaire's tap dancing drives George crazy (R542).

D149 Burns and Allen. Audiocassette. Radio Reruns, R263, 1985.
This March 21, 1944 Burns and Allen radio show features "George the Genius" with guest stars Rita Hayworth and Orson Welles (R547).

D150 Burns and Allen. Audiocassette. Radio Reruns, R264, 1980.
"Gracie Tries to Join a Literary Club," their April 11, 1946 radio show, is featured. **SEE R635.**

D151 Burns and Allen. Audiocassette. Radio Reruns, R265, 1980.
A recording of George and Gracie's May 15, 1947 radio broadcast in which "Gracie Repents by Treating George Like a King" is included (R679).

D152 Burns and Allen. Audiocassette. Radio Reruns, R266, 1980.
"Gracie Buys Everything" (R718) in this classic skit which finds Gracie having trouble saying "no" to door-to-door salesmen and George trying to break her of the habit. This was their May 13, 1948 radio broadcast.

D153 Burns and Allen. Audiocassette. Radio Reruns, R267, 1980.
The March 14, 1946 radio broadcast of "The Matrimonial Bureau" (R631) and another show titled "Gracie Goes Into Business" are featured.

D154 Burns and Allen. Audiocassette. Radio Reruns, R268, 1980.
The "Little White Lies" broadcast from their April 4, 1946 (R634) radio show is featured.

D155 Burns and Allen. Audiocassette. Radio Reruns, R269, 1980.
A recording of George and Gracie's May 8, 1947 radio broadcast, "YMCA and YWCA" (R678) is featured.

D156 Burns and Allen. Audiocassette. Radio Reruns, R270, 1980.
A recording of George and Gracie's May 6, 1948 radio broadcast, "Oil Well Marriage Get Rich Quick Scheme Fails" (R717), is featured.

D157 Burns and Allen. Audiocassette. Radio Reruns, R271, 1980.
A recording of George and Gracie's May 20, 1948 radio broadcast, "Gracie's Mother Doesn't Like George's Work" (R719), is featured.

D158 Burns and Allen. Audiocassette. Radio Reruns, R336, 1982.
One episode of George and Gracie's radio show is featured.

D159 Burns and Allen. Audiocassette. Radio Reruns, R337, 1982.
A recording of George and Gracie's October 17, 1944 radio broadcast, "The Wrecked Car" (R569), is featured.

D160 Burns and Allen. Audiocassette. Radio Reruns, R338, 1980.
Gracie remembers when guest star Jack Benny was courting her in "The Cheapskate" episode of their radio show (R749).

D161 Burns and Allen. Audiocassette. Radio Reruns, R339, 1980, 1985.
"H & R Blockhead" (R785), George and Gracie's March 1, 1950 radio broadcast, is featured.

D162 Burns and Allen. Audiocassette. Radio Reruns, R437, 1986.
"Santa's Workshop" (R451) finds Gracie dreaming of a visit to the North Pole in this 1941 radio broadcast.

D163 Burns and Allen. Audiocassette. Radio Spirits, RS 73, 1979.
Gracie has George's handwriting analyzed and discovers he should have been a surgeon in this radio broadcast. **SEE R744.**

D164 Burns and Allen. Audiocassette. Radio Spirits, RS 336, 1979.
Two episodes from George and Gracie's radio show are featured: one with guest star Walter O'Keefe (R702) and the second with Gracie deciding to prepare George's income tax (R785).

D165 Burns and Allen. Audiocassette. Radio Spirits, RS 760, 1979.
A holiday show from a Burns and Allen radio broadcast in 1937 is featured.

D166 **Burns and Allen**. Audiocassette. Radio Spirits, RS 981, 1989. Two episodes from George and Gracie's radio show are featured: one with guest star Mickey Rooney (R756), the other with Gracie wanting to make a doctor of George (R744).

D167 **Burns and Allen**. Audiocassette. Radio Spirits, RS 982, 1992. The February 5, 1948 (R704) and May 12, 1949 (R755) Burns and Allen radio shows are featured.

D168 **Burns and Allen**. Audiocassette. Radio Spirits, RS 983, 1992. The February 15, 1944 (R542) and September 28, 1949 (R763) Burns and Allen radio shows are featured.

D169 **Burns and Allen**. Audiocassette. Radio Spirits, RS 984, 1992. The November 18, 1948 (R730) and January 6, 1949 (R737) Burns and Allen radio shows are featured.

D170 **Burns and Allen**. Audiocassette. Radio Tape Library, C-108, 1979.

D171 **Burns and Allen**. Audiocassette. Radio Yesteryear, n.d. This is a recording from the February 3, 1941 Burns and Allen radio show with special guest Mayor Kelly of Chicago. **SEE R432.**

D172 **Burns and Allen**. Audiocassette. Radio Yesteryear, 10, 1989. This tape consists of a collection of short routines from George and Gracie's radio shows.

D173 **Burns and Allen**. Audiocassette. Radio Yesteryear, 12, n.d. A short routine from a World War II era broadcast which has Gracie talking about her brother Willie, who has been called up by the Army, is included on this cassette.

D174 **Burns and Allen**. Audiocassette. Radio Yesteryear, 13, n.d. George and Gracie perform some of their vaudeville routines, including "Lamb Chops."

D175 **Burns and Allen**. Audiocassette. Radio Yesteryear, 14, 1989. Gracie acts the part of *Sadie Thompson* from **Rain**, with assistance from the rest of the cast. This January 15, 1936 broadcast is one of the earliest episodes available on tape. **SEE R191.**

D176 **Burns and Allen**. Audiocassette. Radio Yesteryear, 16, 1989. Gracie performs her "Concerto for Index Finger" in this episode.

D177 **Burns and Allen**. Audiocassette. Radio Yesteryear, 36, 1986. The December 4, 1947 (R695) and the September 30, 1948 (R723) Burns and Allen radio shows are featured.

D178 **Burns and Allen**. Audiocassette. Radio Yesteryear, 438, n.d. Gracie's old boyfriend returns in one episode and the Burnses host guest star, singer James Melton, in Boston, Massachusetts (R573) in another.

D179 **Burns and Allen**. Audiocassette. Radio Yesteryear, 485, n.d. Cesar Romero and Cary Grant guest star on two different Burns and Allen radio shows.

D180 **Burns and Allen**. Audiocassette. Radio Yesteryear, 517, n.d. The episode in which Gracie wants George to be more romantic is coupled with their radio show from March 17, 1949 (R747).

D181 **Burns and Allen**. Audiocassette. Radio Yesteryear, MR1169, n.d. Two episodes from George and Gracie's radio show are featured: the February 20, 1947 (R667) broadcast with guest star Al Jolson and one from December 4, 1947 with guest star Bing Crosby (R695).

D182 **Burns and Allen**. Audiocassette. Sights and Sounds of America, 34C, 1977.
Contains what is advertised as a "classic radio program."

D183 **Burns and Allen/The Bob Hope Show**. Audiocassette. Yesteryear's Radio Program, No. 5, 1979.

From the Burns and Allen radio show, an episode about Bill Goodwin's movie offer (R612); it's paired with an episode of **The Bob Hope Show** featuring guest star Frank Sinatra.

D184 **Burns and Allen/Eddie Cantor**. Audiocassette. Radio Memories, 101, 1990.
Two shows include a "George Wants to Look Younger" broadcast from the Burns and Allen radio show. Eddie Cantor and Von Zell are kidnapped on the Cantor entry. Harry Von Zell appeared on Burns and Allen's radio and television shows as announcer/actor, but for many years he worked with Cantor.

D185 **Burns and Allen/Jack Benny (Golden Age Radio Holiday)**. Audiocassette. Metacom, GT219, 1987.
The tape contains "Santa's Workshop" from George and Gracie's radio show (R451) and a **Jack Benny Program**, "Christmas Headache," from December 19, 1950.

D186 **Burns and Allen/Major Bowes' Original Amateur Hour**. Audiocassette. Radio Memories, 132, 1990.
George and Gracie plan a USO tour on their radio show. The second radio program features amateur performers trying to win "a chance at the big brass ring."

D187 **Burns and Allen On Radio**. Audiocassette. Nostalgia Lane, NLC 5002, 1978.
Broadcasts of the November 1, 1945 (R612) and November 8, 1945 (R613) Burns and Allen radio shows are featured.

D188 **Burns and Allen (Radio Classics**, Vol. II). Audiocassette. Great American Audio Corp., 45009, 1992.
Gracie interviews guest star Ronald Reagan in one episode and cons George in another in these entries from their radio show.

D189 **Burns and Allen Show**. Audiocassette. Memorabilia, MLP-722, 1974.
A December 4, 1947 (R695) Burns and Allen radio broadcast with guest star Bing Crosby is featured.

D190 **Burns and Allen Show**. Audiocassette. National Recording Company, CC-5900, 1978.
A Burns and Allen radio show from November 29, 1945 with guest star Jack Benny (R616) and a 1940's show with guest star Bing Crosby are featured.

D191 **Burns and Allen Show**. Audiocassette. National Recording Company, CC-9802, 2, 1989.
The Burns and Allen radio broadcasts from February 20, 1947 with guest star Al Jolson (R667) and May 19, 1949 with guest star Mickey Rooney (R756) are featured.

D192 **Burns and Allen Show**. Audiocassette. National Recording Company, 397, 1979.
The "George Goes Hollywood" (R613) and "George Replaces Bing Crosby" (R695) episodes from their radio show are featured.

D193 **Burns and Allen Show**. Audiocassette. Nostalgia Sounds, 368-2, 1984.
The Burns and Allen radio broadcasts from June 13, 1944 with guest star Dinah Shore (R559) and November 2, 1943 with guest star Jack Benny (R527) are featured.

D194 **Burns and Allen Show**. Audiocassette. Old Time Radio, 497, 1988.
The Burns and Allen radio broadcasts from January 8, 1948 with guest star Jack Benny (R700) and February 17, 1949 with guest stars James and Pamela Mason (R743) are featured.

D195 **The Burns and Allen Show**. Audiocassette. Pastime Products, 114, 1976.
Two Burns and Allen radio show episodes, "They Hire a New Cook" and "Gracie's North Pole Dream" (R451) are featured.

D196 **The Burns and Allen Show**. Audiocassette. Radio Memories from the Attic, 1985.

The Burns and Allen radio broadcasts from September 30, 1948 (R723) and May 19, 1949 (R756) are featured.

D197 **The Burns and Allen Show**. Audiocassette. Radio Memories from the Attic, 1985.
These two broadcasts from their radio show in 1949 feature Gracie wanting George to become a doctor (R744) and Gracie wanting Bill Goodwin to get married (R739).

D198 **Burns and Allen Show/Amos and Andy**. Audiocassette. Sights & Sounds of America, 69C, 63C, 1979.
The Burns and Allen radio broadcast of May 19, 1949 with guest star Mickey Rooney (R756) and an **Amos 'n' Andy** radio show of October 10, 1948 are featured.

D199 **Burns and Allen Show/Fibber McGee & Molly**. Audiocassette. Sights & Sounds of America, 69C, 70C, 1977.
The May 19, 1949 broadcast of **The Burns and Allen Show** (R756) and the October 24, 1949 **Fibber McGee & Molly Show** are featured.

D200 **Burns and Allen Show/My Friend Irma**. Audiocassette. National Recording Co., CC4313, 1974.
One episode from their radio show has George trying to buy a vacant lot. **My Friend Irma**, starring Marie Wilson, is another radio show that later transferred to television.

D201 **The Burns and Allen Show. Original Radio Broadcasts**. Mark 56 Records, LP-614, 1973; Audiocassette. Warner Audio Publishing, 88221, 1973.
The Burns and Allen radio broadcasts from February 24, 1949 (R744) and January 20, 1949 (R739) are featured.

D202 **The Burns & Allen Show: They Hire A New Cook**. Audiocassette. Audio Archives, 1984.
A recording of one of George and Gracie's 1940's broadcasts is featured.

D203 **Burns and Allen, Their Greatest Radio Shows**. Murray Hill, 898047, n.d.
A collection of recordings from George and Gracie's December 4, 1947 (R695), October 10, 1944 (R568), November 18, 1941 (R446) and January 20, 1949 (R739) radio shows are featured.

D204 **Canned Laughter**. Audiocassette. The Mind's Eye, 508-7, 1985.
Seven canisters include fourteen cassettes of radio comedy shows. The set features four Burns and Allen programs: "Gracie Wants to Make a Doctor Out of George" (R744) and shows with guest stars Mickey Rooney (R756), James and Pamela Mason (R743) and Jack Benny. **SEE D137.**

D205 **The Comedians**. Audiocassette. McCoy's Recording Inc., n.d.
This is a six tape collection with excerpts from various comedians' routines, including Burns and Allen.

D206 **Comedy**. Audiocassette. Metacom, GT 213-216, M3501, 1991.
This collection contains four cassettes from the golden age of radio comedy, including two Burns and Allen radio shows.

D207 **Comedy Classics**. ERA Records, BU 3890, 1983; K-TEL International, BU7584, 1987; Compact Disc. 1992.
This is a collection of famous radio comedy programs including Burns and Allen with their "Broken Back" skit. Other artists are Myron Cohen, Abbott and Costello, George Carlin, Rodney Dangerfield, Redd Foxx, Richard Pryor, Lily Tomlin and Jonathan Winters.

D208 **Comedy III**. Radio Yesteryear, 15, 1987.
These radio show recordings feature **The Burns and Allen Show** of May 19, 1949 (R756) and episodes from **Amos 'n' Andy**, **It Pays to be Ignorant** and **The Fred Allen Show**.

D209 **Comedy Tonight (Silver Sounds of Radio)**. Audiocassette. Perfection Form Co., 1979.
Two radio shows, **The Great Gildersleeve** and **The George Burns and Gracie Allen Show**, are featured on this cassette.

D210 A Damsel in Distress/The Sky's the Limit. Curtain Calls, CC 100/19, 1970, 1978.
This recording features two motion picture soundtracks. **A Damsel in Distress** (F30) stars Fred Astaire, George Burns, Gracie Allen and Ray Noble and his orchestra. Side one includes a Burns and Allen comedy routine as well as the "I've Just Begun to Live (Put Me To the Test)" song/dance routine by Fred Astaire and Burns and Allen and the song "Stiff Upper Lip" as sung by Gracie Allen.

D211 Dizzy. British Columbia. PT. 1 WA-10729; PT. 2 WA-10730, DB-286, 1930.
Burns and Allen perform their vaudeville routine "Dizzy" in this October 3, 1939 British recording.

D212 Door-to-Door Salesman. Audiocassette. Radio Reruns, 1987.
Gracie can't say no to door-to-door salesmen in this entry from their radio show. **SEE R718.**

D213 Dulcy. Audiocassette. Center for Cassette Studies, 38992, 1978.
This is a recording of the broadcast of the March 29, 1937 **Lux Radio Theater** (R838) with Burns and Allen in the featured roles. Other members of the cast include Elsa Maxwell and Hedda Hopper, who spoke during intermission. The play **Dulcy** was an adaptation of a 1923 motion picture comedy by the same name.

D214 Eddie Cantor Show. Audiocassette. National Recording Co., CM 6643, 1984; Radio Tape Library, C114, 1979.
Burns and Allen were guests on Cantor's January 31, 1945 show celebrating Eddie's 53rd birthday (R926). The November 5, 1948 show with Dinah Shore as Cantor's guest is also included.

D215 Fibber McGee & Molly Christmas Show of 1949/The Burns and Allen Christmas Show, 1940's. Audiocassette. National Recording Company, CC-9009, 1984.
Two of radio's most popular comedies are featured together on this tape. Side two contains the Burns and Allen radio program in which Gracie dreams of traveling to the North Pole (R451).

D216 The First Fifty Years of NBC. PT. 3. Westinghouse Broadcasting Co., 1970.
This is a recording of the November 21, 1976 NBC television show which features voices of the performers who had appeared on this network's shows, including Burns and Allen. Information for the television show indicates this was Part IV rather than Part III. **SEE T498.**

D217 The Five Funniest Hours in the History of Radio. Nostalgia Lane, 5 NLR150, 1977.
These five radio shows include Burns and Allen broadcasts from November 1, 1945 (R612) and November 8, 1945 (R613). The other four shows star Abbott and Costello, Jack Benny, Fibber McGee & Molly and Groucho Marx.

D218 Follow the Fleet/A Damsel in Distress.
SEE D4.

D219 Frank Bresee Presents the Golden Days of Radio. Mark 56 Records, 713, 1975.
A history of radio with excerpts from many radio shows, including Burns and Allen performing one of their routines.

D220 The Frank Sinatra Show (Songs by Sinatra). Audiocassette. Radio Spirits, n.d.
Burns and Allen were guests on the May 14, 1947 show (R954). One side of the cassette features Jane Powell, dated January 15, 1947.

D221 George Burns and Gracie Allen. Columbia, 152410, 2780-D, 1933.
A recording of Burns and Allen's vaudeville comedy routines, recorded on June 9, 1933.

D222 George Burns and Gracie Allen. Mark 56 Records, 614, 1973.
Two broadcasts from their February 24, 1949 (R744) and January 20, 1949 (R739) radio shows are featured.

D223 George Burns and Gracie Allen. Mark 56 Records, 735, 1976.

Recordings of the Burns and Allen radio shows from October 7, 1938 (R324) and December 23, 1936 (R240) are featured.

D224 **George Burns and Gracie Allen**. Audiocassette. McCoy's Recording Inc., 38, n.d.
Two shows, including their February 10, 1941 (R433) radio broadcast, are featured.

D225 **George Burns and Gracie Allen**. Audiocassette. McCoy's Recording Inc., 39, n.d.
The February 17, 1941 (R434) and March 24, 1941 (R439) broadcasts of George and Gracie's radio show are featured.

D226 **George Burns and Gracie Allen**. Audiocassette. McCoy's Recording Inc., 40, n.d.
An undated Burns and Allen radio show and a collection of Burns and Allen's ending routines are featured.

D227 **George Burns and Gracie Allen**. Audiocassette. Radiola, 1169, 1990.
The February 20, 1947 (R667) and December 4, 1947 (R695) broadcasts of George and Gracie's radio show are featured.

D228 **George Burns and Gracie Allen**. Top Ten, 109-11, 1947.
Recordings of the "Sugar Throat Sings Again" and "The French Long Underwear Maker," Part II Burns and Allen routines are featured. **SEE B31, B20.**

D229 **George Burns and Gracie Allen**. Top Ten, 110-112, 1947.
Recordings of "The French Long Underwear Maker," Part I and "Gracie Discovers a Movie Star" Burns and Allen routines are featured. **SEE B20, B23.**

D230 **George Burns and Gracie Allen**. Top Ten, 113-116, 1947.
Recordings of the "What Every Old Husband Should Know," Part I and "What Every Young Bride Should Know," Part II Burns and Allen routines are featured. **SEE B31.**

D231 **George Burns and Gracie Allen**. Top Ten, 114-115, 1947.
Recordings of the "What Every Old Husband Should Know," Part II and "What Every Young Bride Should Know," Part I Burns and Allen routines are featured. **SEE B31.**

D232 **George Burns and Gracie Allen: 1940's**. Memorabilia, MLP M4-722, 8 track M8-722, 1974.
A recording of George and Gracie's December 4, 1947 radio show with guest star Bing Crosby is featured. **SEE R695.**

D233 **George Burns and Gracie Allen Show**. Audiocassette. Radio Yesteryear, 445, 1986.
Two episodes from George and Gracie's radio show broadcast in 1945 are featured, one with guest star Alan Ladd (R582), the other with Gracie trying to get *Tootsie Sagwell* married (R583).

D234 **George Burns and Gracie Allen Show**. Audiocassette. Radio Yesteryear, 456, 1986.
The tape features two of George and Gracie's radio shows from the 1940's: one with guest star Rita Hayworth and Orson Welles (R547); in the second one Gracie is trying to protect Bill Goodwin from a golddigger (R567).

D235 **The George Burns and Gracie Allen Show**. Radiola, MR-1028, (Comedy Series No. 10), 1974.
This is a recording of George and Gracie's November 18, 1941 (R446) radio show and some of Burns and Allen's vaudeville routines as recorded from their television show.

D236 **GI Journal/Bergen and McCarthy Show**. Audiocassette. Sights and Sounds of America, 35C, 36C, 1977.
An episode of **The Charlie McCarthy Show** is coupled with one of **GI Journal** (n.d.), featuring an appearance by George and Gracie. **SEE R908, R1026.**

D237 **GI Journal Goes to France/The F.B.I. in Peace and War.** Audiocassette. Sights and Sounds of America, 30M, 35C, 1979.

Two radio broadcasts are featured. The first is a 1944 broadcast for the U.S. armed forces with George and Gracie, Robert Young and Mel Blanc (n.d.). Side two has "The Traveling Man" episode from a CBS crime drama series broadcast on June 10, 1953. **SEE R908.**

D238 **Golden Age of Comedy**. Evolution, 3013, 1973, Nostalgia Lane, NLC 5037; 2 Murray Hill, NH90007, n.d.
A collection of routines from some twenty top names in radio comedy, including Burns and Allen.

D239 **Golden Age of Comedy**. Longines Symphonette Society, LS 210A, SYS 5277-5281, 1971.
This five record collection of early 1960's comedy LP's is narrated by George.

D240 **Golden Age of Radio**. Longines Symphonette Society. 6 LWS, 613-618, 1946.
Selections from several radio shows, including episodes from Burns and Allen's 1946 and 1949 shows are featured, with narration by Jack Benny and Frank Knight.

D241 **Golden Age Radio Blockbusters**. Audiocassette. Metacom, MCM CS 110224, BB431-436, 1991.
Six cassettes from radio holiday broadcasts include Burns and Allen's "Santa's Workshop." **SEE R451.**

D242 **Golden Age Radio Comedy**. Audiocassette. Metacom, n.d.
Four hours of radio comedy include shows from the radio series of Abbott and Costello, Burns and Allen, Jack Benny and **The Bickersons**.

D243 **Gracie's Old Boyfriend**. Audiocassette. Mr. Media Productions, 1980.
A broadcast of a 1949 Burns and Allen radio show and the March 5, 1940 broadcast of **Fibber McGee & Molly** on which Gracie broke in to talk about her Presidential campaign. **SEE R861.**

D244 **Gracie's Old Boyfriend/Gracie's Relatives**. Audiocassette. Sights & Sounds of America, 34C, 1979.
This tape contains an episode from George and Gracie's radio program in 1949 and excerpts from Burns and Allen's routines about Gracie's relatives.

D245 **Great Comedians of the Century: The Voices of the All-Time Comedy Greats in Their Funniest Moments**. Columbia Transcriptions, TV 25925, TV 25926, 1957.
Eddie Cantor is the narrator of this collection of famous comedy routines as performed by Burns and Allen, Will Rogers, Weber and Fields and George Jessel.

D246 **Great Moments in American Radio**. Columbia, CSM-1245, 1970.
A collection of songs and excerpts from radio programs from its golden age. Burns and Allen are heard performing one of their skits.

D247 **Great Moments in Show Business**. Epic, FLS-15105, 1966.

D248 **The Great Radio Comedians**. Audiocassette. Book of the Month Club, 84-3192, 1984.
Program recordings from radio comedy shows include those starring Fred Allen, Jack Haley and Burns and Allen. **Baby Snooks** (Fanny Brice) and the **Aldrich Family** are also featured.

D249 **Great Radio Comedians**. Audiocassette. Radio Yesteryear, LCO-14, 1988.
The Burns and Allen radio program with guest star Brian Donlevy from September 14, 1943 (R520) and their June 13, 1944 (R559) broadcast are featured.

D250 **The Great Radio Comedians**. Murray Hill, 5-A, 1979; Radio Yesteryear, 1988.
Recordings of the October 24, 1946 (R650) and February 24, 1949 (R744) Burns and Allen radio shows are featured.

D251 **The Great Radio Comedians**. Murray Hill, 931699, n.d.

Five hours of radio recordings include **The George Burns and Gracie Allen Show**, **The Lucky Strike Program (The Jack Benny Program)**, **The Charlie McCarthy Show**, **The Pabst Blue Ribbon Show (The Eddie Cantor Show)**, **Duffy's Tavern**, **The Jimmy Durante Show** and **The Great Gildersleeve**.

D252 The Great Radio Comedies (Original Broadcasts From Radio's Golden Age). Audiocassette. Great American Audio Corp, 1993.
Four cassette tapes of radio comedy shows include a broadcast from **The Burns and Allen Show.**

D253 Great Radio Humor. Audiocassette. The Minds Eye/AVC Corporation, 488-9, 1992.
A boxed set of twelve cassettes of the great radio comedians includes Burns and Allen.

D254 Great Stars of Vaudeville. Columbia Special Products, CSS 1509, 1970.
Featured in this recording is a comedy skit by Burns and Allen and songs and monologues by performers Rudy Vallee, Clayton, Jackson and Durante, W. C. Fields, Al Jolson, Morton Downey, Baby Rose Marie, Arthur Tracy and Victor Borge.

D255 Greatest Original Radio Broadcasts 1944-1948. Martin P. Zacharius, M. F. Distribution Co., MF 215/3 1978.
Recordings from the Burns and Allen radio shows broadcast February 15, 1944 (R542), March 21, 1944 (R547), April 4, 1946 (R634), May 8, 1947 (R678), May 20, 1948 (R719) and May 6, 1948 (R717) are featured.

D256 Group W Presents the First Fifty Years of Radio. Audiotape. Priceless Sound Productions, 1006, n.d.
A 1930's segment includes excerpts from various radio shows, including Burns and Allen.

D257 Guest Star. Audiocassette. Radio Yesteryear, 15, n.d.
The Burnses were the guest stars on this show promoting war bonds. George and Gracie do a routine where they go door-to-door trying to sell the bonds. (George and Gracie made several guest appearances on this program; **SEE R950, R956, R963**).

D258 I Love Her, That's Why!. New Disk for Simon and Schuster, 1956.
A single recording by George and Gracie as a promotion line (non-retail) for George's book by the same name. The song was written by Dick Manning and Al Hoffman. **SEE B34, T178.**

D259 Jack Benny, Abbott & Costello, Burns & Allen (Triple Features in Sound). Audiocassette. Center for Cassette Studies, 1979.
Three original radio broadcasts from the Jack Benny, Abbott and Costello and Burns and Allen programs are featured.

D260 Jack Benny Presents Golden Memories of Radio. Audiocassette. Sandy Hook Records, 4CSH-1, 1989; Longines Symphonette Society, 613-618, n.d.
This collection of original radio broadcasts covers all aspects of radio programming such as newscasts, commercials, sports and comedy shows, including excerpts from those starring Burns and Allen, Jack Benny, Eddie Cantor, Amos 'n' Andy, Bing Crosby's show for Philco and others.

D261 Jack Benny Program. Audiocassette. BRC, 1618, 1987.
Jack's April 4, 1937 and April 11, 1937 radio shows are featured. George and Gracie appeared on the April 11 show. **SEE R839.**

D262 Jack Benny Program. Audiocassette. BRC, 1639, 1987.
Jack's January 5, 1947 and January 12, 1947 radio shows are featured. George and Gracie appeared on the January 12 show. **SEE R946.**

D263 Jack Benny Program. Audiocassette. BRC, 1852, n.d.
Jack's February 28, 1943 and March 7, 1943 radio shows are featured. George and Gracie substituted for Jack on the March show. **SEE R896.**

D264 The Jack Benny Program. Audiocassette. Old Time Radio Co., 1841, 1989.

Two broadcasts from Jack Benny's radio show with guest stars George Burns and Gracie Allen from March 7, 1943 (R896) and the April 18, 1943 show with Loretta Young are featured.

D265 **Jest Like Old Times**. Radiola, MR 1001, n.d.
Original recordings of "radio's most famous funny men" (Bert Lahr, Jack Pearl, Stoopnagle and Budd, Ed Wynn, Amos 'n' Andy, Edgar Bergen and Charlie McCarthy, Joe Penner and Abbott and Costello) also features George Burns and Gracie Allen and comedienne Fanny Brice.

D266 **Kraft Music Hall**. Audiocassette. Priceless Sound Productions, 1980.
Burns and Allen join George Jessel on Al Jolson's variety show (correct date of November 4, 1948). **SEE R969.**

D267 **Laughter From the Golden Age of Radio, Volume I**. Audiocassette. Great Tapes, 1988.
Twenty-four original radio broadcasts are featured in this collection. A Burns and Allen show from 1946 is included.

D268 **Laughter Is Still the Best Medicine**. Camco Enterprises, 1989.
One hundred stories and jokes from comedians include Burns and Allen in a short skit and routine about their next door neighbors.

D269 **Legends of Jolson, Durante, and Cantor**. Ambassador Artists, 1003-3, n.d.
George and Gracie are heard briefly in this collection of work by some of the world's legendary entertainers. Eddie Cantor was especially prominent in Burns and Allen's early years in radio.

D270 **Maxwell House Coffee Time, Starring George Burns and Gracie Allen**. Audiocassette. Radiola, MR 1169, n.d.
Two broadcasts from George and Gracie's NBC radio show are featured: February 20, 1947 with guest star Al Jolson (R667) and December 4, 1947 with guest star Bing Crosby (R695).

D271 **Mighty Memory Mobile Presents 1942**. Audiocassette. Cinema Sound, M420, 1976; Metacom, 1984.
Hosted by Garry Moore and Bob Maxwell, this program features historical facts and broadcasts from 1942. Burns and Allen talk about Gracie's brother going into the Air Corps.

D272 **Milton Berle's Mad, Mad World of Comedy**. Audiocassette. The Publishing Mills, 1992.
Comedian Milton Berle introduces this recording of comedians who played the RKO Palace Theatre. A conversation with George Burns is featured with performances by Burns and Allen and Jack Benny and George Burns. Other artists include Smith and Dale, Jimmy Durante, W. C. Fields, Will Rogers and Fred Allen.

D273 **The Most Memorable Moments in Broadcast History**. Nostalgia Lane, NR61; Audiocassette. NLC 51, n.d.
In this six recording set from comedy's golden age, Burns and Allen are featured on side four.

D274 **The Nature of Satire**. Audiocassette. Audio-Text, 12256, n.d.
A survey of a sixty year history of American satire in literature and performance analyzed by John Dodds. Includes Burns and Allen, Fred Allen, Charles Chaplin, James Thurber, Jules Feiffer and Shelly Berman.

D275 **The New Burns & Allen Show**. Radiola, CMR 1142, 1983.
These recordings are from their October 21, 1941 and December 16, 1941 radio shows, "The Insurance Exam" and the "Post Office." **SEE R442, R450.**

D276 **The 1948 Rose Bowl**. Audiocassette. Sights & Sounds of America, 67C, 69C, 1979.
Radio broadcasts from Jack Benny's show of January 4, 1948 and the Burns and Allen radio show of May 19, 1949 with guest star Mickey Rooney are featured. **SEE R756.**

D277 **The Nostalgia Lane Treasury of the Best of Old Time Radio**. Audiocassette. Nostalgia Lane, NLC 50, NLR 60, n.d.

Four cassettes feature excerpts from radio performers, including Burns and Allen.

D278 Nostalgia Radio. Compact Disc. Metacom, CD0700439, 1994.
Four hours of radio shows on four discs include "George Inherits $5,000" (R615) and "Jack Benny and George at College" (R616). Abbott and Costello, Jack Benny and W. C. Fields radio shows are also featured.

D279 Nostalgia Trip to the Stars, 1920-1950. Vol. 1. Monmouth Evergreen, MES 7030-31, 1973.
Various artists perform songs and comedy skits. Burns and Allen's vaudeville routine, "Dizzy," is excerpted.

D280 The Old Time Radio Classic Collection. Vol. 2. Audiocassette, Radio Spirits, n.d.
A nine hour collection of radio shows includes a Burns and Allen show, "Gracie's Old Boyfriend Visits."

D281 Old Time Radio (Newsweek Remembers Radio). Columbia Special Products, CSP 104, 154, 1962; CBS, P2M5287, D472, 473, 1968; BT 20092, 1979.
This collector's edition recording of radio performances from popular entertainers of the 1920's, 1930's and 1940's includes Burns and Allen, Rudy Vallee, Will Rogers and Bing Crosby. The recordings were narrated by Warren Moran.

D282 Our World. "The Long Winter and Short Spring of 1937." Audiotape. Pt. 1. With Linda Ellerbee and Ray Gandolf. ABC. New York.
A recording of the May 21, 1987 television documentary series which featured, on this broadcast, the subjects of radio comedy in 1937 (including Burns and Allen) and historic facts from that year. **SEE T592.**

D283 Our World. "Spring of 1954." Audiotape. Pt. 2. With Linda Ellerbee and Ray Gandolf. ABC. New York.
This November 6, 1986 television broadcast of the documentary series centered on historical events of 1954 and included an overview of popular television shows of that same year, including **The George Burns and Gracie Allen Show. SEE T589.**

D284 Radio Reruns on Cassette. Audiocassette. Radio Reruns, 1987.
This is a set of twenty-one sound cassettes of radio show broadcasts which includes Burns and Allen's show, "Gracie's Mother Doesn't Like George's Work" (R719).

D285 Radio YesterYule: Christmas Cassettes, Vol. 2. Radio Yesteryear, 1989.
A collection of Christmas stories as broadcast on several radio programs has been gathered on one tape. **The Burns and Allen Show** of December 23, 1936 is featured. **SEE R240.**

D286 Radio's Famous Theme Songs. Longines Symphonette Society, LW 525/526, 1966.
Twenty of the best known radio theme songs are featured in this instrumental recording, including "The Love Nest," Burns and Allen's theme song.

D287 Radio's Greatest Comedians. Audiocassette. Compact Disc. MMP International, PTN-724 (1-5), 1992.
A set of five original broadcasts from radio shows of the 1930's, 1940's and 1950's. From the Burns and Allen (Vol. 4) program are the shows "Gracie Wants George to Become a Doctor" (R744), "The Happy Postman," "Jack Benny Pays for Lunch", "George is a Frustrated Singer," "Gracie Gets a Letter From Her Sister" and "Gracie Becomes a Business Executive." Also included in the set are programs from the Fred Allen (Vol. 1), Jack Benny (Vol. 2), Edgar Bergen and Charlie McCarthy (Vol. 3), and Red Skelton (Vol. 5) shows.

D288 Radio's Most Famous Sitcoms. Audiocassette. Great American Audio, 1993.
Original broadcasts from radio's golden age includes a Burns and Allen show.

D289 Remember Radio. Audiocassette. Remember Radio, Inc., Reels 214, 215, 418, 1960.

Radio broadcasts from historical events and radio programs are captured on tape; the first one in the series includes a Burns and Allen skit.

D290 **Remember the Golden Days of Radio, Volume I**. Narrated by Jack Benny and Frank Knight. The Longines Symphonette Society, SY5183 (LW447), n.d.
This recording includes performances by great radio comedians (including Burns and Allen) and daytime radio programs and commercials.

D291 **Salute to the Hollywood Canteen**. Stanyan Records, 2 SR-10066, 1973.
George and Gracie were among the stars who hosted and entertained armed forces personnel in Hollywood at the Hollywood Canteen during World War II.

D292 **Screen Guild Theater**. Audiocassette. Radio Yesteryear, 23046, n.d.
A recording from the February 26, 1939 show featuring "The Shining Hour" with Rufe Davis, Shirley Ross and Burns and Allen as guest stars. **SEE R847.**

D293 **66 Flashbacks**. 2 Recar, PCA-5001, n.d.
A compilation of sixteen radio programs with twenty-six performers, including Burns and Allen.

D294 **The Smithsonian Collection of Old-Time Radio: All-Time Favorites**. Audiocassette. Compact Disc. Smithsonian Institution, 1994.
This is collection of radio shows from the past includes Burns and Allen's November 7, 1946 (R652) show.

D295 **The Smithsonian Collection of Old-Time Radio: Comedy Favorites**. Audiocassette. Compact Disc. Smithsonian Institution, 1994.
A collection of twelve complete and original radio broadcasts includes Burns and Allen's show from January 2, 1947 (R660). The five hour set includes a booklet about radio history with an introduction written by George Burns.

D296 **Superstars of Comedy**. Audiocassette. Great American Audio Corp., 7004, n.d.
Famous Radio Comedy Teams, the title of this entry, includes Gracie Allen in a routine with guest star Ronald Reagan and series regular Bea Benaderet. Possibly from R780.

D297 **Superstars of Comedy**. Audiocassette. Great American Audio Corp., 7005, n.d.
Another entry titled **Famous Sitcoms** features excerpts from radio programs **The Burns and Allen Show**, **The Aldrich Family**, **Ozzie and Harriet**, **The Goldbergs**, **My Friend Irma** and **The Life of Riley**.

D298 **Superstars of Comedy**. Audiocassette. Great American Audio Corp., 7006, n.d.
Side one features **The Comedy Superstars of Radio** with radio's favorite comedy teams' running gags and famous feuds. George Burns and Gracie Allen do skits about Gracie's assorted relatives, including her sister Bessie and brother Willie Allen (the "Broken Back" routine).

D299 **Superstars of Comedy**. Audiocassette. Great American Audio Corp., 7121, n.d.
Comedy teams from the late 1940's includes Burns and Allen, Phil Harris and Alice Faye, Fibber McGee & Molly, Bob and Ray and Amos 'n' Andy in two cassettes.

D300 **The Swing's to TV**. World Pacific, 1002, n.d.
This compilation of television theme songs includes George and Gracie's familiar "The Love Nest."

D301 **Telephone Answering Machine Outgoing Messages: Comedy Edition.** Audiocassette. Radio Shack, 1983.
Comic fifteen-second impersonations by ten personalities (including Burns and Allen) for use on telephone answering machines.

D302 **Television Theme Recordings**. Audiocassette. The Television Museum Archives, New York, 1985.
Included in this collection of songs is Burns and Allen's theme song "The Love Nest."

D303 **The Three Funniest Hours in the History of Radio**. Murray Hill Records, M58047, 1970; Nostalgia Lane, 1977.
Featured are several radio programs, including Burns and Allen, Abbott and Costello, Jack Benny, Fibber McGee & Molly and Groucho Marx.

D304 **Tony Martin**. Audiocassette. Radio Spirits, 1060, n.d.
Burns and Allen appear on Martin's April 13, 1947 radio show (R953); another episode guest stars Bob Hope.

D305 **The Very Best of Golden Age Radio**. Audiocassette. Metacom, 1992.
Within this collection of forty cassettes from radio broadcasts, Volume II includes Burns and Allen in "The Literary Club" (R635) and "H & R Blockhead" (R785).

D306 **The War Years**. Audiocassette. Great American Audio Corp., 7138, n.d.
A history of World War II features historical radio recordings of the time, including Burns and Allen.

D307 **You Ain't Heard Nothing Yet! Al Jolson Radio Rarities**. Radiola, 3MR-2, 1985.
Six radio shows from the master showman, Al Jolson, one with guest stars Burns and Allen. The correct date of their appearance on his **Kraft Music Hall** show was November 4, 1948. **SEE R969.**

Addendum

D308 **Burns & Allen**. Metacom, 1995.
Twelve radio shows date from 10-6-42 through 12-22-42.

D309 **Burns & Allen**. Metacom, 1995.
Twelve radio shows date from 12-29-42 through 3-30-43.

D310 **Gracie Allen for President**. Metacom, 1995.
A set of twelve Burns and Allen radio shows from 1940 when Gracie ran for president. The live show from her convention in Omaha, Nebraska, is included. The dates are 2-28-40, 3-6-40, 3-13-40, 3-27-40, 4-3-40, 4-10-40, 4-17-40, 4-24-40, 5-8-40, 5-15-40, 5-22-40, 5-29-40.

D311 **The Life**. Ira Gasman, lyrics; Cy Coleman, musical score. RCA Victor, 1996.
Recorded in 1995, George sings "Easy Money" on this album of songs.

~~~~~
~~~~~

VIDEOGRAPHY

This section includes films, television shows, concerts, specials, compilations and special interest material which is available on (primarily) videocassette and/or laserdisc. Information includes distributor, product number and year of release.

Gracie Allen

VG1 **Two Girls and a Sailor**. Videocassette. Laserdisc, MGM/UA Home Video, M200852, 1990.
The 1944 motion picture (F35) in which Gracie plays her "Concerto for Index Finger."

George Burns

VG2 **The Big Time Variety Show**. Videocassette. Video Yesteryear, n.d.

VG3 **A Conversation with George Burns**. Videocassette. ERGO, 438, n.d.
Monty Hall interviews George about his Jewish roots and his philosophy of life.

VG4 **18 Again!** 100 min. color. Videocassette. New World Video, A88006, 1988. Starmaker, 90002QEPV, n.d. Also available on laserdisc.
After an automobile accident George's character suddenly finds himself in the body of his eighteen year old grandson. **SEE F45.**

VG5 **The 50th Barbara Walters Special**. Videocassette. MPI Home Video, 6127, 1990.
In this compilation of interviews Walters has done for her ABC television specials, George is seen in a very short portion of a soft shoe routine with Walters and from his May 29, 1979 appearance. He says "Say good night, Barbara," to which she replies "Good night, Barbara." **SEE T528.**

VG6 **Forgotten Eyes**. Music video. 1990.
A video tie-in with the audio single for retinitis pigmentosa, which was participated in by a number of celebrities, including George. **SEE D28.**

VG7 **George Burns: His Wit and Wisdom**. Videocassette. Life, LS74994, 1988. VidAmerica, Inc., Vistar International, 7160, 1989.
A look at George's daily routine includes his morning exercises done at home, one of his concert performances and visits with Morey Amsterdam, Army Archerd, Red Buttons, Carol Channing, Emma Samms and Yakov Smirnoff. **SEE B284.**

VG8 George Burns in Concert. Videocassette. USA Home Video, 203-505, 1985.
George Burns' 1982 one-man concert before a live audience is captured for posterity.

VG9 The George Burns Show. Videocassette. Video Yesteryear, n.d.
This tape features an episode from George's 1958-1959 NBC television series in which guest star Carol Channing sues him when she believes he dented the fender on her new car. The company marketing the video refers to it as "The Hollywood Television Courtroom," but it's better known as "Carol Channing Guests" (T310). The tape includes the original commercials.

VG10 Going in Style. Videocassette. Warner Home Video, Inc., 1030, n.d.
The 1979 film (F41) in which George stars with Art Carney and Lee Strasberg.

VG11 Hollywood Palace. Videocassette. n.d.
Discount Video Tapes in Burbank, CA at one time offered up this last broadcast of **The Hollywood Palace**, hosted by Bing Crosby, that includes a retrospective of past show business greats. George, who had appeared on the program several times during its six years on the air, both as guest and host, is included. **SEE T455.**

VG12 Jack Benny I. Videocassette. Shokus Video, 213, n.d.
Three complete Jack Benny television shows include the March 21, 1954 show with George Burns, Bing Crosby and Bob Hope (T376), one from 1953 and a 1965 show.

VG13 Jack Benny/Milton Berle: Legends of American Comedy. Videocassette. Avon, n.d.
Two shows from the 1950's. George appears with Bing Crosby and Bob Hope on the Jack Benny program. **SEE T376.**

VG14 The Jack Benny Show. Videocassette. Concord Video, CTV 724, n.d.
George Burns, Bing Crosby and Bob Hope guest on Jack's television show, dancing and singing in an old vaudeville routine called "Goldie, Fields and Glide." **SEE T376.**

VG15 Movie Movie. Videocassette. Warner Home Video, Inc., 11789.
George performed narrating duties in this film from 1978 (F40).

VG16 Oh, God! Videocassette. Laserdisc; Warner Home Video, Inc., 1010.
George plays the title role in this 1977 film co-starring John Denver. Warner Home Video, Inc. also released this under the title **Dios, Mio!** in a Spanish-dubbed version in 1987 (#6009). **SEE F38.**

VG17 Oh, God! Book II. Videocassette. Warner Home Video, Inc., 1044.
The second film in the series, released in 1980. George's co-stars include David Birney and Suzanne Pleshette. **SEE F43.**

VG18 Oh, God! You Devil. Videocassette. Laserdisc; Warner Home Video, Inc., 11418.
Ted Wass joins George in the third and likely last entry in the **Oh, God!** series, released in 1984. **SEE F44.**

VG19 Rowlf's Rhapsodies with the Muppets. Videocassette. 1985.
George was a guest star on **The Muppet Show**, and this tape consists of musical bits culled from the series, including his appearance. **SEE T501.**

VG20 Sgt. Pepper's Lonely Hearts Club Band. Videocassette. MCA, 55013; Laserdisc. MCA, 17004.
George's first musical since teaming with Gracie in MGM's 1939 film, **Honolulu** (F39). This time it's with the Bee Gees and Peter Frampton. **SEE F39.**

VG21 Sounds of the Seventies: The Darin Invasion. Laserdisc; Videocassette. View Video, 1320; 3320 PAL (United Kingdom), LV7320, 1990.
This was singer/actor Bobby Darin's first and only television special. George Burns and Linda Ronstadt guest. **SEE T462.**

VG22 The Sunshine Boys. Videocassette. MGM/UA Home Video, M600014;

Laserdisc.
George won the Best Supporting Actor Oscar for this 1975 film. **SEE F37, T495.**

VG23 Two Of A Kind. Laserdisc. CBS/Fox 1339-80; Videocassette. AVID, 51048.
SEE T540.

VG24 Vintage Television. Love that Bob, II. Videocassette. Shokus Video, 275, 1993.
Four 1958 television shows with Bob Cummings, Ann B. Davis, Dwayne Hickman and Rosemary De Camp. George Burns appears as himself in "Bob Butters Beck...Beck Butters Better." **SEE T394.**

George Burns and Gracie Allen

VG25 The Best of 50's Comics. Videocassette. Parade Video, DP-1312 (522, 523), 1990.
Comedy skits and routines collected from early television shows comprise this two volume set. Volume 1 (#522) includes Jimmy Durante, Jack Benny and Milton Berle. Volume 2 (#523) has excerpts from Red Skelton, Bob Hope and George Burns and Gracie Allen. In an approximately seven minute excerpt from **The George Burns and Gracie Allen Show**, Gracie is giving a wedding for the daughter of a woman who has done her a favor, and George remarks on attending a wedding in Beverly Hills. **SEE T26.**

VG26 Broadway Highlights. Videocassette.
The original **Broadway Highlights** was a series of 1930's shorts narrated by Ted Husing featuring New York City after dark (Husing worked as an announcer for a time on George and Gracie's radio show). Four films have been captured on video for today's audiences who may never have had the chance to see them in their original form. In one entry George and Gracie are seen at the opening of **Jumbo** on Broadway. **SEE F15.**

VG27 Burns and Allen. Videocassette. Congress Video Group, 1987.
Two episodes from George and Gracie's television series are featured: November 9, 1950 (T3) and April 26, 1951 (T16).

VG28 Burns and Allen. Videocassette. RCA Columbia, 1985.
Two episodes from George and Gracie's television series are featured: December 11, 1952 (T62) and January 22, 1953 (T68).

VG29 Burns and Allen Christmas. Videocassette. Columbia Tristar, 92763, 1992.
Two episodes from George and Gracie's television series are featured: including "Christmas in Jail" (T225).

VG30 Burns and Allen Five Hour Marathon. Videocassette. Star Video. n.d.
This tape contains ten episodes from the George Burns and Gracie Allen television show.

VG31 The Burns and Allen Show. Videocassette. Concord Video, CTV 703, 1987.
Neighbor Emily Vanderlip is staying at the Burnses' while her parents are away from home in "Teen Visit." The offerings from Concord Video consist of one episode per videocassette. **SEE T16.**

VG32 The Burns and Allen Show. Videocassette. Concord Video, CTV 725, 1987.
Gracie and George's home is the setting for the "Wedding Party." **SEE T26.**

VG33 The Burns and Allen Show. Videocassette. Concord Video, CTV 901, 1987.
The "Meet the Mortons" episode from the Burns and Allen television show is featured. **SEE T1.**

VG34 The Burns and Allen Show. Videocassette. Concord Video, CTV 902, 1987.
Gracie thinks she has dented the family car in "Car Accident." **SEE T3.**

VG35 **The Burns and Allen Show**. Videocassette. Concord Video, CTV 903, 1987.
Gracie has trouble with her finances in the "Checking Account" episode. **SEE T5.**

VG36 **The Burns and Allen Show**. Videocassette. Concord Video, CTV 904, 1987.
Gracie tries to understand the Burnses' "Income Tax". **SEE T12.**

VG37 **The Burns and Allen Show**. Videocassette. Concord Video, CTV 905, 1987.
"The Beverly Hills Uplift Society" meets again at the Burnses'. **SEE T28.**

VG38 **The Burns and Allen Show**. Videocassette. Concord Video, CTV 906, 1987.
Gracie's "Nieces Visit" from San Francisco in this episode. The title used to identify the show is a misnomer; although the young girls in the episode call Gracie "Aunt" it is only because she's a good friend of their mother (played by Sarah Selby in the role of *Mamie*). **SEE T44.**

VG39 **Burns and Allen Show**. Videocassette. International Film Forum, 3008, 1990; TV Gold, 1990.
Three episodes from George and Gracie's television series are featured, including "Teenage Girl Spends Weekend" (T16).

VG40 **Burns and Allen Show**. Videocassette. Video Treasures, 1987.
This tape contains one episode from the television version of **The George Burns and Gracie Allen Show**.

VG41 **Burns and Allen Show, I**. Videocassette. Shokus Video, 226, 1985.
Four early episodes have been transferred to video: George and Gracie's first television program from October 12, 1950 (T1), "The Teenage Visit" from April 26, 1951 (T16), "Beverly Hills Uplifting Society" (T28) and "Gracie Takes a Fall" from August 17, 1953 (T92).

VG42 **Burns and Allen Show, II**. Videocassette. Shokus Video, 240, 1985.
Four episodes of George and Gracie's television series are featured: "The Checking Account" from December 7, 1950 (T5), the "Tax Audit" from November 9, 1950 (T3), "Return of the Kelly Kids" from May 22, 1952 (T44) and "Gracie's Driver's License" from November 1, 1954 (T137).

VG43 **Burns and Allen Show, III**. Videocassette. Shokus Video, 257, 1988.
Four episodes of George and Gracie's television series are featured: "George's Hmm, Hmm Day" from January 4, 1951 (T8), "The Health Kick" from August 2, 1951 (T23), "The Wedding" from September 13, 1951 (T26) and "The Life Stories" from March 29, 1954 (T118).

VG44 **Burns, Allen and Benny Christmas**. Videocassette. TV Classics. 1993.
"Eight Cold Christmas Gifts" from **The Burns and Allen Show** and an episode of **The Jack Benny Program** from December 27, 1953 comprise this holiday offering.

VG45 **Cepacol Classic Comedy Hour: The Golden Age of TV Comedy**. Videocassette. Merrell Dow Pharmaceuticals, Inc., 1990.
Cepacol mouthwash celebrated its 50th anniversary with the release of this tape, which features several appearances from the great television comedians, including Burns and Allen.

VG46 **A Christmas Compilation**. Videocassette. Shokus, 718, n.d.
Four shows from the 1950's include the December 20, 1951 **Burns and Allen Show** (T33), **See it Now** (one entry from a series of documentaries hosted by Edward R. Murrow), **The Paul Winchell-Jerry Mahoney Show** and **The Adventures of Ozzie and Harriet**.

VG47 **Classic Movie Comedy Teams**. Videocassette. Goodtimes Home Video Corp., 8010, 1986.
This feature narrated by Steve Allen consists of short film clips from the films of various comedy teams, including Burns and Allen.

VG48 **College Swing**. Videocassette. MCA Universal Home Video, 1993.

The 1938 film with Burns and Allen and Bob Hope (F31). This release is part of **The Bob Hope Collection**.

VG49 Comedy and Kid Stuff, I. Videocassette. Shokus Video, 201, 1985.
This various artists tape includes an episode of the Burns and Allen television show from 1952 (with a correct date of June 5), a 1952 episode of **I Married Joan** starring Joan Davis and Jim Backus and 1953 episodes of **Winky Dink and You** starring Jack Barry and **Carson's Cellar** with Johnny Carson and Jack Bailey. **SEE T45.**

VG50 Comedy and Kid Stuff, II. Videocassette. Shokus Video, 202, 1989.
A compilation tape includes an episode of Burns and Allen's "Christmas at the Burnses'" from December 20, 1951 (T33), a 1953 version of Abbott and Costello's most famous skit, "Who's on First?" from **The Abbott and Costello Show**, a 1955 episode of **Howdy Doody** and a 1967 episode of **The Lucy Show** with guest Jack Benny.

VG51 A Damsel in Distress. Videocassette. Republic Pictures Home Video, 7135, 1988; Laserdisc. IEI, ID7054TU.
The 1937 motion picture starring Fred Astaire, Joan Fontaine and Burns and Allen has been made available on videotape. **SEE F30.**

VG52 The Ed Wynn Show/Burns and Allen. Videocassette. Moviecraft, MC-18, n.d.
Two live shows from the early 1950's comprise this hour-long video tape.

VG53 50's TV Classics. Video Cassette. Concord Video.
SEE VG29-VG36.

VG54 George Burns and Gracie Allen (Legends of American Comedy). Videocassette. PPI Entertainment Group, 1990.
This tape features "The Comedy Hour" episode from Burns and Allen's television series.

VG55 The George Burns and Gracie Allen Show. Videocassette. CBS Columbia House Video Library, 1990.
Columbia House packages selected episodes of several vintage television series and offers them to the public via subscriptions garnered from full-page ads placed in popular publications and from notices to audio/video club members. This time the company presented a collection of fifteen boxed videocassettes of **The George Burns and Gracie Allen Show**, each containing three episodes advertised to be from the 1952 and 1953 seasons.

VG56 The George Burns and Gracie Allen Show. Videocassette. CBS Video Library, 5957, 1990.
Three episodes of George and Gracie's television series are featured: "Harry Loves Gracie" from January 8, 1953 (T66), "Stay Neighbor Stay" from January 15, 1953 (T67) and "Wedding Bell Blues" from January 22, 1953 (T68).

VG57 The George Burns and Gracie Allen Show. Videocassette. Christmas Classics, CCV-212, 1987.
Contains one of George and Gracie's Christmas shows.

VG58 The George Burns and Gracie Allen Show. Videocassette. Goodtimes Home Video, 3015, 1986.
Contains a broadcast of their December 20, 1951 (T33) show.

VG59 The George Burns and Gracie Allen Show. Videocassette. Madacy Music Group Inc., TVC-6-1102, 1992.
Four episodes of George and Gracie's television series are featured. This appears to be the taped version of a portion of **The Golden Years of Television**. **SEE T752.**

VG60 The George Burns and Gracie Allen Show. Videocassette. Madacy Music Group Inc., TVC-6-1114, 1993.
A quartet of George and Gracie's television shows are featured: "Vegetarian Plot" (T23), "Gracie Gives A Wedding" (T26), "Property Tax Assessor" (T3) and a Christmas episode.

VG61 The George Burns and Gracie Allen Show. Videocassette. Parade, 521, n.d.

VG62 The George Burns and Gracie Allen Show. Videocassette. Video Yesteryear, 648, n.d.
One of their early live shows dated December 20, 1951 (T33) is transferred from kinescope to videotape.

VG63 The George Burns and Gracie Allen Show/Heaven for Betsy. TV Classics, Vol. 5. Videocassette. MPI Home Video, 1317, 1986.
This tape contains the debut **Burns and Allen Show** episode from October 12, 1950 (T1) and one from a 1952 series featuring Jack Lemmon and Cynthia Stone.

VG64 The George Burns and Gracie Allen Show, Volume I. Videocassette. CBS Columbia House Video Library, 60537, 1985.
Episodes of George and Gracie's television series that aired December 11, 1952 (T62) and January 22, 1953 (T68) are showcased.

VG65 George Burns Twice.
One episode of **The George Burns and Gracie Allen Show** and one of **Wendy and Me** are juxtaposed, hence the title.

VG66 The Great Radio Comedians. McGraw Hill. n.d.
Stills and newsreel footage capture a number of famous radio entertainers, including Burns and Allen, Bob Hope, Eddie Cantor, Fred Allen, Jack Benny and Mary Livingstone, Fanny Brice, Eddie "Rochester" Anderson, Kate Smith and W. C. Fields.

VG67 Honolulu. Videocassette. MGM/UA Home Video, M202828, 1993.
The 1939 film (F32) starring Eleanor Powell, Robert Young and Burns and Allen is now available on the home video market.

VG68 I Married Joan/The Burns and Allen Show. Videocassette. International Historic Films, VC-10, 1983; Video Sig, 12880, 1989.
Two television shows from the early 1950's, one starring Joan Davis, the other with George and Gracie, are presented together.

VG69 International House. Videocassette. MCA, 80512; Laserdisc. MCA, 40512.
George and Gracie co-starred with W. C. Fields in this 1933 film. **See F20.**

VG70 The Kennedy Center Honors. Archival Videocassette. Peabody Recording Center, 1990.
The December 4, 1988 production televised by CBS on December 30, 1988 in honor of the 11th annual Kennedy Center awards held in Washington, DC has been preserved and housed in the Peabody Collection at the University of Georgia. George Burns was one of the recipients given an award for his career excellence. **SEE T623.**

VG71 Legends of American Comedy. Videocassette. Wood Knapp's Special Interest Video, PD 038, n.d.
Included are some excerpts from Burns and Allen's television show.

VG72 Radio Days (The In Times Past Series). Videocassette. GHI Media Productions, 1992.
This is a collection of radio personalities and excerpts from radio shows, including Burns and Allen.

VG73 TV Variety XXVI. Videocassette. Shokus, 473, n.d.
A television special produced by CBS, **Stars in the Eye**, was broadcast the evening of the dedication of the network's new production facility in Hollywood, appropriately named Television City. Burns and Allen appeared along with other guests, including cast members from **Amos 'n' Andy, I Love Lucy** and **Our Miss Brooks**. The second show on this cassette is an episode of the live musical variety program, **Shower of Stars**, from November 1, 1956. Some sources indicate the broadcast occurred on November 15, 1952, including this tape, but the UCLA archives reveal it was November 11, 1952. **SEE T375.**

VG74 Video Encyclopedia of the Twentieth Century. Videodiscs. CEL Educational Resources, 1986.
Six minutes of black and white newsreel clips of Burns and Allen from 1934 and 1936 include two seasonal bits: Gracie serving George Thanksgiving dinner and George dressed up like Santa Claus. Other clips show them on

a cruise liner talking to reporters and photographers in 1934 (R819), at a Red Cross rally in New York for the USO, again in 1934, and attending a Hollywood premiere with Jack and Mary Benny in 1936. Some are silent, some contain an audio portion.

VG75 Vintage Sitcoms I. Videocassette. Shokus Video, 208, 1980.
Four early television shows include **The George Burns and Gracie Allen Show** originally broadcast on July 6, 1953 (T86), an episode of **The People's Choice** from 1955, a 1949 episode of **The Life of Riley** (when it starred Jackie Gleason, prior to William Bendix taking over the role) and a 1952 episode of **My Little Margie**.

VG76 Vintage Sitcoms VIII. Videocassette. Shokus Video, 266, 1985.
Another entry in the Shokus series includes the November 23, 1950 episode of **The George Burns and Gracie Allen Show** (T4) as well as ones culled from **The Bing Crosby Show**, **The Three Stooges Show** (1949) and **Date with the Angels**, starring Betty White and Bill Williams.

VG77 We're Not Dressing. Videocassette. MCA Universal Home Video, 1994.
The 1934 film starring George and Gracie, Carole Lombard and Bing Crosby. It's available in **The Bing Crosby Collection**. **SEE F23.**

Addendum

VG78 George Burns: 100 Years of Comedy. Videocassette. Stone Entertainment, 1995.
Subtitled **The Best of George Burns** these two tapes are a video biography of his life. Several excerpts from the Burns and Allen television show are included.

VG79 Radioland Murders. Videocassette. Laserdisc; MCA/Universal Home Video, 1995.
George Burns had a cameo in this, his last film.

~~~~~
~~~~~

APPENDIX A: AWARDS AND HONORS

George and Gracie received a voluminous amount of awards and honors during their lengthy careers. Some of Gracie's awards were awarded posthumously. George's own career guaranteed a seemingly never-ending series of accolades. He received so many and was such a popular recipient that it appeared some organizations established awards for the purpose of being able to present him with one!

Emmy nomination dates for **The Burns and Allen Show** and Gracie Allen are listed under the season for which they were nominated. George's Emmy nominations are listed on the date the nominations were announced.

1932 December 3 — George N. Burns and Grace Allen are guests of honor at a midnight dinner hosted by the Saturday Night Boys of the Friars Club in New York City, officiated by toastmasters Eddie Cantor and George Jessel.

1936 May 13 — George and Gracie receive a medal for "Outstanding Merit" from **Radio Guide Weekly** for their performances in radio.

May 19 — Students at the University of Southern California vote Gracie the "most intelligent actress" in Hollywood.

1937 February 10 — The Hearst Radio Editors Poll of 1936 lists Gracie as the most popular comedienne and Burns and Allen the year's most popular radio team for 1936.

December 10 — Gracie is voted one of the 10 best comediennes in **Motion Picture Daily**'s annual radio survey.

ca. — In other poll ratings for the year, Burns and Allen rate third among the top half hour evening radio programs, fifth in radio personalities (**Radio Daily** poll) and sixth among the best radio shows.

1938 February 7 — The Second Annual Hearst Newspapers' Radio Editors Poll names Gracie as the leading comedienne and Burns and Allen the leading radio comedy team.

June 5 — Burns and Allen appear in the **New York Daily News** Favorite Radio Performers Poll.

ca. — In other 1938 polls, Gracie is voted eighth in **Radio Guide**'s best comedians poll, Burns and Allen's radio show is voted fourth best on the air, New York University's poll votes Burns and Allen as number six among the most popular personalities in radio. **Fortune Quarterly**'s survey on radio favorites places Burns and Allen as twelfth and the Seventh Annual **New York World-Telegram** Newspaper Editors Radio Poll places Burns and

Allen as fourteenth among favorite programs and fifth as comedians.

1939 October 7 Burns and Allen are named among the honorary sponsors of the National Better Parenthood Week (the week of October 23, 1939).

December 22 Gracie is named Hollywood Director of the National Dunking Association.

1940 February 22 Los Angeles voters sign petition to support Gracie Allen for President.

April Gracie throws out the first ball of the season at the Hollywood Ballpark in Hollywood, California for the Pacific Coast League during a game for the Hollywood Stars, a minor league baseball team in which she and George shared ownership with other entertainers.

April 9 Gracie receives 63 votes in the Wisconsin State Presidential Primary.

April 20 Gracie is named a Commodore of the State of Texas.

May Gracie is the subject of Indian tribal honors during her Surprise Party convention in Omaha, Nebraska, including being given the name of an Indian chief (translated it means "she who says funny things") and being made an Indian princess.

May 22 Gracie is made Honorary Mayor of Boys Town, Nebraska.

1941 December 20 Gracie is named one of the best comediennes on radio.

1942 ca. Gracie is chairman of the American Women's Voluntary Service.

1943 April 10 Gracie is made an honorary member of Local 47 of the Los Angeles Musicians' Union.

1944 April 9 Honorable mention for Most Outstanding Script, Comedy, is given to the Burns and Allen radio show in the first **Radio Life** magazine awards. The award is presented for the 1943 episode in which Frank Sinatra guests.

1945 April 15 Honorable mention for Most Outstanding Script, Comedy, is given by **Radio Life** to the Burns and Allen radio show for the November 28, 1944 episode.

1946 February 7 Burns and Allen are named as Hollywood's ideal married couple.

April 14 **Radio Life**'s third annual Distinguished Achievement Awards gives honorable mention for comedy scriptwriting to George and Gracie's radio show.

1947 ca. George is named to the ten best-dressed men in America list.

1949 February 17 George is "roasted" by the Friars Club.

April 21 The National Safety Council uses Gracie's name in their home safety campaign slogan, "Don't be a Gracie Allen." Gracie is also elected national president of the "Don't Be A Gracie" club.

1950 February 22 George and Gracie receive the National Safety Council's Award of Merit for 1949.

1951 **The George Burns and Gracie Allen Show** is nominated for an Emmy for Best Comedy Show.

	May	George and Gracie receive Sylvania's Pioneer Award for their work in radio and television.
1952		**The George Burns and Gracie Allen Show** is nominated for an Emmy for Best Situation Comedy.
1953		**The George Burns and Gracie Allen Show** is nominated for an Emmy for Best Situation Comedy.
1954		**The George Burns and Gracie Allen Show** is nominated for an Emmy for Best Situation Comedy Series.
		Gracie is nominated for an Emmy for Best Actress Starring in a Regular Series.
	May	George and Gracie receive an engraved copper likeness of themselves on a plaque presented by the cast and crew of their television series at the wrap party. The plaque contains the inscription "Thank you, thank you, thank you. From the gang."
	September	George receives the "Bard Award" from the International Shakespearean Students Association for popularizing the soliloquy through his monologues on his television show.
	September 24	Gracie is named Best Dressed Woman in Hollywood by the New York Stylists Association.
1955	January 23	George and Gracie are feted at the First Mr. and Mrs. All-Charities Testimonial Dinner by the Friars Club at the Biltmore Bowl, Los Angeles, California. The event raises $100,000.
	February	**The George Burns and Gracie Allen Show** is named top all-around family program on television by the Boy Scouts of America.
	March	The Burns and Allen exhibit is set to open at the Museum of American Comedy in Riviera Beach, Florida.
	March 18	George receives the "Man and Boy" award from the Boys Club of America.
	ca.	George and Gracie receive the Television Champion Award for Best Comedy Team from Quigley Publications (publisher of the **Motion Picture Almanac** and another title, the **Television Almanac**).
		Gracie is nominated for two Emmys, one for Best Actress and the other for Best Comedienne.
	ca.	Gracie is placed on the West Coast Designers' Ten Best Dressed Women list.
	ca.	Gracie is named Best Dressed Woman on Television by The Fashion Coordinators.
	ca.	George Burns is #6 on Dinah Shore's 12 Top Pinup Boys of TV.
	ca.	A library at the Hollywood Boys Club is named in Gracie's honor.
	ca.	A Burns and Allen commercial for Carnation won the first special award given by the American Society of Cinematographers for "outstanding photographic quality and excellence of star endorsement."
	ca.	**Television Today** and **Motion Picture Daily**'s poll names Burns and Allen the top television comedy team, outdistancing Lucille Ball and Desi Arnaz.

	September 28	George is the honoree of the season opener of the television series, **This Is Your Life**.
1956		Gracie is nominated for an Emmy for Best Continuing Performance by a Comedienne in a Series.
1957	October 29	The Cigar Smoker of the Year Award is presented to George by the Cigar Institute of America and filmed at General Service Studios, where his and Gracie's television series is also filmed.
	ca.	George and Gracie again receive the Television Champion Award for Best Comedy Team.
		Gracie is nominated for an Emmy for Best Continuing Performance (Female) in a Series by a Comedienne, Singer, Hostess, Dancer, MC, Announcer, Narrator, Panelist or any Person Who Essentially Plays Herself.
1958		Gracie is nominated for an Emmy for Best Actress in a Leading Role (Continuing Character) in a Comedy Series.
	October 26	Carnation gives Gracie an informal luncheon and presents her with a sterling silver pitcher.
1960	February 9	Official ground breaking ceremonies for the Hollywood Walk of Fame are held to commemorate an initial en masse placement of over 1,500 terrazzo and bronze stars dedicated to show business luminaries in the sidewalks of Hollywood's main thoroughfares. In his lifetime, George received two stars: one located at 6510 Hollywood Blvd. for his work in television; the other at 1637 Vine St. for motion pictures. Gracie received one star at 6672 Hollywood Blvd. for her work in television.
1978	April 2	"How We Laughed!", a dinner tribute to Gracie, Harpo Marx and Ed Wynn is held by the Friends of the USC Libraries in Los Angeles, California.
1989	Aug.-Sept.	The UCLA Film and Television Archive and The Academy of Television Arts and Sciences Foundation presents a tribute to George and Gracie and Jack Benny in Los Angeles, California.
1992	October 2	The cross street near the George Burns Theater for the Performing Arts in Detroit, Michigan is named Gracie Allen Street.
1994	October 12	The street intersecting George Burns Road near Cedars-Sinai Medical Center is renamed Gracie Allen Drive by the Los Angeles, California City Council.
	November 11	**The Burns and Allen Show** is inducted into the Radio Hall of Fame at the Museum of Broadcast Communications in Chicago, Illinois along with Red Skelton, Garrison Keillor, Gary Owens, and Gordon McLendon.

George received the following awards and honors after Gracie's retirement and in the years following her death.

1959	January 7	George is voted one of entertainment's best dressed by the California Men's Apparel Club.
1960	August 13	George Burns Day is celebrated in Los Angeles, California.
1964	June 15	George cements his footprints in a block in the forecourt of Grauman's Chinese Theatre in Hollywood, California.
1965	March 22	The Broadcast Pioneer award from the National Association of Broadcasters is presented to George.

1966	June 8	George receives the Humanitarian Award from the National Conference of Christians and Jews, 16th Annual Brotherhood Testimonial of Southern California Region's Apparel and Textile Division.
1972	May 13	A New York Friars Club Testimonial Dinner honoring George Burns and Jack Benny as Entertainers of the Year is held in New York City.
1975	January 25	George is given the Will Rogers Humanitarian Award from the American Academy of Humor in a televised ceremony.
	September 29	George is dubbed Star of Tomorrow by the National Association of Theater Owners.
	November 23	George is sole honoree at the annual Television Academy of Arts and Sciences Ball at the Century Plaza in Los Angeles, California.
	December 12	George is named Star of the Year at the Pacific Theater during the 19th Annual Christian Luncheon.
	December 21	George receives an award for his role in **The Sunshine Boys** at the Entertainer of the Year Awards, which will be telecast January 11, 1976.
	ca.	The New York Friars Club gives a testimonial dinner for **The Sunshine Boys** co-stars George Burns and Walter Matthau at the Americana Hotel. Nearly one thousand people pay one hundred dollars per ticket to attend.
1976	January 14	George is declared to be the New Star of 1976 by the Variety Club of Southern California.
	February 8	Israel's Sword of the Haganah is presented to George during the Annual Israel Dinner of State of the Entertainment Division for Israel Bonds.
	March 29	George receives an Oscar for Best Performance by a Supporting Actor for 1975's **The Sunshine Boys** at the 48th Annual Academy Awards held in Los Angeles, California.
	October 15	George is honored at the Friars Club Charity Foundation 30th Anniversary Dinner held at the Beverly Hilton Hotel in Los Angeles, California.
	ca.	George is nominated for a Golden Globe award by the Hollywood Foreign Press for Best Performance by an Actor in a Motion Picture Comedy/Musical for his role in **The Sunshine Boys**. The film itself was also nominated for Best Comedy Motion Picture.
1977	October 4	The first annual Jack Benny Memorial Award is given to George at the Beverly Hilton Hotel in Beverly Hills, California under the aegis of the March of Dimes.
	Fall	George receives an honorary elementary school (P.S. 22) diploma from the New York Board of Education at New York's City Hall in New York City.
1978	February 2	The dedication of the George Burns Stage at Hollywood Center Studios (formerly known as Hollywood General Studios and as General Service Studios) in Hollywood, California is held.
	May 17	George is the guest of honor on tonight's televised **Dean Martin Celebrity Roast**.
	August 10	George's 1977 special, **The George Burns One-Man Show**, is nominated for an Emmy for Outstanding Special--Comedy-Variety or Music.

1979 January 17 The Musicians' Union Local No. 47's special award for contributions to live music is given to George.

April 24 George is named Entertainer of the Century at the Showarama in Kansas City, Missouri.

November 11 George is named an Honorary Fellow of Cardiovascular Surgery.

November 25 George's hand and shoe prints, along with that of a cigar, are again immortalized in cement outside Mann's (formerly Grauman's) Chinese Theater in Hollywood in position 69.

1980 ca. George is made an honorary member of the Jack Benny Fan Club, which began January 1, 1980.

ca. George is nominated for a Grammy as best country vocal-male for his single, "I Wish I Was 18 Again."

February 12 The Motion Picture and Television Fund award of dedication to entertaining the world is given to George.

February 15 George is elected to the National Association of Broadcasters Radio Hall of Fame for a significant and lasting contribution to the radio industry.

April 11 George is named Best New Male Artist in the country and western music field, awarded by the nation's disk hockeys.

April 27 George is the Motion Picture nominee to the Hollywood Hall of Fame.

October 23 George is voted the Film Advisory Board's Special Award of Excellence.

December 14 The Louella O. Parsons Award for projecting a favorable image of Hollywood to the world is given to George.

ca. George is the oldest person (84) ever to appear on the United States' country music record charts.

ca. A poll ties George with Bob Hope as the most popular man in America.

1981 April 30 George receives the Social Achievement Award from the Academy of Country Music.

ca. A facility at the University of Israel is named the George Burns Medical Center.

1982 September 9 George is presented with the Man of the Year Award (of the United States Magazine Awards) by the editors and publishers of United States magazines.

November 4 The University of California Los Angeles' 6th Annual Jack Benny Award for Excellence in Entertainment is presented to George.

1982 ca. The George Burns Tribute Plate titled "Young At Heart" by artist Mike Hagel is issued as a limited edition with a $45 price tag.

ca. George is named one of America's ten sexiest men by **Playgirl** magazine.

1983 February The first King of Comedy Award from the Improvisation Club in Hollywood, CA is bestowed upon George during the week of February 6.

May 2 George receives the Actors Fund Medal at the Palace Theater in New York City.

	ca.	George is named one of America's seven sexiest bachelors by **Harper's Bazaar** magazine.
1984	August 2	George is nominated for an Emmy for Outstanding Individual Performance in a Variety or Music Program for his 1983 special, **George Burns Celebrates 80 Years in Show Business**
	November 8	George receives his third star on the Walk of Fame in Hollywood, California, this one given for live theater. It is located at 6670 Hollywood Blvd., next to Gracie's star for her work in television.
1985	October 28	The Motion Picture and Television Hospital of Woodland Hills, California dedicates the George Burns Intensive Care Unit.
	ca.	George is named one of **Good Housekeeping Magazine**'s "50 Most Eligible Bachelors."
1986	January	George is honorary chairman of a fundraising drive for Cedars-Sinai Medical Center in Los Angeles, California.
	April	A two block thoroughfare adjacent to Cedars-Sinai Medical Center in Los Angeles, California is renamed George Burns Road (it was previously called Hamel Road).
	June 2	The announcement of George receiving the Public Service Award of the California Association of Homes for the Aging is published, naming George because of his "support of fullest enjoyment of life regardless of age."
	September 16	George is announced as America's 9th favorite male star, receiving 9% of the votes in a nationwide poll for "Star of the Century" conducted by **Star** magazine.
1987	January 6	George is one of America's ten most eligible bachelors in a poll conducted by **Globe** magazine. Columnist Cindy Adams, Man Watchers, Inc. founder Suzy Mallery, and author Stephanie Brush are responsible for the list, and Brush notes, "He (George) still talks about Gracie, his late wife and partner, with incredible affection and loyalty."
	January 24	Los Angeles Mayor Thomas Bradley designates every January 20th in Los Angeles, California henceforth as George Burns Day, the first time such an ongoing honor has been bestowed. The announcement is made in conjunction with a belated birthday dinner this night designed to raise funds for the Cedars-Sinai Medical Center. To commemorate George's birthday, the hospital commissioned a limited edition painting by Billy Al Bengston called "The 91 Moons of George Burns."
	April 7	One of the 10 Best-Dressed Short Men in America according to fashion commentator, Mr. Blackwell, is George Burns.
	June 17	The announcement is made that a poll of members of the Cigar Association of America names George Burns as the man who has done the most for the image of the industry; he wins with 22.5% of the vote.
	ca.	George is voted King of Comedy in a poll of one thousand comedians.
	ca.	George and Bob Hope tie as readers' favorite well-known American in a **People Weekly** magazine poll
	ca.	George is named Man of the Year by readers of **US** magazine.

1988 March 31 — An honorary Doctor of Humanities degree is awarded to George by Connecticut's University of Hartford.

May 17 — George receives the Life Achievement Award at the American Comedy Awards.

November — George receives the American Image Lifetime Achievement Award.

November 13 — George and Gracie (posthumously) are announced as inductees into the Academy of Television Arts and Sciences' Television Academy Hall of Fame. The awards are to be televised January 23, 1989.

December — **Gracie: A Love Story** appears at the top of **The New York Times** best seller list. George is the oldest author ever to appear on this list.

December 4 — The Kennedy Center Honors Award for Lifetime Achievement is presented to George at The Kennedy Center, Washington, D.C. The actual announcement was made on August 4, 1988 with the program taped on December 4, 1988, to be televised December 30, 1988.

1989 March 20 — The Burns and Allen Chair in Cardiology Research is named at the Cedars-Sinai Medical Center in Los Angeles, California.

May 24 — The Ben-Gurion University of the Negev facility for support and medical research is now called the George Burns Medical Educational Center.

November 5 — A tribute to George Burns from the Museum of Broadcasting is held at the Plaza Hotel in New York City.

1990 ca. — George is nominated for an Emmy for Outstanding Performance in Informational Programming for hosting **A Conversation with George Burns** for the Disney Channel in 1989.

September 16 — George wins the Emmy for hosting **A Conversation with George Burns**.

1991 February — George is acknowledged as the recipient of the Grammy Award for spoken word or non-musical recording for **Gracie: A Love Story**.

August 14 — George is named "Sexiest Man of the Century" by **Muscle Training Illustrated Magazine**.

December 10 — George is inducted into the **Broadcasting Magazine** Hall of Fame in Washington, D.C. during the organization's 60th anniversary celebration.

1992 January — Entertainers Siegfried and Roy announce they are naming one of their famous tigers "George" in honor of George Burns.

January 24 — The George Award from the New York Friar's Club is given to George (first honoree). The award is made at the Riviera Hotel and Casino in Las Vegas, Nevada during George's engagement with Pia Zadora.

Spring — George is honored by the United Jewish Fund for his aid to Russian Jews.

Fall — George receives an award from the National Institute on Aging.

October 2 — The George Burns Theater for the Performing Arts is dedicated in Detroit, Michigan on a street renamed George Burns Avenue.

	ca.	A theater in Livonia, Minnesota is named for George.
1993	June 24	An honorary Doctor of Humane Letters degree is conferred upon George by Brandeis University in Waltham, Massachusetts.
	August	George is inducted into the Comedy Hall of Fame at the 11th annual Just for Laughs Montreal Comedy Festival (the International Comedy Festival) in Montreal, Canada. The Canadian museum was recently opened.
	November 24	George is named as an inductee into the (American) Comedy Hall of Fame at a program taped August 29 in Los Angeles, California. The awards ceremony was the first of a planned annual event.
1995	February 25	George receives the Screen Actors Guild's 33rd annual Life Achievement award in its first televised ceremony, which he attends.

APPENDIX B: PERSONAL APPEARANCES

George and Gracie made many personal appearances after their days in vaudeville had come to a close, taking to the road again to appear at theaters to promote their radio shows, often broadcasting from those cities as well. They were guests at a number of other events, where their presence was a foolproof method of attracting an audience. Like most of their fellow entertainers, Burns and Allen joined wholeheartedly in the war effort by visiting a number of camps and hospitals and participating in bond drives.

1929	June	Burns and Allen begin a fifteen-week tour of Great Britain which will include personal appearances and radio broadcasts.
1930	September	George and Gracie return to England for a second time to appear on radio for the British Broadcasting Company (BBC) and, presumably, some additional theatrical appearances.
1931	October 30	Gracie and George Jessel pass out 10,000 apples in front of the Palace Theater in New York City.
1932	May 2	George and Gracie appear for one week at the Paramount Theater in New York City with Guy Lombardo.
	December 3	Burns and Allen appear at a Friars Club Dinner.
1933	February 1	The Chicago World's Fair in Chicago, Illinois features an appearance by George and Gracie.
	May 31	George and Gracie dedicate the new General Cigar building at the Chicago World's Fair. Gracie christens the building (named for the company's White Owl brand) by (accidentally) throwing a bottle through the door.
	July	Burns and Allen open their stage show revue, "Where's My Brother?" at the Paramount Theater in New York City with James Melton, Mitzi Mayfair and Cardini.
	July	George and Gracie appear at the Loew's State Theater in New York City with Gene Marvey, Ben Blue, Mary Lynn, Cardini and the Stone and Vernon Foursome dancers.
	July 30	Gracie appears at Griffith Stadium in Washington, D.C.
	December 15	George and Gracie go to the Shrine Auditorium in downtown Los Angeles, California for the **Los Angeles Examiner** Christmas Benefit.

	ca.	George and Gracie make their first appearance at a program for the National Recovery Act.
1934	May 20	George appeared alone at the New York City Friars Frolic on this date.
	Summer	George and Gracie spend an undetermined length of time in London, England, making appearances that include the Palladium Theater.
	September 20	Burns and Allen appear at the Night of Stars for Officers of the United Jewish Appeal at Yankee Stadium, New York City.
	October 4-6	George and Gracie make a three day appearance at the Capitol Theater in Scranton, Pennsylvania.
	October 10	George and Gracie are guests of honor at the Central Park Casino in New York City.
	October	George and Gracie make an appearance at the Earle Theater in Philadelphia, Pennsylvania.
	November	A testimonial dinner for entertainer Sophie Tucker draws an appearance by Burns and Allen.
	November 12	George and Gracie attend a dinner at the Waldorf-Astoria Hotel in New York City with George Jessel for Jim Farley.
1935	June 11	The Capitol Theater in Washington, D.C. hosts an appearance by Burns and Allen.
	June 28	George and Gracie join George Jessel for an appearance at the Paramount Theater in Los Angeles, California.
	November 23-30	George and Gracie appear at Public Hall for the Cleveland, Ohio Auto Show.
	December 27	The Burnses make a one week appearance in Minneapolis, Minnesota.
1936	January 3	George and Gracie make a one week appearance at the Chicago Theater, Chicago, Illinois.
	January 17	Burns and Allen are booked for one week at the Metropolitan Theater in Boston, Massachusetts.
	January 24	George and Gracie make a week's worth of appearances at the Loew's State Theater, New York City.
	February 2	George appears at a dinner in honor of Eddie Cantor.
	February 4	Vice President Garner's dinner for President Franklin D. Roosevelt and his Cabinet is held in Washington, D.C. with Burns and Allen in attendance.
	March	George and Gracie again appear for one week at the Paramount Theater in Los Angeles, California.
		George and Gracie appear at the Golden Gate Theater in San Francisco, California with Ben Blue and the Jacques Renard Orchestra.
	August 10	Hollywood's Music Box Theater plays host to an appearance by Burns and Allen.
	September 3	George and Gracie are part of the opening festivities for the Mayflower Doughnut Shop in Los Angeles, California.

1937 January 6 — A **Los Angeles Examiner** Benefit at the Shrine Auditorium in Los Angeles, California again draws an appearance by the Burnses.

October — The Banshee Club is the venue for a New York City engagement by Burns and Allen.

November — George and Gracie make a return visit to New York City at an undetermined venue.

1938 February — George and Gracie are guests of the Clover Club's President's Ball.

March 29 — George and Gracie attend the annual April Fool Masquerade Ball for the American Artist Congress in Los Angeles, California.

April 20 — George and Gracie are invitees of the Tri-Guild Ball along with their friend, Jack Benny.

May 24 — George and Gracie attend the premiere of the film, **Alexander's Ragtime Band**.

June 5 — Gracie speaks at her niece's (Jean Boyston) high school graduation exercises at the Star of the Sea Convent School (Gracie's alma mater) in San Francisco, California.

September 21-22 — Kansas City, Missouri's Jubilesta celebration draws an appearance by Burns and Allen.

ca. — The Burnses make another Shrine Auditorium appearance in Los Angeles, California.

1939 May — George and Gracie are in New York City for a visit to the World's Fair.

Gracie is guest speaker at the National Women's Designers Luncheon at the Biltmore Hotel in New York City.

June 15 — George and Gracie are in New York City to participate in the Christian German Refugee Benefit.

August 11 — A sales meeting for Hinds Honey & Almond Cream (their radio show sponsor) features an appearance by the show's stars.

October 5 — George and Gracie make a short trip to the Beverly Wilshire Hotel in Los Angeles, California for a personal appearance.

1940 March 7 — Treasure Island in San Francisco, California hosts Burns and Allen.

March 9 — Gracie visits the U.S. House of Representatives in Washington, D.C.

March — Gracie is a guest of the National Women's Press Club in Washington, D.C.

April 21 — Gracie appears at a Variety Club banquet in Dallas, Texas, at which she gives a speech concerning her campaign for president.

April 26 — George and Gracie headline the annual Summer Camp Jamboree Show at the Hollywood High School Auditorium in Hollywood, California.

May 15-18 — The Ak-Sar-Ben Coliseum in Omaha, Nebraska is the site of Gracie's Surprise Party presidential convention.

May 22 Gracie gives another speech as an official presidential candidate in Hollywood, California.

May 25 George and Gracie attend a Temple Israel Benefit at the Pantages Theater in Hollywood, California.

May 28 The World's Fair on Treasure Island in San Francisco, California draws an appearance by one of that city's favorite daughters and her husband, Gracie Allen and George Burns.

May Gracie's "campaign" for the U.S. Presidency takes her on a "whistle stop" train tour from California to Nebraska.

June 13 George and Gracie appear at the Golden Gate International Exposition at Treasure Island in San Francisco, California.

June 15 The Hormel Aquacade Party features Burns and Allen.

June 22 The All Star War Relief Show to aid the Red Cross Drive, is held with the assistance of George and Gracie and many other stars at the Warner Bros. Sunset Studios in Hollywood.

July 22 George and Gracie attend the Democratic Convention in Chicago, Illinois.

October George and Gracie star in a revue at the El Capitan Theater in Hollywood, California with host Jack Benny.

December 3 Gracie "delivers" 5,000 men trainers to the United States Navy at San Diego, California. The attendant broadcast is heard by 170,000 members of the Navy around the world.

1941 January 25 George and Gracie travel to the KNX radio studio in Hollywood, California for a March of Dimes radio fundraiser.

February George and Gracie appear at Fort Sheridan on their way to Chicago, Illinois.

February George and Gracie may have made a personal appearance in Toronto, Canada since they did appear on a radio broadcast from there on February 14.

March 1 The Waldorf-Astoria Hotel in New York City welcomes Burns and Allen to a special luncheon.

May 9 George and Gracie attend a dinner held in Jack Benny's honor.

1942 January 24 George and Gracie are at another California Naval Training Station to help boost enlistment.

March 31 Camp Haan in Riverside, California plays host to Burns and Allen.

April 28 George and Gracie make a personal appearance at the NBC studios in San Francisco, California for their radio broadcast.

May 13 Gracie is the luncheon speaker at the Hotel Astor in New York City for the American Women's Voluntary Service, a group for whom she serves as chairman.

May 27 Gracie is at Camp Elliot in San Diego, California.

June 9 George and Gracie continue their war work by appearing at the Naval Training Station in San Diego, California.

	July 28	A two day Victory Rally at the New York City Public Library is uplifted by a visit from Gracie Allen.
	July 30	George and Gracie are in New York City to kick off a new radio show, **Stage Door Canteen** (CBS, 1942-1945).
	November 10	George and Gracie visit Camp Elliot in San Diego, California.
	December 6	George and Gracie are guests at the Army Air Forces West Coast Training Center in Santa Ana, California.
1943	March 16	Gracie's concert is held at New York City's Carnegie Hall featuring her "Concerto for Index Finger."
	April 4	George and Gracie visit the Ontario, California Army Air Field.
	April 27	March Field in Riverside, California is another of George and Gracie's stops during their regular visits to military camps.
	July	George and Gracie embark on an Army camp tour.
	December 7	George and Gracie pay a visit to the Naval Air Station, Terminal Island, California.
	ca.	Gracie's concert at the Hollywood Bowl in Los Angeles, California is held.
	ca.	Gracie holds another concert, this time at Symphony Hall in Boston, Massachusetts.
	ca.	Gracie's appears in concert at Philadelphia, Pennsylvania's Convention Hall.
	ca.	Gracie makes a concert appearance at the Philharmonic Auditorium in Los Angeles, California.
1944	January	Gracie and Ginny Simms appear at a party for the 32nd birthday of the San Francisco Symphony Orchestra at San Francisco's Civic Auditorium.
	April 4	George and Gracie continue their tour of military camps at another visit to the Ontario, California Army Air Field.
	June 13	The Fifth War Loan Drive at Municipal Auditorium in Kansas City, Missouri is kicked off with an appearance by Burns and Allen.
	July	Burns and Allen are in Chicago so Gracie can report on the Democratic National Convention, a task she also performed for the earlier Republican Convention.
	November	George and Gracie attend the United War Fund Rally at Symphony Hall in Boston, Massachusetts with the Boston Pops.
	November 27	Gracie christens the tanker S.S. Hubbarrton at the Sun Shipbuilding and Dry Dock Co. in Chester, Pennsylvania.
	November 28	George and Gracie appear at Convention Hall in Philadelphia, Pennsylvania.
	Winter	George and Gracie are off on another War Bond tour.
	ca.	George and Gracie make an appearance at a Lever Brothers sales meeting (their radio show sponsor).
1945	Summer	A camp and hospital tour is part of George and Gracie's plans for their time off from the radio show.

1947 March — The Damon Runyon Fund (location unknown) benefits from an appearance by Burns and Allen.

1948 April 4 — George attends a Friars Club dinner in Beverly Hills, California for George Jessel.

ca. — Gracie is in New Orleans, Louisiana.

1949 April 16 — George appears at the Friars Club Frolic; this one benefits the Motion Picture Relief Fund Home and Hospital.

August 16 — Burns and Allen headline a soldout performance at the Palladium in London, England. There was eventually talk of another planned appearance in 1954.

October 22 — George appears at the Friars Club Frolic to benefit the Variety Club's Blind Baby Nursery.

1950 July 1 — George and Gracie have been in Texas and are at the Shamrock Hotel in Houston for a personal appearance and radio show.

July 8 — Houston's Shamrock Hotel plays host to Burns and Allen for the second week in a row.

1951 April 14 — George and Gracie collect contributions for the Saints and Sinners Milk Fund for two hours by stopping motorists on the Golden Gate Bridge for donations.

The annual Newspaper Frolic is held by the San Francisco-Oakland Newspaper Guild at the Civic Auditorium in San Francisco, California with Burns and Allen in attendance.

November 9 — George attends the New York City Friars Club salute to Jack Benny.

1953 April 29 — Gracie is in San Francisco, California.

1954 ca. — George appears with Carol Channing at the Dunes Hotel in Las Vegas.

September — Gracie is a guest at the Friars Club.

1955 March 3 — Carnation (their television show sponsor) holds its sales meeting at the Biltmore Hotel in Hollywood, California. George and Gracie are there with other members of their show.

October 15 — George and Gracie travel to the formal opening of the Blue Skies Trailer Village (of which they are shareholders) in Rancho Mirage, California, ten miles southeast of Palm Springs.

November 1 — George and Gracie are in London to publicize the premiere of their television show on the BBC.

November 7 — George and Gracie autograph **I Love Her, That's Why!** at the May Company department store in downtown Los Angeles, California from 1:00-2:00 P.M.

1956 April 21 — Gracie goes to San Francisco to help open the Association of Interior Decorators' convention.

George reinvented his career after Gracie's retirement by returning to the stage in a variety of venues, including these:

1957 February 14 — George attends a Los Angeles Friars Club tribute, possibly for Jack Benny.

1958 November 23 — George attends a Los Angeles Friars Club tribute for Lucille Ball and Desi Arnaz.

1959	June 11	Sahara Hotel, Las Vegas, Nevada in a multi-week engagement.
	November 8	George attends a Los Angeles Friars Club tribute to Dean Martin.
	ca.	Harrah's, Lake Tahoe, Nevada with Bobby Darin.
	ca.	New York World's Fair with Carol Channing.
1960	ca.	Harrah's Club, Lake Tahoe, Nevada.
	mid-August	Greek Theater, Los Angeles, California with Bobby Darin.
	December	The Congo Room at the Sahara Hotel, Las Vegas, Nevada.
1961	June 6	Las Vegas, Nevada.
	October 22	George attends a Los Angeles Friars Club tribute to Mervyn LeRoy.
	November 8	George attends a Los Angeles Friars Club tribute to Gary Cooper.
	ca.	Greek Theater, Los Angeles, California.
	ca.	Toured with Carol Channing.
	ca.	Sahara Hotel, Las Vegas, Nevada with Ann-Margret.
	ca.	Command performance at the Palladium in London, England with Jack Benny.
		George tells **TV Guide** (November 18-24, 1961) that he is performing for six weeks yearly in Las Vegas and Lake Tahoe, Nevada.
1962	February 10	The Players Club, New York City.
	June	The Seattle World's Fair with Carol Channing.
	June 30	Dunes Hotel, Las Vegas, Nevada with Carol Channing.
	ca.	George continues a multi-week theater and nightclub tour with Carol Channing.
1963	January	George attends a party in Washington, D.C. to celebrate the second anniversary of President Kennedy's inauguration.
	May 9	Riviera Hotel, Las Vegas, Nevada with Dorothy Provine for a four-week engagement.
	August 14-21	The Nugget in Sparks, E. Reno, Nevada with Dorothy Provine.
1964	June 7	The Nugget in Sparks, E. Reno, Nevada.
	June 15	Riviera Hotel with Jane Russell, Connie Haines and Beryl Davis in Las Vegas, Nevada for a five-week engagement.
	Summer	Las Vegas, Nevada with Connie Stevens.
	October 12	USO Tour with Connie Stevens.
	October 14	Harrah's, Lake Tahoe, Nevada with Connie Stevens.
	November 8	Annual Palace Day, Cocoanut Grove, Los Angeles, California.
	ca.	The Cave in Vancouver, B.C., Canada with Dorothy Provine and the Lettermen.

1965	January 10	Friars Club, Hollywood Palace Night.
1968	February	The Palmer House, Chicago, Illinois.
1972	May 13	George and Jack Benny are feted by the Los Angeles Friars Club.
1973	February	Lincoln Center in New York City.
1974	June 16	Shubert Theater, "An Evening With George Burns," Los Angeles, California.
	ca.	Fontainebleau Hotel, Miami, Florida.
1975	Fall	Oxnard II Hotel, London, England.
	December 9	Hollywood Palladium, Los Angeles, California.
1976	February 27	Reopening in Buffalo, New York, of the 50 year old Shea's Theater.
	February 28	C. W. Post Auditorium, Long Island, New York.
	February 29	One-man show at Carnegie Hall, New York, New York.
	April	Two-week engagement in Las Vegas, Nevada.
	June 13	Royal Charity Show (command performance for Princess Margaret) at the Palladium Theatre, London, England.
	Summer	Concert-nightclub tour.
	July 5	Garden State Arts Center, Holmdel, New Jersey.
	August 16	Westbury Music Fair, Long Island, New York.
	September 7	The New Greek Theater, Los Angeles, California with Carol Channing.
	October 15	Friars Club Charity Foundation Dinner, Los Angeles, California.
	October 20	Two-week engagement at the Sands Hotel, Las Vegas, Nevada.
1977	February 1	Sands Hotel, Las Vegas, Nevada with The Captain and Tennille.
1978	ca.	Sands Hotel, Las Vegas, Nevada.
1979	September 22	The Concord Resort Hotel, Catskills, New York for the American Heart Association.
	November 25	Mann's Chinese Theatre, Hollywood, California.
	December 12	Concord Hotel, the Catskills, New York.
1980	August	Spent a month touring New England, including the Melody Fair Theatre, North Tonawanda, New York with Connie Stevens.
	September 25	Universal Amphitheater, Los Angeles, California with John Denver.
1981	May 22	The Regency, Atlantic City, New Jersey.
	June 8	Caesar's Boardwalk, Atlantic City, New Jersey.
	Summer	On tour of various venues.
	December 20	Hamilton Place Theatre, Ontario, Canada.

1982	March 4	Barbican Center, entertainment complex opening in London, England.
	October 22	Bally's Park Place Hotel and Casino, Atlantic City, New Jersey.
	November 4	Royce Hall, University of California Los Angeles (California); half hour appearance to coincide with his receipt of the Jack Benny Award.
	ca.	Royal Gala in London, England for Prince Charles and Lady Diana.
1983	January	Ladies Only Show, Bally's Park Place Hotel and Casino, Atlantic City, New Jersey.
	February 17-21	Sahara Hotel Congo Room, Las Vegas, Nevada (first appearance since 1961).
	February 27	President and Mrs. Reagan's party for Queen Elizabeth and Prince Phillip of England, 20th Century-Fox Studios, Hollywood, California.
	May 27-30	Sahara Hotel Congo Room, Las Vegas, Nevada.
	August 3	Sahara Tahoe with Bernadette Peters, Lake Tahoe, Nevada.
	September 18	Aladdin Hotel, Las Vegas, Nevada.
1984	January	Caesar's, Lake Tahoe, Nevada.
	January 20	Second Annual Ladies Only Show, Bally's Park Place Hotel and Casino, Atlantic City, New Jersey.
	ca.	Brown's Resort, the Catskills, New York.
	ca.	Galesburg, Illinois for a St. Jude's Hospital benefit.
	ca.	Resort hotel in Lake Tahoe, Nevada.
	ca.	Purdue University, W. Lafayette, Indiana.
	Fall	10 days of one-nighters on the college circuit and in various other venues.
	Fall	Two days in Las Vegas, Nevada.
	December 27	George appears with Diahann Carroll at Caesar's Palace in Las Vegas, Nevada.
1985	February	Benefit for a hospital in Jacksonville, Florida.
	March	Caesar's Hotel and Casino, Atlantic City, New Jersey.
	July 9	Caesar's, Lake Tahoe, Nevada.
	September 10	Carlton Celebrity Room in Minneapolis-St. Paul, Minnesota for six days.
	ca. October	Caesar's Palace, Las Vegas, Nevada.
1986	Jan-Feb.	Caesar's Palace, Las Vegas, Nevada (not the entire two month span) with Gloria Loring.
	ca.	George's performances featured guest appearances with the singing trio, the McGuire Sisters.
1987	January 24	Fundraising dinner for Cedars-Sinai Medical Center in Los Angeles, California.
	January 30	Caesar's Palace, Las Vegas, Nevada with Peggy Lee.

	February 19	Our Lady of the Lake Foundation Fund in Baton Rouge, Louisiana.
	March 23	Omaha, Nebraska for a one week engagement.
	April 11	Hershey Park Arena, Hershey, Pennsylvania.
	October 15	Minot State University Dome, Fargo, North Dakota.
1988	March 2-7	Caesar's Palace, Las Vegas, Nevada with Susan Anton.
	June 23	Fox Theater, Atlanta, Georgia.
	December 3	George attends the State Department reception in conjunction with the Kennedy Center Honors, Washington, D.C.
1989	October 1	"179 Years of Comedy" with Bob Hope at Madison Square Garden, New York City.
	November	Lafayette, Louisiana.

George also made appearances in Las Vegas, Stateline, Nevada and Atlantic City, New Jersey per his contract with Caesar's.

1990	March 17	Kellogg Arena, Battle Creek, Michigan.
	June 14	Caesar's Paradise Stream, Mt. Pocono, Pennsylvania.
	October 6	Proctor's Theater, Schenectady, New York.
	November 2	50th Anniversary of Sun City, Arizona with Bob Hope.
1991	January 18	Appearance for the "high rollers" at Caesar's Palace, Las Vegas, Nevada.
	January 19	Appearance for the general public at Caesar's Palace, Las Vegas, Nevada.
	April 18, 19,21	Riviera Hotel and Casino, Las Vegas, Nevada with Pia Zadora.
	ca. Spring	The National Booksellers' Convention in New York, New York.
	May	Riviera Hotel and Casino, Las Vegas, Nevada.
	July 1	Yellow Ribbon Celebrity Golf Classic, Monroe, New Jersey.
	Oct 31-Nov. 3	Riviera Hotel and Casino, Las Vegas, Nevada with Pia Zadora.
1992	January 23-26	Riviera Hotel and Casino, Las Vegas, Nevada with Pia Zadora.
	February 5	Long Beach, California Terrace Theater with Pia Zadora.
	June	Peoples Comedy Festival, Toronto, Canada.
	July 3-5	Caesar's Palace, Las Vegas, Nevada.
	July 18	The Concord Resort Hotel, the Catskills, New York.
	ca.	Livonia, Michigan with Florence Henderson.
1993	January 15-17	Caesar's Palace, Las Vegas, Nevada with Florence Henderson.
	February	Improvisation Club, Hollywood, California to accept the "King of Comedy" award.

	February 17-21	Sahara Congo Room, Las Vegas, Nevada.
	March 13	Cerritos Center for the Performing Arts, Cerritos, California.
	August 1	George headlines the Just for Laughs International comedy festival in Montreal, Canada.
	August 12, 13,15	Caesar's Palace, Las Vegas, Nevada with Florence Henderson.
1994	January 20-23	Caesar's Palace, Las Vegas, Nevada.
	June 13	14th annual gala to benefit the St. Jude Children's Hospital in Memphis, Tennessee.
	n.d.	San Antonio, Texas.
	n.d.	Houston, Texas.
1995	January	George makes his last public appearance on the eve of his 99th birthday at the dedication of Gracie Allen Drive at Cedars-Sinai hospital.

APPENDIX C: RESEARCH CENTERS

The following is a list of the major research archives on the performing arts including vaudeville, radio, film and television. The amount of material on George Burns and Gracie Allen in each location is indicated. The general public enjoys very little access to it due, in some part, to its fragility. Some museums listed here encourage membership.

Academy of Motion Picture Arts and Sciences
Margaret Herrick Library
Special Collections
333 S. La Cienega Boulevard
Beverly Hills, CA 90211

This library houses one of the world's most extensive collections relating to motion pictures including the Paramount Collection, the Louella Parsons Collection, clipping files and photograph archives.

American Museum of the Moving Image
35th Avenue at 36th Street
Astoria, NY 11106

This museum houses materials associated with New York early film history at the Astoria Studios, one of the first film studios in America. The collection has photograph files of performers, including Burns and Allen from Paramount film shorts they made at this studio in the early 1930's. **Going in Style** (F41) with George Burns was filmed at the renovated studios in 1979.

The Billy Rose Theatre Collection
The New York Public Library for the Performing Arts
40 Lincoln Center Plaza
New York, NY 10023-7498

This library maintains an extensive collection of scrapbooks, programs, playbills, scripts, photographs, prints, motion picture and television titles and over two million clipping files of performing artists in radio, stage, television and vaudeville.

Broadcast Pioneers Library (SEE The National Public Broadcasting Archives)

Department of Special Collections
University Research Library
University of California, Los Angeles
405 Hilgard Avenue
Los Angeles, CA 90024-1575

Included in this extensive archival collection are those of Jack Benny and Eddie Cantor and papers from RKO Radio. There are a few photographs of Burns and Allen in the collection.

Louis B. Mayer Library
The American Film Institute
P. O. Box 27999
2021 N. Western Avenue
Los Angeles, CA 90027

This collection contains over 75,000 clipping files on the motion picture and television industry.

Motion Picture, Broadcasting and Recording Sound Division
Library of Congress
Thomas Jefferson Building, Room 338
2nd Street and Independence Avenue, SE
Washington, DC 20540

This department was formed in 1978 to organize the Library of Congress collection of motion pictures and recordings. Housed in this collection are over 1,700,000 recordings, including the National Broadcasting Company's (NBC) radio collection, films from 1894 to date and recordings from Armed Forces Radio and Television Service (AFRTS) broadcasts.

Museum of Broadcast Communications at River City
800 S. Wells Street
Chicago, IL 60607-4529

This museum has a library of historic radio and television shows and commercials.

Museum of Modern Art
Film Department
11 W. 53rd Street
New York, NY 10019-5498

This art museum also houses a collection of motion picture film and video from 1880 to the present.

Museum of Television and Radio
25 W. 52nd Street
New York, NY 10019

Founded in 1976 by the late CBS chairman, William S. Paley, this non-profit collection contains over 30,000 radio and television programs, scripts, films, kinescopes and videotapes. Formerly known as The Museum of Broadcasting, it opened at its current location in 1991. There are very few Burns and Allen broadcasts in this collection. The archives had maintained thousands of disks from the NBC radio collection but these were donated to the Library of Congress. There are 96 consoles available to visitors to view or listen to materials in the collection.

The National Public Broadcasting Archives
University of Maryland College Library
Special Collections
College Park, MD 20742

This library has recently been the recipient of the collection from the Broadcast Pioneers Library in Washington, D.C. There are over 10,000 volumes and hundreds of periodicals on radio and television broadcast history. There is also a large collection of audio cassettes of various radio programs, an oral history collection, scrapbooks and scripts.

Oral History Collection
De Golyer Library
Southern Methodist University
Dallas, TX 75275-0396

Interviews given by many show business entertainers are housed in this collection whose innovator was Ron Meyer, Professor of History at the University. Several interviewees worked with Burns and Allen in their radio and film careers.

Pacific Pioneers Broadcasters
1500 Vine Street
Hollywood, CA 90028

This non-profit association is made up of members who worked professionally in radio. Part of its purpose is to preserve radio equipment and recordings. A small library related to radio includes a complete run of **Radio Life** magazine. The members of the association are a valuable resource.

Theater Arts Library
University of California, Los Angeles
Los Angeles, CA 90024

This library has an extensive research collection on the theater. There are some Burns and Allen radio scripts (1944-1945) as well as some of their television shows preserved on videotape.

University of California, Los Angeles
Film and Television Archive
Archive Research and Study Center
46 Powell Library
405 Hilgard Avenue
Los Angeles, CA 90024-1517

The largest film and television archive collection west of the Rocky Mountains. Several Burns and Allen short subjects and Paramount films are in the archives.

University of Southern California
The Cinema-Television Library and Archives of Performing Arts
Edward L. Doheny Memorial Library
University Park
Los Angeles, CA 90089-0182

The main collection of Burns and Allen memorabilia is housed in this library. The entire collection of their radio scripts (1932-1950) and television scripts (1950-1958) are in 139 bound volumes. There are 43 boxes of miscellaneous materials including a two-volume joke index, stage, radio and television scripts, correspondence, publicity, photographs, awards and scrapbooks covering their careers from 1923-1958 and some material on Gracie Allen's death in 1964. Various office files from the 1950's to 1960's and correspondence and production information for **The George Burns and Gracie Allen Show**, McCadden Productions, Banda Productions and Laurel/Laurmac Productions are included. There are approximately 650 transcription recordings of their radio shows from 1934, 1936-1950, and other miscellaneous recordings, 220 16mm films and kinescopes of the Burns and Allen television show, **The George Burns Show** and **Wendy and Me**.

The following organizations maintain lending libraries from which members may borrow scripts, cassettes and reels of radio programs, magazines and other items of interest:

North American Radio Archives (N.A.R.A.)
134 Vincewood Drive
Nicholasville, KY 40356

S.P.E.R.D.V.A.C. (Society to Preserve and Encourage Radio Drama, Variety, and Comedy)
P. O. Box 7177
Van Nuys, CA 91409

BIBLIOGRAPHY

This annotated bibliography is separated into works by Gracie Allen, (mostly ghostwritten), works by George Burns and books and articles about George Burns and Gracie Allen individually and as a team. Also included are publications which aid the reader in understanding the historical eras of the various media as they relate to Burns' and Allen's careers.

Works by Gracie Allen

B1 Allen, Grace. "Are You the Dreamer Type?" **Hollywood Woman**. October 1937: 7.
This article is rather typical of the ubiquitous but innocuous publicity pieces written in and about Hollywood celebrities of the day.

B2 ---. "Being Mrs. North Is More Exciting." **Lion's Roar**. January 1944: 1-5.
This is a publicity article about Gracie acting in the MGM films, **Two Girls and a Sailor** (F35) and **Mr. and Mrs. North** (F34).

B3 ---. "George's Delight." **TV Digest**. February 3-9, 1951: 20.
Gracie offers up two recipes to the readers of this Philadelphia magazine and assures them that they can be taken seriously.

B4 ---. "Gracie Allen Reporting." **News-Tribune** (Tacoma, Washington). February 13, 1945.
An example of Gracie's "contributions" to the world of journalism, as she nominates her choices for Academy Awards in various categories, all of them revolving around the real-life drama of World War II. For example, she nominates Benito Mussolini for the worst supporting performance of the year and, for best comedy writing, she suggests "almost any communique from the Japanese propaganda office."

B5 ---. "Gracie for President!" **Modern Screen**. ca. 1940: 46-47.
Subtitled "Nine Good Reasons Why This Little Lady Belongs In The White House," this article features Surprise Party candidate for President Gracie Allen expressing her views on the issues, including press conferences, farm problems, fireside chats, and state dinners. Those views are disseminated by a series of captioned photos taken at her Beverly Hills home. Typical of the photographs is Gracie in her kitchen at a "cabinet meeting."

B6 ---. "How I Would Doctor the Beauty Business if I were a Beauty Doctor." **Hollywood Mirror**. October 1936: 15.
A typical "Gracie" article, which was written by Burns and Allen's scriptwriters.

B7 ---. **How to Become President**. Prepared by the Gracie Allen Self-Delusion Institute. New York: Duell, Sloan and Pearce, 1940.

Gracie gives her advice to other presidential candidates and outlines her own campaign positions and platform ("redwood trimmed with nutty pine)." The book was written by Charles Palmer and the illustrations are by Charles Lofgren. Gracie donated all of the proceeds from her book to the Red Cross.

B8 ---. "How to Get into Radio." **Radio Life**. February 7, 1943: 34-35.
Gracie notes that getting to be a radio performer isn't easy and that once you are in, it is a continuing effort to stay on the air. She credits her husband for making it much easier as he handles all of the team's business.

B9 ---. "Miss Gracie Comes to Town." **The Commentator**. January 1938: 61-64.
An article about Gracie's current life and career.

B10 ---. "My Mother Complex." **Movie-Radio Guide**. November 30, 1940.
Gracie tells her feelings about being a mother and wonders how her children will look at her as they get older when they realize that their mother is "a comic that no one takes very seriously."

B11 ---. "One Finger Virtuoso." **Lion's Roar**. April 1944.
Gracie's role in the MGM film **Two Girls and a Sailor** (F35) is mentioned in which she plays the piano in "The One-Finger Concerto" while accompanied by an orchestra.

B12 ---. "Our Trip Abroad." **Radio Stars**. January 1934: 46+.
Gracie tells of the vacation trip to Europe that she and George made, sailing on the S.S. Rex. This trip was mentioned in their radio series.

B13 ---. "Pic-ings." **Pictorial Review**. April 1936: 79.
As guest editor, Gracie Allen's column consists of Burns and Allen jokes and one liners.

B14 ---. "Portrait." **Pictorial Review**. April 1933: 42.
A look at Gracie Allen as a personality.

B15 ---. " 'Remember the Banana', Gracie Warns in Accepting Nomination." **Omaha World Herald**. May 18, 1940: 9+.
Gracie's acceptance speech she gave as the Surprise Party's nominee for President of the United States, at the Omaha, Nebraska convention.

B16 ---. **Smart Sayings by Gracie Allen to Comin' Through the Rye**. 1933.
Gracie "wrote" this book for Guy Lombardo as an anniversary gift on his fourth year on radio. **SEE R53.**

B17 ---. "Why America's Next President Should Be a Woman." **Liberty**. June 29, 1940: 45-46.
After announcing her candidacy, Gracie writes an article explaining why a woman would make a good President of the United States.

Works by George Burns

B18 Burns, George. **Dear George: Advice and Answers from America's Leading Expert on Everything from A to B**. New York: G. P. Putnam's Sons, 1985.
Based on his expert advice, George answers fictitious letters from the public on a variety of subjects. **SEE B27.**

B19 ---. **Dr. Burns' Prescription for Happiness: Buy Two Books and Call Me in the Morning**. G. P. Putnam's Sons, 1984.
George offers advice on how to be happy in life and he includes prescriptions written for each weekday and a list of nine definitions for happiness. Although the book is meant to be humorous, there is a truth of reality in the humor which one can use to live a happy life. Included are several photos. **SEE B27, D26.**

B20 ---. **French Long Underwear Maker: A Dramatic Composition by George Burns, Gracie Allen, Paul Henning and Keith Fowler**. London: Samuel French, 1947.
This is a publication of a Burns and Allen routine. **SEE D228, D229.**

B21 ---. "Getting There is Half the Fun." **Saturday Evening Post**, January/February 1985: 14+.
George writes about traveling and why some people seem to be happiest when they are traveling away from home.

B22 ---. **Gracie: A Love Story**. New York: G. P. Putnam's Sons, 1988.
George's loving account of Gracie's life story and of their life together from their first meeting in the Union Hill Theater in New Jersey in 1922 to her death in 1964. There are several quotations from Burns and Allen radio scripts which may appear to the reader to be actual quotes from Gracie Allen. This book, written with author David Fisher, made the **New York Times** best seller list for many weeks, making George the oldest author ever on the list. George does give some insight into the "real" Gracie Allen. **SEE D40.**

B23 ---. **Gracie Discovers a Movie Star: A Dramatic Composition by George Burns, Gracie Allen, Paul Henning, Keith Fowler**. London: Samuel French, 1947.
A routine for Burns and Allen written by George and his writers. **SEE D229.**

B24 ---. **How to Live to be 100--or More: The Ultimate Diet, Sex and Exercise Book *.* At My Age, Sex Gets Second Billing**. New York: G. P. Putnam's Sons, 1983.
George offers his opinions on the key to longevity. Using jokes to tell his story, he includes photos and descriptions of the ten exercises he does daily, diet meals for a week and comments on the importance of family, doctors and retirement. **SEE D42, D43.**

B25 ---. "**I Love Her, That's Why.**" **Coronet**. April 1956: 82.
Excerpt from George's first book, **I Love Her, That's Why!** (B34).

B26 ---. **Living It Up, or They Still Love Me in Altoona!** New York: G. P. Putnam's Sons, 1976.
George writes about his life in show business and how he looks at life in general, mentioning show business friends he has known throughout his career and facts on how he and his writers worked to prepare scripts for Burns and Allen radio and television shows. There are reprints of parts of George's opening monologue for his first show at Harrah's Club in Lake Tahoe, Nevada in 1959 and a routine with Carol Channing in 1962 from their joint personal appearance. This book had at one time been tentatively titled **Confessions of a Happy Hoofer**. **SEE B27.**

B27 ---. **The Most of George Burns**. New York: Galahad Books, 1991.
A collection of four of his books in one volume, includes **Living It Up** (B26), **The Third Time Around** (B32), **Dr. Burns Prescription for Happiness** (B19) and **Dear George** (B18).

B28 ---. "My Favorite New Year's Eve--So Far." **The New York Times**. December 31, 1988, Sec. L: 23.
George recalls his most memorable New Year's Eve as being January 1, 1926, only days after Gracie had agreed to marry him and just prior to their marriage on January 7, 1926.

B29 ---. "My Wife--Gracie Allen." **Look**. December 25, 1945: 60-65.
An amusing article in which George attempts to answer the question "What's it like to be married to Gracie Allen?" Gracie comments on his answers by writing marginal notes. There are some photos of the Burnses at home with their children, Sandy and Ronnie.

B30 ---. "She's Running for President, or Gracie Allen as I Know Her." **Independent Woman**. July 1940: 198+.
George explains Gracie's continuous appeal as an entertainer and "how she gets that way." He explains how his wife came to the conclusion that she should run for President of the United States in 1940.

B31 ---. **Sugar Throat Sings Again: What Every Husband Should Know, What Every Bride Should Know. Composition by George Burns, Gracie Allen, Paul Henning, Keith Fowler**. London: Samuel French, 1947.
This is a Burns and Allen script in book form. **SEE D228, D230, D231.**

B32 ---. **The Third Time Around**. New York: G. P. Putnam's Sons, 1980.

George tells the story of his life and he includes some information on Gracie and her family in San Francisco. He admits that not everything he says is true, so the reader never knows if the story is to be believed. The book reprints the encore Burns and Allen performed on stage at the London Victoria Palace in 1929, their first performance outside of the United States and also includes a routine from their first film short. The title is "The Salesgirl" but seems to be similar to the script for their film short **100% Service** (F6). **SEE B27.**

B33 ---. "What's Funny About a Cigar?" **The Hollywood Reporter**. 1957. George joined the list of celebrity contributors to the popular entertainment industry tradepaper when he submitted this piece about using his cigar as a timing device for his jokes. He also mentions having recently received the honor of "Cigar Smoker of the Year" by the Cigar Institute of America. **SEE B500.**

B34 Burns, George and Cynthia Hobart Lindsay. **I Love Her, That's Why!** New York: Simon and Schuster, 1955.
George's first book in which he tells the story of his life before and after he met Gracie and formed the vaudeville team of Burns and Allen. Included is a "Prologue" by Jack Benny, many family and publicity photos, and a script for a 1955 **George Burns and Gracie Allen Show** (T153). In later interviews, George admits that only the first half of the book is true, the second half a lot of lies, leaving it to the reader to decide which parts are factual. **SEE B25.**

B35 Burns, George and David Fisher. **All My Best Friends**. New York: G. P. Putnam's Sons, 1989.
George has written a history of show business in the twentieth century in which he tells about some of his show business friends (including Gracie). He provides details like the importance of the selection of vaudeville spots on a bill. Some of the early performers, like Frank Fay, will be unfamiliar to contemporary audiences. There are several photos but the book lacks an index.

B36 Burns, George and Hal Goldman. **Wisdom of the 90's**. New York: G. P. Putnam's Sons, 1991.
In ten sequences, George rambles around giving monologues on various subjects. He offers lists of the "Ten Wisest Men and Women," grooming tips and repeats some stories from his other books. Included are several photos taken at his home in Beverly Hills.

B37 Burns, George and Kenneth Turan. "Lessons I Learned from TV." **TV Guide**. September 15-21, 1984: 35-38.
In a cover story tie-in with his upcoming special, **George Burns 'How to Live to be 100' Special** (T567), George notes that television was the hardest medium he has ever worked in, talks about taking **The Burns and Allen Show** from radio to television and discusses his television work after Gracie's retirement.

Additional Works

B38 Adams, Joey. **Here's to the Friars: The Heart of Show Business**. New York: Crown Publishers, 1976.
A history of the New York City and California Friars Clubs by comedian Adams. Chapters include recounts of the George Burns and Jack Benny dinner in 1972 and the 1975 Friars Roast of "the sunshine boys," George Burns and Walter Matthau.

B39 ---. **Roast of the Town**. New York: Prentice Hall Press, 1986.
Adams reveals quips made at the private Friars Club roasts, including those from the one given in honor of George's 90th birthday.

B40 Adams, Val. "Just a Couple of Performers: Burns and Allen Take Their TV Success in Stride." **The New York Times**. October 22, 1950, Sec. 10: 13.
Burns and Allen talk about preparing for their new CBS television show which premiered on October 12, 1950 (T1).

B41 "Air Act's Ace Ballyhoo." **Variety**. May 4, 1940: 24+.

This show business trade paper printed several articles on Burns and Allen's careers, centering on Gracie's presidential convention this month in Omaha, Nebraska during the Golden Spike Days celebrations.

B42 Albert, Dora. "Gracie Allen is Really Scared to Death." **Radio Mirror**. March 1935: 22.
Albert reveals that Gracie, like many performers, is often fearful of appearing in public but forces herself to overcome her fear.

B43 ---. "Her Adopted Children Remade Gracie Allen's Life." **Photoplay**. April 1937: 45+.
A story about George and Gracie's thoughts on parenthood and how they adopted their two children, Sandra and Ronald, from The Cradle in Evanston, Illinois. Albert names Gracie as "one of the finest, most honest and candid people in Hollywood."

B44 Albert, Katherine. "Anticipating a Blessed Event." **Modern Screen**. September 1935: 64-65.
An article about George and Gracie's plans to adopt another child.

B45 Albert, Stephen and Diane L. Albert. **The TV Collector**. Vol. 13. 1978.
A publication geared toward collectors of television shows. The subjects of this issue are Burns and Allen and includes a list of titles of their television shows in syndication.

B46 Albin, Len. "George Burns: His Fire is Still Lit." **50 Plus**. December 23, 1983: 60-62.
This article reviews George's book on how to live to be 100 (B24) and how he follows his own advice.

B47 Alexander, David and Bea Weiss. **Season Ticket**. August 1980: 18-19+.
An interview with George just prior to the release of **Oh, God!** (F38) reveals that a recent poll resulted in a tie between George and Bob Hope as "the most popular man in America." He's also asked if he would consider returning to television on a regular basis, to which he replies, "No, no, no. I would never do that. I'd never do a weekly show..." This interview was obviously conducted some time before he was approached about appearing in **George Burns Comedy Week**, although his participation in that program was limited.

B48 Alleman, Richard. **The Movie Lover's Guide to Hollywood**. New York: Harper & Row, 1985.
This fascinating guide can be used to locate George and Gracie's former apartment in Hollywood, George's current home, one of the studios where their radio show originated, the studio lot where their television show was filmed and the crypt in Forest Lawn in Glendale, California, where Gracie was laid to rest in 1964.

B49 Allen, Steve. **Funny People**. Briarcliff Manor: Stein and Day, 1981.
The multitalented Allen presents a portrait of selected comedians, including his friend, George Burns. The chapter on George describes him as a man who is "funnier in person than on stage."

B50 Alvarez, Max Joseph. **Index to Motion Pictures Reviewed by Variety, 1907-1980**. Metuchen: Scarecrow, 1982.
A title index to film reviews appearing in the show business newspaper **Variety**. Short subject films and re-releases are included in the indexing.

B51 Amory, Cleveland. "Celebrity Register." **McCall's**. May 1963: 136.
A short biographical portrait of Gracie Allen.

B52 "And Here Are George Burns, Gracie Allen!" **House and Garden**. June 1937: 61.
This is a short article on the Burnses and their house in Beverly Hills, California, the only home they ever owned.

B53 Ann-Margret with Todd Gold. **Ann-Margret: My Story**. New York: Putnam, 1994.

This popular entertainer tells the story of her life including how George Burns hired her for his act in Las Vegas in the 1960's, which helped start her successful career in show business.

B54 Archer, Gleason Leonard. **History of Radio to 1926**. New York: The American Historical Society. 1938. New York: Arno Press, 1971.
This is a reprint of an earlier edition which details the history of the early years of radio.

B55 Archerd, Army. "Just for Variety." **Daily Variety**. December 14, 1989: 2.
An Archerd column entry notes that George is the radio and TV pitchman for a new Pepsi product, a flavored sparkling water called H-2-Oh!, with Denver, Colorado, as the test market. If successful in the test market, spots and the product will be distributed nationally.

B56 "Art." **The New York Times**. September 27, 1938: 29.
This short article describes Gracie's one-woman art exhibition at the Julian Levy Gallery on East 57th Street, New York City which runs from September 26 to October 4, 1938.

B57 "Audience Gives Burns 'Vitality'." **The Hollywood Reporter**. January 15, 1993: 46.
A trade paper article timed to coincide with George's upcoming 97th birthday, in which he recalls that his fondest memories in life always include Gracie. George also notes that his greatest achievement is "The fact that I'm still around," and, when asked what he would do if he were eighteen again, finally says, "I would try to find another Gracie."

B58 "Babies Wanted." **Radio Stars**. November 1935: 22.
A short piece about Burns and Allen and other entertainers' adoption of children.

B59 Baker, Gretta. "Backstage with Burns and Allen." **Senior Scholastic**. April 19-24, 1943: 20.
In an interview with George and Gracie in their dressing room at the CBS Radio Theater in Hollywood, California, the couple discusses the types of books they like to read (George likes biographies and Gracie enjoys mystery fiction and novels), art they enjoy and their tastes in music and plays.

B60 Ball, Aimee Lee. "George Burns: Reading Between the One-Liners." **Redbook**. October 15, 1980: 29+.
This writer attempts to find the "real" George Burns, but he doesn't reveal anything new that hasn't been printed previously in other publications.

B61 Barber, John and Ashley Geddes. "Growing Old with Style." **Maclean's**. October 6, 1986: 58.
An interview with George in this Canadian weekly contains his explanation of his conduct of life.

B62 Barnouw, Erik. **The Golden Web: A History of Broadcasting in the United States, 1933 to 1953**. Vol. 2. New York: Oxford, 1968. 3 vols. 1966-70.

B63 ---. **The Image Empire: A History of Broadcasting in the United States From 1953**. Vol. 3. New York: Oxford, 1970. 3 vols. 1966-70.

B64 ---. **A Tower in Babel: A History of Broadcasting in the United States to 1933**. Vol. 1. New York: Oxford, 1966. 3 vols. 1966-70.
A comprehensive three volume history of broadcasting in the United States from the formation of the networks to the moon landing. The volumes include photographs and some excerpts from television scripts and describe how historical events influence broadcasting.

B65 ---. **Tube of Plenty: The Evolution of American Television**. New York: Oxford, 1975.
This one volume update based on the author's three volume work on the history of broadcasting updates the sections on television history to the 1970's.

B66 Barth, Jack. **Roadside Hollywood**. Chicago: Contemporary Books, 1991.
This self-proclaimed "travel guide for movie lovers" lists state-by-state attractions for the film buff and includes information on the Burns and Allen connection to Rancho Mirage, California.

B67 Beckles, Gordon. "Humorist Meets Allen and Burns." **The New York Times**. August 19, 1934.
A British writer interviews Burns and Allen in London, England, upon their return from their summer vacation, which ended in Moscow, Russia. As usual, the team reveals very little of their true natures, and all the writer gets in return for his questions is a couple of one liners from Burns and Allen's routines.

B68 Benjamin, Sandy Stert. "George Burns: Still Going Strong at 92." **Bonus**. June 1988: 4-6.
George confirms his lack of interest in looking back at his life, preferring to concentrate on the future.

B69 Benny, Jack. "My Adventures in Hollywood." **Radio Stars**. November 1936: 17.
This brief article mentions Burns and Allen as friends of Jack Benny.

B70 Benny, Jack and Joan Benny. **Sunday Nights at Seven**. New York: Warner Books, 1990.
Joan Benny has written a biography of her comedian father, Jack Benny, which he had started to write but never completed. Because the Bennys and Burnses were the closest of friends, the book has several references to Gracie, George and their children (Joan Benny and Sandra Burns were the best of friends during their school years). Although George has written the introduction to the book, and Joan Benny has many positive things to say about him, she interestingly writes very little about the "real Gracie Allen," although she admits people have asked her many times.

B71 Benny, Mary Livingstone, Hilliard Marks, and Marcia Borie. **Jack Benny**. Garden City: Doubleday and Company, 1978.
This biography of Jack Benny written by his wife and brother-in-law includes his strong friendship with George Burns but barely mentions Gracie Allen.

B72 Bensman, Marvin R. "Obtaining Old Radio Programs: A List of Sources for Research and Teaching." **Journal of Popular Culture**. 12 (1979): 360-367.
The history of radio program collecting in the United States is overviewed and there is a list of available sources on how to obtain radio programs for educational purposes. Also included is the history of the development and use of records to record sound with an explanation of the electrical transcription disk.

B73 Beranger, Clara. "How Dumb is Gracie Allen?" **Liberty**. September 1, 1934.
The author claims that Gracie is not dumb at all but is a "charming, vital young woman" who is "simple and untheatrical." In the interview, Gracie explains that she is Irish, not Jewish, as many people believe. Burns and Allen tell of their beginning years in vaudeville and continue up to their current career in radio (two years) and in motion pictures.

B74 "Berle, Burns, Hope Look at TV Comedy." UPI Wire Service. May 25, 1986.
This article purports to be a lament by the three veteran comedians (Milton Berle, George Burns and Bob Hope) about the death of the television variety show, and perhaps it was before it was edited. All that remains are comments by Berle.

B75 Best, Katharine. "Nitwits of the Networks." **Stage**. (4) May 1, 1939: 35+. May 15, 1939: 29+.
These two articles cover the early days of George and Gracie as vaudeville performers, including how they met and how they began working as a comedy team. Gracie talks about her work with other partners before meeting George. Their entrances into the fields of radio and motion pictures bring the article up to date, ending with the mention of Gracie starting work on **The Gracie Allen Murder Case** (F33).

B76 Beville, Hugh Malcolm, Jr. **Audience Ratings: Radio, Television, and Cable**. Hillsdale: Laurence Erlbaum Associates, 1985.
This is the story of audience rating services and their importance for advertisers, notably radio's Archibald M. Crossley's Cooperative Analysis of Broadcasting and ending with Clark Hooper Services' Hooper ratings. Ratings continue to have an impact on which programs are aired, and this book helps the reader to interpret the ratings of radio shows in the past, such as Burns and Allen's.

B77 Biddle, Mary. "Beauty and Gracie." **Radio Stars**. April 1938: 92+.
Another story about the actress Gracie Allen.

B78 Biederman, Patricia Ward. "'God' of Movies Blesses His Peers with $1 Million." **Los Angeles Times**. October 5, 1985, Valley ed., sec. 2: 5.
A story about George's donation of one million dollars to the Motion Picture and Television Country House and Hospital in Woodland Hills, California.

B79 "**The Big Broadcast of 1937**." **Radio Stars**. November 1936: 48.
Coverage of the new film with Burns and Allen (F28).

B80 **Billboard**. October 21, 1933.
Gracie and George are featured on the cover of this entertainment trade magazine.

B81 Blanc, Mel[vin Jerome] and Philip Bashe. **That's Not All Folks**. New York: Warner Books, 1988.
In his autobiography, the American actor and voice specialist relates his experiences as a cast member of many radio shows, including those of Burns and Allen. He notes that Gracie off stage was an extremely witty woman and unlike the "dumb Dora" character she portrayed.

B82 **Blue Book of Radio Entertainers**. Bridgeport: General Electric Co., 1935.
Burns and Allen are included in this work of biographical sketches and photos of radio performers. Noted is the fact that they once received 360,000 fan letters in four days.

B83 Blum, Daniel. **Pictorial History of Television**. Chilton Co., 1959.
This history centers on the evolution of television programming since 1930, with many photos, coverage of television performers and programs.

B84 Blythe, Cheryl and Susan Sackett. **Say Goodnight, Gracie!: The Story of Burns and Allen**. New York: E. P. Dutton, 1986.
A history of the George Burns and Gracie Allen television show which includes several interviews with persons who worked on the show. The epilogue includes the names of the main cast members of the show and their careers after it went off the air in 1958. Appendices include a synopsis of each show arranged by episode number and background information on the supporting cast. Text contains some factual errors. Includes photographs.

B85 Bookbinder, Robert. **The Films of Bing Crosby**. Secaucus, New Jersey: The Citadel Press, 1977.
This work on the films which featured singer/actor Crosby includes cast credits, songs, film running time, synopses of films and reviews including **The Big Broadcast** (F19), **College Humor** (F21) and **We're Not Dressing** (F23), which also starred Burns and Allen.

B86 Booraem, Hendrik J., Jr. Taped interview. Hendersonville, North Carolina. Fall 1991.
A director of **The Burns and Allen Show** during the time it was sponsored by Swan Soap recalls some of his experiences working with the comedy team in 1942 and 1943 and draws remarkable verbal pictures of the world of show business prior to the advent of mass-audience television.

B87 Bradbury, Ray. "George, Marlene and Me." **Life**. July 1991: 91.
Science fiction writer Bradbury relates how, as a young boy in Los Angeles in 1934, he met George Burns and Marlene Dietrich on separate occasions. He convinced George to let him attend the Burns and Allen radio broadcasts (this was prior to studio audiences) and started to submit jokes to be

considered for the broadcast. One of his jokes was first used to close a 1936 show.

B88 Brady, James. "In Step with: George Burns." **Parade Magazine**. January 1, 1989: 16.
George talks about his latest book, **Gracie: A Love Story** (B22), and his future plans in an interview conducted in New York City.

B89 Britt, George. "Gracie Allen Succeeds in Being Funny Only When She's Natural, Team Agrees." **New York World-Telegram**. August 30, 1932.
This interviewer notes that the dark haired Gracie Allen doesn't look so dumb in person. Gracie relates that the type of comedy she does fits her style and interestingly notes that she wouldn't mind retiring if she had the money (Gracie and George will continue to work together for another 26 years before she retires). At the time this article was written, Burns and Allen had been appearing weekly for six months on Guy Lombardo's radio show.

B90 Brooks, Tim. **The Complete Directory to Prime Time TV Stars**. New York: Ballantine Books, 1987.
An alphabetical listing of more than 8,500 television performers (including George and Gracie) from 1946-1987 includes birthdate and birthplace (when known), limited credits, biographical sketches and several helpful appendices. Gracie's birthdate is given as July 26, 1902, with a footnote that some sources list 1906. Both are incorrect (she was born in 1895). Most interesting is the statement that Gracie became "increasingly depressed" in the 1960's and that both she and George knew she was dying.

B91 Brooks, Tim and Earle Marsh. **The Complete Directory to Prime Time Network TV Shows: 1946-Present**. 5th ed. New York: Ballantine Books, 1992.
Probably the most comprehensive one volume encyclopedia of television shows which have aired on American television in "prime time" (7:30-11:00 P.M. EST). Entries include the first/last telecast, broadcast history, cast and synopsis. Co-author Brooks contributes a valuable essay titled "A Short History of Network Television." Eleven appendices include prime time network schedule charts for each network season, Emmy Award winners by year and top rated shows according to the A. C. Nielsen Company. There is a detailed personality index of nearly 14,000 performers.

B92 Browar, Herbert. Personal interview. Beverly Hills, California. July 27, 1991.
The production manager for the **George Burns and Gracie Allen Show** provides insight into how the show was staged for television and information on those who worked on the series.

B93 Brown, Sheldon. **Official 1985 Price Guide to Radio-TV and Movie Memorabilia**. Orlando: House of Collectibles Inc., 1985.
A brief history of film, radio and television precede suggested price ranges of various forms of popular media collectibles, including celebrity autographs. Some photos.

B94 Burnham, Bob. **Listening Guide to Classic Radio Programs**. Redford: BRC Productions, 1986.
Information is provided for collectors of classic radio programs and radio equipment. There is a section of names and addresses of currently active collectors from which one may purchase materials. The Burns and Allen shows are on a list of favorite radio shows which the author suggests a collector should consider collecting.

B95 "Burns". **New Yorker**. March 15, 1976: 29-30.
An interview with George about his recent Carnegie Hall "highly creditable" debut. George and Goodman Ace also recount stories about working in vaudeville.

B96 "Burns, Allen and Burns." **TV Guide**. August 25-31, 1956: 24-25.
A story about Ronnie Burns starting work as a television actor on his parents' show.

B97 "Burns & Allen." **TV Forecast**. January 27-February 2, 1951: 8-9+.
George and Gracie are featured on the cover of this Chicago television

guide. While the article states that "Most Chicagoans agree: they look and act the way they sound," strangely little attention is given to their television show in the ensuing paragraphs.

B98 "Burns and Allen Arrive on a Busman's Holiday." **New York Post**. October 11, 1937.
Coverage of the Burnses' arrival in New York City with their two children which has the team gagging the moment they appear in front of reporters and their trying to make their children part of the act. This might have made an impression on Burns and Allen, which led to a unusually (for them) serious interview they gave three days later to a reporter (B466).

B99 "Burns and Allen Hit New York." **Time**. December 9, 1944.
A photograph of George and Gracie attending a CBS radio publicity party with a caption in which the interviewer remarks on how young the Burnses look "like they are thirty."

B100 "Burns and Allen May Adopt Child." **Los Angeles Times**. May 15, 1934.
Reprints a rumor concerning the possible adoption of a child by George and Gracie, noting that "It's a custom that occasionally prevails in the movie profession." George and Gracie did adopt their daughter, Sandra, that year and one year later adopted their son, Ronald.

B101 "Burns and Allen Set a Zany Pace." **New York Cue**. January 5, 1951: 13.
This article illustrates the Burnses' work and hectic schedule they follow to produce and act in their television series.

B102 "Burns and Allen: Their Children Tell About Them." **Televiewer**. July 17-23, 1954.
A rare article in which Ronnie and Sandy talk about their parents, revealing that their mother is a nervous type of person and their father is always firing the gardener.

B103 "The Burns and Allen Tuesday Night Riot." **The Movie-Radio Guide**. November 29-December 5, 1941: 38-39.
A behind-the-scenes look at the first Burns and Allen radio show in which George and Gracie appear as husband and wife, broadcast for Swan Soap. The text is accompanied by photos.

B104 Burns, Ronnie and Sandra Burns. "Life with Father...and Mother." **Radio Life**. December 9, 1945: 4-5.
George and Gracie's children talk about life with their parents. The article includes photographs of the family at home in Beverly Hills, California.

B105 "Burns Without Allen." **Time**. March 3, 1958: 46.
The announcement that Gracie Allen had made the decision to retire from show business is accompanied by a recounting of her career.

B106 Buxton, Frank and Bill Owen. **The Big Broadcast 1920-1950**. Rev. ed. New York: Viking Press, 1972.
An expanded edition of their earlier work, **Radio's Golden Age**.

B107 ---. **Radio's Golden Age: The Programs and the Personalities**. New York: Easton Valley Press, 1966.
A reference book about early radio which lists major shows, their casts, themes and production credits with photographs.

B108 "Cadets Give Concert and Ball." **San Francisco Chronicle**. January 31, 1914: 5.
A photograph of Miss Grace Allen is featured as one of the hostesses who assisted the League of the Cross boys school in entertaining their guests at their concert and ball.

B109 Cahn, William. **The Laugh Makers: A Pictorial History of American Comedians**. New York: G. P. Putnam's Sons, 1957.
A brief history of American wit and humor beginning with the comedian Thomas Wignell in 1787 with several photos and illustrations.

B110 ---. **Pictorial History of the Great Comedians**. New York: Grosset and Dunlap, 1970.

This is an updated version of **The Laugh Makers**.

B111 Cahn, William and Rhoda Cahn. **The Great American Comedy Scene**. New York: Monarch Press, 1978.
An update of his earlier book, **Pictorial History of the Great Comedians**, this book was completed and published posthumously by the author's wife.

B112 Campbell, Robert. **The Golden Years of Broadcasting: A Celebration of the First 50 Years of Radio and TV on NBC**. New York: Charles Scribner's Sons, 1976.
An historical picture of the development of early radio and television programming at the National Broadcasting Company (NBC).

B113 "Candidette." **Time**. March 18, 1940: 36.
An outline of Gracie's race for the Presidency a week after she has been breaking in on other radio shows to talk about her campaign. The writer illustrates that Gracie's "dippiness" is just an act and that offstage "she is not always so dippy."

B114 Cantor, Eddie and Jane Kesner Ardmore. **Take My Life**. Garden City: Doubleday, 1957.
Entertainer Cantor's autobiography tells of Gracie's first radio appearance on his show in 1932. **SEE R804.**

B115 Cantril, Hadley and Gordon W. Allport. **The Psychology of Radio**. New York: Harper & Brothers, 1935.
A look at radio programs with a psychological approach to determine how listeners respond to different content broadcasts such as drama, comedy and the news.

B116 Carpentier, Fran. "George Burns: The Show Goes On." **Parade Magazine**. December 28, 1980: 4-5.
The interviewer reveals that George keeps on working in his first love, show business. The previous summer he was playing before live audiences by touring in New England for a month. In talking about his marriage, George says that reason it worked was that he and Gracie "both had the same mistress--show business."

B117 Carroll, Carroll. **None of Your Business or My Life With J. Walter Thompson (Confessions of a Renegade Radio Writer)**. New York: Cowles Book Co., 1970.
Autobiography of a comedy writer who was assigned by his advertising agency to work with Burns and Allen on their radio show. Carroll began working with the comedy team in the early 1930's at the time they were still touring in vaudeville shows with Guy Lombardo, just prior to their going to Hollywood to begin their first movie. Carroll relates personal stories of Burns and Allen as well as other performers. He continued to write for other shows after he left Burns and Allen.

B118 Carter, Betsy and Peter S. Greenberg. "A Ray of Sunshine." **Newsweek**. March 1, 1976: 57.
In an article printed a week after George was nominated for an Academy Award for Best Supporting Actor for his role in **The Sunshine Boys** (F37) (which he is favored to win), George admits that the success of the film has changed his life. The writers conclude after interviewing George that the "funniest thing about Burns is that he doesn't think that he is funny."

B119 Castleman, Harry and Walter J. Podrazik. **Harry and Wally's Favorite TV Shows**. New York: Prentice Hall, 1989.
An annotated guide to television series which have aired on American television. Included is a cast index and an index of programs available on videocassette.

B120 ---. **The TV Schedule Book (4 Decades of Network Programming from Sign-On and Sign-Off**. New York: McGraw-Hill, 1984.
American television schedules by year are reproduced with details on the morning, afternoon and evening programming.

B121 Cerf, May. "Come to a Party with Burns and Allen." **Radio Stars**. July 1933: 8-9+.
Cerf is a reporter who was a recent guest at a party given by George and Gracie at their 36th floor apartment in the Essex House in New York City,

located across from Central Park on W. 59th Street. She notes that Gracie is a perfect hostess.

B122 Champlin, Charles. "George Burns: Almost 90, Still Slayin' 'Em." Datebook, **San Francisco Chronicle**. November 11, 1984: 18+.
This article, published at the time of the opening of **Oh God! You Devil** (F44) and the publication of **Dr. Burns' Prescription for Happiness** (B19) retells many of George's old stories but does offer information on how George stopped a ratings slide during their radio days. He realized that having Gracie flirt with others on the program was a mistake (since the audience knew they were married in real life); once they changed the show's premise, their ratings recovered.

B123 ---. "The World's Youngest 92-Year-Old Man." **Los Angeles Times**. April 3, 1988, Calendar sec.: 21+.
Timed to coincide with the opening of his latest film, **18 Again!** (F45), this article is typical of most written about George in later years. They serve their purpose of promoting his most recent project but offer little if any fresh insight into the man (and never any fresh quotes!), shortcomings that may not always be the fault of the writer.

B124 Chandler, Charlotte. **Hello, I Must Be Going**. Garden City: Doubleday, 1978.
A biography of Groucho Marx, with many interviews with Marx and some of his peers. The author was a friend of Groucho's and was able to meet with him and others over a period of years in which she documented these conversations. A dialogue with George Burns is included in which he and Groucho talk about their days in vaudeville. George mentions that Groucho first met Grace Allen when she was working in vaudeville in the early 1920's with Larry Reilly.

B125 "Chapereau's Way." **Time**. December 19, 1938: 12.
Background article on the convicted criminal, Albert Chapereau, and how George Burns and Jack Benny became involved with him and were themselves found guilty of smuggling jewelry into the United States.

B126 Chase, Francis, Jr. "My Friends and Fellow Candidates." **Movie and Radio Guide**." May 11-17, 1940.
An interview with Gracie concerning her Presidential campaign. Included are details of her Union Pacific special train stops in thirty towns, from Hollywood on its way to Omaha, site of her Surprise Party's convention.

B127 Cheatham, Maud. "When It's Mr. and Mrs." **Radio and Television Mirror**. December 1940: 22-23+.
This writer gives an overview of Burns and Allen's career and personal life as a married couple in show business.

B128 "The Children's Hour." **TV Guide**. February 2-8, 1957: 8-11.
Ronnie Burns is mentioned as one of the many children of famous television stars who also work in show business.

B129 Christon, Lawrence. "Burns: Down to the Essentials." **Los Angeles Times**. December 30, 1979, Calendar sec.: 42+.
In trying to analyze George's audience appeal, the author concludes that the comedian has a special style and that the audience thinks that George is playing himself. George states that "he is not a comedian, but a humorist."

B130 Christopher, R. "Tip of the Old Toupee." **Maclean's**. August 20, 1979: 10-11.
A short article on George Burns and his current career in films and on stage.

B131 Christy, George. "Architectural Digest Visits: George Burns." **Architectural Digest**. August 1982: 64-69.
Photographs (by Mary E. Nichols) and a description of the remodeling of George's home in Beverly Hills by interior designer R. Paul Berry.

B132 Churchill, Allen. **Remember When?** New York: Golden Press, 1967.
Data on the golden age of radio includes pictures of some of its performers, including Burns and Allen.

B133 **City Directory**. San Francisco, California. Annual. 1895- .

These directories include the names and addresses of the city's residents and businesses, including the Allen and Darragh families.

B134 Clarke, Gerald. "Going in Style with George Burns." **Time**. August 6, 1979: 59+.
George answers questions about his latest film, **Going in Style** (F41), and other projects. He notes that "film acting is not hard work." The author feels that George "puts himself down" when he says Gracie made him successful. Clarke feels that the "truth is that George also made it for Gracie."

B135 Collins, Frederick L. "The Man in Gracie Allen's Life." **Liberty**. Winter 1972: 74-75+.
Originally published in the December 10, 1938 issue of **Liberty**, the author recalls the saga of "the trouper who fell in love with the girl who stole his act." The reading time of the story, incidentally, was proclaimed to be "15 minutes 40 seconds."

B136 Colt, George Howe and Anne Fadiman. "Why Do We Love Dogs: Why Do We Love Cats?" **Life**. October 1994: 77-88.
In this article written by husband and wife writers, famous pet owners advocate which is a better pet, cats or dogs. George Burns is photographed with his cat Willie at the dining table.

B137 "Comedian Escapes Year's Prison Term." **New York Post**. January 31, 1939.
A report of the fines and suspended prison sentence George received after pleading guilty to charges of buying smuggled jewelry. The piece notes that George could be called as a government witness against Jack Benny, who pleaded not guilty to similar charges. It is equally interesting that a news article would describe George as "straight man and spouse of goofy Gracie Allen," as if "goofy" was an apt description (which it wasn't) of the real Gracie instead of her fictional character.

B138 Connolly, Mike. "Subject Is Gracie." **Newark Evening News**. September 6, 1964.
Connolly, one of Gracie's pallbearers, recalls his friend in this article written shortly after her funeral. He includes a remark attributed to celebrated actress Lynn Fontanne, "'With all due respect to Ethel Barrymore, Helen Hayes, Kit Cornell, Tallulah Bankhead and the rest of us, THE great lady of the American theater is Gracie Allen.'"

B139 Cook, Alton. "Burns and Allen Get Brave." **New York World-Telegram**. May 3, 1934.
Returning to New York City after a long stay in Hollywood broadcasting their radio show before audiences, Burns and Allen note that they have lost their fear of the microphone in the broadcast studio, which haunted many of the first radio performers. But they conclude that they still do not want audiences when they are broadcasting.

B140 ---. "Burnses Introduce 'Sandy'." **New York World-Telegram**. September 26, 1934.
A story of the adoption of their daughter Sandy and how it has changed George and Gracie's life as a family.

B141 ---. "Gracie Allen Real Actress." **New York World-Telegram**. October 20, 1939.
Gracie stepping outside her best-known character to play someone else always made news, as evidenced in this announcement of her upcoming role on **Screen Guild Theater** (R851). Cook also notes that radio is giving Gracie a chance to "demonstrate her unexpected talent," referencing her earlier appearances on **Lux Radio Theater** (R838) and **Information Please** (R850).

B142 Cooper, Arthur. "George Burns (A Candid Conversation with a Promising Young Comedian, Actor and Singer)." **Playboy**. June 1978: 85+.
George recounts his life in show business ending with his current second career as an actor in films and his nightclub and concert appearances. He reflects on other entertainers and his life with Gracie. A few lines from their "Lamb Chops" vaudeville routine is quoted. This is the first article in which George revealed that he had at least one extramarital affair, which was a surprising admission to readers at the time.

B143 ---. "George Burns: Still Sexy After All These Years." **Family Weekly**. June 19, 1983: 4-5.
George talks about Groucho Marx, Jack Benny and George Jessel and how he has become a sex symbol at the age of 87.

B144 Cooper, Arthur and Katrine Ames. "Playing Old." **Newsweek**. May 19, 1975: 89-90.
A review of the making of the film **The Sunshine Boys** (F37).

B145 "The Courtesy Kick." **TV Guide**. December 1-7, 1956: 8-9.
Subtitled "George Burns Picks His Funniest Monolog For **TV Guide** Readers," George explains the pros and cons of extending little courtesies to women. George and Gracie are on this week's cover, "courtesy" of an Al Hirschfeld caricature.

B146 Coville, Gary W. "Gracie Allen's 1940 Presidential Campaign." **American History Illustrated**. November/December 1990: 62+.
Highlights of Gracie's 1940 campaign for the Presidency and how it helped bring humor to a nation in a depressed economy just prior to the start of America's entrance into World War II. Photos of Gracie's campaign are included.

B147 Cox, Stephen and Parl Corkery. "End of an Era." **TV Guide**. May 9-15, 1992: 10-21.
George joins other celebrities in saying farewell to **Tonight Show** host Johnny Carson upon his retirement. As can be imagined, George advises against it (retirement).

B148 Creelman, Eileen. "Picture Plays and Players." **New York Sun**. May 15, 1933.
Interview with the "shrewd, honest and friendly team" of Burns and Allen. George tells of their experiences in Hollywood in March when they were filming **International House** (F20). He said that during the filming they experienced an earthquake but while everyone ran outside the building, Gracie stayed inside the studio and hid under an elevator--not realizing that it was a prop elevator until George came back inside to look for her.

B149 Culbertson, Judi and Tom Randall. **Permanent Californians**. Chelsea: Chelsea Green Publishing Company, 1989.
This guide to California cemeteries includes Gracie's final resting place in Glendale's Forest Lawn.

B150 Cummings, Robert. Interview. Dallas: Oral History Collection, De Golyer Library, Southern Methodist University. July 22, 1974.
The lead actor in the television show, **The Bob Cummings Show,** has some recollections on George Burns, who was one of the financial backers of the show.

B151 **Current Biography Yearbook**. New York: H. W. Wilson, 1940.
"Gracie Allen" is included in the first edition of this annual which contains biographical information on contemporary figures of the period. The article has incorrect factual information such as the wrong birth dates for George and Gracie (1898 and 1905 rather than 1896 and 1895) and their debut in England on the BBC (1929 not 1930). Included is a portrait of Gracie and a description of her physical attributes, noting that she is "simple, unaffected, untheatrical" and that "her voice is mellow and entirely unlike the high pitched voice she uses in her act."

B152 ---. New York: H. W. Wilson, 1951.
This article on "George Burns and Gracie Allen" updates the 1940 article on Gracie. Noted is their recent success of their television series.

B153 ---. New York: H. W. Wilson, 1976.
A "George Burns" article retells the Burns and Allen story and updates the 1951 Burns and Allen article with details of George's career since 1958 when Gracie retired.

B154 Darbyshire, Martha B. "Radio Stars Build a Home." **Arts and Decoration**. August 1938: 25+.
This article details the architecture and interior design (H. W. Grieve) of Burns and Allen's new home they built in Beverly Hills on North Maple Drive. There are photographs by Fred R. Dapprich of the home's interior and exterior with signatures of George and Gracie on the first page of the

article. This was the only home the Burnses ever owned, and George has remained in the home after his wife's death in 1964.

B155 Darin, Dodd. **Dream Lovers: The Magnificent Shattered Lives of Bobby Darin and Sandra Dee**. New York: Warner Books, 1994.
The son of singer Bobby Darin and actress Sandra Dee tells his parents' story. George Burns introduced Bobby Darin as a singer in Las Vegas, where he started on his road to success. George and Bobby (who died in 1973) became very close, almost like "father and son."

B156 Davies, D. "Films of Gracie Allen." **Films in Review**. January 1965: 57.
The title says it all for this list of Gracie's films.

B157 Davy, Kate. "An Interview with George Burns." **Educational Theatre Journal** 27 (1975): 345-355.
Doctoral student Davy interviews George Burns in 1974 in a question/answer format. George responds to questions on his early days in small time vaudeville, and he relates how he started working with Gracie, their acts "Sixty-Forty," "Dizzy" and "Lamb Chops," and in their films and radio shows. This is one of the few articles in which George answers the interviewer's questions seriously without gag lines.

B158 de Cordova, Fred. Interview. Dallas: Oral History Collection, De Golyer Library, Southern Methodist University. August 10, 1982.
Mr. de Cordova responds to an interviewer's questions regarding his career in television, including his work as producer-director of **The George Burns and Gracie Allen Show** from 1953-1955.

B159 ---. **Johnny Came Lately**. New York: Simon and Schuster, 1988.
This is an autobiography by former **Tonight Show** executive producer de Cordova, who had previously worked on **The Burns and Allen** television series.

B160 Debenham, Warren. **Laughter on Record: A Comedy Discography**. Metuchen: Scarecrow, 1988.
A list of comedy recordings available on phonodisc.

B161 **Dictionary of American Biography**. Supplement 7. New York: Charles Scribner's Sons, 20 vols. 8 supplements, 1928-1988.
An article on Gracie Allen is found in this biographical dictionary of noteworthy individuals.

B162 Diehl, Digby. "A Man for all Media." **Los Angeles Herald**. July 24, 1983: E: 1-2.
The well-known **Herald** book editor discusses the many entertainment fields George has conquered in this article prompted, in part, by the preparation for another of his television specials, the correct title of which is **George Burns Celebrates 80 Years in Show Business**. **SEE T562.**

B163 DiMeglio, John E. "Radio's Debt to Vaudeville." **Journal of Popular Culture** 12 (1979): 228-235.
Background information on how vaudeville performers became headliners in radio. The importance of a reactive audience to these performers led to studio audiences at the broadcasts.

B164 ---. **Vaudeville U.S.A.** Bowling Green: Popular Press, 1973.
A history of the inner workings of American vaudeville as popular entertainment.

B165 "Discreet Silence." **Time**. December 26, 1938: 21.
A short article written shortly after George Burns pleaded guilty in New York to two Federal indictments for smuggling.

B166 "Do Comics Hate Each Other?" **TV Guide**. August 14-20, 1954: 5-7.
This article notes that the relationship between comedy teams is not always amicable, but Burns and Allen are one of the exceptions.

B167 Douglas, Susan J. **Inventing American Broadcasting 1899-1922**. Johns Hopkins Studies in the History of Technology. Baltimore: Johns Hopkins University Press, 1987.
A history of radio broadcasting in the United States with an extensive bibliography.

B168 Dumont, Lou. "Historical Tape Recordings: George Burns & Gracie Allen." **Hobbies.** September 1979: 78+.
A reprint of the George Burns and Gracie Allen radio program of December 2, 1941 (R448).

B169 Dunning, John. **Tune in Yesterday: The Ultimate Encyclopedia of Old-Time Radio, 1925-1976.** Englewood Cliffs: Prentice Hall, 1976.
A narrative dictionary of United States radio programs. The entries list players of major roles, sponsors, cast, crew, writers, premiere dates and the network on which the program aired.

B170 "The Durable Ones." **Newsweek.** June 24, 1957: 94.
This article looks at why Burns and Allen's television show was renewed for the season and over 55 others dropped. George says that the success of their show is that "Gracie and I don't try to get all of the laughs."

B171 Eaton, Mick. "Television Situation Comedy." **Screen.** Winter 78-79: 65-68.
A comparison of television situation comedy with the British variety-theatre. **The Burns and Allen Show** is analyzed as one of the first television comedies to use characters originally developed in vaudeville. George Burns has remarked that Burns and Allen throughout their careers were really just vaudevillians who continued their act successfully in radio and television.

B172 "Economics of Entertainment." **Radio Guide.** July 30, 1938: 20-21.
Coverage of a birthday party for Mary Benny with the Burnses in attendance.

B173 Eells, George. "George Burns...The Improbable Tycoon." **Look.** March 18, 1958: 34-38.
A look at George Burns as a very successful businessman as head of the McCadden Corporation which produces the George Burns and Gracie Allen television show, as well as others.

B174 Eichberg, Robert. **Radio Stars of Today or Behind the Scenes in Broadcasting.** Boston: L. C. Page and Co., 1937.
Biographical sketches of radio stars, including Burns and Allen, with a list of radio stations and 275 illustrations.

B175 Eisner, Joel and David Krinsky. **Television Comedy Series: An Episode Guide to 153 TV Sitcoms in Syndication.** Jefferson: McFarland, 1984.
A limited number of United States comedy programs, their plots and themes are included, with titles and story lines for the Burns and Allen television series.

B176 Eliot, Marc. **American Television: The Official Art of the Artificial Style and Tactics in Network Prime Time.** Garden City: Anchor Press, 1981.
The story of the development of television and its relationship with radio and motion pictures. Included are charts of weekly prime time television shows by year which aired on the major networks (Dumont, CBS, NBC and ABC).

B177 Endres, Stacey and Robert Cushman. **Hollywood At Your Feet.** Los Angeles: Pomegranate Press, Ltd., 1992.
Ceremonies surrounding one of Hollywood's supreme tributes--placing hands, feet, and other well-known body parts (and props) into cement into the forecourt of Mann's (formerly Grauman's) Chinese Theatre--are described in detail. George placed his prints (including cigar) there on November 25, 1979 (the book first lists the ceremony date as January 25, 1979 but newspaper reports say it was November 25 and the book, in fact, later mentions that the square contains the November date), in Ceremony #144, to coincide with the release of his current film. The inscription: "Ted--I'm 'Going in Style.'" (F41).

B178 Enge, Charles. "Just a Dumb Englishman." **Radio Life.** October 18, 1942: 5-6.
This article is about the orchestra leader and songwriter, Ray Noble, who was a part of the Burns and Allen radio show in the late 1930's and for a partial season in 1940 and appeared with them in the film **A Damsel in Distress** (F30). The article also reviews the first show of their current

season, noting that "last season's show was one of the most intriguing the pair has ever had."

B179 Everson, William K. **The Detective in Film**. Secaucus: The Citadel Press, 1972.
A look at the part the detective film has played in motion pictures provides information on **The Gracie Allen Murder Case** (F33) from its inception as a book until it was made into a film vehicle for Gracie Allen.

B180 Eyman, Scott. "Legend's Wit Proves Timeless." Syndicated. December 6, 1993.
The author conducts a telephone interview with George as he looks back on ninety years in show business.

B181 Farley, Ellen. "Inauguration Day to Also Star George Burns, Age, 85." **Los Angeles Times**. January 18, 1981, Calendar sec.: 6-7.
An article about George's 85th birthday party, a tribute whose proceeds will go to Ben Gurion University Medical Center in Israel. George recounts how he got started in show business and his life with Gracie and show business friends. Includes a page of photographs from his career.

B182 Federal Writers Project. **New York City Guide**. American Guide Series. New York: Hastings House, 1939.
A guide to the points of interest and historical background of the five boroughs of New York City by the writers of the Works Progress Administration (W.P.A.). The description of the Times Square District has a map and key of the area indicating the names and locations of the theaters in 1939. Many of the vaudeville theaters in which Burns and Allen appeared were still in existence at the time this book was published.

B183 Fein, Irving. **Jack Benny: An Intimate Biography**. New York: G. P. Putnam's Sons, 1976.
Jack Benny's personal manager tells the story of his employer. Included is information on how Jack and George Burns met in New York in 1921. Fein became George Burns' manager after Benny's death.

B184 **Film Review Annual**. 1981- . Englewood: J.S. Ozer, 1982- .
An annual publication which reprints complete film reviews of motion pictures released in the United States. Citations from other publications with reviews of the films are noted.

B185 Firestone, Ross, ed. **The Big Radio Comedy Program**. Chicago: Contemporary Books, 1978.
Scripts from radio shows from 1932 to 1945 are reprinted, with two Burns and Allen radio show scripts from the 1940's.

B186 Foster, Inez Whiteley. "Gracie Isn't So Dumb Off the Air." **Independent Woman**. October 1947: 292-294.
An interview with Gracie, when she and George are on vacation in New York City. Foster writes about the "real" Gracie Allen who is "keen as a razor" and only resembles the radio "Gracie" in that she talks nearly as fast and jumps about from one subject to another. She also finds Gracie "extremely quickwitted." Included are photos of the Burnses with their children, Sandy and Ronnie.

B187 Franklin, Joe. **Joe Franklin's Encyclopedia of Comedians**. Secaucus: The Citadel Press, 1979.
George Burns and Gracie Allen are included in a look at the men and women of the twentieth century who brought their humor and entertainment to the American public.

B188 Frick, John W. and Carlton Ward. eds. **Directory of Historic American Theatres**. Westport: Greenwood Press, 1987.
Information on American theatres, including many vaudeville theatres, constructed during the years 1800-1915.

B189 "Gallery of Stars: Gracie Allen." **Radio Mirror**. January 1935: 25.
Gracie Allen is featured on the cover of this magazine.

B190 Gaver, Jack and Dave Stanley, eds. **There's Laughter in the Air!: Radio's Top Comedians and Their Best Shows**. New York: Greenberg Publishing, 1945.

Biographical sketches of the careers of some of the best-known radio comedians. A complete radio script for each is included. The section on Burns and Allen is titled "Be Dumb, Sweet Maid" and includes two radio scripts from their show, November 30, 1943 (R531) and April 11, 1944 (R550).

B191 Gehman, Richard. "With them, it's Jack and Natty." **TV Guide**, December 19-25, 1964: 15-18.
The author spends the afternoon with the two old friends in Benny's Beverly Hills home, where they discuss how they met, their early years in show business, their work schedules today and the challenge of television.

B192 "George Burns Talks About His Special and Retirement." **TV Guide**. November 20-26, 1976.
The subject of the article is George's upcoming television special (T498) with his co-star from **The Sunshine Boys** (F37), Walter Matthau. The word "retirement" has, of course, been exorcised from George's personal dictionary, but that doesn't stop writers from questioning him about it.

B193 "George, Gracie Burns Set Comedy Record." **San Francisco Chronicle**. July 1, 1956.
The George Burns and Gracie Allen Show is acknowledged as the longest continuously running situation comedy show on television--six years--with the beginning of the new season.

B194 Gerdes, Lesta W. "George Burns and Gracie Allen at Home." **Better Living**. May 1941: 11-12.
A description of the Burnses' home and life in Beverly Hills, California, which notes that their home's interior is decorated in soft greens, rich tans and warm rose colors.

B195 Geri, Ruth. "Have You Met Mrs. George Burns?" **Radio Stars**. March 1936: 44+.
This article introduces the readers to Gracie and her career. The Burnses and their two children are still living in New York City but will soon move to California at the end of the year.

B196 Gilbert, Douglas. **American Vaudeville: Its Life and Times**. New York: Whittlesey House, 1940. New York: Dover Publications, 1963.
The history of American vaudeville and the entertainers who were a part of that world from 1881 to 1930.

B197 Gittelson, Natalie. "George Burns at 92." **McCall's**. June 1988: 73.
Using the thesis that George Burns is a living legend, the author talks to George about his latest movie, **18 Again!** (F45), and his zest for life.

B198 Goldberg, Lee. **Unsold Television Pilots, 1955-1988**. Jefferson: McFarland & Co., 1990.
Annotated listings of television shows that never made it past the pilot stage, including an adaptation of **The Sunshine Boys** (F37), the film that pushed George's career into overdrive all over again.

B199 "Golden Gate Has Alice Brady in Condensed Play." **San Francisco Chronicle**. July 7, 1924: 11.
A list of the vaudeville acts which would be appearing this week at the Golden Gate Theater in San Francisco is accompanied by a photo of Grace Allen with a caption that Burns and Allen would be appearing after Grace's five week stay in the hospital (for appendicitis).

B200 Gordon, Gale. Interview. Dallas: Oral History Collection, De Golyer Library, Southern Methodist University. June 17, 1975.
Actor Gale Gordon played the part of "Tex" Judson on the Burns and Allen radio show. In this interview about his career and the various roles he played in radio, Gordon explains how that part was developed for the Burns and Allen radio show in the 1940's. Gordon is perhaps best known for his roles in several of Lucille Ball's television series.

B201 Gould, Jack. "How Comic Is Radio Comedy?" **The New York Times Magazine**. November 21, 1948: 223-225.
The radio and television editor of **The New York Times** writes an article on the decline of radio comedy. Gould believes comedy shows seem to be repetitious because of the writers' tendency to repeat what has been

successful in the past. He concludes that radio is at fault for not adapting a long range plan, contending television is going to come in and fill that void.

B202 ---. "TV's Top Comediennes." **The New York Times Magazine**. December 27, 1953: 16.
A story which includes Gracie Allen as one of the first among the few successful television comedians.

B203 "Gracie Allen." **Radio Guide Mikeroscope Album and Log Book**. Chicago, 1935: 8-9.
A biographical sketch of Gracie Allen, with a full page photograph, in which she mentions her personal likes and dislikes.

B204 **Gracie Allen and George Burns 1991 Calendar**. Novato: Landmark Calendars, 1990.
This 1991 calendar has a full page photo of Burns and Allen for each month with line captions by George.

B205 "Gracie Allen Dead: Comedienne was 58." **The New York Times**. August 27, 1964: 1+.
The announcement of Gracie Allen's death includes a biographical sketch and a history of Burns and Allen as "one of the greatest husband and wife comedy teams of all time." The headline reported Gracie's age incorrectly. She was 69 at the time of her death.

B206 "Gracie Allen Decides to Quit After 50 Years." **New York Daily News**. February 19, 1958.
An account of Gracie's announcement to retire from show business, made on February 18, 1958, in Hollywood with a brief review of her career.

B207 "Gracie Allen Denies Paying." **San Francisco Chronicle**. October 22, 1933.
A press story from Chicago, Illinois stating that George Burns had to pay money to prevent the kidnapping of his wife for ransom. George denied the story was true.

B208 "**Gracie Allen Murder Case**." **Radio Mirror**. February 1939: 38+.
An article on the motion picture written for and starring Gracie Allen (F33).

B209 "Gracie Allen's Will." **Variety**. September 9, 1964.
The terms of Gracie's will, dated December 10, 1957, name George as executor of her estate and gives him her interest in their Beverly Hills home as well as all of her personal belongings. The balance of her estate, which is estimated to be more than $50,000, is being left in trust, although George can draw upon the trust to receive up to "$50,000 a year when added to his own income." The estate will be divided between the couple's two children upon George's death. The article states that Gracie gave her age as 55 at the time she signed the will, making her 62 at the time of death rather than 58. (However, Gracie was actually born in 1895, making her 69 at the time of death).

B210 "Gracie Ends Act with George." **Life**. September 22, 1958: 87-93.
A cover story of the final appearance of Burns and Allen as a comedy team during the filming of their last (first run) television show (T293). This marked Gracie's retirement from show business and was her final show business appearance.

B211 "Gracie Fiddles While George Burns." **TV Forecast**. September 13-19, 1952: 10-11.
The announcement that George and Gracie's television show will appear weekly beginning this season prompts one Chicago writer to remind viewers that Lucy and Desi aren't the only talented married couple on television.

B212 "Gracie Made Cupid Dizzy Too." **Shadowplay**. March 1935: 33+.
Another story of how George and Gracie met, became vaudeville partners, and of their eventual marriage and success in show business.

B213 "Gracie: Madness is her Method." **New York Sunday Mirror**. November 26, 1944: 23.
An exhibition of one of Gracie's surrealistic paintings to raise funds for China Relief prompted this article. It also contains an admission by

Gracie that, even after a number of years on radio, she still gets mike fright. "My hands are cold and clammy; my face is hot; and sometimes I fumble lines miserably."

B214 "Gracie Started Dancing." **San Francisco Chronicle**. February 20, 1939: 9.
This short article mentions that Gracie got her start in the theater as a child dancer in San Francisco.

B215 Green, Abel and Joe Laurie, Jr. **Show Biz from Vaude to Video**. Garden City: Permabooks, 1953.
An overview of the history of American show business (1900-1950) and its performers, by two men who knew most of them and had viewed their performances. Green was an editor of **Variety**. Laurie was a **Variety** columnist who had been a successful vaudeville performer as well as a writer for radio shows (Eddie Cantor and Al Jolson), motion pictures and plays. Burns and Allen are mentioned as part of this history.

B216 Green, Stanley. **Hollywood Musicals Year by Year**. Milwaukee: Hal Leonard Publishing Corporation, 1990.
A selected chronological listing from 1927-1989 of some of Hollywood's most popular movie musicals. The author includes limited production and cast credits, song titles, year of release, running time, a synopsis and commentary, as well as the film's availability on audio and/or video. The index is divided into categories (film title, composer/lyricist, cast, etc.). Several of the films in which George and Gracie appear are included.

B217 Green, Stanley and Burt Goldblatt. **Starring Fred Astaire**. New York: Dodd Mead and Co., 1973.
Text and over 800 photographs on each of Astaire's films, including **A Damsel in Distress** (F30), with Burns and Allen. Astaire noted that RKO borrowed the team from Paramount for this film.

B218 Greenberg, Peter S. "The Sunshine Boy." **American Way**. June, 1977: 28-32.
George admits to occasionally watching reruns of **The Burns and Allen Show** and states emphatically that Gracie "was not a comedienne; she was a great actress...She never did comedy before I met her."

B219 Greenfield, Thomas Allen. **Radio: A Reference Guide**. New York: Greenwood Press, 1989.
The chapter on "Radio Comedy and Variety" includes an excellent overview of other sources of information on the subject of radio and discusses George's first book, **I Love Her, That's Why!** (B34).

B220 Grote, David. **The End of Comedy: The Sit-Com and the Comedic Tradition**. Hamden: Shoe String Press, 1983.
The author discusses the popularity of the situation comedy television format and how it grew from radio series into a new form of comedy. "The most complex and sophisticated of all the comedy series in the 50's was **The Burns and Allen Show**." A list of the most successful television comedies is included.

B221 Gurman, Joseph and Myron Slager. **Radio Roundups: Intimate Glimpses of the Stars**. Boston: Lothrop Lee and Shepard Co., 1932.
This book consists of short entries with illustrations of the radio stars of the day. Gracie Allen's article says that "she began to wax side-splitting when she was forced to fill in for Burns on occasion when he was unexpectedly incapacitated." George has noted that, at times early in their career, he would go out on stage and would not be able to say his lines due to stage fright. Gracie would then pick up George's lines as well as her own.

B222 Gussow, Mel. "In Movies Again, George Burns is Still All Sunshine." **The New York Times Magazine**. May 29, 1975: 28: 1.
An interview with George while filming **The Sunshine Boys** (F37) in New York City.

B223 Hadfield, Edwin. "4,000 Whooping Whiskerinos Carry Torches for Gracie." **Omaha World Herald**. May 17, 1940: 1+.
An outline of the celebrations to be held in conjunction with Gracie Allen's Presidential convention in Omaha, Nebraska.

B224 ---. "Puns for Planks--That's Gracie's Campaign." **Omaha World Herald**. May 16, 1940: 1+.
A description of the Burns and Allen broadcast of their weekly radio show from the Ak-Sar-Ben coliseum in Omaha during the Surprise Party Convention. Gracie explains her party's platform.

B225 Hall, G. "Interview." **Movie Classic**. May 1934: 56.
An interview with Gracie about the Burnses' private life.

B226 Hall, Leonard. "Nat and Googie." **Screenland**. Fall 1934: 16+.
The story of George and Gracie's summer vacation trip to Gibraltar, France, Italy, the Balkans and the Soviet Union. Shortly after their return, they adopted their daughter Sandy.

B227 Hamamoto, Darrell Y. **Nervous Laughter: Television Situation Comedy and Liberal Democratic Ideology**. New York: Praeger, 1989.
Television and liberal democracy are jointly analyzed. Noted is the debut of **The George Burns Show** (1958) as an indication that the "situation comedy was in need of renewal."

B228 Hamilton, Sara. "By the Grace of Georgie." **Photoplay**. April 1938: 27+.
The author explains that in real life George and Gracie's roles are reversed from their stage, film and radio roles. George is always funny and ready for a laugh while Gracie is restrained and more interested in her role as wife and mother than joking.

B229 Handman, Stanley. "Life's One Long Gag." **Weekend Magazine**. 7.21 (1957): 13-16.
The article, while routine in several areas, does include several paragraphs lifted from George and Gracie's television show and contains some insight into the writing process.

B230 "Hands Tell the (Funny) Story." **TV Guide**. November 6-12, 1954: 4-6.
George notes the importance of an actor's hands during his performance. George smokes a cigar so he has something to do with his hands onstage, while Gracie doesn't have a problem and "never does the same thing twice." There are photographs of George imitating other comedians.

B231 Harding, H. "The Death of Gracie Allen." **TV Guide**. September 1964.
A short entry notes the passing of Gracie Allen.

B232 Harkness, John. **The Academy Awards Handbook**. New York: Windsor Publishing, 1994.
A year-by-year listing of nominees and winners in the film, directing and leading and supporting acting categories since the awards' inception, the text includes winners in other areas that receive less attention from the general public. A valuable reference for anyone looking for succinct information and interesting commentary.

B233 Harmon, Jim. **The Great Radio Comedians**. Garden City: Doubleday, 1970.
Sections of radio performers' comedy routines from their shows. Included are script lines from a recording of Burns and Allen and W. C. Fields.

B234 Harrison, Paul. "Gracie Allen." **Screen and Radio Weekly**. September 11, 1937.
Harrison writes that Gracie Allen in private life lets her husband do the talking to the press for the team.

B235 ---. "Gracie Allen Isn't Only Dumb-bell in the Family." **New York World-Telegram**. February 1, 1939.
Despite the title, which refers to George's admission of buying smuggled jewelry, this is a sympathetic article that veers away from George's legal troubles after the third paragraph.

B236 Hartley, Katherine. "In Each Other's Hair." **Radio Mirror**. August 1935: 16-17+.
Another story on Burns and Allen's life and career in vaudeville and radio.

B237 "Have You Heard This One?" **TV Guide**. August 24-30, 1957: 22-23.
Seven television comedians, including George, share their favorite story with readers. George's favorite, ostensibly, was a brief bit between him and Gracie in which she tells him she used to be a lion tamer.

B238 Hay, Peter. **Canned Laughter: The Best Stories From Radio and Television**. New York: Oxford University Press, 1992.
A collection of anecdotes from the history and personalities who made up radio and television. Burns and Allen are included and one story notes that, after doing a radio routine on old light bulbs, their apartment was filled with bulbs mailed to them by radio fans.

B239 Hayes, Barbara. "How Gracie Took It." **Movie Mirror**. January 1939: 33+.
Coverage of the first Burns and Allen radio show after George's indictment for smuggling jewelry.

B240 Heldenfels, R. D. **Television's Greatest Year: 1954**. New York: Continuum Publishing Co., 1994.
The author, a television critic for an Ohio newspaper, contends that 1954 was the greatest year in the history of the medium, arguing that it was television at its most ambitious. The work makes a number of references to Burns and Allen.

B241 Hellman, Jack. "British Radio Discovered B & A." **Variety**. May 8, 1940: 24+.
A detailed look at Burns and Allen's careers in vaudeville which led to their first appearance on radio with the British Broadcasting Corporation while they were entertaining in England in 1929.

B242 Helm, Harvey. **It's Murder, But it Could Be Worse (A Mystery by Gracie Allen)**. 1935.
Helm, one of Burns and Allen's scriptwriters, wrote a short mystery which was given to their sponsor, Campbell Soup Company.

B243 Henderson, Amy. **On the Air: Pioneers of American Broadcasting**. Washington, DC: Smithsonian Institution Press, 1988.
This book, based on an exhibition at the National Portrait Gallery from October 7, 1988-January 2, 1989, has a chapter on the pioneers of radio. There are biographical sketches of radio performers with photographs and illustrations, including Burns and Allen.

B244 Henkel, David K. **Collectible Magazines: Identification and Price Guide**. New York: Avon, 1993.
An illustrated guide to the market value of various popular periodicals, including an extensive section on **TV Guide**.

B245 Henning, Paul. Interview. Dallas: Oral History Collection, De Golyer Library, Southern Methodist University, July 19, 1975.
A writer for ten years with Burns and Allen in radio and television, Henning reveals how George Burns worked and his important contribution to the success of their television show. Henning is best known as the creator, writer and producer of one of television's most successful programs, **The Beverly Hillbillies** (CBS, 1962-1971). He was also the producer of **Petticoat Junction** (CBS, 1963-1970) which starred **Burns and Allen** alum Bea Benaderet and executive producer of **Green Acres** (CBS, 1965-1971).

B246 Henning, Ruth. Interview. Dallas: Oral History Collection, De Golyer Library, Southern Methodist University, July 23, 1975.
The wife of Paul Henning as well as a script writer, Mrs. Henning talks about the personal side of Burns and Allen during the 1940's radio years when she sometimes traveled with the Burnses to a show away from the studio. She describes the Burnses as a "very close couple" and "very nice people."

B247 Hickerson, Jay. **The Ultimate History of Network Radio Programming and Guide to All Circulating Shows**. Hamden: Jay Hickerson, 1992.
A log of radio show titles and the dates of their broadcasts with notes on which shows which are in circulation. This is a valuable resource for identifying program titles and dates of broadcast. Sponsors and names of performers are indicated in the entries.

B248 Hickman, Dwayne and Joan Roberts. **Forever Dobie: The Many Lives of Dwayne Hickman**. New York: Carol Publishing Group, 1994.
The former child actor and television network executive recalls his career to the present, including his relationship with George Burns, one of the producers of **The Bob Cummings Show** (alternating between NBC and CBS, 1955-1959), which featured Mr. Hickman as a young adult, and the owner of the rights to Mr. Hickman's starring vehicle, **The Many Loves of Dobie Gillis** (CBS, 1959-1963).

B249 Hilliard, Robert L. and Michael C. Keith. **The Broadcast Century: A Biography of American Broadcasting**. Stoneham: Butterworth-Heinemann, 1992.
A history of radio and television (from its inception to 1991) which relates broadcasting history to "events, issues and people" of the times. An historical date chart is at the top of each page noting world events which assists the reader in relating how broadcasting fit into historical time frames. Photographs, tables and charts relating to broadcasting are included on almost every page of the book.

B250 Hilton, Pat. "How to Have a Blast in the 90's." **USA Weekend**. November 3-5, 1989: 4-5.
Ninety-three year old George Burns talks about aging, work and marriage.

B251 Hodges, Ann. "Birthday Boy Turns 90." **Houston Chronicle**. January 3, 1986, sec. 4: 1+.
Coverage of a birthday party given by CBS for George which will be broadcast as the **Kraft Salutes George Burns' 90th Birthday--A Very Special Special** (T581).

B252 Holden, Anthony. **Behind the Oscar: The Secret History of the Academy Awards**. New York: Simon and Schuster, 1993.
This book is, in the author's words, "...neither authorized nor endorsed by the Academy of Motion Picture Arts and Sciences" as it goes behind the scenes to ferret out the "real" story from the "reel" one. Rather than a strict year-by-year listing of the nominees and winners (although that information has been placed in an appendix), the volume's bulk is separated into decades or portions thereof (for example, chapter seven is titled "1948-1959: Television to the Rescue"). Appendix B is devoted to honorary Oscars; Appendix C to Oscar facts and figures. There are also source notes, a bibliography and an index.

B253 ---. "Holiday in Hawaii." **TV Guide**. September 26-October 2, 1953: 10.
A look at the Burnses' vacation and their television show.

B254 Hope, Bob and Melville Shavelson. **Don't Shoot, It's Only Me!** New York: G. P. Putnam's Sons, 1990.
The comedian writes about touring worldwide entertaining American military personnel. The last chapter is about Hope's 1989 show at Madison Square Garden with George Burns.

B255 Hopper, Hedda. "Burns and Allen." Syndicated. February 18, 1953.
Entertainment journalist Hopper interviewed George and Gracie at home where they answered questions about their work in show business. George noted that Gracie, being Irish, was very stubborn at times and didn't always listen to his advice--and that times, she was right. He also reveals that Gracie didn't really like show business and for the last twenty years she had talked about quitting.

B256 Houston, Robert W. "Costume Ball Ends Festival." **Omaha World Herald**. May 19, 1940: 1+.
Article and photographs on the closing of Omaha's second Golden Spike Days celebration, with a costume ball held in conjunction at Ak-Sar-Ben coliseum for Gracie Allen, the Surprise Party's nominee for the Presidency. The article notes that neither Burns and Allen nor their company was given monetary compensation for their appearances.

B257 "How Gracie Allen Gets That Way." **TV Guide**. October 8-14, 1955: 13-15.
A look at how George Burns and his four writers work at creating forty scripts a year for **The George Burns and Gracie Allen Show**.

B258 "How to Get Along with Your Family." **This Week**. May 12, 1940: 14.

This article, written by George and his scriptwriters, has Gracie giving her opinions on family life.

B259 Howe, Irving. **World of Our Fathers: The Journey of the East European Jews to America and the Life They Found and Made.** New York: Harcourt Brace Jovanovich, 1976.
A history of the East European Jews who immigrated to the United States and settled on the East Side of New York City. The author speculates as to why so many of America's greatest entertainers come from this background, including George Burns.

B260 Hoyt, Caroline Sowers. "George Burns and Gracie Allen." **Modern Screen.** September 1933: 40+.
An article on the new radio and film stars Burns and Allen.

B261 Hubbard, Kim and Dirk Mathison. "George Burns Writes a Final Loving Tribute to Gracie Allen." **People Weekly.** October 31, 1988: 58-60.
Preceding the publication of George's remembrances of life with Gracie in **Gracie: A Love Story** (B22) by a week, this article recounts the meeting of Burns and Allen, the highlights of their years as a team, how George picked up the pieces after Gracie's death and began a new career at an age when most people have retired and of his monthly visits to her crypt. Photographs are by Harry Benson.

B262 Hurst, Walter E. **Cumulative Copyright Catalog.** 1989.
This volume contains entries on television shows registered with the Copyright Office in Washington, D.C. The copyright date does not always match the date the television show was actually broadcast.

B263 Hyams, Joe. "George Burns Tells Why Gracie Will Retire." **New York Herald Tribune.** February 20, 1958.
In his "Joe Hyams In Hollywood" column, the author recounts the press conference held at McCadden Studios at which George disclosed the reasons for Gracie's retirement from show business and that he has no personal plans to retire. George also announced that his new television series will include members of **The Burns and Allen Show** cast but there are no plans to replace Gracie. Gracie had also appeared at the press conference later and seemed excited about her plans for life after show business.

B264 Inge, M. Thomas, ed. **Handbook of American Popular Culture.** 2nd ed. Vol. 1. Westport: Greenwood Press, 1989. 3 vols.
The chapter on "Stage Entertainment" by Don. B. Wilmeth has information on vaudeville's history as a part of American culture. Another chapter, "Television," by Robert S. Alley looks at commercial television as having gone through four distinct types of comedy ("the earliest was the personality, like Milton Berle and George Burns").

B265 Inman, David. **The TV Encyclopedia.** New York: Putnam, 1991.
Alphabetized entries of over 7,500 television performers and behind-the-scenes personnel and their credits.

B266 Issel, William and Robert W. Cherny. **San Francisco 1865-1932: Politics, Power, and Urban Development.** Berkeley: University of California Press, 1986.
A scholarly but readable history of San Francisco which provides information on its urban development, helpful in understanding the city's population and work force. The reader is given some insight into how Gracie Allen's family fit into the description of the average Irish family in San Francisco in the late nineteenth and early twentieth centuries.

B267 Jacobs, Mary. "This is Gracie." **Screen & Radio Weekly.** October 1939.
An interview with Mary Kelly, who talks about her good friend, Gracie Allen, beginning in 1920's New York City when they shared a $30 a week apartment with Rena Arnold. Mary reveals that Gracie is very particular about her food and loves surprises and shopping. This is one of the few articles written about Gracie Allen from a friend's viewpoint.

B268 Jacobs, Seaman. "The Passion Still Burns." **Remember.** October/November 1994: 72-77.
George, at the age of 98, is interviewed by writer Jacobs, who has worked with him and other comedians, about his life and work as he nears his one hundredth birthday. George mentions his late wife often and says that he

still visits Gracie's grave once a month. He also mentions twice during the interview that he is a very humble man. There are many photos of Burns and Allen taken throughout their careers.

B269 Javna, John. **The Best of TV Sitcoms**. New York: Harmony Books, 1988.
A history and critique of situation comedies with many photographs. Arrangement is by decade (1950's-1980's) with a "best" and "worst" show list. **The George Burns and Gracie Allen Show** is among the detailed articles on best shows of the 1950's.

B270 ---. **Cult TV: A Viewer's Guide to the Shows America Can't Live Without!!** New York: St. Martin's Press, 1985.
A guide to television shows which have a "cult" following by fans. Filled with trivia, historical facts, information on the actors and many photographs and illustrations. **The George Burns and Gracie Allen Show** is listed in the first section, "Cult Classics."

B271 Jaynes, Gregory. "In California: A Place for Curtain Calls." **Time**. February 7, 1983: 8.
A story on George's charitable contribution to the Motion Picture and Television Country House and Hospital.

B272 Jenkins, Dan. "George Burns Contends Comedy is No Longer Stylish." **TV Guide**. June 6-12, 1959.
George believes that **The George Burns Show** was not renewed because the television viewing audience is not interested in comedy shows at the present time. This is proof perfect of the cyclical nature of the popularity of various genres and the fickleness of the viewing public, a phenomenon apparently not exclusive to modern-day programming.

B273 ---. "How George Burns Feels About Riding Alone." **TV Guide**. October 25-31, 1958: 17-19.
George Burns reveals his thoughts about working alone without Gracie Allen. He talks about his new **George Burns Show** which debuted on October 21, 1958, in which he plays the role of a producer. **SEE T295.**

B274 ---. "She's Tired of Being Gracie Allen." **TV Guide**. June 14-20, 1958: 29-30.
An interview with Gracie after the announcement of her intention to retire. She seems surprised at the reaction the announcement generated but admits that she is tired of playing the part of "Gracie Allen" and has wanted to quit show business for the last three years.

B275 Jenkins, Henry. **What Made Pistachio Nuts? Early Sound Comedy and the Vaudeville Aesthetic**. New York: Columbia University Press, 1992.
Jenkins, an MIT assistant professor, looks at the early "less critical" motion picture comedy films and their performers (most from vaudeville) including Burns and Allen. Jenkins names these films, which were produced in the late 1920's and early 1930's as "anarchistic comedy." He looks at Burns and Allen's roles in **International House** (F20), **Six of a Kind** (F22), **Many Happy Returns** (F24), **Love in Bloom** (F25), **Here Comes Cookie** (F26) and two of **The Big Broadcast** films (F27, F28). Photographs which appear to be taken from film frames are included.

B276 Johnson, Catherine E. and Joyce A. Post. **TV Guide: Twenty-Five Year Index, April 3, 1953-December 31, 1977**. Radnor: Triangle, 1979.
This index (by author and subject) to America's quintessential television programming magazine is updated by periodical supplements.

B277 Johnson, Stephen Burge. **Roof Gardens of Broadway Theatres 1883-1942**. Ann Arbor: University Microfilms International, 1985.
An overview of New York City theaters during the heyday of American vaudeville.

B278 Jones, Gerard. **Honey, I'm Home!: Sitcoms Selling the American Dream**. New York: Grove Weidenfeld, 1992.
This volume discusses the importance of the situation comedy as part of American popular culture and how shows are reflective of the history of their times.

B279 Kaye, Jay. "George Burns While Gracie Fiddles." **Pageant**. June 4, 1950: 104.
The author feels that the Burns and Allen act "can stay unchanged and still have an audience."

B280 Keogh, James. "Gracie Arrives, Sees, Conquers 20,000 Omahans." **Omaha World Herald**. May 15, 1940: 1+.
Front page coverage of the opening parade of Gracie Allen's arrival in Omaha, Nebraska, for her Surprise Party convention. There were over 20,000 people who met her at Union Station. Other sections include photographs of Gracie and her entourage arriving via the special Union Pacific train.

B281 ---. "Hilarious 'Unconvention' Nominates Gracie." **Omaha World Herald**. May 18, 1940: 1+.
Coverage of the events of Gracie's political convention in Omaha, Nebraska where she was nominated as the Surprise Party candidate for President in front of 8,000 supporters. Gracie's acceptance speech is also printed.

B282 Kerwin, Bob. "George Burns Says He Talks to Gracie at the Grave." **San Francisco Examiner-Chronicle**. January 15, 1984, Datebook: 33.
George speaks of going to visit Gracie's grave once a month and telling her about his activities, saying it makes him feel she's still alive and with him. He also says, "...really, the only girl in my life was Gracie Allen...Gracie was my best critic...She was a real lady; not too many of them around anymore."

B283 Key, Pierre. **Pierre Key's Radio Annual**. New York: Pierre Key Publishing Corporation, 1933.
The first edition of a radio annual which surveys the history of the year in radio, with lists of the network programs, their casts and time of broadcast.

B284 "Kicking at 93." **Maclean's**. January 16, 1989: 33.
A discussion of George's newest project, a comedy video which follows him through a typical day. **SEE VG7.**

B285 Knapp, James G. "Radio's Golden Age." **The National Journal**. January 1983: 26-28+.
The author discusses a number of stars from radio's heyday, including Burns and Allen.

B286 Koszarski, Richard. **The Astoria Studio and Its Fabulous Films: A Picture History with 227 Stills and Photographs**. New York: Dover Publications, 1983.
Documents with text and photographs the film history of the New York Astoria Studio including several Burns and Allen short films which were filmed at that studio.

B287 Krebs, Albin. "Gracie Allen--Just the Name Evoked a Smile." **New York Herald Tribune**. August 29, 1964: 8.
A tribute to Gracie Allen written only days after her death includes a lengthy overview of her career.

B288 Lackmann, Ron. **Remember Television**. New York: G. P. Putnam's Sons, 1971.
Over 300 photographs and brief descriptions of television shows from 1947 to 1958. The section on Burns and Allen contains several factual errors.

B289 Lahue, Kalton C. **World of Laughter: The Motion Picture Comedy Short 1910-1930**. Norman: University of Oklahoma Press, 1966.
The history of the comedy short from 1910 to its decline in the late 1920's when the sound era began and longer feature films were more popular with the public.

B290 Lamparski, Richard. **Whatever Became of?** New York: Bantam Books, 1976.
This is the first volume of a series which profiles entertainment celebrities no longer in the public eye. This book includes a biographical article on George and Gracie's son, Ronnie Burns. Now out of show business and a businessman, Ronnie is described as a divorced father of three sons who lives in Marina Del Rey, California. Ronnie remains close to his father and pays his late mother a compliment when he tells the

author that "the side of my mother the public never saw was the most wonderful one." Photographs are included.

B291 Landry, Robert J. "Air Acts Ace Ballyhoo." **Variety**. May 8, 1940: 24+.
There are several articles on Burns and Allen's careers and on the planned Golden Spike Days events in Omaha, Nebraska where Gracie will hold her Surprise Party Convention. Several pages of advertisements by Burns and Allen's writers and talent agency supporting her candidacy are included.

B292 Langman, Larry. **Encyclopedia of American Film Comedy**. New York: Garland, 1987.
This is a dictionary of 150 comedy films, comedians, directors and screenwriters from silent films to 1987.

B293 Larsen, David. "76 Years Later, Burns Works Sidewalks Again." **Los Angeles Times**. November 26, 1979: 3.
An account of the previous day's ceremony at which George placed his prints in cement outside Mann's Chinese Theatre in Hollywood.

B294 "Laughter By the Yard." **Radio Mirror**. November 1940: 40-41+.
An article about the Burns and Allen radio show and how the weekly scripts are developed. The article reports that the Burnses' salary is $10,000 a week and their writers' $1,200.

B295 Laurie, Joe, Jr. **Vaudeville: From the Honky-Tonks to the Palace**. New York: Henry Holt and Company, 1953.
An entertaining history of vaudeville, 1881 to 1947, told by the author who knew many of the performers and their acts.

B296 Lazarsfeld, Paul Felix. **People Look at Radio**. Chapel Hill: University of North Carolina, 1946.
A director of the Bureau of Applied Social Research, Columbia University, the author reports on the first public opinion survey of radio conducted by the National Opinion Research Center, University of Denver.

B297 Lazarsfeld, Paul Felix and Patricia L. Kendall. **Radio Listening in America: The People Look At Radio Again**. New York: Prentice Hall, 1949.
The second report on a survey conducted by the National Opinion Research Center of the University of Chicago which looks at radio listeners in America.

B298 Leerhsen, Charles. "Grace After Gracie." **Newsweek**. December 26, 1988: 68-69.
This is an article on George's love affair with show business at the time his book **Gracie: A Love Story** (B22) is number one on the best seller list.

B299 Lewis, Leonard. "Radio Needs A Good Five-Cent Cigar." **Printer's Ink Monthly**. November 1935: 21+.
Personal impressions of radio including comments on the Burns and Allen radio show.

B300 Lewis, Richard Warren. "An Apple Blossom with the Wham of a Bulldozer." **TV Guide**. May 1-7, 1965: 16-20.
This cover story of Connie Stevens was written during the production of **Wendy and Me** and offers some insight into George as a producer. It also compares this latest effort to his and Gracie's television series.

B301 "Like Mother, Like Daughter." **Photoplay**. ca. 1937.
This article includes photographs of Gracie and her daughter, Sandra (Sandy), and their new home in Beverly Hills, California.

B302 Lombardo, Guy and Jack Altshud. **Auld Acquaintance**. Garden City: Doubleday & Company, Inc., 1975.
The orchestra leader's autobiography includes the story of how Burns and Allen were asked to join his radio show, **The Robert Burns Panatela Program**. The Burnses also toured vaudeville theaters with the Lombardo Orchestra in the early 1930's.

B303 MacDonald, J. Fred. **Don't Touch That Dial! Radio Programming in American Life, 1920-1960**. Chicago: Nelson-Hall, 1979.

A history of radio broadcasting in the United States with a look at popular culture during the same time period.

B304 Maltin, Leonard. **Movie and Video Guide 1994**. New York: Signet, 1993.
The granddaddy of all portable film guides, the latest issue contains over 19,000 entries as well as mail-order video sources, a widescreen glossary, index and laserdisc availability.

B305 ---. **Movie Comedy Teams**. New York: Crown, 1976.
Burns and Allen are one of the teams included in this look at comedy teams who worked in films. Their film careers are covered in chronological order. Included is a list of their short subject films and feature films with information including studio, release date, cast members and director. Photos include one from their short film, **Burns and Allen in Lamb Chops** (F1).

B306 Marc, David. **Comic Visions: Television Comedy and American Culture**. London: Unwin Hyman, Inc., 1989.
A look at American popular culture and television comedy. In explaining television comedy Marc describes the early shows as "vaudeville bits for home consumption." The Burns and Allen television show is analyzed with comments from Ralph Levy, the first producer-director of the show. The show is described as having a "dislocated absurdist tone."

B307 ---. "Say 'Explication de texte,' Gracie." **The Village Voice**. June 25, 1985: 39.
An occasionally esoteric review of **The George Burns and Gracie Allen Show** as it appears in syndication, worthy of the expoundings made by the last incarnation of *Harry Morton*. There are "factoids" on actors John Brown, Harry Von Zell and Larry Keating and producer-director Fred de Cordova.

B308 Marc, David and Robert J. Thompson. **Prime Time, Prime Movers: From I Love Lucy to L.A. Law--America's Greatest TV Shows and the People Who Created Them**. New York: Little, Brown, 1992.
A look at writers and producers of successful television shows. The first part of the book discusses the vaudeville style performances of many television actors. The authors also study how the social mores of the time affect the success of a television show.

B309 Mariani, John. "George Burns, the Actor, Tells How He's Survived." **The Village Voice**. November 17, 1975: 140-141.
This writer contends that George Burns and Jack Benny were the only vaudevillians whose acts are still funny, possibly because Burns and Allen's humor, like Benny's, was verbal and their acts well constructed.

B310 Marill, Alvin H. **Movies Made for Television: The Telefeature and the Mini-Series, 1964-1986**. New York: Zoetrope, 1987.

B311 Marschall, Rick. **The Golden Age of Television**. New York: Gallery Books, 1987.
Over 240 photographs are included in this tribute to television in the United States and the United Kingdom. In the description of **The George Burns and Gracie Allen Show** there is an error in naming Bob Sweeney as one of the actors who played the character *Harry Morton*. The author names the show as one of the "classics" of the golden age of television due to its "inspired writing."

B312 ---. **History of Television**. New York: Gallery Books, 1986.
This history lesson on the world's most powerful medium contains a full-page black and white picture of George and Gracie and recounts how George modified his reactions to Gracie when they moved their show from radio to television by letting the viewer in on the fun.

B313 Marsters, Ann. "Movie Stars at Home." **Chicago American**. June 16, 1939.
An interview with Gracie in which the reporter notes that the comedienne is "not so dumb." She describes the Burnses' home as 13 rooms, decorated in shades of rose and green, and the number of employees who help run the house (cook, upstairs and downstairs maids, gardener, nursemaid, night watchman, pool man).

B314 Martin, Linda and Kerry Segrave. **Women in Comedy**. Secaucus: Citadel Press, 1986.
This volume profiles female comedy stars from the past (vaudeville) and present in all areas of entertainment. The authors note that few of these women began their careers as comediennes, including Gracie Allen, who began as a dancer and dramatic actress.

B315 Marx, Arthur. "The Ultimate Cigar Aficionado." **Cigar Aficionado**. Winter 1994: 60-80.
Ninety-eight year old George Burns talks about his cigar smoking, his life and future career plans. This interview took place after George's brain surgery in the fall of 1994. The text includes several photographs of George and Gracie.

B316 Matthau, Walter. Interview. **Reflections on the Silver Screen**. By Richard Brown. American Movie Classics. Amalgamated Talking Pictures, New York. June 17, 1992.
Professor Brown's interview with Matthau in which the actor reveals that he had been asked by George Burns in the early 1950's to replace Fred Clark as the character *Harry Morton* on **The George Burns and Gracie Allen Show**. Matthau says he did not accept the offer because he wanted to stay in the theater.

B317 "May Pole Dance Feature of Day." **San Francisco Call Bulletin**. April 30, 1909: 9.
This is an overview of the May Day celebrations to be held at the Children's Playground at Golden Gate Park with over fifty young dancers, directed by two of Gracie's sisters, Pearl and Hazel Allen. Pictures of three of the dancers for the May Pole Dance were printed, including Grace Allen.

B318 McCaffrey, Donald W. **Golden Age of Sound Comedy: Comic Films and Comedians of the Thirties**. Cranbury: A. S. Barnes, 1973.
The volume compares major comedians and comedy films of the 1930's, focusing on new talents and the development of comic traditions. Burns and Allen are mentioned only briefly in the section on W. C. Fields, which seems surprising but which may be attributed to the fact they were not considered major film stars. There are many photos and illustrations.

B319 McCall, Michael. **The Best of 50's TV**. New York: Mallard Press, 1992.
Television in the 1950's is dissected according to category in this tribute to a memorable decade of programming. The "Situation Comedies" section contains two pages committed to George and Gracie's television show, giving a brief history of the show, limited cast credits and two photos.

B320 McCollister, J. "George Burns: An American Treasure." **Saturday Evening Post**. May/June 1987: 58-59.
A look at George as an entertainer.

B321 McDermott, William F. "Times Have Changed for Burns and Allen Since Last Appearance." **Cleveland Plain Dealer**. November 24, 1935, Women's Magazine and Amusement Sec.: 1+.
An article about Burns and Allen's prior appearance in Cleveland on a vaudeville bill four years ago. They are now radio and movie stars and are being paid $8,000 for their eight day appearance. The writer says that it was a stage appearance with Eddie Cantor which led to Gracie's first guest spot on a radio show. He feels that Burns and Allen are better on the stage than they can possibly be on radio because the full effect of their comedy depends on their visual image, being fundamentally stage people.

B322 McHarry, Charles. "Good-By to Gracie Allen?" **New York Daily News**. May 5, 1958: 28; May 6, 1958: 80; May 7, 1958: 40.
Three articles written at the time Gracie announced her retirement from show business recount Burns and Allen's background in vaudeville, radio and television. Gracie notes that she is "not exhausted, sick, or mad at anybody but has simply had enough of show business." In reality, she was suffering from poor health and had wanted to retire from show business for many years because of the harsh pace of acting in a weekly television series.

B323 McLean, Albert F., Jr. **American Vaudeville as Ritual**. Lexington: University of Kentucky Press, 1965.
This book gives an historical overview of American vaudeville as part of the popular culture of the United States. There are tables of the seating capacity of New York City theaters in the early twentieth century and the price range of tickets. Source notes on the history of vaudeville theaters are included.

B324 McNeil, Alex. **Total Television**. New York: Penguin Books, 1980.
Information on 4,700 television series, arranged in the following sections: an alphabetical listing of series by titles, a chronological listing of special programs and broadcasts, primetime schedules of CBS, NBC, ABC and Fox, as well as Emmy and Peabody award winners and top-rated series from each season.

B325 Mellencamp, Patricia. "Situation Comedy, Feminism and Freud: Discourses of Gracie and Lucy." **Studies in Entertainment: Critical Approaches to Mass Culture**. Theories of Contemporary Culture 7. Bloomington: Indiana University Press, 1986.
This article, part of a series of writings about mass media, culture and women, begins with the premise that in early 1950's comedy television shows, women such as Gracie Allen and Lucille Ball portrayed female characters who were seen as "helpless" and childlike. The author discusses Sigmund Freud's published views of jokes, comics, humor and male-female roles, seen as "perhaps ...another policy of potential containment for U.S. women."

B326 Menken, Harriet. "Laughs from the Ladies." **The Delineator**. August 1936: 64-65.
Biographical sketches of successful radio comediennes of the thirties, Mary Livingstone, Gracie Allen, Agnes Moorehead, Portland Hoffa, Beatrice Lillie and Fanny Brice. The article describes their different personalities and includes childhood and contemporary photos.

B327 ---. Radio Personalities." **San Francisco Chronicle**. September 22, 1935.
An interview with radio star Gracie Allen, who reveals what makes a successful comedienne and how to be a successful wife and mother.

B328 Miller, Harlan. "The Land of Make-Believe Reaches the Age of Maturity." **The New York Times**. July 11, 1937.
This article on the wealth of the stars who live in Hollywood notes that "Burns and Allen have one of the quietest and most sedate homes of all."

B329 Miller, Holly. "George Burns: Red Hot and Spicy." **Saturday Evening Post**. September 25, 1979: 88+.
Interview about George's new movie with Brooke Shields, **Just You and Me, Kid** (F42). The writer meets with George in New York City where he is appearing on **The Dick Cavett Show** (T522). George says that he never kept a joke file, writes most of his material and "delivers it off the cuff."

B330 "Miss America Helps Fete George Burns on Birthday." **Jet**. February 6, 1984: 10.
Remarks on George's appearance with Miss America on his 89th birthday.

B331 Mitz, Rick. **The Great TV Sitcom Book**. New York: Perigee Books, 1983.
Situation comedies from 1949-1983 are listed by year. Some shows are emphasized as "front runners" and have in-depth articles, such as **The George Burns and Gracie Allen Show**. The book includes photographs, cast of characters, list of Emmy winners, ratings, top rated sitcoms for each year and the longest running sitcoms.

B332 Moore, Jacqueline. "The Burns and Allen You've Never Heard About." **Movie Mirror**. June 1934: 27+.
A short article on the "real" Burns and Allen.

B333 Mordden, Ethan. **Movie Star: A Look at the Women Who Made Hollywood**. New York: St. Martin's Press, 1983.
A categorical history of women in film, Gracie's character is examined in a section that also includes Marie Dressler, Carole Lombard, Marion Davies, Lucille Ball and Eve Arden. The author notes that Gracie Allen

"became an American institution...but missed out on the revered phase of fame" due to her death in 1964.

B334 Morgenstern, Joseph. "George Burns Refuses to Say Good Night." **Los Angeles Herald Examiner**. January 25, 1981: F1+.
An interview by a freelance writer which took place at the Hillcrest Country Club in Los Angeles. George reveals that he constructs his stage act from real-life situations and then elaborates on the event to develop a routine.

B335 ---. "Sunshine Boy at 85." **The New York Times Magazine**. January 25, 1981: 27-29.
This article is probably based on the above interview. George talks about the former members of the Round Table at the Hillcrest Country Club, comedians Jack Benny, Danny Kaye, Groucho Marx and others. The author concludes that "Burns is a prodigy and he knows it and he knows that we know it."

B336 Morino, Marianne. **The Hollywood Walk of Fame**. Berkeley: Ten Speed Press, 1987.
Block by block locations of the terrazzo squares with their bronze stars that line the streets of Hollywood, paying tribute to the famous and occasionally obscure personalities from motion pictures, television, recordings, radio and live theatre. The book includes a map and addresses (including those of George and Gracie's stars) as well as brief biographical information.

B337 Morris, Jane Kesner. "Gracie Allen's Own Story: Inside Me." **Woman's Home Companion**. March 1953: 40+.
The most complete interview in print given by Gracie Allen, in which she talks about her childhood and family in San Francisco, touring with her sisters in vaudeville and her introduction to George through a mutual friend and her marriage and career. She gives all of her success as a credit to him. There are several photographs.

B338 Morris, Ruth. "Uncommon Chatter." **Variety**. November 3, 1931: 47.
The reviewer notes that "Shy Grace Allen, with a nice new dress that doesn't fit as expertly as its demure predecessors, remains the most facile and subtle of all vaudeville dumb ladies." Burns and Allen were currently playing in the nine week record-breaking performance with Eddie Cantor and George Jessel at the Palace Theatre in New York City.

B339 Morrison, Patt. "Star Stuck: George Burns' Popularity--Marked Again--in Hollywood Walk of Fame." **Los Angeles Times**. November 9, 1984, pt. 1: 3+.
George receives his third star in the 6600 block of the Hollywood Boulevard portion of the Walk of Fame.

B340 Moss, Violet. "Things You'd Never Guess About Gracie." **Radio Life**. November 9, 1941: 11.
Moss tells readers what kind of woman Gracie is like when she isn't standing in front of a microphone.

B341 Muir, Florabel. "Behind Hollywood's Silken Curtain." **New York Daily News**. February 14, 1955: 22.
An overview of the January 23, 1955 testimonial dinner given for George and Gracie by the Friars Club at the Biltmore Bowl in Hollywood. The $100 a plate dinner, which raised $103,000 for charity after expenses, was attended by many of the industry's luminaries. Photos of the honorees and several guests accompany the article.

B342 Murphy, Mary. "Have You Heard the One About George Burns?" **Los Angeles Times**. April 3, 1975, part 4: 1+.
Written during the filming of **The Sunshine Boys** (F37), the article is refreshingly free of that "let's just rewrite the Burns' bio" mentality that eventually began to permeate so many stories about George. The article benefits, of course, from being written at the beginning of the most celebrated part of George's career, and some of its appeal today lies in the knowledge of things to come and the impact the film's release would have on George's future.

B343 Murray, Ken. Interview. Dallas: Oral History Collection, De Golyer Library, Southern Methodist University, August 10, 1981.

The American actor who started in vaudeville talks about the vaudeville circuits and what is was like to work in that era of show business.

B344 Museum of Television and Radio. **Jack Benny: The Radio and Television Work**. New York: Harper Perennial, 1991.
A book published in conjunction with an exhibition at the Museum of Television and Radio in New York City. There are many photos of Benny's career with titles and descriptions of his network shows. Included is the "Gracie Bit" from March 9, 1952 in which Jack dressed up as Gracie and took her place in a Burns and Allen routine.

B345 Nalven, Nancy. **The Famous Mister Ed**. New York: Warner Books, 1991.
A history of the popular television series includes an interview with George Burns, who produced the show's pilot and appears in episode number 46. **SEE T413.**

B346 Nash, Jay Robert and Stanley Ralph Ross, eds. **The Motion Picture Guide**. Chicago: Cinebooks, Inc., 1985.
A multi-volume set which analyzes motion pictures through the decades. There are annual updates to this publication.

B347 "Nat & Googie." **Time**. January 30, 1933: 40.
Commentary on Burns and Allen's radio season which places them in fifth place in the ratings. The reviewer doesn't like the show and considers it the "most annoying broadcast on the air...climax of sub-moronic radio drivel" but admits that the gags sell the sponsor's product, cigars. He guesses that the Burnses' radio salaries are $2,000 a week and their vaudeville profits an additional $5,000 a week. Repeated is a story that Gracie Allen is getting frustrated in becoming personally associated with the radio "Gracie" she portrays so convincingly.

B348 "National Affairs--Crime." **Time**. December 19, 1938: 12.
A short piece on Albert Nathaniel Chaperau's indictment with George Burns for smuggling $4,885 worth of diamond bracelets and a ring into the United States.

B349 **National Vaudeville Artists**. New York: NVA, May 11, 1924.
This book was published for the National Vaudeville Artists' (NVA) eighth annual benefit held at the Friars Club in New York City. Included in the volume are ads from vaudeville agencies. In the full-page ad for Rialto Vaudeville Representatives, Inc. (Thos. J. Fitzpatrick, manager) are pictured four of the agency's performers--Geo. N. Burns and Grace Allen, Jack Benny and Harry Holman.

B350 Neale, Steve and Frank Krutnik. **Popular Film and Television Comedy**. London: Routledge, 1990.
This volume analyzes British and American comedy in films, radio and television and places **The George Burns and Gracie Allen Show** as "an example of upper middle class sitcom."

B351 Neibaur, James L. **Movie Comedians**. Jefferson: McFarland, 1986.
A history of movie comedians from the silent era to the present with a short entry on Burns and Allen's work in motion pictures.

B352 **The New York Times**. February 25, 1944, sec. 2: 7.
A letter from a Chicago listener who "had always enjoyed George Burns and Gracie Allen" but "was tired of their announcer making continuous references to soap throughout the show" (i.e. Bill Goodwin for Swan Soap).

B353 **The New York Times Film Reviews, 1913-1968**. 6 Vols. New York: New York Times and Arno Press, 1970; **Supplement 1969-1970**, 1971; **Supplement 1981-1982**, 1984.
A multi-volume set of reprints of film reviews from the pages of **The New York Times**.

B354 Nightingale, Suzan. "Q&A." **Los Angeles Herald Examiner**. November 8, 1981: A-1+.
In this article timed to coincide with his upcoming television special, **George Burns' Early, Early, Early Christmas Special** (T544), George talks about how ideas for specials come about, his reading habits, Ann-Margret, his own show business hero, how he started in the industry, his daily routine and his advice to young people.

B355 Norback, Craig T. and Peter G. Norback, et al. **TV Guide Almanac**. New York: Ballantine, 1980.
The history of the weekly guide to American television with photographs of all the magazine's covers.

B356 Nugent, Frank S. "Calling All Clowns." **The New York Times**. February 14, 1937: A1.
Takes a look at what has become of comedy and comedians with a negative view of "Burns and Allen...whose lunatic pattern can be prolonged until it becomes more deadly than the Chinese Water Torture."

B357 Nussman, Albert. "Funny Man: An Interview with George Burns." **Take One**. March 1977: 26-28.
A short piece on George's career in show business.

B358 Nye, Russel Blaine. **The Unembarrassed Muse: The Popular Arts in America**. New York: Dial Press, 1970.
A study of music, drama and literature in American mass culture with information on comedy in films, radio and television.

B359 "Off To Query Gracie Allen on Smuggling." **New York Daily News**. January 20, 1939.
Assistant United States Attorney Joseph L. Delaney left New York by train for Hollywood in order to question Gracie Allen in the smuggling case against Jack Benny. Gracie's name had not been closely associated with the scandal previously, although George was involved and had pleaded guilty to smuggling charges.

B360 "Oh, George!" **Hollywood Reporter**. July 27, 1993: S-10+.
George looks back on ninety years in show business in the days prior to being inducted into the Comedy Hall of Fame, part of the festivities surrounding the 11th annual Just for Laughs Montreal Comedy Festival. This was a special comedy issue of the well-known trade paper.

B361 Okon, May. "Grandma Gracie, Grandpa George." Personalities in the News, **New York Sunday News**. October 2, 1955: 4.
George and Gracie discuss their children, Ronnie (who has just joined the cast of their television series) and Sandra (who has recently made the couple first-time grandparents). Gracie, who prefers to talk about her children over show business, says "'for years now I've been going to quit show business any minute, but George keeps signing those contracts.'" The article also mentions how they spend their time away from the television series and their friendship with Jack Benny and his wife, Mary Livingstone. Gracie plugs the show (to George's wry amusement) and he plugs his book, **I Love Her, That's Why!** (B34).

B362 "Old Burns & Allen Stage Gets Reprieve." **Hollywood Reporter**. December 21, 1990: 45.
Announcement that an agreement has been made by preservation groups and studios not to change or destroy the "George Burns Stage" at the old Hollywood Center Studios without joint approval. The sound stage is one of four structures affected by the agreement.

B363 O'Leary, Susan. "The George Burns and Gracie Allen Show: Life in a Domestic Comedy." **Emmy Magazine**. January/February 1984: 44-50+.
Writer Sid Dorfman and producer-director Fred de Cordova delineate the reasons for the success of **The Burns and Allen Show** in this cover story article. Mr. Dorfman explains the importance of having well-developed characters and recalls how deeply George was involved with the show. Mr. de Cordova gives much credit to Gracie the actress and discusses the careful craftsmanship of the show. The article also contains script excerpts.

B364 O'Neil, Thomas. **The Emmys**. New York: Penguin Books, 1992.
Details of forty-three years of Emmy Awards are documented in the first book in more than twenty years to do so. Included are a history of the awards, a year by year survey of what went on behind the scenes as well as in front of the cameras and nominees (and winners) by category.

B365 "Orpheum Actress is San Francisco Girl." **San Francisco Chronicle**. May 15, 1924: 15.
A short article noting that Gracie Allen of Burns and Allen would be appearing next week at the San Francisco Orpheum Theater. Unfortunately,

Gracie became ill with appendicitis and had to cancel the team's appearance.

B366 Page, Brett. **Writing for Vaudeville**. Springfield: Home Correspondence School, 1915.
The author describes the process of writing for vaudeville performers. The text also includes stage diagrams of some theaters and explains the different uses of the stage by performers such as "in one," the very front of the stage, which was used by Burns and Allen.

B367 Pan, Hermes. Interview. Dallas: Oral History Collection, De Golyer Library, Southern Methodist University. January 12, 1983.
The movie choreographer talks about Burns and Allen's dancing in the movie **A Damsel in Distress** (F30). Pan won an Academy Award for his dance direction in the "fun house" segment from the film which featured George, Gracie and Fred Astaire.

B368 Parish, James Robert and William T. Leonard. **The Funsters**. New Rochelle: Arlington House, 1979.
This book on famous comedians includes a chapter describing George Burns and Gracie Allen's careers in show business and lists several of their films. The authors believe that "film was not the perfect medium for Burns and Allen as Gracie was not a very energetic performer...radio (in which Burns and Allen worked for 18 years) was not a demanding medium."

B369 Parsons, Louella O. "Burns and Allen." Syndicated. January 23, 1955.
Columnist Parsons, a friend of the Burnses, interviewed them in their home prior to their being honored at the Friars Club Testimonial dinner in Hollywood. Gracie says that she liked doing their television show when it was on every two weeks but her husband disagreed, saying that "she needed the momentum." But his wife states that she didn't agree with him. Gracie ends the interview by inviting Louella upstairs to see her new dress for the dinner while George frets about the interruption in the interview. Gives insight to the fact that George Burns always was thinking about his work while Gracie wasn't that interested in talking about herself and her career to reporters.

B370 ---. "Gracie Allen--Darling Dimwit." Syndicated. ca. Spring 1958.
Three-part series of articles written after Gracie's announcement that she was quitting show business. Parsons, a personal friend of Gracie's, had made the initial announcement in her column but says Gracie had indicated to her a year earlier that retirement was on her mind.

B371 **People Weekly Extra: Television's 50th Anniversary**. Summer 1989: 90.
This special edition salute to fifty years of television includes a bow to George and Gracie in "The Glory Years: 1950's" section.

B372 Pine, Arthur and Julie Houston. **Just Don't Let it Hit You**. New York: Delacorte, 1994.
George's literary agent authored this self-improvement book on overcoming adversity and offers up some tips from some of his well-known clients, including George.

B373 Pitts, Michael R. **Radio Soundtracks: A Reference Guide**. 2nd ed. Metuchen: Scarecrow Press, 1986.
Lists radio shows and entertainers' performances available on records.

B374 --- and Louis H. Harrison. **Hollywood on Record: the Film Stars' Discography**. Metuchen: Scarecrow, 1978.

B375 "Playing it Straight: George Burns Has 'A Nice Family Arrangement.'" **TV Guide**. December 25-31, 1953: 5-7.
An interview with George about being a straight man and how he and Gracie work together as a team onstage. George, as the straight man, delivers lines which Gracie reacts to--and thus gets the laughs. George says that "the first impression of a joke is the best." (In 1953 **TV Guide** began its weekly coverage on Fridays rather than Saturdays).

B376 "Portrait." **Parents' Magazine**. December 1937: 42.

A baby picture of Gracie Allen appears in this series of photos of famous people entitled "who is she today?"

B377 Prouty, Howard H., ed. **Variety Television Reviews**. New York: Garland Publishing, Inc., 1989.
A fifteen volume set which reprints nearly 37,000 television reviews written for the weekly entertainment industry trade newspaper, the New York-based **Variety** from 1923-1988 (experimental television began in the 1920's) and for its sister publication, Hollywood-based **Daily Variety** from 1946-1960. The set includes an index.

B378 Rader, Dotson. "The Jewish Comedian." **Esquire**. December 1975: 106+.
Interview with George while on location for **The Sunshine Boys** (F37) in New York City. The article notes a little of George's true personality. George tells the reporter that the cat's eye ring he wears was given to him by Gracie after they were married.

B379 "Radio." **The New York Times**. January 15, 1933: 10X.
A weekly section of the paper titled "News and Gossip of the Studios" writes about the success of Gracie Allen's search for her "lost" brother and her breaking in on other radio programs. The writer notes that the idea is not a new one but was used in vaudeville when actors "strolled through the various acts after his own performance." He feels that listeners like the idea of Gracie's informality in interrupting other shows.

B380 **Radio Annual**. New York: Radio Daily. 1938-1949.
A yearbook publication of the year's events and performers in radio. Included is information on radio stations and radio polls of favorite performers and shows with advertisements and photos.

B381 **Radio Annual and Television Year Book**. New York: Radio Daily-Television Daily. 1950-1956.
A revised title of **Radio Annual**, which now includes information on television stations, programs and performers.

B382 **Radio Life**. September 15, 1940: 3-5.
In this review of the new season's Burns and Allen radio show, Gracie talks about her high-pitched voice. "I've always had what might be called a ripply voice. On the air I merely accentuate it a little, because comedy calls for elaboration."

B383 **Radio Mirror**. May 1939.
An article stating that the Burnses' film careers are dependent on how moviegoers react to **The Gracie Allen Murder Case** (F33). If successful, Paramount will make a series of Burns and Allen films and, if not, Gracie Allen's contract will not be renewed. George Burns' contract had already ended.

B384 **Radio Mirror**. July 1940.
Gracie's campaign song "Vote for Gracie" is printed. Words and music are by Charles Henderson.

B385 **Radio Times**. June 14, 1929; September 26, 1930.
This weekly listing of radio shows broadcast by the British Broadcasting Corporation (BBC) cites Burns and Allen's June 17, 1929 (R798) and September 30, 1930 (R802) appearances on the program dates.

B386 **Radioland**. November 1, 1933.
Coverage of the new Burns and Allen film, **Many Happy Returns** (F24).

B387 "A Ray of Sunshine." **Newsweek**. March 1, 1976: 57.
A review about George's role in **The Sunshine Boys** (F37).

B388 Raymond, Jack. **Show Music on Record: From the 1890's to the 1980's**. New York: F. Ungar, 1982.

B389 Reagan, Ron. "The Unretiring George Burns." **Ladies Home Journal**. December 1984: 68+.
George talks about his career in show business, daily routine of exercises and work and of his life with Gracie with the son of an old Hollywood friend.

B390 Rochlin, Margy. "Golden Oldie: How George Burns, Almost 93, Was Reborn in a Town Obsessed by Youth." **Los Angeles Times Magazine**. January 8, 1989: 9+.
This article relates George's current show business career as a single act and film actor and why he has remained popular despite his age and number of years in show business. Photographs are by Rosemary Kaul.

B391 Rockwell, Donald Shumway, ed. **Radio Personalities: A Pictorial and Biographical Annual**. New York: Press Bureau Inc., 1935.
This is the first edition of a biographical and pictorial annual with personality sketches of radio performers.

B392 Rogers, Gail. "They Fell in Love at Fifth Sight." **Movie Mirror**. August 1935: 48-49+.
A movie magazine story of how George and Gracie first met and their eventual marriage after teaming as partners in vaudeville for three years. George and Gracie tell of their first opinions of one another when they first met, which were a little negative.

B393 Roman, Shari. "George Burns, Humor's Elder Statesman." **Video Magazine**. July 1989: 14.
Another biographical article on George Burns.

B394 Rothstein, Mervyn. "George Burns is Still Letting (Letting?) Gracie Allen Steal the Show." **The New York Times**. November 2, 1988: B1.
An article about George's soon to be printed book about Gracie Allen, **Gracie: A Love Story** (B22). George notes that the idea for the book came from freelance writer David Fisher.

B395 Rouse, Sarah and Katharine Loughney, comps. **3 Decades of Television: A Catalog of Television Programs Acquired by the Library of Congress 1949-1979**. Washington: Library of Congress, 1989.
An annotated record of television programs housed in the Motion Picture, Broadcasting, and Recorded Sound Division in the Library of Congress, Washington, D.C. The citations are under **The George Burns and Gracie Allen Show**.

B396 Rubin, Benny. **Come Backstage with Me**. Bowling Green: Bowling Green University Popular Press, [1973?].
An autobiography by actor/entertainer Benny Rubin which reflects on his life and friends in all areas of show business, including Burns and Allen, whom he first met when they worked in vaudeville. At one time, Rubin was good friends with Benny Ryan, who was once engaged to Gracie Allen. Forewords are by Steve Allen, Jack Benny, George Burns, Frank Capra and Arthur Treacher. Printed is an edited interview by John E. DiMeglio illustrating what it was like to work in vaudeville.

B397 Rust, Brian A. L. **The Complete Entertainment Discography from 1897 to 1942**. 2nd ed. New York: Da Capo, 1989.

B398 Sackett, Susan. **Prime-Time Hits: Television's Most Popular Network Programs (1950 To The Present)**. New York: Billboard Books, 1993.
One of the co-authors of **Say Goodnight, Gracie!** (B84) surveys the most popular television programs for every decade since the 1950's. Unfortunately, since **The George Burns and Gracie Allen Show** never made it to the Top Ten list in any of the years it was on television, it is relegated, albeit lovingly, to the "But What About...?" section of the book's appendixes.

B399 Safire, William. "The Man With the Pictures." **The New York Times Magazine**. June 18, 1989: 14.
This article on death and the terms applied to it mentions George's description of death as "the man with the pictures," which is a term from vaudeville. When you were canceled in vaudeville, the manager would give you back your pictures which had been posted in the front of the theater to advertise the theater bill.

B400 Samuels, Charles and Louise. **Once Upon a Stage: The Merry World of Vaudeville**. New York: Dodd Mead and Co., 1974.
Former vaudevillians tell of their lives as performers on the stage and provide a personal insight on what it was like to work in vaudeville. The authors note that Gracie Allen was a member of the vaudeville act "The

Three Allen Sisters," in which she appeared with her sisters Bessie and Hazel.

B401 Sandomir, Richard. "Ghost Stories." **Los Angeles Times**. May 11, 1990, sec. E: 1-2+.
The career of ghostwriter David Fisher, **Gracie: A Love Story** (B22) and **All My Best Friends** (B35) is examined in this account of the man behind two of George's most well-received books and how thirteen words won him his first assignment with George: "'For forty years, my act consisted of one joke. And then she died.'"

B402 Schneider, John F. "San Francisco's Network Radio Broadcast Centers of the Thirties." **Antique Wireless Association Review** 5 (1990). Rpt. in **Radiogram**. March 1992: 3-24.
Informative article that tells of the importance of San Francisco as a major network production center for NBC and CBS from 1927 to 1937. The history of the development of the NBC Red, Blue And Orange networks is explained as is the building of studios in San Francisco and Los Angeles. Provides a history of the Don Lee Columbia Broadcasting System, owner of KHJ (the CBS affiliate in Los Angeles), where much of the programming from the West Coast originated, including the Burns and Allen radio shows.

B403 Schraub, Susan. "George Burns: From Vaudeville to Nashville." **Harper's Bazaar**. December 1980: 81+.
An interview with George after his debut as a country singer on NBC's special from the Grand Old Opry in Nashville, Tennessee, **George Burns in Nashville???** (T535). George remarks that "work is no strain and when people come to see you perform it gives you vitality."

B404 Schuster, Mel. **Motion Picture Performers: A Bibliography of Magazine and Periodical Articles. Supplement I, 1970-1974**. Metuchen: Scarecrow, 1976.
Quite valuable as a starting point for locating celebrity articles.

B405 Schwartz, Lloyd. **Goodnight, Gracie**. Chicago: University of Chicago Press, 1992.
A collection of original poetry and prose which centers around the theme of man's mortality. The title of the book is also the title of one of the poems, which is dedicated "for Gracie Allen, 1906-1964." The prose consists of lines from Burns and Allen's routines and a quote from George's book, **Gracie: A Love Story** (B22).

B406 Seldes, Gilbert Vivian [Foster Johns]. "Comical Gentlewoman." **Saturday Review**. May 2, 1953: 37.
Television and radio reviewer Seldes praises the Burns and Allen show as "above its competition... pretty special." This was achieved, he thinks, due to their talents and also because they were able to carry over their successful radio show to television because their comedy was verbal.

B407 ---. **The Great Audience**. New York: Viking Press, 1951.
Focuses on the business side of motion pictures, radio and television and how each influences audiences' tastes. Tells the story of how CBS was able to convince many NBC comedians like Burns and Allen to switch networks in the late 1940's when television was just beginning to develop its programming.

B408 Senelick, Laurence, Barbara Sicherman, Carol Hurd, et al, eds. **Notable American Women: The Modern Period**. Cambridge: Belknap Press, 1980. Updated volume to the 3 volume **Notable American Women, 1607-1950: A Biographical Dictionary**.
These volumes provide the life stories of American women of achievement. The entry on Gracie Allen is documented with source notes and is the first publication to print her actual birth date of July 26, 1895.

B409 Sennwald, Andre D. "Miss Allen and Mr. Burns at Home." **The New York Times**. May 6, 1934.
This interview took place at the Burnses' apartment in the Essex House in New York City. The writer says that Gracie is not at all the "lunatic young woman" she plays on the radio and George doesn't want many to know that because he believes that the radio "Gracie" wins the sympathy of audiences with her dumb answers. George states that he writes all of the dialogue for the team, both in radio and in their films.

B410 Settel, Irving. **A Pictorial History of Radio**. New York: Citadel Press, 1960.
The history of 1930's and 1940's radio performers and programs accompanied with captioned photographs. There are excerpts from Burns and Allen radio scripts from the 1940's.

B411 Shalit, Gene, ed. **Laughing Matters: A Celebration of American Humor**. New York: Ballantine Books, 1987.
A collection of selected works of American humorists with a section titled "Say Good Night, Gracie." Burns and Allen's routine as they performed it at their first appearance at New York City's Palace Theatre in 1926 is reprinted with a few lines from some of their other performances throughout their years in show business. The book cover is a reproduced drawing by Al Hirschfeld, representing various American humorists, including Burns and Allen.

B412 Shanley, J. P. "People on Television: Burns and Allen. **The New York Times**. July 17, 1955.
George gives an interview in the New York City borough of Manhattan while he and Gracie are in the city on business. He discusses the new television season, which will have the show "located" in New York City, and how the program has recently been including vaudeville-type routines at the end of each episode.

B413 Shaw, Ellen Torgerson. "Jack Was a Quiet Riot." **TV Guide**. January 31-February 6, 1981: 24-27.
George joins Johnny Carson and Bob Hope in recalling the life of Jack Benny as a prelude to the upcoming television special, **A Love Letter to Jack Benny** (T539). In this cover article, George remembers what made Jack laugh, his concern for details (including when he imitated Gracie) and how much George still misses him.

B414 "Should Comedy Shows Use Phony Laughter?" **TV Guide**. October 23-29, 1954: 7.
A poll of several situation comedy stars about the wisdom of inserting "canned" laughter into their show's sound track resulted in varying responses. George notes that television viewers hear actual preview audiences' reactions and goes on to say, "We don't insert laughs we don't earn."

B415 "Show Business Marriages." **TV Digest**. April 12-19, 1952.
Described by the writer as having "one of the happiest" marriages in show business, this Philadelphia television magazine includes a claim by George that having different interests has made him and Gracie closer.

B416 Shulman, Arthur and Roger Youman. **How Sweet It Was!** New York: Bonanza, 1966.
A pictorial look at television with photographs from the shows, including **The George Burns and Gracie Allen Show**.

B417 Siegel, Scott and Barbara. **The Encyclopedia of Hollywood**. New York: Avon Books, 1990.
Over seven hundred entries covers Hollywood from A-Z: its history, stars, films, filmmakers, studios, anecdotes and terminology. The text includes photos.

B418 Silden, Isobel. **Family Weekly**. July 29, 1979: 4-5.
An interview with George talking about his personal life and his current work in motion pictures.

B419 ---. "George Burns at 89: Sage Advice on Outliving Your Doctor." **Star**. October 14, 1984: 3.
This tabloid article details George's "prescription for happiness" which, not coincidentally, is the title of his fifth book (B19) and the reason for this interview.

B420 Simon, Al. Personal interview. Beverly Hills, California. July 27, 1991.
Thoughts and memories from the associate producer of the Burns and Allen television show.

B421 Simon, George T. **The Big Bands**. New York: Schirmer Books, 1967.

As former drummer for the Glenn Miller orchestra and the longtime editor-in-chief of **Metronome**, the author has compiled an easy to use reference work on the history and personalities of the big band era.

B422 Slater, Jack. "Burns Roasted with Love." **Los Angeles Times**. October 18, 1976, sec. 10: 1+.
An account of the Friars Club 30th Anniversary Dinner, billed as George's "first roast" as guest of honor on his 80th birthday. Milton Berle predicted the event would be more aptly compared to a "rib feast," and one of the most memorable lines is a quote by Steve Allen, "Here we are again, Burns and Allen."

B423 Slater, Robert. **This...Is CBS: A Chronicle of 60 Years**. Englewood Cliffs: Prentice Hall, 1988.
An historical narrative of the history of the Columbia Broadcasting System (CBS) where Burns and Allen began their radio careers in 1932 and which later aired their 1950-1958 television series.

B424 Slide, Anthony. **The Encyclopedia of Vaudeville**. Westport: Greenwood Press, 1994.
A guide to vaudeville, this reference book expands on the author's earlier work, **The Vaudevillians**. It contains biographical information on performers with critical information on their acts and sometimes includes a sample of their dialogue/routines. Included in the entries is information on various theaters, vaudeville houses and genres. The Burns and Allen entry has only minor changes from his earlier book. A photograph of Burns and Allen is on the book cover. The work includes a bibliography.

B425 ---. **Great Radio Personalities in Historic Photographs**. New York: Dover, 1982.
A summary of thirty years of radio programs with photographs and short biographies of its stars. The Burns and Allen entry consists of their photo on the book cover and description on the frontispiece.

B426 ---. **Selected Vaudeville Criticism**. Metuchen: Scarecrow, 1988.
A collection of twentieth century review media on vaudeville performers consists of "Part I, Individuals" and "Part II," general comments or reprints of performer's articles. The entry on Burns and Allen consists of a 1926 review from **Variety**.

B427 ---. **The Vaudevillians: A Dictionary of Vaudeville Performers**. Westport: Arlington House, 1981.
Here in one source is found the most complete biographical listing of American vaudevillians to date. Included are some lesser known performers as well as headliners such as Burns and Allen. Preceding the listings is a short chapter on the history of vaudeville. A photograph of each performer is included as well as photographs of New York City's Palace and Hippodrome Theatres.

B428 Smart, James R. **Radio Broadcasts in the Library of Congress 1924-41: A Catalog of Recordings**. Washington, DC, Library of Congress, 1981.
This book lists only five Burns and Allen recordings from this period of time as being in the Library of Congress collection.

B429 "Smile When You Read This, Pardner (George Burns, An Old Cowhand Himself, Spoofs the Westerns." **TV Guide**. September 28-October 4, 1957: 17-19.
The domination of television programming by Westerns is given the comic treatment by George even as he announces that the first **Burns and Allen Show** episode of the new season will be cowboy-themed.

B430 Smith, Bill. **The Vaudevillians**. New York: Macmillan, 1976.
A former critic for **Billboard** interviewed thirty-one former vaudevillians, including George Burns, about their lives and careers in vaudeville.

B431 Smith, Ronald Lande. **Comedy on Record: The Complete Critical Discography**. New York: Garland, 1988.

B432 ---. **The Stars of Stand-Up Comedy: A Biographical Encyclopedia**. New York: Garland Publishing, 1986.

A biographical sketch of George Burns' show business career, including his current success as a stand-up comic. Reprints excerpts of Burns and Allen routines and George's current act.

B433 ---. **Who's Who in Comedy: Comedians, Comics and Clowns from Vaudeville to Today's Stand-Ups**. New York: Facts on File, 1992.
This alphabetical listing of performers in comedy includes an entry for Burns and Allen as well as a separate listing for George Burns. There are short biographical articles and a list of films, biographical sources and audio sources.

B434 Smith, Sally Bedell. **In All His Glory: The Life of William S. Paley**. New York: Simon and Schuster, 1990.
A biography of CBS president William Paley, which includes a history of the development of the network. There are extensive source notes and interview notes. Included is a photograph of Burns and Allen with Jack and Mary Benny and Paley.

B435 Snyder, Robert W. **Voice of the City: Vaudeville and Popular Culture in New York**. New York: Oxford University Press, 1989.
An historical survey of the beginnings of the vaudeville show as a part of the popular culture in New York City from 1880 to 1930. Includes information on the acts of Eddie Cantor, Weber and Fields and Burns and Allen (parts of "Lamb Chops" are quoted) among others. There are descriptions of vaudeville theaters from the Palace in New York City to Brooklyn and the Bronx. Ends with a bibliographic essay and notes.

B436 Soames, Wood. "Burns & Allen." **Oakland Tribune**. October 6, 1934.
In this interview, George explains the planning of the Burns and Allen's sketches, saying that gearing them toward an intimate audience makes it difficult for other performers to copy their style.

B437 Sobel, Bernard. **A Pictorial History of Vaudeville**. New York: Citadel Press, 1961.
An informative history of vaudeville with photographs.

B438 Sochen, June, ed. **Women's Comic Visions**. Detroit: Wayne State University Press, 1991.
Original essays by female writers on women's humor, a subject which until recently was deemed nonexistent by scholars, who seem to write only of men as humorists. This book, part of the series **Humor in Life and Letters**, includes writings on the subjects of comic performers, women cartoonists and "domestic" humorists. Gracie Allen, who is deemed an example of how comic women were portrayed in the past as dumb and silly, and George Burns are mentioned in several of the essays. Lacks an index.

B439 Spitzer, Marian. **The Palace**. New York: Athenum, 1969.
An informative and readable history of the famous vaudeville theater in New York City, from its opening in 1913 to its renovation and reopening in 1966. Spitzer was a press representative who had worked at the theater and was closely associated with the performers and viewed many of their performances.

B440 Spotnitz, Frank. "Comics Pick Comedies." **American Film**. December 1988: 48-50.
Several comedians are asked to name their favorite comedy films. George Burns names two of his own films as his favorite, **The Sunshine Boys** (F37) and **Oh, God!** (F38).

B441 Springer, John and Jack Hamilton. **They Had Faces Then: Super Stars, Stars and Starlets of the 1930's**. Secaucus: Citadel Press, 1974.
This large volume has photographs and brief biographical sketches of many of the actresses of the 1930's, including Gracie Allen.

B442 Staples, Shirley. **Male-Female Comedy Teams in American Vaudeville 1865-1932**. Theater and Dramatic Studies 16. Ann Arbor: UMI Research Press, 1984.
Based on the author's thesis, this book looks at famous male-female vaudeville teams, beginning from their historical background in Europe to the decline of the popularity of vaudeville in the 1930's. There are descriptions of some acts and explanations of why they were popular. The book is well documented and includes many of the teams' routines. The

last chapter is titled "George Burns and Gracie Allen" and includes their "Dizzy" routine.

B443 Stein, Aaron. "Burns and Allen Celebrate Fourth Air Anniversary." **New York Evening Post**. February 6, 1936.
The lead article notes that at the end of their fourth year in radio, the team still seems to be on top with their "mad and merry world" of "absurdities based on logic."

B444 ---. "Series Closes with a Tear." **New York Evening Post**. June 14, 1934.
A review of the last Burns and Allen radio show with Guy Lombardo in which Gracie was serious in her remarks about leaving the show. She ended the show singing "Auld Lang Syne." **SEE R121.**

B445 Stein, Charles W., ed. **American Vaudeville as Seen by its Contemporaries**. New York: Knopf, 1984.
Fifty-eight entries divided by historical periods note the social impact of vaudeville with memories of its stars, like George Burns.

B446 Steinberg, Cobbett. **TV Facts**. New York: Facts On File Publications, 1985.
This volume includes prime time television schedules from 1950 to date, ratings and awards.

B447 Steinem, Gloria. "Here's Gloria and...George Burns." **MS**. February 1983: 28-32.
An interview with George for the **Today Show**'s "Close Encounters" series (NBC). Steinem notes that George is a "male stand-up comic who doesn't use putdowns as humor" and doesn't tell jokes but simply tells of his experiences.

B448 Stern, Lee Edward. **The Movie Musical**. New York: Pyramid Publica tions, 1974.
A brief illustrative history of the movies from the 1920's to 1970's.

B449 "Still Going Strong." **New Choices**. May 1992: 52+.
Comments from seven celebrities, all at least 75 years of age, including George Burns, on how they keep their strength to continue a full life and career.

B450 Stoddard, Maynard Good. "Amazing Gracie." **Saturday Evening Post**. March 1989: 58-59.
An article on George's new book, **Gracie, A Love Story** (B22).

B451 "Straight Man." **Time**. December 13, 1943: 58+.
An article on George Burns, the "most famous straight man in U.S. radio," who was celebrating his 40th anniversary in show business. Notes that vaudeville was still Burns and Allen's mainstay, despite their elaborate radio plots and guest stars on their show.

B452 Stuart, Ray. **Immortals of the Screen**. Sherbourne, 1965.
A portrait of Gracie Allen as one of the motion picture actresses who made an impact on the entertainment world.

B453 Sudler, Culbreth. "I Went to a George and Gracie Broadcast." **Radio Life**. March 14, 1943: 34-35.
A look at a live Burns and Allen radio show. The reviewer notes that George was a "smoothie" and that Gracie was one of the ablest and most finished actresses in the country. She noted that to see the couple in performance was something the at-home radio audiences missed.

B454 Sullivan, Ed. "Take the Stand, Burns and Allen." **New York Daily News**. January 4, 1938.
Newspaper columnist Sullivan (prior to his own hugely successful television career) interviews Burns and Allen about their backgrounds and how they met and started working as a comedy team.

B455 Surmelian, Leon. "The Private Life of Burns and Allen." **Motion Picture**. April 1938: 33+.
The writer interviews the Burnses at their Beverly Hill home and tries to get to the serious side of the couple. He reveals that their lives are centered around their two children. Burns and Allen tell of their start

in show business as very young children, their meeting and marriage and success in show business.

B456 Swanson, Pauline. "The Comic Tragedy of Gracie Allen's Real Brother." **Radio Mirror**. September 1935: 22-23+.
A history of how the radio search for Gracie's "lost brother" affected her real brother, George Allen, who lived in San Francisco, California. He was so harassed by reporters and friends that he left work for a month's vacation to escape.

B457 Swartz, Jon D. and Robert C. Reinehr. **Handbook of Old-Time Radio: A Comprehensive Guide to Golden Age Radio Listening and Collecting**. Metuchen: Scarecrow Press, 1993.
This 806 page guide to American radio shows (1926 to 1962) includes a short history of radio, category logs, program descriptions and other information helpful for researchers and collectors. The "Burns and Allen" entry was found to be lacking in detailed information, and the length of the description of their shows is equal in print to other shows which were on radio for only a few years. For example, Burns and Allen are listed as having appeared on radio from 1932 to 1950 and only one of their show's sponsors is listed. The authors note that music was by Ray Noble and Meredith Willson and leaves the impression that they had continuous appearances for the 18 years Burns and Allen were on the radio, which is incorrect. Although this entry was found lacking, the volume is still worthwhile in its attempt to name and provide general historical information on most of the American radio program series broadcast by the major networks.

B458 Taylor, Glenhall. **Before Television: The Radio Years**. New York: A. S. Barnes and Co., 1979.
A collection of anecdotes and reminiscences by the author, who began working in radio in the 1920's and later in television. He was the producer and/or director of hundreds of radio shows, including **Burns and Allen** (as producer). Describing his stint on the show as one of his "most pleasant assignments," he recalls George's off-stage behavior and his friendship with orchestra leader Paul Whiteman. Taylor was replaced in his position by Hank Booraem in the early 1940's.

B459 Terrace, Vincent. **The Complete Encyclopedia of Television Programs 1947 to 1979**. 2nd revised ed. 2 vols. Cranbury: A.S. Barnes, 1979.

B460 ---. **The Encyclopedia of Television: Series, Pilots and Specials, 1937-1973, Volume I**. New York: New York Zoetrope, 1986.
The first volume of a multi-volume set on television is an alphabetical listing of program names with a synopsis, partial cast and production credits, network, running time, broadcast dates and, in the case of series, number of episodes produced.

B461 ---. **The Encyclopedia of Television: Series, Pilots and Specials, 1974-1984, Volume II.** New York: New York Zoetrope, 1986.
An updated edition brings the total number of programs detailed to nearly 8,000.

B462 ---. **The Encyclopedia of Television: Series, Pilots and Specials, Vol. III**. New York: New York Zoetrope, 1986.
The index to Volumes I and II, this entry in the series lists alphabetically the television credits of performers, producers, directors and writers who worked in the medium between 1937 and 1984 and cross-references it to the volume in which they appear.

B463 ---. **Radio's Golden Years: The Encyclopedia of Radio Programs 1930-1960**. New York: A. S. Barnes and Co., 1981.
Titles of over 1,500 programs, including **The George Burns and Gracie Allen Show**, with brief type, format, cast, announcers, orchestra, program length, network and broadcast information.

B464 ---. **The Ultimate TV Trivia Book**. Boston: Faber and Faber, 1991.
The George Burns and Gracie Allen Show is accorded the equivalent of an entire page in this book of little-known or overlooked trivia from a number of television series. Mr. Terrace states that Bob Sweeney was one of the actors to play the *Harry Morton* role, along with Larry Keating,

John Brown, and Fred Clark when actually, it was Hal March. Mr. Sweeney did appear on the show from time to time, but in other roles.

B465 Terrace, Vincent and James Robert Parish. **The Complete Actor's Television Credits 1948-1988**. 2 vols. Metuchen: Scarecrow, 1990.
A list of actors' appearances on television programs during the years noted.

B466 Thirer, Irene. "Extra!--Burns and Allen Chat Like Sane People." **New York Post**. October 14, 1937.
The interviewer is surprised that Burns and Allen answer her questions in a normal, serious manner (when conducting interviews they usually answer in lines taken from their act or in their radio personas). The Burnses are in New York for a three week vacation with their children. They have just finished filming **A Damsel in Distress** (F30).

B467 Thomas, Bob. "Benny and Burns--Comedic Masters." **Los Angeles Times**. December 25, 1974, sec. 4: 30.
In an exclusive interview long-time friends George Burns and Jack Benny talk about how they first met in New York in the 1920's. Benny believes that no one stole jokes from him and George because they didn't use one liners in their acts. They were basically story tellers. This interview was printed the day before Jack Benny's death.

B468 "Toast to Two Funny Old Pals." **Life**. May 26, 1972: 78-79.
Jack Benny and George Burns are honored as "Entertainers of the Year" at a New York Friars Club testimonial dinner.

B469 Took, Barry. **Comedy Greats: A Celebration of Comic Genius Past and Present**. Wellingborough: Thorsons Publishing Group, 1989.
A collection of portraits of people who are in the business of making people laugh. George Burns talks about Gracie and is seen as "one of the most refreshing people you could possibly meet on or off the stage...His talent is that of an excellent editor of script material."

B470 Toronto Film Society. **Film Buff Series**. Toronto: Toronto Film Society. January 8, 1984; November 23, 1986.
Members of the organization contribute film notes which include production credits, cast, a synopsis, review and commentary.

B471 Torre, Marie. "Gracie Allen To Turn Intelligent." **New York Herald Tribune**. February 11, 1958.
This column publicizes two upcoming episodes of **The George Burns and Gracie Allen Show** on television to be broadcast on February 24 (T274) and March 3, 1958 (T275), in which Gracie is hypnotized into becoming the smartest woman in the world and appears on a quiz show--and wins! Columnist Torre is (tongue-in-cheek) aghast at the thought.

B472 Treadwell, Bill. **Fifty Years of American Comedy**. New York: Exposition Press, 1951.
There is a biographical entry on George Burns and Gracie Allen included in this overview of American comedy.

B473 Trent, T. H. "The Truth About the Burns-Benny Smuggling Case." **Radio Guide**. April 22, 1939: 2-3. Rpt. **Old Time Radio Digest**. May/June 1990: 4-10; July/August 1990: 4-12.
An account of how George Burns, Jack Benny and Mrs. Elma N. Lauer, wife of New York Supreme Court Justice Edgar Lauer, were found guilty of smuggling jewelry with Albert N. Chaperau.

B474 Tuska, Jon. **The Detective in Hollywood**. Garden City: Doubleday & Company, Inc., 1978.
This work provides a history and criticism of the detective and mystery motion picture film as it has been produced in Hollywood. The story of the inception and production of the book and film, **The Gracie Allen Murder Case** (F33) by Willard Huntington Wright (S. S. Van Dine), is traced.

B475 "Two Of A Kind." **TV Mirror**. June 1954: 56-57.
Nine captioned photos of George and Gracie at home, at work and with their children, Sandra and Ronnie. One photo shows Gracie as an unintentional but remarkable Gloria Swanson look-alike.

B476 "Unforgettable Gracie Allen." **Reader's Digest**. April 1990: 97-102.

Condensation of **Gracie: A Love Story** (B22) by George Burns with an accompanying illustration by Ann Neisel.

B477 United States Copyright Office. **Catalog of Copyright Entries: Motion Pictures 1912-1939; 1940-1949; 1950-1959; 1960-1979; 1980-** . 19 vols. plus machine readable data file. Washington: Library of Congress Copyright Office, 1951- .
Each entry includes information necessary for a motion picture to be registered with the Copyright Office. Listed for each entry is the title of the motion picture, date of production, number of reels, source of story, credits and the name of the company owning the copyright.

B478 United States Department of Commerce. Bureau of the Census. **Census of Population.** 1880, 1890, 1900, 1910, 1920. Washington: Government Publication Office, 1972-1993.
The Federal Population Census for the United States is released 72 years after the data is collected. The Allen, Darragh and Birnbaum families can be traced, although there is some confusion with names and birthdates from census to census, most notably with the ages of Gracie Allen and her sisters after 1910.

B479 Unterbrink, Mary. **Funny Women: American Comediennes, 1860-1985.** Jefferson: McFarland and Company, Inc., 1987.
Gracie Allen is featured in the section titled "Funny Women of Radio." This is one of the few books which looks at women in comedy separate from their male counterparts and partners. A photograph, biography and description of each comedienne's career makes up each entry.

B480 Vallee, Rudy. Interview. Dallas: Oral History Collection, De Golyer Library, Southern Methodist University. October 4, 1975.
Vallee is interviewed about his show business career and his work in the early days of radio and the performers.

B481 Vallee, Rudy and Gil McKean. **My Time Is Your Time: The Story of Rudy Vallee.** New York: I. Obolensky, 1962.
In this autobiography Vallee tells of his entrance into show business. He admits that he cannot take the credit for selecting personalities like Burns and Allen for his radio show for Standard Brands (**Fleischmann Yeast Hour**). They were among the performers to go on to success in radio after their appearance on Vallee's show.

B482 Van Dine, S. S. [Willard Huntington Wright]. **The Gracie Allen Murder Case: A Philo Vance Story.** New York: Charles Scribner's Sons, 1938.
The American author of the Philo Vance mystery series, has written another book which this time involves Gracie Allen in a murder mystery. George Burns is a character in the book who is a perfume smeller and is Gracie's sweetheart. This book was made into a motion picture which starred Gracie Allen and was the first time a motion picture was named after an actress (F33).

B483 **Variety Film Reviews, 1907-1980.** 16 vols. New York: Garland, 1983-1985.
This multi-volume set consists of reprints of motion picture film reviews from **Variety** (which began publication in 1905), the official weekly newspaper of show business. Beginning in the summer of 1927, short films are not included in the film reviews, and thus none of Burns and Allen's short films are included in this publication.

B484 **Variety Obituaries 1905-1986.** New York: Garland Publishing, 1986.
An eleven-volume set (including index) of facsimile reproductions of more than 90,000 obituaries originally printed in **Variety** over a span of nine decades. Gracie Allen's obituary appeared in the trade paper on September 2, 1964. An error that occasionally appears in other sources concerns George's former male partner, Billy Lorraine, whom **Variety** refers to as a female, "Billie Lorraine."

B485 **Variety Radio Directory.** New York: Variety, 1937- .
Compiled by **Variety** writers, this annual directory gives facts on that year's radio business and performers, program ratings and awards.

B486 **VideoHound's Golden Movie Retriever.** Detroit: Visible Ink Press, 1991.

Reviews and ratings of 20,000 videos (primarily films) available for rental or purchase are listed, with future editions planned. The rating scale is based on a "four bone" system (although really bad movies are merely given a "Woof!"). Far more professional than this would at first glance indicate, the volume also contains five indexes: captioned, awards, foreign film, category and cast/director. Although the entries do include year of release and running times, they do not contain source material.

B487 Walker, Leo. **The Wonderful Era of the Great Dance Bands**. New York: Da Capo Press, Inc., 1990.
This unabridged republication of the author's 1964 work partially defines the hugely popular entertainment phenomenon by explaining the importance of other media in its growth and decline: records, radio, television and film. Contains many photos.

B488 Waller, Judith C. **Radio: The Fifth Estate**. 2nd ed. Boston: Houghton Mifflin, 1950.
A revision of the author's 1946 work in which she attempts to survey the historical field of radio and television and offers advice to those working in these fields. This book is based on the author's work with the National Broadcasting (NBC) Summer Radio Institutes to assist in the training of broadcasters. Looks at the different types of radio programs, such as comedy shows.

B489 Walters, Barbara. "Best Interviews." **Ladies Home Journal**. Special Edition. Summer 1994: 42.
In the "Legends" section of Ms. Walters' best interviews is an excerpt from her May 29, 1979 television interview with George Burns. **See T528.**

B490 "Wanted: Babies." **Radio Stars**. November 22, 1934: 90+.
A story about show business personalities, like Burns and Allen, who have adopted children.

B491 Weaver, John D. **Carnation: The First 75 Years (1899-1974)**. Los Angeles: Anderson, Ritchie & Simon, 1974.
The history of the Carnation Company and its founder, E. A. Stuart. Carnation sponsored/co-sponsored **The George Burns and Gracie Allen Show** television show for eight years.

B492 "A Week in the Life of Burns and Allen." **TV Guide**. March 13-19, 1953: 6-7.
This New York edition of the television magazine contains photographs and commentary illustrating what goes on in the lives of Burns and Allen in a week's preparation for their television show. (In 1953 **TV Guide** began its weekly coverage on Fridays rather than Saturdays).

B493 Weisblat, Tinky. "Will the Real George and Gracie and Ozzie and Harriet and Desi and Lucy Please Stand Up? The Functions of Popular Biography in 1950's Television." Ph.D. diss., University of Texas at Austin, 1991. Abstract in **Dissertation Abstracts International** 52/04 (1991): 1402.
The George Burns and Gracie Allen Show, The Adventures of Ozzie and Harriet and **I Love Lucy** were popular television shows of the 1950's whose stars also produced their programs. The author maintains that biographical narratives published in the popular press of the time, in conjunction with the television shows, carried over a fictitious picture of these couples as "happy housewives married to offbeat tycoons."

B494 Wertheim, Arthur Frank. **Radio Comedy**. New York: Oxford University Press, 1979.
This book follows the evolution of American radio comedy from the 1920's to the 1950's and its relation to the social history of the times. Some chapters are devoted to individual comedians, such as Amos 'n' Andy. Burns and Allen are discussed in a chapter titled "Scatterbrains," which has excerpts from some of their vaudeville routines ("Lamb Chops"), Gracie's appearance on the **Chase & Sanborn Hour** with Eddie Cantor in 1931 (R804) and other radio routines. There are detailed bibliographic notes and photographs.

B495 West, Robert. **So-o-o-o, You're Going On the Air! and the Radio Speech Primer**. New York: Rodin Publishing Co., 1934.
Advice is given to those wanting to audition for radio. One chapter, "Comics of the Ether," looks at the successful radio comedians and

analyzes the nature of comedy and how it is created for radio. There is a list of broadcasting stations in the United States and Canada.

B496 Wiener, Leigh. "Portraits: The Great Comedians." **Los Angeles Times Magazine**. August 1987: 104-113.
A collection of photojournalist Wiener's photographs of comedians which were taken in the 1950's and 1960's. The portrait of George was taken on the set of **Wendy and Me** in August 1964, the month and year in which Gracie Allen died.

B497 Wilde, Larry. **The Great Comedians Talk About Comedy**. New York: Citadel Press, 1968.
Sixteen of "the funniest people of our time" are interviewed. Each talks about what they believe makes people laugh and what they find personally funny. There are brief biographical sketches and samples of the comics' humor. George is profiled and a Burns and Allen routine is included.

B498 Wilk, Max. **Golden Age of Television: Notes from the Survivors**. New York: Delacorte Press, 1976.
Television writer Wilk tells the history of the early years of American television, incorporating stories of performers, writers and production people.

B499 ---. **The Wit and Wisdom of Hollywood**. New York: Warner, 1973.
This collection of Hollywood lore includes a story told to the author about an earthquake during the filming of **International House** (F20) and of his efforts to have the story corroborated by George.

B500 Wilkerson, Tichi and Marcia Borie. **The Hollywood Reporter**. New York: Coward-McCann, Inc., 1984.
Excerpts about the entertainment world and its performers, including Burns and Allen, from the venerable trade paper. There is a reprint of a special article, "What's Funny About A Cigar?", written by George for the paper in 1957. **SEE B33.**

B501 Wilkins, Barbara. "A Star is Born--George Burns Lights Up the Screen (And His Stogie) in 'Sunshine Boys.'" **People Weekly**. December 1, 1975: 34+.
The success of **The Sunshine Boys** (F37) is beginning to make George "new" again to the public, and at least one writer comes to a savvy conclusion even while she dutifully records George's observations and the requisite background information. She says, "When George Burns gives an interview, it's a one-man vaudeville turn by the greatest surviving practitioner of the art. The problem is that most of the story sounds created by his writers."

B502 Wilmut, Roger. **Kindly Leave the Stage! The Story of Variety 1919-1960**. London: Methuen, 1985.
The story of English variety entertainment, including vaudeville and radio. Noted is the radio success of Burns and Allen on the British Broadcasting Corporation (BBC) beginning in 1929 with their first broadcasts on radio.

B503 Wilson, Liza. "New Backdrop for George and Gracie." **The American Weekly**. January 11, 1953: 8.
George and Gracie's life as vaudeville performers is contrasted with their relatively new role as owners of a successful television show.

B504 Winship, Michael. **Television**. New York: Random House, 1988.
A history of television with many photographs. In his description of television comedy, the author states that **The George Burns and Gracie Allen Show** was "part situation comedy and part variety show." Included is a synopsis of Paul Henning's career as a writer (he was with Burns and Allen from 1942 to 1952) and creator of the television show, **The Beverly Hillbillies** (CBS, 1962-1971).

B505 Wixen, Joan. "I Still Tell Gracie Everything." **Detroit News Sunday Magazine**. December 7, 1975: 16+.
In an interview prior to the release of **The Sunshine Boys** (F37), George tells how he is constantly working out routines and thinking of new lines for his act. He lists what he thinks are his good points and what makes a good comedian. He describes Gracie as a "quiet, honest, meticulous,

dainty, wonderful lady" who never wanted the limelight that their success brought them.

B506 Wolfe, Rusty. "The Mistress of Illogical Logic." **The Golden Years of Radio & TV**. Spring 1983: 12-14.
George and Gracie are on the cover, but the emphasis is on Gracie in this article that traces her life and career. The author credits Gracie with being the inspiration for later "dizzy" television characters.

B507 Wood, Carlyle Leo. **TV Personalities: Biographical Sketch Book**. St. Louis: TV Personalities, 1954.
The book includes portraits of George Burns and Gracie Allen.

B508 "Would Gracie Allen Make a Good President?" **TV Forecast**. February 2-8, 1952: 5.
In an article in this Chicago "pre-national" television guide ostensibly penned by George, he admits to not knowing if she would make a good President but describes how Gracie "managed" her Uncle Sidney's campaign for the Presidency.

B509 Wylie, Max. **Best Broadcasts of 1939-1940**. New York: McGraw Hill, 1940.
Scripts from various radio broadcasts are reprinted, including "Vote for Gracie," based on Gracie Allen's convention in Omaha, Nebraska.

B510 York, Pat. **Going Strong**. New York: Arcade Publishing, 1991.
Interviews and photographs of men and women over 74 years of age who still contribute to society. George Burns expresses his belief that it is his full and busy life which keeps him young.

B511 Ziegler, Ronald. **Celebrity Sources: Guide to Biographical Information About Famous People in Show Business and Sports Today**. New York: Garland, 1990.
An annotated bibliography with entries on how to find biographical information on entertainers and athletes.

B512 Zolotow, Maurice. "...Say Good Night George." **Los Angeles Times**. December 1979: 256+.
A look at the three main cast members of the film, **Going in Style** (F41), George Burns, Art Carney and Lee Strasberg. George comments that "acting for him is easy."

Addendum

B513 "And for the Next 100." **Time**. 22 January, 1996: 71.
Covers the opening of the Burns and Allen Research Center at Cedars-Sinai hospital.

B514 Burns, George. **100 Years, 100 Stories**. New York: G. P. Putnam's Sons, 1996.
George's last book released the month of his 100th birthday is a collection of what he considered his 100 best and funniest stories. It was still on the **New York Times** best seller list at the time of his death.

B515 "Burns Keeps Fellow Comics in Stitches." **USA Today**. 19 January, 1996: D1-2.
A tribute to George Burns on his 100th birthday.

B516 Clinton, Bill. "Statement on the Death of George Burns." **Weekly Compilation of Presidential Documents**. 18 March, 1996: 462.

B517 Fairhurs, James. "The Burns and Allen Show." **Ireland's Own**. Spring, 1995: 48.
Profiles Gracie Allen's Irish heritage and her career.

B518 Gabler, Neal. "Long Ago, When Burns Wasn't So Lovable." **New York Times**. 24 March, 1996: Sec. 2: 36.
The author writes about George Burns' humor and his television shows.

B519 **George Burns: The First 100 Years**. New York: Communications Inc., 1996.
A collectors edition which covered George's life and career.

B520 Gottfried, Martin. **George Burns and the Hundred Year Dash**. New York: Simon and Schuster, 1996.
The author of this biography interviewed George and his children, friends and colleagues over a seven year period. There is no documentation.

B521 King, Larry. **The Best of Larry King Live: The Greatest Interviews**. Atlanta: Turner Pub., Inc. 1996.
The television interview with George Burns on November 10, 1989 is included in this book of King's best interviews.

B522 Krebs, Albin. "George Burns, Straight Man and Ageless Wit, Dies at 100." **New York Times**. 10 March, 1996: 1+ .
Front page story of George's death the day before at his home in Beverly Hills. The article reviews his life and career and that of Burns and Allen.

B523 Lacayo, Richard and Danelle Morton. "Into that Good Night." **People**. 25 March, 1996: 44.

B524 "Light Up a Stogie for His Next Century." **US News and World Report**. 29 January, 1996: 20.

B525 Natale, Richard and Timothy M. Gray. "George Burns--Death and Burial." **Variety**. 18 March, 1996: 53.

B526 Oliver, Myrna, et al. "George Burns, Comedy's Elder Statesman, Dies." **Los Angeles Times**. 10 March, 1996: 1+ .
A tribute to George Burns the day after his death includes color photos of George and Gracie. There are statements of appreciation by President Bill Clinton and comedian Milton Berle.

B527 **People Weekly**. 12 February, 1996: 174-75.
This special double issue of the greatest love stories of the century covers the marriage of Burns and Allen.

B528 Sauter, Michael. "' God is Dead': George Burns Gave Us the Laughs of the Century." **Entertainment Weekly**. 22 March, 1996: 14.

B529 "Special Tribute to George in His Own Words." **TV Guide**. 30 March-5 April, 1996: 32-35.
A collection of **TV Guide** front page covers through the years on which George and Gracie appeared. An insert entitled "Tributes to a Trouper" has various comedian's remarks on George Burns.

B530 Zoglin, Richard. "Good night, George." **Time**. 18 March, 1996: 99.

INDEX

The index numbers refer to page numbers in the biography section and chapter introductions and to the following enumerated sections: "V" (Vaudeville), "F" (Filmography), "R" (Radio), "T" (Television), "D" (Discography), "VG" (Videography) and "B" (Bibliography). Items in bold-face are titles of books, magazines, radio shows, plays and television shows. Fictional character names and "see" references are in italics. Song, article, and episode titles are in quotations.

About the Authors

CYNTHIA CLEMENTS is the Collection Development Librarian at Richland College, Dallas County Community College District, Dallas, Texas.

SANDRA WEBER is a free-lance writer.

Titles in
Bio-Bibliographies in the Performing Arts

Milos Forman: A Bio-Bibliography
Thomas J. Slater

Kate Smith: A Bio-Bibliography
Michael R. Pitts

Patty Duke: A Bio-Bibliography
Stephen L. Eberly

Carole Lombard: A Bio-Bibliography
Robert D. Matzen

Eva Le Gallienne: A Bio-Bibliography
Robert A. Schanke

Julie Andrews: A Bio-Bibliography
Les Spindle

Richard Widmark: A Bio-Bibliography
Kim Holston

Orson Welles: A Bio-Bibliography
Bret Wood

Ann Sothern: A Bio-Bibliography
Margie Schultz

Alice Faye: A Bio-Bibliography
Barry Rivadue

Jennifer Jones: A Bio-Bibliography
Jeffrey L. Carrier

Cary Grant: A Bio-Bibliography
Beverley Bare Buehrer

Maureen O'Sullivan: A Bio-Bibliography
Connie J. Billips

Ava Gardner: A Bio-Bibliography
Karin J. Fowler

Jean Arthur: A Bio-Bibliography
Arthur Pierce and Douglas Swarthout

Donna Reed: A Bio-Bibliography
Brenda Scott Royce

Gordon MacRae: A Bio-Bibliography
Bruce R. Leiby

Mary Martin: A Bio-Bibliography
Barry Rivadue

Irene Dunne: A Bio-Bibliography
Margie Schultz

Anne Baxter: A Bio-Bibliography
Karin J. Fowler

Tullulah Bankhead: A Bio-Bibliography
Jeffrey L. Carrier

Jessica Tandy: A Bio-Bibliography
Milly S. Barranger

Janet Gaynor: A Bio-Bibliography
Connie Billips

James Stewart: A Bio-Bibliography
Gerard Molyneaux

Joseph Papp: A Bio-Bibliography
Barbara Lee Horn

Henry Fonda: A Bio-Bibliography
Kevin Sweeney

Edwin Booth: A Bio-Bibliography
L. Terry Oggel

Ethel Merman: A Bio-Bibliography
George B. Bryan

Lauren Bacall: A Bio-Bibliography
Brenda Scott Royce

Joseph Chaikin: A Bio-Bibliography
Alex Gildzen and Dimitris Karageorgiou

Richard Burton: A Bio-Bibliography
Tyrone Steverson

Maureen Stapleton: A Bio-Bibliography
Jeannie M. Woods

David Merrick: A Bio-Bibliography
Barbara Lee Horn

Vivien Leigh: A Bio-Bibliography
Cynthia Marylee Molt

Robert Mitchum: A Bio-Bibliography
Jerry Roberts

Agnes Moorehead: A Bio-Bibliography
Lynn Kear

Colleen Dewhurst: A Bio-Bibliography
Barbara Lee Horn

Helen Hayes: A Bio-Bibliography
Donn B. Murphy and Stephen Moore

Boris Karloff: A Bio-Bibliography
Beverley Bare Buehrer

Betty Grable: A Bio-Bibliography
Larry Billman

Ellen Stewart and La Mama:
A Bio-Bibliography
Barbara Lee Horn

Lucille Lortel: A Bio-Bibliography
Sam McCready

Nöel Coward: A Bio-Bibliography
Stephen Cole

Oliver Smith: A Bio-Bibliography
Tom Mikotowicz

Katharine Cornell: A Bio-Bibliography
Lucille M. Pederson

Betty Comden and Adolph Green:
A Bio-Bibliography
Alice M. Robinson

Al Jolson: A Bio-Bibliography
James Fisher

William Shatner: A Bio-Bibliography
Dennis William Hauck

Margaret Webster: A Bio-Bibliography
Milly S. Barranger

Ginger Rogers: A Bio-Bibliography
Jocelyn Faris

Joan Fontaine: A Bio-Bibliography
Marsha Lynn Beeman

Harold Lloyd: A Bio-Bibliography
Annette M. D'Agostino

Montgomery Clift: A Bio-Bibliography
Mary C. Kalfatovic

Roscoe "Fatty" Arbuckle:
A Bio-Bibliography
Robert Young, Jr.

Audrey Hepburn: A Bio-Bibliography
David Hofstede

George Sidney: A Bio-Bibliography
Eric Monder

Eleanor Powell: A Bio-Bibliography
Margie Schultz

Spencer Tracy: A Bio-Bibliography
James Fisher

Jayne Mansfield: A Bio-Bibliography
Jocelyn Faris

Bing Crosby: A Bio-Bibliography
J. Roger Osterholm

Rock Hudson: A Bio-Bibliography
Brenda Scott Royce

Robert Wise: A Bio-Bibliography
Frank Thompson

David Niven: A Bio-Bibliography
Karin J. Fowler

Gregory Peck: A Bio-Bibliography
Gerard Molyneaux

Lee Remick: A Bio-Bibliography
Barry Rivadue

Liberace: A Bio-Bibliography
Jocelyn Faris

John Barrymore: A Bio-Bibliography
Martin F. Norden

Tony Richardson: A Bio-Bibliography
Don Radovich

Howard Keel: A Bio-Bibliography
Bruce R. Leiby

James Dean: A Bio-Bibliography
David Hofstede

ISBN 0-313-26883-5
90000>
EAN
9 780313 268830
HARDCOVER BAR CODE